Memorial (Yizkor) Book of the Jewish Community of Novogrudok, Poland

Translation of
Pinkas Navaredok

Edited by Rabbi Helen Cohn

Originally Published in Hebrew and Yiddish Tel Aviv in 1963
Edited by:

Dr. Eliezer Yerushalmi, David Cohen, Dr. Aharon Mirsky, Moshe Sarig (Steinberg), Menashe Rabina, Yehoshua Jaffe, Yacov Rudnicki, Yacov Kivelovitch, Shlomo Kamin — Israel. Edna Cogan, Chaim Noah Leibovitch — U.S.A.

Published by JewishGen

An Affiliate of the Museum of Jewish
A Living Memorial to the Holocaust
New York

Memorial (Yizkor) Book of the Jewish Community of Novogrudok, Poland
Translation of *Pinkas Novogrudok*

Copyright © 2013 by JewishGen, Inc.
All rights reserved.
First Printing: May 2013, Sivan 5773
Second Printing: August 2019, Av 5779

Editors: Rabbi Helen Cohn, Joel Alpert and Ilene Weiner
Image Editors: Jan R. Fine, Dr. Larry Gaum, Max Szmekura and
    Jerry Isenberg
Image Scanner: Sandy Malek
Cover Design: Nili Goldman
Publicity: Sandra Hirschhorn
Indexing: Jonathan Wind

This book may not be reproduced, in whole or in part, including illustrations in any form (beyond that copying permitted by Sections 107 and 108 of the U.S. Copyright Law and except by reviewers for public press), without written permission from the publisher.

Published by JewishGen, Inc.
An Affiliate of the Museum of Jewish Heritage
A Living Memorial to the Holocaust
36 Battery Place, New York, NY 10280

"JewishGen, Inc. is not responsible for inaccuracies or omissions in the original work and makes no representations regarding the accuracy of this translation. Digital images of the original book's contents can be seen online at the New York Public Library Web site."

The mission of the JewishGen organization is to produce a translation of the original work and we cannot verify the accuracy of statements or alter facts cited.

Printed in the United States of America by Lightning Source, Inc.

Library of Congress Control Number (LCCN): 2013933042
ISBN: 978-1-939561-03-9 (hard cover: 796 pages, alk. paper)

"This book is a moving testimony to a world that no longer exists. It documents the savage destruction of this Jewish world. It includes stories of extraordinary bravery and survival"

Jack Kagan

Survivor

JewishGen and the Yizkor Books In Print Project

This book has been published by the **Yizkor Books in Print Project,** as part of the **Yizkor Book Project** of **JewishGen, Inc.**

JewishGen, Inc. is a non-profit organization founded in 1987 as a resource for Jewish genealogy. Its website [www.jewishgen.org] serves as an international clearinghouse and resource center to assist individuals who are researching the history of their Jewish families and the places where they lived. JewishGen provides databases, facilitates discussion groups, and coordinates projects relating to Jewish genealogy and the history of the Jewish people. In 2003, JewishGen became an affiliate of the **Museum of Jewish Heritage - A Living Memorial to the Holocaust** in New York.

The **JewishGen Yizkor Book Project** was organized to make more widely known the existence of Yizkor (Memorial) Books written by survivors and former residents of various Jewish communities throughout the world. Later, volunteers connected to the different destroyed communities began cooperating to have these books translated from the original language—usually Hebrew or Yiddish—into English, thus enabling a wider audience to have access to the valuable information contained within them. As each chapter of these books was translated, it was posted on the JewishGen website and made available to the general public.

The **Yizkor Books in Print Project** began in 2011 as an initiative to print and publish Yizkor Books that had been fully translated, so that hard copies would be available for purchase by the descendants of these communities and also by scholars, universities, synagogues, libraries, and museums.

These Yizkor books have been produced almost entirely through the volunteer effort of researchers from around the world, assisted by donations from private individuals. The books are printed and sold at near cost, so as to make them as affordable as possible. Our goal is to make this important genre of Jewish literature and history available in English in book form, so that people can have the personal histories of their ancestral towns on their bookshelves for themselves and for their children and grandchildren.

Lance Ackerfeld, Yizkor Book Project Manager

Joel Alpert, Yizkor Book in Print Project Coordinator

This book is presented by the
Yizkor Books in Print Project
Project Coordinator: Joel Alpert

Part of the
Yizkor Books Project of JewishGen, Inc.
Project Manager: Lance Ackerfeld

These books have been produced solely through volunteer effort of individuals from around the world. The books are printed and sold at near cost, so as to make them as affordable as possible.

Our goal is to make this history and important genre of Jewish literature available in English in book form so that people can have the near-personal histories of their ancestral towns on their bookshelves for themselves and for their children and grandchildren.

Any donations to the Yizkor Books Project are appreciated.

Please send donations to:
Yizkor Book Project
JewishGen
36 Battery Place
New York, NY 10280

JewishGen, Inc. is an affiliate of the
Museum of Jewish Heritage
A Living Memorial to the Holocaust

Title Page of Original Hebrew and Yiddish Edition

Title Page in English of Original Hebrew and Yiddish Edition

PINKAS NAVAREDOK

MEMORIAL BOOK

From the Original Yizkor Book

Edited by :

Dr. Eliezer Yerushalmi, David Cohen, Dr. Aharon Mirsky, Moshe Sarig (Steinberg), Menashe Rabina, Yehoshua Jaffe, Yacov Rudnicki, Yacov Kivelovitch, Shlomo Kamin — Israel. Edna Cogan, Chaim Noah Leibovitch — U.S.A.

Published by
Alexander Harkavy Navaredker
Relief Committee in U. S. A
and
Navaredker Committee in Israel

Printed in Israel
1963

"ACHDUTH" COOP. PRESS LTD., TEL-AVIV, ISRAEL

Acknowledgements for the

Publication of the English Translation

The publication of the English translation of the Novogrudok Yizkor Book (*Pinkas Navaredok*) was a labor of love for large group in order to make it a reality. The original yizkor book (*Pinkas Navaredok*) was edited by. E. Yerushalmi and published in 1963 in Tel Aviv by the Alexander Harkavy Navaredker Relief Committee in the USA and Israel. It was originally in Hebrew and Yiddish with 419 pages.

This publication came about through two distinct efforts. First was the translation effort, corrdinated by Oskar Delatycki z"l, with the support and permission of Dov Cohen of the Novogrudok Landsmannschaft in Israel. Secondly was the publication effort, and for that we acknowledge the following people: Rabbi Helen Cohn, Joel Alpert, and Ilene Weiner served as the text layout editors; cover design was by Nili Goldman; Sandy Malek scanned all the images of the book so that the images in the book are now higher quality than they would have been had we used the files that on the Yizkor Books web site; Jerry Isenberg, Larry Gaum and Max Szmekura processed the images further for best reproduction in the book.

Special gratitude goes to Jack Kagan, a survivor of the town, who, in addition to writting his own book on Novogrudok, has helped provide corrections and additions to this volume.

Joel Alpert, Coordinator of the Yizkor-Books-In-Print Project

Note to the Reader:

It should be mentioned that the town is also known by alternate names: Navahrudak [Belarus], Novogrudok [Russian], Nowogródek [Polish], Navaredok [Yiddish], Naugardukas [Lithuanian], Novaredok, Novogrudek, Novohorodok, Novradok, Nowogrudok, Nowogradek, Navharadak, Nawahradak.

Before World War I it was know as Novogrudok in the Russian empire, between the wars it was know as Nowogrodek in Poland, after World War II until the end of the Soviet Untion, it was known as Novogrudok in the Soviet Union, and today as Navahrudak in Belarus.

TABLE OF CONTENTS IN THIS BOOK

Translated by Solomon Manischwitz
and edited by Judy Montel and Oskar Delatycki

Note: [H] stands for Hebrew and [Y] for Yiddish

Title Page of the Original Hebrew Edition		vi
Title Page in English of the Original Hebrew Edition		vii
Acknowledgements for Publication		ix
Note to the Reader		ix
Table of Contents		x

Introduction to the book

Introduction	the editors	[H]	1
The prologue	the editors	[Y]	4

History of the City [H] 7

The history of the Jews in Novogrudok	Yaakov Goldberg	[H]	7
The history of the town		[Y]	19
The Rabbis of Novogrudok	Rabbi V.Ch. Kancipolski	[Y]	30
The Musar movement	Mordechai Ginsburg (Montreal)	[Y]	46
What I remember of Novogrudok	Shlomo M. Gutman (Argentina)	[Y]	58
Leaders and ordinary members of the community	E. M. Yerushalmi	[Y]	63
The Bund in Novogrudok	H. Kaplan and Y. Maslow	[Y]	82
Memoirs from before the First World War	Wm Uris (New York)	[Y]	85
Old Novogrudok	Shimeon Yosifun	[Y]	96
Reminisces of Yischok Gurwitz: Rabbi Nachman Getzovhttp		[Y]	111
The Tailors' Synagogue		[Y]	114
The Seder night that was disrupted		[Y]	117
Dr. Benjamin Einhorn	Yaakov Gershovski	[Y]	120
Without a hammer, shears and a saw	Menashe Unger, US	[Y]	124

Alexander Harkavy	Prof. Nosun Ziskind, US	[Y]	125
Avrohom Eliyahu Harkavy		[Y]	133
The "eelui" (exceptional students of Tora) from Novogrudok (in memory of Reb Kalman Aharon Midler)	Chaim Noy	[H]	134
The big fire (blaze) in Novogrudok	Yaakov Gershovski	[Y]	137
The Jewish Souls (from the Old Pinkas Navaradok)	Dr. Eliezer Yerushalmi	[Y]	138

Between the Two World Wars [Y] 142

Hebrew education in Novogrudok	Moshe Steinberg-Sarig	[H]	142
The kindergarten	Sima Yonas-Portnoy	[H]	162
Music in Novogrudok	Menashe Rabina (Rabinovitz)	[H]	164
Politico-Communal life in Novogrudok	Shmuel Openheim	[Y]	171
The Novogrudok orphanage			182
The history of the orphanage		[Y]	182
Memories	Aharon Srebranik	[Y]	188
The first child in the orphanage	Aba Rutkovski	[Y]	191
The orphanage (1917-1919)	Shalom Cohen	[Y]	192
Shokdey melocho (the trade school)	Chaim Leibovich	[Y]	194
Volunteer Fire brigade	A. Shochor (Czarny)	[Y]	198
The theatre in Novogrudok	Zahava Rabinovich-Engel	[H]	199
Chaluts (Zionist scouts) movement	Yehoshua Brook (Kibbutz Negba)	[H]	202
Personalities	Shmuel Openheim	[Y]	217
The last of the Rabbis	Yehoshua Jaffe	[H]	225
People and Images	Yehoshua Yaffe	[Y]	228
Jewish Gardeners	Boruch Sapotnicki	[Y]	235
Peculiar types of people	A. Yerushalmi	[Y]	237
The public bath	A. Y.	[Y]	240
Schloss gass – a distinct township	Eliezer Berkovitch	[Y]	242
Yiddishe gass	Miriam Lipchin Negrevitski	[Y]	245
United Jewish Artisans Association	Samuel Nikolayevski	[Y]	247
The Professional Movement	Eliyahu Berkovitch	[Y]	250

"TOZ" (a Jewish Health Organization) activities	Majrim Ginzburg	[Y]	251
Aid for Jewish prisoners	Aharon Rudnicki	[Y]	257
Village Jews	D. Cohen	[Y]	259
Benjamin Kotlover	W. Uris	[Y]	265
Weekly papers in Novogrudok	Yehoshua Yaffe	[Y]	266
A native of Novogrudok in the Herzelia Gymnasium	Yishayahu Avi-Amots	[H]	267
Zeydl Bushelevits	Ch. Leibovitch	[H]	268
Extinguishing the fire of hatred	Noach Avni (Kamenitsky)	[Y]	269

Those Whom We Remember [Y] 272

Edna Kagan	Baruch Yakov and Meir Kagan	[Y]	272
Louie Zlotnik	Chaim Leibovitch	[Y]	273
Ilia Aranovitch Gumener	Ch. L.	[Y]	275
Shmuel Solomon	Ch. L.	[Y]	275
Yitzchak Gurvitz	a fellow townsman	[Y]	277
Vager Family	Ch. L.	[Y]	278
Grandmother slept (in memory of the old woman Etl Goldberg)	D. C.	[H]	279
Alter Kamenetzki	N. K.	[Y]	281
Shmuel Goldberg	Lyuba Cohen	[H]	283
Yehuda Kaplinski	Lyuba Rudnicki	[Y]	284
My mother and sisters	Lyuba Valkin	[H]	287
Hersh Ostashinski	a fellow townsman	[Y]	287
With the coffin of Rabbi Yosef Yoyzl Hurvits in Israel		[H]	288

The Surroundings [H] 290

Karelich	Ch. T.	[H]	290
How I remember Selib (Wsielub)	Y. Y.	[Y]	295
My Shtetl Selib	Liba Shmulevits	[Y]	297
My shtetl Selub	Sara Shmulevits	[H]	300
Tsemach The Coachman (A type from the shtetl Selub)	Yehushua Yaffe	[Y]	301

Novoyelnie	Chana Kamin (Kaplan)	[Y]	303

Our Sisters and Brothers in the USA

		[Y]	304
The Alexander Harkavy Navaredker aid committee in US	Ya'akov Maslow	[Y]	304
Novogrudok Progressive Branch 146	B. Seltzer	[Y]	307
Yaakov Maslov	L.Ch.	[Y]	309
Committee of Emigrants from Novogrudok in Israel	Lyuba Rudnicki	[H]	313
About the editorial staff of the Pinkas Novogrudok (Yizkor) book	the Editors	[H]	317

Poetry and Prose in Novogrudok

		[H]	320
The song of Beseeching	Aharon Mirski	[H]	320
The Holy Ark Falls	Chaim Grade	[Y]	325
Mickiewicz and the Jews of Novogrudok	Prof B. Marc, Warsaw	[Y]	329
Adam Mickiewicz and his attitude to Jews	S. L. Shnayderman	[Y]	335
A Preacher in Siberia	Dr S. Shabbat	[H]	340
My home, poem	Bertha Kling	[Y]	344
A Friday in Novogrudok	Fruma Kamieniecki	[Y]	345
The first Rosh Hashona of the survivors of the Holocaust	Chaim Leibovich	[Y]	348
Three Kol Nidrei's	Chaim Leibovich	[Y]	351
Legends and fables	David Cohen	[Y]	355
The path to riches	David Cohen	[Y]	355
Belief in the Messiah	David Cohen	[Y]	358
"We will do and obey"– a legend	David Cohen	[H]	363
An Ethrog for Succoth	David Cohen	[Y]	364
A "Din Torah" a Jewish court	David Cohen	[Y]	367
Yitschok "Yom Suf"	David Cohen	[Y]	369
"Boze moyi"		[Y]	372
Letter from a mother	Edna Kagan	[Y]	375
The Shloss-barg	Dr. Avraham Ostashinski	[Y]	381
My home town	Emanuel Efron	[H]	386

Shoah and Bravery [Y] 398

Shoah [Y] 398

I fear and dread the consolation (poem)	Mirsky	[Y]	399
On the threshold of the shoah	Yaakov Kivelevich	[H]	399
A sea of troubles	Eliyau Berkovitz	[Y]	417
A. Under the Soviets			417
B. The Tunnel			418
Under the German Yoke	Lyuba Rudnicki	[Y]	423
Outside of the Ghetto	Lyuba Rudnicki	[H]	432
In the days of annihilation	Shmuel Openheim	[Y]	441
In the Nazi hell			441
The slaughter in Horodyszcze			446
The 52 martyrs	Yehuda Slucki	[H]	453
The slaughter	Eshke Shor Levin	[Y]	455
The First Slaughter	Sima Yanos-Portnoy	[Y]	457
Slaughters	Chaim Kravets	[H]	463
Under the German whip	Sula Rubin-Wolozynski	[Y]	477
They burned the town	Yehoshua Yaffe	[Y]	480
The great destruction	Chaim Leibovitz	[Y]	498
A. How 300 Jews saved themselves			498
B. The last Passover			507
C. Three who were burned to death	(told by Chana Kirshner)		510
D. Escape through the tunnel			512
E. The heroic death of Berl Yoselevich			514
How I survived	Idl Kagan	[Y]	517
The Ghetto in Peresike	Frume Gulkovitz-Berger	[Y]	522
Chapters from the Holocaust	Y. Yaffe	[Y]	525
A. Escaping from the slaughter			525
B. The second slaughter			533
C. The final wandering			546

D. The tradesmen's Ghetto			551
E. The tar and pitch factory in the village of Karnyshi			559
Surviving the Holocaust with the Russian Partisans	Jack Kagan		563
The latest Kaddish (a poem)	Zelig Limon	[Y]	583
No Yahrzeit candle (a poem)	Nechama Layzerovski	[Y]	585
Where is my home? (a poem)	Miriam Ninkovski-Berkovich	[Y]	586

And the Bravery [H] 558

The partisans' company of Tuvia Belski	Samuel Amarant	[H]	588
Jewish revenge	Chaim Leibovich	[Y]	620
A. Fight of the Jewish partisans			620
B. The Jewish Hero			625
C. Commander Shmatovich			626
Memories	Reyzl Volkin	[Y]	628
Jewish Partisan Intelligence	Moshe Reznick	[Y]	631
Jewish Bravery	Yehoshua Yaffe	[Y]	632
A. The first Jewish partisans			632
B. The partisans avoid slaughters			635
The four mass graves	Miriam Ninkovsky	[H]	637
People of Novogrudok after liberation	Yehoshua Yaffe	[Y]	638
Partisans of Novogrudok who fell in action	S. Openheim	[H]	641
Such were the Jewish partisans	Y. Yaffe	[H]	646
My brother Meir	Yaakov Rudnicki	[Y]	654
In memory of my father, Asoel Belski	Asoella	[H]	655
How does Novogrudok look now?	a townsman	[Y]	656
The Conclusion		[H/Y]	663

The Blood Bond with the Land of Israel [H] 665

To Those Who Fell For Their Country		[H]	665
Osher Gorodisky	Ya'akov Ginenski	[H]	665
Yekuti'el (Kushi) Solchinski	Bilha	[H]	667
With Kushi in his last days	Shlomoleh Shvartz	[H]	668

Ruven Openheim	Shmuel Openheim	[H]	675
Eliezer Kriner	by a friend	[H]	679
Luka Shapiro	by a friend	[H]	681

A List: We will remember the Names of the Martyrs of Novogrudok, the Vicinity and Korelich [H] 683

Novogrudok 687
List of citizens of Novogrudok 721
A list of Jews from Novogrudok, including members of the Bielski partisan group 735
Killed by the Poles soon after liberation 735
List of Jews from Novogrudok who were arrested or deported on the night of 19/20 June 1941 and died during the war with Russia 735
List of the Bielski Partisans Killed 736
Karelich 737
List of the Jews in the Ghetto of Karelich 744

Table of Contents of the Original Hebrew and Yiddish Book 753

Index 757

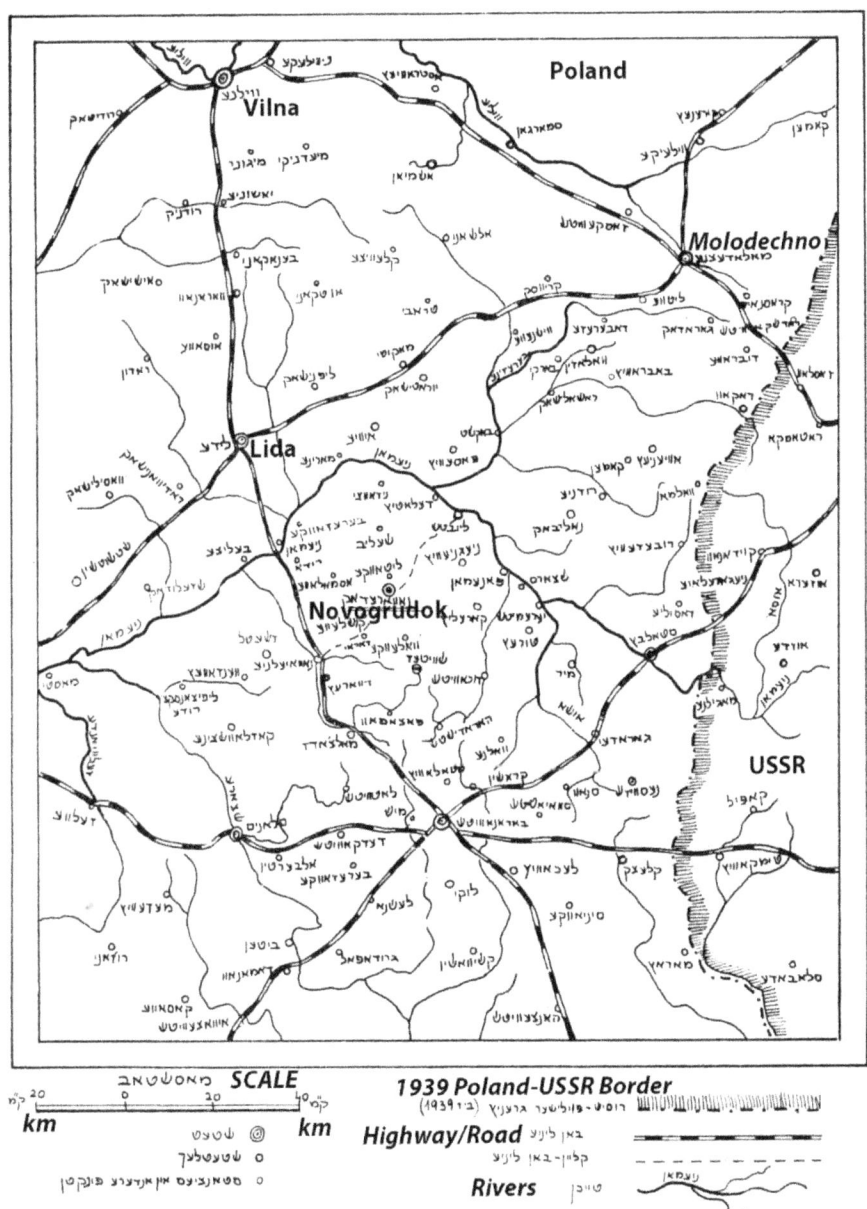

Area Map from Original Yizkor Book in Yiddish with Novogrudok identified in English

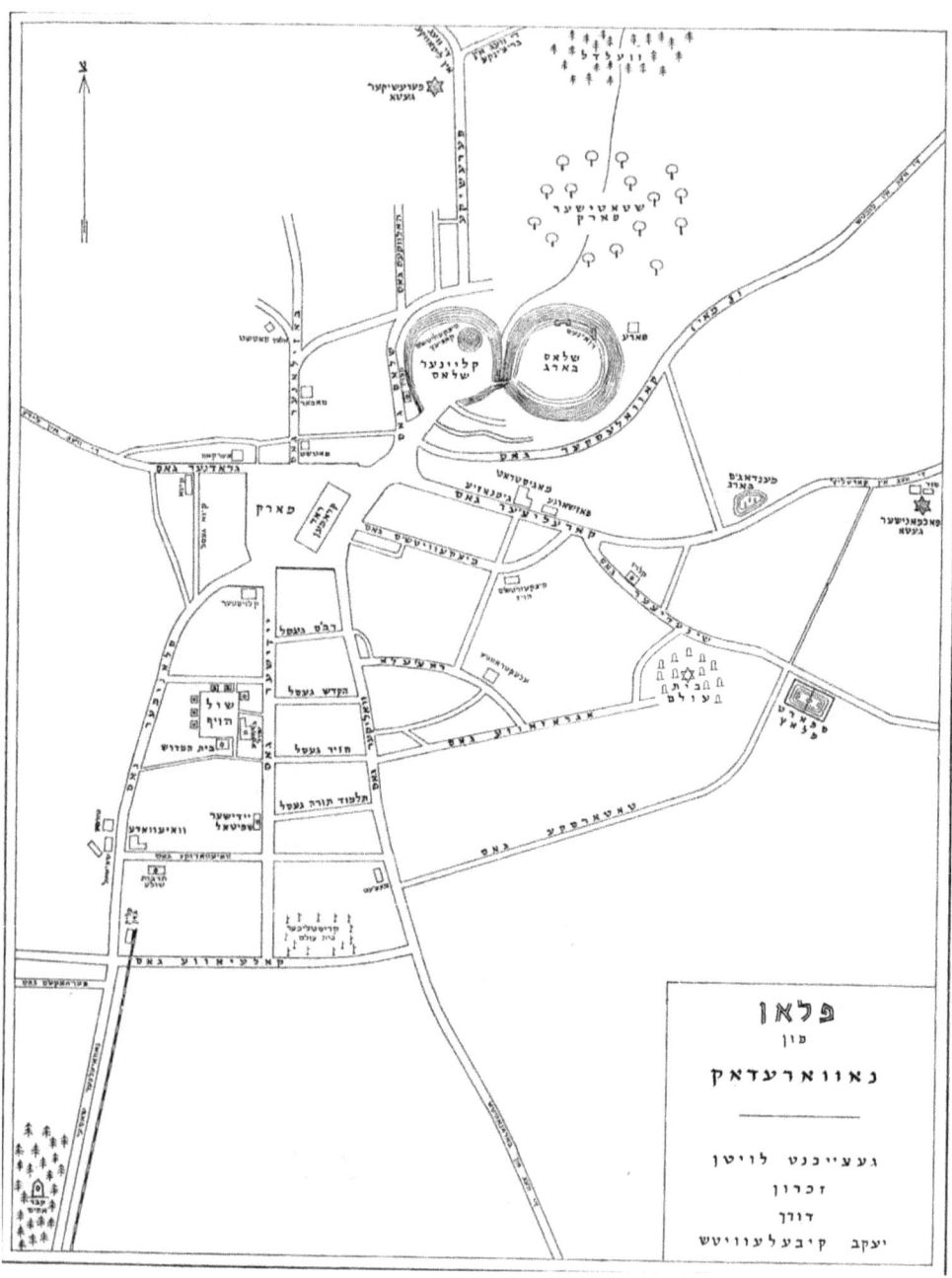

Local Town Map from Original Yizkor Book

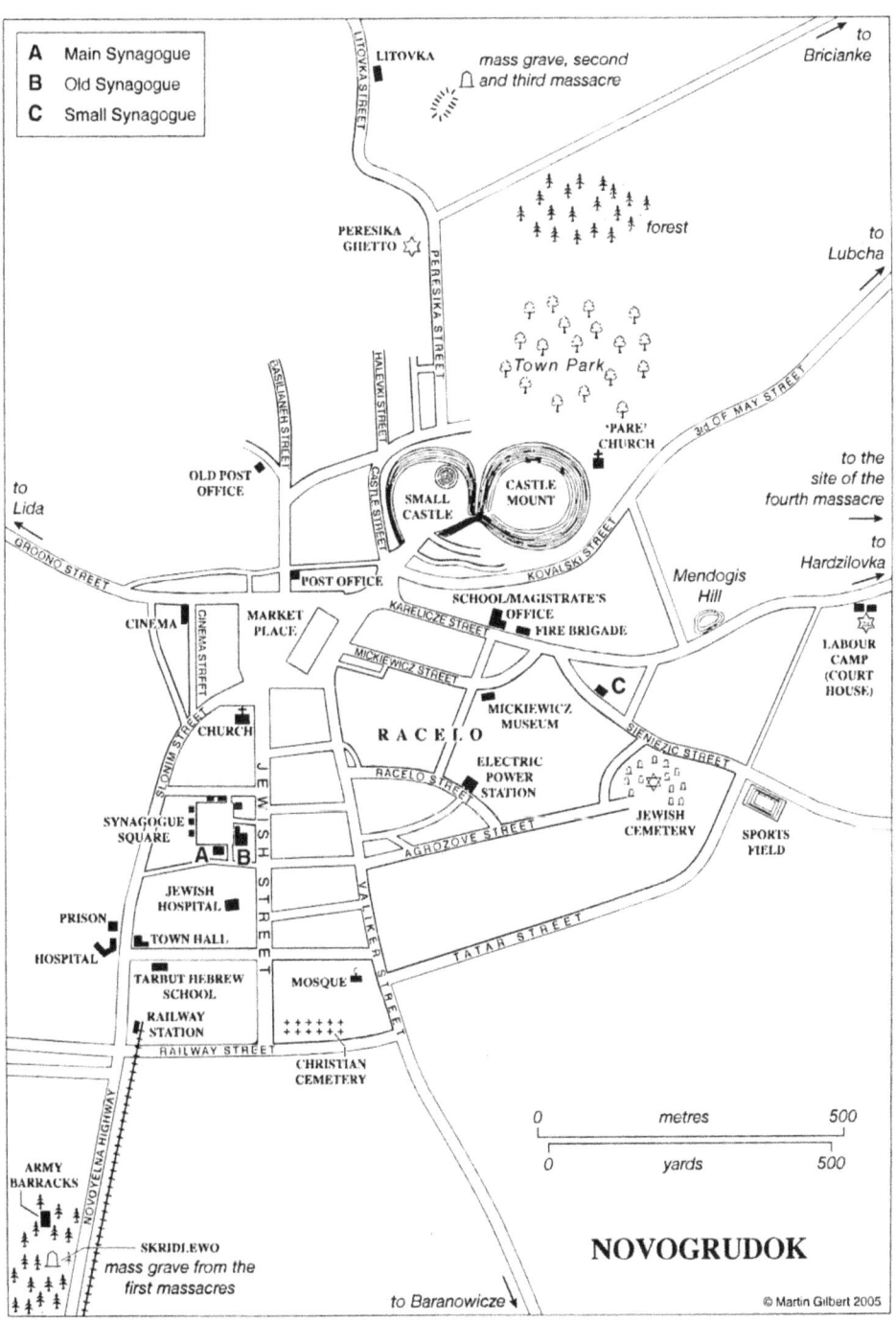

Local Town Map Translated
Provided Courtesy of Sir Martin Gilbert
First appeared published by Vallentine Mitchell

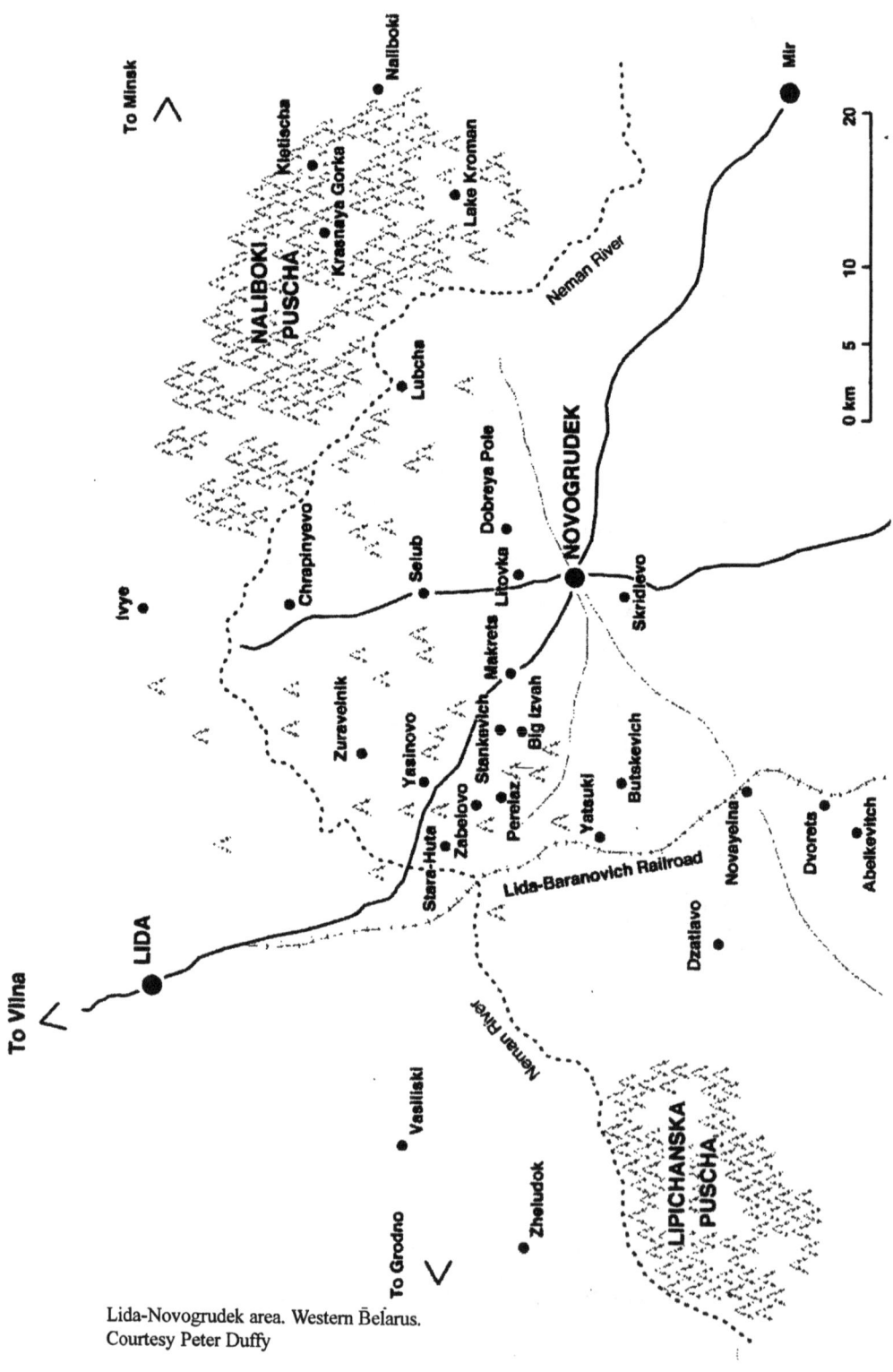

Lida-Novogrudek area. Western Belarus.
Courtesy Peter Duffy

Novogrudok and Vicinity
Provided Courtesy of Sir Martin Gilbert
First appeared published by Vallentine Mitchell

Novogrudok within Poland
Provided Courtesy of Sir Martin Gilbert
First appeared published by Vallentine Mitchell

Synagogue in Nowogrodek, 1939
Courtesy of the Yad Vashem Archive, Photo Collection 204EO9

THE GATE TO THE NOVOGRUDOK CEMETERY

Donated by Judith and Yitzchak Gurevitz in 1929

Family Notes

[Page 10]

Introduction to the book

Introduction

Translated from Hebrew by Aviva Kamil

The creators of Pinkas Novogrudok.
Sitting from right: Dr. Eliezer Yerushalmi. Dovid Cohen. Dr. Aharon Mirski.
Standing from right: Shlomo Kamin. Jehoshua Jaffa. Moshe Steinberg. Yaakov Rudnicki and Yaakov Kivelevitz
God bless their memory.
[Above Photo was not in the original Yizkor Book]

Past and recent generations look upon us from the pages of Pinkas Novogrudok. We consisted of generations of different types of Jews: Great Torah scholars and ordinary Jews, Mitnagdim and Chasidim, workers, scholars from the Yeshiva "Beit-Yosef" and academic scientists, Zionists and revolutionaries. All of these Jews left their impression on the institutions that they had built up: on the Yeshivot, the Hebrew and Yiddish schools, and other establishments and institutions.

All schools were filled with kindergarten children and studious Jewish pupils. All cut down, exterminated, woe to our loss!

Novogrudok took a place of honour in the cultural life of the Jewish people for over 500 years. It was uprooted and exterminated, along with all of European Jewry, by the murderous Nazi Germans, may an eternal curse befall them and their descendants forever!

The Pinkas is a type of link in the chain of Pinkasim that were customary in Jewish communities. They consisted of reports and documents of all the happenings in the community. They were vessels of tears and blood, of the few celebrations and the many sorrows that people experienced, as well as comments about good deeds. Devoted hands wrote the Pinkas in a simple language and with pure intentions, a testimony and a memorial to the Jewish communities.

The present Pinkas, the Novogrudok Pinkas, is here to tell the orphaned generation and generations to come all that the community experienced from its very beginning hundreds of years ago until its terrible destruction. The Novogrudok community was over many generations a warm nest for Jewish life and culture. Only a few were saved from the monstrous fire, a few who showed great heroism, who lived in the forests or in concentration camps and later were scattered around the world: U.S.A, Latin America. Only a few reached the safe shores of the liberated and independent Israel.

Some survivors and their brethren, although they left the town many years ago, still carried in their hearts a love for their hometown. They all dreamed of establishing a memorial for their mothers, fathers, sisters, brothers, a memorial for the children and youths, who were cruelly murdered and buried in brotherly graves, to preserve for eternity the history of that splendid town in a memorial book, and for it to be a "Kadish" and a testimony for generations to come. It was a dream with many obstacles: they did not know if they would be able to find the material, the means and the dedicated people needed for the sacred task of publishing such a book. On annual memorial days in Israel and America, the day of the first slaughter, Yod Chet of the month of Kislev, the survivors expressed their wish to undertake that task, to publish the book. It took them twenty years to bring the project to fruition. Three years ago, at a memorial evening, the task was given to the members: David Cohen, Yaakov Kivelevich, Shlomo Kaminietzki (Kamin), Moshe Shteinberg-Sarig, who was the principal of "Tarbut" school in Novogrudok, Yehoshua Yaffe, Dr. Aaron Mirski, Menashe Rabina and Yaakov Rudnitzki, the representative of the committee of ex-Novogrudoker. Their task was to collect the material, and to be the editors of the "Yizkor" book. The Israeli committee of ex-Novogrudoker financed the initial stage of the project. A contact was made with the U.S.A committees and some people from the U.S.A joined the editorial staff: The famous personality Edna Kagan, who came, when young to the U.S.A, but kept a warm place in her heart for her home town Novogrudok had contributed greatly to this project. Our friend Chaim Leibovich, a holocaust survivor, joined the editorial staff. The two committees, in Israel and U.S.A, headed by the dear patriarch Mr Maslov, gave their blessings and their help to the editors.

Be blessed all you who wrote with bleeding hearts about all that they and the town went through. And be blessed all of you in Israel and overseas who contributed articles to this book.

After a year of collecting the precious material, following the request of our friends in the U.S.A, the editors turned to Dr. Eliezer Yerushalmi, an author and a teacher, a native of Novogrudok, to accept the post of technical editor. The editorial committee accepted his suggested title for the volume as "Pinkas Novogrudok" and the following chapters:

> A. The history of the town and its Jewish community from its beginning to World WarII, including a chapter about great people, and one chapter from the old Pinkas.
>
> B. The town and its Jewish life between two World War s: businesses, culture, daily life, personalities and images.
>
> C. The life of the town and its people mirrored in poetry, prose, legends and tales.
>
> D. The holocaust and heroism during the days of the evil oppressors, may their name be erased.

To end with memorial candles to the holy and pure souls that went up in flames of the holocaust and the destruction. Many photos were included in the Pinkas.

The editorial committee presents with awe "Pinkas Novogrudok" to the natives of the town in Israel and the Diaspora, with a prayer in their hearts: let the words of this Pinkas be kept in our hearts and the hearts of our descendants'. "Ya'aleh Ve'itkadash" the memory of our beloved martyrs who were cut down by a cruel hand from the land of the living. *"Yitgadal Ve'itkadash"*

We end the introduction of the Pinkas with sorrow. Two of our faithful and dedicated members of the editorial committee passed away.

The kindly Edna Kagan from the U.S.A, who dedicated her last years to the collection of the relevant material for the Pinkas, and inspired the editorial committee with her enthusiasm.

Dr. Eliezer Yerushalmi, for whom Novogrudok was a source of inspiration for his literary creativity. He helped faithfully in the editing of the Pinkas.

Both of them did not live to see the completion of the Pinkas. Their memory will be kept in the pages of the Pinkas.

The Editors.

Prologue

Translated from Yiddish by Oskar Delatycki

Many generations look at us from the pages of Pinkas Novogrudok, generations of various types and classes of people: famous religious scholars and simple toilers, mesnagedim and chasidim, Musar scholars from Reb Yoysl's Yeshiva, enlightened people and men of science, Zionists and those who opposed them. All of them left their imprint on the many learning institutions of the town. There were primary (cheders) and advanced (yeshivas) religious schools, trade schools for the poor (Shogdey Melocho), the Hebrew school Tarbut and Yiddish schools. All the schools and educational institutions were filled with very dear Jewish children. And then the time came when the community, which had existed for hundreds of years, together with thousands of other Jewish communities in the whole of Europe, was exterminated by the German vandals and their supporters.

Pinkas Novogrudok is a link in a long chain of similar books which describe the lives of Jewish communities over hundreds of years. They are the chronicles of the few moments of happiness and the many years of anguish in the lives of the communities. It was a vessel filled with blood and tears but also with noble deeds and *kiddush hashem*. The compilers of the Pinkas books have described many deeds over the generations. Our Pinkas gives an account of the end of our town. It is the last Pinkas of Novogrudok. The book was not written by many or by hired hands. It was the work of the few survivors, the last remaining members of our community.

A rich and multicoloured community, hundreds of years old, was wiped out. Thousands of Jews young and old, hundreds of children are buried in the four deserted mass graves. Only few survived by super human bravery and ingenuity. They dwelled in the forests and they took revenge for the spilled innocent blood. After the war, the survivors remained for years in refugee camps. Later they were dispersed to all corners of the earth. Some came to the welcoming shores of Israel.

The survivors together with others who had left their native town a long time ago, but had never forgotten their roots, have decided to initiate a project to perpetuate the memory of their dear fathers and mothers, brothers and sisters and their innocent children who were exterminated in a most barbaric manner. Thus the idea of compiling a Yizkor [memorial] book had arisen. Such a book would also serve to describe briefly the past of the famed, ancient town and the personalities who lived in there over the epochs.

We were dreaming and striving but we had doubts whether we would be ever able to fulfill our aims. We did not know if any of the documents accumulated over many centuries, which we would require for our work, had been saved. We had doubts regarding the availability of the necessary financial resources. We did not know if we could find people who would be willing and able to write the book. Each year we would meet to commemorate the fallen on the anniversary of the first slaughter (8/12/41) and each year we would restate our desire to publish but we took it no further. Three years ago [1960] we finally decided to commence working on the project. We selected an editorial committee consisting of Dovid Cohen, Jakob Kivelevich, Shlomo Kaminiecki (Kamin), the former director of the Tarbut school Moshe Steinberg-Sarig, Yehoshua Yaffe, Dr A. Mirski, Menashe Rabina, and a member of the Novogrudok committee Jakov Rudnicki and gave them the task of collecting manuscripts for publication. The committee of the Novogrudok Landsmanshaft [compatriots] in Israel got in touch with the Novogrudok Landsmanshaft in USA. It was decided to set up a parallel editorial committee in the States, which consisted of Edna Kagan, who left Novogrudok many years ago but had never forgotten her birthplace, our friend Chaim Leibovich, a survivor of the Holocaust, and our old and devoted friend Maslov. They all helped with their deeds and words in the work of the editorial staff. Many survivors and other fellow countrymen were of great help. They told and have written down their tragic stories. They also related the tales of the better times before the war. Thus we collected the rich material. We are grateful to all contributors.

The editorial committee had nominated as the technical editor, our fellow townsman, a teacher and writer Dr Eliezer Yerushalmi. He suggested the name of the book, Pinkas Novogudok.

The book contains four chapters:

> Chapter 1: The story of Novogrudok and the Jewish community from its foundation until the first World War.
>
> Chapter 2: The town and the Jewish community between the two World Wars, the economic and cultural existence. A sub-chapter on Personalities and Images.
>
> Chapter 3: Novogrudok as portrayed in the literature.
>
> Chapter 4: Novogrudok during the slaughters under the rule of the evil beings and their helpers.

In each chapter there are literary works, both poetry and prose. And there are many photos.

At the end is a section "Yohrzeit Candles"

With much hesitation and uncertainty we are putting this volume into the hands of the readers in Israel and in all lands where our townsmen are now living. Our prayer is that the Pinkas should exist in our and our children's hearts and it should remind us of our holy martyrs.

V'iscadal and hiscadash.

We finish the prologue to this volume with the names of two of our dear collaborators, who passed on: Edna Kagan, the dear and devoted lady who dedicated the last years of her life to collect material for the Pinkas and was a shining example to us all; Dr Eliezer Yerushalmi, who spent his youth in Novogrudok and who drew his inspiration from his memories of the town. He did his editorial work tirelessly. Both have not lived to see the Pinkas finished and in the hands of the readers. Let their names and our memories of them be ever parts of our existence.

The Editorial Committee.

[The task of translating of Pinkas Novogrudok turned out to be much more complex than could be imagined when the task has began. It would have been impossible to get anywhere without dedicated help from many quarters. Let me mention just a few:

A great deal of immaculate work was put in by Freda Salter. I could not thank her enough.

Aviva Kamil translated all Hebrew articles and did more besides. Many thanks, Aviva.

My wife Jeanette read and helped to correct every word in every article. She is best at finding the right word when all dictionaries failed. I will be forever grateful.

Minia Lipkes helped a lot, particularly with articles on religious themes.

My brother Jack was of much help. He remembers the past much clearer than most people I know.

Jack Charney, who remembers every man and every house of Novogrudok between the wars, was an inspiration.

I could go on and on... O.D.

[Page 11]

History of the City

The History of the Jews of Novogudok

by Yaakov Goldberg

Translated from Hebrew by Aviva Kamil

Novogrudok was situated in the Great Duchy of Lithuania and after the Polish-Lithuanian union it was under the rule of Poland.

Novogrudok was established around 1116 CE by the Galich-Volhynian principality and in the middle of the XIIIth century, as a result of a few small wars, came under the rule of Lithuania. A number of historians consider that the town was founded in 1044 by Yaroslav the Wise, a Kievien Prince, who was, at the time, on a military expedition in the region. Other historians, the best known among them was Narbutt, name Yaropolk, the son of the famed Kievien Prince Vladimir Monomach, as the founder of Novogrudok in 1116. Other dates and name have also been mentioned. The evidence obtained by the archaeological expedition of F. D. Gurevich (1957-1984) shows that there was a settlement where Novogrudok now stands, at the end of the Xth century and a town with a citadel on the Zamok mound 50 years later. This evidence would support 1044 as the likely date the Novogrudok citadel was built. Who was the founder of the town has not been established beyond doubt. How Novogrudok came to be ruled in the XIIIth century by the Lithuanian Prince Mindovg (d. 1263) is also subject to many interpretations]

The language and culture of the inhabitants were preserved and to a great extent were adopted by the conquering Lithuanians. On arriving, the Jews took up the language of the local population, so that to the end of the XVIIIth century their common tongue was Belorussian. After the union of Krewo in 1385, two districts were established in Lithuania with administrations located in Vilno and Troki. Novogrudok was in the Vilno district, but the association with Vilno's governing body was weak. In 1569 the alliance between Lithuania and Poland was strengthened by the union of Lublin.

The new district of Novogrudok included the towns of: Slonim, Kletsk, Volkovysk and the principality of Slutsk.

The administrative arrangement, which was instituted in the XVIth century, lasted until 1795, i.e., until the third and final partition of the Polish State by Russia, Prussia and Austria. In the second partition, in

1793, Russia occupied the eastern part of the district of Novogrudok with the town Nesvizh.

The district of Novogrudok was re-established after World WarI, when Poland regained its independence.

Novogrudok was an important town in the old days of the Polish State. Bi-annual sittings of the high court of the Great Duchy of Lithuanian took place there since 1581 [on alternate years it sat in Minsk]. But Vilno was, of course, the permanent location of all the high offices. The sittings of the Tribunal were of great importance to the Jewish community. Its leaders took part in the deliberations, which concerned not only local matters.

In 1775 the seat of the tribunal was transferred to Grodno. It happened, most likely, because Grodno was the center of the political life in those days. but that change occurred towards the end of the existence [of Poland and] the tribunal. Novogrudok was host to the Lithuanian tribunal for 200 years. Novogrudok retained local courts.

The sources of information about the Jews in Novogrudok are very limited, therefore we'll deal with only a few aspects of the Jewish life there.

The concentration of Jews in the eastern part of the Great Duchy of Lithuanian started in the XVIth century. They arrived mainly from the Jewish communities of Brest, Grodno and Pinsk and fewer came from other parts of Polese and from Volhyn.

At the same time Jews from Belorussia were also arriving in Novogrudok. The reason for that movement was economic.

In the XVth-XVIth centuries the Jews of Novogrudok earned their livelihood working for the government, [collecting] taxes and custom duties].

For a long period Russian Jews were not allowed by law to be traders.

Novogrudok was not situated on the main trading routes of the country. The trade routes from Krakov and Warsaw went through Minsk. Two routes led from Grodno to Smolensk, one through Vilna and the other through Novogrudok and Minsk.

This is the reason why towns such as Pinsk, Troki or Brest attracted more Jews.

All matters of collection of taxes and customs in the Lithuanian Duchy were in the hands of Jews. One of them, the well-known and wealthy Michael Aspovich was a favorite of King Zigmunt the Old (1506-1548), who bestowed on him in 1507 a high title [knighthood]. It was the only known case of such a title having been awarded to a Jew. Aspovich's brother, who was also awarded that title, was a convert.

In 1514 the King appointed Michael Aspovich to be head of the Jewish community of Lithuania. Other Jews, who were also collecting taxes, were: Agron Mehaimovich, Isak Pashovich and Shachna Golevich. It is not clear if they were living in Novogrudok, but they must have spent a lot of time there, as did Michael Aspovich, who, because of his connections, was able to help other Jews, like the people mentioned above, to earn their livelihood in Novogrudok.

There are indications that the Jewish community started to grow in 1529 with the help of Aspovich. In a governmental document of the Great Duchy of Lithuanian, dated 1529, a few towns, with Jewish populations are listed: Novogrudok, Brest, Grodno, Slutsk, Machislav (?), Pinsk, Slonim, Troki, Tichotin, Lachovich and Vladimir. Our information of the events in the XVIth century is limited only to Novogrudok. The sources are trade documents and court cases. The size of the businesses in Novogrudok was smaller than that of the Slutsk and Vladimir, but was greater than the businesses of the Vitebsk Jews.

Novogrudok Jews traded mainly with Lublin, where they were supplying furs, honey, fish, milk and the like. Some Jewish names started to appear in the documents of 1540. One Jew, for example, Yeheskiel Shmoilovich sued Mosihek Itzkovich, whom he accused of breaking a trade agreement. In the first few decades the economic status of the Jews improved and thus grew their importance in Lithuania. Of course they sometimes had disputes and quarrels with their Christian neighbors, and some serious clashes occurred with the "Shlachta" [landed gentry]. One of these erupted in 1551. Two Christians, Ivan Kmiticz Stratovicz and Lukasz Stanislavovicz Drabski blamed the Jew Yankl Pashovich of arranging burglaries. They were two of his victims [they claimed]. Yankl Pashovich defended himself vigorously and sued them for libel. The accusers did not appear in court and Yankl Pashovich was awarded a sum of money for the libel. Monetary compensation was an accepted method [of redress] and it was paid in accordance with the person's status, Jewish peasants were low on that scale. Yankl Pashovich did not take the money and was satisfied that he was cleared of the charge. It could be that fear prevented him from taking the money or that the sum of money offered was only nominal. As far as we know there were not many occurrences such as this.

Quarrels and disputes with the common people were prevalent. In 1559 a dispute broke out between the local governing body and Yaakov Yehilevich from Brest and Nisan Haimovich from Grodno, who leased the breweries at Novogrudok. The local people maintained that the local brewery should be leased to local people, for that was their right. They presented their case to the King and lost. The king's council decided that there were no privileges in that matter. But there was another case in 1568, when the Jew Nathan Nairovich from Grodno sued two citizens of Novogrudok for beating and injuring him. He thought that the witness, who was one of the gentry, would assist him at the trial, but he did not appear. The court found against him.

There were disputes between the Orthodox Church and the Jews in the first century of Jewish settlement in Novogrudok [the Jewish settlement in Novogrudok had probably begun first in the XI or XII century, when such disputes were unlikely]. Those were individual disputes [as opposed to clashes between communities]. In the courts Jews had to swear on the Bible. As it happened, in 1541, the head of the Orthodox Church refused to accept the oath of a Jew named Metatshiz. The Jew complained to queen Bona. The outcome [of the case] is unknown to us. Disputes and antagonism spread. In 1567, the plebeian Franciszek Kasziszovski (?) from Novogrudok attacked the house of Shaya Lazerovich wounding him and his wife and robbing them of their valuables. The situation of the Jews in Lithuania was fair, in comparison to the situation in the Polish ethnographical areas, but it was fast deteriorating. There were persecutions of the Jews as a whole. The locals wanted to limit the number of Jews in Novogrudok. They wanted them out of the center of town, so that they would not be a competing with the local Christian traders.

On the 30th of September 1563 a delegation of the locals to King Zigmunt [Sigismond] August obtained a special order from him to create a Jewish Ghetto in Novogrudok. The King appointed the governor of the district Pavel Spieha [one of the nobility] to execute the order, and he in turn appointed another aristocrat Bogdan Spieha as a special town supervisor. The latter, with the help of the locals, decided which streets to allocate to Jews. The King's order was that the Jews should live in separate streets, which he named. It is hard to identify now the streets of XVIth century Novogrudok. They carried the names of towns in Lithuania which they led to. [pre 1939-45 war most streets which radiated from the central market square carried the names of the towns they led to and some of the streets retained these names to this day, e.g., Grodienskaya, Minskaya]. The order also marked the topographical position of the streets Jews had to live in. By that order, they had to move from the center of town, even if they owned houses there, and relocate outside of the citadel.

Despite the expulsion order the Jews stayed put. The Christian residents obtained a second order [a year after the original order]. They insisted on severe sanctions for the disobedience and for staying in the houses in Podolska Street. An official was appointed, from the Byelorussia aristocracy, Jan Jorvich Bogomatka. He was instructed to destroy every house that owners refuse to vacate. Christian citizens also demanded a high penalty: 1600 gold ducats. They considered Jewish houses on Podolska Street an affront to their sovereignty. The Christian residents needed some documents to attain their aim, but they did not have any. The Jews of Novogrudok did not accept the order to create a Ghetto. They turned to the crown court in Warsaw and presented a claim against the local government in Novogrudok, which wanted to oust them from Podolska Street. The crown court was a King's chamber, which dealt with matters relating to the King's towns as opposed to privately owned towns [owned by the landed gentry and the church]. The Warsaw court favored the King's towns. The same court found in favor of the Jews when the brewery dispute occurred, and the Novogrudok Jews turned to it again with the Ghetto order. The procedure this time was much more difficult and expensive, authorized people had to be sent time and again to court sessions in Warsaw. The representatives were chosen: Mandel Gershonovich, Shmuel Mandelevich, Lazer Shmuelevich and Yankl Pashovich. The date of the hearing was the 25th of November 1564. Because of hardship on the way, the fear of robbers and Polish soldiers, who did not hesitate to rob too, the representatives arrived very late. The court ruled in favor of the Christian residents, it ruled that the Jews had no right to live in Podolska Street and ordered them to relinquish their homes and gardens to the Christians. The court based its judgment on the fact that the representatives did not bring any documents with them to prove their ownership. The reason the Jews did not bring the documents was the fear of being robbed of them, as events like that were a common occurrence in those days, especially by their litigants, who wanted to rob them of proof. The outcome of the dispute is not known, but it must have finished in favor of the Jews because, as we know, they went on living in Podolska Street. It was by no means the end to their troubles. When the Christian residents could not remove the Jews from favorable locations in the town, they tried to limit their commercial activities. In 1598 they forbade the Jews to sell meat at the market and so on, but the Jews persisted and succeeded. The Jews in Novogrudok fought for their right of residence and trade. It is a pity that not much information is left about the first century of Jewish existence in Novogrudok [but see note above]. We don't know much about their struggle to survive.

With the establishment of a Jewish autonomy and the Committee of the Lithuanian Jews in the Polish State, the Jewish leadership was resident in Brest. There was always a close relationship between the Jews of Novogrudok and Brest and it lasted until the termination of the autonomy in 1765. The nature of the relationship was in matters of tradition and religion. "The Answers" by Rabbi Shlomo Luria [16th century] deserves a special mention. Rabbi Luria settled in Brest and then moved to Lublin. He discussed many problems in his "answers."

He mentions the small young Jewish community of Novogrudok and deals with an incident when a Jewish man insulted a Jewish woman because she refused his invitation to dance with him and so on. The Renaissance reached Poland and Lithuania and influenced the Jews there to a certain degree. They knew of light entertainment such as games and dance and cultural performances were not rare events in their community.

It is impossible to find out the exact number of Jews in Novogrudok in the XVIth, XVIIth and XVIIIth centuries, but by comparing the taxes in certain towns we can conclude that the Jewish population was small. The Jews in the Great Duchy of Lithuania had to pay tax of 4000 "kopas" groshes in 1563. Of that sum the Jews of Pinsk had to pay 600 "kopas", Slutsk only 15 and Novogrudok not much more then 30 "kopas" groshes, [kopa means 60 in polish].

In 1765 the number of Jews in the whole of the Grand Duchy was approximately 12,030. Their number in Novogrudok is unknown. We can assume that judging by the number of people and houses it was an average size town. The earliest statistics we have are for 1790. We know that in Novogrudok there were 394 buildings and approximately 3000 residents. In that year there were in the towns of that district 8932 houses, of which 2401 belonged to Jews, which is 27% of the real estate in the towns of that district. At that time there were 1424 buildings in Vilna, 1108 in Grodno and 602 in Brest. Novogrudok was the fourth in size [in the Great Duchy of Lithuania], and a large part of the population was Jewish. In the first hundred years they managed to achieve some sort of stability, but disasters struck in the first half of the 17th century, when fire, robbery by soldiers, and the plague of 1630 took many Jewish lives. Twenty years later a huge fire destroyed a great part of the city, the town hall, churches, shops and residential houses went up in flames. The market place burnt down and, as Jews lived around it and traded there, we can assume that they suffered greatly as a result of the fire.

Another shock came when the Swedes attacked the Polish State. The Swedes did not conquer Novogrudok, but as a result of the Polish-Russian war of 1655 the Russians invaded Novogrudok and looted it. In 1659 the Polish army under the command of hetman Pavel Spieha retrieved the area. A year later the Russians invaded Novogrudok again under the command of Prince Chubanski, who stayed there until June 1660. Then the Prince, before leaving, appointed a governor and gave a clear instruction to the soldiers to treat the population well. But to no avail, they kept on robbing people. After a few months the Polish army returned under the command of the same hetman Spieha and the famous Polish commander Stefan Czarniecki. The situation did not improve, as far as we can tell the opposite happened.

The Polish army and its commanders considered themselves the defenders of their faith, Catholicism. They fought the Protestants and Swedes but the Jews were their first victims. So we can assume that the fate of the Jews in Novogrudok was not different to the fate of Jews in other Polish places.

The disasters of the XVIIth century, being so numerous, retarded the recovery rate. As a result, the Polish Sejm issued in 1676 a special law for the towns Novogrudok, Lida and Orsha. Part of it was that in order to assist the recovery of these towns all the residents were exempt from a number of duties including the support of the army [Magdeburg law]. Many Russian towns and villages were granted similar exemptions. The first time Novogrudok received such a benefit was by the 1652 law passed by the Sejm. They were given relief because of the great fire of 1650. Generally these laws were not for the Jews, but those exemptions would indicate that the Jews suffered great loses in the second half of the XVIIth century. They could not repay their loans and taxes. Cases were brought before the Tribunal of the Great Duchy of Lithuania, which sat at Minsk, Vilno and Novogrudok. In the years 1670-1699 one of the landed gentry Yozef Brzozovski sued Baruch Smuelevich, Shimon Tubishovich, Hanan Yudkovich, Laib Haimovich, Abraham Movshovich and Yosef Robinovich, the Jewish community representatives, because he claimed that the community owed him the large sum of 1490 zloty.

Those sued never replied to the court order and never appeared before it. By doing so they hoped to postpone the time of payment of the money they did not have and would be forced to pay it by any means. Being in debt was a common occurrence in Jewish communities in Poland of the XVIIIth century. And it was no different in Novogrudok. The Jews protested against all sorts of taxes that were imposed on them. In 1702, after the Swedes conquered Vilno, the governing body tried to bring back the taxation system that existed before the exemption given in 1676 [Magdeburg law]. A tax collector from Minsk by the name of Damien Shishko sued a number of Jewish merchants from the Great Duchy of Lithuania for not paying their taxes. From the Jews of Novogrudok he asked 365 zloty. The Jews based their opposition to it on the rule of the Sejm, which released them from the payment of that tax in 1676. In the XVIIth century there were also times when the Jews set out to protect their interests even by using force. In 1667 the residents of the town--Aaron Gushkovich, Yuchel Izraelovich, Shlomo Pashovich and Izik Shlomovich--attacked on a market day the servant of the aristocrat Azrovich, took his horses and a certain sum of money. It's possible that it was their only way to get back whatever the Count owed them and was reluctant to pay. Anyway this little story tells us that some Jews were far from being obedient and ready to surrender. The Jews could not only present themselves well at the courts but also, in certain instances, could use force.

Through the age of the Reformation, in the second half of the XVIIIth century, the persecution of the Jews intensified in Novogrudok. A committee of Poles and Lithuanians--"a police committee of two nations"--took care of Jewish affairs. Its task was to protect the King's towns.

In 1792 Jewish representatives brought a complaint to the attention of that committee. They asked for justice to be done in their quarrels with the Christian communities of Novogrudok, Grodno, Shavli and other cities. There are no historical documents to find out the grounds for those disputes, but it is possible to deduce that the Christians wanted the Jews debarred from commerce.

Events like that happened everywhere and they were discussed in high places and echoed in the Polish papers of those days. The central Jewish Autonomy ceased to exist, but a few chosen representatives [from Novogrudok too] dealt with the problems of the Jewish community.

In the XVIth century Jews looked for protection of the court and King. But in the late XVIIIth century they appeared as a unified body and asked for recognition and justice. At that time something else arose in Novogrudok, which had no precedent in any other town in Poland or even Europe. It was the financing of the army by the Jews. The first laws and privileges given to the Jews spoke about the Jews financing the army [a certain numbers of soldiers]. Prince Aleksander Jagiellonczyk in the second half of the XVth century ordered the Jews to finance 1000 horsemen, but he cancelled it. By the order of King Zigmunt [Sigismond] the Old in 1514, the Jews, like anyone else, had to provide accommodation etc as long as the army was in town. The situation changed completely in the 80s and 90s of the eiighteenth century. Conscription was introduced for young people from villages and state towns [to differentiate them from privately owned towns?]. In Novogrudok most of the households belonging to the landed gentry or to Jews and so the people residing in them were not subject to the conscription law. The town council turned to the police and they decided that every household should be subject to conscription. Therefore, the Jews also had to provide their quota of conscripts. That made them, as far as we know, the only Jewish conscripts in the State of Poland. But the conscription of Jews was not executed after all.

After a few months there was a change of rules - at the Confederation of Targowica (14 May 1792) they decided to reduce the size of the army. [The pro-Russian Confederation of Targowica was formed with the support of the conservative gentry and with the connivance of the

Empress Catherine of Russia. They opposed the Polish constitution of 1791 {the 3rd of May constitution}. After the invasion of Poland by Russian troops {May 1792} and the installation of a Russian client regime {July 1792} – the Confederation of Targowica – many opponents of the invasion fled abroad.]

Relations in the feudal Republic endangered the Jews, who were threatened by the locals, but they could cope with them. But aristocracy was a different matter: difficult to stand up to because of their power and wealth.

The Jewish merchants in Novogrudok were in close contact with the court of the Princes Radziwill; they did business with them since the days of old. In Novogrudok, their main supplier at the beginning of the XIXth century was a Jew by the name of Kalman Movtovich. In this town like in other state towns an enclave was created [a special area in the town which belonged to Prince Radziwill with rules of its own, not under the jurisdiction of the local municipality]. It was called "Radziwillian juridical."

The area behind the castle [zamek] was the one, which in the XVIIth century they wanted to turn into a Jewish quarter. It was a "juridical" too, but by the rule issued by the Sejm in 1641 it became part of the municipality.

The Radziwills had "juridicas" in Vilno, Grodno, Minsk and Brest. Large concentrations of Jews were found in towns, which were owned by the Radziwills such as: Nieswiez, Slutsk, Korelicze and more. Some Jews lived in the "juridical" of Novogrudok; they paid taxes and enjoyed the protection of the Princes. In that "juridica" was a street called Korelicka, which lead to Korelicze, a town which belonged to the Radziwills and was famous for its textile industry. Included in the "juridica" were the streets Podlaska and Kowalska [one of them was called in the XXth century Troitzka (?)]. At the beginning of the XIXth century the streets Korelicka and Sieniezycka were part of the "juridical."

In the fourth decade of the XIXth century the "juridica" passed from the hand of the Radziwills to Prince Wittgenstein.

The "great sejm" in its sessions between the years 1788-1792 cancelled all the "juridicas" in the Polish Republic, but the one in Novogrudok existed until the mid-XIXth century.

After the division of Poland, when Novogrudok was under Russian rule, the "juridica" still existed under the ownership of that powerful family. The administration did not act against them, and even awarded some of them titles in the court of the Russian Tsar.

The "juridica" was only cancelled in 1861. The Radziwills protected the Jews in their "juridical." In the second half of the XVIIth century, the army tried to settle in houses in the "juridical." The Radziwills interfered and the commanders responsible to that deed were punished severely. Incidents like these occurred mainly under the rule of the King Ian Sobieski III in years 1678-1679.

A table of the number of Jewish and Christian families who resided in the Radziwill "juridica" between the years 1759-1859.

Year	Christian families	Jewish families	Year	Christian families	Jewish families
1759	5	13	1805	5	11
1771	6	9	1806	11	8
1778	7	8	1834	3	9
1781	9	6	1851	3	8
1782	8	6	1859	3	9

The "juridica" families, Jews and Christians, paid special taxes to the Prince, but were exempt from any other taxes that the other town residents had to pay. They were freed from serfdom by paying the Prince a certain sum of money.

As a rule the Jews paid higher taxes then the Christians. In 1702 they presented a complaint to the Prince and asked him to lighten their load.

For a few years, in the second half of the XIXth century, they did not pay duty.

With the passing of the "juridica" into the hands of Prince Wittgenstein, the Jews tried to change the assessment of their duty payments because the existing tax was far beyond their capacity to pay. Most of the Jews who resided in the town in the XVIIIth and XIXth centuries were poor and the taxes that they paid to the Radziwill and the Wittgenstein administrations made them even poorer.

Some Jews managed inns and sold brandy. It was a common occupation in the Polish Republic.

The Jews, sometimes, had disputes among themselves in the "juridical," and on different occasions it attracted the attention of the clerks at Prince Wittgenstein administration. One such dispute broke out in 1842, between two residents, Movsha Murdoch and Nochim Izraelovich. The former was an owner of a house in Troitzka Street. He received permission from the management of the Prince's estate to buy another lot of land in the same street. But his rival Nochim Izraelovich protested and complained to the Prince's representatives, they in turn advised the management: "As it is known from here and there that Movsha Morduch is in dispute with Nochim Izraelovich who owns an inn and accommodation which borders with the above mentioned lot, it is worthwhile to attract attention to the matter that by giving permission to buy an allotment of land—not to give the nearby residents a just reason to complain." It was typical of the "juridica" owners always to try to solve their residents' problems on their own; they did not want outside interference.

Apart from the closed area of the "juridica" there is in Novogrudok the old palace of the Radziwills which lost its importance in the end of the XVIIIth century, which was due to the political activities of Prince Karol Radziwill, who was nicknamed "panie kochanku" [my beloved sir], which was his manner of addressing all and sundry. [The Confederation of Bar formed in Feb. 29, 1768, was a league of Polish nobles and gentry that was formed to defend the privileges of the Roman Catholic church and the independence of Poland from Russian encroachment. Its activities precipitated a civil war, foreign intervention, and the First Partition of Poland. Prince Karol Radziwill was one of the ardent supporters of the Confederation.] He stayed after the fall of the Confederation of Bar (1772) outside the country as a political refugee.

In his absence the palace fell into ruin. The Prince was an eccentric. He was light hearted with all people: peasants, Jews and the town residents. Shlomo Maimon, the known Jewish philosopher, who stemmed from the estate of the Radziwills near Niesviez, said that in spite of his unusual character [or perhaps, because of it] he did not show any hatred towards the Jews. At one time there was a Jew who was the manager of the palace and he lived there with his family. It was at the beginning of the XVIIIth century. The palace bordered with the town hall and with the wall of the Dominican church.

The irony is that in 1808 two Jews of Novogrudok, David Ariovich and Ale Laibovich bought the ruined palace from the Radziwills and used its bricks to build new Jewish houses.

In the first half of the XIXth century the places of abode of the Jews changed. Between the XVIIth and XIXth centuries most of them were concentrated in the market square. In the XIXth century they concentrated in the Jewish street and Volevska Street . In the writings of I. Yatskovski we read: "In the mid XIXth century one came to Novogrudok and climbed up the streets to the center of town. The town was built on a mountain, on top of which there was a great flat area called The Market Square. On the square were built diagonally two rows of Jewish shops. It reminded one of the time when 'bnei dat Moshe' [sons of the Moses] crossed 'yam-suf' [the Red Sea] and erected their tents."

The houses on the Market Square belonged to well established Christian residents and the town officials.

In the second half of the XVIIIth c. the economic importance of Novogrudok diminished because of its unfavorable geographic position.

In 1881 there were in Novogrudok three small breweries, beehives and a factory making bricks and ceramic, which employed altogether a few dozen people. A few things hindered development: shortage of water, few connecting routes and an undeveloped local market.

Export to great Russia was in the hands of other industrial towns, so a large part of the Jewish population was in small trade and craft. In Novogrudok, development was minimal in the last century. The population did grow, but it was considered to be an average town in the Lithuanian-Byelorussian region.

In the first half of the XIXth century the Jewish population suffered most from the hands of the soldiers of the Russian army that camped there. They found a special enjoyment in taunting the Jews. Many Jews sympathized with the Polish liberation movement. One of them called Perez was sentenced to prison in 1863 for helping a known commander from the days of the uprising of January 1863, Vitold Mildovski, to escape.

It is hard to assess how the "Hasidut" and "Haskala" influenced the Jewish community in Novogrudok, though they were not far from the center of those movements. The strong political and social trends among the Jews of Novogrudok in the XXth century was inspired by centuries of struggle and fight for their livelihood and existence. Theirs was a life of tradition and culture, which is no more.

With their lives, most sources about their past were destroyed too, and it is impossible to believe that they are lost.

The ruins of the Zamok (citadel)

History of the town

Translated from Yiddish by O. Delatycki

The town of Novogrudok is the capital of the sub-district (uiezd) Novogrudok and was before the First World War part of the Minsk gubernia. The town is situated 143 km southwest of Minsk, close by a small stream, which flows into the river Neman. Novogrudok is surrounded by many well-known towns and townships. North of Novogrudok, at the same distance as from Minsk, is Vilno. Novogrudok is situated on a mountain. Within the city there is a mound, the Zamok, which was thought to have been erected, but it looks as if it is natural [it is natural, though the ravine around it was probably dug out]. The nature around this mountain is very beautiful, particularly in the summer, when the trees and fields around present a splendid vista. Around the fields is a dark ring of pine forests which is miles wide. A large part of the town is located in the valleys, such as the historical Rachelo. It is said that there the Grand Prince of Lithuania Mindog [Mindaugas] was crowned as the king of Lithuania. He obtained the title from the Pope, because he had converted to Catholicism. Mindog was the first ruler of Lithuania and Novogrudok was its first capital.

In the center of Novogrudok is a big market square, from which radiate the main streets of the town. In the center of the square is "the row of shops" built in a very nice style [actually a long rectangle, with a plurality of small shops arranged on all four sides]. The houses around the square are the nicest buildings in town.

The remarkable monuments of the town are: the Zamok [citadel] mound with the ruin of the citadel of the ancient Lithuanian princes, old Jewish memorials include the old synagogue which was built in a pleasing style, the Mohammedan mosque on Valiker Street, two Russian churches, one of which, named Borysoglebski, is very old [XII century], two Catholic churches, of which the Fara (parish church) is very old and well known. There is also the house in which the great Polish poet Adam Mickiewicz was born and brought up [Mickiewicz was born in the family estate in Zaosie].

The climate of the Novogrudok area is moderate in summer and cold in winter. The air is dry and clear. Around the town springs abound, which provide good quality water. Particularly good and healthy is the water from Brichinke [Brecianka], which was used for cooking and making tea in samovars.

Economically Novogrudok was dependent on the farming population. Mondays and Thursdays were market days and several times a year there were large fairs: in January and March as well as in the summer before the harvest. The merchants of Novogrudok obtained their wares from Vilno and Warsaw [and many other centers, notably Lodz and Bialystok].

Novogrudok was the cultural center of the surrounding district. The high school was established in the distant past and there was a good library, which was taken over by the Jewish community after the First World War. Since then the library distinguished itself as a source of excellent books.

The population of Novogrudok consisted of Jews, Belorussians, Poles and Tatars and in the past Karaites. In 1888 the population of Novogrudok was about 12,000, of which there were 8,270 Jews, 2,200 Poles, 470 Belorussians, and 1,160 Tatars.

By the year 1897 the number of Jews was reduced to 7887. From then on the Jewish population of Novogrudok continued to decline. Before the First World War there were 5000 Jews in Novogrudok. The immigration to the United States and Western Europe had attracted a large proportion of young Jews.

This was the appearance of Novogrudok

The market place

The founding of the town

Novogrudok is a very old town. It existed in the XII century. It has not been determined when the town was founded, but it is assumed that one of the Kievian princes established it. It may have been Yaroslav the Wise, who built a fortress to defend the borders from the Yatviags, a bloodthirsty and savage tribe, which was threatening to overrun the whole region. [The history of Novogrudok is now better known due to the discoveries of the archaeological expedition of F. D. Gurevich, which worked in Novogrudok for 25 summers after the II World War. In the late X century there was a settlement on the site of Novogrudok. Yaroslav the Wise may have been in Novogrudok. About that time - middle of the XI century - the Zamok mound was fortified by a bank. Some historians consider it the beginning of the town of Novogrudok, as opposed to the early settlement.] The history of Novogrudok in the era of the Galich Volhynian prince Daniel Romanovich and the Lithuanian prince Mindog, who had converted to Catholicism and was crowned as king of Lithuania by the papal Nuncio, is better known. Mindog had given the town to his son Voisalk. In the year 1277 the Galich Volhynians with the help of the Tatars had tried to take Novogrudok from Lithuania. The siege ended with the Tatars burning the town and killing the inhabitants. [The Zamok, where the inhabitants took refuge, was not taken by the invaders]. Since that time, under the Grand Prince Gedimin [1315-1340], [who moved the capital of Lithuania from Novogrudok to Vilno] Novogrudok was again in the possession of Lithuania, which was governed by Gedimin's children and grandchildren, who were orthodox and russified.

In the year 1314 the Grand Master of Prussia's Teutonic order Hinrich von Plozke had attacked Lithuania and Belorussia. He captured and burned Novogrudok, but the population of the town fled to the citadel, where they defended themselves and repulsed all attacks. Later they emerged from the citadel, expelled the Teutonic invaders and pushed them back to the river Neman, where they defeated the aggressors. The Teutonic knights retreated in disorder to their country, having lost on the way many warriors due to hunger and sickness.

In the year 1323 the Lithuanian Grand Duke Gedimin had granted the Franciscan order a large property in Novogrudok. The order built a monastery, which spread Catholicism in the district.

At the end of the 14-century Novogrudok had became part of the Grand Duchy of Lithuania governed by Witold [Vytautas] the Great. The next ruler was the Grand Duke Jagello, who later became the king of Poland.

The market from the east side

In the year 1394 Novogrudok was attacked again by the Teutonic knights. The town was burned down, but the attacker could not retain it and had to retreat to Drohichin. In 1451 Witold rebuilt Novogrudok.

In the same year the orthodox Patriarch had called a consistory in Novogrudok of all the elders of the churches of Russia, among whom were the bishops of Chernigov, Polock, Luck, Chelm, Vladimir, Smolensk, Tchervensk and Turov. At the consistory the metropolit of Kiev was elected. He resided in both Kiev and Novogrudok. From that time Novogrudok had become the seat of the Kiev metropolit and the center of the orthodox church of all Russia and the Ukraine.

Large festivals took place in Novogrudok. In the year 1422 the fourth son of the Polish King Jagello married a Holshtin princess. The wedding was celebrated in Novogrudok. [On the wall of the Fara church in Novogrudok a plaque reads that in 1422 king Wladyslaw Jagello (and not his son) married (his fourth wife) Zofia, princes of Holsztyn. The marriage produced the Polish kings Wladyslaw Warnenczyk and Kazimerz Jagellonczyk, who in tern produced a line of Polish and other kings.] In 1426 the Grand Duke Witold had a great victory over the Russians and celebrated his success in Novogrudok.

In the year 1444 the king of Poland and the Grand Duke of Lithuania Casimir had bestowed on Novogrudok the Magdeburg rights (this was the name of the privilege which bestowed on a town the right of self-government with an elected mayor and city council, with its own police force and court). The Magdeburg rights had released the inhabitants from the duty to perform physical work for the king and pay taxes, which the peasants were obliged to do. Magdeburg is the name of a German town. Its laws set an example for all laws in Europe. The Polish nobility, who were opposed to the extension of any rights to the inhabitants, had protested at the Lublin sejm which sat in 1447, against the extension of any benefits granted to the city of Novogrudok. In answer to this protest the King had recalled the Lithuanian sejm in Novogrudok and confirmed the granting of the privileges.

The above-mentioned session of the Lithuanian sejm was not unique, it was sitting frequently in Novogrudok. One such sitting occurred in 1537. At the same time the Polish sejm was sitting in Lwow (Lemberg). In the year 1581, King Stefan Batory had convened the highest tribunal in Lithuania. He conducted the sittings alternately in Novogrudok and Minsk. The archives of the tribunal were kept in Novogrudok.

In January 1638 the archives were granted a special constitution. A high official was appointed to look after the archives. At the same time in the Franciscan monastery in Novogrudok an archive of the Catholic Church was founded. In the year 1662 the Tsarist army under the command of Prince Trubeckoy occupied Novogrudok. On the 1 May 1751 a large fire enveloped Novogrudok. 67 homes were destroyed as well as the building of the archives. In 1776 the remains of the archives were transferred to Grodno. In the year 1676 king Jan Sobieski granted the city of Novogrudok the following privileges:

1. It was exempt from the duty to provide quarters for the king's army.

2. It was given the privilege of a free town (it would appear that the Magdeburg rights granted by King Casimir in the year 1444 and

confirmed by Zygmund the Old in 1511, had in time been abolished or were reduced and Jan Sobieski had renewed this privilege).

The old synagogue

The bimah in the old synagogue

In the XVII century Novogrudok had eight Catholic and Orthodox churches. Among them were two monasteries, a Franciscan and a Dominican one. There was an Orthodox monastery in the vicinity of Novogrudok, which was built on land granted by the commanding officer of the Lithuanian forces, Hetman Constantin Ostrogski, in Bykowicze of the Tsyrin sub-district. The monastery was called Borysoglebsk and was in existence until the year 1830.

Under the Polish rule, Novogrudok was the capital of the Novogrudok wojewodstwo. Under Russian rule Novogrudok was degraded to a powiat town, but even then it was one of the biggest powiats in Tsarist Russia. According to the census of 1897 the population of the Novogrudok sub-district was 247,000 of which there were 30,043 Jews. In that census the following figures were obtained for the population in the towns of the Novogrudok sub-district listed below:

Shtetl	Population	Jewish population
Novogrudok	7.887	5.015
Lubcha	3.374	2.463
Stolovichi	929	515
Vselub	1.306	645
Goradzeya	754	668
Goradzishcha	2.631	2.108
Deliatichi	1.439	461
Yaremichi	865	258
Korelichi	2.559	1.840
Kroshin, Yurzdyka, Scheda	966	151
Mir	5.401	3.319
Mysh Novaya	2.995	1.764
Nechnevichi	610	276
Polonka	645	549
Rozvodava	4.692	2.171
Snov	707	526
Strelova	529	66
Turets	1.616	737
Tsyryn	649	144

In total the population in the towns (not counting Novogrudok) amounted to 32, 657. This included 18,658 Jews, which is over 60% percent of the total population. In fact the towns and townships were totally Jewish, since the non-Jewish population was engaged largely in agriculture such as gardening, dairy, chicken farming, and fruit production. Other tasks in the towns were only performed occasionally.

The Jewish town councils (kehila)

The kehila in Novogrudok was one of the oldest in Lithuania. A Jewish institution in Novogrudok is mentioned first in a document in 1484, when the Polish King Casimir Jagellon leased the customs duties of the town to Ilia Moiseyevich, Rubim Sakovich, Avram Danilovich, and Eska Shelemovich, Jews of Troki. Novogrudok is mentioned in two documents of 1529. On Jan. 21 of that year the Jews there, with those in other Lithuanian towns, were made subject to the payment of a special military tax. On March 4, of the same year, King Sigismund ordered the wojewoda of Novogrudok to render all necessary aid to the collector of taxes, Michael Jesofovich, in the collection of customs duties throughout the whole district. In a document of 1531, Novogrudok is mentioned among the cities which were exempted from the payment of the special tax called the 'serebschizna' (tax on silver). In 1551 the Jew Jankel Pejsachovich from Novogrudok was sentenced for having been accused slanderously by a landholder Kmitich. His case was dealt later in the crown court which set him free. From another source we learn that the above named Jankel Pejsachovich was the tax collector of Novogrudok and the district. He was also one of the eminent members of the Jewish community in Novogrudok.

In the year 1559 the king Sigismund August had ordered the city authorities not to place obstacles in the way of the Jewish leaseholders Jacob Ikhelovich of Brest-Litovsk and Nissan Khaimovich of Grodno in their work of collecting custom duties.

In the year 1563 the Jewish kehila is mentioned in a list of the towns of the Brest district, which payed the 'head' tax. The tax was 30x60 groshes. In the same year Grodno paid 200x60 groshes, Pinsk 600x60 groshes that is Pinsk paid 20 times more tax than Novogrudok. At that time 12,00 Jews were paying head tax in the Pinsk district. We must assume, therefore that there were 20 times more Jews living in Pinsk than in Novogrudok. It follows that at the time there were 500-600 Jewish taxpayers in Novogrudok.

In the year 1665, i.e. a hundred years later, there were in Novogrudok and district 12,031 taxpayers. In the town there were 893 taxpayers. It would seem that in the 100 years the Jewish population of Novogrudok had grown a little. Until the year 1563 the Jews lived in

Novogrudok among the Christian population that is in the Podlasie Street. But on the 30 September 1563 king Sigismund August announced to the head of the sub-district, the mayor of the town and the members of the city council that he ordered the kings official Bogdan Teodorowich Sapieha to remove the Jews from the Podlasie street and settle them outside the Zamok (citadel) mound in the Vilno and Trumco streets, so that the Jews would be separated from other citizens of the town. The Jews appealed against this order. At the same time the non-Jews appealed to the high court. Both appeals were to be heard on the 20 September 1564 in the high court, when both parties were to appear, but the high court could not reach a verdict and transferred the case to the crown court. The crown court was to hear the submissions of both parties on the 11 November 1564, but if one side would not appear the case would be considered in its absence. On the appointed day the four representatives of the town appeared, but the Jewish party was absent. The case was heard in the absence of the Jews. The Christian representatives have presented the order of the king of the 20 September 1563 to the wojewoda Pawel Ivanovich Sapieha. The court passed the verdict. In the new order it was decided that the Jews must move to a place, which was provided to them. At the same time the king ordered his representatives to demolish the Jewish homes in Podlasie Street, if the Jews would not obey the royal order. In addition the Jews had to pay 1600 gold ducats for the land of the Christians, which they have occupied.

Old Cold synagogue bombed by the German in 1941
It was built by the Karaites in 1648 when Novogrudok was a Karaite centre.
[Not in original Yizkor Book]

Inside the Old Cold synagogue
[Not in original Yizkor Book]

Two weeks after this final decision there appeared in court H. Gershenovich, Shmuel Mendelovich, Lejzer Shmulovich and Jankel Pejsachovich and argued that they did not appear in court because the king's soldiers prevented them from doing so. Because they could not prove their case and had no convincing documents to support their arguments the king has given all their gardens and other lands to the Christians.

The kehila of Novogrudok is mentioned in many documents of the XVI century, from which it can be seen that it occupied a reputable place among the kehilas of the time.

In the XVIII century Novogrudok is mentioned frequently in connection with rabbinical matters, because it was a "mother town" among the Jews (ir vam be Isroel), which was the home of famous rabbis and learned men.

In olden days Karaites lived in Novogrudok, a fact which is little known, but which is supported by documents found in the Tzar's library in St Petersburg. It can be deduced from some of these documents that at the beginning of the XVII century Karaites were already well settled in Novogrudok. It follows from the writings of the

XVIII century that Novogrudok was a center of the Karaite gatherings. In 1740 deputies from Troki, Zytomir and other places came to Novogrudok to discuss the matter of taxes (Adolf Nayboyer of the St Petersburg library "Presentations and documents of the Karaites" Leipzig 81,73,1866). There is no earlier documentary evidence to indicate when the Karaites have settled here. It is possible that they arrived together with the Tatars at the end of the XIV century, when the Lithuanian Grand Duke Witold settled Karaites and captured (prisoners of war?) Tatars in Lithuania.

The ruins of the Novogrudok castle

[Page 25]

Rabbis of Novogrudok

Rabbi V.Ch. Kancipolski (Brooklyn)

Translated by Minia Lipkes and Oskar Delatycki

The first Rabbis

Rav Aba Mairi

As far as it is known the first rabbi in Novogrudok was the Rav Aba Mairi. In his days there was in Novogrudok a sizable Jewish community. There were also many *lomdim* (scholars). One of them, Reb Yosef, became a rabbi in Brest. Rav Aba Mairi married a woman from Zalkevy.

Reb Shmuel Vilner

Reb Shmuel Vilner was born in Slutsk. His father was Reb Shmelke. He was a son-in-law of Reb Dovid Koidanower, whose brother was *MHRSH"K* (Rav Shmuel Koidanower), the *mechaber* (author) of *Tiferes Shmuel* a *perush* (commentary) on the *RA"SH*. The two were rabbis from 1690 till 1720.

Reb Arie Leib

Mechaber (author) of the *Sefer* (book) *Divrei AR"I*. Arie Leib was the rabbi from 1740. He died in 1771.

Reb Naftali Hertz

He was a grandson of the first rabbi, Reb Aba Mairi. His son Reb Chaim was a rabbi in Zetl, a town close to Novogrudok.

Reb Mordechai Markl

His legal ruling can be found in the books of the year 1793.

Reb Yakov Zvi Hirsh

He is mentioned in the *Sefer Toldoys Odom* printed in Hereford in 1805.

Reb Isroel ben Reb Yehuda Leib

He was a *goen* (genius) in Torah and studied languages and science. He later assumed the surname of Libel. His previous rabbinical post was in Mogilev. From there he was invited to Novogrudok. He was a great *darshn* (preacher) and distinguished himself by his battles by both word and in writing with the Chasidim. He wrote several books: "*Sefer Havikuach*" printed in the year 1799, also a book in German "*Nachrichtn auf eine neue Sekte zwischen die Juden in Polen, welche ruft sich Chasidim*" printed in Frankfurt in 1799. This book was translated later into French by the *geistlichn* (clergyman) Gregoire in his renowned book about religious sects. Reb Isroel's books were confiscated, but he managed to have the ban rescinded. He was also a big *ascan* (activist) in the town.

Reb Moishe

Not much is known about him.

Reb Dovid ben Harav Moishe *Mi Kleck* (from Kleck)

Reb Dovid was appointed a rabbi at the age of 25 years in 1798. He become renowned in the world as one of the greatest *goanim* (geniuses), the mechaber (author) of the famous book *Sefer "Gallia Maseches"* in two parts, of which one is "*Sheiles ve Tsuves*" (response) and the second is "*Drush and Hespeidim*" (exegesis and eulogies). Among the last can be found the following *Hespeidim* (eulogies): about his father-in-law Hare Reb Eliezer from Brestovic and his brother-in-law Reb Elijahu, about the rabbis of Vilno Reb Shoulke Kacenelenboign and Reb Abele Pasveler, about Reb Chaim Voloziner and Reb Efraim Zalmon Margolit of Brod, also of his first rabbinic adjudicator Reb Note, who was a great *lamdan* (scholar) and *Bal Hora* (educator). He died at the age of 80 and was buried next to Reb Dudl. The book "*Gallia Maseches*" was printed in Vilno in 1844. In his days Novogrudok was an exemplary *Kehile* (community) with all *Klei Koidesh* (religious institutions). The town appointed as *magid* (preacher) Reb Chanoch Zundel from Nai Zogel , who was a famous *darshn* (preacher) and a *mechaber* (author) of the books "*Kanaf Rananim*" and "*Motot Knafaim*", a *sefer* (book) of *Drosh* (commentary) and a *sefer* on "*Shmos Nirdofim*" (a book on synonyms). Many of the inhabitants of the town were great *lomdim* (scholars) and knew who to select as their *Rav* (rabbi), judging by their subsequent selections. *Harov* Dovid was a very *tokev beda'ato* (forceful in his opinions) and never gave in to another rabbi in a *psak haloche*(legal ruling) even if the opponent was the greatest in the *dor* (of his generation), but had a different opinion. But he gave *mechabet* (respect) to every *talmid chochom* (eminent scholar), he respected especially a great personage *(adom godl)*. Reb Shapti, the rabbinic judge of Novogrudok, tells the story that at one time the rabbi of Razanov, *hagoen*(genius) Reb Mordechai Zahakis, announced that he was coming to Novogrudok. Reb Dovid ordered that the *Shul heif* (the courtyard in front of the synagogue) should be spread with yellow sand, as it was the habit to spread sand for honoured guests, and on the eve of Sabbath in the house, since Reb Zahakis would come to stay in the Bet ha Rav (house of the rabbi) in the *Shul heif*. Reb Dovid with the *dayanim* (religious judges) and other *nichvadim* (important persons of the town) were waiting in the Shul heif to *mecabl ponim zajn* (to welcome) the eminent guest.

Reb Dovid varied the determination in a case concerning ritual slaughter. The problem was an abnormal adhesion in the lung of an animal, which Rama judged to make the meat *traif* (not kosher). This ruling was accepted in all Jewish *kehiles* (communities) at the time, but Reb Dovid *paskend* (adjudged) the meat to be kosher, and this had became the rule followed in Novogrudok. The later rabbonim accepted the lenient ruling.

Reb Dovid received a weekly allowance of three roubles, but not regularly. A transient visitor asked once what was his weekly allowance. He answered that it was three roubles this week. Asked why he said "this week" and not "a week", he answered that it means "this week and not last week and I am not certain if I will be paid next week". The reason was that there was no steady income to provide a regular allowance and the great rabbi and his family suffered poverty. But that did have no effect on his conduct in town nor his scholarship and his dealings with the great ones of his generation.

His situation had improved by a curious set of circumstances. Reb Dovid was approachable to the congregation. He used to socialize with the people of the town. He would comfort them and amuse them. Having come one day to the synagogue he told the story that though nobody could outwit him in a ruling, his wife presented him with an argument for which he had no answer. The story goes as follows: it was a severe winter with exceptional frosts and snow falls and his family was suffering from illnesses and poverty. He was in debt and Passover was approaching. His wife asked him why they had to suffer so much. She burst into tears, which she had never done before. She was reproaching him strongly for not being concerned about the deprivation of the family and for not looking for relief. He answered that the town could not pay him regularly because they had no means to do so. She should have been well aware of this. She answered that she knew it but she also knew that she could be a wife of a rabbi in a larger town such as Minsk of Vilno. "Is it my fault", said she, "that you can not secure such an appointment". Reb Dovid was astonished by the logic of her argument. He put on his fur coat and went to the synagogue to recount to the members of his congregation how his wife confounded him with her complaint. The story quickly spread around the town. A meeting was rapidly called, the rabbi's stipend was increased by two roubles in addition to his previous allowance of three roubles. They established a reliable source for obtaining the money to make sure that payment would in the future be regular. In addition, 50 gold coins were given to him to repay all his debts.

In his old age Reb Dovid suffered much anguish, because the tsarist government was contemplating the introduction of military service for Jews. The Jews were distressed by the proposed edict, because it would mean that they would be sent for many years to serve in the depth of Russia, made to eat non-kosher food and forced to forget their origin. The Jews considered it a terrible edict. Reb David took it to heart, was perpetually sick and told his visitors that he was disconsolate by the Jewish sorrows. He anticipated his demise. He died at the age 73 at *taf cuf cadic chet.*

Reb Alexander Ziskind Harkavy

Following Reb Dovid's death, the town engaged a Rabbi who was a *landsman* (a local man). He was a *goan* (genius) in Torah and a businessman, Harav Alexander Ziskind, the son of Rav Gershon Harkavy and a brother of the wealthy Reb Moshe Harkavy. Initially he did not want to take on the position of a Rabbi in his home town, despite the fact that his large and influential family wanted him to do so. Only after his financial position deteriorated did he agree to become a Rabbi in Novogrudok, and remained in that position for approximately 12 years until 1850.

Ha Rav Yitzchak Helhonon Spector (1851-1864)

Novogrudok was privileged to have a rabbi for 14 years, who was a great person. He was a genius among geniuses. He was known everywhere as the "rabbi of all people of the Diaspora" "the rabbi of the Jewish nation" and a possessor of great knowledge. He was loved and treasured as a national leader. In many Jewish homes his picture was displayed on the wall. Many hundreds of rabbis called him by his many titles and wrote to him asking him to rule on difficult questions of law. He would reply in all cases by return post. Later his responses were published in three books "*Be'er Yitzchak*" (1858), "*Nahal Yitzchak*" (2 vols. 1872-1874) and "*En Yitzchak*" (2 vols. 1889-1895). Such was Reb Yitzchak Helhonon Spector. Having come to Novogrudok, he began taking part in all concerns of the community and he became the recipient of all communications concerning Jews. When it was necessary to contact high officials or the government in St Petersburg he was always the voice that was asking for improvement in the conditions of the Jews in Russia. He was often successful.

Early Years

Reb Yitzchak Helhonon was born in 1817 to the eminent rabbi Reb Isroel Iser and his wife Rochl, in the township of Rozhanka, near Volkovysk. As a youth, Reb Yitzchak Helhonon studied with his father and became known for his diligence, dedication and great talent. At the age of 12 he was offered a bride, a daughter of a businessman of Volkovysk. They brought the young man to the house of the future father-in-law for an assessment. Scholars discussed with him his learning, questioned his knowledge and spoke of many tractates. Young Yitzchak Helhonon answered all questions well. As he spoke he partook in the prepared refreshments, various fried sweetmeats on the table, without taking notice of what he was doing. The bride-to-be observed this through a curtain. She said to her mother: "I don't like him, he has no respect and I don't want him for a husband". Her mother agreed. Nothing came of the marriage proposal. (the bride-to-be became a shopkeeper of a small shop in a small township, she died before the first World War . Ed.) Having heard of the event, the eminent businessman Reb Eliezer and his wife Blume snatched Reb Yitzchak Helhonon up like a precious stone and said that the Torah is even sweeter when it is derived from him. He married their daughter Reizl.

Some time later, when Reb Yitzchak's name was well known in the world and everywhere he went he was mobbed--they thought it a privilege to shake his hand and to see him--he came to Volkovysk and Rozhanka to visit his ancestral graves. Large crowds came to see him. An old, crumpled woman insisted on seeing him and asked him to bless her so that her fate would improve and her misfortunes would come to an end. Reb Yitzchak recognized her, it was his first proposed bride, who told her mother that she did not like him.

After he married he was on *kest* (also called *esen kest*, a custom of sustaining a young couple by the parents of the bride for an agreed period to allow the young husband to finish his studies) for 6 years and continued to study with diligence and dedication. At that time came to Volkovysk as a prospective bridegroom a well known young scholar Reb Boruch Mardechai Lipshits (later a rabbi in Novogrudok). He came to see a wealthy family in Volkovysk. He was envious of Reb Yitzchak's Helhonon diligence. On occasions, after Reb Yitzchak left the synagogue Reb Boruch would stay back and continue to study for a few hours. Once, after the Yom Kippur fast, Reb Boruch Mordichai thought: "By now Reb Yitzchak must be asleep. I will go to the synagogue to study." But having come to the synagogue he found that Reb Yitzchak was still there, having prayed for the past hour. "I will not exceed his diligence" Reb Boruch Mordichai decided. And thus it was. Reb Yitzchak Helhonon developed to be the *goen* (genius) of his generation who was knowledgeable in everything in *SHAS* (acronym of *Shisha Sedarim* of *Mishna* or *Talmud*) Babylonian and Jerusalem *reshoinim* and *achroinim* (early and late authorities on Jewish law from 11 century to *Shulchan Oruch* 1564-1565) and became a leader of his generation. Whilst eating *kest* he studied in a learning circle which included the son of Reb Binyamin the rabbi of Volkovysk, with Reb Yeshiva Leib Diskin (who was later the *goen* of Brisk and later of Jerusalem).

Reb Yitzchak Helhonon was tall, had soft dark eyes, rosy cheeks and a smile. He spoke softly and delicately using short, refined sentences, in a thin soprano voice. He could never be made cross or curse anyone. He gave everybody the benefit of doubt. On his way from home to the synagogue he would be the first to greet everyone, Jew or non-Jew, big or small, poor or rich. Others were always waiting to meet him because they believed in the power of his blessing. They waited to hear his greeting and believed that this would secure them a good day.

His first rabbinical appointment

When Reb Yitzchak decided that he was on *kest* long enough, he took up his first rabbinic appointment in the town of Isabelin in the Volkovysk district. This was the year 1837, he was then 20 years old. His stipend was 5 gilden a week (75 kopicks, 38 cents US). Later, because the town was very happy with his work, 15 kopicks were added to his stipend. Thus he lived a very frugal life. The greater his deprivation the greater was his dedication to learning. His father-in-law sent him a chala and meat for every Sabbath. Thus he had at least one good day a week. He found it difficult to sustain the needy existence. He decided that he should befriend some eminent rabbis, who might recommend him for a better position. He borrowed a set of better clothing and travelled to Karlin. At the time there lived the famed Rabbi Yakov of "*Mishkenos Yakov*". As Reb Yitzchak came into his dwelling, the rabbi was engaged in an important discussion with some rabbinic judges about a divorce. They paid no attention to the young rabbi Yitzchak Helhonon. As he listened to their discussion he was able to identify the chapter and verse of the divorce law they were discussing. At that he was greeted and asked who he was. He said that he was the rabbi of Isabelin (Zabelin). To which Reb Yakov said that he received from Reb Yitzchak a letter on a point of law. After this introduction Reb Yitzchak was asked to sit down and participate in the discussion. In the course of this they saw that, though he was young, with no beard, he was a *goen* in matters concerning the Torah. They included him in their circle. He stayed with the rabbi for three weeks. The citizens of Karlin gave him a present of 40 roubles, almost a year's stipend. Reb Yakov Karliner found for him his next position in Bereza. There he was paid a rouble a week. At the time they were building highways, one of which went through Bereza. The contractors opened an office in Bereza. The contractors Reb Yom Tov Bramson and Reb Yidl Sheroshevski from Grodno were dropping in to have discussions with him and brought him valuable presents. He was also asked to settle disputes in surrounding townships: Mulch, Antifalie and others. Reb Yitzchak had a good friend Reb Nochim of Kaltinyan (Kovno gubernia) who knew him well and understood him. He believed that Reb Yitzchak would be very famous one day. He persuaded the people of Neswiez to engage Reb Yitzchak as their rabbi, since they needed to appoint one. They sent an offer to Reb Yitzchak. But when the people of Bereza heard that he had an offer from another town they said that they would not release him. Having heard that, Reb Nochim sent a horse and cart to fetch Reb Yitzchak from Bereze. When they arrived in Neswiez the citizens of the town were surprised that they engaged as a rabbi such a young man without a proper beard. Should he occupy the honoured rabbinic seat of Neswiez? But when he started reciting Torah and discussed matters of law with them they realized that they had engaged a *goen* and they confirmed the rabbinic appointment and granted him a stipend of 4 roubles a week. From Neswiez he came to Novogrudok in 1851 in the month of *Iar* (April or May).

Reb Yitzchak's method of dealing with questions of Jewish law

Following his arrival in Novogrudok he accepted all the traditions and laws according to "*Galia Masechet*". He was approached frequently on matters of "*Aguna*" (the problem of the status of women unable to obtain a proper divorce). In some cases he eased the position of forsaken women. During his stay in Novogrudok, a citizen of Novogrudok drowned in a ship. The rabbi was asked by his widow for permission to remarry. After a laps of time he gave the woman permission to remarry. Next day it had become known that the body of the drowned man had been washed up on the sea shore and he was identified by a bundle of keys found on his body. This was considered to be a miracle.

In 1858 he went to Koenigsberg to print his first book of "Be'er Yitzchak". Two rabbis came to visit him in his hotel to discourse and study. They were the famous *goen* Reb Isroel Salander and the *goen* Reb Yakov Tzvi Mecklenburg, the rabbi of the town. At the same time arrived the well known businessman from Minsk, Reb Heinach Eisenstadt. Having seen such eminent persons forgathered, he said to them that he had a request. He told them that in his district lives a woman who needs *chalitse* (release according to the levirate marriage law) but her brother-in-law is an apostate, who once studied Judaism but has converted and is now a priest in Germany. "I saw him recently", he said. "He refuses blankly to give *chalitse*. He said that there is no explicit law in Talmud which obliges an apostate to give *chalitse*. Only the later judges have reinstated this law. He told me that if I can show him an appropriate law in Talmud he will oblige". The wealthy man from Minsk was imploring them to find an apposite ruling in the Talmud. Rabbi Yitzchak Helhonon exclaimed "Yes, I know of proof in the Talmud, it is in the *Gemarrah Gittin* page *ajen daled alef*," and brilliantly he deduced from it that an apostate is obliged to give *chalitsa*. The other rabbis were astounded. Heinach Eisenstadt went to the priest, who consented to give the woman *chalitsa*.

In issues concerning "*Aguna*" he was usually correct in his legal determination. He worked very hard day and night until he found the foundation for his positive judgment. This was because he was by nature kind and soft hearted. He would say "I am sorry for the poor '*Aguna*' all that is possible must be done to save her from an unfortunate life". And that is how he treated everyone. Charity he would dispense with an open hand. When he travelled he would tip the servants as a rich man. He paid the coachman double that which the normal passenger would pay and he would thank warmly the inn keeper for all his kindness.

When he was the Rav in Novogrudok a dispute broke out in the Volozyn yeshiva between the Rav Hirsh Berlin (father of Reb Meier Berlin) and the *goen* Reb Josef Ber Soloveichik, who was at the time the deputy head of Reb Hirsh Laibl's yeshiva. There was also a big dispute among the students. The well known rabbis Reb Dovid Tevel Minsker, Reb Yosef Fimer (twin) Slutzker, Reb Velvel, rabbi of Vilno and Reb Yitzchak Helhonon were invited. They were asked to settle the dispute. They did settle the matter and they introduced *takkanot* (regulations) in the yeshiva. Whilst the rabbis were in Volozyn, the students of the Yeshiva asked the rabbis to give them a lecture. This would be highly valued by the students. The rabbi asked Reb Yitzchok to give the lesson and said that they were too old to have discussions with the protégées of Volozyn. "You are still a young man (he was 40 at the time), you could cope with them better". He accepted the commission and gave a lesson on the *Gomorrah* of *Bava Batra* ("Last gate"- laws pertaining to the sale, acquisition etc of real estate), which they studied at the time. The lesson was a success. Later Reb Yosif Ber had become the Rabbi of Brest. There was also an argument in the Mir Yeshiva between the rabbi Reb Dovid and the head of the Yeshiva. Reb Yitzchak settled the matter. At the time when he was the rabbi in Novogrudok, the enemies of the Jews in Russia and the Polish landowners were inciting the Russian government against the Jews.

The outcome was the policy of the Russian Government to expel the Jews. They prohibited the Jews to live in villages, they drafted twice the number of Jews that they were obliged to, and often they did not for some years, draft non Jews from the western regions, where the Jews lived. They took Jews instead. They were intending to introduce a law that Jews would not be allowed to live within 50 *viorst* (53 kilometres) from the German boarder. They were planning to forbid kosher slaughter. They were planning to reform the curriculum in Jewish schools by forbidding the study of the Talmud. They wanted to introduce a government examination in the Jewish schools and introduce many other prohibitions. But the rabbis, among them Reb Yitzchak Helhonon, were conducting frequent meetings with Jewish community leaders (this was in the second and third year after his arrival in Novogrudok), activists were elected, who lobbied the government in St Petersburg and frequently they managed to forestall the introduction of a hostile decrees. Reb Yitzchok travelled frequently to Vilno and St Petersburg and, whilst he was a rabbi in Kovno, he was travelling frequently on matters concerning the Jews and was acting on communal matters. Whilst he was the rabbi in Novogrudok he heard that Tsar Nicholas I (1825-1855) was coming to Mogilev to attend a wedding of the son of *Graf* (Earl, Count) Pashkevich. He contacted communal workers and a delegation, which consisted of Rav the *goen* Barit of Vilno, Yitzchak Zelkind, Shmuel Lurie of Mogilev and Lipe Zelzer from Vitebsk. They went to Gomel and handed a petition to the Tsar. Two activists Mr Nisen Katzenelson from Bobruisk and Mr Fivel Freedland from Dvinsk were sent later to St Petersburg to petition the government. The Tsar gave them a friendly reception and promised to do something about the situation.

During the outbreak of the pogroms in the 1880's, Yitzchak Helhonon founded committees which were helping the victims. When whole townships were burned to the ground, he undertook to collect money to rebuild the ruined towns. He alone collected more than a million roubles. As it is known, the pogroms of '81-'82 in the south of Russia, which were characterized by their enormous spread (204 communities) and exceptional cruelty (the event was known in Jewish annals as the hurricane of the south). The pogroms were conducted by tsarist officials and the military (for example in Elizavetgrad). The dark tsarist reactionaries were frightened by the revolutionary movement that embraced all levels of the nation. They wanted to use the Jewish people as scapegoats to divert the suffering of the people. The pogroms had also the aim to force the Jews to convert or to emigrate. The chief adviser to the Tsar, the chief prosecutor of the Holy Synod, who was the spiritual leader of the tsarist government, had made his meaning openly known. He said that the Jewish problem in Russia would be solved in the following way: a third would be killed, a third would convert and a third would emigrate. He added that the western boarder was open.

And indeed tens of thousands of Jews were making their way to the border. The border towns of Brody and Lemberg and the harbour towns of Rotterdam, Amsterdam and Hamburg were full of Jewish refugees. Thus began the great Jewish emigration which was increasing year by year and which brought millions of Jews from Eastern Europe to America. The Minister of the Interior, Graf Ignatiev, had issued his "temporary" May decrees, to make Jewish life more bitter still. These decrees were kept in force until the fall of the tsarist regime. Tens of thousands of Jewish families were uprooted from their land and expelled from their homes. Their places of habitat were continuously reduced and further hundreds of thousands of Jews were expelled into the overflowing Jewish towns. The Jews were restricted in all their rights.*

At that time RebYitzchak Helhonon got in touch with prominent personalities abroad such as Dr Asher, the Secretary of the committees of the communities in London, the Chief Rabbi Tsadok in Paris, HaRav Hilf of Memel and others. They organized protest meetings with the participation of bishops, members of parliament and ministers, where the barbaric behavior of the tsarist state was condemned. The press had written about it at length. Contact was made with the Danish king, who was the father-in-law of the Tsar. He had written to the Tsar that the pogroms were giving a bad impression of Russia. The protests had some influence, because the tsarist government was in need of support from their European allies. The vicious Graf Ignatiev was dismissed (though his "temporary" law had, as mentioned above, remained). The wave of the pogroms had temporarily come to a halt.

RebYitzchak Helhonon became sick in *jud chet adar* 1894. He had inflammation of the kidney and his heart was weak. Whilst sick he was still engaged in ruling on difficult issues and came up with *hidushshei Torah* (original interpretations of passages in the Torah). Professors from Koenigsberg and St Petersburg were invited, but they did not give much hope for improvement because of his considerable age. People were reciting everywhere *tehilim* (psalms) for him. But to no avail. He died in *beit alef adar* 1897 *tav nun tzadic bet'h* (may his sole rest in peace).

Reb Boruch Mordechai Lipshits

Reb Boruch Mordechai Lipshits was a Rav in Novogrudok from 1834 till1844. He was a great *goen*. He was a friend of Yitzchak Helhonon in Volkovysk. They were pupils of the Volkovysk Rov Benyamin together with the Rov's son, Reb Yehoshua Leib Diskin. Reb Boruch Mordechai arrived in Novogrudok after Reb Yitzchak Helhonon left for Kovno. The town's people looked after him and honoured him. He was previously the rabbi of known communities, such as Semiatych and Volkovysk. Reb Boruch Mordechai was the author of *Seifer Brit Yakov*. He did not reach the world fame of his friend Reb Yitzchak Helhonon, however he too was one of the *goen's* of the generation. After 10 years in Novogrudok he was induced to go to the larger town of Sedlec.

Ha Rav Yechiel Michl Epstein (original German spelling Eppstein)

He was the rabbi in Novogrudok between 1874 and 1908. *Hagoen* (genius) Rav Yechiel Michl Epstein was the child of Reb Aron Yitzchak and Rashke of Bobruisk. The Epsteins were a large, eminent family known over many generations. According to records they stemmed from the exiles from Spain, expelled in 1492. And previous to that, in the ancient times, they stemmed from the exiles from Jerusalem, who were taken by Titus to Rome after the destruction of Jerusalem. In Spain the family lived in the vicinity of Seville and Toledo, where their name was Ben Venashti. After the exile from Spain the family was divided. A part of the family went to Turkey to Salonica and Constantinopol. Others went to Ismir. The second part of the Ben Vanashti family went by sea to Germany via France. They arrived to the town Eppstain. The town gave them a friendly reception and granted them right of residence. In gratitude they changed their name from Veneshti to Epstein.

Ha Rav Yechiel Michl was born in Bobruisk into a large interconnected family who lived in wealth, honour and prominence. They were men of the Torah and men of charity. This is how Yechiel Michl was brought up. He could have also grown up to be a man of letters and wealth, however he was destined to become a *goen* of his generation and a rabbinic scholar of law. After he married the daughter of Reb Yakov Berlin of Mir he started a business, which was conducted by his wife. He was immersed in studying. His wife started a textile shop and employed people. This was the way they earned their living. The letter of patent for the shop was in his name and when an inspector would call to check the patents Reb Yechel used a hired man to show him the way to his shop. Thus he would be present in the shop when the inspector came.

At that time there was a rabbi in Bobruisk Rav Elijah Goldberg, a *goen*, a pupil of Reb Chaim Volozyner. He met the young scholar, Reb Yechiel Michl and recognized his substantial capabilities and great potential in the young scholar, because of his great talents and logical mind. He called on Reb Aron Yitzchak, the father of Yechiel Michl and he said: "You have gifted children who assist you in your extensive enterprises. Why don't you let one of them become a *Godl be Isroel?*" (a great one among his people). And that was Reb Yechiel Michl. His father agreed to the suggestion and Reb Yechiel Michl remained a student of the Torah without being disturbed. He began to lecture to gifted students and had become known as a great scholar in the town.

He obtained his first appointment as a rabbi in Novozivkov in the Mogilev gubernia. Most of the Jews in town were Lubavich Chasids. Having seen the great respect of the chasids to their rabbi Reb Mendele of Lubavich, whom they called the *Tzemach Tzadik*, he decided to visit the renowned *goen*. He travelled to Lubavich. The Rabbi gave him a friendly reception and despite their age difference they became firm friends. The Rabbi soon gave his guest a rabbinical degree. Every day they would discuss and study matters of functioning as a rabbi, how to be in turn lenient and strict depending on the nature of the matter in hand. This advice left a life long influence on Reb Yechel Michl. Reb Mendele shared with Reb Yechiel some personal confidences, for example, that he had great respect for the *goen* of Vilno. The *Shulchan Oruch* with Beor Hagra (which is the *goen*'s of Vilno *perush* (commentary) on *Shulchan Oruch*) was always on his table and he did not budge without them. "The Chasids should be thankful to the *goen* and his students, because if it was not for their persecution of the Chasidim, who knows how far the Chasidim would have strayed in their new ways of learning by defying the hidden Torah and not being scrupulous in the study of the revealed Torah." This is why the *Baal ha Tania* had written his *Shulchan Oruch* because he used it to demonstrate to the Chasidim the need not to abandon the practical laws according to *Shulchan Oruch*. The foundation of Judaism is to live every minute according to the *Shulchan Oruch* and not to delve into the mysticism which is hidden.

Reb Yechiel Michl had his rabbinic style which was different from that of his predecessor. He was by nature not effervescent but was studious and contemplative. It was a pleasure to discuss matters and exchange information on lots of matters of history and politics. He was a good speaker. He kept things in order and supervised all matters in the town. His writings were in good order and were clear and well formed. Every name was spelled correctly. Concerning issues of the practice of slaughter in Novogrudok he confirmed all the existing rules. He always searched for a lenient ruling according to the law. His opinion was, as written in the *RASH*, that he who wants to be stringent must provide evidence, because to be stringent for its own sake meant wasting people's money. Once some people came to him on the seventh day of Passover with the following problem: they found a cooked grain of wheat in some soup. He did not want to rule on the matter on the spot. He postponed making the decision twice till evening came, which was the beginning of the eighth (last) day of Passover. A different law applies to this problem on the last day of Passover, because during the seven days of Passover the ruling according to Rabbenu Tam applies that any *chomets* during Passover is all *chomets*, but on the eighth day of Passover there is a rabbinic rule for the Diaspora to which the 60% rule applies, and everything can be used. Rabbi Yechiel Michl did not want to cause anguish to a Jewish family and found a solution to the problem.

In his personal life, Rabbi Yechiel Michl conducted himself without allowing concessions, strictly without lenience. He gave an example of a train. The passengers can sit in the carriages and enjoy themselves. They can walk and look in all directions. But the train driver must look intently at his engine and in the direction the train is going. Thus the rabbi must be the ruler of his community. In relation to the people of his community he was kind hearted and if anyone asked him for a favour he obliged regardless of whether the person was deserving or not. He was often interceding with the city authorities and always succeeded, because he was respected. Every day and night he was available as a soldier on duty in service to everyone. He considered himself wealthier than a Moscow millionaire because he lived a complete spiritual life.

His first book was "*Or leishorim*", which he had printed. His second book which made him world famous was the "*Oruch hashulchan*" in nine parts. The book was written according to the method of "*Baal halvushim*" Reb Mordechai Yaffe, who died 400 years ago. In the "*Arba'ah helkey shulchan aruch*" he explained every law according to *SHAS* and *reshoinim and achroinim* (former and latter) until the last judges and he wrote the last legal ruling. The book was accepted by all Jewish communities. It became a book that every rabbi kept on his table, so as to see what the latest judge said. It was printed in large numbers and had several additions, which was a sign of its great importance.

Reb Yechiel Michl had arranged in Novogrudok that Sabbath should commence an hour before sunset. The reason for this was as follows: he was going one Friday evening to the synagogue at candle lighting time, when he saw that the shops in the marketplace were beleaguered with Jews and non-Jews and the shopkeepers were occupied with cashing in money and no attention was given to the time to close the shops. And all the pleadings that it was nearly sunset were disregarded. He caused the announcement to be made that from the next Sabbath the evening prayer in every shul would be conducted before sunset which would be followed by the immediate commencement of the Sabbath. And so it was. But the shopkeepers did not believe that the new ordinance would stand. But when they came to shul at the usual time, they found that the service was over and the shul was closed. After that they complied with the ruling so as not to desecrate the Sabbath.

Reb Yechiel Michl fell ill and passed away in the winter of 1908. The funeral was attended by most rabbis from the surrounding towns as well as many Jews from the neighboring towns to mourn the passing of the great genius.

Following the seven days of mourning the community wanted to make an offer of the rabbinic position to his son, the *goen* Reb Boruch Epstein, author of the famous books "*Torah tmima*" "About *Humash*" and the book "*Makor Baruch*". He refused, however, to accept the rabbinical position in Novogrudok. He preferred to retain his position as an accountant in a bank in Pinsk.

Reb Yichiel Michl took as his son in law the famous rabbi and the head of the Yeshiva of Volozyn (the Natziv-pillar) Reb Naftoli Tzvi Berlin, who was 64 years old at the time and his bride was 16 years old. They had a famous son, the well known Mizrachi activist Reb Meyer Berlin OBM. The young Rebetzn was conducting the affairs of the Yeshiva with much understanding and was a great help to her old husband.

The time had passed and Novogrudok was looking for a suitable rabbi. They made an offer to the Tavriker rabbi the eminent Rabbi Harav Avraham Burshten, who later went to Israel. He could not have been an active rabbi in Novogrudok, because previously he had written in the newspapers "Ha Melitz" "He Chaluts" and "Ha Sfira" agitating against the Musar movement. He was an avid opponent of their method. This led to a great conflict in town. Reb Yoisl and his supporters harassed him. He had to leave the town. He was replaced later by the eminent Rabbi Menachem Krakowski who later went to Vilno as the town preacher.

Rabbi Menachem Krakowski

*(On March 1, 1881, in St. Petersburg, Alexander II was mortally

wounded by a bomb thrown by student I. Grinevitskii, a member of the revolutionary organization "The National Will, ending his policy of conciliation toward the Jews of Russia and inaugurating an oppressive reign under Tsar Alexander III.

Within months after the assassination, the Russian minister of the interior, Count Nicolai Ignatiev, announced that, since the tolerant policies of Alexander II had failed, harsh measures against Russian Jewry were now in order. The notorious pogroms, anti-Jewish riots under thinly-veiled government sponsorship, soon followed, with the loss of many Jewish lives and the extensive destruction of Jewish property. Next came a series of anti-Jewish decrees, termed "temporary regulations", which came to be known as the "May Laws" since they were placed into effect on May 3, 1882. These "temporary" laws were so repressive and restrictive on Jewish life that, by the year 1900, nearly 40% of Russia's Jews were dependent upon charity. The combined effect of the pogroms and the May Laws drove the Jews of Russia, in desperation, to seek relief in whatever direction it could be found.)

[Page 33]

The Musar movement

by Mordechai Ginsburg, Montreal

Translated from Yiddish by O. Delatycki and Aviva Kamil

[The founding of the Musar Movement in Novogrudok represents a glorious chapter in the history of the town. For those who are unfamiliar with Musar we enclose a short introduction by Mr. Gurevitch, the Principal of Yeshiva Beit-Rivkah.]

A little about the Musar Movement

There were in those days' two main streams of [religious] thinking:

    1. The Chasidic movement with Ba'al Shem Tov its founder.

    2. The Lithuanian movement with the Gaon of Vilno as its head.

The Musar Movement aspired to be in-between the two; it did not agree with the extremes of the other two movements: the ecstasy of life of the Chasids or the ecstasy of learning of the Lithuanian movement.

The Musar Movement stressed the importance of **INDIVIDUAL SELF**

IMPROVEMENT in every aspect of the human character. Virtues (Midot Tovot) of the individual should be developed to the utmost and bad characteristics (Midot Ra'ot) should be combated and conquered.

[The transliterated Hebrew words in the text are in *italics*.]

A. What did the method *(shitah)* of Musar represent, and who developed its ideology and were its founders?

B. The specific role of Reb Yosef Yoysl Hurovitz and his colossal influence *(hashpa'ah)* on the religious youth of his time.

C. The drastic actions of Reb Yosef Yoysl in order to enter the shrine *(hachpa'al)* of Musar, his great mind and deep understanding *(havanah)* of Musar, great willingness of sacrifice, which he brought on the altar *(misbe'ach)* of Musar

D. Novogrudok was the Mecca of Musar. Musar in Novogrudok was created by Reb Yosef Yoysl.

A. I am beginning with trepidation *(bedchilu urechimu)* the brief recitation of the story of one of the greatest Jewish personalities of our time. We are going to stress here certain characteristics and historical notions of one of the main personalities of the Musar movement - Reb Yosef Yoysl Hurovitz, who has written a golden page in the history of the Russian -Polish Judaism at the beginning of the XX century. Before we start to describe directly the personality of Reb Yosef Yoysl, we will sketch briefly what the whole Musar movement represented, what were its aims, and how it differed from other movements of that time. What brought the Musar method into the Jewish life? How big was its influence on the young generation, which found in Musar a deep ideal and had become devoted to it with their life and soul. We will try to find an answer to these brief questions. Musar meant a method of life, built on preaching and practicing good deeds *(midot tovot)*. Musar meant simply learning, castigating, showing to others that they had left, alas, the path of righteousness, if their dealings, affairs and deeds were not in agreement with the principles of Musar. In our modern language, we could interpret the word Musar to mean ethics, morals or religious behaviour. In fact, *(bedi'avad)*, however, the word Musar is not translatable, just as one cannot translate into another language the word *Torah* or *cedoka* and such like meanings or idioms. As much as one would like to translate the word *gemilat chased* it is impossible to provide a correct and precise translation into another language. The same applies to the word Musar, the root of which is deeper than the words such as morality, righteousness, and ethics. Musar means, first of all, to have a religious foundation, because it is not conceivable to live by the principles of Musar and at the same time be without belief (emunah). Many may think perhaps that it is possible to be an ethical and honest being without a religious base.

Receipt from the Beit Yosef Yeshiva in Novogrudok

However, it is not so with Musar, which includes the religious behaviour (hanhagah) of the individual (yachid). This means that he will observe precisely (b'deiuk) all commandments (mitzvoth) to do or not to do (ta'aseh ve lo ta'aseh), all commandments of the Torah (mitzvot hatorah) and to be aware of sins of a man to God and a man to his fellow man (nizhar averot benadam lamakom ubein adom le'chavero). Surely, the roots of Musar are in the deep religious philosophy, which is concerned with human life on earth, its tasks and obligations, which have to be fulfilled and which are in general the aims of human life. Musar is seeking to get to the basis of the *raison d'etre* of creation (tachlit hayetzirah), why the life of a man is so short and loaded with heavy problems, and in all *(ve al kulam)* - which are the consequences of living on the sinful earth. But the earth is, after all, only a corridor *(prozdor)* to the next world, where a permanent life exists. Musar has addressed all philosophical levels, which we have encountered to this day. The nearest to us, however, is our own *Tanach*, which includes all the foundations *(yesodot)* of the Musar and it is also contained in the *Mishna*, the *Gemora* and, in the recent centuries, in the large number of cardinal Musar works, which have tied our people with the eternal reality *(amitan)*, which is arising from the sources of Musar. Some of the books are: "The obligations of the heart" *(Chovot halevavot)* by *Rabeinu Bakhye:* "Eight chapters" *("Shmona prakim")* by Rmb"m (Rabbi Moshe ben Mimon - Miamonides), "The book of Chasidim" *("Sefer chasidim")* by Rabbi Yehuda Hachasid, "Gates of repentance"*("She'arei Tshuvah")*, "The road of Musar" *("Shevet Musar")*, "Two tablets of the covenant" *("Shin Lamed Hey-Snei Luchot Habrit")* by Reb Yishayahu Horowitz, "The road of the just" *("Mesilat Yesharim")* by Reb Moshe Chaim Lutzato.

B. Let us sketch a chronological picture of the founders and representatives of the Musar movement. Reb Yosef Yoysl Hurovitz was not the originator of the great movement. He joined an existing movement, and he brought to it his great character and determination, which placed him close to the forefront of the founders of Musar. Reb Yosef was a fanatical leader of the Musar. For him Musar was not a method, an idea or an encyclopedia of ethical notions. No, it was a lot more than all of these. Let us however approach the matter gradually *(behadragah)* and describe the Musar movement starting from its first founder and visionary, Reb Israel Salander (whose surname at birth was Lipkin). Reb Israel Salander had established, to begin with *(le'chatchila)*, a Musar Yeshiva in Vilno. Later he founded a Yeshiva in Kovno and one in Slabodka. He has become known as the father of the movement. There are opinions, however, that Reb Israel was not the first to come out with the Torah of the Musar movement *(Torat Hamusar)*. Some believe that he took over from Reb Yosef Sundul Salander, father-in-law of Reb Shmuel Salander of Jerusalem. Obviously, Reb Israel had become acquainted with the Musar literature, which was published at the time in Vilno, such as the book "Improvement of the virtues of the soul" *("Tikun midot hanefesh")* by Reb Shlome ben Gavriel and other works. The first Kovno Musar Yeshiva was established by Reb Israel in the year 1844. It became a centre of the Musar and consisted not only of Yeshiva people and students, but also of a number of business people who joined the movement. Fifteen years later i.e. in the year 1859, Reb Israel moved to Koenigsberg, where he established a new Musar Yeshiva, and from there his influence had reached Memel, where he fired the imagination of many followers. Memel has become a centre of the Musar movement. Similarly, a Yeshiva was established in Berlin and in other places. The movement continued to grow, but at the same time a strong opposition was encountered from the members of the *Haskala* (knowledge) movement (*Maskilim*). At the time some great rabbis and holy men in Russia thought that Musar was a superfluous undertaking. They were adamant that they did not need Musar, not for themselves and less still for others. A sharp polemic started in the Hebrew press of that time (e.g. in *"Hazfira"* and *"Hamelitz"*), and it almost came to a holy war (*milchemet mitzvah*) between the followers and the opponents of the Musar system. It got to a point when threats were made that Musar would create a third orientation in the Jewish life, just as the Chasidic faction had constituted a second orientation. A large movement which opposed the Musar method were the Misnagdim, which included the Rabbi of Kovno Reb Arie Leib Shapiro, the Rabbi of Janov Reb Jehoshua Hashl, the Rabbi of Salant Reb Yeshoel and above all (*ve'al kulam*) the world famous Gaon of Kovno Reb Itschok Elchonon, who had spoken against the Musar Yeshiva, which was created in Kovno by Reb Itschok Bloser, a pupil of Reb Israel Salander. The division grew. Over 40 rabbis came to the defense of Musar. They argued that Musar was not just good but also useful and, which was most important, that it would result in positive outcomes and be of benefit to the Jewish nation.

C. After the closure of the Yeshiva of Volozin, the Yeshiva of Slobodka was considered the outstanding school among the followers of the Torah and 200 students gathered in Slobodka.

As for Reb Yosef Yoysl, he was a distinguished (*muvhak*) pupil of Reb Itschok Bloser and he had already created an important circle of students of religious studies *(kolel),* who were engrossed day and night in the study of Torah and their endeavours (*yomam valailah al hatorah ve'al ha'avodah*) and were totally absorbed in learning. A little later, Reb Yoysl created the famous circle of religious studies in Novogrudok, with the aim of educating young men to become rabbis. But Reb Yoysl was not satisfied with creating only the Bet Yosef Yeshiva in Novogrudok. He had a volcanic nature, and when he undertook something, he was [dedicated to it] with all his heart and soul (*bekol libbo and nafsho*). He created also a Yeshiva in Shavl, later a Bet Musar in Jerusalem with the help of the philanthropist *(nadvan)* Nathan Strauss, who was strongly influenced by the movement.

How did Reb Yoysl view the world? He began with the assumption that it is not enough to be a great scholar, to know all religious laws and traditional laws (*halachot*) of the *Shulchan Aruch* and "Knowledge of Teaching" (*"Yoreh Deah"*), but one should also be aware of bad habits, as for example anger (*ka'as*) and haughtiness (*ga'avah*). How can one reach the high level of Musar? To this Reb Yoysl had an answer - to study and dwell in the famed Musar books (*sifrei*), which we mentioned previously. And even then one is not certain that one would reach the limit of the depths, which exercise a pressure and an influence on the human heart.

Yeshiva students from Beit Yosef

What were the theses of the followers (*ba'alei*) of Musar? For them sufficed, for instance, such an expression as: "you live despite yourself" (*"be'al korchecha ata chai"*) or "know where you came from (Avot)" (*"Da mea'in batah" (Avot)*) and similar basic thoughts, which we could consider to be paradoxes. Reb Yosef Yoysl displayed at all times an appearance of worry and sadness (*atzvut*) (though within himself he was filled with Godly dreams and ideals) and only dreamt of the end of all humanity *(sof kol adam)*(when) one will have to face judgment and to give an account at heaven's court (*beit-din shel ma'alah liten din ve'cheshbon*) of all deeds (*ma'asim*). Reb Yosef Yoysl had always an open ear for every word and he even listened to mundane subjects (*advar-chol*), a voice heard sometimes at the market place, to hear if in the substance (*etzem*) lay a grain of Musar. And, let us add that the amount *(s'chum)* (of findings) with attributes *(midot)*, which have created the cult of Musar was by no means small. Together they were generating a very large field, with seeds of plants of many principles (*ikarim*) of Musar. In them, one was looking for fulfillment *(hashlamah)*. Reb Yosef Yoysl was distinct from all scholars, from all pupils of Reb Israel Salader, and just as the High Priest bore the names of all the twelve tribes on the priestly garments *(chushan ve'ephod)*, so did Reb Yosef Yoysl cast roots of twelve principles *(ikarim)* of Musar, which was the general program of the Musar method. Firstly one must consider the matter of rest *(menucha)*, which meant that one should be calm, have peace of mind *(menuchat-nefesh)* and not be disoriented, bewildered, lose balance. The second characteristic of Musar was *savlanut*, which means simply patience, and was intended to provide a reason why even to suffer troubles one must employ a measure of patience *(midah shel savlanut)*, because otherwise a human being could not bear his heavy destiny. Savlanut meant also to be able to suffer undesirable elements, which one may meet in one's way. To put it simply, one should be able to suffer every kind of misfortune *(pegah-rah)* and not lose one's bearings. The third attribute *(midah)* of Musar is order *(seder)* - to keep things in order, which would save a man much time and many worries when he is orderly. Then follows diligence *(charitzut)*, which means to weigh and measure every step, each deed, and then to do everything with diligence and meaning. To other good attributes belong *(nekiyut)*, cleanliness and tidiness of both the body and soul, both in dress and in habits. A human should have a clear conscience and cleanliness in all his dealings. Another characteristic is *anavah* - modesty and recognition of personal faults *(tauyot,)* and only later to look for faults in others. The other six characteristics of Musar include the notion of *kimutz* - thriftiness, frugality, not to waste assets on unnecessary things. *Zrizut* is yet another attribute, which teaches not to waste time on useless activities, but also not to concentrate on practical and useful things only, either for oneself or for others. With it all one must learn the art of silence, or as it is called in Hebrew *shtikah*. This refers to all human beings, and it means that before one speaks one should consider if it is worth saying. The last two rules *(klalim)* of good manners in Musar are relaxation *(nichutah)*, which means to fulfill *(mekayem)* the attribute that "words of wise men are listened to with pleasure" (*"divrei chachamim be'nachat nishmaim"*) and "the last is the friendliest" (*"acharon chaviv"*), and the truth *(emet)*, which means not to say things that can create a suspicion *(chashad)* that something is not true or whether it is really all true *(kulo emet)*. Reb Yosef Yoysl Hurovitz had strictly followed the teachings of all the recommended books *(se'ifim)* of Musar. He was not satisfied with the opinion *(svarah)*, that he was only better than others *(oleh al kulam)* were. He had his accretion *(hosafot)* of knowledge, which helped him to overcome his previous limitations (*gader*) of the ordinary (*stam*) Musar.

Yeshiva students.

D. Reb Yosef Yoysl was a son of Rabbi Shlome Zalmon Ziv (?), who changed his name later to Hurovitz. Reb Shlome Zalmon was the rabbi of Flugian and from there moved as head of the (religious) community (*marah-de'atrah*) of Kurtuvian, close to Shavl of the Kovno district, where he lead the community (*kehile*) for a period of 20 years. As would be expected, Yosef Yoysl acquired his basic education under the supervision of his father. The great abilities of Yosef Yoysl became obvious, when at the age of 16 years he was reciting the lesson (*hasheur*) in the synagogue of Kurtuvian. He married young, as did many young scholars of those days. After the wedding, he had to engage in commerce (*mischar*) because his father-in-law died before the wedding. However, as it happened, it was this need for his frequent journeys (*nesiot*) to Memel that introduced him to the "holiest of holies" ("*kodshei kodashim*") of Musar. Reb Israel Salander, the founder of the Musar method lived at that time in Memel. No matter how much his soul was attracted to Musar, it can not justify his remarkable determination to leave behind his neglected (*hefker*) wife and children and lock himself up, hidden from the world (*bechadrei chadrim*), to study and plunge into the depth of Musar. This attribute gives a full picture of the character and obstinacy of Reb Yosef Yoysl.

Obviously, almost everyone tried to dissuade Reb Yosef Yoysl from such an undertaking and advised him to return home, but he did not yield until his wife came to him and stayed with him in the circle of religious studies. Even Reb Israel could not persuade him to change his mind and return home to his family. Obviously, all this caused much anxiety to his father and even more to his wife, but the fire of Musar was to prevail (gover) over all. We do not intend to convey here the details (befrotrot) of all the insides and happenings of Yosef Yoysl's life. We are describing here only, based on his conduct (hanhagah), a man of the greatest enthusiasm (hitlahavut). His spirit had a great influence on everybody in Novogrudok. Its Yeshiva created a new way of life and Reb Yosef Yoysl called the tune, and was the guide (moreh-derech) for hundreds of youths and adults, who found shelter under the wing of Musar. How did Novogrudok react to his (Musar) method? What was the attitude to the young people who were in the Yeshiva and the circle? A great many local inhabitants were almost hypnotized by Reb Yoysl and were prepared to tolerate (hanachot) and endure all sacrifices (korbanot) as long as he could continue with his method and create a generation of God fearing and complete (beings) (yere'im ushlomim). There were however a large number of inhabitants who did not agree with all the eccentricities and have quietly, from time to time, protested against his behaviour (hanhagah,), against the epidemic of Musar, and even the heads of the community (mara-de'atrah) of Novogrudok, were initially (lechatchila) protesting against the Yeshiva and against its leader Reb Yoysl. Non-the-less this remained an internal matter and nobody publicized (mefarsem) the dispute (sichsuch). Reb Yoysl was a remarkable character, he was obstinate and would not let anything stop his endeavors. When he had to leave Novogrudok because of divisions of opinions (chilukei deot) with his community (kehile), he found another way of following the method of Musar. But he did not surrender. This characteristic could be observed in his character on each occasion, though in later years he became more flexible. An interesting fact is that when his father died in 1890 and Kurtuvian offered him the position that he would have inherited from his father as head of the community, he did not accept it because he had a sister who was left an orphan and he rejected the rabbinical seat (kise harabanut) in favour of his future brother in law. On the anniversary [of his father's death?] Reb Yoysl decided to shut himself in a room of a blacksmith's house and not allow anyone near him, but sit and immerse (chakirah) himself in Musar. To bathe in, he even made for himself his own ritual bath (mikvah). He showed strength of character, so that on the New Year he did not go to the synagogue to hear the blowing of the ram's horn. This was not done with ill intent, but he preferred to study rather than to pray. Books kept on his table were books on religious laws and morality (*sifrei halachah ve'sifrei Musar*). He studied repeatedly the "*Shulchan Aruch*" (a book of religious laws) "*Orach Chaim*" ("A Way of Life") "*Choshen Mishpat*" (a book of (religious) laws) and other books, which would separate him from the everyday world and change into a sort of asceticism (*nazir*). It is interesting to read in "*Hamelitz*" in No. 18 of the year 1883 (*Tof Rez Mem Giml*) an article (*ma'amar*) by Reb Moshe Yehoshua Halevi Levin, where the author made a joke about Reb Yoysl and called him "*nazir beisrael*" (an ascetic among the people of Israel). He was also exposed to criticism from the Goan of Kovno Reb Itschok Elchonon, who sent for him once and asked him "why did you not appear to listen to the blowing of the ram's horn?" Reb Yoysl was not fazed by this question and replied that "First comes avoidance of the bad (*sur mera*) and only then comes the doing of good" ("*ve'ase tov*") by which he meant that it is better to avoid people with their faults (*chesronot*), than to listen to the blowing of the horn. Basically he was a type of an ascetic (*parush*), because asceticism (*prishat*) was his main characteristic, However, in later years he convinced himself that such isolation (*prishat*) is not natural (*lo kederech hateva*) and he began to mitigate his principles.

E. The ways of Reb Yoysl have disappointed even his teachers (*Rabeim*), Reb Simche Zisl from Chelm and also Reb Itschok Bloser. To their aid came Reb Itschok Elchonon, a giant of his generation (*Gdol Hador*) and they all were looking for a solution or tricks (*tachbulot*) to extract him from his lethargy and his solitude (*hitbodedut*). For entire two years they conducted discussions with him to convince him to abandon his isolation, until in the end he had to give in and re-enter the open world. Giving up the isolation (*prishut*) meant that he admitted that the time of seclusion had ended for him. Now he could teach others so as to recompense the multitude (*lezakot et harabim*). Leaving his seclusion had altered his new way of life, he entered the era of spreading the learning of the Torah and this had become his obsession, and again with the same zeal (*kanaut*) as he displayed in his previous solitude (*hitbodedut*), he engaged in creating small circles of learning (*kolelim*). He could not be satisfied with Novogrudok alone, but he entered the wide world with the same teaching of Musar and zeal (*kanaut*). He created a circle (*kolel*), a sort of branch of Novogrudok, in Lubch and established a big new network of circles in Dvinsk, Minsk, Warsaw, Berdichev, Lida, Zetl etc. He insisted that the head of the movement should be the famous leader of Musar, Reb Itschok Bloser, who was at the time (*be'et*) the main strength of the Musar movement (*tnuat Musar*) and carried Reb Yosef Yoysl on his shoulders. Notwithstanding all the branches and circles, the Novogrudok house of the big Yeshiva Yosef (*bet Yosef Yeshive Gdole*) was his main centre, his spiritual arsenal, from which he has drawn inspiration for himself and for others. Later he endeavoured to centralise all small Yeshivot (*Yeshivot ktanot*) in the Yeshiva of Novogrudok and dozens of students from many towns of the district came to Novogrudok. Some come from as far as Caucuses and other alien places, to study in Novogrudok. And many chasids have sent their children to study the Torah and Musar in the Centre Yeshiva of Yosef in Novogrudok (*Merkaz Yeshiva Novogrudok bet Yosef*). The Rabbi of Novogrudok Reb Yechiel Michl Epshtin helped Reb Yoysl to succeed. Reb Epshtin was the author of the book "*Aruch Hashulchan*" (a book of religious laws, using the title of the famous "*Shulchan Aruch*" in reversed order). Reb Epshtin did not follow the method of Musar, but had respect for Reb Yoysl and approved (*haskamot*) of his followers (*meshulachim*). A letter from Reb Epshtin of Novogrudok exerted at that time a large influence. Also, the lay world respected the young men who received permission (*heiter hora'ah*) from Reb Yechiel Michl Epshtin to teach. At that time, the Centre Yeshiva of Yosef had about (*karov*) three hundred students in addition to the large number of young men in the circle, which together amounted to four hundred students of the Torah. Reb Yoysl had put all his body and soul into the circle of Novogrudok. He endeavoured (*mishtadel*) to influence the military authorities to exempt his pupils from military service, so as not to interrupt their study of the Torah. He was, however, the one in charge ("*moshel bakipa*") in the Yeshiva and in the circle. He did not allow anyone to interfere in the affairs of the Yeshiva. He alone was the head of the Yeshiva, he alone recited the lesson and he alone set the innovations to the Torah *(chidushei Torah)*. To be better prepared for the task (*mlachah*) he spent some time in Brest, where he gained much from the teachings of Reb Chaim Soloveichik the head of the (religious) community of Brest. When the workload had become too big for one man, he divided the Yeshiva into groups, according to the level of knowledge of the pupils. He involved his brothers-in-law Reb Alter Shmulovich, Reb Eruchim Varhaftig and Reb Simche Sokolovski to help with the load. Reb Alter did not assist for long, because of differences of opinion with Reb Yoysl and, at that stage, his son-in-law Reb Avrom Yaffe undertook the task. This was actually the best period in the history of the Novogrudok Yeshiva, because it was crammed with studies (*sugiyot*), problems, justifications, chatter and discussions. The main input of Reb Yoysl was the fundamental principle of teaching Musar, because this was the highest aim of his life. Reb Yoysl was at his happiest when he heard the pupils arguing (*nitvakeyach*) at a difficult study or discussion and he did not leave until the matter was settled (Reb Dov Chof Cadic wrote about this subject in his book *"Tnuat Musar"* ("The Musar Movement") p.199). Naturally it was a long process until the Novogrudok bet Yosef Yeshiva obtained its "citizens' rights", because it was a new type of a Yeshiva, a Musar industry with which, to begin with, the common people *(hamon ha'am)* were not familiar. As I remarked before, I do not pretend to have exhausted the full picture and all characteristics of the great Reb Yoysl. Even after the publication of two books by rabbi Chof Cadik and rabbi J.L. (Jud Lamed) Nekrit, many characteristics remained that were not yet not explained to this day (*ad haymow*) and have not been investigated. Reb Yoysl was a colossally great personality and in proportion to his greatness he was also a great possessor of faults *(bal chesronot)* and immensely obstinate and the obstinacy robbed him of a great part of his life and of his appeal. His worries regarding the building of the Yeshiva and the physical well being of his pupils, the continuous battles with the surrounding opponents and jealous people (*be'alei kinah*) , the disorganised family life and other problems have shortened his life. At the time when the first World War started, he was left a shepherd without a flock (*k'eroeh bli tzon*) . The pupils had departed, fled. The living conditions had become very difficult and that was his second bitter calamity, because in 1905 he lived through a big catastrophe, when many pupils have been exposed to evil influences (*le'tarbut ra'ah*). The Russian revolution had brought to an end his woes and battles, though he thought that the revolution will result in strengthening Musar. Let a future Jewish historian look at Reb Yoysl's difficult battles in Novogrudok, which he later lost, because the public opinion (*da'at haklal*) turned against him. There were also thousands of other details (*pratim*) which must be left for the future. It is a rich canvas of many colours, but not everything can be accommodated in one article (*ma'amar*), even if it were somewhat longer. The book about Novogrudok that should serve as a monument to the past Great Novogrudok community should provide space for many other matters, with an apology to the respected reader (*ve'im hakore hanichbad haslicha*).

[The Yiddish writing (particularly of religious texts) of those days was intermingled with many Hebrew words. Their translation is a hazardous task. We include the transliterated Hebrew words next to the translations for each to select a translation that pleases him best.]

[Page 39]

What I Remember of Novogrudok

by Shlomo M. Gutman (Argentina)

Translated from Yiddish by O. Delatycki

Harav Cvi Hirsh Gutman

My memories of Novogrudok are connected with a time before the First World War , when our town was renowned for its famous Yeshiva led by Reb Yosef Yoysl Hurovitz ZLB. The Yeshiva took on the specific 'derech Hamusar' (the way of the Musar), which had become known as the Novogrudok derech (way). My father Reb Zvi Hirsh Gutman ZL was a principal of the Yeshiva and at the same time he travelled to various towns in southern Russia as the representative of the Yeshiva.

Reb Yosef Yoysl, who was later the head of the Yeshiva, and the founder of the new derech (way), had a significant past. I will try to relate a number of events that are known to me as well as to others.

Reb Yosef Yoysl was born in 1850 in the small town of Kurtuvian close to Shavl in Lithuania. His father, Shlome Zalmon, was the Rabbi of the town. His father was considered a great scholar and a God fearing man. Yosef Yoysl had three brothers and four sisters. He had distinguished himself as a young man of great abilities and keenness to study. He joined the Chelm Yeshiva when he was still very young. At the age of 18 he married in the township of Svechne, which was on the German boarder. His father-in-law to be was a businessman. However, he died before the wedding took place, having left a wife and eight children. Yosef Yoysl took over the task of caring for the whole family. He undertook to continue his father-in-law's business. He was successful. Because of his business commitments he was a frequent visitor to Memel, where Reb Isroel Salander was the Rabbi at that time. There are several versions of the story of how Reb Yosef Yoysl met Reb Isroel Salander. I was told the following account: once, as Reb Yosef Yoysl was walking rapidly in a street of Memel in pursuit of his business, a pupil of Reb Isroel Salander, Reb Itschok Bloser (later known as Reb Itchele Peterburger), stopped him. Reb Itschok asked him where he was rushing to. Reb Yosef Yoysl answered that he was in a hurry, because he was about to buy stock for his business. Reb Itchok, seeing that he was speaking to a learned (ben Torah) young man, said that he should give up business and turn to studying Torah and Musar. Reb Yosef Yoysl replied: 'Yes Rabbi, but how will I get my livelihood?' Reb Itchok had allegedly replied: 'Why are you concerned what you will live on, when your concern should be what you will die with. A Jew must be concerned with what he will accomplish before he dies.' Reb Yosef Yoysl said that those words had left a deep impression on him and gave him no peace. He sent back home the money he had on him, remained in Memel and took up studies with Reb Isroel Salander.

He became one of the scholars who began spreading the learning of Musar in the Yeshivas. He established a Yeshiva in Berdichev. When that Yeshiva was functioning well and had 200 students, Reb Yosef Yoysl went to other towns to bring together young men and establish other Yeshivas. On one of his journeys he met a wealthy Jewish merchant, Reb Gershon Sazyner, who owned estates around Zetl. Reb Yosef Yoysl asked Reb Gershon to build for him a hut in his forest, where he would be able to study without interruptions. Reb Gershon built the hut. It had become known that the hut was built with the assistance of a wealthy man named Lachman, from Berlin.

Reb Yosef Yoysl lived in that hut for 9 years. My father was the principal of the Yeshiva, when it was created later. In our house, a number of stories were told about the time of Reb Yosef Yoysl's solitude. One story was that Reb Yosef Yoysl sat in a room, with the door locked. The room had two openings through which food was served to Reb Yoysl. One opening was for milchik (food based on milk) and the other for fleishig (food made with meat). This is why Reb Yosef Yoysl was called the man of the gash.

After Reb Yosef Yoysl had spent 9 years in seclusion, he, together with other students of Reb Salander, went into the world, to towns and townships, where they created organisations for young people. The purpose was for them to collect money to make it possible to study Musar. The youth who joined were young men who left their homes and took up full time studies. Such organisations were created in the towns of Novogrudok, Zetl, Lubch, Shavl, Dvinsk and Lida. Young people were studying everywhere. They were supplied with food from a special kitchen and were given 6 roubles per month by the communities they lived in, which the students passed on to support their families. Reb Yosef Yoysl travelled to all the schools, stayed for a while, taught the students and was implanting the way of the Musar. He would stay in a place for no more than a month before going on to the next place. Once a year, in the month of Elul, a get together of the students from all the schools would take place. The venue would change from year to year. One year they assembled in Novogrudok, the next year in Slonim and so on.

Finally Reb Yosef Yoysl had decided to establish a Yeshiva. He has chosen Novogrudok as the preferred place. At that time the Rabbi of Novogrudok was Reb Yechiel Michl Epshtin the author of the book *Aruch Hashulchan*, who was the father-in-law of the head of the Yeshiva in Volozyn, Reb Naftale Zvi Yehuda Berlin, known as the NZYB of Volozyn. Reb Yechiel Michl was supportive of the initiative of Reb Yosef Yoysl. A number of local inhabitants helped. Thus, in 1896 the Yeshiva was created. It was the first of hundreds of Yeshivas of Musar, which were created subsequently. They all assumed the name of Novogrudok Yeshivas.

At the beginning, Reb Yosef Yoysl created in Novogrudok a circle of learning. Later he assembled in Zetl all members of the circles, about 50 young men. He than found suitable spiritual leaders and created a Yeshiva. However, a division occurred in respect of the way of the Musar. A number of Rabbis had declared their opposition to the Yeshiva and insisted that the citizens of Novogrudok should not support it. The Yeshiva had, however, its supporters, foremost among them the Rabbi Epshtin. He supported the Yeshiva and its management.

Let us mention some of the other supporters. I remember well some of them. They were: Leib Kabak, Yehoshua Leib Harkavy (father of Alexander Harkavy), Eliohu Faigenberg, Shmuel Krasnopiurka, known as Reb Shmuel Matuses, Eliezer Levin, Velvl Movshovich and others.

The opposition to the Yeshiva had come to public notice in the paper Hazvira. The struggle subsided only after the Rabbi of Novogrudok, Reb Yechiel Michl Epshtin had openly denied in the Hazvira all inventions and suspicions expressed about the Yeshiva and its ways.

At that time Reb Yosef Yoysl had summoned my father, Reb Cvi Hirsh Gutman ZLB, who was at the time the Rabbi of Tshelba in Crimea. My father travelled to the towns and townships of Southern Russia to create there Yeshivas modelled on the Yeshiva in Novogrudok. My father, influenced by Reb Yosef Yoysl, created Yeshivas in Cherson, Mohilev-Podolsk, Kamieniec-Podolsk, Berdichev, Nikolaev, Balty, Odessa and other places. Reb Yosef Yoysl sent young scholars to lead the Yeshivas. The connections with those Yeshivas were of big importance during the First World War , when the teaching of Musar was concentrated mostly in the Ukrainian towns.

In 1908 the Rabbi of Novogrudok, Reb Yechiel Michl Epshtin, died. The town wanted to appoint a suitable Rabbi as a replacement. Among the prospective candidates were Harav Burshtain from Tavrik in Lithuania and Reb Itzchok Jankef Reines from Lida. Both candidates were unsuccessful. They opposed the way of the Musar of Reb Yosef Yoysl. Yosef Yoysl and his friend did everything to prevent the appointment of these two Rabbis. The town was for a long time without a Rabbi.

The story of the development of the Yeshiva, which was a model for many Yeshivas in the world, was of great interest. A condensed version of the history of the Novogrudok Musar Yeshiva can be found in a collective book. It was written by Rabbi I. L. Nekrich, who is at present the head of the Novogrudok Yeshiva in Brooklyn.

I would like to add a few details about the family of Reb Yosef Yoysl. He had three sons-in- law: Reb Alter, Reb Isroel Yankef Lubchanski and Reb Avrom Yoffe. Reb Alter was a renowned scholar and was a follower of the education by 'derech hapilpul' (by way of conversation). After each of his lectures the students discussed the topic amongst themselves for a long time. He was not a follower of Reb Yosef Yoysl's way of Musar. This led to frequent altercations between father-in-law and son-in-law. In the end Reb Alter left Novogrudok and he became the head of the Yeshiva in Schuchin. Reb Isroel Yankef followed the direction of his father-in-law. He was the supervisor of the Yeshiva in Baranovichi 'Oil Torah' which followed the way of Musar. In later years (from 1921) Reb Alter Wasserman was the head of the Yeshiva. My father Zvi Hirsh Gutman was the principal till the last day of its existence. Reb Isroel Yankef Lubchanski and my father were killed by the Nazi (may their name be erased) together with the Jewish community of Baranovichi.

Reb Avrom Yoffe was the head of the Novogrudok Yeshiva in Bialystok, the biggest Yeshiva in Poland between the two World War s. This Yeshiva 'Beit Yosef', which was the name of all Novogrudok Yeshivas in Poland, supervised 30 other Beit Yosef Yeshivas. Reb Avrom Yaffe survived by a miracle. After many tribulations he came to the United States, were he established the Novogrudok Yeshiva. At present he is the head of the Beit Yosif Yeshiva in Israel.

The 8 December is the anniversary of the Kehile Gdoyshe in Novogrudok. This is the date of the first slaughter in Novogrudok, in which 5000 victims were killed. Novogrudok was destroyed in this and subsequent actions. The town was famed before the war of having great and wise men as well as good and honest Jews. It was changed from a Kehile Gdoyshe into a Kehile of the dead IZAV Ibone Zion Veureu (let it be rebuilt in Zion and its towns).

There was once a habit among the Jews that when in a document the name of the community was written the words HID Hashem Incom Dumom were added (my G-d take revenge for their innocent blood).

I don't know how the habit had begun. Maybe this contained a premonition that if a community would be destroyed the Jewish spirit would not be eradicated. The destroyed settlements will be rebuilt in Zion.

Perhaps this will be a certain consolation for the big catastrophe, which occurred.

Shiniezits Street

[Page 42]

Leaders and ordinary members of the community

by E.V. Yerushalmi

Translated from Yiddish by O. Delatycki

(The help in translation by Les Kipen is acknowledged).

All we know about the history of our town before the beginning of the XIX century, are stories about the Rabbis. From that time onwards we have information about the lives and habits of ordinary people and leaders of the Novogrudok community. The sources of that information are grave stones in the Novogrudok cemetery, written sources and the memories of persons who are still alive. The oldest of the prominent Jewish inhabitants, whose legible grave stone remained, was Reb Eliahu Bar Gershon, who was the brother of Rabbi Alexander Ziskind and Reb Moshe Harkavy, who both played prominent parts in the life of our town. The grave stone is dated 1822. Of the householders who lived in town from the forties to the late eighties of the XIX century, the biggest influence on the life of the town was exerted by two families: the Harkovies and the Kabaks. Two brothers were particularly prominent: Rabbi Alexander Ziskind, who died in 1850, and his brother Moshe Kabak. (Reb Moshe was the grandfather of the famous Hebrew novelist Dr Kabak, the author of *Bmishol hatzar* and other works). Rabbi Ziskind is mentioned in the chapter on Rabbis. We will now describe, among others, two prominent townsmen Reb Moshe Harkavy and Reb Yoysef Kabak.

Reb Moshe Harkavy

He was raised on the Torah, as were all his brothers, but he was an enterprising man and had chosen to become a merchant. He had a large wine and grocery store, which was well known in the whole district. One could buy there the dearest wines and the best delicatessen. The customers were mainly landowners from the surrounding district, who used to come often to Novogrudok to enjoy themselves and attend balls. He conducted himself in a modern manner: beautifully polished rooms, the merchandise arranged in good order with bookkeepers and salesmen in attendance, not at all as in a provincial town. His *achnose* (income) was considerable and he lived affluently. His demeanour was always that of a Jew and he always wore a yarmelke and was well dressed and tidy in his habits. Being a man of the world, he gave his children a worldly education, which was, non-the-less, in tune with a Jewish upbringing. He took a considerable interest in the affairs of the community and in matters of charity, to which, as a townsmen said, he gave a tithe of his *achnose*.

Reb Moshe Harkavy. Rabbi in Novogrudok from 1838 to 1850

He maintained his own *kloyz* (small synagogue) where the "aristocrats" of Novogrudok prayed, as did learned men and *maskilim* (followers of Haskala, meaning modern intellectuals). On the Sabbath, after the prayers, anyone from the *kloyz* who so desired, could come to his house for a *kidish* (a traditional drink). The tables were readied for them with all of the best. He was much esteemed and Reb Movshe's name had the sound of authority in the town. He was also respected by the Russian officials and the land owners of the district. His contacts enabled him to be of help to the Jewish community (about his character see "*Otrivki, vospominania*" (Excepts, recollections) by Vladimir Harkavy in "*Perezytoie*" (Experiences) volume 4 pp 271-272.)

Bread was often distributed from his house to poor families. His wife Etl was in charge of the household expenses. She was the daughter of Reb Benjamin from Shereshov, of the Grodno gubernia. Reb Moishe died in 1877 at the age of 72. His wife died 5 years later.

Reb Yousef Kabak

It was said about him in town that he stemmed from a poor family. He worked his way up to wealth. It is not known if he had an education in his youth, but later, when he came to a *maamed* (position, status, class) he spent time studying Torah. He was dealing with land owners and had succeeded remarkably well. He was in his day the richest man in Novogrudok. Just as Reb Moshe Harkavy, he was loyal to his town and he was devoted to the community. Apart from his usual donations to charities, he was concerned about a special obligation - to provide three meals on every Sabbath for each needy family. He had his own *kloyz* (small synagogue), where every Saturday food was laid out on tables and served to anyone present. He died at an old age in 1880. His grave stone tells of his good deeds.

Apart from the Harkavies and the Kabaks, there were the Zamkovys, the Bailins, the Pikers, the Rabinoviches, the Chishins, Sapotnickis, the Israelits, the Sostkoviches, the Vagers and the Metropolitanskis.

Reb Moishe Frumkies Sapotnicki was of particular merit. He was one of the leaders of the town. He guarded the piety of the community, he made sure that the pupils of the Yeshiva and of the Talmid Torah did not waste time and did not get off the path of righteousness. He died in old age in 1898.

Pupils and teachers of the Torah

In the XIX century the study of the Torah in Novogrudok was at its summit. The whole youth of Novogrudok studied in the Talmud Torah and in the *cheders* (primary religious schools). There were also Yeshivot in Novogrudok, where local and out of town youths were studying. The students from other towns had "eating days" (i.e. they ate, by arrangement, in different houses on each day of the week). Many householders were learned. There were poorer people, who had no opportunity to study in their youth. They made an effort to study in their later years. There were those who with will to learn and *hatmode* (diligence), achieved the level of a learned person. The whole town was steeped in the study of the Torah. The Rashi Yeshivot lectured every day. The teachers taught children *mikra*, *mishna* and *Gemora*. Those desiring to learn were studying the Torah day and night in synagogues and *kloyzn*. People who were engaged all day in business and trade, had, after work and early in the morning, devoted many hours to the study of the Torah. Of the learned of Novogrudok and *gdoilim* (literally - great, eminent), it is appropriate to mention the following personalities:

HeyGiml"Reiz Maishe Mordichai

A giant in the study of the Torah, who died in 1847. He is mentioned in the book "*Kehilat Yankof*" by Reb Yankof the Rabbi of Karlin.

Harav Efraim Mordechai Epshtein

The *mechaber* (author) of the books "*Mira dchiya*", a *pirush* [a commentary] on "*Pirkey Avot*" and "*Machane Efraim*", a *pirush* on *Maharsha*. He published responsa in the journal "*Haflas*" year B.

Reb Gershon Harkavy

A brother of the well known scholar the orientalist Dr Abram Eliahu Harkavy (about him see further). For a long time, until the end of the 80's (i.e. 1880's) he was the head of the Yeshiva. He lectured in the Great Synagogue. In about 1890 he left for Erets Israel, where he later took over the position of his father Reb Yankef (who died in 1894) as the head of the Yeshiva "*Etc Chaim*" in Jerusalem.

Reb Zelig Azriel

The head in the Yeshiva of the third class of the Talmud Torah (about him see a notes by Yosif Vaiter).

Reb Isser the *Masmid* {Diligant} (surname Horovitz)

He was one of the nicest persons in town. He spent his time studying the Torah both by himself and with others. He distinguished himself by his tolerance of the young and the modern generation. The source of his income was a small grocery shop, which was managed by his wife, and from teaching the Talmud. He was teaching *Gemora* to older children of the wealthy and enlightened householders, who valued him for his mild nature and his teaching skill. Reb Isser belonged to the *kloyz* of Moishe Harkavy, of whom he was a favourite. The name "*masmid*" (diligent) speaks for itself. He was given it for his outstanding diligence in learning. He was very pious but not a fanatic. He was tolerant of the endeavours of the younger generation of the *Haskola* and was popular among them.

In 1880 Reb Isser went to live with his daughter in Roznoyi, Grodno gubernia, where he remained until 1903. From there he moved to his second daughter's home in Slonim. In the same year in *Shmini Hazeret*, he died aged 88 years.

Reb Hendel the *Melamed* (surname Obelinski)

Rabbi Obelinski taught Biblical history according to the methods of the German-Jewish philosopher, Moses Mendelsohn.

He was a teacher of *Tanach* and was known as a follower of *Haskola*. At that time, when all these that learned *Tanach* were studying it with the *perushim* (commentaries) of *Rashi* and with other accepted *meforshim* (commentators), Reb Hendel taught *Tanach* of Beor, using the German translation of Moshe Mendelson and his pupils. He was an exceptionally gentle and honest man. He was particularly liked by the younger generation.

Reb Nechemia de-Lion

He was a grandson of Leizer Bruchovich de-Lion, the chief contractor of powder and arms for the Russian army in the time of Tsar Alexander I. De Lion was also a member of a Jewish committee together with the contractor Zanenberg. At the time of Nicholas I, Leizer Bruchovich lost all his contracts.

Reb Nechemia de-Lion, his grandson, was the main contractor of a large Catholic monastery. He supplied all the needs of the monks and nuns. He would purchase from Moshe Harkavy 120 roubles worth of candles for a festival day. He was so trusted in the monastery and he could enter the cells of the monks and nuns unannounced. In the family de Lion, (later Yerusalemski - Yerushalmi), the following story is related: on one holiday evening Reb Nechemia de Lion entered the monastery and found the monks and nuns together, drunk and *michutz leagader* (literally - outside the fence, beyond the pale). He started to reprimand the monks and the nuns and said "how would you look if one of the landowners, who donates thousands of roubles to the monastery, would come now". But the drunk and lewd monks and nuns did not understand a word he said. Then de Lion took off his belt, gave them a belting and locked them up in their cells. He did not release them till the next morning. The monks and nuns were very grateful to him.

The land owners used to place with Reb Nechemia tens of thousands of roubles of *shalish* (trust) money. He was a *boirer* (mediator) among them and his authority among the priests was higher than of the senior hierarchy.

On a particular market day, his son Reb Yoshe Cyres, asked him for a loan for the day. His father refused. "But you have *shalish* money" his son reminded him. Reb Nechamia was angered and said "Do you expect me to take other peoples *pikdoines* (deposited) money?" and he did not lend money to his son.

One day, after Reb Nechamia died, an old monk was passing the de Lion house and saw Reb Nechamia's daughter in law, Cyre Reb Yoshes, mending the roof. The monk told her "Your father in law could have filled this house with gold, but he was too honest".

His son Yoshe son of Nachamie or Reb Yoshe Cyres, (because his mother was famous as an *eishes chail*) was more of a *yshev ohel* (literally - sitter in a tent, meaning one who was sitting and learning) a Jew a *lamdan* (a man of learning). Business was conducted by his wife, Cyre. When Reb Yitzchak Elchanan left Novogrudok in 1864, he was asked by his *mikorvim* (followers) "Rabbi, who are you leaving behind in charge of the town?" Reb Yitzchak Elchanan answered "I am leaving here two honest Jews Reb Iser Masmid and Reb Yoshe the son of Nechemie". Reb Leib, the *shoiched* (ritual slaughterer), was a son of Reb Yoshe (about him and his children see the memoirs of Yosef and William Uris, who were grandsons of Reb Leib). Leon Uris, the author of "Exodus" is the son of William and the great grandson of Reb Leib).

Enlightened citizens, *maskelim* and learned man.

Novogrudok was prominent not only as *makom* (place) of the Torah (i.e. place of learning), but also as a place of enlightenment and the *haskole* starting with the time of the enlightened Rabbi Reb Israel Leibl. From the end of the XVIII century the spirit of *haskole* and secular education was manifest there. From that time the learning of Hebrew and European languages, particularly German, had spread. It was not just the less observant, even the orthodox youths were studying general subjects. Reb Sa'adie the *mohel* (one who performs circumcisions) can be seen as an example. He was fluent in the Russian language.

Of the Novogrudok *maskelim* of the XIX century, who excelled in their education and learning we will mentioned the following personalities:

Reb Yoisef Bezalel Harkavy (the son of the above mentioned Reb Eliahu)

A merchant, a man of learning, *maskiel* and a communal benefactor. He was a son in law of the eminent Reb Shmuel Strashun of Vilno, who established the world renowned Strashun library. At that time, Reb Yosif Bezalel had become the head of the well known printing house Ram. He died in 1873 at the age of 60.

Wladimir (Wolf) Harkavy

The son of Reb Yosif Bezalel, a man of learning and a *maskil*. He gained a university degree and was a prominent lawyer in Moscow, where he was a distinguished public figure in Jewish circles. He died on the 8th of September 1911. He wrote memoirs about his home town and his student days, which appeared in the Russian-Jewish annual "*Perezitoe*" (Experiences) (vol.4, pp 270-278).

Dvora Ram

The daughter of Reb Yoisef Bezalel and sister of Wladimir Harkavy. She married Dovid Ram, the son of the famous *madpis* (printer). Reb Yoisef Rubin Ram of Vilno. When her husband died she managed the business which assumed the name "*Haalmanah vehaachim*" (The widow and brothers) Ram. She died in 1904 in her 70's.

Dr Avrham Eliohu Harkavy

Born in Novogrudok in 1835, died in 1919 in St Petersburg. He lived in Novogrudok in his youth. He had a religious education. He was attracted later to the *haskola*. He entered the Vilno Rabbinical collage, which he completed in a short time by skipping years and enrolled in the St Petersburg University. (his detailed biography is in a book "*Dor vechachamav*" by Moshe Reinem, Krakow 1890 and in the Jewish Encyclopaedia vol. 6 pp 235-236).

Gershon Harkavy (The son of Reb Moshe Harkavy).

Self-educated, he combined the knowledge of the Torah with wisdom. Was versed in "*chochmat Israel*", knew several European languages (Russian, German and French) as well as oriental languages (particularly Arabic and Aramaic). He had an extensive library, which was available to anyone who craved for knowledge. All the young *maskilim* of the town who endeavoured to acquire an education gathered in his house. Gershon died in 1875 aged 52 years. In the "*Hamagid*" of that year (November 20) an obituary appeared written by the official Rabbi of Novogrudok, Chaim Yelin.

Jakov Harkavy

A son of Reb Gershon. An educated man and an activist, who participated in the works of the friendly society *Shokdey Melocho*. His aim was to educate the Jewish youth in the old Jewish spirit. He had written a brochure on this issue under the title "A few words about our upbringing and education". He died in Vilno in 1919 aged 58 years.

Chaim Jelin

The official Rabbi of Novogrudok from the beginning of the 70's to the late 80's of the XIX century. He was a man of letters and foreign languages. Apart from his official job, he taught both Jews and landowners from the surroundings German and French. He was a retiring and likable man.

Reb Sa'adia the scribe and the *moel* (Kantorovich) (A brother of Reb Nachemie de Lion).

A remarkable personality. He was both orthodox and worldly. Regardless of the fact that at in his days it was considered sacrilegious for pious Jews to learn a foreign language, he knew Russian, in which he wrote *"proshenes"* (petitions) for his fellow townsmen. He had, among other *hashlamos* (accomplishments), an aptitude for drawing. He wrote the Novogrudok *"Pinkas hakahal"* and also *"Pinkas Shogdey Melocho"*. On the front page there is one of his beautiful drawings *"Sha'ar"*. The booklet about the town was written by Reb Shmuel Matis, the booklet of *Shogday Melocho* by Avrohom Chasovschik. He was also a *moel*. His main income came from bookkeeping and writing of petitions. He died in the 1890's.

Reb Sa'adia the scribe and the *moel* (Kantorovich)

Arke the *melamed* (teacher)

A teacher of Hebrew and German. He was a *boki beshas* (expert in Talmud) in Halachic authorities and responsa and books on philosophy. He was conversant with German literature. He was considered to be an *apicoires* (non-believer) and the older generation shunned him. But the young people turned to him. He taught them German and Hebrew and planted the spirit of *hascola*. Young pupils who came to him to study, did so *beshtike* (in secret, on the quiet) from their pious parents. One of his pupils was Reb Shaptai Rabinovich a son of Reb Avreml, who lived in Boston. Arke was paralysed in his old age, but this did not stop him teaching.

Zvi Hirsh Shteihoise (Hirshele Shmae's')

A popular *maskil*. He was considered to be an *apikoires*, because he read modern Hebrew literature and made merry at the expense of the fanatics and *batlonim*. He was a hero of the youth and there were stories told of his pranks, when he was a student at the Yeshiva. In his late 70's he moved to a village and tilled the soil. He kept his good humour and inquiring mind till the last.

Oizer Fidler (Oizerke or Oizer the *klezmer*)

He played at weddings, and was an extraordinary performer, it is not known if he read music, but when he was playing he spoke to the soul. Tales were told about the magic performed on his fiddle. It was said that his fiddle cried, laughed and teased. It was said that he valued his talent. There were stories that he studied his art in Vilno.

Oizerke was *shem dawar* (well known) beyond the boundaries of the town and he was engaged to play at wealthy weddings in the whole district. He was liked by all, the intelligentsia and simple folk, the rich and the poor. Without him weddings were not celebrated. He died in 1898 at the age of 78 years.

Yehoshua (Jules) Butenski

The son of Chackel the carpenter. A famed sculptor. As a child he learned how to carve and form figures. At the age of 13 he went to Pscov where he studied in the science high school. When he was in the fifth grade he was banished from Pscov, because the town was outside of the Pale of Settlement (ie outside of the area were Jews were allowed to live). At the age of 17 he went to Vienna to further his studies of sculpture. Later he moved to Paris, where the famous Jewish sculptor Antokolski took an interest in him. In Paris and later Barcelona he won prizes for his work. In 1904 he went to the States. He settled in New York where he opened a studio. He was a sculptor of Jewish subjects. Among his works were: a sculpture "The world peace" (or Eshayahu), which the New York Metropolitan Museum of Art had purchased, "The eternal wanderer", "Jehuda Halevy" "Noson the wise" and others. One of his sculptures depicts the soul leaving the matter. Butenski was an ardent Jewish patriot and Zionist. He was born in 1871.

Notte Grodzienski

The son of Reb Uri, Shmul Rabke's son in law. A portrait painter. He had a studio in Berlin.

Unusual characters.

Reb Shepsl the *lekach* (pastry) cook.

Who in our town did not know the good tempered and always smiling Reb Shepsl the *lekach* cook? Who among us does not remember the scene on a Friday night on the eve of Sabbath, when Reb Shepsel surrounded by a few dozen Yeshiva students, *Talmud Tora* pupils and other needy youths, was going from the Great Synagogue to the smaller houses of prayer looking for anyone who would take home one of the students for a Friday night's meal. His face beamed with pleasure, if he could place all students with hosts who would feed them. Having entered a *shul* with his *machane* (band) he would know with whom to place each of his *oirach* (guest). He knew which prospective host was looking forward to feed a *choshevn oirach* (an important guest, in this case a senior student) and which would prefer a *talmud Toire* (in this case a junior pupil). For some tens of years he secured a good Sabbath meal for all needy youngsters. This breed of a Jew disappeared with him.

Reb Avrom Yedida the tailor

Few of us in Novogrudok remember still the winter nights of yore and the early Sabbath mornings when they were lying in bed, snugly buried in their doonas, dreaming sweet dreams when suddenly a sweet, sad tune would wake them: "Jews get up, get up to *avoidas haboire* (serve the Amighty) . That was Reb Avrom Yedida the tailor, who took it on himself to wake the *Thilim* (Psalms) fraternity early on Sabbath and pray *Thilim,* and at the same time wake up everybody to *avoidas haboire* Even in the coldest frosts and blizzards, even if it was dangerous to venture outside the house, Reb Avrom Yedida would go from one end of town to the other and wake everyone with his sweet voice. Nothing would stop him, not even if he was ill and should have stayed in bed he woke the people. Reb Avrom Yedida was also a famed *machnis orchim* (provider of hospitality) . On Friday nights 5-6 students from the Yeshiva sat at his table. During the week 2 pupils from the Talmid Torah ate at his table every day. When he died nobody replaced him. That sort of a Jew died out.

Pinie the water carrier (as described by A.I.)

A broad, solidly built man, radiating physical strength, who, it was said, could lift an ox. He was a man of few words and was considered to be a mysterious person. Some even spoke of a connection with the world beyond - among the dead. Legends were spread that after midnight he would be summonsed by the dead for an *aliya* (call up to the Torah) in the big cold synagogue.

Nobody knew how old he was, his looks never changed. Nobody knew if he ever had a wife or children. Nobody knew where he lived. He was always seen bent under the weight of the yoke with two buckets, carrying water from the well to the houses. In the evening he would come to the Todres kloyz, take his seat behind the oven and stay till late at night.

Nobody would notice him, nobody was interested in him. People were shunning him, he was very dirty and was giving off a bad odour of decay. Nobody knew what he was muttering under his breath. Only seldom at the prayers would he suddenly come up in his wheezing sharp voice with an "amen" or *baruch hu we baruch shmoi* and fall silent again. As he got older he did not have the strength to carry water and he was replaced by Leitovich, the brigand from the forest, who was delivering water for tea in a barrel on a horse driven vehicle, from a stream in Peresike. At that time Pinie was sitting all day and all evening behind the oven in the kloyz. Some objected to the evil smell that he spread, but the old timers did not allow anyone to expel him. "He is alone and a student of the Bible, we can not toss him into the street", they argued. That he was lonely I had no doubt, but I could not see how he could be a "student of the Bible". But I was proven wrong. One day, after the prayers, father, as was his habit, stayed back in the kloyz and had a lively discussion on a religious subject with the Rabbi Ajzenberg, a *musmach* [man of the book] and a big *maskil* (man of knowledge), and Nachman Getzvan (a colossal *lamdan* (learned man) and a linguist, the *mechaber* (author) of the famous at the time *siddur "Al Naharod Barel"* (at the river of Babylon).

They were all pondering, because they were missing [or they were short of] *maamar chazal* (talmudic learning), which they could not find, no matter how they tried. They were all searching and looking through the mountain of prayer books that were lying before them on the table. I was waiting impatiently for the end of the discussion, so that we could go home to eat. Suddenly Pinie came up from his seat behind the oven, moved with his heavy footsteps to the three man engaged in the discussion, recited briefly a *miomer* (Talmudic except) and returned to his seat. The three looked at each other astounded, grabbed a book, looked up a certain paragraph and exclaimed "this is a real *yerushalmi*". On the way home I asked father how Pinie could know things like that. "My child", father said "Pinie knows the *shass barli* (complete Babilonian Talmud) and is *yerushalmi* in all *psokim* (chapters) in philosophical books by heart. There is no other learned person and *mashgiel* (knowledgeable person) in town like he..."

Later he was admitted by Polonski to the old people's home. They kept him there in separate quarters. In his corner he studied day and night. In the late hours of the night he murmured his prayers by heart.

Jewish Water Carriers in Poland

A Jewish water carrier with his son by the well at the "Shulhoif" (The backyard of the Synagogue) of Navaredak (Novogrudek) a town in north Poland. The photo was taken by J.Vinik at the beginning of the 1920s during an expedition over a line of Jewish Shtetlakh in Poland. From the archives of YIVO Vilna.

"Crazy" Yisroel

In his youth he was a carpenter, but, as he was lazy, he gave up work. To tell the truth, he was not crazy, but, to be able to exist he pretended to be simple and did crazy things. With all that, he was thought to be appealing by the people of the town. He did not have a family life, and survived by doing occasional chores and from a pension, which he received from the town. One of his tasks was to bring a stretcher from the dead for which he was given a *gildun* or more [from *gulden* - a coin in imperial Germany and Austria]. He claimed the ownership of the coal, which was left in the ovens of the synagogues. He would sell it to the households for fuel in samovars. He would appropriate the *misher* (a tithe) of a bake. When the housewives were baking bread they had to bake a bun for Isroel. He kept promising, that in recompense he would make for them rolling pins, but this was seldom if ever done. On religious festivals he would invite himself to various households. Hospitality was never refused. In return he would *mehane zain*(entertain) with his crazy *toires* (stories), which were amusing. Here are some samples of his stories: "It is said in the *Tehilim* (psalms): happy is the man who does not follow the*eice fun di rashoim* (advice of the evil ones) and did not stand or sit in the path of the sinners. Do what Zishe did." And he would answer his own puzzle: "He hung". He would say: "It is written in *Pirkei Avot* (ethics of our fathers): the one who accepts the *oll Toire* (burden, yoke of learning) is relieved of the *oll malchut* (yoke of the secular State) and the one who rejects the *oll Toire* is burdened with the *oll malchut*". Isroel used to mix up the quotes and would say: "The one who accepts the *oll Toire* is free of *oll malchut.*, and the one who accepts *oll malchut.* is free of *oll Toire*". And he would ask: "what if he did not want to accept either *oll Toire* or *oll malchut*?" Those listening to him would wonder what *harifes* was he about to display? But Isroel would let forth "If he does not want to accept the *oll Toire* and not the *oll malchut* he will knock his head on the wall (meaning "he will do himself injury to no avail"). Isroel was also a joker, just like Motke Chabad (a legendary wit, who mocked the rich and favoured the poor). It was told that once, when there was no death in town, Isroel put up the *mitta* (bier) in the middle of the market place and left it there. Passers by asked him in astonishment "who is the bier for?". "It is for the town", answered Isroel "I keep hearing that the town is dead, let it lie down and I will take it away". Once, at a Sabbath meal, the host asked him how he liked the food. "Very good" answered Isroel "I wish you that when you will be invited for a meal your Sabbath repast would not be worse".

I heard the following stories about Isroel. On one occasion he disappeared from Novogrudok and nobody knew where he was. Some time later a young man from Novogrudok was passing through a town in Volyn and stopped there to celebrate the Sabbath. He noticed some agitation in town, Jews were running to the large Chasidic synagogue, all were in a hurry to meet a "good Jew". The young man asked the owner of the *achsania* (inn) who the newcomer was, the owner looked at him *bitul* (askance) as if to say "what does a dry Litvak know of the pleasures of the Chasidim?" and replied that a famed good Jew came to town for the Sabbath. The young man became interested and wanted to see the "good Jew". He went to the inn, fought his way through the throng and saw a familiar face. The stranger looked at the young man and also recognised him. The "good

Jew" winked at him and led him to a detached room. The Chasids stood outside wondering why the Litvak deserved such an honour. When they faced each other, the young man said to the "good Jew" Isroelke (a dimunitive and somewhat belitteling form of Isroel), what are you doing here? But the other, instead of answering, poured out rude curses at the young man, who thought that Isroel was out of his mind. "No, brother, I am not crazy, I am only making up for lost opportunities. For all those years I did not have anyone to open my heart to".

Arie Mes-Mitzvah

A middle aged, of medium sized, dressed in torn trousers through which one could see dirty legs, a military jacket and an uncovered brown chest, always with a butt of cigar in his mouth - this was the person. His name was given to him because of his occupation. He was the provider of information for the *Chevre Kadishe* (Burial Society). If somebody died, Arie would appear in the market place and would cry "go to the *mes-mitzvah*", with the voice of an heroic tenor that was often similar to the sound of an old goat, but was heard over kilometres. Housewives with frightened faces would appear in the open doorways and would ask "Arie, who died?" Arie replied "Such and such died". His "office" was at the door of Leipuner's restaurant. Here he was always given a surfeit of bread, sausage, pork and, most importantly, half a bottle (of vodka), and boxes filled with butts of cigars from the mouth of the owner of the restaurant, the fat Leipuner.

Reb Tritl the *soifer*

Praying on Sabbath was always difficult for me. It occupied the best part of my only day of freedom. After the prayers were concluded, there were my father's conversations, which sometimes lasted for hours and caused me pain and anger. But when Reb Tritl the *soifer* was praying at the pulpit the time seemed to pass rapidly. He was not a *chasn* (cantor), nor a *bal tfile* (leader of the praying) he was a bal bechi, who brings on tears. He was praying by reciting the prayers, he was explaining every word, every *posl*, such that the words found their way to the hearts of the congregation and awakened the consciousness and the nicest feelings. Reb Tritl was particularly good at interpreting the prayers about Zion. He could be compared to the great poet Yehuda Halevy. It was not only *metikes* (pleasantness), it touched all feelings. This is why during his prayers even the biggest *davronim* (talkers) were silent. Even children set silently. Reb Tritl spoke to their soft hearts. But, when praying the *Kol Nidre Maariv* (the evening Kol Nidre prayer) Reb Tritl exceeded himself. The long, narrow Tadres synagoge was filled with the flames of hundreds of candles. The air was saturated with their holy smoke and the fear of the *Yom ha Din* (Day of Judgment). But when Reb Tritl's pleading, speaking voice would spread, everybody recovered and was of good heart. And not just at *Kol Nidre* but also at the *sliches* (Prayers of Pardon) which were said at the end of *Maariv* (evening prayer). He would put in this prayer all his soul. Because of his *sliches*, we, the children would remain in the synagogue till the end of *Maariv*. Some of the members of the congregation would leave the synagogue in a better mood and hope. Such a prayer must open the *Shaare Rachamim* (gates of mercy). After completing his *Shliches Tzibur* Reb Tritl would retreat quietly to his corner, next to the pulpit, so as not to be overwhelmed by the calls of *Yise Koyach* by the congregation, though they meant it sincerely. He was almost unnoticed in the synagogue, he seldom spoke, and even more seldom took part in political discussions. But when there was discussion about Israel, Reb Tritl could not hold back and would quietly join the participants and listened attentively. After the prayers he would often accompany my father and ask of news "from over there" from Israel, of the new settlers. My father would chat with him willingly and share all the news, which he obtained by reading and listening. I also benefited from these talks. All conversations with Reb Treitl took place on the way home. Because of the talks, father would not be detained in the synagogue. Once I had the pleasure of seeing Reb Treitl in our home. Father came back with a group of Jews, among them Reb Treitl. The guests were in a festive mood. Father served liquors, which he obtained together with Vysocki tea and sugar three times a year for Kriyat Hatora (reading of the Torah scrolls) and cake. At that time he produced an assignation of Jewish *oises* (letters), which he showed to his guests and each held them by the tips of their fingers and read with tears in their eyes the words "Anglo-Palestinian bank". The guests drank some more and spoke wishing each other the same *geule* .

As he grew old Reb Tritl moved to the *Meishev Zkeinim* (Old Peoples home), which was rebuilt after the fire in the Yiddishe street. There too, he occupied a place of honour and presided at the table on the Sabbaths and holidays. His praying was remembered in the Todres kloyz for many years. In my memory he remained as one of the great personalities of my old, dear Novogrudok.

Reb Yoshe Hertzkes.

He lived in a small dilapidated house in the *Chaser* (Pig) lane. In the small quarters lived also his two daughters and their children. Thus, except for the long table, where we, the pupils, sat, there was no room to move in. In time he had to move to the Todres kloyz. When I joined his *cheder* (primary religious school) he was already old. I think that he was weak and that may have been his final term. He had no teeth left in his mouth. It was difficult, therefore, for me to understand his speech. And yet my best memories of my childhood were of the years in the cheder of Reb Yoshe. He was a *melamed* (teacher), who was doing God's work with faith. He looked upon his task as a *heilige schliche* (God sent) which was filled with *mesires nefesh* (total dedication). It was considered a *schoos* (a privilege) to attend his cheder, because he would admit only 10 pupils. Once, by mistake, two more pupils were enrolled. He did not admit them and asked for a *Din Torah* (religious court hearing) by the Rabbi to decide the issue. The Rabbi *hot gepaskend* (has given the verdict) that he should accept both pupils. He was a teacher of God's *genod* (blessing). He educated each pupil such that he would be able to reach a level where he could understand by himself a *blat Gemore* (a section of the Talmud). He would work systematically and easy. He would start by teaching his pupils the difficult Aramaic expressions. Then he would visualise and explain in a lively manner the *sugia* (problems which were the subjects to be studied) and by using the dialectic method, asking fitting questions he would lead the pupil to the right answer. At the same time the pupils would be guided to self education and would prepare the *blat Gemore* for his *sheur* (lesson). He would only correct the mistakes and would further the depth of knowledge of his pupils.

Apart from *Gemore* he taught *Nikud* (punctuation). He was known as the best *menaked* (authority on punctuation) in town. There was no *tiych* (interpretation) or *peirush* (translation) in *Radak* or *Eben Ezara* which Reb Yoshe could not explain. He would, with his pupils, interpret according to the *klalim* from *dikduk* (rules of grammar) of the Tanach. He taught Tanach in the hours before lunch when the pupils were already weary. And he would arrange it such that he would embrace all the rules of the *dikduc*. At the same time he would introduce them to accept the *Sifre dikduc, Talmud loshen Ivrit* and *More ha Loshon* (teaching of the language). Reb Yoshe Hertzke's teaching in *dikduc* served me later in my studies of philosophy at the University. But, more than with his pedagogic virtues, he served his pupils with his *Mides Tives* (good deeds). One never heard from him a bad word about any Jew. He would not tolerate *rechiles* (vicious, malicious gossip). He would *farcitert vern* (tremble) at an oath. My father said of him that he has never sworn on anything, even if it was the truth. He was never involved in a *Din Toyre*, accept for the case mentioned above. The following story was told of him: He suffered much from a bad neighbour, but he never reciprocated. But the longer he kept silent the more the neighbour pursued him, till he altered his neighbour's attitude by his decency. A landlord owed money to Reb Yoshe's neighbour. But the neighbour was never allowed to get near to the landlord to redeem his money. One day Reb Yoshe saw the landlord in town and told his neighbour about it. The neighbour got back his money and from then on he became Reb Yoshe's best friend. Later Reb Yoshe moved to the *Mashev Zkienim* (old people's home). I used to visit him there and I liked his hearty *Musar verter* (moral words). On my last visit, before I left the town, he taught me *Derech Eretz* (respect) for a Jew with these words: three things should a Jew not have in excess but of the fourth he may have any amount: too much wealth which brings plenty of worries; too much wisdom, a Jew should not be too smart, because from too much *chacires kumt men zu apikorses* (if one is too smart one can become an unbeliever) and a Jew should not be too healthy for this is *a esic far an akshen* (a thing for the stubborn), but a Jew should study a lot of Torah as it is said: he is blessed who concentrates day and night. Even if I did not follow all of Reb Yoshe's dictums, his dear memory has remained for a long time in my mind.

[Page 52]

The Bund in Novogrudok

by H. Kaplan and Y. Maslow

Translated from Yiddish by O. Delatycki

Novogrudok, as is well known, is located in a deserted corner of Byelorussia, a long way from a railway line. It had no industry. For this reason, the workers movement developed later than in larger towns. Due to the influence of the intelligentsia of the town, Novogrudok not only joined the movement, but it became the centre of its activities in the district. The organizations of the Bund, SS and RSR were outstanding.

It all started by accident in the year 1902. In the autumn, when young men were called up for army service, H. Kalpanicki from Vilno was among those who had to appear for the call up, because he was registered in Novogrudok. The young man was a student. Previously he was brought up in a traditional manner and studied in a cheder and the Yeshiva. Later he joined the Haskola, when he prepared himself and was admitted to the University. At the same time he joined the workers movement. One day, as he was weary of the call up, he felt like visiting a synagogue. The time was between Minche and Miriv and all synagogues were immersed in darkness. Only the kloyz Mitaskim was lit. There Reb Yosef Yoysl preyed Musar. Kalpanski entered and was astonished to find a friend of his childhood inside. He was Avrom Kaplan, who was also known as the Grodno porush. After a long chat he discovered that his friend was not only a conscientious follower of the Musar movement but also a dedicated follower of the Bund. They decided on the spot to establish a branch of the Bund in Novogrudok. As it happened, Kalpanicki remained in Novogrudok since he had no money to return to Vilno. He stayed and became a teacher of Russian and, secretly, an instructor in the Bund. In a short time, a large proportion of the working population joined the movement. The first members came from Zalatucha, where many of the workers lived. They readily accepted the ideal of socialism. A short time after the birth of the organization, systematic work had begun. In Novogrudok were several sizeable clothing stores, each with an attached workshop. The working conditions were frightful. The women worked from 7 o'clock in the morning till late at night. And in season i.e. between Purim and Shavuot and between the high holidays and Sucot, they worked through the night, catching a nap at work for a couple of hours. A relative told me that the owner or a member of her family was watching the workers at all times. They were making sure that no one would fall asleep for even an instant. The workers tried by all means to avoid the evil eyes of the supervisors and catch a doze. One of the devices was to pretend to be looking for a lost needle under the workbench and having a brief nap in the process. I did not see my relative during the high holiday season, not even on a Sabbath, because on Sabbath she slept from the time of the blessing of the candles to the end of Sabbath. After Sabbath she worked the whole night. After Passover I met her and could not recognise her. In the three months the sixteen year old healthy girl changed into an old woman. I.L. Peretz describes it in the song "The three maiden" "the eyes red, the lips blue, the blood has vanished to the last drop, the back is bent". She described to me her work and her hurt.

In the year of 1903 the Bund organised a strike of the workers in the tailoring shops, among them in the largest enterprise, that of Hirsh Shimen Israelit. Two hundred workers went on strike for two months and finally prevailed. Since than the image of the town had changed. The Yiddish Street, which was deserted from one Sabbath to the next, was lively each night after Mincha. The population started to treat the Bund and its members with respect. The son of Kivelevich, who was a student, worked next to Chaim Japoniec (a nickname given to him because of his short stature, his surname was Lageza), Chaim Dovid the student as well as Yores and Pinchas Lintz. The owners at heart hated the Bund, but in the open they displayed a tolerant attitude.

On the 1 May 1904, the Bund and other socialist parties requested that all shops should be closed for the day. The following curious event occurred: that evening the verger of the Beth Din knocked on the doors of the leaders of the Bund. When asked who he was looking for he answered that the Rabbi sent him to find out if the religious schools and the Talmud Torah could remain open - he wanted to know how to behave. Kalpanicki allowed these institutions to continue functioning.

The second big and important strike was in the matzo factories, Novogrudok was the centre of matzo production. The matzos, nice, round, thin and brittle were sent to all the big towns and abroad to all corners of the world. The matzo factories would begin production after Hanukkah and would continue until the eve of Passover. The exploitation of the workers was frightful. The work would start at 2 in the morning and finish at midnight. The pay was 60 kopeks a day. The Bund organised the matzo makers and declared a strike. The workers won. The working day was reduced to 12 hours and the pay was substantially increased. With the arrival of 1905 the workers movement came out into the open, the movement in Novogrudok joined in. There were daily demonstrations. The local police, who in the past behaved towards the Bund in an indifferent manner, realised its mistake. A company of Cossacks was brought in creating a fear in the population. However, the movement had become more revolutionary. The members saw that notice was being taken of them and this brought them courage. The historical day of the 17 of October 1905 had arrived when the declaration of new liberties by Tsar Nicholas II was announced. On the next day the news reached Novogrudok and from the early morning masses of people started moving into the Market place. Young and old were anxious to know what changes the declaration would bring to the people. At the time all were happy. People were hugging and kissing each other. The police knew little about the changes to the constitution proposed by the Tsar and they did not know how to react. Should they disperse the demonstration? Suddenly Dovid Zamshnik appeared in the Market place and read the constitutional amendments to the people. The Bund called a mass meeting in the big synagogue and for the first time the general public heard the socialists speak. And for the first time they discovered that the quite, respectful Abram Broido was a socialist. The behaviour of the officials was remarkable. Before the meeting, the ispravnik (chief of the district police) asked to see the representatives of the workers organizations. He told them that the Cossacks, who were not familiar with the constitutional changes, may behave in the same manner as the bloodhound Krylov in Minsk. He asked the representatives of the workers parties to give an undertaking that they would ensure public order. If the promise to keep order would be given, he would prohibit the Cossacks from interfering. Such an undertaking was given and the meeting was allowed to proceed without interference. But the happy mood brought about by Nicholas's declaration did not last long. The press each day brought mournful news. Here were attacks on Jews, there assaults on worker's associations. Blood was spiled. The population of Novogrudok was in a mournful mood. There were rumours circulating that Novogrudok would not escape the fate of other towns and the Jewish population was afraid. The ispravnik was advising the workers to take on the defence in case of a pogrom. All parties have united. Bund, SS and RSS formed a defence force Hagana. At a meeting, the householders together with the Rabbi contributed 200 roubles for the purchase of arms. A mobilisation was proclaimed. Anyone who could hold a stick was called to duty. Secret meeting places were named for the units, and a headquarters for the leaders. Patrols were moving through the town and surroundings. Because of a pogrom was avoided. The Bund was also in contact with farmers in the villages. The members of the movement from Zalatucha were handing out proclamations to the villagers. On market days they placed literature in the farmer's carts. The work was conducted with great dedication. Thanks are also due to the members of the intelligentsia, who were enlightening the population and giving free lectures. They were Avrom

Broido, Chaim Hershl Kalpanicki, Avrom Kaplan, Itzchok Maslovaty, the student Itzchok Mircelevski, Chaim Dovid Moskovski, Mojshe Kivelevich, Eliahu Moskovski, Mandl Wagier and Mojshe Broido. We are grateful to a number of people, including Mr Ostashinski (Soker), Mr. Shimonovich, his wife Batsheva and Mr Feigenberg's children for their financial help to the Bund.

A group Zionist Socialist in Novogrudok, 1905
Standing, first on right, is H. Bunder, who later lived in New York

[Page 54]

Memoirs from before the First World War

by William. Uris (New York)

Translated by O. Delatycki

Viewed overall, Novogrudok displayed a unique appearance. It was positioned majestically on a mound, the surrounding valley was covered by thick woods, which spread for miles, and its streets were wide, though in parts not paved. Each house had a small tidy garden or a small orchard, which yielded some support for its upkeep. Novogrudok had a significant non-Jewish population, which consisted of Poles and Byelorussians. And though the town was considered to be Byelorussian, it was dominated by puffed up Polish landowners.

Novogrudok did not have an industry. The Jewish population had gained its livelihood from commerce and craft workshops. They were all waiting for the market day on a Sunday, when the farmers came to town to sell their produce and buy the goods they required.

In those days there was no railway line to Novogrudok. One had to travel to Novoyelnia to catch a train or to collect goods that were delivered by train. The conveying was done by a large number of coach drivers, who were taking passengers and goods to Novoyelnia and other localities. Some of them travelled as far as Slonim and Grodno.

In the late hours of the night one could hear in the surrounding streets the crying and yammering of the scholars of the Musar yeshiva who were studying Gomorrah. Some must have yammered to bemoan their fate. As Avrom Reisen used to sing: 'to eat "days" and swallow tears'.

Novogrudok had a well developed cultural life. The religious Jews were proud of their rabbis: such outstanding leaders as Reb Itzchok Elchanon and Reb Yechiel Michl Epshtin, the author of the book *Aruch Hashulchan*. But the town produced also many maskilim [from *Haskola* - knowledge] such as Alexander Harkavy, Shmuel Lidski, Nachman Getzov etc. The famed Polish poet Adam Mickiewicz was born in Novogrudok.

My father Yoisef, or as he was known, Reb Jashe, was a bookish Jew and an honest man. He was an intensely devoted Zionist and a good public speaker. He was imbued with the spirit of Haskala. He defied bitterly Reb Yoysl, the father [spiritual leader] of the Musar movement in Novogrudok.

When I read Mendele Meicher Sforim's book 'The Taxi', I imagined that 'the grandfather' was describing the Novogrudok 'karobke'. [the reference is unfamiliar to me, which makes the following sentence inexplicable OD] The income from the meagre slaughter-house had to support 3 butchers and their equipment, but the town's rich were not concerned with the paucity of earnings of the butchers.

Well, father had to look for additional income from other sources, such as selling of skins (they had to be dried on our oven at home), inscribing lettering on grave stones and helping with the studies of sons of rich parents. He was known as a student of the Tanach, which he knew by heart. In this atmosphere of clerics, Haskola and poverty, I studied in Novogrudok until I was 16 years of age.

Education among Jews was always a high priority. The poorest Jew would save on food and clothing to give his child an education. Apart from studying 10 hours a day in the cheder [Jewish religious primary school], I studied at home Hebrew, dictation, Jewish history and

Russian, because my father was of the opinion that his 5 children would not be content to be butchers. There was a need, therefore, to prepare them for different occupations. I was not a great performer at school. I did not like the narrow four walls of the not too clean class rooms and the fierce discipline of the teacher. On the other hand, I liked studying Hebrew and Russian.

Since I was a young boy, I have been imbued with nice memories of Novogrudok. The legendary Castle hill, which brought to mind the colourful historical past, was the place where we boys played in the spare time. Standing on the mount one could see for miles the splendid panorama of the fields of wheat and dense forests. Behind the Castle hill on the way to Brichinke [Brecianka] was the small forest where we would go to pick berries. I also remember well the city park, or orchard, as they used to call it. In the summer a troupe of artists used to act in Russian. I remember how we, the young boys, used to indulge in all manner of tricks to get into the park. We would break a board from the fence or creep over it. The Market place in the centre of the town was very pretty. Father and I used to stroll there on Saturday evenings.

The Matzo contracts (podryad)

I wrote above that Novogrudok did not have an industry, did not have factories. But one product made in Novogrudok was known all over the Jewish world and that was Novogrudok matzo, which were famous in the whole world. They were thin, well baked and brittle. From Chanukah the town would change in a matzo bakery. The owners of the bakeries were known as podryadchiks. Young girls, elderly wemen and young boys from surrounding townships would come to Novogrudok to work in the matzo podryads. The men were 'redler' [presumably, those who inserted small cuts with a serrated redl (small wheel) in the raw matzos] and 'setzer', who would insert the raw matzos in the oven and remove them when they were baked. The women would knead the dough and roll it out into matzos. The matzos were packed into boxes and sent all over the world where Jews lived, all over Europe, to America and even to Australia and South Africa. The export of matzos continued until the beginning of the second World War . The workers toiled in the podryads 16 to 18 hours a day with short breaks for meals. There was no work on Sabbath, but immediately after the havdole the work would recommence. When one passed a podryad one could hear the workers singing folk tunes. The air carried a smell of freshly backed matzo. The boys would venture into the bakeries to snatch a piece of matzo. [It is sad to think that the tiny shipment of matzos which is now delivered for Passover to the few surviving Jews of Novogrudok probably comes from the United States].

The big fires

Summer was the season for fires in Novogrudok. The population always lived in a state of fear, not knowing where and when a fire would break out. The equipment of the firemen consisted of a few hand pumps and half a dozen barrels to convey water from the wells. When a fire would start, people would pray that the wind would not cause the fire to spread. On a nice summer night in the year of 1911 a fire started in a barn in Waliker Street. A strong wind blew the flames and in a blink of an eye the sparks started fires in houses and burns, one after another. Obviously, the firemen were helpless facing such a large conflagration. Balls of smoke and fire covered up the sky. After a night of dreadful hell more than half the town was wiped out by the fire. Our house was also burned down. For several days we were encamped in the orchard of Grasbowski next to the hospital, till we received permission from our relative Branicki, who was at the time abroad, to occupy a few rooms in his large house in Waliker Street. Another fire, which I remember well, occurred on Yom Kipur [Day of Atonement]. The fire also started in Waliker Street in the house of the glazier. A mentally ill woman lit the fire with a candle. In few minutes the sky was red. Tongues of flame were stretching upwards and the timber homes caught fire, one after the other. Men and women were speechless: how can such a calamity happen on Yom Kiper? This is a punishment of God. Jews were commenting that they never heard of such a calamity on Yom Kipur. Next morning, after the fire was extinguished, the streets which did not suffer from the conflagration were filled with chattels and furniture saved from the burned houses. People were resting on their belongings exhausted, drained. In the evening parents left the children to look after their possessions in the street and went for prayers in the synagogue. I will never forget the heart wrenching wailing of the supplicants as they prayed.

As the summer passed the townsmen gave a sigh of relief. In time Novogrudok began looking prettier and more prosperous, as it was being rebuilt in brick.

Call up in Novogrudok

Soon after the autumn holidays young men from villages and townships began arriving in Novogrudok in large numbers for the call up. This continued for several weeks. The town was lively; the streets were full of passers by. The taverns were packed with villagers who brought their children for the call up. The shops in the centre of the town were filled with customers. The stalls in the market place were selling lots of bread. Those that were drafted to serve were allowed to return home for a few weeks. Later, they returned to town, from whence they were sent out to all parts of the empire. The army barracks were filled with soldiers, who came to pick up the recruits. The recruits were quartered in private homes. The new soldiers who were distressed for having been torn from their families for four years, decided to live it up. They were drinking, singing and dancing in the streets. They were turning their scorn on the Jews. They were upturning the tables of the poor street vendors, they were breaking windows in shops, breaking into Jewish homes, robbing and leaving behind them Jewish victims. This continued until people – butchers, coach drivers, shoe makers, tailors and other craftsmen - fetched from the farmer's carts: poles, steel crow-bars, axes and chased the recruits away from the market place.

Jewish recruits had specific reasons for dreading the call up to serve the Tsar. Jews were subject to restrictions and persecutions. When the time came for a Jewish boy to face the call up there was sadness in the house. Parents looked for ways for their sons to avoid the 4 years of service. Those that had no means were resigned, but deeply saddened. Tragic was the moment of parting with the parents, friends and loved ones. The recruits were taken to Novojelnia on foot. Hundreds were following the recruits who they were accompanying on their way. As they walked, there was heart rendering crying by the accompanying women, till the police would let the families go no further.

The tsarist authorities would expose the Jewish community to punishments. The parents or brothers were liable to pay a penalty of 300 rubbles if a son was abroad when he was called up. If the fine was not paid, domestic chattels, including bedding, were seized. I remember when a policeman was leading the Russian officials to our house to sequester household goods, because my father had brothers in America, who left before they were called up. We would take the bedding and the better clothing to friends to hide. The few pieces of furniture were valued on the spot by an official and my father payed up, that is he bought back his own possessions. Some managed to negotiate in advance with the officials and pay them off with a bribe. For months, while the go-between was negotiating with the officials, paid him the bribe and arranged for a time when the official would come, we would sleep on bare boards and sit on broken benches. This was the order of things we lived under until we left for Volkovysk.

The burial of the rabbi Reb Yechiel Michl Epshtin

The news of the death of the rabbi spread quickly in town. People of were immersed in sorrow. Couriers were sent with the news to neighbouring towns to invite the rabbis to the funeral and grieving.

Funeral in Synagogue Square

On the day of the funeral all shops in town were closed and the workshops were idle. All religious schools were closed. It was a wintry, frosty day, but large crowds filled the synagogue square where the body of the rabbi was brought. Men and women, young and old were standing for hours listening to the many orations. The main oration was given by the Minsk preacher (magid) who gave a fiery eulogy, like a real people's orator, with a strong voice which reverberated throughout the whole synagogue square. But the greatest impression was made by the speech of the rabbi's grandson, who was at the time 18 years old. He became later the well known Rabbi Berlin. After several hours of speeches, the cortege moved to the cemetery. It was led by selected youngsters, who were formed in two rows. I was among them: 'the righteous will walk before you and he will put on the way truth'. The body was carried by rabbis and personalities of the town. The cortege moved very slowly. It took some time for us to reach the cemetery. It was quite dark when the funeral came to an end and the people started to disperse. I did not eat that day. When I came home I went to sleep. Next day I had a cold and a temperature. My mother fetched a doctor, who, after having examined me, declared that I suffered from having consumed an excess of food.

I became a Musarnik for a while

For a time I studied in Lithuania in the yeshiva of Reines. After a while I had to return home because father could not afford the fees. There was a rule in the yeshiva that the students were not allowed to eat "days". Accommodation and food had to be paid for and that caused a difficulty for my father. Therefore, I returned to Novogrudok and enrolled in the yeshiva of Iche Leib. There I studied exclusively Gomorrah. A boy had to know a page [meaning presumably any page] of the Gomorrah with the addendums. The pupils in Iche Leibs yeshiva were 13 to 15 years old. I was 14 years old. Reb Iche Leib was an interesting type of man among the holy men of Novogrudok. He was considered a great scholar of the small print [of finer points]. He was a small man with a short black beard, rotund and very pious. The yeshiva was located in a small house, which was built onto the great synagogue. The boys were seated around two long tables. Reb Itche Leibe was standing at a pulpit in the middle of the room and supervising. If a boy tried to have a chat with his neighbour – woe and behold. Reb Itche would spank him mercilessly. Musar was not taught in the yeshiva. But Reb Iche Leib would encourage us to slip into the synagogue when the musarniks were talking with each other about Musar and listen to their high level discussions. Once I went to the Musar yeshiva. A muscarnik approached me. He was a youth of about 20 with nice burning eyes and a black mane. He was clad in modern dress. I was told that he came from the Ukraine and was a son of rich parents, who were supporters of Reb Yoysel's yeshiva. We would meet daily and speak about Musar. He frightened me because of all the sins that I had committed in my life and instructed me in what I had to do to placate the wrath of the Almighty.

This did not last long. I had become disappointed in the preachings of the Musar and gave up our meetings. My father favoured this outcome because he did not support the teachings of Reb Yoysl. After I left Reb Iche Leib's yeshiva, my father studied Gomorrah with me. Each morning I studied Hebrew and Russian, for which I paid from my earnings at the bank, where I worked half days.

Jewish Characters in Novogrudok

Dr. Epshtin

There was one Jewish doctor in Novogrudok. His name was Epshtin. He was also the only doctor in the Jewish hospital. I don't know where he came from. His behaviour was stiff and unbending. He spoke Russian, but if it was necessary he also spoke a good Yiddish. He also sang Yiddish tunes very nicely. His father was a chasen [cantor]. He was quite a likable person and treated the poor patients with care. Dr

Epshtin was a friend of our family, and my father was a frequent visitor in his house. My father arranged the match between the doctor and a girl from Hancewicz and they soon married. The name of Epshtin remains in the list of our martyrs, because the doctor's son died a heroic death fighting the Nazis in the forests near Novogrudok.

Tritl the soifer

I don't know if Tritl is a Jewish name, but Tritl the soifer was known in Novogrudok. He was an elderly man of medium hight, stately in appearance with a thick grey beard. He was a man of the book, a great singer. His praying at the pulpit of Musar on the New Year and Yom Kippur was a pleasure to listen to. His 'bearing of his heart' before G-d in his prayers caused me to tremble. He knew the prayer books for all the festivities by heart. He conducted the prayers at the small or Todres synagogue. He was prized for his praying. As he got older he became blind. He lived in the old people's home and though he was old and his voice was not as strong, he was still praying at the pulpit in the synagogue at the old people's home. The sweetness of his voice could be heard every Sabbath and holy day. We lived close to the old people's home. I used to pop in for a chat with Reb Tritl. He sat on a bench and recited prayers or studied mishnot. When he heard my voice he would stop his praying and tell me some pleasant stories of the past. Reb Tritl died of old age surrounded by many friends.

Nachman Getzov

Nachman Getzov was a great man of letters and a maskil, fluent in a number of languages and the author of the book 'By the waters of Babylon', a historic investigation of the Babylon Talmud. He was a very modest man. I would often visit him when my mother would send me to buy sugar and tea at his shop. He would begin by asking me about me studies and whether I was applying myself to the study of Hebrew. If there were no other customers in the shop, he would ask me searching questions on Talmud and history. I was very encouraged by his interest in my studies. His house was the centre for Jewish intelligentsia in Novogrudok. Obviously, Getzov deserves a more thorough account of his achievements. Let this brief note serve as a remainder that there were many learned Jews in Novogrudok. Getzov was one of them.

Sholim the pincher

A melamed (teacher) of beginners, he worked fairly for his scant piece of bread. He tried to show the fathers how well he taught their sons. But, alas, he had one failing – he liked to pinch the cheeks of his pupils. He not just pinched them, but hurt them when he did so. It was accepted by the parents that the malamdim were beating their pupils. But if a child would return home bloodied by the teacher's strikes, even the lenient parents would not tolerate it. Sholim the melamed had his troubles. A parent would often remove his son in the middle of the term and transfer him to another melamed. Sholim lived in the synagogue square in a squat house with a few rooms. There was the kitchen, the dining room, bedroom and the school room. The sanitary conditions of such schools were not brilliant. If there are anywhere heirs of Sholim the melamed, who will read this note, I must ask them to forgive me for my critic of the melameds of Novogrudok. It was not their fault that they were not great educators. But they were honest and they worked hard for their scant income.

Yachke the teacher

There were lots of rumours in town about Yachke. She did not stem from Novogrudok and some said that she was sent to Novogrudok to direct a worker's party. Other said that she left her native town Zeludok, because she was suspected by the Tsarist government of revolutionary activities. Her father was initially the rabbi of Zeludok and later of Moscow. Her brother was known to be a fiery revolutionary. He belonged to a terrorist group. Yachke was a teacher of Russian. Though she kept her head slightly inclined to one side, she was a rear beauty. She had black eyes and a curvaceous figure. Her voice was soft and tender. Her age -20 odd years. She taught Russian to beginners. She taught me three times a week. In the short time she lived in Novogrudok, from memory 2-3 years, she had become a favourite of the educated Jewish youth. But the older people treated her with suspicion. Her father the rabbi had a number of daughters and it would seem that they were all involved in the revolutionary movements. Frequently Yachke was dispatched with a parcel to one of the sons of Moshkovich and I would bring back a parcel. What was in the parcel I never knew. Yachke was a very intelligent and sympathetic woman and if she was connected with a worker's party, she certainly was useful to the worker's movement in Novogrudok.

Some time later there appeared in Novogrudok a young man who was also a teacher of Russian. He lived with the family Stocker, who were candle makers. The young man wore a black cape and he walked everywhere without a head cover, which was a rarity at that time. He spoke Yiddish with a peculiar accent. He was also my teacher. His name was Simonov. In his youth he was a rabbi in a Jewish colony in Crimea. Later he sat for an examination, obtained his matriculation and became a non believer and a revolutionary. After a raid by the police on the activists of the workers' parties a number of people were arrested. At that stage the young man disappeared from Novogrudok and I never saw him again.

Yike the reife (medical attendant)

Yike the reife was an institution in Novogrudok. Who did not know him? He was, one could say, the only reife in town, who everyone trusted. Yike was a short person , an elderly man with red cheeks, he did not grow a beard. He was a very likable man. Day and night he would go around visiting and curing the sick. His charge for a visit was 5 kopecks. He was not greedy and he would spend a long time at the sick bed until he felt and knocked about the patient thoroughly. He was keen on a bitter drop [i.e. vodka], but he never exceeded his measure. He liked telling stories about the times when snatchers would catch children and pass them on to the army, where the children would serve for 25 years. They were called Nikoley's soldiers. He was one of the children who were taken away by a snatcher from his father arms. But his father, with the help of a friend managed to save him. He lived with his wife in the Yiddishe (Jewish) street. They had no children. He was very honest in his profession. When the patient was seriously ill he would suggest that a doctor be called. He did not want to take on himself the responsibility. Both doctors in town respected Yike. One day the news was passed on all over town that his wife hung herself. Nobody knew the reason. This had a strong effect on Yike. He felt dejected. Later at the age of 80 he married a young woman. In my memory, Yike the reife remained as rare type of the old school.

Benjomin Kotlower

A considerable number of Jewish settlements were spread in the surrounds of Novogrudok, where Jews were leasing the land from Polish landlords. In the Tsarist days Jews were not permitted to own land [nor in the Polish days after the First World War]. One of the leasers of land was Benjomin Movshovich in the village of Kotlowo, 14 verst from Novogrudok. Benjomin Kotlower was an interesting man with a unique character. He was strongly traditional and deeply religious, but at the same time he was a follower of the Haskola movement. All his children, including his girls, received a traditional but worldly education. He was ready to help others and was a great entertainer of guests. No one who stopped at his house was allowed to leave without a meal. Benjomin and his wife Simka made certain that every person who passed by left satisfied. Benjomin was a man with a big Jewish heart. He was very saddened by the troubles the Jews were exposed to under the tsar's anti-Semitic rule and was hoping to live to see a Jewish state in Israel. Benjomin was a close associate of my father and a devoted friend of our family. I had a particularly close bond with him. Often he would take me to the country. And though he was a strict disciplinarian, I was allowed complete freedom in the country and I could do whatever I pleased, even to go horse riding. The good hearted Simka saw to it that I should eat well and drink a lot of milk. The two Jewish families who lived in Kotlowo, Benjomin Movshovich and his partner Brine, were the only Jews in the place. Though their financial position was quite good, they suffered much due to anti-Semitic incidents. Brine and her children left for America and Benjomin moved with his family to Novogrudok.

Benjomin died when he was getting ready to join his children in America. Only one daughter Maryashe remained in Novogrudok. Among those killed by the German fascists is Maryashe with her husband and four children.

The above are only a few stories of Novogrudok, which I remembered from my youth before the First World War . This was the town in which I obtained my initial traditional Jewish education. This was the place where several generations of my forebears have made a contribution to the cultural life of the town. Let these few notes be my small contribution to the monument for the slaughtered Jews of Novogrudok, and for those who died a heroic death fighting the murderers of Jews. We will never forget our fallen and their murder will never be forgiven.

The center of the town

[Page 61]

Old Novogrudok

by Shimen Yosifun

Translated by O. Delatycki

I stem from a Chasidic family and therefore I can tell the story of the lives of the Chasids in Novogrudok. A prominent member of the movement was my grandfather Reb Izek Zalmon OBM. My father's name was Yankl Izek Zalmon's and I am called Shimen Yankl Zalmon's. There were no surnames at the time. They were not necessary. Another Jew who was at the head of the Chasidim of the town was called Shloime the Malach (Angel), not because he stemmed from angels, but because he had a soul of an angel. The mutual bond between the Chasidim was beyond description. They were part of one family. If there was a celebration in one household, a wedding or a circumcision, all turned up to the last man. And if there was a misfortune in a family all participated in the sorrow. In the "shtibl" (small synagogue) of the Chasidim only a small congregation prayed during the week. But on Saturdays the shtibl was full to the brim. On Saturday a Chasid was unrecognizable, for instance Shloime the Angel, who made his living by manufacturing axle grease for carts, was dressed the whole week in a capote smeared with grease, but on Sabbath he shone like the sun, which emerged from the clouds. The other Chasidim were equally impressive. Friday, after washing in the city bath, followed by the mikva, adorned in their Sabbath attire, the divine presence rested upon them. Following the Friday night prayers (kabolot Shabbat) the people would sing together and the passers by listened in awe. After Mairiv the congregation went to Leah's winery that was next door to the Chasids' shtibl, where they took wine for the Sabbath blessings. It was a very tasty grape wine. By the way, Leah the wine maker had a son named Mordche, who subscribed to Shachar a newspaper from Smolensk (a paper would cost 20 kopeks). I contributed 2 kopeks and he allowed me to read the paper. That reading had a great influence on my future life.

On the Sabbath, at the prayers, which was filled with Chasidic enthusiasm and fire, one could sense the holiness of the day.

On the Sabbath afternoon, following the Sabbath repast, at Minche each one of us brought a small chala for the Sholosh-sudes. It was a pleasure to hear the Chasidic tunes which inspired one. For the Havdola one would buy from Yashe Michl in the Synagogue Square, next to the water well, a drink called under-beer. Selling of the beer provided Yashe Michl with an income. As Succoth approached one esrog and one lulav were purchased for all those attending the shtibl. On the first day of Succoth, before blessing the esrogs, one had to go to immerse oneself in the ritual bath. One slept in the Succoth for all the 8 days of the festival. During Succoth, each night one would visit a different house of a Chasid to sing Simchat beit Hashoeiva. On the eve of the sixth day of Succoth, which is called the Shana Raba, the people went to the shtibl to pray and say Tehilim, so as to secure a good outcome (which was called quitl). Anton (antonovka) apples were purchased for the night and kept in the attic of the shitibl. They were distributed at the reading of the T'chila to keep the congregation awake. On Sabbath Chilemoid the Chasids would visit each other and assist in removing the kugels (baked potato cake) from the ovens. On the eve of Simchat Torah all would sing on entering the shtibl. All the worries of the year were forgotten. Having sang the piut (a Simchat Toyre song) they would turn to Ato'hoteiso and to the hakofes. Who is capable to describe the joy of the Chasidim at the hakofes? After each hakofe they would indulge in a jig. The singing shook the walls. Among the Chasids was an impecunious man by the name of Moshke Yankl son of Eliahu the tobacconist. He had a shop in the market square (rad kromen). His stock consisted of half a bag of salt, a dozen boxes of matches, a bundle of candles and a few cords. That was his source of income from which he paid the school fees for his children. He was usually the sixth to be called up for the reading of the Torah (Oizer Dalim – help the one who helps paupers). But sometimes they would forget. On such occasions they would start reading the Torah from the beginning to avoid a quarrel. On the morning of Simchat Torah the shul would be overflowing with singing. After an alia (call up to the Torah) everyone was given a glass of vodka and a slice of honey cake. The congregation would contribute generously to the community chest. Money was also collected for the purchase of kerosene for lighting of the Chasidim's shul. The Yomim Naroim (the holy days of Rosh Hashonah and Yom Kipur) were spent by many Chasidim together with the Slonim Rabbi. Not everyone could afford the cost for the trip, so some walked. It was a matter of a Mitzvah; they all wanted to visit their Rabbi. On the Sabbath night after the first slicha everyone brought his bundle to my grandfather's house. The bundles contained a rye bread, a hard cheese and a special outfit for the celebration of the holiday. They walked cheerfully, singing and chatting along the '21 wiorst (22 km) to the nearest railway station. Many continued on foot all the way to Slonim. In the Yomim Naroim (in the holy days there was hardly a minyan left (it was hard to gather a minyan) in Novogrudok. Having returned home after the Yomim Naroim, the people looked as if they were dreaming. When they came to, everyone started to tell of the wonders of Him (meaning the Slonim Rabbi) may he live long: how he prayed, how he read the Torah, how he immersed himself in the mikva before blowing the Shofar, in one word - nisim ve nefloyes (wonders and miracles). The headmaster of the Talmud Torah was Reb Zelik ZC"L (zeicher cadik lebrocho - the name of the tzadic be blessed). I was one of his pupils. The Rabbi gave each day four lectures. The first one from 6 to 9am including the prayers, the second from 9 to12 midday, the third from 12 to 3pm and the last from 3 to 6pm. After the lessons he studied by himself. He taught until he was very old and lived till he was 90 years old. He died in 1900 on Sabbath eve on Shovuot. Every Thursday he examined the older pupils, who studied Gomorrah with the commentaries, to assess their knowledge of the matter that was studied during the week. He was very strict and a pupil who did not know his work was punished physically... The pupils knew the Rabbi's weakness and those who felt that they did not know the work were certain to bring with them a cigar. And with the cigar the matter finished better than anticipated... If a pupil was not quite up to scratch, yet did not bring a cigar, the Rabbi would pinch his cheek and say: 'you deserve a punishment but I forgive you this time'.

The exams took place in the big Bat-Medresh. The young were on the look out to create mischief. The stands of the leading citizens of the town were moved from the eastern wall and exchanged for the stands of the poor. In the morning there was disquiet: who dared swap over the stands in the big Synagogue? It was decided that it was done by the riff-raff overnight.

On Thursday night we would make mischief with Bine the water carrier. He slept in the women's Synagogue. The boys would roll up a long piece of paper and would push it into the nose of the sleeping Bine. He would wake up in a panic. We would disappear. He thought that it was the work of the devil.

On Friday evenings Reb Zelik would walk with his stick along the street lined with shops and would shout: 'Jews, it is the Sabbath, close the shops'. As soon as the shopkeepers saw Zelik there was banging of the doors and shutters and the shops would be closed. Sometimes somebody was not quick enough and Reb Zelik would give him a remainder with a stick over his back.

The town's *Balebatim* (important personalities, masters, hosts)

Moshav Zekeinim (Old peoples home)

There was in Novogrudok a small Moshav Zekeinim that was maintained by the great benefactor Reb Hendel Chisin from Moscow, who was born in Novogrudok. He supported also the poorhouse supplying money, medication and equipment. The Harkavys, who lived in St Petersburg, supported the Jewish hospital and the poor. There was in Novogrudok an organization called Shogdey Melocho. They placed the children of poor families with craftsmen to learn a trade. They were placed with tailors, bookbinders, carpenters etc. depending on the inclination of the youth. The apprentices were given some decent clothes and medication. The parents of the apprentices were also assisted with small loans. To support this project the Jews of Novogrudok were giving a weekly donation of 1 to 10 kopeks. Money was collected from the Harkavies, the Kabaks the Rabinoviches etc. There was also a society that collected clothing for the poor. There was another society that provided for the poor interest free loans. There was a society that provided anonymously food for the Sabbath. Another society existed which supplied bread for the needy. The societies were supported by the families of Chisin, Harkavy and Kabak.

Rabbi Echiel Michl Epshtein

There were two butchers in town Ele and Itche, who slaughtered an animal with a defect. They turned to the Rabbi and told him that they borrowed money at a high interest and would be bankrupt if they would not be able to sell the meat. The Rabbi inspected the meat and asked 'Reb Ele and Reb Itche do you pray every day?' 'Yes, we do' they answered, 'only occasionally do we miss a prayer when we are in a village among the gentiles.' 'The meat is kosher' the Rabi declared. 'You can sell the meat and repay the loan. Your wives and children need food. God is merciful'. That was how the Rabi Echiel Michl ZL" made his verdict.

The story about Gamliel the coachman illustrates the piety of the ordinary people of Novogrudok. It was during the days of the First World War . The trains did not circulate as frequently as in the pre-war days. I came to Novogrudok for the Sabbath to see my parents. On Saturday night I had to travel back. I went with my brother in law Jankef Dobrin to Zalatuche at the end of Waliker Street to see Gamliel the coachman to order a coach for the evening. When we went in to the house of Gamliel he was seated at the table studying Sefer Mnoira Hamaor. On the table stood a clay jug wrapped in a scarf to keep the water warm. The family was drinking tea and enjoyed the Sabbath. We wanted to book the wagon for Sabbath night to take me to the train. He answered that on a Sabbath he does not discuss such things. I had to find another coachman and Gmalilyel travelled to the train with an empty coach. Such were the simple Jewish folk in Novogrudok. I lived in Novogrudok until the year 1900. After that I went to Warsaw and later I lived in Central Russia and other places. I used to return to Novogrudok for the holidays to see my family. My dear birthplace – Novogrudok, I could not forget you. I am interpolating the words of the prophet Ermiyahu Hanovi: 'My dear birthplace Novogrudok. How can I forget you? Me itan royshi mayim, we eyni dima, we eveke yomam we laylam at chleley ir Novaredok (who will give me the water for my head and tears for my eyes to make me cry day and night for the fall of Novgrudok).

The good deeds of Itzchak Horovich

Let these words be a monument on the grave of my best friend Itzchak Horovich, the son of Osher and Asna, who left this world in his best years.

Our friendship developed in Tel Aviv. I did not know him well in Novogrudok, though we lived close by. It could be that this was because I stemmed from a Chasidic family and I wore Chasidic garb and he was from the Mesnagdim and was dressed differently. We were both educated in the Mir Yeshiva, when Reb Chaim Laib ZLB was the head of the Yeshiva. We sat often at the same table and I noticed often that he hid under the Ghemorah another book. In the Yeshiva this was considered treif posl (not kosher). It could have been the reason why we were not friends. I must confess that I was jealous of him, because he was an all round person. He knew the Tanach, he knew and comprehended a blat Ghemoreh with commentaries, and he spoke and had written well Hebrew. He knew European languages, which he learned by himself without teachers.

When he left the Yeshiva he started looking for Tachles (something of purpose). He began learning butchering – killing poultry and he quickly became an expert. At the same time I learned to be a watchmaker and I went to Warsaw and later to central Russia, where I worked in my trade. Years later we met in Tel Aviv and thus started our friendship. We used to meet each other and share the memories of our childhood, of Mir yeshiva etc. We studied together Ram Bum's 'Me ore Livoichim' (the blind will see) and a chapter of Tanach. When the Alia (emigration) from Poland increased, his house had become a place where advice was sought by the people from Novogrudok. He helped the newcomers as much as he could.

When the Second World War started and Jews went to Russia, to Kazachstan, Uzbekistan, Ural and Siberia to save themselves, letters would come from Jews of Novogrudok asking for help: food, clothing etc. I, together with Izik Horovich and Shloimo Israelit, from Novogrudok collected money for that purpose. The people were glad to contribute money, clothing and food, which was packed and sent to the people from Novogrudok in Russia. As a parcel had to weigh no more than 3 kg we looked for a solution to increase the value of a parcel. We would buy towels, sew them into sacks and pack the goods inside. For those who received the parcel the towels were valuable. We would send soap, salt, needles, razor blades and even buttons. Those were all things which were needed by the people in Russia. We sent to some people as many as two or three parcels a week. Three of us were sending the parcels, but the initiator of that activity was Izchak Horvitz. He was also the one who went to the post office to send the parcels. We received many letters thanking us for the parcels. Those letters gave us a lot of pleasure. We made certain that the hungry were fed, those wearing rags had clothes to wear. The help sustained those who would not have survived.

When the war ended, Itzchak Horvitz died suddenly. It seems as if after he had fulfilled his duty on the sinful earth he was called to the family up above to be rewarded for his good deeds. He had in him a spark of a holy man. May his memory be blessed.

The 'thirty sixers' (referring to 36 holy men)

In Novogrudok was a Jew, who was called by all 'Isroel the crazy'. He was a quiet man, he spoke with no one. In summer and winter he always sat in the big synagogue next to the oven, which was clad in tiles. He slept in the home for old people, for his pillow he used his fist and old rags. How he descended to this level and how he came to Novogrudok nobody knew. On Sabbath he ate in various households. On Friday he would come and say to my mother: 'Eske, if you give me 5 kopeks, I will eat at your place tomorrow'. He liked our food. He ate in our household one Sabbath a month. My father asked him once: 'Isroel, do you think that our food is good?' Isroel answered: 'Jankl, I wish that if you will have to eat at a stranger's home, they will feed you food not worse than the food you feed me'. The answer was not what one would expect to hear from a crazy man. After he would finish, he would take a bag and go to households where he collected bread and chala for the rest of the week. Women used to maintain that he must be a "thirty sixer".

**Awaiting the arrival of Alexander Harkavy in 1931.
In the background is the Main Synagogue.**

Chasens, learned men, clever pupils and learned people

Of the chasens of Novogrudok I remember Reb Berche. Following his death, he was replaced by his son Avrom. There were also two other chasens, Gershonovich and Skobelev. They were learned, G-d fearing men. Of the learned people and the Rabbis, the foremost was Reb Zelik ZLB (see more about him above). I was privileged to have been one of his pupils.

The other teacher in Talmid Torah was Reb Ber, a man with a ginger beard. He was pious and clever and could explain cleverly a difficult chapter of Gemorah. Reb Ber was a son-in-law of Reb Jashe Miches, who was the producer of a drink, which was known as under-beer. This beer was drunk for the Havdole. The sale of the beer provided his income. He lived in the Synagogue square, opposite the water well. It was rumored that Reb Ber went to Israel. I met in Israel a son of his, Shimon. As well as the Rabbis, there were in Novogrudok men of substantial learning. One was called Reb Berl Jashe and the other Reb Mojshe Vishniover. I was one of their pupils. There was also a great man of learning Jankel Katz. His house stood opposite the big synagogue. The house was old and sunken into the ground, so that his windows were at the level of the footpath. He was my first teacher. Another teacher was called Michl the verger. He taught me Chumash and Rashi and instilled in me the love of Torah.

There were also two young teachers who were sons in law. After they married they endeavored to make a living. They were hired by Jews who lived on estates, which was called 'condition'.

There were also modern teachers who taught writing and arithmetic. One of them was Mendel Mojshe Eliash, who had a nice handwriting of a calligrapher. Another was called Jankl. He wrote nice letters for brides and bridegrooms, who were not capable of writing letters themselves. There was also a teacher called Arie, a tall, thin man with a ginger, pointy beard. He had always a cigarette in his mouth. He taught six pupils including myself. The schoolroom was in a rented house. This teacher would beat pupils with a stick. We were no longer children, we were twelve-year-old boys. One day we decided amongst ourselves that when the teacher would start beating a pupil with his stick, we would attack him, remove the stick and beat him. Should we not succeed in removing the stick, we would hit him on his head with a Gemorah, so that he would not forget us. We would also empty his tobacco pouch onto the floor, which would hurt him more than the beating. In other words we planned a revolution. And it happened as we planned when we were taught Baba-karma. The teacher said thus: you may know that there is a baba mecia, which starts with the following words: shanim orsim betalit (we have held on for many years to the tales). Having said that he caught a pupil by his ear and shouted: shanim orsim be oznaim (to hold on for years by the ears). He started to pull viscously the pupil's ears. The boy was wriggling and shouting from great pain. We, the boys, did not wait long, we got up, took the Gemorah books and started to hit the Rabbi. We emptied his tobacco pouch on the floor. The disoriented Rabbi endeavored to hit us. We all escaped from the chider, each to his own house. At home we told the whole story. We decided not to return to the Rabbi's school and the parents supported us in this decision. All this happened in

July, in the middle of the term. What were we to do now. We had no Rabbi. Should we roam around aimlessly? We, all six of us, went to Rabbi Selig and we told him the whole story. We brought him also a packet of cigars. He gave us a friendly reception and examined the state our knowledge. He promised to teach us for one hour per day under the condition that we should behave and not punish a Rabbi. We accepted gladly his suggestion. In Reb Relic's class we got on well and learned a lot. Quite soon we learned to study by ourselves Gemorah, Rashi and the additions, without a Rabbi.

Having completed Reb Relic's chider we dispersed each on his own way. Some went to school and some went to learn a trade. I went on to study watch making. My nearest friend Shleime Izraelit went to study in a Russian school. He was a son of a wealthy textile merchant. After I learned my trade I went to work in Warsaw. My friend, after finishing his school had gone to Lodz, where he became an agent in the textile trade. We were in constant contact by letters. Later Shleime married a girl from Bialystok. They were very hospitable. Their door was always open to all in need. Years later, when I went and settled in Israel, I persuaded him to join me. In Israel he commissioned the writing of a Holy Scroll. He built a house in the Maze St. in Tel Aviv. We met frequently. Eight years ago he died suddenly in his home. I will remember him for as long as I live.

In Novogrudok there was a Rabbi named Reb Leizer Leizerovski. He conducted a school in his small apartment in the Brazilian lane. He had four children, three daughters and one son. They were nice and peaceful people. They never complained, yet they must have been quite poor. His children studied Russian and Hebrew. The three girls went to live with an aunt in the United States, where they learned trades. They worked during the day and at night they wrote. They were able writers and had their work published in Jewish American journals.

The son of Lizerowski, Natkie met my sister Chaia and they married. The wedding took place in the village of Solomianka at our uncle Reb Hersh Zuchovicki's home. After the wedding the young couple went to live in Warsaw. It was the time of 'Brothers and Sisters', which was the anthem of the Bund. Both husband and wife joined the Polish Socialist Party (PPS), where they were active members. The Warsaw police kept an eye on them. During the years 1903-1905 they were arrested several times and kept in the Pawiak. After the collapse of the revolution the couple went to England, where my sister give berth to three sons, and named them after the names of the prophets Yermeahu and Ishaiahu and after a member of the first apprising, Matitiahu. The first son, Yermeahu is now a professor of medicine at the London University. Matitiahu is a professor of history and

Ishaiahu was a military physician, where he was highly decorated. The English newspapers wrote that the mother and the town that produced such an important person should be blessed. Ishaiahu left the English military service at the time of the Israeli war of independence. Our government invited him to come to Israel to arrange the medical services of the country. After the first armistice, the enemy planes bombarded Sedera. Ishaiahu was tending the injured under the fire of the enemy. He died in the bombardment. Having been told the sad news, I with my whole family went to the funeral. It took place on the 11 June 1948 in Afula. The husband of my sister Natke is now known as Dr Natan Morris. He is one of the most important scientists in England in the field of Judicia. He is the author of the book 'The History of Education of the Israel Nation' published by Emanut, Tel Aviv. The book was also published in English.

Of the people who stem from Novogrudok, it is worth mentioning a professor of medicine. In Seieniezyc Street lived a Jew with the surname Harbuna. He was very poor, yet he found money to educate his children.

I remember the excitement in town when on Passover eve there arrived in town the son of Harbuna from St Petersburg. He was a professor of medicine. People gathered and looked at him as at an apparition. But the professor behaved in a modest and simple way. He was asked to visit some of the sick and he did not refuse anyone. He would come with a local doctor, he spoke a nice Litvak Yiddish. He did not accept any money. He even gave some money to the poor to buy medicine.

The town did not know how to thank this wonderful man. Harbuna the father had acquired great popularity in town, because of the excellent upbringing of his children.

Butchers and craftsmen of Novogrudok

I remember three of the Novogrudok butchers. Reb Leibe the butcher, who was knowledgeable in the Torah and Shas. The butcher Broine was also a pious Jew. The third butcher was called Reb Hertzl. His grandson, who has his grandfather's name, lives in Israel.

The cows were butchered in the yard of the house of the well-known man of substance, Reb Shapiro, the timber merchant. His house stood in a small lane at the end of the Yiddish street.

The ritual killing of poultry was done in a house behind the Butchers synagogue. The house was let for a year at a time. At the time that I remember the house was let to Reb Lejzer Larenski. In the winter Larenski also sold timber for heating in partnership with my father OBM.

Bakers

My father, Reb Yankl Izek Zalmon's, was one of the bakers in Novogrudok. The others were Leizer Chertok, his son-in-law Nate Pinchuk, Bejle Wenze, Shleime Dovid, Shimke and Manie Fus.

There was also a bakery that specialized in bread made of wheat (that means that the others baked rye bread). This baker was called Benche. He lived opposite the row of shops (rad kromen) next to the house of Leibe Dworches' on the right hand side. On the left side was the house of Reb Hirshl Winer, who sold kiddish wine made of raisins (blessing of the wine). He also sold, for a kopek, tea served in glasses. This was the source of his income. His son lived in Israel, where he died.

There was also a bakery that produced sweet products, biscuits, cakes and honey cakes. The baker was called Shaftiel, the honey cake maker. He had a nose like an elephant. He displayed his products in the passage of the row of shops. His daughter and her husband lived in Israel and they both died ten years ago.

There were other bakers in Novogrudok. They baked bagels, kuchns and pleclach (the last two were fancy flat breads). They sold them from tables opposite to the row of shops at the entrance to the market place. I don't remember the names of these bakers.

There were physicians and assistant physicians (feltchers) in Novogrudok. Their names were: Pinchas, Welvl and Ruve. There was also a doctor (about Jeke the physician see I. Jaffe).

Tailors

I can remember only three tailors: Shmaie, a tall, deaf man. His home was situated between the synagogue Chai Adam and the synagogue of the carriers. Shmaie was dressed mainly in long coats (like dressing gowns). The Thilim were always on his bench. He would make a stitch with the needle and would read a portion of Thilim. This is how he worked.

There was another tailor called Welvl. He lived in the Yiddish street next to Pinchas the physician. He worked mainly for pious clients.

Another tailor was called Dovid Bashes (son of Bashe).

Yisroel from Vilno

Isroel from Vilno was a modern tailor. He lived in Valiker street, where he shared the house with the Chasn Rabinovich. He had a salon. On his door was a picture of an elegant man. He made garments for men and women, the richer people of the town. I studied with his son at the pious teacher, Sholim Merke Pesies. His son told me that his father was a revolutionary. He was a member of the Bund and was arrested in 1905. In my days Isroel from Vilno was an even tempered, solid citizen, who prayed every Sabbath and, at times also on weekdays in the Tailors synagogue.

The above is not a complete list, but this is all I remember.

Shoemakers

I will mention two of them. I would like to show the modern reader that there were some refined characters among the working people of Novogrudok.

One of them was called Shie the small one. He lived in the Hegdish (home of derelicts) lane. Next to his working bench he attached a special shelf where he kept a book of the Laws of Israel, from which he read each week the portion for that week, parts of the Havtorah (portions of the Torah), also the Zohar and a chapter from Thilim. I saw Shie working on a shoe and at the same time reading the Havtora and Thilim. At the same time he would call with a sigh; 'Oh G-d Almighty'. What that sigh signified I don't know. He was not a poor man. He may have been unhappy because his work was not considered a skilled occupation.

He had two sons. The older was, like his father, a shoemaker. The younger, named Chackl, studied with me in the cheder, until I left to learn a trade. We both studied Talmud. Chackl applied himself to his studies. He sat days and nights in the Shoemaker's synagogue and studied. Sometimes he did not go home to eat. His mother would bring him food to the synagogue. My dear friend of my youth, may your memory be blessed.

There was another shoemaker. He was the son-in-law of Chaje the shoemaker. His wife was called Mirke. He was a tall man with a ginger beard. I don't remember his name, but I remember well his good deeds. He was a pious man and he respected the Torah. He was very hospitable. Two pupils of the Yeshiva ate at his table every day. He would also bring home after the Sabbath prayers travelers who found themselves in our town on Sabbath. He had on his table chalas (pleated white bread), fish, meat and a strong drink too. The Sabras (Israeli born Jews) should know that, before the Holocaust, we were very hospitable to strangers. People were feeding the students of the Yeshiva. When I recollect the life in our town, I shed a tear.

The shoemaker and his wife went to the States. I hope that he is alive and will read the Yizkor book. If he will read it, he should know that this was written by Shimon Yankl Izik Zalmons, the baker. We lived in a house three doors from his mother-in-law.

Synagogues and prayer houses of Novogrudok

The Synagogue Place in Novogrudok was round. In the centre of the place stood the Big Synagogue. Around the Big Synagogue were smaller houses of prayer, which carried the names of the trades of those praying there. The main entry to the Synagogue Place was from the Yiddisher Street at the back fence of the Catholic Church. There were other narrow entries to the Synagogue Place. Not far from the Synagogue Place lived Reb Meyer the dien (a religious arbitrator). There was also another dien in Novogrudok named Reb Mordchai Hirsh, who lived in Waliker Street. In case of a religious dispute, both diens were called in. My sister Chana married Reb Mayer the daien's grandson. He was called Michl. The third house in that lane belonged to my father, where our bakery was. Nearby was the synagogue of the shoemakers. The building was narrow and long. One entered the synagogue through a long, dark corridor. The members of the synagogue were all shoemakers. Between Mincha and Miriv the Rabbi studied with the congregation a short version of the Shulchan Oruch. Before a holy day they studied the laws of that holiday.

Across to the right was a synagogue, which was called Metaskim, which meant the Burial Society. The gaby (chairman of the lay committee) of the synagogue was a member of the Kivelevich family. Their son lives in Israel.

The verger of the synagogue, named Michl drew three incomes: as a verger, a teacher and he baked also buckwheat pancakes. The income from all three was quite meager.

Between Mincha and Miriv a Rabbi recited Ain Yaakov with those praying in the synagogue.

A little further along was the synagogue Chai Adam. The synagogue was in a small timber building. Here, between Mincha and Miriv a Rabbi recited Chai Adam.

A little to the right was the synagogue of the carriers. Those praying there were the carriers of the death- beds of the Chevre Kadishe (Burial Society). Here, between Mincha and Miriv a Rabbi recited Mnorat Hamaor (the candelabra of light), on a Sabbath Chovat Halivavot from Rabeinu Bechai.

A little to the left of the synagogue of the carriers was the Koidanover shtibl (small house of prayer). In that shtibl prayed a Chasid named Hirsh Dobrin, who baked, under supervision, matzo for Passover. This was his income for the year. One can imagine how wealthy (ironically) he was. Dobrin was a tall, thin man with a long, pointed beard. He was a G-d fearing man of the book.

The Big Synagogue was built of bricks and had windows in all four walls. Inside the thick walls stood bookcases filled with books. Two tiled ovens warmed the synagogue in the winter. After the prayers a 'blat Geromorah' was read. The people who prayed in the Big Synagogue were the prominent citizens of the town. Among them were Reb Yoine and Reb Moshe Frumkes OBM. Other members of the congregation of the Big Synagogue were Rabinovich, Kabak, and Harkavy.

The Big Synagogue also housed a cheder, where young men were studying. Their teacher was Reb Moishe, a great scholar and a clever man. I had the privilege to be one of his pupils.

On a Sabbath I had the pleasure of seeing how our Rabbi, the brilliant Reb Yechiel Michoel Epstein, the author of Oruch Hashulchan, walked from the big synagogue in his Sabbath dress, a nice round hat and a long satin coat. And eminent members of the community, Jewish patriarchs, watched the Rabbi go all the way to his home in Yiddishe Street, across the road from the Catholic Church. All walked slowly with measured steps, whilst conducting a discussion about a difficult paragraph in the Gemorah. The Rabbi had the look of a Jewish king and my heart was full of joy as I looked at him.

At right angles to the big synagogue was the cold synagogue. One entered that synagogue by going down four steps. This gave credence to the expression 'I am calling to you from the depth, G-d'. In that synagogue on a big table stood a copper menorah. In a corner an opening was formed in which a perpetual oil light burnt.

There were legends about the cold synagogue. One story had it that in the depth of the night the dead prayed there. Children were frightened to walk past that synagogue at night. Nata, the verger, when he had to go into the synagogue early in the morning, would knock three times on the door with a stick and would shout: 'Bar minan minuchot' (the dead go to rest).

In the cold synagogue was a cheder 'Sheva korim', which means that on Sabbath only seven people are called up to read the Torah.

On both sides of the synagogue were 'Esrot nashim" (a sanctuary for women), where women prayed on the Sabbath.

A small, narrow building was built onto the synagogue. This was the Tailor's synagogue.

On winter nights, when Reb Avrom Edida OBM, a small thin man, would go around the town, knock on the shutters and shout: 'Get up to do the work of the Creator'. The Jews that were woken up in the middle of the night would get up and say Thilim in the Tailor's synagogue. That gave them a special satisfaction. Outside it was bitterly cold, but inside it was warm and bright and they prayed with fervor a chapter of Thilim.

Next to the tailor's synagogue was a small house. That was the synagogue of the butchers. My wife's father, Reb Avrom OBM, a good and G-d fearing Jew, would pray mishnot with the butchers between Minche and Miriv.

On the left of the tailor's synagogue was the Todres synagogue. A man by the name of Todres built this synagogue at his own expense. This synagogue was frequented by learned people that were fluent in the Torah. Reb Abele, a fur merchant, delivered a lesson each day in the Todres synagogue. The most learned people of the town would come to listen to his lessons. Reb Abele had a shop in the row of shops. His merchandise consisted of thin leather straps, which the farmers would buy to make laptes (home made open sandals). In his shop lay a copy of Ein Yaakov. He spoke with the customer and looked into Ein Yaakov, so as not to interrupt his study of the Torah.

Outside of the synagogue square were other synagogues in Novogrudok: in Shloss Street, Siniezits Street, in Zalatuche, at the end of Valiker Street and other synagogues where people prayed, studied and spoke about the Torah.

There were also groups of ten or more, who prayed in private homes. The family Harkavy, who had a house in the Market Place, had a separate building for prayers. In that building they prayed only on Sabbath.

As can be seen, there was in Novogrudok a considerable activity in praying and religious learning. The income of the people of Novogrudok was scant, but there was great involvement in religion. This gave them a lot of pleasure and made their lives more satisfying.

On Fridays after the bath, people would change into festive clothes and would meet the Sabbath. On the tables lay festive chales and stood bottles of wine. Those who could not afford a chala prayed using two whole matzot. The worries and the tasks of the whole week were forgotten. Every Jew felt like a king, the wives in their best clothes were like queens and the children were princes.

This is how Novogrudok looked on the eve of the greatest catastrophe, which wiped out thousands of Jewish communities, and among them the community of our beloved town of Novogrudok.

The invaluable assistance of Mr. David Grynberg, Jack Delatycki and Jeanette Delatycki is acknowledged.

[Page 70]

Reminisces of Yischok Gurwitz:

Reb Nachman Getzov

Translated from Yiddish by O. Delatycki

In my memory are imprinted those Sabbath eves when I held high the pleated, thick Havdola candles and my father ZLB started to sing the tune 'I am certain of my salvation and I have no fear' and he emphasized especially 'I am certain' and 'I have no fear'. Following the singing I drank with particular pleasure dear Dvoira's wine. Mother's blue tiled oven was hot. I liked to bake potatoes in it. Father would put hot charcoal into the samovar He used his boot to get the charcoal burning. Shortly after, two friends of father's would arrive. One of them later taught me Tanach and the other told me about Zionism. They were Reb Yosef Goldfine and Reb Nachman Getzov. We all sat down at the table. Mother served tea. In the mean time my potatoes were ready. Half of them were burnt and the other half was raw, but to me they had a delicious taste.

At the table a long discussion was conducted about a certain Shlomo ben Aderet and Osher ben Yechiel. Both Reb Nachman Getzov and Reb Yosef Goldfine were in a state of high animation, they spoke rapidly and angrily. It was obvious that both of them were excited and were indignant in regard to Shlomo ben Aderet, and Asher ben Yechiel. On the other hand, my father was remarkably controlled in that matter and smiled into his long beard. 'Drink your tea' urged mother. To no avail! The conversation continued for hours, till father took from a shelf the chess set and suggested that they should play chess. Reb Yosef Goldfine started to play the game, which continued, as I remember, for the rest of the evening. Reb Nachman Getzov left soon after.

'Mother, who is that Shlomo ben Aderet?' 'I don't know my child, he is probably a famed Rabbi or a tana (teacher of the Mishna).' 'No, he must be a bad man, because our visitors were very cross with him,' said I.

Years like an eternity have gone by. I spent those years in cheders [religious primary schools], with my Rabbis, I studied by a small lamp, which was always smoking. Later I studied in the large Talmid Torah of Reb Zelik ZLB. I passed through all grades in the building which, many years' later, savage people destroyed and with it destroyed every sign of the past, they flattened every mark of the old tradition, where many generations lived and thousands of children were educated.

Later, I lived in foreign lands, in Yeshivot and I ate 'days' in many homes. Only than did I find out that Reb Shlomo ben Aderet was actually no other than RASBA (Rash'ba) (the head of a Yeshiva) and Reb Asher ben Yechiel was also RASH (Ra'sh). They were two Goens (men of great learning), one of whom came from Germany and the other from Spain. They played an important part in the moral, political and economic life of the Jewish people. Now I began to understand why Reb Nachman Getzov was so excited on that Sabbath eve in my father's house when I was very young.

Now we come to the essence of the story – who was Nachman Getzov? He was one of the many shopkeepers in Novogrudok. He sold tea and sugar in a small shop. But those who knew him better realized that, firstly, Nachman Getzov was a pious, G-d fearing Jew, who kept exactly to all the mitzvoth of the Torah, secondly, Reb Nachman was enlightened in Gomorrah and its judgments. He was also enlightened in all the Jewish literature. He knew foreign languages and specifically German literature. Apart from the book 'On the rivers of Babylon', which Nochem Sokolov printed as a gift for the readers of "Hazfirah," he was also knowledgeable in the history of the ancient world, specifically in the period of the Tnaim Amoraim (teachers of Mishna and teachers of Talmud). He knew very well and was absorbed in the life of every single Goen (teacher of Mishna), starting with Shmaye Vaftalion to Rabbi Rav Ashi.

He knew and described the life of everyone, and the influence of each one on the community, and he explained it in great detail in his book 'Hatana'im Ve'ha'am' ('Teachers of Mishna and the People'), a manuscript which regrettably, was never published. Should the Jerusalem University obtain at present such a book as 'Teachers of Mishna and the People', they would receive it gladly and would print it for all to read. I, in particular, know how to value the pearls, which Reb Nachman used to embellish the works of every single man of learning and he had drawn it from the right sources, from the real one – from Talmud of Babylon and Jerusalem.

In the era of political Zionism, when Dr Hertzl's book 'The State of the Jews' had appeared, our unforgettable Nachman Getzov had turned with his whole heart to Zionism. Reb Nachman was not a talented speaker, yet for years he never ceased to speak up for Zionism. Initially, his friends, the pious Jews of the Todres synagogue, did not take him seriously. Nevertheless he became their main orator. He spoke in all the synagogues and his speeches were replete with Jewish history, with Jewish blood and tears from every epoch. He raised a large circle of followers, particularly among the pious. The youth were also among his admirers. Reb Nachman had become a symbol of Zionism – he became a keen supporter of the people and their citadel, the place where the people were gathering every Sabbath to listen to Reb Nachman's sermons. The Talmid Torah had become a place which brought to the people of Novogrudok, and particularly the youth, worthwhile ideals and clear perspectives. Reb Nachman opened their eyes and gave them pride and courage. People acquired a different outlook of themselves. He was not only preaching, he was the first to sell shares of the Colonial Bank, the so called Treasury of the Jewish settlers in Israel, which changed in time to an ordinary, wealthy bank named the Anglo-Palestinian Bank (more about it elsewhere).

And remarkably, Reb Nachman found enough time to study. He was a great matmid (a person who constantly studies the Torah) with a good head on his shoulders. He read the latest literature in foreign languages - Russian, German. He liked philosophy and adored RAMBAM. He studied conscientiously the 'Strong hand'. In his spare time he dwelled deeply into 'Moreh nevuchim' (A Guide to the Perplexed) by Moses Maimonides (RAMBAM). He liked greatly the Tibbonim; Yehuda Ibn-Tivon, Shmuel Ibn-Tivon and Moshe Ibn-Tivon.

I remember a summer's day when Reb Nachman came into our shop, bought ink for a penny and said to me: "if you are available come with me to Slonim St., we can have a chat". We went some way out of town. Reb Nachman spoke of Yeduda Ibn-Tivon with ecstasy: 'What would we be without copiers, without translators? Who would translate for us from the Arabic the great book 'The duties of the heart' by our Rabbi Bechii? Who would translate for us 'The book of morals' and 'Selected pearls' by Rabbi Shlomo Ibn-Gvirol, 'Sefer Hakuzari' by Yehuda Halevi? And who would translate 'Seifer HaRikma' (Grammatical world) by Yonah Ibn-Ganach? Who would translate the book 'Beliefs and opinions' by Rabbi Sa'adya Gaon? Only they, the translators. The Tibbonim led us into a nice world. In the world of the spirit we have the pleasure of looking in and thinking of the magnificent books translated into Hebrew. It is true that the Hebrew is a bit fractured, but none-the-less it can be well understood'.

This conversation allowed me to understand better this unique man and I looked for opportunities to converse with Reb Nachman. I benefited from that contact greatly. I learned a lot from him. As well as everything else he had good habits. He liked to tell the truth. I remember a small episode. When the citizens of Novogrudok appointed a new Rabbi from Tavrig, Reb Nachman was opposed to the choice. But after the Tavrig Rabbi gave the first sermon, which was well remembered by all his followers – this was the story of two Kohanim – Reb Nachman told me 'I have to confess that his sermon was sweeter than honey'. He used to say 'Why am I a small shopkeeper? I am tied forever to a bit of sugar. Is that what I have been created for?'

I, as a man born in Novogrudok, cannot point to anyone I could compare him with. Within him were combined the Torah and the fear of G-d in philosophy and they acted together. One did not exclude the other. Now sitting in my house in Tel Aviv and writing this article, I can see him walking with his talles and tfilim to the Todres synagogue.

The invaluable assistance of Jack Delatycki and Aviva Kamil in translating the above article is acknowledged

[Page 72]

The Tailors' Synagogue

[Shtibl – a small house of prayer]

by Shimeon Yosifun

Translated from Yiddish by Minia Lipkies and Oskar Delatycki

Why have a tailors' shtibl? Are there not many other shtibls and synagogues in town? The answer is that there are, but the Tailors' was quite special.

The tailors' shtibl, or, as it was called in the old days, "afun shtibl" [at the shtibl], has a very special history. If a young man was asked "where do you pray?" or "where do you study?" [referring to religious studies] it was a matter of pride to reply "at the shtibl". I like to remember particularly the shtibl, which was the cradle of my childhood and youth. In that small shtibl grew up and lived generations of personalities and rare types of people. I will not describe everyone who attended the shtibl. I will write about the congregation as a whole.

It happens quite frequently, when I stroll in the evenings along the streets of Tel-Aviv, and my eyes are filled with images of the large, well lit up shop windows, with cars rushing one way and the other way, crowds of young people walking leisurely, numerous languages spoken by the many newcomers to this country. In the new suburbs, from the new houses with the large balconies one can hear singing and music of radio stations from the entire world.

And in this babble of noises I close my eyes and in my memory come up pictures of the past, of my small town and the small shtibl and I see before me images of a Friday night. It is winter and the streets are covered in snow. It is 2 o'clock in the early morning. All is still. Only one person, an elderly Jew, is fighting his way through the deep snow. Rapt in his fur coat and boots, the old tailor Avrom Yedida is singing in his thin, squeaky voice. The street is empty. His voice is heard on and on. It penetrates into the Jewish homes and Jewish hearts and soles. Little children wake up and rouse their parents. "Father, mother-listen, the old man is singing. Get up, get up to worship the creator." My father rinses his hands in a finger bowl, dresses me warmly and takes me to the shtibl for the psalms. On Friday night, Jankl, the verger, had heated well the damaged blue oven with the long brick flue which served as a bench on the western wall. By the time we arrived in the shtibl the flue was already filled. In front sat old Berl Notkes, a man in his nineties with red eyes, no eyebrows, staring into his prayer book without glasses. Next to him Tevie the tailor, Heshl, Hershl, Shimen, and others. On the flue sat Jankl Yosl the verger with his two sons: the older Ichke and the younger Meishke with twisted fingers. Next to them sat Tritl the scribe with his three sons: Tevie, Leibe and Aron. All were chatting quietly. Shortly the shtibl was packed solid with people. The lanterns were smoking, there was no seat left, but who was worried about such details? Aron Motke the furrier banged on the podium and Berle Kefkes, a man in his mid thirties, short with a thick black beard, approached the podium and recited by rote, with heart and sole, the beginning of psalms. The large crowd recited with him, paragraph after paragraph, with ecstasy, one endeavouring to shout louder than his neighbour. And this went on, one paragraph after another, chapter after chapter, with many mistakes and omissions as long as the intentions were good. But when it came to chapter seventeen, we, the young ones, had to smile at Berl's rendition of the paragraph. When I asked my father: why does Berl say the prayer by rote and not by reading it from the book, father answered that he makes fewer mistakes when he does not read the book. But, anyway, Berl is a fine fellow so let him pray as he likes. And that was the way we prayed every Friday night from Ashrei ha ish to Kol ha nishomo tehalel ya [from the beginning to the end of the psalms]. Afterwards we would walk home and drink tea with milk covered with a thick skin and then back to the stibl for more prayers.

This time the shtibl seemed to be different. Seats were still not available, but the lanterns were not bellowing smoke and the crowding was not as dense. They still stand in front of my memory – the praying people, the dear Jews from the small shtibl. The eastern wall was fully occupied. Here is Reb Shepsl Zeliks, a man of the Book, slightly megushmedicer [worldly], broad boned with long hair on his eyebrows – they nearly covered his eyes. I remember that after the prayers my father would invite Reb Shepsl to share a drink (kiddish). Father would open a bottle of vodka and pour in half a glass of pepper into the bottle. That's how he liked it. Reb Shepsl would praise highly my mother's kichl [brittle pancake shaped biscuit] and tzimes [diced cooked carrots]. Mother used to repeat the same phrase each time after he left "I had the biggest honour when he sat at our table".

Reb Meier Tsires, a learned and clever man, my late father, Reb Asher Kopls, my dear teacher Reb Yosif Kaldfine, who was known as Yosl Leibke Wagers, Reb Sholim Chaim Berls, Reb Meilach Skakun, Hershl the tinsmith, Shier the dyer, Heshl Avrom Iches, Iche Purkuls with his sons Avrom Ber and Akiva, Yoshe Kirshner and the permanent cantors: Wisel for the morning prayers, Mashe Chananies for the evening prayers, the permanent gabay Aron Motke the furrier and the permanent opposer Moishe Yankl Kirshner and other memorable Jews who prayed with a will. Who would look at the young shnekes – Dovid Shmerkovich, Yehuda Litvin, Yudl Eliyahu Vilenski or the younger still generation Shmerl Kisner, Alter Yosl Chananies, Dov Malchacki and I, the author of this article.

I enumerate many names of the prayer group for another reason: they were not only participants in the tomchey yedidim [supportive friends] which existed for 50 or 60 years. I doubt if the majority of the people of Novogrudok ever knew that such a circle existed. The duty of the circle was to help unobtrusively worthy people in need with small donations. I will not say much more about this circle and will only mention that they had a regular annual meeting on a specified day when the weekly portion of the Torah "beshalach" was read. The members of the circle looked forward with anticipation to the meetings. Four weeks prior to the meeting Shneer the dyer would exclaim "thanks God we are approaching the portion of the Torah "beshalach". As the expected Shabes beshalach came around, all the members of the circle had to pray in the shtibl. Each of them was called up to the Torah. When the turn of Yoshe Kirshner would come, he would stumble over the blessing and all the boys would burst out laughing. Quite often I was given a smack by my father for laughing at an old man because he had made a mistake.

For years, after the prayers, there was a Kiddush at our house for the members of the circle. There were big slabs of honey cake. We were given the cake twice a year; once at tomche yedidim, when the portion of beshalach was read, the second one at Sholem Yoine which was read by Aron Motke of the group of psalmist, when the portion of the Torah was nesa. The actual general meeting took place on Saturday night. Yankl Yosl the verger would organise the provisions which included a package of Istanbul tobacco and a bundle of cigarette paper and everyone could roll thick cigarettes and smoke to his hearts content. There were baskets of apples and there was tea for one and all.

The permanent secretary, bookkeeper and reporter was Tritl the scribe. He would read out the list of income and expenses, but the recipients of the assistance were not named. That was the secret of the committee. The committee was elected for a year. They were opposed by the troika Moshe Yankl Kirshner, Chonon Leibovich and Yehoshua the boot maker. The troika was always arguing the same thing – they wanted the secretary to read out the names of the people who received assistance – but that was never done, unless the opposition would be elected to the committee, which never happened. The argument continued till midnight when a compromise was reached and everyone departed expressing a wish that next year the money in the treasury would remain untouched, because nobody would need support.

The circle was dissolved probably during the World War [i.e. the first World War]. I don't know where the books and the archive of the circle are. I believe that only Dovid Shmerkovich and Yudl Eliyahu Vilenski would know that.

In the noise and whirl of the new life on the shores of the Mediterranean sea emerge memories of long ago, of times that will never return, of events that existed in the far away land of Novogrudok, where the vanished generations of our parents and grandparents lived. They had their worries and their happiness. They prayed and sang in the distant past.

[Page 74]

The Seder night that was disrupted

by Yischok Gurwitz

Translated by Oskar Delatycki

The story I want to tell you happened in the recent past – about 35 years ago in the year Tof Rez Samach [1900], when the pupils at the Reb Yiovzl's Yeshiva were the best students from Kovno and Slobodka, genuine talmid chochims [clever students]. Among them, many became famous scholars. Their voices could be heard emanating from the big synagogue through the nights.

The population of Novogrudok was treating the students with great friendliness and respect and especially by the women, who fed the young people with the very best. If a student could not come on the appointed day, the food was taken to his lodging. I remember one student named Reb Yosef. He was a young man from Galicja. He was tall with a round friendly face and a short black beard. He was pleasant and was good at his studies and had a thorough understanding of the subjects he studied. He knew thoroughly three books of Gemora, was clever and a hard worker. It was a pleasure to converse with him. His depth of understanding and sharp mind had beguiled me. I first met him in my father-in-law's house where he was stationed. He was fed by 'days' by the neighbours. My mother used to bring her pot on Sundays, my mother-in-law on Mondays, and Tzivie, daughter of Isroel from Vilno, on Tuesdays. When Tzivie would bring her pot and put it in the oven to keep the food warm, a sweet smell would permeate the house. On a certain Tuesday I came for a chat with Reb Yosef. I found him sitting at the table, eating his food. 'Good appetite' I said 'how do you like the food'. 'Very good' said he 'all is in good order'. 'This is so tasty' said I 'because a good looking woman cooked it'. The expression on the young man's face changed, it was obvious that he was angry. He said 'I don't know her, I don't know who brings me the food'. 'That is the problem' I answered 'if you knew who brought the food you would have even more pleasure from it'. The young man's face darkened, he looked at me angrily, but it was obvious that he would not dare to rebuke me for my indiscretion and he changed our conversation in another direction.

On the Sabbath, Reb Yosef ate at the house of Reb Hirshl Shimon Israelit, the richest man in town. Reb Yosef would say after he retuned home 'It would seem that Reb Hirshl Shimon is an ordinary person, he can be very friendly to his fellow men. I feel that I am welcome in his house. I don't deserve the respect that he shows me'.

Reb Yosef had one blemish however – he was too pious. His extreme devotion could lead to untamed excesses. I would like to tell you about one such incident. The time was a couple of weeks before Passover and in those days the preparations for the holiday were quite advanced in every Novogrudok household. The tables, the chairs, the kitchens and the dishes were thoroughly scrubbed and washed. The women were up to their necks in work. In the last week before Passover we were walking on sawdust, straw and matting in my mother-in-law's house. The benches and tables were put out in the house. We were eating in a corner. My father-in-law was walking around discontented muttering and complaining. My mother-in-law was very pious, even her name was Frume [pious] and despite her husband's discontent everything was scrubbed tenfold.

When the time came to cleanse the oven, Reb Yosef appeared. He asked my mother-in-law to allow him to cleanse the chimney. Even my mother-in-law had never reached the level of piety which involved cleaning the chimney. She was very interested to observe how a chimney is prepared for Passover. Reb Yosef did it quite simply: he brought in a large handful of straw, pushed it well into the oven, lit it and almost burned down the house. But the chimney was thoroughly prepared for the festival. When father-in-law heard about it he was most upset. He blamed Reb Yosef and kept asking: where did he learn about the law to cleanse chimneys? 'One day you are going to be a rabbi of a town which will be devastated if it follows such laws'. Reb Yosef said nothing. He was just smiling forlornly as if to say: the deed is done and we can do nothing about it.

Between Purim and Passover the house of Hershl Shimon was a beehive of uninterrupted activity. The 8 hour working day did not exist in those days. Normally the girls worked till midnight and Sorre Ester made sure that they worked fast. But between Purim and Passover they worked the whole night through without interruption. Sorre Ester had two duties: to watch the girls in the workroom to make sure that nobody fell asleep and to prepare for Passover at home. The servant, a Jewish girl, had a hard task because Passover in the house of Hershl Shimon had to be prepared in grand style.

On the eve of Passover Reb Yosef made preparations, he went to the bath house and had barely eaten; it was neither every day fare nor Passover food. It felt as if he was overlooked. My mother-in-law brought a plate of mashed potatoes with mushrooms. Reb Yosef ate it without appetite. He said to me pondering 'I find Passover eve tedious'.

When the evening came we all went to the synagogue and the atmosphere improved. Having come back with Hershl Shimon to start the Seder, Reb Yosef was in a good mood. The big table was splendidly arranged with the big chandelier and big candle sticks. With panache and according to tradition all sat around the table and listened to the blessing of the wine by the host. The youngest son asked the traditional Passover questions, but when Reb Yosef started reading the Haggadah – just the first few sentences starting with 'avodim hoinu' [we were slaves] – Hershel Shimon and Sorre Ester both fell asleep. Reb Yosef, who was engrossed in reading the Haggadah, did not notice it initially, but when he heard the snoring of his overworked hosts, who for weeks did not have enough sleep, he felt compassion for them. He started to read the Haggadah loudly to see if that would wake them. But the louder and with more feeling he read the Haggadah the deeper his hosts slept. The children also fell asleep. Reb Yosef finished reading the Haggadah and sat there not knowing what to do next. Reb Yosef started pacing the house. He began thinking of his home, his wife and child and tears ran down his face. He was thinking: this was the way of the Torah. He put on his overcoat, got out from the warm house, closed the door and went away - where to? He found himself at the house of my father-in-law where I was invited to the first Seder. We just started eating. We asked him 'What is the matter Reb Yosef, did you finish so early?' He told us the whole story and he sounded deeply disturbed. I, wanting to cheer him up, asked him 'could you not get your food from the servants?' He answered to my jest in all seriousness 'in the kitchen lay the kitchen maid with, if you will excuse me, her bottom up and was snoring like an ox, next to her lay the serving girl crouched, her hair tossed about, their snoring reminded me of a wild tune, I ran from the kitchen.' 'Sit down at the table' my father-in-law said 'I forgave you the cleansing of the chimney.' Reb Yosef shed his overcoat, sat down at the table and we had a festive meal and conversation. Reb Yosef told us stories from Galicja, I spoke of Saratov and so on till midnight.

That night we had shmire, we did not sleep. Every 2-3 hours we would check if all was well at the house of Hershl Shimon. In the morning we went into his house. As we opened the door the following sight greeted us: the big lamp was still shedding a low light, the setting on the big table with the candelabra, the cups still filled to the brim with wine were still untouched, Hershl Shimon dressed in a frockcoat and sash, with a broad, wild beard, scull cap on his head seating in his chair at the head of the table fast asleep. He looked like the head priest in his priestly attire. Sorre Ester was also asleep, with her left arm resting on the table and the right hand supporting her chin.

When we woke them up with words: 'the time had come to say the morning prayer', they were very confused, they asked our pardon and begged us to keep the matter secret. I promised to do so. But, you be the judges, how long can one keep a secret?

I think that 35 years is long enough.

[Page 76]

Dr. Benjamin Einhorn

by Yaakov Gershovski

Translated from Yiddish by Oskar Delatycki

Novogrudok, though a uvezd [sub-district] of the Minsk gubernia [district], was at the time an isolated backwards corner. A Byelorussian small town with a substantial Jewish majority, Novogrudok did not have a train connection either to the capital of the gubernia Minsk, with which it was bound administratively, or to Wilno, the centre of the Haskola movement and of commerce, where the township's shopkeepers were buying their supplies. The means of communication consisted of large horse drawn carts in the summer and sleighs in the winter. The vehicles belonged to Rafael the commissioner. He was conveying to Wilno young men to study in the yeshivas and other educational institutions, or any young man in search of a tachles (essence). He took back various goods, according to the lists that the shopkeepers gave him.

The two Jews in town with degrees: Dr. Lubchanski and the pharmacist Shtrik, had an attitude of alienation towards the Jews, which was characteristic of the intelligentsia of that time, because they tried to distance themselves from the masses. If they came to the synagogue for half an hour on the New Year or Yom Kippur it was a veritable event, and was being discussed as something extraordinary. Children and others would gather around them and observe their every movement, every step. They looked on them as if they came from another planet. However they were well known the whole year around. What an event! The doctor and the pharmacist in the synagogue!

Now, can you imagine the sensation in town and the effect it had on one and all when in the early 80's of the last (i.e. XIX) century a middle aged Jewish doctor settled in town, and not just an ordinary doctor but a military one with the rank of Colonel. And that's not all, because the military doctor Benjamin Einhorn came to the synagogue for the prayers draped in a woolen talles (prayer wrap) and big tfilim (phylacteries). He also came to pray at Mincha (afternoon service) and Maariv (prayer at night, after sunset). He prayed piously, with inspiration. After prayers he would sit down and study 'a page of Gomorrah' with great perseverance. The excitement in town was extraordinary: a military doctor with the rank of Colonel was wearing a beard and sideboards and behaves like a most observant Jew! The Jews were most impressed. In no time the event became known to the police officer. I don't remember the name of that police officer stationed at the time in Novogrudok, but the Jews in town called him among themselves Haman (enemy of the Jews, see the Book of Esther). He was a great persecutor of the Jews, the difference between him and his namesake from the days of Achashverosh was that the historical Haman had no respect from Mordechai and was prepared to spend money to get rid of Mordechai and his Jews, whereas the Novogrudok Haman had lots of respect from the Jews of Novogrudok, if he was seen at a distance they would hastily take off their hats and bow reverently, and they were prepared to give him money – if only he would accept it - 3,5 or even 10 rubbles, and gifts like heads of sugar, geese and so forth. And if he did not want to accept the bribe himself, thus indicating that the alleged breach of law was so great that even a bribe would not erase the guilt, on those occasions money was offered to Haman's wife. She never refused. She would make extensive purchases in Jewish shops and put the bill on her husband's account.

Having found out about Dr. Einhorn from the Jews, who wanted to show off that they had among them a Jewish doctor who was a Colonel, Haman decided that something was wrong, that the doctor must be a swindler or a major criminal, or possibly a meshumed (convert), possibly even a doctor who managed to prosper because he converted to Christianity and now he wants to return to Judaism. And because this is forbidden he is hiding out in the township in a synagogue. He was triumphant in advance assuming that he would cause troubles to the Jews, by making them responsible for hiding a felon. On the following Saturday morning when the Jews were going to the synagogue, Haman took with him four armed policemen and went with them to the guesthouse where Dr.Einhorn was staying. On the way he stopped a few Jews who were on the way to the synagogue and took them with him to serve as witnesses. At that stage several curious Jewish onlookers joined the throng. They were eager to know what was happening and where Haman was going with the armed policemen. Having entered the guesthouse, Haman stationed two policemen at the door to be certain that no one could escape and with the other two and the witnesses he went in to the room to investigate. Einhorn was dressed for the Sabbath and was about to leave for the synagogue. Having seen in front of him a Jew with a beard and with a talles in his hand, Haman became courageous. He looked at Einhorn from top to bottom and he shouted at him 'who are you, where are your documents'. Einhorn showed no concern. He took out the documents from the wardrobe and gave them to Haman, who started examining the documents, first with disdain and later he started flipping through them. He noticed that they were authorised with state seals. The colour of his face started to change, he became paler and paler, his hands shook. He put down the documents and started sliding out of the room. However Einhorn stopped him and said to him in a strong voice: 'How dare you treat me like this? Do you know who you are dealing with and what my rank is?' He took out from the wardrobe a handful of medals from the Turkish war and he spoke to him firmly 'Do you see how the State honoured me for my endeavours during the war. According to my rank you must salute me, and not treat me with such brutality and gall'. Haman remained standing for some minutes as if frozen, after which he stretched ridged, saluted and in a low and depressed voice answered 'My fault, your highness, I was given wrong information by the Jews'. Einhorn was furious 'Be quite', he shouted, 'get out of here or I will report you to your superiors. How dare you blame the Jews'? Haman disappeared in a hurry, worried, with a bent head. He was so distraught that he forgot to call off the policemen who he had put at the door. He also forgot to disperse the onlookers, who in the meantime gathered in numbers and blocked the entrance to the guesthouse and half the street. And instead of unsettling the Jews on the Sabbath and do them ill, Haman was defeated (Haman's mapole).

It was thanks to this story that Dr Einhorn became popular. His practice increased. His popularity also increased because he was not greedy. He treated poor patients without payment. He was also not concerned how much rich patients paid him. He became known as a specialist in eye diseases. He cured patients who could previously not be healed by radical treatments such as spring water 'reines art' [I am puzzled by this, the English expression 'spring water' is sometimes translated into German as 'reines Wasser ', this is the best I can do] or even water that was used to cleanse a corpse.

Though he now had a busier practice he did not neglect the synagogue. He studied with great perseverance. On Sabbath he would not write prescriptions. If it was urgent he would go to the pharmacy and order the prescription. Despite of this, his success was not long lasting. His practice shrank and did not provide him with a livelihood.

The attitude of Jews towards him had become more indifferent and lacked respect. The richer patients took advantage of the fact that he never bargained and never counted the proffered fees. The patients would pay him using low denomination copper coins instead of silver money. The potential patients decided that his mode of living and his pious behaviour were interfering with his professional duties. Some even suggested that his head was not functioning well. Some thought that he could not be trusted with patients. His practice continued to diminish. He was short of money and he moved to Korelich. There was no doctor in Korelich. In Korelich Dr Einhorn did not change his way of life. He sent his children to the cheder and yeshiva. His son Dovid (the renowned poet Dovid Einhorn born in Korelich) was sent as a boy to study in the Ramal yeshiva in Wilno.

It is worth mentioning a characteristic of his life. For most of the year Dr Einhorn kept to himself, and that included his behaviour at the synagogue when he studied. He shunned company. He behaved like a hermit. He seemed worried, apprehensive. He appeared to be hard-pressed. But when Simchas Torah came he seemed to 'put on a new skin' as the saying goes. He was of a sudden full of joy and most active. He danced and sang in a circle, whilst holding on to a scroll. It made no difference if he was among young or old, rich or poor. And yet, though he was the only doctor in Korelich, [apart from him there was only a medical assistant (feltcher) and a nurse], he could not earn enough to live on. Here too did his patients take advantage of him, they cheated him. Again, copper coins instead of silver, wrapped in paper would be given to him. They took advantage of the habit that payment was given to a doctor wrapped in a piece of paper.

Not being able to survive in Korelich, Dr Einhorn moved to another township. But again the story repeated itself. In the end he gave up his profession and moved to Wilno. There he did not work as a doctor. He studied in the synagogue of the chasid Goyen. He lived off charity from his relatives. During the First World War he was cut off from his family. He survived for a short time, lonely and in great poverty. He died in the autumn of 1914. He was given an honourable place of burial in the cemetery.

Why did Dr Einhorn, a military doctor and a Colonel, suddenly become strictly religious? Various stories about it circulated. Dr Einhorn was a son of very pious parents from the small town Ivie. Naturally, he was given an orthodox upbringing. Whilst at the yeshiva he was influenced by the Haskola movement. He gave up his studies at the yeshiva and took up a conventional education. In time he achieved a university education and later studied in the military academy. In the time of the Turkish-Russian war he was promoted to the rank of a Colonel. His pious parents were quite unhappy about this. At that time Dr Einhorn persuaded his younger brother to drop his yeshiva education. This caused further anxiety to his parents. Einhorn promised his parents that he would do all he could to bring back his brother to religion. His brother, however, having finished his studies, converted to Christianity. His parents were shattered. They could not face the shame and shortly after died. The death of his parents shattered Dr Einhorn. He suffered for a time a mental collapse. He left the army and moved to small towns, where he lived remote from the world and followed the dictates of religion.

[Page 78]

'Without a hammer, shears and a saw'

by Menashe Unger, US

Translated from Yiddish by Oskar Delatycki

Josef Bruksman from Brooklyn describes a Chevre Kadishe for living orphans, which was established in Novogrudok 82 years ago.

In 1872 in the big city synagogue a large meeting of presidents and members of all the synagogues took place. It was decided to form an organization which would provide better living conditions for abandoned orphans, for homeless and poor children and the poor who walked the streets. The accepted resolution at that meeting was signed by the 88 persons present. The first among them was Gershon Harkavy.

The resolutions were written in Hebrew and consisted of 18 points. The most important points were: the society, which will be known as 'Chevre Kadishe Shokday Melocho' will look firstly after total orphans, next after half orphans. Care will also be extended to children whose parents beg in the streets. The society will hire teachers for the above mentioned three categories of children, will study with them, particularly on the Sabbath and holidays the Torah or Chai Adam (the life of man) and other religious works suitable for children. The children should be also given an elementary secular education. In addition, the children should receive instructions in acquiring trades. Every child should learn a trade to be able to build in the future an independent life and not require the help of strangers. Anyone could be a member of the Chevra Kadisha by making a contribution of two kopeks a week. Women have the full right to be members of the Chevre Kadishe, have the right to vote and be elected, to have a say regarding the activities. They must belong, however to a separate group and have their own books. On Saturday, after the festival of Shavuot the annual meeting must take place. The accountants must have two meetings per year: between the holy days of Pesach and between the holy days of Sukot. The minutes of the meetings must be displayed in all synagogues. The emblem of the original organization will be 'a hammer, a shear and a saw'. The 'Chevre Kadishe Shogdei Melocho' had grown well over the years and influenced other Jewish centres to create such organizations in Lida and Zetl.

[Page 79]

Alexander Harkavy

by Prof. Nosun Ziskind, US

Translated by Oskar Delatycki

The Jewish nation is 'am ha seifer' [the people of the book]. We created the 'seifer ha sforim' [the book of books] the Tanach, which is the greatest and the best.

We are in the position to appraise, therefore, Alexander Harkavy and place him in his due place among our great teachers. He took part in many activities. Alexander was born in 1863 into a family which could claim among its forebears a long line of rabbis, scholars, maskilim [members of the *Haskala* (knowledge) movement], modern scientists, researchers and the renowned publishers Ram of Vilno, which supplied prayer books and literature to the Jewish world. He continued in the family tradition. He participated in new intellectual developments with the best minds of his generation. He was a pleasant young man, a maskil, a member of the intelligentsia who was thirsting for knowledge, determined to find the truth, was intent on improving himself the world. And though he was orthodox, he had achieved the highest level of education and learning. As they say in English: a self-educated, self-made scholar. As he was an idealist he joined 'Am olam' [the nation and the world] and joined a group of young men from Vilno, who were planning to create a utopian colony in the new world, so as to improve themselves and the society. In the end, however, he worked his way from a labourer to being a leader and a communal worker, he assisted the emigrants through HIAS (Hebrew Immigrant Aid Society), was a lecturer with the Board of Education, an adviser on education to the city of New York, an activist in the Jewish school movement, an actor in the theatre, a translator and popularizer of books, a philologist, a writer, an editor of newspapers and books. But, as well as all that, Harkavy was foremost our rabbi (teacher). For about fifty years he was teaching the Jews of the United States his Torah shebal-pe (by word of mouth). To this day his teaching of the Torah bi ktav (written) influences his generation.

He taught the Jewish masses, the poor migrants, sweatshop workers and labourers, peddlers and shopkeepers and the radical intelligentsia. First and foremost he taught them the language of the land – English: speaking, reading and writing, so as to integrate them into the society. He followed this with teaching the history of the United States, its Constitution, the laws of citizenship and more, much more. To educate the masses, Harkavy published text books. He started with the traditional letter writing texts in Yiddish and English. He published a book in English – 'The teacher of English'. He continued to improve his books with each new edition. This was followed with English-Yiddish text books and English spellers. Then he wrote books on basic mathematics, advanced bookkeeping and geography, Tanach, history of the world, Jewish history, world literature, and aesthetics. And even a cookbook in Yiddish. His journalistic and publicist activities, his creating and editing of newspapers, journals and calendars was in totality mass education in the best meaning of that word. But his most popular creations remain his dictionaries, which ran into 30 editions.

Alexander Harkavy

To assess fully the influence of Harkavy, or, to put it more succinctly, his part in the education and development of Jewish immigrants, it is impossible and probably useless to gauge how much more difficult it would have been without Harkavy's help for immigrants to assimilate in their new home, to adjust and to Americanise and to widen their horizons of their general education. I made an attempt to establish, even approximately, the print run of all his teaching books, but I was not able to establish it to date. Some of his editions don't exist anymore. The most important publisher of his works, who is still printing his books, Hebrew Publishing Co. of New York, gave me a great deal of information, but the figures we were looking for were not available, not the overall number of books published nor the number of copies of individual books or the number of editions of the individual books. We only obtained the dates of the latest editions of every book. Through Ms Edna Kagan, secretary of the Novogrudok Relief Committee, we found out that Harkavy's wife used to complain that he allowed his publisher to enrich himself from his books and did not see to it that he obtained enough income for his needs. Having taken stock of the numbers of his books which are kept in the various libraries, I came to the conclusion that Mrs Harkavy was right. I estimated that hundreds of thousands of his books have been sold. It is certain that there is hardly a Jew who at one time did not consult one of his teaching books. The majority of his Jewish readers were those who read his "citizen" books, which were manuals to prepare them for the examination prior to obtaining their American citizenship. It would be no exaggeration to state that almost all Jewish immigrants had gained knowledge from his books, from the ordinary common Jews to the intelligentsia.

All investigations undertaken to date are showing that the first generation of Jewish migrants learned English from Hakavy's teaching books. I can serve as an example. My parents arrived in the States in 1912. They had to leave behind their children. In 1914 the First World War started and the children joined them in 1921. I was 15 years old at that time. I found in my parent's home Harkavy's books 'Learning at home' and the dictionary. My parents were learning English in government public evening classes. They must have considered it insufficient and were studying at home using Harkavy's teaching books. I was enrolled into the Yeshiva of Rabbi Itchok Alchanan and there I learned English for 4 hours a day. But for a long time I also studied at home using Harkavy's books. I think that it will not be an exaggeration to state that we, Jews of America, were all students of Harkavy. The fact that Harkavy was the foremost teacher of English of the Jewish immigrant generation in America would be a sufficiently big achievement.

Actually an English text book was published before Harkavy's in the 1870's. The book was written with Yiddish characters but the language was German, not 'deichmerish' [a germanised version of Yiddish], but simply German, which was meant for German Jews. With the appearance of Harkavy's works, this book disappeared for good.

If one looks deeper into the books of Harkavy, it becomes clear why he had such a great influence. Harkavy was obsessed with the desire to help and improve his fellow men. To teach, to educate was for him a melocho hakodesh [holy duty]. More than his genius and his ability as a populariser shine through his ethic, his desire to improve and humanise the world around him, and in particular to better his brethren. This was the secret of the unique success of his blessed activities, the continued love of his task. Though we don't know as yet the number of books Harkavy published, we know that whilst Harkavy endeavoured to earn a living from his work, his main aim was to publish regardless of his income. For example, he published by himself in 1925 his dictionary in three languages: Yiddish-English-Hebrew. When the book turned out to be successful, the Hebrew Publishing Company took over the publication of his books. Professor A.R. Heshl characterised in a lecture our goens and he said that in every period they understood what their generation was in urgent need of and undertook to satisfy those needs. This could be said about the works of Harkavy. He too had recognized what his brethren required and he created that which was needed or he made certain that others did so. This is why he went to the trouble of translating a cookbook to make it easier for a Jewish housewife, who only knew Yiddish, not to be disadvantaged compared to her non-Jewish neighbour and to have the same chance to excel in cooking. For that reason he also translated the then popular book by Prof. Brown. Another example was the absence on the market of a good quality translation into English of the Tanach for the English speaking Jews. The translation by Lazar was too unwieldy, the translations by non-Jews were not kosher with inserted erroneous Christian ideas. He could not undertake to translate anew the whole of the Tanach (because even 25 years later the Jewish Publishing Society was forced to engage a whole assembly of learned specialists to compose a new English version of the Tanach for Jews, based on the King James version). But there was a need at that time for a kosher Tanach in English. Harkavy, by removing the rejects from the modern "Revised Version", obtained an acceptable kosher translation for Jews. The same impulse to serve the spiritual needs of the Jews motivated Harkavy to collaborate on a Spanish language phrase book for Jews (1929) and to compile a Hebrew-English dictionary for the holy books for the English speaking Jews. But Harkavy the *maskil* had not neglected his first love – Hebrew. As early as 1894 he published an English-Hebrew vocabulary "Torah language in English" for the talmid chochim (clever scholar), which satisfied his desire of making accessible Hebrew books. Characteristic was also the change in the spirit of the time when in 1900 appeared the last edition of the Hebrew – English language tuition book. The Yiddish tuition book is still in existence (last edition 1956). Because of the demand in Israel, he had produced for Yiddish speakers in America the three language dictionary English -Yiddish – Hebrew. This enabled the Yiddish speaker to converse or correspond with both his English speaking children in America and with his Hebrew speaking brothers in Israel. It is significant that Harkavy started learning English with the Jewish migrants and finished by teaching their grandchildren Yiddish. In 1921 his practical lessons of English were still printed in Forward for Yiddish speakers. In 1932 he was publishing lessons of Yiddish for English speakers in the Morning

Journal. As we said, he was our universal teacher.

It is most interesting to note that in the Hebrew Tribune Harkavy proclaimed, even at that time, the importance of Yiddish. He declared his readiness to forgo all his previous efforts and to create a complete universal grammar of all Yiddish dialects. His early articles and books are polemic writings to show that Yiddish is a language equal to all others. It is possible to follow the development of Yiddish in the last 70 years by following the development of Harkawy's Yiddish style. Clearly, he was advancing from simplified Yiddish, putting in the effort to liberate Yiddish from imitation and copying from German. He endeavoured to make Yiddish independent and to make it shine with its native beauty instead of dressing it up in the dead feathers of German. When he started writing Yiddish the German migration was at its peak. The rule prevailed: the more 'deichmerish' the better, the nicer, the more elegant and the more intelligent. Even Harkawy called one of his early works "Handwoerter buch der Englischer sprache with the translation of the English words". In three consecutive editions the book was called:

> Firstly: Yiddish-English dictionary (1898)
>
> Followed by: English-Yiddish dictionary (1900)
>
> And finally: Yiddish-English-Hebrew dictionary (1925)

In the newspaper Forward (1921) his article was called Englisch Lektionen [German for the English lessons] but in the Morning Journal of 1932 it was called Englische Lekcies [Yiddish for English lessons, 'lekcies' is actually from Polish 'lekcje' OD], and his last book 'A werterbichl fun kreivishe werter' [A wordbook of related words].

In the end: Harkavy's book closest to his heart was his 'Peoples dictionary of the Yiddish language'. In the first volume, 'IVO papers' (1931), is a Yiddish dictionary where everything is explained in Yiddish without the help of any other tongue. Alas, Harkavy did not live to finish his work. But even the part that he did finish was lost by the publishers (I was given by the 'Committee for the Big Yiddish Dictionary' the mission of find the manuscript, but the publisher could not find it).

His most important works still remain: his multi-language special dictionaries, his 'Yiddish-English-Hebrew dictionary", which is still the largest compilation of translated Yiddish words. Harkavy must have been a saint, because work was for him everything, to which the young 25 year old Harkavy wanted to dedicate his whole life. Shtuchko has given us the full treasure of the Yiddish language and created now the instrument which is compiling the 'Big Yiddish Dictionary' (it would have been worthwhile for the editors of the dictionary to review his methods of phonetic transcription and his inventions of the terminology of grammatical terms. We can not enter here into a discussion of technical matters, but Harkavy was in that field innovative and created things which are worthwhile and useful to emulate.)

The next task is to realize Harkavy's dream. Maks Winrich, who is working assiduously on the history of the Yiddish language, Yochevet Yaffe, who created a method to study Yiddish dialects and Ariel Winrich, who collects and records perfectly prepared samples of Yiddish dialects from the whole world. Be happy, sage Harkavy, glow and shine in our sky among the shiny stars, be exultant about our nation, among our heroes are the rabbis: from Moshe Rabanu to Ezram, Hilel, Rashi, Rambam – to the eternity.

Alexander Harkavi at the cemetery of Navaredok

[Pages 82]

Avrohom Eliyahu Harkavy

Translated from Yiddish by O. Delatycki

Avrohom Eliyahu Harkavy, a famous Jewish man of letters and orientalist, died in Russia in March 1919 aged 84 years. He was born in 1835 in Novogrudok. Harkavy studied initially in the Volozyn yeshiva. Later he graduated from the Teacher's Institute in Vilno. In 1843 he enrolled at the University of St Petersburg and completed a master's course majoring in history. He continued his studies in Berlin and Paris. In 1876 he was appointed head of the oriental division in the St Petersburg library and held this position for the remainder of his life. He collaborated in many Jewish-Russian publications. He also wrote many papers, which made him famous in learned circles. In 1910 the scientific world celebrated Harkavy's 75th birthday by issuing a memorial book. The contributors were the world's best known scientists in Judaica and orientology. Attached to the book was a list of 399 works by Harkavy. Harkavy reviewed the entire literature of the Middle Ages, specifically of the Arabian era, the history of the Jews in the middle ages (with the emphasis on Jews in Slavonic and Balkan countries), Hebrew epigraphy etc. Harkavy continued to work during the last 10 years of his life. His death was a loss to both the Jewish community and the worldwide scientific community.

Welcome party for Alexander Harkavi

[Page 83]

An *Eelui* (Brilliant Scholar) from Novogrudok

(In memory of Kalman Aaron Midler)

by Chaim Noy

Translated from Hebrew by Aviva Kamil

A narrow, tall dwelling, in the style of the houses in Hanseatic towns, stood in the "long market", in the centre of Danzig. At the entrance a sign in English said: "Midler's Academy Of Languages". An occasional visitor climbed up the many stairs to the Academy on the top floor, where there was a small room adjoining a huge attic, from which all the roofs of the town could be seen. The room was stacked from floor to ceiling with books. The only member of staff was a Jew wearing a moustache, a pipe in his mouth, his one eye almost blind from too much reading. Shabbily dressed, he lived the life of an old bachelor, of thriftiness and neglect.

But anyone who climbed those steps to learn a language or to procure a translation never ascended in vain.

What languages did the lone man master? Almost any language you may name: all European and many Asian languages and even some useful African tongues; and, without a doubt, all the old Classical languages of the West and East.

When you entered his room you would see on his desk three printed items: a book for studying the Polish language, a volume of Sh"S (6 Sidrei Mishnah) and the latest edition of the German newspaper "Die Welt am Montag" in which its editor, von Gerlach, fought, between the two World War s, a desperate and hopeless one man battle for freedom, justice and peace.

If you wanted to learn a language, Reb Kalman Aaron took it lightly, teaching languages was for him just a matter of earning his livelihood (and a poor one at that), but if it was the Sh"S you wanted to discuss, or "The World on Monday", he would not let you go until he told you about his interpretation of a certain "Sugiyah" (Misnnaic problem) or about the pleadings of von Gerlach every Monday in his newspaper, about one latest atrocity or another that occurred in a forsaken corner of the world. And if you arrived at an opportune time he would read to you poems of his two beloved authors Yehudah Leib Gordon and his friend the German poet Nikolaus Linau, or play for you on his old gramophone music by the cantors Kvortin and Sirota. Kalman Aaron

Midler concentrated his main interests on three things: studying the Talmud and Midrash according to the principles and wisdom of western Judaism, composing sermons in the style of east European Jewry and scrutinizing the wars for justice, wherever they occurred in the world. And lucky were the few who were rewarded by listening to him articulating his concepts of Torah and morality! Such a mix of knowledge and acumen! A brilliant command of all the sources, a clear and exact scientific method, a Jewish way of learning with the knowledge of Asian and European cultures, clarity of mind with warmth, cleverness and naivety, courage and modesty. One could find all of these gifts, only in one person in a generation and he was that person.

And with all of these many interests he was not at all a recluse, he loved to mix with people, was joyful and sharp-tongued, overflowing with wisdom and jokes. "King Arthur's Court" (as the grain and produce stock exchange was called, which was the daily meeting place of the Jews of Danzig) was only a few steps from his apartment. (If only King Arthur knew who were his knights of later days!). All the affairs of the Jewish community of Danzig, a free city and a crossroad between east and west Europe, were discussed there, and Kalman Aaron Midler being a man of morals and arguments in the style of Y.L. Gordon, could not tolerate wrong doings, and did not keep quiet about it.

Who was that strange man, and how did he arrive in Danzig? There was no one in the city that knew accurately his life story. My knowledge is fragmental too and is based on a small number of hints, which he gave me.

Kalman Aaron Midler was a man from Novogrudok, he was born in 1870 or thereabouts. In his childhood he was known as an "Eelui" (a brilliant student) and as a young man he was ordained as a Rabbi. And then the "Eelui" of Novogrudok went through the crisis of "Haskalah" (the Jewish enlightenment movement). "Bederech hayam, derech eretz Plishtim" (the journey by sea leads to the land of the Philistines) a road, which was familiar to the "Maskilim" (those belonging to the enlightenment movement) from Lithuania. His destination was the University City and the queen of wisdom of Judaism, Berlin. He went from Lithuania to Memel, from Memel to Koenigsberg, from Koenigsberg to Danzig and there he was stranded in the middle of his journey and stuck for the rest of his life. He found his livelihood wherever he could: as a preacher (Darshan) in the synagogue, as a porter at the sea port, a Bar Mitzvah teacher or a swimming instructor, a composer of epitaphs on tombstones or economics reporter for a Russian newspaper. Somehow he managed to accumulate books, learn languages and an understanding of different cultures (when he came to Germany he studied for a time in a German primary school, as a 20 years old amongst kids!). Somehow he managed to buy an apartment and open his Academy which had a single teacher, one who was equal to a collage of instructors.

But he did not find satisfaction in his work. The curse "Lemi ani amel" (for whom do I labour?), which troubled his idol Y.L.Gordon, tormented him too. No one wanted to hear about the integration of Judaism and "Haskalah". The world continued in its old ways, some assimilated and others became more pious, (Goyim on one side and crazy on the other - said Midler), or the world has found new ways, which Midler viewed with sympathy, but could not follow: Socialism and Zionism. Secular Jews saw him as one of the old generation and laughed at his naivety and the orthodox Jews saw him as an atheist, freethinker ("apikores") and made his life bitter. Here too he remained at the cross roads.

All his work, the Academy, teaching at school, the "Darshanut" (preaching) on Yom Kippur, contributed towards a very modest living. Conscious of the fact that he would not be able to support a family, he never married, lived thriftily and was sometimes hungry. From time to time he brought home some vegetables and mushrooms to eat with his bread. He died alone from a stomach ailment at the age of 60. His corpse was found in his apartment among the many books and articles that were never published.

Kalman Aaron Milder left this world before he could see the destruction of the European Jewry.

And what about his articles, notes, his life's work, a treasure to a researcher of Judaism?

My mother and my aunt kept all his writings and looked after them with great care. They took them when they escaped from the Germans. The writings of the "Eelui" from Novogrudok are where the bones of their guardians are buried, under the ruins of the Ghetto of Otwock.

[Page 84]

The Big Fire in Novogrudok

by Yaakov Gershovski

Translated from Yiddish by O. Delatycki

The two things that a man should fear most when he goes to sleep are, firstly, that he may be robbed while he is asleep and, secondly, that there may be a fire during the night. It would seem that the Jews of Novogrudok could sleep soundly. It was impossible for them to be robbed. The rich Jews, who had things worth stealing, lived in the centre of the town in the Market Square or in the nearby streets. Their houses were patrolled the whole night. The watchmen walked around the row of shops in the Market Square and in nearby streets and would thump their "kalakotkies" [a timber stick with a cut along its length, when the stick was thumped it would issue a penetrating sound]. The sound indicated that the watchmen were awake and doing their duty.

As to fire - the citizens felt that they were well protected from it and could sleep peacefully. Reb Itschok Elchonon, when he left Novogrudok, where he was a famed rabbi for some years, had blessed the town and expressed a wish that there should not be a fire in town. The blessing seemed to be effective. For more than 20 years, there were no fires in Novogrudok. The fire brigade, which was located in Beilin's house and consisted of 3 or 4 firemen, had nothing to do. Their only work was to guard a few prisoners who were held in the detention cell - a small room with iron bars in the same house as the fire brigade. The detention cell was not used for holding dangerous prisoners. The prisoners who were kept there committed minor thefts or were drunks who were held in the cell until they were sober. Having sobered up they would be released, but not before they drank a glass of vodka with their jailers, the firemen [this is called in russian "na pochmiel'e", an alleged cure for a hangover]. Next to the fire station, under an overhang, stood a few empty drums on two wheels. Next to them were a few hand pumps with long hoses for pumping and spraying water. A small metal plate was affixed to each house with instructions of who should come out in case of a fire and what equipment they should bring. The instructions have become illegible over the years. As it turned out, the blessing of Reb Elchonon must have ceased to be effective. However, the fire, when it erupted in the early 1880's, had started in a non-Jewish area outside the town. A farmer lit his oven to bake bread. The day was hot and the straw roof burst into flame. Presently the rest of the timber house caught fire followed by the houses of neighbours. After ten houses were set alight, the fire had become violent and burned both Jewish and Christian homes. In the middle of the night there was a great panic. The watchmen started knocking on the blinds, waking everyone. The bells in the churches started ringing, the streets were full of scantily clad people of all ages. Young people hurried to the pumps, others started to fill the drums and fetch water. Women dragged their belongings: bundles of linen, bedding, jewelry, silver cutlery, candelabras etc. Old people were running to the synagogues to save the sacred articles such as silver goblets, crowns and other decorations of the Holy Scriptures (Sefer Toras). When the fire spread into the narrow, densely built up Jewish streets it moved with a renewed ferocity. At that stage more than half the town was on fire. But at that moment, the Power above us must have remembered Reb Elchonon's blessing. The sky opened up and rain gushed down, and flooded many homes, extinguishing the fires and saving the rest of the town. This was the end of the fire but hundreds of families remained homeless and without means to survive.

I would like to mention the admirable deed of my mother OBM. The fire burned on Thursday night until Friday morning. Our house did not burn down. First thing in the morning, as soon as the rain stopped, my mother put up long tables outdoors, borrowed a few samovars, bought as much bread, rolls, potatoes etc as she could and fed the victims of the fire for the rest of the day. As Friday night was approaching, mother secured the help of friendly Christian neighbours, who served tea to all comers for the entire Sabbath. Naturally, the Christians drank their cups of tea first to indicate that they made the tea for themselves and not for the observant Jews.

[Page 85]

The Jewish Souls
(from the Old Pinkas Navaradok)

by Dr. Eliezer Yerushalmi

Translated from Yiddish by O. Delatycki

It happened in the year 1863. The Polish uprising in the Novogrudok district was at its height. The Polish insurgents were concealed in the forests. Cossack troupes were surrounding the forests. The Jews were between a hammer and an anvil and suffered from both parties.

In those days there lived in Novogrudok a wealthy man, a money-lender, Reb Avrom Skleser. He was a G-d fearing scholar. Two daughters of his brother lived with him. He kept them under his strict supervision and did not take his eye off them. In those troubled times Reb Avrom seldom let them out of the house. Who knew what could happen in times like that to young Jewish women.

On a certain day, on a Sabbath after the Cholent was eaten, when Reb Avrom went to visit the grave stone of Sheine Bashke, the girls went out for a walk. Having walked around the market place, they were tempted to go on to the green Shloss (Castle) Street. From there it was but a step to the Castle mound with an outlook onto Mickiewicz St. The girls took courage and directed their steps to the Mickiewicz mound, close to the countryside. As they wandered, time had passed and they became distressed. The girls were afraid to walk back. Quite suddenly it got dark and they were frightened. Not knowing what to do, the girls hid in a shelter – and they did not leave it.

In the mean time Reb Avrom got up to go to Mincha. When he returned home to Shalashudes he discovered that the girls were not home. Naturally, he was perturbed. As it was Sabbath, he could do nothing and he returned to the synagogue. After Miriv the girls were still not home. Reb Avrom quickly recited the Havdole and went out to look for them. After he had enquired from all the relatives and friends and could not find them the whole town became alarmed. Everyone started searching everywhere. The girls had disappeared without a trace. Another search was organized in all parts of the town. No wonder, the missing were Jewish girls and the nieces of Reb Avrom. But all searchers came back disappointed. It was assumed that a tragedy had taken place and the town was in a state of panic.

Next morning Reb Avrom went to see the Russian spravnik and the Polish marshal. Reb Avrom was known to all the officials of the town. But he could not find out anything. Next the Orthodox Priests were approached. They made inquiries in all their Churches and monasteries. They got no results.

The Jews gathered at Rabbi Yitzchak Helhonon. They sat with him days and nights. Reb Avrom brought all the money he possessed, 70,000 roubles, to the Rabbi and said: 'Rabbi, I will give all the money I have to save my nieces. What will I say to my brother when we meet in the better world and he will ask about his family'. He started to cry and with him cried the whole community.

Money was given for charity. Bribes were given to all the policemen and their superiors, to all church officials. A rumour was spread that the girls were hidden in a church or monastery. But how can one know if this was true, since there was no one to ask.

The old cemetery

It seemed as if there was an agreement among the Poles not to disclose anything to the Jews. It was assumed that the girls were not in town anymore, but were taken elsewhere. Where? How could one find out? Reb Avrom gave the marshal of Novogrudok, the representative of all the landowners of the district, some money. The marshal promised to do his best. He gave Reb Avrom a letter he had written to the Minsk marshal and said that the marshal in Minsk knew where the girls were and he would help.

Reb Avrom sent couriers to Minsk and told them to hurry and contact the marshal of the gubernia and give him the letter. The Minsk marshal sent a letter with the couriers to the marshal in Novogrudok, but Reb Avrom was told nothing.

Reb Avrom went to Minsk and was given another letter. He said to the marshal 'Give me a clear answer, where should I turn to and no more letters. The letter was thick, filled with paper, why was there so much to write?' But you could not ask that of an important person. Reb Avrom returned to Novogrudok and brought the letter to the Rabbi.

The Rabbi called an assembly and sought advice from the community on how to handle the letter. They sat the whole night and expressed different opinions. Some said that the letter must be passed on to the recipient as it was. Others maintained that the letter should be opened to establish what was in it.

After many arguments, they decided to open the letter. The letter from the Minsk marshal, who was the head of the uprising in the whole gubernia, contained a plan with instructions of how to conduct the Polish uprising. It was addressed to the marshal of Novogrudok, who was in charge of the Novogrudok uprising. There was not a word in it about the Jewish girls.

It was decided that the girls must by saved by using force. Reb Avrom rented speedy horses, usually used by the nobility and state couriers and took off to Petersburg to speak to a minister. It is a long story to tell how Reb Avrom got to a minister. A Jew was not allowed to enter the capital. But Reb Avrom went there regardless.

He waited for the time when the minister would return home and he went into his palace. The doorman stopped him, beat him up and took him away. Reb Avrom started to shout. The minister heard it and came out. That gave Reb Avrom an opportunity to say to the minister that he had something important to tell him. The minister received him and Reb Avrom passed on to him the letter of the Minsk marshal.

What happened to the marshals is not part of this story. It was told that the Minsk marshal escaped, but the Novogrudok marshal was apprehended. The minister ordered the Catholic Church to release the girls. They were found in the Sluck monastery, where they were being prepared for conversion.

All could have been well, but the girls did not want to return. They were ashamed to return to the Jewish community. The older one maintained that the uncle would punish them, nobody would talk to them and they would not find a husband. There was talk that one of the sisters ate non-kosher food.

It was impossible to force them to return. They were both old enough to decide for themselves. The Poles were also aroused and they swore that they would not release the girls. It had become a matter of pride to convince the girls to convert. Two landlords offered to marry them. One of them was the Graf of Wsielub, Arik and the other the landowner of Novoelnya, Jundzl. The girls were both good looking. The weddings were to coincide with their conversion.

But the Jewish community had not given up. Rabbi Yitzchak Helhonon sent out match makers to find for them suitable suitors. Both were splendid scholars and maskils (members of the *Haskala* (knowledge) movement). One of them came from Danzig.

The girls agreed to return. On the eve of Succoth they were brought back from Sluck. The whole town including the Rabbi came out to welcome them. The famous klesmer Oser with his band provided the music and they were taken to their wedding ceremony. Rabbi Yitzchak issued a cheirim, prohibiting mention of the incident.

But the scribe of the Jewish community had entered the story into the Pinkas.

[Page 89]

Between the Two World Wars

Hebrew Education in Novogrudok

by Moshe Steinberg-Sarig

Translated from Hebrew by Aviva Kamil

Hebrew education in Poland and in neighboring countries, in between the two World War, was the focal point of every organized Jewish community. It was also the centre of interest for all the institutions and establishments of the world (Jewish) nationalistic movement, which included different streams and political parties. The leaders and advocates of the future state, especially the deep thinkers who were immune to illusions of miracles and short cuts in history, put their trust in the Hebrew School. They saw in the national education[al] institutions the most efficient instrument for bringing to fruition the tremendous and responsible mission: education and formation of the face of the new generation and its ability to fulfill the special national tasks in our historic era.

Therefore, I will allow myself to broaden a little the backdrop, and in the prologue to my exposition I will provide a short general view, which will reflect the historic background and the objective conditions for the development of the nationalistic education and its influence on the life of our people in the Diaspora.

The Secret Existence of our People in the Diaspora

With sacred feeling and deep admiration we observe now, from the pinnacle of happiness, because of the national and political independence in our country, the sorry life of our brethren in the Diaspora, all its peculiarities and differences, its horrors and awful fears.

We are wondering and are amazed at that strange phenomenon, unique in the history of humanity, and we ask what was the marvel and secret of our people's survival in such strange and unnatural conditions that prevailed for two thousands years.

Only in our time, the time of the third temple, the time of bringing together all of the Diasporas, its absorption and blending, can we properly appreciate the enormous physical and mental powers that our brethren displayed in all of those generations in foreign lands, their strong will for survival, their immense belief in the victory of justice and the approaching redemption.

Yes, there is a God of this nation; there is pure spiritual culture, supreme moral values, purpose in life and a vision for the future.

The burning bush - "The bush burned with fire, and the bush was not consumed" - is not only a wonder and a legend but also a nice and telling symbol of our history.

Bnei-Israel survived the Diaspora thanks to their various institutions: public, religious, cultural, nationalistic, which they established wherever they went in their eternal wanderings. Those institutions were substitutes, in part, for self-rule, a hiding place and a castle of their cultural independence, a frame and a fence of their national uniqueness.

They were fertile spiritual nurseries for the creation of a special folklore, way of life, customs and habits common to the whole community. In those institutions was woven slowly the spiritual tradition of a people, a tradition that was passed on from generation to generation. Those institutions assumed, on and off, different forms. They were needed to provide, at times, a certain contribution, as the times changed, but they were and still are safe bastions for the spirit and the culture of the nation, true vessels to preserve the wine....

National Education and its Task

There is no doubt that among the establishments which the Jews built in the Diaspora the most important were the educational institutions in their different forms: "Cheders" and the "Chadarim Metukanim", Yeshivas and Batei-Midrash, Kindergartens and Hebrew schools. The young generation was educated in them, and was taught to live in the spirit of the time.

In its healthy sense the people felt, without a special explanation or propaganda, without law enforcement, that the education of the young was the secret of its survival among the "Goyim", that the educational institutions were the places where the nation's soul was created.

The educational institutions were never detached from the life of the people. The educational and didactic plan reflected the people's political, economic and cultural situation, and was in accord with the social aspirations of the nation. In order to fulfill its main purpose in life, to ensure the continuation of the existence of the people and its culture, the national education had to adapt to the special conditions in every country and establish accordingly its institutions.

In the period of our isolation, forced or otherwise, behind the walls of the physical or spiritual Ghetto, at that time the task of the education was mainly to keep "the coal burning", the burning coal which remained after the destruction of our political and national independence; the Cheders, Yeshivas and Beit-Midrash fulfilled, no doubt, a very important task in the life of the Jewish people. From that source our slain brethren drew courage and spiritual strength, to die sanctifying God, they drew solace, unlimited endurance, hope, security and belief in the coming redemption.

The command of educating was then: wait a minute for the storm to pass...

Our great national poet praised those "houses of learning" (batei hatorah) and their place in the life of the nation.

With great love he sings about the super heroes and the unpretentious "Matmidim" (Torah students), who gave their soul to the Torah and kept the smoldering burning coal (of the Jewish spirit) alive.

But a song was not sung yet about the new Hebrew school, which was established between the two W.W, and about its redeeming task in the days of world destruction, days of illusions about idols who failed and the betrayal of nations.

The splendid story of the new educators, who created a revolution in the education of the people and its life, is yet to be told. They brought out from its hidden place the smoldering "burning coal", fanned it with a gigantic force and turned it into a flame burning with the fire of longing for a complete and real redemption, for a new "pillar of fire" which lights for the redeemed their long road to their motherland, for a creative and urging power for action and deeds, for training and self realization.

The uniqueness of the New Hebrew education was its rebellious spirit against the stagnant reality of the Diaspora and its negative characteristics, war against apathy and "happy go lucky" attitude in its daily life, vision of a future, of a new and healthy life in the historic motherland of the people. The command of the new education was: not to live by the charity of other nations, and "im ein ani li mi li?" (Who is going to help me if not myself?).

Though those schools did not reward their students with matriculation or any other certificates and did not teach them how to earn a living, the children of Israel still learn with love and steadfastness Torah (knowledge) for the sake of Torah and self realization.

From those educational institutions came out the creators of the national and cultural renaissance, the Hebrew poets and authors, teachers and spiritual guides of the nation.

The pioneers, who laid the foundations for the redemption of the land and conquering the work in Eretz-Israel, came out of those institutions. They, also, gave their blood and soul in the War of

Independence and the establishment of the Hebrew state.

The Jewish centers survived in Europe for 1000 years. In that long period the Jews established, working like ants, their public and cultural institutions. They created a wealth of spiritually and culturally valuable material, which influenced and contributed to the general enlightenment of the European nations.

The fates and fortunes of the Jews in that big continent over the generations were many and varied. Sometimes it looked as if they sent strong and deep roots into the land that they drenched with sweat and blood for hundreds of years.

But the eternal curse of the long Diaspora did not skip even those established centers. The last bloody holocaust cruelly exterminated almost all the Jews of Europe, and erased to the ground all its wonderful achievements, material and spiritual, the fruit of work and creativity over twenty generations.

That is how the blossoming isle of European Jewry sunk into the depth of the ocean and not even a slight foam remained on the surface of its cruel waters.

The Hebrew Education in Novogrudok

I accepted willingly the task that the Pinkas editors allotted to me, to write about the Hebrew education in Novogrudok.

I had the great privilege to work in Novogrudok, fifteen years as the principal of the "Tarbut" school in the name of Ch.N.Bialik, and during the time of the Soviet rule, in the years 1939-41, as the principal of the new Jewish Gimnazjum [see comments in the chapter "The school during the Soviet regime in 1939-41"].

There were in Novogrudok several "streams" of institutions of [Jewish] education: Chadarim, Yeshivot, a religious Hebrew school, which was established by the "Mizrachi" movement and the "Tarbut" school.

Though Novogrudok was close to Vilna, the center of activity of Tsadik Yod Shin 'Alef, there was no Yiddish school in Novogrudok. The reason was that the Jewish community of Novogrudok was mainly Zionist and permeated with a nationalistic-Hebrew spirit. There were in Novogrudok a few Yiddish activists; most of them were not natives of the town, like the lawyer Gumener, Dr. Marmurstein, the teacher Salomon and more, but over time they "assimilated" into the Nationalistic-Zionist movement of the town and educated their children in a Hebrew school.

I intend to concentrate in my article, specifically, on the story of the Ch. N. Bialik "Tarbut" Hebrew school for two reasons: firstly, it was the big and central educational institution of the town, it put its mark and influenced the whole education system of the Jewish youth in Novogrudok, secondly, I do not want to encroach on the area of other educators who should be the ones who would write about the schools that they worked in.

The Hebrew school in Novogrudok was established, as it is shown in a few documents, in 1919, at the end of World War I.

That transitory period, when rulers and regimes changed in the western provinces of the former Russian Empire, was a suitable and easy time to advance and develop the independent Jewish education system.

The Germans left the Russian occupied land and returned to their country.

The Polish regime, which did not distinguish itself, not at the beginning or in the end, for a special liking of their Jewish citizens, started to rule the liberated areas.

The Jewish intelligentsia, active in communal and cultural life, was educated in Russian schools before the war, and it was natural for them to be attuned to the Russian language and its rich literature. Apart from that, in those days the Jews had serious doubts as to the longevity of the new Polish government.

In order to avoid unwanted suspicions from the political antagonists and not to place ourselves between the rival cultures, the Jews decided to establish for their children independent Jewish schools where the teaching language was Hebrew or Yiddish.

At the beginning, the education in those schools was general-nationalistic and politically neutral. At that time various political parties and ideologies started to evolve among the Jewish population. For a short period the school was like an educational syncretism, coexistence in peace of the two languages, Yiddish and Hebrew, in an agreed upon curriculum. But that peace did not last long. It was hard to promote neutral education in an ideologically stormy era around the globe and especially in the Jewish world: the social revolution in Russia with all its promises and illusions, made waves around the world and, of course, did not skip the Jewish streets. On the other hand, it was the spring and glory of our national movement and the beginning of the building of our national home following the Balfour Declaration. Jewish education could not stay apathetic to the immense social and political changes, which excited the Jews everywhere.

Every school had to find its identity and take a clear stand regarding the burning questions of the era. The teachers and the administrators of the school as well as the pupils' parents did not hesitate for a moment, when the time of "self-identification" arrived, they decided in one voice to join the school organization "Tarbut".

The Hebrew school "Tarbut" in the name of Ch. N. Bialik was a day school comprising seven grades, and its pupils were released of the duty of education in a government school. The language of teaching from the first grade was Hebrew, but history and geography of Poland were taught in Polish. Recognizing the value of the Yiddish language for the people and the importance of its literature, I introduced the teaching of that language from grade 5. Near the school was also a Hebrew kindergarten for children 4-6 years [old] of age.

The Kindergarten by the "Tarbuth" school

The School Curriculum

The curriculum in the school was similar to the one in the Hebrew schools in Eretz-Israel. The education of the pupils and the maturing students, which was conducted by the school, was Zionistic - Chalutz (pioneer), permeated with Jewish spiritual awareness, and based on work ethics, self governing within the children's community, training towards alia to Eretz-Israel and self - awareness in the new surrounding.

Classes were conducted from 8 a.m. to 2 p.m. At 5 p.m. some pupils and few of the teachers returned to the school for educational activities in a number of "circles" (study groups) and for changing books at the school library.

Subjects Taught at the School

1.	Hebrew language and literature.
2.	Bible.
3.	Mishna and legends.
4.	Jewish and general history.
5.	Nature studies.
6.	Geography.
7.	Arithmetic and Geometry.
8.	Yiddish.
9.	Polish.
10.	Polish history.
11.	Polish geography.
12.	French.
13.	Gymnastics.
14.	Music.
15.	Drawing.
16.	Agriculture.
17.	Craft.

The education in all "Tarbut" schools, including our school in Novogrudok, was distinguished not by the curriculum or hours of study, though they were important too, but by its invaluable good educational atmosphere that prevailed in every school.

An atmosphere of nationalistic ideals and spiritual values, and the spirit of vision and purpose filled the hearts of the teachers and their students. The teachers were devoted, heart and soul, to their sacred work. But their cheerful influence did not stop at school; it penetrated the parents' homes and various public establishments. The teacher was an educator to the students, a guide to the youth and a leader to the adults. The school doors were open all day long, and, of course, in the evenings, because after the mid-day break there were different sorts of additional studies under the guidance of the teachers.

There were many and varied kinds of study circles.

Pupils of the "Tarbuth" school

The School Choir and its Performances at "*Oneg-Shabat*"

The school had a large students' choir and an orchestra. The conductor of the choir was the music teacher Mr. Eliezer Rabinovich of blessed memory. Thanks to his abundant energy and special talents in his profession, the choir became an important cultural asset in town. The choir performed at all the assemblies and festivals that were conducted at school, and also took part in other cultural activities, which were instigated by the public institutions in town.

The custom of celebrating "Oneg-Shabat" and "Yom-Tov" at school started thanks to the initiative of Mr. Rabinovitch. It was very popular amongst all levels of society in town. History, literature, education and current affairs were the subjects of lectures at those assemblies. The choir appeared after the lectures with folkloric and national songs in Hebrew and Yiddish. The melodies and songs that were heard on "Oneg-Shabbat" at "Tarbut" have become known in town and were often sung on other occasions.

All sang and hummed the songs of "Oneg-Shabbat", the students during the school breaks, the workers at work and the housewives by the stove in their kitchens. And many mothers put their babies to sleep humming the tunes.

Tarbut School

Work in the School['s] Garden

All school students from grades one to seven worked in the garden, under the guidance of the teacher of nature studies, Chana Levin-Feigin of blessed memory.

The purpose of children's work in the garden was:

1. To bring the children close to nature.

2. To develop their sense of aesthetics by growing flowers, and the love of working on the land.

3. To make the studies of nature tangible.

The children liked to work in the garden, they considered it a training for their future work in the fields of their country, Eretz-Israel.

The students' committee kept an accurate account of expenditure and income of the garden and at the end of the year they published a detailed balance sheet in the school newspaper "Beit-Sifrenu" (our school). All the above details were copied from that newspaper.

The Jewish school

Children with the kindergarten teacher Sima Portnoi

The School's Workshops

One of the principle efforts of our education, like in all "Tarbut" schools, was to instill in the students the high value of work. A carpentry workshop for boys was opened for that purpose on the 30.5.37 under the guidance of a qualified teacher, as was a dressmaking workshop for girls.

The school's carpentry workshop was situated temporarily in the hall of the building of "Shokdei-Melacha" (craftsmen). Work at the workshop, 4 hours a week, was a duty for all the boys starting at grade 5. The teachers worked there with the students, too.

Work for the "Blue Box"

Work for the "Blue Box" took an important place in our school, and was an integral part of the school curriculum.

Studies about Eretz-Israel, its geography and collecting for the "Blue Box" were much loved by the pupils, because it brought them in touch with current affairs in Eretz-Israel, which were close to their heart.

In every classroom there was a corner for the "Blue Box" and in the center of it was the map of Eretz-Israel. The "Blue Box" appeared in all the classes' gatherings and the big assemblies at school. I would not exaggerate if I say that our students knew the tracks of the Valley (of Israel) and Galilee of Eretz-Israel better than they knew the roads in Polesie and Galicia in Poland.

In the school library there was a collection of the "Blue Box" literature. The teachers and students liked especially the magazines "La'noar" (For the Youth). The Hebrew school in Poland was, in a certain way, an Israeli island in the Diaspora, in its way a cultural appendix of the Jewish State.

I remember one visit of the Polish Supervisor to our school. He had a long, leisurely walk around the classrooms and hall, looked at the decorations, the "Blue Box" corners, saw the nice pictures of the Hebrew poets and authors, showed interest in the contents of the written articles and banners on the walls. Before leaving he expressed his admiration for all he saw at school, but he commented that he felt as if he was in a beautiful and neat school in Palestine.

And one could not sneer at the money that the school raised for the "Blue Box".

The student's committee report of the school's donations for the "Blue Box", which was printed in the school newspaper "Beit-Sifrenu" in (Taf Reish Tzadik 'Zain) 1937.

Stamps in the children's booklets	124.32 zloty
The "Blue Box"	119.50 zloty
Afforestation and plantations	20.89 zloty
The Children's Book	13.00 zloty
The project "Hagalilah"	72.95 zloty
Miscellaneous	127.49 zloty
Total	**478.15 zloty**

In the year 1935-6 the teachers and students entered the school's name into the "Gold Book" of the "Blue Box" (Keren Kayemet Le'Israel).

The School Libraries and Student's Reading.

Special attention was given to developing the school library, to organize efficiently the student's reading and the constant checking of reading proficiency. For that purpose there were monthly [student assemblies in the classes, when the students gave accounts of their reading during the month. At that time, the teacher was checking the reading records, where the children noted their impressions of the books they read. In Pinkas Novogrudok we are publishing an article about "Reading Books and the Library in Our School" by the schoolteacher Binyamin Leikin of blessed memory, who was murdered by the Nazis, Hei, Yod, Daleth (God avenge his blood).

We copied the article from our school newspaper "Beit-Sifrenu" of 1937.

Number of loans of library books in 1938-9, on the eve of the destruction:

			Grades					
Language	**Teachers**	**Former students**	2	3	4	5	6-7	**Total**
Hebrew	229	145	214	183	176	131	323	1401
Polish	175			154	147	101	198	775
Total	404	145	214	337	323	232	521	2176

The School-Paper and Wall-Journals at School (*Iton-Kir*)

An important tool in the hands of the educators were the "Wall-Journals": the class "Wall-Journal" and the school "Wall-Journal". In addition, by the end of the year "Beit Sifrenu", the school newspaper, was published.

That writing for the newspaper helped the teachers and educators of the school to promote and develop the skills of independent work and self-expression among the students. The editors of the school newspaper were the student representatives of the higher classes under the guidance of the teacher B. Leikin of blessed memory. In that newspaper the school administration and teachers published a detailed account of the situation in the classes and the school and, also, the school plans for the coming year. The students and their parents participated as well in the production of the newspaper.

The teacher Elchanan Levin of blessed memory published in the paper of 1937 an important and detailed article about the production of the newspaper at school. We are publishing it in this book (Pinkas Novogrudok) with some abridgment. The teacher Elchanan Levin, of blessed memory, was murdered by the Nazis.

The Students' Club (*Moadon*)

Connected to the school was the students club under the direction of the student's committee and the guidance of the teacher Sonya Wolf-Nimenchik of blessed memory, who was murdered by the Nazis.

The aim of the club was:

    1. To develop the social sense of the students.

    2. To create brotherhood and friendship among the students.

    3. To create a special atmosphere and easy conditions to hasten the process of "Ibur" (to become Hebrew) in the life of the students.

The Club contained three rooms: Reading room, Playroom and Dancing room. In the Reading room were all the Hebrew journals and newspapers for the students, which appeared in the Diaspora and Eretz-Israel. There were also monthlies and newspapers in Polish. Books from the library were leant to all who asked for them. In the second room was a number of student games among them "A'avorah na ba'aretz" (passing through the land; Eretz-Israel). At the end of the reading and playing rooms was the dancing hall. The following is a paragraph which gives the impression of one of the teachers about that room: "Arms on shoulders, light feet, sparkle in the eyes, flying movement. Innocent and free laughter fills the air, the kids are delighted. Music, song and dance and happiness no end...."

Outline of the School Work

In order to introduce order and discipline into the work and the study at school, the pedagogic community created a frame of work: the Pedagogic Committee.

Once a fortnight the Pedagogic Committee met to discuss school matters.

During the year there were special meetings, if needed, to discuss extra matters if they had arisen. The presidents of the parents' committees took part in all the meetings, they were: Asher Parsman, Chaim Maslovaty and Itzchak Orlinski of blessed memory.

The educational work was shared between all the members of the committee, such that every part of the students' activity had a teacher to guide it. There was a students' self-rule at school.

The following are the names of the principals, the teachers and the kindergarten teachers who worked in the school at various times from the day of its foundation to the day of its closing.

1919-1939

The members of blessed memory who fell, sanctifying God and nation and whom the cursed Nazis murdered.

Shmuel Lidski	Binyamin Leikin
Eliezer Rabinovich	Sonya Wolf-Nimenchik
Shlomo Wolfovich	Shmuel Salomon
Shlomo Krant	S. Prisitzki
Mrs. Gumener	M. Lis
Elchanan Levin	A. Bitanski
Chana Levin	S. Cohen

And long life for:

David Cohen	Tamar Sensentus-Efron
David Bogatin	Luba Mordechovich
Koren	I. Piltski
Moshe Steinberg-Sarig	Menucha Yelin
S. Gutswort	Sima Portnoy
S. Rabinovich from Vilna	Langleben
I. Shalita	Chava Lipski
Ch. Koshlen	S. Manusevich
S. Milchiker	

The Sponsors and Promoters of Hebrew Education in Novogrudok

In those days before the establishment of the Jewish state, when there was no department of education and the local authorities in the Diaspora worked against the interests and aspirations of the Jewish communities, Jewish educators and parents carried the heavy burden of education; they supported and promoted the organization of national education. These unknown heroes deserve the highest of honors!

With their devoted and faithful work they established the splendid institution of national education, despite the resistance and hostility of the government and despite [the] material hardship, which was the situation of most of the parents.

The educational institutions, the training of teachers, the supply of books and other learning tools, were built and maintained with their creative initiative and generous help. They covered the constant deficits of the school by establishing new and diverse sources of income; the students' fees never covered more then half of the school expenditure. They organized balls, parties and flower-days, established a branch of "Tarbut" and collected money from the members, for education; from time to time they passed "a special action" among the friends of the school. As far as I can remember not even one year passed without that "special action" for the benefit of the school.

The following are the names of all the faithful sponsors who during many years dedicated their time and energy for the betterment of Hebrew education and the "Tarbut" school" during its twenty years of existence, (1919-1939):

The members of blessed memory who sanctify God and nation and who were murdered by the cursed Nazis:

Asher Parsman	The chairman of the branch "Tarbut".
Chaim Maslovaty	The chairman of the parents' committee.
Yehuda Kaplinski	"
Itzchak Orlinski	"
Nachum Gordon	"
Yaacov Lubchanski	"
Malbin, community Rabbi	"

Shlomo Efron
Eliyahu Shlosberg
Binyamin Efron
Chana Nachumovski

Yitzchak Ibinitzki
Moshe Dunitz

Israel Goldshmit — Shalom Efroimski
Shalom Bencianovski — Yosef Chiz
Yerucham Israelit — Fridman
Tzipora Shlosberg — Duba Lutski
Mrs. Parsman — D. Harakavi
Bezalel Makoliveski — Kaplanski
Alter Kaminetzki — A. Litovski
N. Sukarski — Y. Rabinovich
Golda Rabinovich of blessed memory.

Long life to:

Avraham Ostashinski
Kaplanski
S. Openheim
Nachumovski.

12 years of the "Tarbut" school in Novogrudok

Calendar year	School year	Graduates		
		Boys	Girls	Total
1927	1	4	16	20
1928	2	5	12	17
1929	3	6	5	11
1930	4	9	10	19
1931	5	3	9	12
1932	6	8	2	10
1933	*			
1934	7	5	8	13
1935	8	3	11	14
1936	9	13	10	23
1937	10	11	15	26
1938	11	14	17	31
1939	12	18	25	43
Total		99	140	239

* School closed for construction of the new building.

The social composition of the students' parents in 1938-9.

Commerce	41.3%
Tradesmen	40.2%
Labourers	5.5%
Clerks	3.3%
Farmers	3.0%
Working Intelligentsia	1.5%
Industry	0.9%
Orphans	4.3%

The New School Building

For many years the school suffered from very poor accommodation, in rented houses and in an unwanted and undesirable neighborhood next to the Byelorussian Gymnasium. This situation had an adverse effect on the learning and educational work and hindered the potential development of the school. The idea and the need to expand this establishment and establish a central high school could not be accomplished because of the lack of a suitable building.

Building of a new school was an important issue for the Jewish people of Novogrudok. It is interesting to note that even people, whose children were past the school age, and those who had no interest in the Hebrew education in "Tarbut", all supported the idea of erecting the building. It was discussed for many years at many meetings of the Parent's committee and the Branch Committee. At long last a happy solution was found.

At one of the meetings of the two committees a small Building Committee was elected, its head was the known Zionist personality Avraham Ostashinski, who was then the Deputy Mayor, and they started acting immediately. Mr. Alter Kaminetzki was invited to be the manager and supervisor of the building.

The first step was to find a suitable piece of land. There were many arguments and opinions about it. Some wanted to buy land anywhere as long as it would not cost a lot of money, there were many offers of this kind of land.

Eventually the school principal's suggestion was accepted and a nice piece of land was bought from the family Zipert. It was in Slonim St., at the heart of the beautiful district where the Polish high society [the Polish public servants] lived, opposite the Voyavodstvo. I still remember my impressions of the last meeting before buying that parcel of land.

We did not have a cent in our cash-box, and we had to pay quite a big sum in cash, people started to "donate" jokes instead of money, one more clever then the other, they did not manage to raise even the small sum needed to take out a security bills (mortgage) which were needed to obtain a loan from the bank. Eventually the security bills were bought and signed by the committee members, we received a loan from two Jewish banks: the Commerce Bank and the Tradesmen Bank and paid the family Zipert for the land.

In the purchase contract was a special note to say that the school committee has the first option to buy the second half of the land within three years and in the meantime the land would be leased to the school.

The happy news about buying of the land and the commencement of the building spread quickly and caused great enthusiasm among the public and especially the parents and students.

The committee started immediately to collect a school fund. The first results surprised even the most pessimistic. The town residents donated readily, some more and some less, but there were almost no cases of refusal. The committee members worked wonders with the fund raising. Of special note was the chairman of the committee Mr. Avraham Ostashinski.

The building work progressed according to plan, without delay and holdups. The work supervisor, Mr. Alter Kaminetzki made certain of that. He managed to get in time all the materials needed, even though there was not one cent in the committee's cash-box.

The building "operation" justified the saying that not the budget but the man influences the result.

After a year the building was completed, and on Sunday Caf' Daleth of Sivan, Taf Resh Tsadik 'Gimel (1933) the new school "Tarbut" in Novogrudok was dedicated. This event was celebrated by the whole Jewish community. The celebrations lasted three days.

There was a public assembly in the morning at the town's theatre, and it was packed with students, parents and invited guests from a number of organizations

The chairman of the building committee, Mr. Avraham Ostashinski, due to whose tireless effort the school was built, opened the assembly.

Mr. Tremble, who came especially from Vilna to take part in the celebration, passed on the good wishes to the assembly in the name of the "Tarbut" organization.

After the many short congratulatory speeches by the representatives of various organizations the school choir sang under the direction of Mr. Eliezer Rabinovich. In the evening there was a big party in the school halls.

A new era began in the life of the new school, energetic and rich in potential, in the fateful year of 1934, on the threshold of the catastrophic and cruel holocaust, which brought annihilation and destruction to our brethren in Europe and also to our town.

The School During the Soviets Regime in 1939-41

With the coming of the Soviets to Novogrudok the teaching language at the school was changed [by the authorities] to Yiddish.

By the instructions of the Soviet administration for education, all the Jewish schools in town were united into one ten year school [desetiletka] and it was located in the building of the past Polish gymnasium in the name of A. Mickewicz. [It is probable that the Yiddish school was located in the new building completed by the Poles in the summer of 1939 at the end of Zamkowa St (Shloss Gass). It was probably meant to be the new Polish primary school. Under the Soviets the Jewish desetiletka shared the building with the new Russian desetiletka. There were two shifts in the building - morning and afternoon. Each school conducted classes in one of the shifts.] All teachers who worked in the different [Jewish] schools were transferred to the combined school; there were 30 teachers and over a thousand students [quite impressive for a town with a Jewish population of 6000]. Apart from the teachers from Novogrudok, Jewish teachers from Russia were brought in too, among them the Jewish poet Lis from Minsk.

Children and teachers

I wanted to resign from the management of this big school. I argued with the Administration of Education that a different person is needed to supervise the teachers and to educate [the] Jewish youth under the new circumstances.

My request was rejected and I was told that the workers of the town considered me to be the right and deserving person for the job [who ever asked "the workers" anything?]. I managed the school until the Nazis attacked Soviet Russia, which was the beginning of the holocaust and the total destruction of European Jewry.

Like a thunderbolt from a clear summer sky came the news of the betrayal by the evil and criminal Nazi government of its former ally,

Soviet Russia. Its loathsome soldiers with their armory crossed the temporary border between the two states and made their way east.

Dread and panic took hold of all the Jews, who during the division of Poland in 1939 had the good luck to find themselves under the Soviets rule. But, before they had the chance to recover from the horrific news of the coming catastrophe, German planes appeared in the sky above Novogrudok bombarding the town and surrounds...fire, destruction, horrors and death.

Bitter and awful fate was the fate of Novogrudok, which drank to the last drop from the poisonous cup like all her sister towns of Poland and Europe.

Where are you, our Jewish Novogrudok, the beautiful and attractive town, a great "mother" town in the Byelorussian Diaspora, a town full of Jews; working people, innocent and honest, God fearing, hungry learn the Torah and knowledge and aspiring for redemption!

Where are you the Kindergarten children, dear and loved children of Israel, and you working and studying youths, the pride of our people!

Still kept in my memory are the sad and pleasant tunes of your yeshiva students, I can still hear the echoes of the joyous songs of the kindergarten and school children; I still hear the stormy discussions of your many associations, parties and organizations. How the cruel reaper, the destructive Satan put them to dust and ashes.

Earth, do not cover their blood, the blood of the sanctified and the pure!

The bitter and terrible cry of parents, sons, daughters, brothers, and sisters all bereft, will forever rise to heaven-WHY?!

Tel-Aviv, Av Taf Shin 'Caf (1960)

[Page 97]

Kindergarten

by Sima Yonas- Portnoy

Translated from Hebrew by Aviva Kamil

The Kindergarten was established many years before I started to work there. A few teachers worked there before me. Ms. Brikner, who established the kindergarten, was the first teacher in the kindergarten. In 1933, when I started my work at the kindergarten, which was at

Pilsudski (Valiker) Street, in the house of Shlosberg, about 25 children attended.

There were three rooms: two small ones and a big one. They were furnished with white furniture made for the use of small children who played most of the day, sang and did some craft.

The Kindergarten was part of the "Tarbut" school, but its financial situation was more precarious, and always caused anxiety as to whether it would continue to exist. Mr. Steinberg, who was the school principal (of Tarbut), tried to improve the situation.

I remember the children on festivals; their happy laughter resonated through the rooms, no one thought about the imminent horrifying disaster.

I saw them on the Saturday morning, in the winter of 1941 at the yard of the district court, where the Germans brought them together with their parents. They stood all day long shivering in the cold and were hungry. Afterwards I saw a few of them jammed in an open truck, which took them on their last journey.

Kindergarten

Sima Portnoy with her kindergarden children, 1935

[Page 98]

Music in Novogrudok

by Menashe Rabina (Rabinovich)

Translated from Hebrew by Aviva Kamil

Novogrudok had a number of musical bodies which included: Kleizemers, a cantor with a choir, solo cantors, amateur cantors, professional "Ba'alei-Kriah", Chasidim with their specific tunes, the band of wind instruments of the fire brigade, school choirs, and Yeshiva students with their incessant Gmarah tunes. It would seem that the town was permeated with music.

And if we add ringing of bells and the sounds of organs that were emerging from the churches every Sunday and every Christian festival, then we can understand that every resident of Novogrudok was absorbing, willy - nilly, many sounds. We, the people of Novogrudok, were not aware of some of the music. To us it was just a normal part of our existence. But it created an atmosphere of emotions as nothing else could. But today, when our town exists only in our memory as part of a distant, yet dear to us, past, it is clear to all who understand the influence of music, just how rich our town was in musical experiences.

Singing lesson in the orphanage

Every book about the history of music of any country talks extensively about the period when music was performed by amateur performers, who were often called "local blowers", who were enriching festivals with the sounds of their instruments. A harp player was instructing members of a church choir in carol singing. We, the Jews in the small towns, did not have brass bands, because of a persistent lack of money. We also did not have a special liking for wind instruments, because their sound was loud and spread widely. This did not suit the quite and inward looking life of the Jewish communities in small towns. But as far as a song, a melody, a sincere tune, a sing along or listening to the voice of a messenger - the Jewish town excelled in all of those. And the musical life of Novogrudok was proof of this.

The Kleizemers of Novogrudok were not respected; their trade was not revered among the Jews because the musicians kept too close to the bottle, and more often then not, had the habit of emptying it. They cannot be blamed, that was their trade. But the treatment of the Kleizemers on a wedding day was different. The Kleizemers, with the help of the celebrant's family, were well presented and I could add that they even created an artistic mood. A wedding without Kleizemers would have turned into a quick meal. Our band of Kleizemers consisted mostly of: two violinists, a clarinettist and a drummer. The guests, and in particular the children, were greatly impressed. This was musical education by means of popular music. I remember two violinists of a Kleizemer band. One was short with a gentle face full of bitterness. It could be that he dreamt of a musical career in a concert hall or at least in a known band, and there he was, an unappreciated Kleizemer in a small town. He was a violin teacher and because of him I stopped playing the violin and started to learn the piano. There is a story in that, which needs retelling:

As I mentioned above, the musician, whose name was Archik the Kleizemer, was a bitter man and he poured his wrath on us, his pupils. Once, out of anger at one of his pupils, whose playing was abysmal, he lifted the bow and instead of applying it to the strings he smashed it violently on my fingers, because I was standing close to him. In a fit of chagrin I dropped my violin (purposely?) on the floor. That was the end of the violin.

But I did not get out of music lessons by doing so; I changed the instrument but not the profession.

The second Kleizemer looked, at the time, young to me. His name was Shimon the Kleizemer. He had an accentuated limp, yet was joyful and with a little drink in him he delighted everyone. If I want to visualise a Kleizemer, his figure comes to mind.

The Kleizemers of Novogrudok fulfilled their musical mission not only at weddings but also, as I remember it, by accompanying the Sefer Torah to the synagogue. Though I cannot remember the melodies, it was clear that the playing influenced all those who took part in the celebration including those in my age group.

Cantor and teacher Eliezer Rabinovitch

I remember one musical event that created a "revolution" in our town. It was a public party. If I remember rightly it was a Chanukah celebration. The public was invited to the "Kalte shul" [Cold (unheated) Synagogue], a choir conducted by my father ZL and a few instrument players took part in the event. Long discussions (sometimes furious ones) followed that revolutionary step - singing and playing in the synagogue!

At this point I would like to digress and say a few words of the activities in the field of musical education in Novogrudok of my father ZL, Leizer (Eliezer) Rabinovich. My father always performed with his choir. He belonged to those cantors whose strength was in the depth of their prayer and their comprehension of the words, but not in the quality of their voices, and above all he recognised the importance of a choir performing in the synagogue. The choir of the cantor Leizer Rabinovich was an established body. They sang in four different voices. Many of them could read music, as they had been taught by the cantor.. Father had a music library of partitas. Most of them he copied in his nice handwriting and bound them into very thick books. He composed a few works and later wrote songs for the school. He was a disciplinarian with his budding choristers and was proud that parents from the Ukraine (his birth place) sent their sons to receive a music education from him. They knew that they would get a good education and guidance as well. Father knew Hebrew and subscribed to "Yarchon Hachazanim" (Cantors' Monthly, I have two volumes from his library) and other Hebrew newspapers. On Sabbath evenings he used to read to us from the Hebrew newspaper for children (if I am not mistaken it was "The World of Children").

Towards the "Yamim Noraim" he worked hard to prepare the choir and he considered his work to be a very important mission. It could be said that his mission was as much to serve the community and art, as for the sake of religion. During prayer he used a Kammerton and not a small tube that the Rabbis resented.

The cantor used to appear with his choir at public celebrations, Chanukah parties and, because he was an active Zionist, at Zionist social events.

Some of his pupils became known cantors. They were mentioned in the book "Kultur traeger von der judischen liturgie" by Eliyahu Zalodkovski.

There were more cantors in Novogrudok, but with no choirs. One, by the name of Moshe Bruk, was a professional singer and, like my father, was also a "geler" (red head). There were also amateur cantors; the foremost among them was the lawyer Shwartz. His daughters inherited his inclination to music and drama. Their home was a meeting place for "apikores" (should it be plural "apikorsim"?) who were craving for the theatre, the folk songs and even Russian literature. Yes, the music of Novogrudok was multifaceted.

I don't want to imply that the musical endeavours in Novogrudok were different from those of any other Jewish town. I did not visit those towns and I don't know about them. But it is clear to me today that for a town of 8000 residents in Russia of those days, a town that was very far from any big city (one had to ride a horse-drawn cart from Novogrudok to Novoyelna to catch the train) the popularity of music was great, and it is important to note that everyone was exposed to it.

The number of Chasidim in Novogrudok was substantial and their influence on Jewish life was extensive. Many used to go out to welcome a Rabbi, when one came to town. The tradition was to put up the Rabbi in a private home. The Sabbath party in that home was full of music, which was heard far and wide and involved every Chasid and Mitnaged (opponent to Chasidut).

While talking about the influence of music without the real need to take part in the actual event, I want to mention another instance, which was outstanding in the life of our town. That occurrence was characteristic of Novogrudok, the town where Reb Yozl established his Yeshiva. Every event in that Yeshiva was accompanied by music. I recall the loud tunes that came often from "Waremer Beit-Hamidrash"

(Warm Synagogue) at the twilight hours, with the reading, shouting of chapters of "Musar" by the "Musarnikim". In the houses and the streets erupted those strange, crying, screaming tunes, which frightened children and bewitched them with their strangeness and depth.

Yes, Reb Yozl was a great pedagogue. He knew how to appeal to the hearts of his students. He invented new and very original ways to create the right atmosphere in order to penetrate to the soul of his students and to leave in them memories of deep moments that they would never forget. It was during the ten days of repentance, when every one in fear of the coming days. Reb Yozl rented a house that stood alone in a garden (to me it looked a huge garden). On the left was the "Beit-Olam" gasl (the cemetery lane). To me it looked a very steep lane. Reb Yozl asked his pupils to come to that lonely house, far from town, near the cemetery. A prayer service was conducted there. I will never forget the moment of suspense, when the pupils finished their prayer and there was silence. They waited for Reb Yozl to start a new prayer and for them to join in. He stood at his stand, silent. Outside the trees rustled, autumn, wind, the darkness of twilight and Reb Yozl was still silent. The pupils were frightened, their hearts full of dread. Suddenly he issued a terrible scream and began to pray. All the pupils followed their Rabbi with screaming and reading the prayer loudly. It was a very impressive crescendo, which one remembers many, many years later.

And now from the sacred to the mundane. The fire brigade band of Novogrudok. I would not assume that they could play better then other bands of the same kind, but they did blow their instruments with vigour.

And on another theme - there were many church bells in Novogrudok, they rang with confidence and strength. Passing by the church on a Sunday morning your ear absorbed the sounds of singing and music. And even if you whispered secretly to yourself "timah" (uncleanliness) or expressed resentment towards the splendid building and the happenings within its walls -you did hear and appreciate that they sang nicely, and the music was also nice.

I was in close contact with one of the musicians from the church. When I stopped my violin lessons I was sent to a piano teacher, one who was playing in the church in "Pochtgasel" (post lane). He was a habitual drunk and always smelt of liqueur. His hands were big, soft and careless. The drunkenness left deep lines on his, once handsome, features. He knew nothing about pedagogy and his attitude towards the student was naive, primitive and often rude. But he loved music and that love attracted a small number of pupils.

When the Germans occupied the town in World War I, a tremendous change occurred in the musical life in Novogrudok. Good wind instrument bands appeared in town and they often played in the market square. Once even a symphony orchestra came to town with strings, wind and percussion instruments playing in harmony. It was a great event. That orchestra played in the officers' Casino, which was on the second floor of the hotel "Loshok" in Valiker street, opposite the house of the family Shocher. We met at the Shochers to listen to all kinds of military bands. It was there that I first heard a Philharmonic Orchestra.

With the conquering army came soldiers who could play the piano well. One of them gave me lessons for a while. He taught me the Piano Sonata of Hayden. I know that the soldier-pianist had more pupils in the town. There were other soldiers who were good pianists.

We had gifted children in our town. I remember the sounds of the quartet that emanated from the home of Solomon Lubchanski (in Israel: Shlomo Chavivi). The son, the youngest of the family, played the cello; the daughters played the violin and the piano; and their father, who was their teacher and guide, played the second violin.

There was music in Novogrudok. And when one takes into account the period that I am talking about, when the gramophone was in its infancy and a rare commodity; the radio did not exist; travel was burdensome and expensive, the number of conservatoria in Russia was limited and they were concentrated in the large cities, taking all of these points into account we will appreciate the significance of the musical awareness of the residents of the town. They sang and sang a lot: In the synagogue; on Saturdays around the dinner table; at parties, as Sabbath was fat an end and at community celebrations. They sang Jewish songs, Russian romances and Chasidic melodies. They played the piano, the violin and the wind instruments. Considering the period that I am talking about (I left town in 1918) and the number of residents, it would not be an exaggeration to say that the musical standard was significant and of great importance in our lives.

[Page 100]

Politico-Communal life in Novogrudok

by Shmuel Openheim

Translated from Yiddish by O. Delatycki

Shortly after the First World War the Jewish population of Novogrudok began to develop a broad, multifaceted political and communal life. Old institutions were renewed and reorganised, among them the Jewish hospital, the old people's home as well as other bodies. New organisations, institutions, associations and political parties were created. New talents were discovered; people became devoted to the communal work heart and sole.

Orphanage

As a result of the war there were many orphans in town. An orphanage was created. This meant that the children were not left in the streets. The orphanage accepted all orphans, as well as children of impoverished parents. The children had to be of school age. The orphans were provided in the orphanage with all needs for their development and it was made possible for them to become worthwhile human beings. The atmosphere created in the orphanage was such that the children felt that they had become part of an ordinary household. They attended a school [Tarbut]. There were several volunteers who devoted all their efforts to the orphanage. It was due to them that the orphanage continued to exist until the beginning of the Second World War in 1939. When the Soviet Government occupied the town, they took over the running of the orphanage, because in the Soviet system the government was running such institutions. They amalgamated all orphanages in town and the Jewish orphanage ceased to exist, it was transformed into a different institution. The person who was the most outstanding participant in the development and running of the orphanage was Chana Bloch.

Shogdey Melocho

As mentioned above, the orphanage accepted only children of school age. There were, however, orphans and children of impoverished parents who exceeded the school age, and could not be accepted in the orphanage. There were also children who finished their schooling whilst they were in the orphanage and required further education.

Shogdey Melocho was created to meet that demand. The institution taught the children to be tradesmen. A boarding house was created to provide accommodation for the orphans where they were given the same care as in the orphanage. Children with parents, who were not in a position to look after them, were given help in various forms such as part time work, clothing etc. The institution took total care of its pupils. The pupils were sent to Jewish tradesmen to learn specific trades. Shogdey Melocho signed contracts with the tradesmen, they supervised the progress of the pupils as well as and the attitude of the masters to the pupils. A few years later, the institution created its own furniture workshop. A good instructor was found. The workshop produced good quality furniture. It had become a habit in town that when a young couple got married or decided to buy new furniture it was they purchased it from Shogdey Melocho. They made it their task to satisfy the customers. Most pupils in the workshops were boys. The workshop did not send out work to outside carpenters.

Prior to the Second World War a small subsidy was extracted from the city council, which, though unwilling, could not refuse some help. Shogdey Melocho was also supported by the Vilno district committee of YEKAPA. Shogdey Melocho existed until the Soviet occupation in 1939.

There are several people in Israel who were brought up in the orphanage and they learned a trade in Shogdey Melocho after they had left the orphanage. They are now independent and work in the trade they learned in Novogrudok.

Most of the expenses of the institutions were met by membership fees. Each institution had its volunteer collectors who would visit every month the members i.e. practically all Jews in Novogrudok, and collect the membership dues. Nobody refused unless they were not in a position to pay. Thus all Jews in Novogrudok were members of all Jewish institutions in town and had the right to vote at all meetings.

Jews from the nearby villages were also supporting the Jewish institutions. One of the big supporters was the owner of a flourmill in Slobodke Itzchak Izik Kagan. He was supporting not only institutions, but also needy people in town. Itzchak Izik would never refuse help to anyone, be it an institution, a needy person or a Zionist cause. He gave generously. When the war started and the Nazi beasts arrived, there was hunger in town. Itzchak Izik was still in his mill at the time and he helped many Jews. He was providing flour and other produce. Everyone knew him and some made use of his generosity.

לְהָאָדוֹן הַנִּכְבָּד
שבתי בן אברהם רבינוביץ
סופר ומזכיר חברתנו.

החברה שׁוֹקְדֵי מְלָאכָה בהכירה לטוב
ובהוקירה את פעילותיך הנעלות לטיבתה התכבד
לברכך בזה לרגלי ברית ־ האירוסים הכרותה בינך ובין
העלמה הכבודה

שרה בת פסח

ואנחנו תפלה לה' בעל הגמולות כי יאמר
לדבק טוב ויברך אתכם באריכת ימים עושר
ואושר ברוב טוב וענג לשמחתנו ולטובת חברתנו
הואיל נא אדון נכבד לקבל את ברכתנו זאת
לאות תודה על פעילותיך בחברתנו עד היום ולאות תפעננו
ובקשתנו כי תוסיף לשקוד על מלאכתך גם לימים הבאים

ברגשי־כבוד

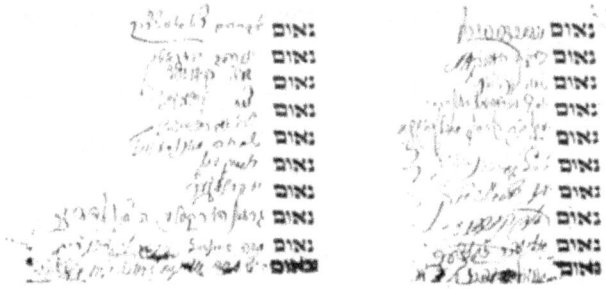

Translation below:
The Society for supporting the Trade School (*Shokdei Melakha*)
To the honorable mister
Shabtai ben Avraham Rabinovitz
Writer and secretary of our Society
The Society **Shokdei Melakha** acknowledging your activities for it's favor
is honored to congratulate you to your engagement with the dignitary maiden
Sarah bath Pesakh
and we wish you with God's help long life, wealth an happiness.
Honorable Sir, please receive our congratulations and this as a thank for your
activities forour society until now and as our wishes for your continuing work
on the coming years.
With respect (20 signatures)
This is a document from the "Shokdei Melakha" Society in 1898.
(The signatures are ffrom the members of the society in this time)

Schools in Novogrudok

Elders by a Gemara page (Studying Talmud)

At the same time a modern school, which was called Beit Seifer, was established,. The name gave a good indication of the type of school it was. Later, when the Tarbut movement was created in Poland, Beit Seifer became one of the Tarbut schools. The school existed until 1939. When the soviets came they converted Tarbut to a Yiddish school, but retained Moshe Steinberg, as the school principal.

For a time, there was also a Yiddish school of CISA headed by the teacher Solomon. After a few years the school was closed.

There was also a Mizrachi school in town. It was a private school which belonged to Shloyme Wolfovich. In time the school was modernised, it joined the Mizrachi "tushia" and employed a few teachers. But the school still belonged to Wolfovich and was commonly called the Wolfovich school.

A "melamed" [old fashioned teacher of religious texts] was still available to teach junior students – this was the Menaker school in Rachelo.

Professional unions

After the first World War professional associations were created in Novogrudok.

1. Needle workers. The head office in Warsaw was connected with the Bund.

2. Leather workers. The head office was communist.

3. Tobacco workers. The head office was connected with PPS [Polska Partja Socjalistyczna – the Polish Socialist Party].

All the unions were located in one building. There was a great deal of functional and cultural activity. There were meetings, lectures mostly of an anti-Zionist nature. A number of young activists created a group of Zionist metal workers. The other associations have allowed us the use of their premises. They were also helping us. But when it came to legalising the metal workers union it was refused because I, the secretary of the union, was a member of Poalei Zion and the other members on the committee were our supporters. The head office in Warsaw was Bundist. They rejected our application to join the union, though formally we were eligible to do so, since we fulfilled all of their requirements. Many letters of support were of no use, nor were my two trips to the head office in Warsaw. They did not reject us, they just told us that they were looking into it. But in the end we were never made official members. The union could not exist without legalisation. Thus a metal workers union was never formed in our town. Some of our members created a provisional group in the professional union. This group created a worker's library. We collected money for its creation. We catered at all festivities and weddings. We were organising entertainment parties. The library was growing well. It was located in the building of the unions. As long as there were three unions of three different kinds, the few Zionist youths who created and ran the library were not rejected, though we did not trust each other. The tobacco union was abolished when the production and retail of tobacco was monopolised by the Polish government. Some of the leaders of the leather workers union have become independent manufacturers and suppliers of leather goods. This left only the Bundist needle union. They decided to close us down. They locked the premises, and as the library was in the premises it was also closed. After a time they found new premises and the library remained in their possession.

Workers union and workers bank

The Jewish workers began to join associations. The guiding spirit of the movement was Jankel Lubchanski, who owned a shop selling sewing machines. All Jewish independent workers joined the union. They set up nice premises, where the comrades would gather every evening. Newspapers, checkers etc were available. There were also cultural events, for example readings of Professor Graetz's "History of the Jews from Oldest Times to the Present". The largest effort of the administration was in the area of interceding with various institutions, first among them was the taxation office, and others were the city hall, sub-district office, district office, and the workers division. There was never a shortage of cases of mistreatment of Jews. There was need for registering tradesman, obtaining of diplomas, examinations etc. Jankel Lubchanski and his cossacks, as the followers of Lubchanski were called in town, have occupied an important place in the Jewish society of Novogrudok. The delegates of the tradesmen's union were represented in all organisations in town. Some were deputies in the city council. The union also helped poorer members. They were providing flour for Passover matzoth and organized the baking of matzoth. The profit was used to provide matzoth and other foods for poor workers. Help was given to the needy before all holidays.

At the same time as they created the tradesmen's union, they also opened a cooperative tradesmen's bank. It was called "The Tradesmen's and Small Business Bank". The director of the bank was the same Jankel Lubchanski. For a considerable time the bank was the only financial institution in town. Later a commercial bank was created. The value of the tradesmen's bank to the customers need not be described. One could always obtain a loan on favourable conditions. In time the bank developed well. It existed until the war of 1939. But the tradesmen's union and bank were troubled over the years by perpetual quarrelling. Among the tradesmen were members of the Bund, of the Peoples party (folkistn), and just anti-Zionists. They knew that as long as Jankel Lubchanski, who was a Zionist, was the leader, they would not have any influence among the tradesmen. They directed, therefore, all their efforts to combat Lubchanski, until they won and he left the union and the bank. Only then did the winners elect a management team consisting of their insiders. For chairman they elected the photographer Yankef Vinnick, who was a Zionist. They had two reasons for this: firstly he was well known, accepted in the government offices and secondly he served as a paravane. But their domination did not last long. The Poalei Zion party had increased its strength and influence. They managed to put into the management team two members of the party: one was the treasurer [the author of this article Openhim] and Alter Chesly was the secretary. The presidium consisted of the chairman Vinnick, a Zionist, Openhim and Chesly, Poalei Zion, were treasurer and secretary. Only the vice-president Mojshe Fajwelevich was not a Zionist. The tradesmen's union existed until 1938, when the Polish government closed the central office in Warsaw and all branches.

Hashomer Hatzair

Many years ago two young men were on holidays in Slonim. They came back very impressed by the Hashomer Hatzair in Slonim. They soon gathered a group and now we had the Hashomer Hatzair in Novogrudok. They brought with them the statute of the organization which I copied on my typewriter. In those days a typewriter was a rarity. I was repairing typewriters and there was always a spare one in my workshop. Hashomer Hatzair had developed greatly since its inception. The organisers of Hashomer Hatzair in our town were all my school friends and were close friends at that. That is why I took part in the organization of the Party. Later I was told that in a closed meeting my problem was discussed: could I remain as a member of Hashomer Hatzair since I was a worker? According to its statute, Hashomer Hatzair could not accept workers. Questions were asked in the higher echelons of the party. As an exception, I was allowed to stay. When I found out about it I withdrew from the Party. Hashomer Hatzair went through the entire evolution and developed well. It conducted an extensive education program among the youth. It was one of the strongest youth organisations in town. They participated actively in all Zionist actions. Later, when the league of workers for Eretz Israel was formed, they participated actively in the sale of shekels [bonds for Israel] and in the elections. They existed in our town until the outbreak of the Second World War in 1939.

"*Hekhalutz*" in Navaredok

Hachalutz and Hachalutz Hatzair

The first cell of Hachalutz was formed at the end of 1920. The movement was not big, but it continued to grow. The meetings were conducted in the women's section of the Shloss Gass Synagogue. The Hachalutz existed as long as there was an alliya [emigration to Eretz Israel]. When restrictions on alliya were eased, the recruitment to Hachalutz grew. After the disturbances in Jaffa in 1921 alliya was stopped and Hachalutz stopped its activities. When in 1923 hope had arisen of the resumption of alliya, Hachalutz renewed its activities. At that time Chatskel Rabinovich came from Slonim (he lives at present in the kibutz Lochame haghettaot). He renewed the activities of the Poalei Zion Party by drawing on the membership of Hachalutz. At the same time a committee was elected for the purpose of organising the political party activities in town. It would appear that the persons who were the leaders in Hachalutz had to lead the party. As they had no experience in party work, they neglected the task. The activities of the Hachalutz were not legalized in our town. As long as the membership was small it was possible to meet occasionally in the women's section of a synagogue, at other times in a private home. But when the membership increased another solution had to be found. There was a sudden increase in engagements, weddings and other functions. Members would report to the police, as the law required, an engagement party or a wedding. Tables were covered with drinks and food and the meeting would proceed. When the movement grew still further, the membership was divided into cells of 5-6 members and they continued with the cultural work. Newspapers such as "Haolam" and "Hapoel hatzair" from Israel were read. The leaders of the Vilno district of Hachalutz were at the time Josef Bankaver and Biber. The work was illegal. It was not easy. People were frightened, because the events in Pinsk were fresh in minds of many. When the Polish army occupied Pinsk, they found a number of Zionist youths in a hall. They took 40 of them outside and shot them. Hachalutz decided to organize Hachalutz Hatzair in town. Later, after the event of 1926 in Israel, Hachalutz ceased to exist. Only Hachalutz Hatzair continued its work. It grew well, conducted extensive cultural activities and sent many young members on hachshara [work experience preliminary to alliya to Eretz Israel]. Hachalutz hatzair continued its work until 1935, when it amalgamated with Freihit [Freedom].

In 1925 Hachalutz established in town two harshara facilities, one for forest work near Selub the other in town at Berek Chiz in Sieniezyc street making concrete products. Hachalutz participated in all Zionist work. In 1925 the first blue boxes appeared in Jewish homes. The first collection of money from the blue boxes occurred at Purim. All the known Zionist activists including the senior members of Hachalutz participated. This was a big event. A blue/white box was to be seen in almost every Jewish home. The first collection from the blue boxes brought in nearly 1000 zloty. Another event was the opening of the university at Har Hatzofim on the 1 April 1925. A march through the streets of Novogrudok was organised to celebrate the occasion. In 1929 the league of the workers for Israel put up their own list for election to the city council. The candidate was Pilecki [S. Prisitzki?] a teacher in Tarbut and a leader in Hashomer Hatzair. He missed being elected by a narrow margin.

Frihit [Freedom]

Frihit was established in 1933 and it developed well. It was legalised from the beginning. Accommodation was obtained and an active educational and cultural program was conducted. To maintain a venue, to heat it and conduct cultural work was not easy for the working youth. In winter a time table was established and every day an appointed member had to find the timber for heating the premises. Some members could not afford to supply timber. But no one failed to heat the offices on the appointed day and the daily scheduled meetings and education programs could be maintained. Each week cultural meetings were conducted. A large gathering of youth would be present, including some who were not active in the Zionist movement, such as the communists. Each summer Frihit organised accommodation and seminars in Novoyelnia. As mentioned above, Hachalutz ceased to exist. At that time Haoved was created. Its membership consisted mainly of adults, some with families. The membership was not able to participate in harshara. Young Zionists had to work in harshara before they could emigrate.

The general Zionists had created a similar organization, which was called Chaluts ba mlocha. It was possible to cooperate with the general Zionist movements. Firstly the general Zionists in Novogrudok were of the Al Hamishmar [on watch] kind, which was Grinbaum's variety. Bet lebanot [Time to build] practically did not exist in Novogrudok. Secondly, our general Zionists were liberals, their head was the Deputy Mayor of the town, Abram Ostashinski. He was the chairman of all shekel [Zionist bonds sold in support of Eretz Israel] and election commissions and a Deputy Chairman of the League (workers for Eretz Israel). We established good relationships with them, particularly with Avrom Ostashinski.

Members of the Poalei Zion Party

Poalei Zion

In 1934 a few members of Poalei Zion together with a few members of Frihit had renewed the existence of Poalei Zion and elected a committee that began to conduct extensive activities. Representatives of the new party were placed on the committee of the league of workers for Eretz Israel. They immediately occupied their proper place on the committee and in time they had practically taken over the running and influence of the committee. Previously the league was run mainly by members of Hashomer Hatzair. Representatives were also placed in Vaad Haoved. The influence of the party had become apparent. The party distributed the paper Dos Wort and increased its circulation. It became apparent in town that Poalei Zion was reborn. In 1935 on the eve of the 19th Zionist congress the party put in an extra effort in distributing shekels and later in preparing for and conducting the elections. In the elections to the congress, the league gained about 55% of the votes. In the elections to the institutions in town, some members of the party were elected. Two members of the party, Jakov Rabinovich and I, were elected to the parent's committee of the Tarbut school. In the elections to Shogdey Melocho [board of management?] members of the party were also elected, namely I, Chaim Novach Leibovich and others. In the elections to the Kehila [Jewish city council] in 1937 the party presented its own list. We were short of two votes to have our representative elected.

A welcome of the Revisionists in honor of Meir Grossman

At this time came the end of the bubbly political and social life in Novogrudok, which started after the First World War. In 1939 the Second World War started. The Soviets came and after 22 months of a relatively peaceful life time the Germans attacked on the 22 June 1941 and brought total devastation to Novogrudok.

[It would be remiss not to mention that the above article does not list all, or perhaps even most, organizations in Novogrudok of the 1920's and 30's. There must have been several religious parties apart of Mizrachi, such as Aguda (two varieties?). Among the Zionist parties the right wing party of Jabotinsky's Revisionists must be mentioned. Jabotinsky visited Novogrudok in the early 1930's to a tumultuous reception. Many wore Betar uniforms. There were Communists in Novogrudok, though the party was illegal. The Friland movement (Freeland league) headed by the lawyer Gumener was small but significant. Bund is mentioned above in passing. There must have been a party in town. The Musar movement had for a time its headquarters in Novogrudok. Though it was on the decline in the 1930's there must have been followers who were still active. I am certain that the list is incomplete. The Jews of Novogrudok, many of them poor, were looking feverously for a solution to their many problems, but not the one that meant extermination.]

[Page 107]

The Novogrudok Orphanage

The history of the orphanage

Translated from Hebrew by Aviva Kamil

A. The foundation of the institution

In 1917 the situation of the Jewish community in Novogrudok was very difficult. The town had been under German occupation since 1915 and was close to the front line. The population of the surrounding towns, such as Karelich, Lubch etc, moved to Novogrudok. The circumstances of hundreds of children, specifically those of the orphans whose parents had been killed or had died during the war, was particularly difficult. In September 1917 it was decided to establish an orphanage. The founders were David Cohen, Sholem Cohen, Benjomin Metropolitanski, Josef Izraelit, Chaim Ajzikovich, Izchok Volfkind and Zorach Chasovshchik. An appeal for funds from the Jewish population was published. The occupation forces were also approached. The German officer in charge gave permission for the project. The following people joined the organising committee: Rabbi Meir Abovich, Reb Sh. Eizenberg, Nachman Vasserman, Meir Eicher, Avrom Chasovshchik and Rivke Shvartz. The Jewish community, which had itself suffered greatly, extended willingly their help. Initially, 22 boys and girls aged between 5 and 7 years joined the orphanage. On the 28 November 1917 there was a festive ceremony at the orphanage to declare it open and the sum of 4825 marks was donated by those present. In addition, the town's people donated cloth, apparel and bedding. On the 4 December 1917, ten more children joined the orphanage. Income was derived from membership fees, occasional donations, the German administration, the food centre, various spectacles and amusements as well as lotteries. New members joined the committee. On the 26 August 1918 the orphanage moved to its own premises and 28 additional children were admitted and joined 11 other children, who had been admitted previously. In January 1920 assistance was obtained from the Jewish community council (Kehila) and in June, with the help of Dr Alexander Harkavy, the orphanage received 80,000 mark.

B. The life of the institution till 1925.

On the 25 April 1921 Mr Yelen arrived from the United States and brought $400 with him for the orphanage. Many children were transferred gradually out of the orphanage to learn a trade. On the 5

November 1921 Mr Eizikovich went to Vilno to discuss the situation of the orphanage. Systematic help started to arrive from "YEKAPA", which had begun previously to support the institution. At that time orphanage branches of DDK had started their activities in Poland.

C. Building of a new dwelling.

In 1922 a building containing a kitchen was added to the orphanage. In 1923 building of a new dwelling had begun. The orphanage had at its disposal $200 and the Kehila contributed $100. Shortly after, construction came to a halt due to the lack of funds. In 1923, $100 was contributed by the American Relief organization and a further $25 from the Kehila. In 1924, Mr Gumener a representative of the DDK organization, visited the town. He took an interest in the construction of the new building. With the help of "YEKAPA" and the drive of the orphanage committee the building was completed. A festive inauguration was held to launch the new building and those present included M. Shalit and M. Yecerov who were representatives from "YEKAPA" as well as the representative of DDK, H. Gumener. In all, the cost of the building was $1951, derived from the following sources: the resources held by the orphanage, Kehila, the American Relief, "YEKAPA", the building committee, collection at the inauguration and from the Chevra Kadisha (burial society). On average, by 1925 more than 50 children lived in the orphanage. The manager was Joisef Izraelit. Teachers helped in the running of the orphanage.

D. The transition.

The completion of the new building was the swan song of the members of the old committee, who worked tirelessly over the years. Gradually the help of "YEKAPA" was reduced and for a time ceased and DDK had begun to liquidate its activities. The local activists, tired and disheartened, began to leave the organisation. A serious deficit began to accumulate. The situation was catastrophic. At this stage a breakthrough occurred. An organisation to take care of the orphans was formed and took over the management of the institution. A new management team was elected and took over the task. The chairman was the former representative of DDK, Mr Gumener. The committee consisted mainly of women, who were very dedicated. The women were: Chana Bloch, Chaia Delatycki, Rabbi (Rebezn) Wolobrinski's wife, Roze Zamkowe, Cipe Klubok and Sora Karenski. Initially Mr Wolfkind, Mr Wager and Mrs Benzianowski-Wager supported the work. Mr Eliezer Rabinowicz, the Chasan assisted the committee. The new committee started with great enthusiasm to bring back financial viability to the institution. Money was collected in Novogrudok and the surrounding towns. They sought and obtained help from "YEKAPA". For the first time support was obtained on a regular basis from the

Sejmik (district council), city council and the provincial government (wojewodztwo). A systematic replacement of older children was undertaken. Some unsuitable children were removed from the institution. Gradually the building was repaired. A new experienced manageress from Warsaw was hired. Step by step the orphanage assumed the image of a "normal" institution. It was not easy, however, to arrive at this transformation. It took 5-6 years of perpetual battles to achieve the change. Many hours of waiting by members of the committee in the offices of the Sejmik and the city council were required till fractions of the subsidies were paid. Often, performances were arranged, but eventually the members of the committee had to pay the entertainers. But nothing seemed too difficult for members of the committee. Gradually, the deficit created by the old committee, which had been incurred since 1925, was repaid. A bookkeeper was engaged. Money was kept in a bank and payments made by cheque. For those times these changes were revolutionary. Not only was the financial situation very difficult but also the institution was very neglected and it was necessary to rebuild it and normalise relationships with the children. Those who were unsuitable had to be removed and those who reached maturity had to be placed into apprenticeships and work. The buildings were insured. The children were given personal documents. More care was taken of the medical needs of the children. The management had taken on a more serious and social character. Discipline was introduced and the orphanage had become a model institution. Nothing was too difficult for the management, and specifically for the women. To observe the women at festivals was a wonder to behold. It was not just the provision of a home for the children or a feeling of pity for them that were their motivation, but it was also love and devotion to the lonely children.

E. The financial position of the institution

The first period.

Despite the difficult times, the population was assisting the orphanage. Time was available and spent on activities for the orphanage. The German occupation isolated the town from the rest of world and there was a lot of interest in the well being of the orphanage. The German forces were of some assistance.

The second period.

The district became part of Poland. Representatives from the American Relief organization and the DDK had appeared. Regular assistance was provided by "YEKAPA" of Vilno. The Polish-American Committee provided help. Clothing was given. Businesses were reopened and more money became available.

Third period.

The economic crisis of 1925 began. DDK stopped its contributions. "YEKAPA" reduced its input. The activists of the past quit their positions.

The following support was received:

Sejmik	2,400 zloty per annum
Wojewodstwo	2,400 zloty per annum
City council	3,500 zloty per annum
Membership fees	3,000 zloty per annum

Later the contribution of "YEKAPA" was increased. From time to time the American Relief organization sent in donations. Enterprises also gave significant contributions. The consequences of the economic crisis were less severe than it was feared.

The last period.

The situation becomes more difficult. From 1930 all donations were gradually reduced. The income from membership fees was reduced by half. The Sejmik provided only 150-300 zloty. The city council reduced its payment to 1,000 zloty, and even that amount was not paid in full. The income from "YEKAPA" and a reduced contribution from the wojewodstwo were still available. The financial situation was becoming more and more difficult. But life went on. There was hope that better times would come.

Statistical data of the children in the orphanage.

Over the years 119 children lived in the orphanage, 55 boys and 64 girls. Of them 28 had no parents and the remainder had one parent.

The children came from:

Novogrudok	38 orphans
Novogrudok sub-district	70 orphans
other sub-districts	11 orphans

Of the children listed above 69 children had acquired the following trades:

tailors	14
dress makers	26
carpenters	13
hair dressers	3
technicians	4
type setters	2
mattress makers	2
saddlers	3
watchmakers	2

Thirteen children migrated to the following countries:

USA	8
Israel	2
Cuba	1
France	2

Seven children were learning a trade at Shogdey Melocho.

Of the 119 children 41 returned to their relatives, and 30 became independent. The others learned a trade while they lived in the institution.

Overall characteristics of the institution

In the institution there were girls and boys in the age group of 7 to 14 years, that is of school age. The institution consisted of 7 rooms: a dining room, 2 dormitories, a classroom, an office, a room for the teacher and a room for the cook. There was a separate bathroom. The walls of the dining room and the bedrooms were painted in oil paint. The number of children in residence at any time was 15-20. The majority were from Novogrudok and the surrounds. In the institution the family system predominated, which meant that the children were growing up, as far as possible, in a family atmosphere. The members of the management committee visited the institution quite often. Most children were educated in the Tarbut school (there was no Yiddish school in Novogrudok). A few boys studied with Rabbis and in the Talmud Torah. When the children finished their primary education they were placed in Shogdey Melocho, where they were trained in for specific trades. Previously, the members of the management committee were placing the children with tradesmen to learn trades. Medical care was provided by the Jewish hospital headed by Dr I. Marmurshtain. All children were provided with all necessary documents. The food for the children was modest but healthy; bread (on Sabbath chala), meat, butter, sugar and vegetables. Bread was baked on the premises. The rooms were clean and warm. The children were supplied with clothing. The personnel of the institution consisted of a teacher and a cook. Laundry help was hired when necessary. A bookkeeper was employed. The money was kept in the Jewish Peoples Bank.

The Children's Home with the management

Life in the institution

The children would get up at 6.30am. Every child was responsible for making their bed, washing the top part (to the belt line) of the body and cleaning their teeth. Breakfast, lunch and dinner were served by the supervisors. The children attended school from 8am till 2pm. Lunch was served at 2.30. After lunch was a rest period. Later homework was done in a separate room, and then the children participated in recreational games (in the summer outdoors) until dinner time. There was a children's library. Selected children were responsible for the issue of books as well as being responsible to see that the borrowers read the books. Games played in the institution were carefully selected. Talks were conducted. In the summer, the children were taken frequently for walks. In the winter the children participated in winter sports. The games were chosen by the children. The children had an elected governing body. When necessary a mock court was conducted.

The pedagogic arrangements in the orphanage.

Initially the manager was a person without qualifications for the *position*. By 1927 a specialised educator was engaged (M. Lipshits). It was something new and different and it was difficult to arrange. As was mentioned previously, the atmosphere in the orphanage was similar to that of a private family. There were, of course, children who did not fit in with the life style of the orphanage. On the whole, however, there were no major complications either in the orphanage or at school. It was interesting to note the changes in children a few months after they were admitted to the orphanage. They changed from frightened, apprehensive children to children full of life and song. The most difficult task was the creation of a friendly atmosphere. Some children could not understand why they should work, but in time the children became attached to the institution. In town and at school, the children from the orphanage were considered to be disciplined and well educated.

> *[The above article was written before Wold War II and at the end of Jewish Novogrudok. The unknown author, and all of us, did not foresee the tragic end.]*

[Page 110]

Memories

by Aharon Srebranik (a child from the orphanage)

Translated from Yiddish by O. Delatycki

After the first World War , dozens of orphaned children were roaming the streets of Novogrudok. They had no place to call their own. I remember and will never forget people stopping me and asking "why do you drag yourself around in the streets, go home, it is terribly cold and you have no shoes". It was easy to say "go home", but there was no home to go to. We would spend the nights in the synagogues, or more likely in "klizlach" [small synagogues frequented by particular groups, such as those of specific trades] on the Shul Heif [Synagogue square]. It was warmer inside. Sometimes a miracle would happen - somebody would offer a child a bed for the night and give him a meal. But nobody could afford to keep a child permanently. As is usual after a war, everyone had his own worries.

But suddenly, without warning, all strays were gathered together into a house, which was called "children's home" [kinderhoize]. A better name would have been orphanage. Many families wanted to send their children to that institution, but only orphans were admitted. When I write about the foundation of the orphanage, I cannot forget the first "father" of it, Joisef Izraelit, who devoted his entire life to the children.

The diminutive "Josele" was a Jew of little formal education, but was full of verve and reacted with good humour to the capricious behaviour of the children. As is usual with children - one would laugh another would cry, others would play, one would behave this way, the other would behave that way. Not all things were trifling matters, but he managed to arrange these as best as he could. The children loved him dearly. I remember the occasion, when at a meal, he spoke and asked that nobody should call him "father", because he was father to all children. Naturally, the children did not appreciate the value of their orphanage. But in later years, when the children had grown up and some had found relatives, such as older brothers and sisters, they began to understand the value of the orphanage.

In the early years, there were great difficulties in maintaining the orphanage, since the burden fell on the shoulders of the people of Novogrudok who were impoverished by the war. But the good people of Novogrudok would not neglect the orphans. As the years went by, the orphanage improved in every aspect. Later a specially trained teacher, Lola Lipshits, was brought from Warsaw. The blossoming of the orphanage coincided with her presence. She was full of stamina. She was never resigned to the fact that all expenses of the orphanage had to be met by the impoverished citizens of Novogrudok. She went to the starostwo [sub-district office] and wojewodstwo [district office] and explained the needs of the orphanage. The officialdom began to take note of the existence of the orphanage.

Since then the orphanage was subsidised by the two institutions. From 1926, the lawyer H. Gumener was helping with the official contacts. He devoted a large part of his life in helping the orphanage. Some of the untiring workers were Mrs Chaja Delatycki and Mrs Sora Korenski, who now lives in Israel and is interested to this day in the fate of the surviving orphans. "They are still my children", she says when she meets them. And concerning Chana Bloch, no matter what is said or written about her will never describe her. She was the permanent mother of the orphans of Novogrudok. I have written about her previously, but I think that she should be portrayed by a great writer, who will be able to describe the fine, devoted, faithful and good-hearted Jewish mother of the Novogrudok orphans - Chana Bloch. I believe that the whole community will know how to value her memory, and will realise that I am not exaggerating. She was devoted to the orphanage with all her heart and nothing was too difficult for her, despite her advanced years. I used to imagine that she was born in the orphanage. There is no one who was brought up in the orphanage who does not remember Chana Bloch. She remains deep in our hearts.

The Children's Home

Due to the devotion of the citizens of Novogrudok to the orphanage, we wanted for nothing. I believe that many children did not receive as much support in their own homes as the children of the orphanage. All who could would render support. I remember the celebrations of "Chanukat habait" of the new building in the presence of Mr Shalit. The building was erected with the help of YAKAPA of Vilno. There was happiness all around, the orphanage had at last its own house. It is impossible to describe the satisfaction of everyone. I believe that there had never been a bigger celebration by the children and by the people of the community at large. It was also, come to think of it, the biggest celebration in a very long time. Even greater than the Pesach or Chanuka concert when Chasan Rabinowicz would conduct the children's choir. The board of management together with many guests and friends of the children would come to the concert. It was a lively performance, which continued until late at night. As it is written: "the one who spreads the word of the exodus from Egypt is to be commended". All was done in good taste and with love

The children of the orphanage were given a good general education and were taught a trade. They studied at the Hebrew school Tarbut under the guidance of the director of the school Mr Moshe Steinberg, who was constantly helping the children of the orphanage. The trades were taught at either Shokdey melocho or by private arrangement. The survivors from the orphanage are spread throughout the world. Most of them live in Israel and help to build the free Jewish State, a State of love and happiness for all Jews around the world, who are gathering from all the lands of the Diaspora.

[Page 112]

The first child in the orphanage

by Aba Rutkovski

Translated from Yiddish by O. Delatycki

Having been told that the management is intending to publish a book to mark the fifteenth anniversary of the existence of the orphanage [1932], I would like to contribute my story to the book. I was the first, literally the first child to come through the doorway of the orphanage in 1917, when it was first opened.

I would like to describe briefly what the orphanage meant to me and for many other children. When all inhabitants were expelled from Lubch during the war, my mother was sent to Novogrudok. I was 4 years of age at the time, with both of my legs crippled. My father had gone before the war to America (I have not met him to this day). Father alienated himself from us. Thus, broken hearted, mother was left carrying me in her arms, with no place to rest her weary head. She was hoping to find shelter for her crippled son so as to be able to earn a crust of bread.

However suddenly one evening, I remember it as if it happened today, the door opened and in the light of a stub of a candle two young men entered our room. They came to view our tomb like accommodation. They asked mother to send an application to Dovid Cohen, so that the orphanage would accept me. I remember my mother started to cry for joy. She said that God listened to her prayers and now she would be able to work and afford a piece of bread. On the 7 November 1917 a member of the committee of the orphanage Chaim Izikovich took me in his arms and brought me to my new home. My joy was great. I was rid of my mother's beating and cursing and I was given not only a piece of bread, but a piece of cheese with it. And at night, before going to bed, a clean nightshirt was put on me. In this manner I lived in the home for years.

As I grew older and began to understand my situation, I started to ask myself the question: what will happen to me without being able to walk? I was most depressed. The manager would take all the children for a walk and I was left behind. The children went to school and I stayed at home. Not to remain illiterate, a special teacher would visit me. In the summer all children would walk off for a few hours and I could only creep into the yard. On days when all children would march in parades, I would stay in the house alone. It was only due to the good-hearted manager Josif Izraelit and a member of the committee Chaim Itzkovich that I was carried at times in their arms. The management was very interested in my welfare, and each time a doctor would visit the home they would draw his attention to my feet and ask if they could be straitened. Some doctors said that the feet could be cured, but the treatment would cost a lot of money. But money was not available at the time. The influx of new children grew by the day and the expenses grew accordingly.

But fate decreed that I should become a man like others. A delegate from America, Mr H. Yelen arrived in Novogrudok. He brought money for poor families. Among the names on the list was that of my mother. But for certain reasons he did not want to give the money to my mother. At that stage the committee of the orphanage asked Mr Yelen to put aside a sum of money to send me to Warsaw to have the operation performed, and the delegate agreed. When I was told that I was being taken to Warsaw I cried for joy, because I thought hitherto that I was destined to wear boots made of felt for the rest of my days. For a year and a quarter after the operation I suffered great pain. I wore gadgets on my feet. I was told that I should change, without fail, the plaster at set intervals. And it was because of this treatment that I became a man the same as all others.

I spent eight years in the orphanage. I was growing up and I learnt to become a tailor. I started gradually to earn a living and become independent. I, together with all others, am feeling now [1932] the effects of the economic crisis. Yet I am not forgetting and will never forget what the committee of the orphanage did for me. I send them my blessings and the blessings of all the children of the orphanage who were made into independent men.

[Page 113]

The orphanage (1917-1919)

by Sholim Cohen

Translated from Yiddish by O. Delatycki

A. Autumn 1917. Our town, with its 5000 Jews, of which there are hundreds of homeless Jewish families, is under a threatening black cloud. The situation is hopeless: hunger, want and destitution worsen by the day and become more ominous. Epidemic diseases spread with a wild fury and the death rate is frightful. In the cold, wet mornings thin, ragged human shadows move slowly. They are the road menders, mostly women. Their men are in the army or in America. With them are their older children, youths 10 to 12 years of age. While they work, their younger children, some almost infants, are locked in their homes. The infants sit in the unprotected, unheated homes with a piece of dark bread and cold water to quench their hunger. Many are ill and many die.

A group of young people have decided to help the neglected children. They seek advice, make plans and decide to create a home for the abandoned children. They will call it an orphanage. Will they find means to create such an institution in such dreadful times? They hope to obtain help from the authorities and believe that the Jewish society will do all it can.

B. The festive opening of the orphanage on a light, frosty November day of the year 1917. The sun casts its rays through large windows into a large room. This is the bedroom of the orphanage. The invited guests sit at a large, decorated table. They make speeches and pass on greetings, they sign their names in the golden book, and the donations grow steadily. Guests continue to arrive and none comes empty handed. The atmosphere becomes more festive. Well wishes for the success can be heard. In the intervals between the greetings a splendid choir is performing. And at that moment a long line of children enters the room. All are 5 and 6 years of age. The children stop at the tables where the guests are seated. Reisele, who is 5 years old, steps forward. With a ringing child's voice she thanks the assembled company. At that point the choir cuts in with a lively, happy tune, composed specially for the occasion. The children walk out of the room. The moment is festive and everyone is deeply moved.

C. The financial success of the opening ceremony is great. But greater still is the moral achievement. The interest and sympathy that are shown to the orphanage hearten the members of the committee and encourage them to further efforts. Additional children are admitted. All worked with dedication and loyalty. The children are becoming stronger and are regaining a healthy appearance. They also regain their liveliness and joyfulness . The orphanage becomes their real home. It is heartening to see how the children embrace the women who help with the chores and spend many hours in the orphanage. The eyes of the children are twinkling and shining when Dovid Cohen, the head of the committee and the mentor of the children is gathering them around him in the evenings and is telling them stories. In the summer of 1919 we can conduct with pride the member of the Morganthau-mission, Prof Gothard and the representative of the

Polish Ministry of Foreign Affairs Count Zultowski who is accompanying him, through the large, bright, sparkling clean rooms of the orphanage. And we can also tell them that in the two years of the orphanage's existence, infectious diseases were kept out of the orphanage and no life was lost. Yes, the Jews of Novogrudok can be proud of their orphanage.

[Page 114]

"Shokdey melocho"

The Trade School

by Chaim Leibovich

Translated from Yiddish by Oskar Delatycki

The cruel war and occupation by the Germans and the Bolsheviks had finished. Novogrudok, which had passed a number of times from hand to hand between the Germans, the Bolsheviks and the Poles, was greatly impoverished. But as soon as the fighting stopped life began to normalise. The wounds started to heal and communal institutions started to develop again. In the autumn of 1921, due to the initiative of Hirsh Ostashinski and Moshe Shimonovitz, old activists of Shokdey melocho movement, a meeting of youth was called in the Harkavy synagogue. Mr Dovid Cohen outlined the difficult situation facing the Jewish population. Many sources of Jewish livelihood had vanished. He explained that occupations such as Jewish shop keeping, trading and go-between, were defunct due to the war and that the youth must become productive and find other means of income. They needed to learn a trade and thus become useful members of society. After an exchange of views it was decided to renew the activities of the old association of Shokdey melocho, which had a distinguished past in educating many young persons, who became good tradesmen. A committee was elected which consisted of Shkolnik, Perl Klubok, Joselevich, Abramovich, Klachko, Pinski and Sapotnicki. Dovid Cohen was elected chairman and H. Leibovich secretary.

The committee started work immediately. A statute was developed to decide which young men and women would be given an opportunity to learn a trade. Contracts with tradesmen with whom boys or girls would learn trades were signed up for three years. The organisation Shokdey melocho undertook to feed the students for the first year. In the second year the tradesman would pay the apprentice a sufficient sum for him to sustain himself. Shokdey melocho undertook also to clad the apprentices. Contracts were signed up with all kinds of tradesmen: tailors, boot makers, carpenters, watchmakers etc. The girls learned to become seamstresses for dresses, coats and corset making. Evening classes had begun, where teachers taught voluntarily, without pay. Yiddish, Polish, mathematics were some of the subjects. The evening classes were held at the Talmid Torah. A boarding school for boys was set up. It was situated in the house of the Slonim Chasids in Slonim St. A boarding school for girls was situated in the house of the Talmid Torah. The boarding houses were accommodating orphans who had lost both parents. Children from the orphanage, when attaining 13 years of age, would leave the orphanage and enter Shokdey melocho. The committee would visit once a month all workshops, which employed the apprentices, to inquire about their progress. If an apprentice was treated badly by a tradesman, the contract with him would be annulled. If the apprentice was not suited to a given trade he or she would be transferred to an apprenticeship in another trade.

The scheme was supported by the following contributions: support from America, from the Kehila (Jewish council) and membership fees. It was the duty of the members of the board of management to collect the contributions each month. The committee was well organised and worked effectively for a period of some years. Due to the efforts of the activists, the wojewodztwo (governing body of the district) granted an annual subsidy to Shokdey melocho. Street collections and theatre presentations were conducted. Shokdey melocho made considerable advances and became quite popular. People from the neighbouring towns, such as Karelich, Lubch and Selib were sending poor youth to Novogrudok to learn trades. In 1925 the lawyer Gumener arrived in Novogrudok. With his arrival the activities of the organisation had been enlarged. New committee members were attracted and activities were reorganised. A trade school for carpentry and cabinet making was initiated. An instructor from Vilno was hired. Youths aged from 14 to 18 years attended the professional school, obtaining a certification equivalent to the fifth grade of a public school. The course took three years. The main aim of the course was to produce tradesmen with the highest possible qualifications. Sixty four hours were devoted to practical work and a further 32 hours was spent in the workshop. The rest of the course consisted of theoretical studies of literature, geometry, arithmetic etc. Emphasis was placed on the students developing an artistic bent and learning how to draw to enable them to design items of furniture. In time the workshops became known to the entire population of the town, due to the high quality of products made by the workshops.

In 1931, the first exhibition of furniture made at the workshops was held. A big opening ceremony was arranged in the presence of the head of the sub-district administration and a number of officials of the district, including the mayor, Mr Shalit representing YEKAPA of Vilno and Ing. Plebaner of ORT. The exhibition was very successful and attracted the entire population. Many pieces of furniture were sold. The district administration sent a letter of appreciation. The exhibition concluded with a ball, which brought in a considerable return. In 1935 the second exhibition was held under the guidance of the instructor Shniderman. This exhibition was also very successful. All the exhibits and some other pieces of furniture made by the pupils were sold. At the time many institutions in Novogrudok were beset with difficulties. But the trade school and Shokdey melocho were prospering. The progressive intelligentsia was supporting the movement. They were lawyer Gumener, Dr B. Kivelevich, Mirim Ginzburg, A. Izraelit, Ing. Klubok, M. Movshovich, Ch. Delatycki, M. Zyskind, Sh. Solomon, H. Leibovich. In 1936 the Ministry of Commerce and Industry issued a law that each tradesman and apprentice must pass an examination to be permitted to work independently and legally own a workshop. A committee, consisting of tradesmen, was established at Shokdey melocho with the aim of helping young workers to obtain the necessary certificate. Special evening courses were established which were attended by the apprentices, with the objective of obtaining the necessary qualifications to enable them to obtain a certificate. Thus the activists of Shokdey melocho were branching out in the town and the surroundings.

In time many pupils were qualified as tradesmen and many apprentices obtained certificates as qualified workers. But in 1939 the work of Shokdey melocho came to a halt. On the 17 of September the Soviets entered Novogrudok. A delegation from the orphanage and Shokdey melocho visited the executive committee of the town and asked for support for the two organisations. A week later I was asked to see N. Gutertzova, the commissar in charge of education, who appointed me the director of Shokdey melocho and the orphanage. She combined both institutions and ordered us to increase the size of the orphanage. She also ordered that children of all nationalities, including both orphans and the homeless, must be admitted to the orphanage. In a short time, the orphanage housed an extra 220 children. A new orphanage was opened in Kowalewsker Street. I employed a staff of Jewish workers. Jaffe and Erlich were appointed managers in charge of the housekeepers. The work in Shokdey melocho had slowed down, the workshops were empty. There was a shortage of materials. Two months later I was ordered to close the workshops of Shokdey melocho and open a state furniture factory. Various machines were brought into the Reb Yoysl's Yeshiva. All carpenters were registered and worked for the state factory.

Management and the Children of the "Society for Teaching Children a Vocation"

On the 5 January 1940 I was dismissed from my position as the director of the orphanage and was told that I could not be relied upon to bring up the new generation. Things continued in this manner till the 22 June 1941, when the war with Germany began. The German's bombardment of Novogrudok had ruined a large part of the town. The furniture factory, the houses where Shokdey melocho and the orphanage were previously situated were burned. The new building of the orphanage in Kowalewsker St remained intact. The Germans ordered the removal of the Jewish children from the orphanage. By the order of the Judenrat, I together with I. Izraelit removed the children to the house of Israel Delatycki [the family was arrested and deported by the Soviets to Siberia a few weeks previously]. The Judenrat gave them food. But the orphans did not remain alive for long. As is well known, on the 8 December 1941 they put white kerchiefs on the heads of all the girls and took them to the mass grave in Skridlevo.

This was the end of the beloved orphanage and Shokdey melocho, which qualified hundreds of Jewish tradesmen.

Our town was in ruins. The cries of the Jews of Novogrudok were silenced in the four mass graves at four ends of the town. The bubbling life of the Jewish community, together with the institutions of Shokdey melocho and the orphanage were extinguished forever.

[Page 117]

Volunteer Fire brigade

by Arie Shochor (Czarny)

Translated from Yiddish by Oskar Delatycki

My grandfather Leibke Hershl Motkes, whose nickname was "the apple carrier" because he sold apples, was a voluntary fireman. His sons and grandsons also served in the fire brigade. I, Leibke, when I turned 16, ran behind the fire cart, when it was rolled out to attend a fire, and I begged to be taken on as a fireman. I had to wait a few years until my wish was fulfilled and I was taken on as a signalman. My job was to blow a horn all over town when a fire occurred or when the brigade was training. At times I did my job riding on a horse. Later I joined the members of the brigade whose job it was to drag large fire station drums mounted on two wheel trolleys. In that capacity I obtained in time the rank of commander of the trolley pullers. The other commanders were Moishe and Ele Israelit, the sons of Hershl Shimen. As well as the trolley pullers, the fire brigade had two units of firemen, who dragged the water pumps and hoses by hand. There was yet another group of firemen whose job it was to deliver the fire ladders, axes and spare hoses. A horse drawn vehicle was used for this purpose. These firemen would put up the ladders, crawl into the burning buildings and, using their axes, break off the burning planks. They were the most respected members of the fire brigade. They wore brass helmets on their heads. If a fire occurred on a market day, we were allowed to commandeer the farmer's horses.

The members of the fire brigade, almost all Jewish, were utterly devoted to their task, and were proud to be firemen. When summoned in an emergency or for a drill we would turn up clad in our uniforms, which we wore as if it was our Sabbath best. We arranged frequent meetings with the firemen of the neighbouring townships. We felt proud when the Novogrudok brigade was the most efficient in the joint exercises. In 1923 the fire brigade established a brass band. Most members of our family joined the band. My brother was the band leader. Shortly after I made my Alia to Israel. Seven years later, when I returned to visit Novogrudok, the members of the fire brigade arranged a dinner in my honour. We celebrated till midnight. Ten of those present were the grandsons of Leibke Hershl Motkes. Seven of them, praise be to God, survived the Holocaust. Three of us now live in Israel.

Orchestra of the Firemen

[Page 118]

Theatre In Novogrudok

by Zahava Rabinovich-Engel

Translated from Hebrew by Aviva Kamil

I can not recall when the first stage performance of the Novogrudok theatre took place. But two things are firmly engraved in my mind: a) the first play which we staged was titled "The Jewish Heart", b) the people of Novogrudok called our theatre group "triater" [a deliberate distortion of the Yiddish word "te'ater" - the theatre], to indicate how ridiculous, in their opinion, our experiment was.

We did not enjoy this attitude, but it did not weaken our resolve to establish a theatre, perform in it, find an outlet for our theatrical talent and, most important of all, help the needy of our town.

There were many charitable institutions in Novogrudok, but they could not take care of all the needs of the poor amongst us. Conditions worsened as winter approached and many of the town's poor were in need of firewood, clothing and some money to buy matzos. The "mitzvah" of charity at Passover was very important in our town, which was known as the "town of matzos".

July 1928. **Members of the Jewish Theatre.**

The first performance took place in Leizerovski's private home. Its success was obvious, because after a short time we had to find a larger venue. We moved to the "Firemen's Hall". It added to our tasks. Preparations for the evening performance started in the afternoon, all the red firemen's trucks had to be taken out and benches arranged in the hall. Suspense was high and the atmosphere was very much like that of a proper theatre. Interest in the theatre grew.

For the first performances we, the players (we were called "komediantoon" [comedians] by the people of Novogrudok) went from house to house selling tickets, emphasizing the charitable aim of our group as the main motivation.

Later we sold tickets on the premises, and I remember that it was very difficult to buy a ticket for many performances. It became a real theatre, but we remained amateurs and accepted no reward.

Leizer (Eliezer) Rabinovich was our director. He was an amateur and a volunteer. He was also a cantor. Many in town did not look upon it favourably - "should a cantor be connected with a "'triater'"? But many were also against any change in the established order in our town, and many others were unconcerned about any problems of the Jewish community.

It should not be forgotten that the famous yeshiva of Reb Yoyzl [Yosef] was in Novogrudok. The town was a bastion of Jewish orthodoxy. This could have been the reason for the unrest among the youth; we were looking for new activities and spirituality. The cantor, Leizer Rabinovich, always supported the young. He approached his work as a director with great enthusiasm, at times exaggerated. It gave him a lot of satisfaction. Sometimes he was asked to write a piece of music to accompany the play. This pleased him enormously. Once he brought a handwritten play from Warsaw, as yet unpublished--"Der Dorf Yung" [The Village Youth] by L. Kabrin. It impressed him greatly and he wanted us to perform it. We staged it with everyone's help. The artistic and monetary rewards were great. And then came a crisis. We began to regard ourselves as real actors. We demanded that a professional director should be engaged, one who would be able to develop our hidden talents. A director, Madam Domb, was brought from Vilna. She directed the play "The Kreutzer Sonata". Then another director was brought to town. I cannot remember his name.

Not long after, the theatre came to an end. The directors' fees swallowed the income. The main aim of the theatre, which was charity, was forgotten. We matured and the joy of creating the theatre and the charitable ideal evaporated. The group disbanded. Of course there was no shortage of unpleasant incidents, insults and quarrels. The process became tiresome and when it was clear that we could not control it any more, we decided to close.

July 1928. Members of the Jewish Theatre

There were some funny episodes; I would like to relate one of them. It happened after a suspenseful and elated rehearsal. We could not go straight home and went together to the "Shlossbarg" to have fun. Suddenly the policeman, Karshun, appeared, cursing and shouting at us to stop the noise and let decent people sleep. He took down our names and delivered the list to the appropriate authority in order for us to be fined, as the law of the land required. After the intervention of some good souls the "case" was quashed and we were left with pleasant memories.

Here is the list of the amateur actors:

Avraham, Hindl, Sonia ZL* Iviniecki
Yosl Israelit ZL,
Gershonovski ZL,
Itzhak Wolfkind,
Yona Slosberg,
Mania Kivelevich,
Golda, Itzhak Rabinovich,
Chana Shwartz ZL.

[*ZL - zichrono librocho - of blessed memory]

Titles of plays that I remember are: "Jewish Heart", "The Blind Yudeleh", " The Orphan Chasia", "The Unknown", "The Kreutzer Sonata", "Der Dorf Yung".

Many more plays were performed, it was a long time ago and in the meantime... all that is left is to try to remember those distant days in Novogrudok.

[This article describes events that occurred, quite clearly, before the first World War . There certainly was another theatre movement in Novogrudok, which functioned after the First World War . They performed in the old cinema "Pogon" in the market square. There must have been a lot of interest in the theatre, because one can recall many discussions and lively comments after each performance. The word "triater" was still used. The people of our town were nothing if not consistent.]

[Page 119]

Chalutz (Zionist Scout) Movement in Novogrudok

By Yehoshua Brook (Kibbutz Negba)

Translated from Hebrew by Aviva Kamil

Edited by Judy Montel

I can picture in my mind the town of Novogrudok as it was in my early childhood, at the time of the Russian Revolution of 1917 and at the end of World War I , the hard times, the battles raging. I remember very little of the German occupation, but I can recall clearly the battles between the Bolsheviks and the Poles, when the town passed from hand to hand back and forth. Those were anxious days for the Jewish residents of the town. The Jews feared both sides: the Bolsheviks, who considered the Jews to be illicit traders ("speculanty") opposed to the revolution, and the Poles, who proclaimed that all Jews were communists, and thus opposed to the creation of an independent Poland. The Poles would raid Jewish homes to catch youths and force them into the army. The Polish authorities often made public spectacles of catching and publicly flogging innocent Jews. This sowed fear and despair among the Jewish population. Jews suffered no end during the four years of war and were looking forward to peace.

When eventually the Poles took control of the town, life stabilised to an extent and slowly returned to its usual underprivileged existence.

Education

For many years Novogrudok excelled in its religious – Torah - education. The name of the Yeshiva "Beit-Yosef" was famous. An outsider would probably think that the number of Yeshiva students was large, out of proportion to the Jewish population of the town. But hundreds of those students came from the small towns of the district and some came even from large cities. I remember many students; a substantial number of them were lodging with local families. One must not forget that most of the Jewish population of the town was religious, but they were not fanatics and the town was not a perpetual battlefield (as it is sometimes in Israel).

I am a son of a Chasidic family, yet I never felt fanaticism or experienced a rift between the young and old. As to the "mitzvot" (the observance of the religious laws), the conflict between the various factions never reached the level of the present day struggles in Israel.

The Jews were mostly small self-employed shopkeepers and craftsmen. There were few professionals, too few to meet the needs of the town. The town had the now renowned ambience of a "shtetl". The water carriers; I still remember the Jew who carried on his back two buckets of soft water for tea from the cemetery or the spring in Grodno Street. This water was considered especially good. I remember the "balegoles"- the drivers of horses and carts - they must be mentioned too. Things were similar to any small township of those parts.

An important economic support for the town was the village. The Jews waited for the twice-weekly market days, like waiting for the "mashiach" [Messiah].

Apart from the Yeshiva, there was a primary religious school of 4 classes in the Third Lane, (Drite Gesl). I remember three teachers from that school: Gerber, Parnes and Mirski ZL.

When the school was closed down, Gerber and Parnes started their own "cheders". Mirski's home was Zionist and devout. Hebrew was spoken as a matter of course. For us, in those days, it was a wonder to behold.

There was another primary school, which was secular. It was located in the market square, in a building it shared with the Byelorussian high school. The classes were in two shifts: the first shift was the Jewish primary school and the second the Byelorussian high school, where many pupils were Jewish. The Polish high school did not exist at that time.

The primary school was progressive. Religious studies were not a major part of the curriculum. The spoken language was Yiddish, but most books were in Hebrew. Learning Yiddish literature was of particular importance. Our friend David Cohen taught at that school. He still lives with us in Israel and takes an active part in perpetuating the name of Novogrudok.

The Jewish intelligentsia was greatly influenced by the Russian culture. This was particularly noticeable at the beginning of the Polish rule. As usual, snobbishness was evident. All those who spoke Russian saw themselves as the social elite. This trend was evident throughout Polish Byelorussia.

As Polish rule stabilised and Polish schools and cultural centers were established, the influence of the Polish culture increased markedly.

I will not exaggerate when I say, that most of the town's Jews tried to give their children the best education they could afford. I do not remember even one youth who was deprived of education. Of all the teachers in my first years at school I remember two who left a deep impression on me: Peresiecki and Lidski. I think that none of their pupils would forget them. They taught for many years in our town and were experienced in their profession. We learned elementary Jewish subjects: Peresiecki taught Hebrew, Yiddish and History and Lidski taught the Bible.

Members of "Hashomer Hatsair"

The years 1922-23

In the early twenties a wave of political awareness swept the country, which engulfed the Jewish streets of Novogrudok. Parties of all political hues appeared like mushrooms after the rain, and each of them fought for the soul of every Jew in town, especially the young. The "Bund" and the communists excelled in their efforts. The wave which followed the 1917 revolution affected our town, even the religious youths and "Yeshiva" students. The "Bund" was particularly active in trying to reform education and was seeking ways to control this domain.

At the beginning of the 1923 school year the students of the primary school were told that the school would be teaching all subjects in Yiddish, even Jewish history was to be taught using Yiddish books. The students resented this and started to rebel. Those amongst us who supported the retention of Hebrew took that message home to their parents. It became clear that most of the people, even the ones whose Hebrew was only the language of the prayer books, disliked the innovation and wanted Hebrew to be retained in the school.

The arguments went on for two years. Then the Hebrew school "Tarbut" was established, with the help of the central office of the "Tarbut" (culture) movement, and the supporters of the indoctrination of the Hebrew language. The principal of the new school was Koren.

At the same time, compulsory education was introduced by the government. This meant that seven years of primary education would be available free for every boy and girl. The economic situation prevented many from sending their children to "Tarbut", where tuition was paid for by the parents. Therefore, many sent their children to the Polish primary school. Jewish religious study was not part of the state school's curriculum, though it was studied in Jewish schools. Only later was the teacher Bruk, engaged to teach religious studies to the Jewish students of the Polish schools for one or two hours a week.

At this time a Polish high school was founded. This school became over the years one of the best in the region. Many Jewish youths from the town and the district (Karelich, Lubch, Ivie, Selub and others) studied in that school. [In the mid nineteen thirties a limitation (numerus clausus) of 10% was imposed on Jewish enrolment at the Polish high school. At that time 60% of the population of the town was Jewish.] Nonetheless, the number of students attending "Tarbut" was substantial. Many parents preferred their children to learn Hebrew at least at the primary level [Tarbut was a primary school]. It is a matter of pride that the children of the Orphanage studied at that school.

The political life of town

In the early post war years the two anti-Zionist movements - the "Bund" and the Communist party, (the latter was made illegal by the Polish authorities) did not have any serious opposition in the Jewish community. Though most Jews were not supporters of the two parties, the Jewish youth could be influenced by them, especially the younger members of the working-class, who were toiling long hours, fighting for better working conditions and for their very existence.

Political life expressed itself, first of all, by voting in elections, and there were a few of them: for the Polish Sejm, municipality, Jewish community, and the Zionist congress. I was not aware of any active Zionist party, apart from organisations that collected money for Zionist causes. They were represented by people who came from the centre or from Erets-Israel. The party "Poalei-Zion" (the workers of Zion), though it had a lot of sympathisers, did not make an impression on the daily life of the Jewish street.

There was no Zionist body that attracted many youths. I do remember the "Chaluts" movement, to which some young people belonged, but, as I recall, the numbers were small, especially after the crisis and the decline, which followed the end of the "fourth aliyah". Two old Zionist families returned to Novogrudok: Gurevich and Efron. The Gurevich family returned to Erets-Israel with the "fifth aliyah", the Efrons remained in Novogrudok.

I do not remember any extra curricular cultural activities in the early twenties. At that time the "Maccabi" was established and Jewish youth could participate in organised sporting activities. But cultural needs were not catered for. Young people were mostly idle in their free time, they lingered around the market place or the "Shlos-barg", bored. In the summer they walked to the lake for a swim, in winter they went skiing.

The young were thirsty for news. They could pick up some snippets of news in the synagogue. There were always political discussions in Rudnidski's cellar, where soft drinks and ice cream were sold. Newspapers were relatively expensive and not everyone could afford to buy them, but if you passed Michalski's kiosk, you could catch a glimpse of the headlines in the newspapers that were displayed on the front counter.

My story would not be complete if I did not mention the Jewish community library and its head Katrashinski ZL.

Hashomer Hatzair in Novogrudok

The establishment of "Hashomer Hatsair"

One Saturday in the summer of 1927 we were told that an assembly of youth was to take place at the Gordzielovka forest. Only a few knew the purpose of that assembly, but we were starved for things to do and did not ask questions. On the appointed day Jewish youth walked to the forest. I cannot remember who or how many came, but I do remember that the atmosphere was one of unusual curiosity and secrecy.

A member of "Hashomer Hatsair", a "shaliach" (a delegate from Erets Israel) from Baranovich appeared. His name was M. Zuchovicki and he spoke to us in Hebrew. All listened with gaping mouths to every word he uttered. A date was set for the next meeting and the assembly dispersed singing the Socialists Anthem "Tehezakna".

Thus the "Hashomer Hatsair" unit was established in Novogrudok. We still did not know its aims, but the "shaliach", his dress, his manner of speaking, attracted and charmed us from the beginning.

The establishment of the "Hashomer Hatsair" movement in our town was followed by recognisable changes in the conduct of the Jewish youth of the town. It was significant that disparate groups of Jewish youth joined the unit - mostly students, but also some working youths. It was a revolution in those days to bring the two into the one movement. At the head of the unit were Kalman Gordon, Sima Shapiro, Raya Klubok, A.Rakovski, and the leader was the "Tarbut" teacher Piltski, who now lives in Israel.

The organisation of the unit, the division into groups, the activities in the evenings and on Saturdays, the hikes that were held, meetings with units from Baranovich, Lida and other towns, all that brought an atmosphere of activity and interest to the life of the Jewish youth of the town. Only the lack of experienced guides – "madrichim" - prevented a more vigorous growth. At that time the "Young Chaluts" movement was already established in town, it was connected to the general "Chaluts" movement, which was in crisis because of the lack of prospects of early migration to Erets Israel - the "aliyah".

The "Hashomer Hatsair" unit in Novogrudok - as, initially, a scout movement - was approved by the local government as a regional unit that could establish other units in the district without a special permit. Such units were started in Lubch, Zetl, Ivia and other towns. Our activity spread.

Scouting, as the main component of "Hashomer Hatsair" education, constituted the principal attraction for the youth and brought interest to their lives. Youths, who could expect only a depressed life, found their way to the movement and held on to it with great enthusiasm.

One of the elements of the "Hashomer Hatsair" education and its guideline was "rebellion of the sons"- rebellion against the existing traditional life, the boring existence, stagnation and opposition to parents who did not understand their children's desires.

Because of the large number of members who did not know Hebrew, the slogan "learn Hebrew" became one of the important aims of the unit, where all the activities were conducted in Hebrew.

A particular problem in the early period of the movement in Novogrudok, was the relationship between the students and the working youths. Polish high school students considered themselves to be the elite of the youth in town. Work was held in contempt and the workers considered inferior. The threat that a Jewish boy would fail in his studies and become "a cobbler" was still common.

Despite the problems, the work of the unit was expanding, it became an influential body in the Jewish community, and no activity took place without involving the unit. We took part in all Zionist functions in town. For years we were the foremost collectors of the "Blue Box". We were active in the movement "The Working Erets-Israel" (Land of Israel Funds, Chaluts and more). We were responsible for many combined Zionist projects, together with "shlichim" from Erets-Israel or other Zionist centers. We participated in collecting donations, in elections to the Zionist congress and in many other activities.

With the guidance of the cantor, Eliezer Rabinovitch ZL (Menashe Rabina's father) we organised a choir. It became well known in our town, it performed well and with its help many pleasurable Friday evenings ("Oneg-Shabbat") were celebrated. It brought together many Jews who were starved for this kind of activity. Members of the unit looked after the preparations. The camps at "Lag-Ba'omer" were also well known events.

As a legitimate movement we were permitted to organise parades in town. During every festival we congregated in an orderly fashion in the centre of the town and from there marched through the streets of Novogrudok. It was a powerful demonstration and the means of influencing all levels of youth.

"Hashomer-Hatsair" was closely involved in all Zionist activities, including elections to the Zionist Congress, to the city council and other bodies in town. Zionist leaders, who arrived to raise funds or to speak in support of the Zionist cause, always visited the unit for a discussion, for a lecture or just to sing and dance with our members. It seems that the years from 1927 onwards, were the most beautiful years of the Zionist movement in town, especially for the young.

The revolution that "Hashomer-Hatsair" brought to the town - a change in life style - questioning the parent's ideas of what was acceptable, friendship among members of the movement, the awakening of national pride - all that was felt in the town - and despite what people thought of the ideological side of the movement, and objections to it by other circles, all of them had to admit to the benefits which the unit brought about.

The positive attitude to work caused problems for parents, who saw in their son a future "genius" and wanted him to become anything but a tradesman. One incident is memorable; a daughter rebelled against her parents and despite their objections decided to become a shoemaker, she preached to them moral objections to being merchants and of living a life of exploiters. The tension was great and she was forced to leave home. For a few weeks she lived with different members of the unit and in the end she was forced to return home. We came to understand that it was not easy to organise a revolution in the family. It was beyond us to control the destiny of the parent's generation. The revolution could only occur among the young. The daughter eventually went on "Hachshara" and then to Erets-Israel (Rivka Yedidovich).

Erets-Israel was to us, at the beginning, a romantic aim, a dream that we did not know how to fulfill. We had a vision and enthusiasm, but there was no power, which could take advantage of our enthusiasm.

The ideological guidance of the "Hakibbutz-Haartsi" ("Hashomer-Hatsair") was based on three principles: Zionism, Socialism and Communes. The teaching spread by "Hashomer-Hatsair" in the Diaspora followed those guidelines. The time came when every mature member knew that there is no other way but to fulfil the ideal, which meant "Hachshara" and going to Erets-Israel to live on a "Kibbutz".

In the meantime a group of members reached the highest level and became senior members of "Hashomer Hatzair". They had to make one of the most fateful decisions of their lives: to fulfill the ideal and go on Aliyah or to leave the movement. This situation had to be faced by some of the members who studied in the Polish high school or at the Teachers' and Kindergarten Teachers' seminaries in Vilna. They had to address the prospect of discontinuing their studies and going on "Hachshara", which was the necessary step to Aliyah. "Hashomer-Hatsair did not see any alternative for its members but to discontinue their studies. As long as the work in the unit involved every day activities with no future obligations, neither parents nor children interfered with the situation: "let the boys play". The fact is that many parents felt that membership in the movement benefited their children in their studies and well being. Then came the first crisis in the unit. The struggle was hard: many parents did not want their children to remain members of the unit. The excuse was that it interfered with the children's studies. The unit's educators made a special effort to prove them wrong. They maintained that the opposite was true. Some members, out of weakness, surrendered to their parent's wish and left the unit, while others fought tooth and nail to stay.

We had the example of previous "Aliyahs" to Erets-Israel - most of them were students from high-schools and universities - who left their parents' homes and had chosen the new hard way of following their ideal.

Discussions and clarifications went on among the adult members of the unit. It was not easy, and in the meantime the gates to Erets-Israel were closed to "Aliyah".

It was the period of the 1929 riots, the declaration of the "White Paper" by the government of MacDonald and the infamous Passfield laws.

For the first time in the Jewish history of the town, a group of boys and girls went on a one month working–camp ("Moshavah" - settlement). It involved 4 hours of work per day and the rest of the time was taken up by studies and other activities. On the "Moshavah" were the youths from Novogrudok as well as senior members of units from Baranovich, Nesviez, Molchad, Slonim and other towns. The site of the "Moshavah" was 8 km. from Novogrudok on the new road from Novogrudok to Baranovich, which was being built at the time. The contractor was a Jew, who helped us to set up camp. The manager of the "Moshavah" was Piltski, who was assisted by Yaakov Horovits (he is now a member of "Ein-Hachoresh").

I remember an incident: The mother of one of the members was opposed to her son joining the "Moshavah". The son was insisting on staying in the unit. One day his mother came to the camp on foot early in the morning to search for her son and to take him home. The son was hidden, and after a day's search mother left empty handed. But that is not the end of the story. The unit's "madrichim" were students from the Polish high school. Membership in the unit was forbidden by the school. The mother threatened to tell the authorities. After some persuasion, this did not occur and a great harm to the unit was avoided.

In the following year a 3 month summer "Hachshara" was organised during the school holidays. It was an agricultural "Hachsharah" on the farm of a Polish landowner near Nisviez - Lachovich -Baranovich. The proposed task was hard and only a few went. For those who did go it was an unforgettable experience, though working 11-12 hours in the field, for those who were not used to it, was not easy. In the assembly of the senior members of the district a stormy argument erupted between the hesitant and the idealists. The latter visualised a district "Kibbutz" as a first step to "Hachsharah", followed by "Aliyah".

In that period, when "Aliyah" was stopped, arguments were rife in the Jewish communities. There were doubts whether Zionism could fulfil the aim of the gathering of Jewish people in Erets Israel; and if Erets Israel could absorb most of the Jews. This controversy involved our community. Opinions from different sectors of the community were discussed in an assembly. The non-Zionist left was determined to prove that Erets Israel was not capable of absorbing more than half a million Jews. They referred to the Passfield laws and the "White paper". It was particularly difficult to convince people, when the gates of Erets-Israel were closed to "Aliyah". All that occurred, of course, before Hitler's rise to power.

Because of the uncompromising ideal of "Aliyah", it was the duty of every senior member of the unit to belong to "Hachaluts" and participate in the daily work, but they still were free to continue their involvement in units. That brought the different levels of society together and no doubt had a positive effect. When the high school students finished their studies and the moment of decision arrived, many dropped out.

In 1930 the first three senior members went to the "Hachsharah", which was organised by the "Chaluts" (S. Kaminski, Shmuel Dobrin and Yehoshua Bruk). The "Hachsharah" was near Polesie, in one of the big sawmills on the river Horin. But for various reasons that venue had to be abandoned. After staying a month in Baranovich, living on very little and sleeping on benches (they had not a single dime to their name) they were forced to return home. The movement decided that they should join the district group, which was organised at the time.

In 1931 a few members of the unit were asked to go on "Hachshara" with a district group called "Hamefales". The organisation of the venue for the "Hachsharah" was the task of the participants. This proved to be difficult. The search for work included the forest districts of Baranovich, Hancevich and Luniniec, where many sawmills were concentrated. In the event the members from Baranovich, Nisviez and Slonim joined other groups. The group from Novogrudok and the surroundings, which was connected to "Hamefales", was too small. It was hoping to join another group. These changes caused a loss of some members. With no "Aliyah", people started to doubt the merit of continuing. Persistence and patience were needed and the weak dropped out.

From time to time there were some rare possibilities for "Aliyah", through attending the "Eastern fair" and the "Maccabia". Even then it was difficult to arrive in a conventional way. Those were, as a matter of fact, the first attempts to arrange a camouflaged "Aliyah Bet" (illegal entry). This was the way some of our senior members reached Erets Israel. Some others were permitted to come because they were invited by their relatives. Despite the crisis in the Zionist movement caused by closure of the "Aliyah", and the crisis in our unit (many dropped out and some joined the Communist party), it is worth noting that the unit continued to exist and carry out the necessary work. Thanks to the persistence of the remaining senior members the unit was thriving, the youth-groups were strong and guided by good and experienced "madrichim".

The second group of senior members from the district - "Plugat-Atid", also had to confront the decision of joining the Aliyah. In time, they established "Kibbutz Masad" (today Kibbutz Eilon in west Galilee).

The third group of senior members "Baderech" worked within the movement. They formed Kibbutz Hachsharah "Achavah". Today part of this group is in Kibbutz Dan in Upper Galilee and the others in Kibbutz Eilon.

In 1932 "Hashomer Hatsair" decided that the first group of senior members from Novogrudok, "Alizim", would join Kibbutz "Volyn B" which was the district kibbutz of Volyn. It was sent on "Hachsharah" to Chelm and later to Rovno. The conditions in the "Hachsharot" were very hard; lack of money, appalling accommodation, sleeping on benches in crowded rooms, and the very bad supply of life's necessities. There was unemployment, and if some work was found, it was not enough to better the conditions. It is difficult for us today to understand the situation at the time. It is possible that training of young Jews, mostly town's people, to the hard life awaiting them in Erets-Israel, demanded those preparations. After 1933 a considerable change occurred. The "Chaluts" organisation realised that for a prolonged "Hachsharah" better conditions were required: improved accommodation, sleeping arrangements, food and health care. There were also those who were ready to go on "Aliyah", but the long stay on "Hachsharah" weakened them and they needed "recuperation". Special accommodation was built for that purpose near Warsaw.

The closure of "Aliyah" influenced the mood of the movement. With no prospect to go to Erets Israel soon, members changed their plans and sometimes left "Hachaluts". We felt that the situation would be completely different if prospects for speedy departure were better.

In 1933 the senior members of the group "Baderech" went on "Hachsharah", first to one of the big farms near Novogrudok to do agricultural work. After a "Hachsharah" centre was established in town. Accommodation was found with a Tatar family near the football ground, not far from the Jewish cemetery. For the Jewish residents of the town, it was an unusual scene to see Jewish youths doing jobs like felling trees and cleaning the town's square. And, surprisingly, girls took part in the activities too.

The market square, after two market days a week, had to be thoroughly cleaned. Scores of workers (non Jews) were employed by the municipality to do this work. No one thought that Jews would do it. And here was a group of boys and girls from "good families" that demanded this work and fought for it. It was not easy. With the help of the deputy mayor, our friend Avraham Ostashinski, we managed to get the job. Those days (and nights) are well remembered, when the town's people looked with curiosity on the young boys and girls sweeping the market place.

At that time, the task of education in the unit passed to the third group of senior members, the group "Baderech". The rest of the members of "Mefales" and "The Future" later joined the Slonim "Hachsharah". That "Hachsharah" was more stable.

In the same year the writer of this article returned from the "Hachsharah", which lasted, with a few intervals, two and a half years, to prepare for "Aliyah". And in the meantime he started to work again in the unit and in the "Chaluts".

A club named after Haim Arlozorov was established as a joint initiative of the senior members of the unit and the members of the "Chaluts", in the building that once was the "Tarbut" school. The club was opened every evening and many kinds of printed matter could be found there: daily news in Yiddish, weeklies, monthlies and publications from Erets-Israel. The club was of considerable importance. Youths and adults could read a paper or a book, play games and avoid boredom.

In 1934 the writer left for Erets-Israel. A very interesting period in Novogrudok, in "Hashomer-Hatsair" and "Hachaluts" came to an end. With a great deal of interest I followed the happenings in Novogrudok from Erets-Israel.

With the eruption of 1936 riots "Aliyah" was almost completely stopped, and members of the movement were detained in Poland. Their prospects of "Aliyah" had become very slight. At the same time, changes occurred in the structure of the Kibbutzim in Erets-Israel. In the Diaspora the number of members in the "Hachsharah" of every Kibbutz was high, because inevitable rejections and dropouts were unavoidable.

Few people were allowed to come by the "Aliyah". When the early groups arrived they established independent kibbutzim. They were initially temporary kibbutzim, usually in existing "Moshavot". They kept in close contact with their members in Poland, who were sitting on their suitcases waiting for "Aliyah".

In 1939 I had the chance to visit Poland and my home town- Novogrudok. It was an unforgettable event in my life. It was a period of political upheaval in Europe, with the threat of Hitler to Danzig and Poland. We were a small group of kibbutz members on a ship. We had a good time, with our friend Klavoriski ZL. Then we heard the rumour that Fascist Germany had invaded Danzig. We decided that if this rumour was true we would turn back to Erets-Israel the moment we arrived in Constance. On our arrival we found that the rumour was false, but the tension was great and the atmosphere electrified. Fearfully we continued our journey to Poland.

When I arrived, after an absence of 5 years, to the town where I had spent 22 years of my life, I found a great change. Anti-Semitism was rife. The Poles were never friendly and the Polish youths were permeated with virulent hatred of Jews. Jewish residents told me that a short time ago they could not go out at night for 5 weeks because of Polish hooligans in the streets. There was encouraging news of Jewish self-defense. The economic situation had changed too. The local peasants (mostly Byelorussian) were no longer trading with Jews. They used other outlets such as stores, credit institutions, rural banks etc. They were not dependent on Jewish traders. [These may have been the plans for the future, in 1939 the poverty was due to the disastrous ineptitude and anti-Semitism of the Polish government]. Making a living became harder for the Jews; the rug was pulled from under their feet.

Among the youths I found frustration and despair. The atmosphere was saturated with gunpowder from Germany and the unlimited hatred by the Polish population. My friends and acquaintances were astonished that I visited Poland at such an awful time. You could sense danger in the air. I wanted to return to Erets-Israel as soon as possible. My parents pleaded with me to stay longer. Disquiet enveloped me even more. News from Erets-Israel was of bloody riots. My kibbutz went to settle a place in the south called "Negba". I was cruel to my parents by my reluctance to stay longer, but I had the feeling that I should not extend my stay. Two weeks before the eruption of World War II I returned to Erets-Israel.

Whilst I was still in Novogrudok, the members of the unit kept asking me what they should do. There was no "Aliyah". Many people wanted to leave Europe. "Aliyah Bet" was active in Poland, but in those days there was little they could do. I knew that it was difficult. I advised them to be as active as they could, and not to accept that they had to stay there. I had a subconscious feeling of dread of the future. Like anyone else, I had friends and relatives, I feared for their future. I knew that I could not save them.

With the outbreak of Wold War II the doors were closed. With fear and painful longing I followed the events in the town and the fate of my dear family and friends. I still remember the few words that my dear mother wrote to me when the town was held by the Soviets: "for the first time in my life I have to admit that you were right, I thank God that you did not listen to me when I pleaded with you to stay longer, I am happy that you did get away." She still did not know what the cruel future was preparing for them and what fate was awaiting them from the hands of the monstrous Nazis.

So was lost forever the old, rooted Jewish settlement in Novogrudok and its fertile life. A small group was saved from the Nazis, thanks to the partisans who fought, defending their souls and their honour. [It was estimated that 10% of the population of Novogrudok was saved by joining the partisan movement. This was not a "small group" by any measure.]

In 1946 I came as a "Shaliach" to the refugee camps in Germany. Among other things I took it upon myself to trace the survivors from Novogrudok who roamed the sad roads of the European Diaspora. I met some of them in camp Foehrenwald. I found among them members of our movement. In time I met more people from my hometown. In Munich I met Nachman Kirsner, who studied opera singing with a German musician. I think that he is a cantor now in the U.S.A. I received messages about other survivors in West Germany as well as Austria. I am sorry to say that some of them subsequently left Israel. I met Raya Klubok. Sima Portnoy is with us today. I was for some time in the "Ashuga" camp (a refugees camp near Kassel) with my neighbour from Novogrudok, Liza Shwartz and the youngest son of the family Zeshukovski from Koscielna Street. I was glad to meet these people, but it was with mixed feelings of pain and sorrow to know of the hell that they went through and that so few survived.

Activists of "Keren Kayemeth" (LeYisrael)

Often I have a feeling of guilt. Could more people from my hometown have been saved and brought to Erets Israel, as they were saved from other towns? And more: when you look around you and you see many people from your home town that are working in industry and in the kibbutzim (Negba, Eilon, Dan and I think a few in the "Kibbutz Hameuchhad" kibbutzim) and some work in the professions, then you have a pleasant feeling, you feel good.

Having been brought up in "Hashomer Hatsair", I am proud that the time we invested in our work in the unit in Novogrudok was not in vain. A good many of the "Hashomer Hatsair" youths of Novogrudok came to Erets Israel. They preserved the values of our movement. They remembered its aims and the call to create Zionist Socialist Pioneering.

> [This is a narrative of a life devoted to Hashomer-Hatsair and Erets Israel. We hope to add translations of stories of other people and other movements, which also played vital parts in the existence of Novogrudok.]

[Page 126]

Personalities

by Shmuel Openhim

Translated from Yiddish by O. Delatycki

Missis Charne Pressman

Her husband, Asher Pressman was brought to Novogrudok to serve as the head bookkeeper of the Tradesmen and Shopkeepers bank. He was a general Zionist of the Grinbaum kind. She quickly acclimatised in the town and became indistinguishable from a native. She dashed in to communal work, she participated in Zionist work, she led the VICO, gathered money for Keren Kayemet. She was the centre of the Zionist activities of the town. Her house was the location of all Zionist committee meetings, preparation of all Zionist activities, collection of money from Keren Kayemet boxes, she was the leader of Chaluts Baalei Melocho. Zionist work was the main reason for the existence of Mrs Pressman, regardless of the fact that she was not a well woman. Her Zionist work was supported by Avrom Ostashinski. He was the representative of Zionism and she did all the underlying work. She was the actual leader behind the curtains. No task was too difficult for her. She died before the commencement of the war.

Lawyer Eliahu Gumener

Lawyer Gumener was killed by the Nazi assassins in Dvorets. He came to Novogrudok after the First World War and had rapidly become an indispensable activist in the community. He was a typical Jewish man of action. He took charge of a number of institutions. He was particularly interested in the orphanage, of which he was a chairman of the committee of management. There was practically no gathering in which he would not participated actively, other than in Zionist affairs, because he was a member of the leftist workers movement, a follower of Noyach Pryslicki.

Attorney Eliyahu Gumener   **Shmuel Solomon**

Salomon

He was killed by the Nazi beasts on the 26 July 1941 in the Market place, in a group of 52 Jews [50 Jews were picked at random for execution. Yehuda Slutzki in "p.257 The Fifty Two Martyrs" writes that Salomon and one other were not selected, but tried to escape and were caught and killed]. He came to Novogrudok after the First Wold War, the former principal of the Yiddish school of Cadic Yud Shin Alef, which existed for a few years. He participated in communal work, was represented and participated on many bodies and took active part in numerous meetings. He produced many plays and spectacles, which served to augment the budgets of the organisations. He was for a time an alderman in the city council.

Itzchok Izik Kohen

Kohen lived in Slobodke on the fringe of Novogrudok. He was killed by the Germans in the first slaughter. He owned a flour mill. He lived in Slobodke, but he kept a sharp eye on all that has happened in town. Though he did not belong to any organisations, he was of more assistance to them than many members. He knew of institutions and individuals who were in financial difficulties. The first person to turn to for help was Itzchok Izik. Prior to a holiday, particularly Passover, he would provide the needy with flour, produce and also cash. This was a Jew who held his hand in his pocket for all institutions and the needy. All one had to do is to approach him and he would distribute sizable donations without ever asking for whom the money is intended. For him it was adequate to know that a Jew of Novogrudok is asking a donation for someone. Even when the Nazis were in town was he distributing among the needy flower and produce. No Jew who approached him was ever disappointed.

[Page 127]

Meir Aicher, Gershon Ziskind and Judl Bloch

All of the above were killed by the Nazis in the first slaughter. They were all connected with the loan fund which was distributing interest free loans, returnable in small repayments. This was of enormous assistance to the small artisan and small merchant, who would borrow 100 zloty. That would assist him. The three members of the loan fund were always acting in unison, as if they were bound to each other. Most of the Jews raised their income on market days – Mondays and Thursdays. On Sundays and Wednesday afternoons the loan fund was functioning in the Harkavy's kloyz [small synagogue]. I lived close to the synagogue and I never noticed that one of them was ever absent when the fund was opened, unless he was unwell or has gone to another town.

Jankef Lubchansky

He died in Siberia, where he was sent by the Soviets, where he wad deported in 1941, prior to the Soviet-German war. He formed after the first World War the union of Jewish craftsmen, the people's bank of craftsman and small businessman and was the head of both institutions. He was represented in almost all institutions and establishments. He was closely connected with his creations and they often called them Lubchanski's union of craftsmen or Lubchanski's bank. He had many opponents, some political others in business. At the end he was defeated by the opponents and he was pushed aside. That brought him a lot of suffering, because he was used to communal work.

Notke Zubarsky

He owned a sheet iron workshop. He died after the liberation in 1964. He was active in community organizations, particularly in the craftsmen association, he was a member of the Jewish community council, the council of the Jewish hospital, the committee of the old people's home etc. He was devoted to community work.

Notke Sucharsky

Shmuel Kantorovich

He died in 1938. He suffered of ill health, but this did not prevent him from participating in community work. He was one of the key personalities of Shogdey melocho and other organisations. He was a carpenter. He was not well of.

Chasan Eliezer Rabinovich, Cantor and teacher

He was killed by the Nazis in the first slaughter. He was an active, devoted Mizrachi Zionist. He took part in all Zionist activities. He was a member of many institutions. He provided invaluable assistance to the old people's home after the Nazis occupied Novogrudok. The old people's home was destroyed in the first bombardment. The old people who survived the bombardment were placed in the Harkavy synagogue. At that time it was difficult to look after one self. Walking in the streets was dangerous. It was almost impossible to manage any institutions. Nevertheless Rabinovich made it his task to look after old, unwell survivors of the old people's home. He managed to come frequently and brought them some food which he managed to scrounge. I lived at the time close to Harkavy's synagogue and Rabinovich would drop in occasionally. His optimism was infectious and he involved me in the task of helping the sick, helpless old people.

Dovid Cohen

Born in Slabodka, was born in Slabodka, near Novogrudok, in 1892. Dovid Cohen was from an early age interested in folklore and Hasidic stories. As a young man he published these stories in the Yiddish newspapers. In 1924 he joined the Chalutz movement and emigrated to Palestine.

Influenced by Berl Katzenelson, Dovid Cohen was among those who founded the Working Youth organization and accompanied it from its first steps through all the settling and organizing stages. All his life was dedicated to the Working Youth. His family understood of his activities by being patient, they faithfully shared his holy work among the youth.

In his literary book <u>My House among the Young</u> Dovid Cohen's profound value for the love of others is revealed. Also revealed is his special affection for the young generation, in which he saw warmth, purity and the goodness. Dovid was a real artist in telling stories and legends. In later life he was a member of the manager of the organization of those in Israel who originated from Novogrudok, and he contributed to consolidating and strengthening the Novogrudok organization.

[Page 128]

Photographer Yankef Vinnick

He was killed by the Nazis in Zetl in 1942. He was a dedicated Zionist, a devoted worker in community organisations and actively participated in the work of many institutions. He was for many years the chairman of the craftsmen association. He was a representative of the Jewish community in contacts with the authorities. He was often heading delegations, which represented the Jewish community in negotiations with the wojewoda (head of the district). Many meetings, both Zionist and general) were held in his house.

Photographer Moshe Shimanovich

He was killed by the Nazis in the first slaughter. He was a personality. A man of great general knowledge. One could speak with him on many subjects, in which he participated willingly. He was fully committed to his work in various Jewish institutions. Whenever one would visit him one was likely to find in his home members of the Jewish intelligentsia. The discussions were on local and international subjects.

Dovid Ziskind and Mojshe Brojdo

The owned a wholesale grain and flour store. They died in Siberia where they were deported on the eave of the German invasion in 1941 [they died when the soviet-German war started, in an echelon of prisoners on the way from Novogrudok to Saratov]. Dovid Ziskind was the chairman of the Jewish contingent of deputies in the city administration. He participated in a number of communal institutions. Was on the board of management of the Jewish hospital, old people's home, businessman association etc. Mojshe Brojdo was a devoted communal worker. He was an active participant in the work of many institutions, specifically Jewish cultural institutions. The house of Brojdo and Ziskind was the best known in town. People would come there on all manner of errands, both Zionist and not Zionist activities, institutions and when collecting money for the poor. They were always generous. They never refused anyone.

Family Kaplinski

They were owners of forests and had a timber yard. Hershl Kaplinski is in Israel and lives in Bat Yam. Refuel Kaplinski was killed in the second slaughter in August 1942. Both brothers were active social workers. They were represented in many institutions. Refuel Kaplinski was on the committee of the Hebrew Tarbut school and actively participated in the construction of the Tarbut school building. They were the first participants in all actions in town both Zionist and not Zionist. They were always ready to help out with a donation for the needy. They gave generously. No one was refused help.

Zeidl Bushelevich

He was killed by the Nazis. He was the editor of the Jewish weekly newspaper "Navaredker leben". He was devoted to his work for the newspaper. He was not only the editor but also the administrator. He would collect subscriptions, advertisements, births and deaths announcements. He would go around collecting money. He would write assiduously for the paper and encourage others to do it. He would participate in printing of the paper. The paper would appear regularly on time. He was preoccupied with the production of the paper and had no time for other activities.

Zeidel Buselevitch

[Page 129]

The Last of the Rabbis

by Yehoshua Yaffe

Translated from Hebrew by Aviva Kamil

Rabbi Meirovich

On a bright day in the twenties, when I was of school age, I, together with many Jews, went outside the town to welcome our new Rabbi, Reb Meir Meirovich, who previously was the rabbi of Swencian (Swienciany, Svencionys). We took him to the great synagogue with a grand ceremonial where he gave his first "Drasha" and became our Rabbi. He was called "The Swencianer Rabbi" and he quarreled constantly with the "Lubcher Rabbi" (who's previous position was that of the Rabbi of Lubch, a town near Novogrudok). The Chasidim maintained that the Lubcher Rabbi was appointed to be the Rabbi of the town, and that was the reason for the quarrel.

The Polish authority recognised Rabbi Meirovich as the town's Rabbi. He was a studious Jew, erudite in all Jewish subjects; he was a "Maskil" as well, soundly educated in German philosophy and literature. In his speeches he used to mention the names of German classics, mainly those of Goethe. He was a Zionist and fought for the Zionist's cause in town; he was also one of the leaders of the "Mizrachi" in Poland. The Chasidim called him the "Zionistisher Rav". He was proud of the fact that he could exhort Zionists' ideals in the Jewish town. Later on when he was very old and frail, when Hitler came to power and anti-Semitism grew in Poland, he anticipated the coming catastrophe and urged the Jewish youth to go to Eretz-Israel. He did not care if they were religious or "Hashomer-Hatzair", the main thing was to go to Eretz-Israel and there one could decide how to live. In his "Drashot" (speeches) to "Agudat-Israel" he argued: "go to Eretz-Israel first, there you could try to influence the non-believers"...

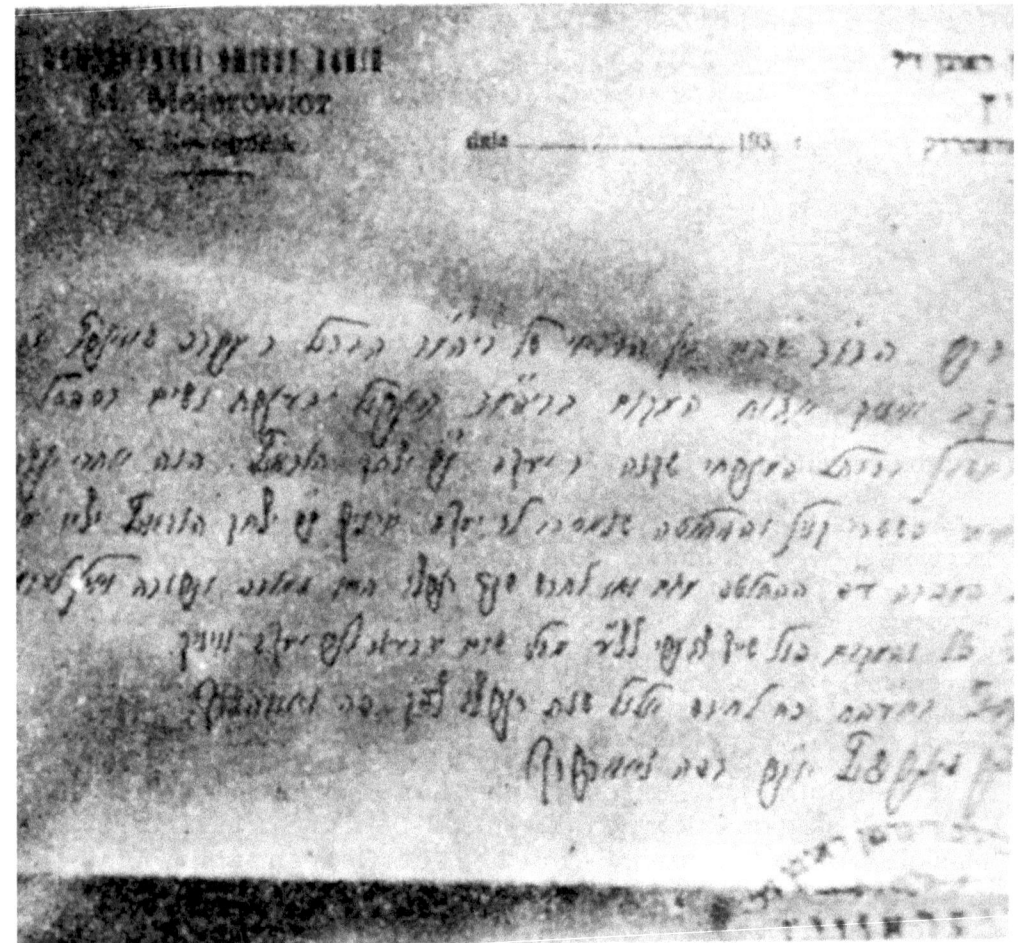

Hand written document from Rabbi Meirovitz

He asked the Polish government to make concessions for the Jews who wanted to go to Eretz-Israel.

In the beginning the dispute between the Rabbis was bitter, a small group of zealot Chasidim and the people of Shlas-Gass (Castle Street) led a strong conflict against the "Zionist Rabbi", but over a period of time the town became a Zionist town, and the sons of the Chasidim "saru miderech hayashar" (left the path of righteousness). The sons of the people of Shlas Gass joined the Zionists of the town, and some of them went to Eretz-Israel. The quarrel between the rabbis weakened and the virtues of Rabbi Meirovich were acknowledged by all in Novogrudok; even the people who disputed his ideas revered him. He died at an old age shortly before World War II.

Rabbi Abovitz

In the 1920's, when the rabbinical seat of Novogrudok became vacant, Rabbi Meir Abovich offered the rabbinical seat of Lubch (which he occupied at the time) to his son in law, Rabbi Weis, and appointed himself the Rabbi of Novogrudok. Most members of the community did not consider it appropriate that the Rabbi of Lubch should inherit the seat of such famous rabbis as Reb Yitzchak Alchanan, and Reb Yechiel Michel Halevi Epstein.

Rabbi Abovich directed the small yeshiva in town, which taught 80-100 pupils. He managed also the "Talmud-Torah", which had three classes and prepared gifted pupils for the Yeshiva. The pupils of the "Talmud-Torah" were mainly poor and their number was small. Among the followers of Rabbi Abovich were the students from the big Yeshiva, which was known as the Reb Yozl Yeshiva. Rabbi Abovich was the head of the committee for the Yeshivas of Novogrudok. Basically it was a bastion of "Agudat-Israel", which conducted a war against Zionism and Eretz-Israel. The rabbi controlled the distribution of yeast and the wives of his followers bought the yeast for Chalot from the Rabanit (rebetzen - wife of the rabbi). Rabbi Abovich was a tall man with an imposing face and a beautiful beard. He was harsh in his rulings, while Rabbi Meirovich was lenient. His son, Yaakov Abovich, did not follow in his father's footsteps; he wanted to study and became a grain merchant in town. Rabbi Abovich died a natural death before the outbreak of World War II.

[Page 130]

People and Images

by Yehoshua Yaffe

Translated from Yiddish by O. Delatycki

Harav Nachemie

In the Hegdish lane, in a small house with narrow windows lived Reb Nachemie, the town's Magid [preacher]. In his youth he was a student at a Talmid Torah. Every Sabbath and Friday night he would pray ain-Jakov in the Katzev [butcher] synagogue. Later he became the town's Magid. In the morning, after shachres, he would teach a 'blat Gemore' [a page from the Gemorah] at the Katzev synagogue and in the evenings, between Mincha and Miriv, he would teach the common folk a chapter of mishnayes and ain-Jakov.

He knew much of midrash and Hagadah. He was liked by the whole town, particularly by the tradesmen, who were busy the whole week, but in the evenings and on Sabbath they used to join him at his table to listen to his stories or hear readings from the books by pious men of the present and from the past or a chapter of the Chumesh with commentaries. He taught people who were not highly educated. They understood him and were pleased with his efforts. On returning home they retold his stories to their wives and they were well received. The tales eased their hard, monotonous lives. Nachemie would also deliver hespeds [funeral orations]. If some one died, the body would be brought to the synagogue square and put on a table in front of the Todres synagogue. Nachamie would deliver the hesped. He did not have to prepare himself to deliver it. He had the orations well prepared in advance. When he was told that such and such died he would find on the spot something suitable for the occasion. All his life he was learning midroshim and he would pass them on to the people. He did not participate in divisions and altercations. He was a quite man and lived in peace with everyone. He died in the 1930's, and with him died the last magid and hesped speaker in Novogrudok.

Reb Benjomin Chaim Gordon

Reb Benjomin Chaim Gordon or Reb Benjomin Chaim of Wojce, as he was sometimes known, was the miller in the village of Wojce. When he became old he moved to Novogrudok. He had a nice home built on the Zamok mound, where he lived with his family. He was a good Jew, quite and calm. He prayed in the Mitaskim synagogue, where he was the gabi. He was a good student of the Torah. In the evenings at

Mincha or Miriv he would read to the congregation 'a page of Gemorah'. He also attracted an audience on Friday evenings in the winter, when he read the Chumash. Most of the listeners were tradesmen and shopkeepers. Some enjoyed the stories he would tell about the forefathers. Others used the opportunity to catch a nap. After the reading of the Chumash, religious tunes were sung. And that was a good beginning to the Sabbath. Leibe the verger of the Mitaskim synagogue was waiting for the start of singing after the Chumash. He was a tall, thin man, with a thin white beard. He had a torn, squeaky voice and as he chanted 'Yismechu bi malchutcha' all present would burst out laughing.

Reb Benjomin's son Mojshe sold flour. He was the cantor at the Mitaskim synagogue. He had a thin, ringing tenor voice, and he was one of the best cantors in Novogrudok. Reb Benjomin's grandchildren studied at a university and were members of the Novogrudok intelligentsia.

Reb Fivel (Leib) Nikolayevsky and his son Bezalel

Reb Nachamie was the gabi of the Katzevs [Butchers] synagogue, and when he died Reb Fivel became the gabi. Early, before the first minyan [session], he read 'a page of Gemorah' for those assembled. He was learned in shas and psukim and could have been a qualified rabbi, should he have wanted. He was a wealthy man. Together with his two sons he dealt in oakum and tow and he had an adequate income. When he became old he transferred his business to his sons and devoted all his time to study. He would also read a 'page of Gemorah' as well as pray Mincha and Mirev in the big synagogue. His family was devoted to Zionism. His son Bezalel was one of the Zionist leaders in town. It was the son's influence that made Reb Fivel a dedicated Zionist and the father saw to it that his son would remain religious. Bezalel prayed not only in the big synagogue but also in the Katzevs synagogue, where he was a cantor.

Bezalel Nikolayevski was one of the organisers of the Zionist movement in town. He was one of the leaders of Keren Kayemet and Keren Hayisod. He was also a member of the committee of the Tarbut school as well as a member of various cultural and social organisations. After the Soviets arrived in Novogrudok Bezalel was in charge of an organisation purchasing oakum and tow. However, he was arrested for participating in Zionist organizations and kept in Soviet jails. He never returned from his confinement.

Sender Kagan

Sender was a tall youth bent as a lulav (branch of a palm tree). He wore glasses – pence-nez – which kept falling off his nose. He studied at the yeshiva and completed his learning by self education. He married in Novogrudok and had a shop in the rad kromen [row of shops, which used to be the Radziwil's stables, in the centre of the market place before they were converted in 1833 into several dozens of narrow shops selling a wide variety of goods]. He lived in Sieniezyc street in a small wooden house.

When we established in 1934 the Ha chaluts ha Mizrachi in Novogrudok he became one of its members. He put his small house at our disposal for meetings. We used the accommodation to conduct cultural work. He wrote philosophical dissertations for our weekly newspaper. Once a month he would lock up the shop in the middle of the day and would collect money for Keren Kayemet. The pleadings of his wife were to no avail. He would tell her: 'For Eretz Isroel I would give my life, not just my small shop'. He read and wrote a lot on philosophical subjects, but his manuscripts were never published. In 1940 the Soviets accused him of illegal trading and jailed him for 5 years. He was never seen again.

Reb Shloime Efron

He was a wealthy man, among the best respected in Novogrudok. He was a learned man, a maskil and an activist. He was the head of the local Mizrachi in Novogrudok. He fought for Zionism and loved Eretz Isroel. He visited Eretz Israel twice and with each journey his love for Israel grew. He was a good and whole hearted Jew. He supported the poor as well as all Jewish institutions in town. All his family were supporters of various branches of Zionism: Mizrachi, General Zionists, Frihite (Freedom) and Hashomer Hatzayir and even Betar.

His children were always arguing among themselves, and their voices could be heard in the street. He was a lively, impulsive, stormy person in the street and in the synagogue. Everywhere and always he campaigned for Israel. He spoke from his heart, with all his soul. In his last years his business was conducted by his children and his wife. His time was taken up in his work for Israel. When the Soviets came they arrested his son Benjomin, who was an ardent member of Betar. Before the outbreak of the German-Soviet war the whole family was sent to the remote regions of the Soviet Union. He died there.

Reb Avrom Yaffe

My father Reb Avrom Yaffe was born in Novogrudok in 1885. My grandfather, Reb Dov was a man of the book, a fanatically pious and sincere Jew who brought up his children in the spirit of devotion. My father studied at the Mir yeshiva and later studied Russian and secular subjects. He was close to the Tivat Zion [love of Zion] movement. During the 1905 revolution he got closer to socialism, but not of the revolutionary kind. He was always opposed to dictatorships. He was preaching the 'vahavta leriecha amocha lo talian shachar sachir otcha ad boker'.

After the socialist revolution of 1917, when the EvSeks [members of EvSec, which stands for Evreyskaya Sekcia- Jewish Section of the Communist Party] were murdering and terrorising the Jewish population and religion and Zionism were prohibited in Soviet Russia, he joined a Zionist organisation. Since than he advocated that the only salvation for the Jewish people was Eretz Israel. He lived his entire life in need and survived on the income from a small food shop. He gave his children a religious Zionist upbringing. He was a communal worker. He was for many years the gabi of the Katzev's [butcher's] synagogue and influenced all who attended there to become Zionists. He was an active member of Mizrachi and on the committee of Keren Kayemet and Keren Hayisod. He was on the committee of the Tarbut school, where his daughter Dvoira was a pupil. He also supported and helped to collect money for the small yeshiva and he also sat in Vad Hayeshivot. He fought the pious fanatics, who opposed the Zionist movement, and tried to induce in the religious populace the spirit of Zionism. If a magid (preacher) or a courier arrived in town, father would endeavour to meet him. He would lock up the shop in the middle of the day and go with the magid to collect money for whatever purpose the magid came to town for. He was the secretary of the businessmen's union in Novogrudok for 15 years. He was an adherent of Harav Mayerovich, who was the Zionist rabbi and kept in contact with Harav Abovich and did much to reduce the tension between Aguda and Mizrachi in Novogrudok. In the last years before the war, as Polish anti-Semitism had become stronger, he worked with Jewish youth to persuade them to go to Israel because the future in Poland was not at all certain. He sent his oldest son, Moshe Zvi on Hachshara of Hachluts Mizrachi. Moshe went to Israel in 1939. In 1940 [1939?], when the Soviets arrived in Novogrudok he wept. He kept saying 'now we are lost, we will be isolated from the rest of the world and we will not be able to go to Israel'.

When in 1941, when the Germans bombarded Novogrudok and burned down most of the town, he separated himself and read Tfilim the whole day. 'The end is near', he kept saying, 'we sinned too much'. Eighteens of Kislev Taf Shin Alef [8 December 1941] they took him to the slaughter together with my mother Rivke Leye, a quite, good and pious woman and their only daughter Dvoire who was then 14 years old. We, the three brothers remained alive. We also survived the second slaughter. During the third slaughter of the 2nd of February 1943 my brother Jankef Yehuda Jaffe was killed, a quiet man, a good mechanic. God will punish them for our blood.

Doctors Menuche and Shimon Kaminiecki

There were two dentists in Novogrudok: Dr Shimon on one side of the market square, close to the Yiddish street and doctor Kaminski on the other side of the market square next to Grodno street. [this is not correct: Shimon and Menucha Kaminiecki's practice was right next to Grodno street and there were other dentists in Novogrudok]. I knew the father of Dr Kaminiecki, who lived on the second floor together with his daughter Petie, the milliner. He was a pious Jew, but not a fanatic. He provided a good education for his children and his son was, as was said, a dentist. But as to the knowledge and study of Judaism he had no pleasure out of his son, the dentist. 'He is totally non-Jewish' his father used to say. Dr Kaminiecki was a Yidishist [a movement which favoured the use of the Yidddish tongue, as opposed to Hebrew]. His children studied at the Polish gimnazjum [high school] and they too were remote from national Judaism. And yet they were good Jews and were known as generous contributors to Jewish charities. They contributed to every cause including the Yeshivas.

On two occasions the family Kaminiecki showed that they were true Jews. Once, when the younger son reached Bar Mitzvah, his grandfather bought him a set of Tfilim. He learned about Judaism, knew about the exodus from Egypt, and about the Land of Israel. He knew about the banishment from the Holly Land. He was also told about anti-Semitism in Poland, which was also a punishment from G-d [it seems surprising that he had to be told of anti-Semitism, which was all around him]. A Jew is born a Jew and must die a Jew, whether he liked it or not. A nation must not be allowed to assimilate, and the best proof was Hitler, who came at that time to power in Germany. The boy experienced anti-Semitism in the Polish school and decided to become a pious Jew. He came home and gave an ultimatum to his parents: 'either you will live as complete Jews, the house must become kosher, you must not work on the Sabbath, or I will leave the house'. The parents complied. The un-kosher dishes were thrown out, they bought new dishes and the house was made kosher. This, however, did not last long. The boy studied in the Polish school. He had to go to school on the Sabbath. For a few weeks he did not write on the Sabbath, but after a while he started writing again. And his period of piousness came to an end.

The second time Dr Kaminiecki was reminded of his Jewishness was when the Germans entered Novogrudok. Our house burned down during the German bombing raids and Kaminiecki gave us a room in his house. It is then that I found out about Kaminiecki the man. Kaminiecki fell ill and he lost a lag. His older son was killed in the Polish-German war. His younger son studied in France, he married a French woman and came to visit his parents. On their way the war started and they could not return to France. Her husband went to the front and never came back and she remained as Ruth Hammurabit with her Jewish in-laws. The Germans considered her to be a Jewess. She was killed with her in-laws in the second slaughter in August 1942.

During the German occupation Dr Kaminiecki was morally depressed. He was disenchanted with his socialist, assimilationist views, the friendship among nations, the unity among the nations etc. When the Soviets arrived in Novogrudok he found a solution for the Jewish nation. Let's intermingle with the Soviet people – he advocated. And after this disappointment, the cultured German nation was eradicating Jews.

Through his window onto the market place he saw how the Germans had arranged 50 Jews in 5 rows of 10 plus two 2 members of the Judenrat and killed them all. They were not human.

He was moving on his one leg from one room to another and could not rest. He was broken morally and was regretting his past beliefs. He regretted that he fought against Israel and Zionism. He regretted that he had denied the existence and future of the Jewish nation. He took the Tilim and started saying: 'blessed is the man who did not follow in the steps of the assassins'. 'I did everything in the opposite way' – he began crying and he gave me back the Tfilim, 'in my dirty hands I dare not hold such a holy book' he told me. 'but if there is a G-d' he looked up 'I ask him for vengeance, from the depth of my heart. I ask for vengeance for our innocently spilled blood. And perhaps there will be someone who will survive. He must tell the future generations about us, about our inhuman suffering and awful death'.

Reb Aren Dovid who was blind in one eye

Reb Aron Dovid was a tall Jew who was blind in one eye. He was quite old. When he was younger, he was a teacher in the Talmud Torah. Later, when his children were married, he lived in a small house at the end of Kowalski street. He was a simple Jew, a good, quite, reticent man. And though he was not a great scholar, he thought of securing his place in the better world by helping others to learn the Torah. His life's aim was to support the poor children of the small Yeshiva, where 40 to 60 children came from the surroundings of Novogrudok.

He made arrangements for the smaller boys to 'eat days' with the local families. A kitchen was set up to feed the older boys. He collected bread and other produce for the kitchen. Reb Aron Dovid would go from house to house to collect food for the Yeshiva kitchen.

He told me once 'I am not an outstanding scholar, I have difficulties in understanding the Gemorah, I would be honoured to see to it that the children would be studying and would grow up to be good, pious Jews. On Simchas Torah he would invite the students of the Yeshiva to his home. His wife would prepare the best delicacies. He used to say: 'This gives me courage to work for another year for the Yeshiva'.

Rabbi Reb Yoisef Epshtein

Rabbi Reb Yoisef Epshtein was the rabbi in the small Yeshiva. He taught the third and fourth class. From morning till night, with a 2 hour break for lunch, he was teaching the students 'a page of Gemorah'. He lived modestly and he did not expect much. He taught time and again the same chapter of the Gemorah till the slowest scholar in the class would understand it. The students valued his efforts and liked him. He never shouted, but patiently and quietly he would explain matters. Every two years he graduated a class of students. His students came from Wsielub, Karelich, Lubch and Delatycz. His pupils went on to study at all Yeshivas of Poland. And those who did not continue with their studies and worked in trades or commerce remembered him and in their minds they preserved his teachings – the elements of the spiritual Yeshiva studies.

His pupils are to be found in Israel. He had a son and a daughter. The daughter was a teacher at the Bet Yakov school and his son, Moshe Epstein taught in the Kleck Yeshiva. From the Yeshiva he went on hachshara through the 'workers of Aguda Israel' with the aim of going to Israel. When the Soviets came to Novogrudok he smuggled himself out through Wilno, because there were rumours that from Wilno it would be possible to get to Israel. This is the last we heard of him.

Reb Judl Kaplanski

The 5th grade in the small Yeshiva was taught by Reb Judl Kaplanski. He was a pupil of the Mir yeshiva. He married young and taught the largest class in Novogrudok's small Yeshiva. His pupils could study independently and were able to understand 'a blat Gemorah'. His pupils were 15 to 18 years of age. He also endeavoured to show to his pupils a path through life. His principle was to speak little, and consider every word before it was uttered from the mouth. He said that every man when born is given a number of words which he will utter in his life. When he reaches the allotted number, the man must die. After the word is pronounced it does not belong to the speaker. He also maintained that a Jew must different from the gentiles, to make it known that the speaker is a Jew, that it should be seen that he is higher, more refined, better, and more spiritual than other people. He prohibited his pupils to ride on bikes, because the others ride on them. One must never offend anyone and must not give cause to another to offend you. To deceive a friend even in speech is a great sin. He prohibited reading newspapers because it leads to 'bitul Torah' [denial of the Torah]. He was a strict, religious Jew, a fanatic and was naïve.

There were some of his pupils who endeavoured to live according to his directions, but they did not succeed, because those ideals were even then against the established norms. Reb Judl Kaplanski, however, was serious in his beliefs. He was honest and he endeavoured to live according to his ideals. As time went on he had fewer and fewer pupils.

[Page 134]

Jewish Gardeners

by Boruch Sapotnicki

Translated by O. Delatycki

It is definitely the wrong image when Novogrudok is represented as a town of shopkeepers, shonky business dealers and airy-fairy arrangements. If we look into the reality and not in the literary criterion, which emphasised a sceptical view of the Jewish existence, we can find a second Jewish town, a productive town of hundreds of artisans of many occupations, who made products for the large population of the countryside. They made clothing and shoes, they built carriages and ploughs and made all manner of tools and dishes for the field and home. Of particular interest is the story of artisan associations, their organisations and their fight against the infamous law, introduced in the interwar period, concerning guilds.

It is also worth mentioning another level, a more modest, little noticeable and seldom mentioned. It is the trade of gardening and the gardeners – people of the land, people who produced flowering field, people which we looked down upon from the height of the town. Most of them were Jewish. The survival of the trade under the prevailing laws is remarkable. How could Jews be able to compete economically with the gentiles, working on hired the land [under the tsarist and Polish law Jews were not allowed to own land other than a building block for a house] and considering the Jewish existence with the emphasis on education, religion and culture compared to the existence of the illiterate, primitive gentile farmers. The difference was the

Jewish entrepreneurship and knowledge. Many gentile farmers were unable to achieve the output of vegetables to satisfy the needs of their own family. Farmers from outlying areas would come to town during the harvest season to buy from Jews cucumbers and cabbage for preserving for the winter. The gentile farmers would employ their young children as shepherds. The Jewish children were sent to a religious school or later to a primary school. The minimum level of education included the ability to prey, read Chumash as well as the ability to read and write. This was achieved by industriousness and frugality. A common sight in sunshine, rain, in mud and snow was a carriage loaded with large containers of milk, trudging up the hill to deliver their products to their customers.

The money earned was used for the education of their children. No matter how poor and restricted their lives the money was found to build a synagogue. Not many town dwellers ever went to the country, where on the crossroads from Brecianka to Litowka stood a synagogue. The old synagogue was taken apart for the building materials and taken to Germany in the first World War. For a number of years after the war the prayers were conducted in private homes, till the time came, which was a real epopee, of how and with what dedication have the poor country Jews began to build the new synagogue. Their efforts resembled that of the ants. In the dark nights they would travel to the state forests, fell the trees and removed the brunches and by dawn the logs were at the building site. Everyone cooperated. Even the Polish forester approved of building of the house of prayers. Everybody worked. Everybody contributed something – some a board, some a brick, some a few zloty [Polish currency]. Even those contributed whose roof was in urgent need of repair. When the synagogue was built they came at least on the Sabbath. Having worked hard during the week, on Sabbath they came with measured steps to the house of prayers. Here they participated in reading of the Torah, each was given a portion. They had a chance to have a chat, to speak of what ailed them. There was always a bit to eat and a cup to drink. There were students of the Yeshiva in town who made it their duty to visit the lonely synagogue. In the summer the windows were opened wide and the summer aroma of the fields would spread. In the winter one had to thread through the deep snow to form a passage. Their own houses were heated with anything to hand but the synagogue was heated with logs of pine and birch.

The nearest suburb to the synagogue was called Peresike, which became a place of infamy. During the German occupation a Ghetto was established in Peresike and it was the place of two mass murders of Jews.

[Page 135]

Peculiar Types of People

by A. Yerushalmi

Translated from Yiddish by O. Delatycki

As in every town, Novogrudok had also its share of peculiar types of people. I remember some of them.

Bejle

That was what she was called. She came to Novogrudok from Lubch and she lived in the synagogue 'Metaskim'.

She wore only patched dresses. Even if she was given a dress without patches she would sew on a few patches of various colours. Her cheeks were always smothered in soot with the edges of the soot painted red. She kept repeating that somebody wanted to poison her and because of this she would not accept food from everyone. But if she was very hungry, she was less choosy and accepted food from whoever gave it to her. When she had her spells, she would shout and curse. She frightened people who came near her on dark winter nights.

Noach the water carrier

Noach the water carrier was a short, thin Jew. He was dressed in well worn, patched clothes. He dragged himself with the yoke on his emaciated shoulders. Two buckets filled with water hung on both sides of the yoke. He slept in the Sieniezyc synagogue. He delivered water to many houses of the merchants. He kept saying that one day he would bring Moshiach and, having done that, he would marry Moshiach's daughter. Noach thought that Moshiach's daughter would look like Miriam the crazy woman, a quiet, lost girl dressed in tatters. She always avoiding him, but he wanted to marry her and bring Moshiach to earth.

Yoshke the 'klipe'

Yoshke the 'klipe' was a quiet, peaceful, poor man. He never shouted or caused disturbances. He walked about with a dirty bag on his shoulder and would collect empty bottles. He considered himself to be a big businessman. He would say 'every day I earn new money'. If he decided that on a certain day he made enough money, he would stop collecting bottles, even if it was midday. Children hid from him, but if they were at a safe distance they would shout: 'Yoshke the klipe'.

At times he would isolate himself and would not speak to anyone. At other times he would be talkative. He was also occupied with political problems. He knew about the situation in Israel, and why not – he was a big merchant of empty bottles.

His only family was his daughter Rifke, a hefty maiden with rosy cheeks and big, expressionless eyes. She gazed at everyone. She went about barefoot in all seasons. She had her customers, where she cleaned their houses. But most often she followed Riva the midwife. She was a quite person and did not bother anyone. But, despite of this, she was called 'Riva the crazy one'.

Ek Mek

Ek Mek was about thirty years of age when he arrived in Novogrudok to join his old mother, who lived in the corner of the Synagogue Square and Yiddisher Street. His mother was a widow. They stemmed from the village of Branik. Ek Mek studied all his life at the Yeshiva. He studied uninterruptedly Musar and Gomorrah till he became crazy. He did not speak to anyone and if somebody asked him something he answered: Ek Mek. No matter what he was told, the answer was: Ek Mek. And that is how he got his name. He prayed in the big Synagogue after all had finished praying. After a while he stopped praying. He became an Apikores [defined as non-believer or perhaps doubter]. At that time, before the 1st of May, when the Polish secret police arrested the members of the Communist Party and Bund, Ek Mek was also arrested. During the interrogation by the judge he answered to all questions 'Ek Mek'. The Polish police gave him a beating, but all he said was Ek Mek. Children followed him in the streets shouting Ek Mek. He would turn to the children and answer Ek Mek and the children laughed.

Grandma (bobe) Tzinke

My bobe Tzinke was about 90 years of age when she was taken to be slaughtered on the 8th of December 1941. Together with her were slaughtered her daughters and sons, tens of grandchildren and eight great grandchildren. The tree of Jewish life was killed and torn out with its roots. A couple of branches have been replanted and have grown roots. A new tree had grown. I am one of the branches.

Bobe Tzinke lived in the small town Wselub, 14 kilometres from Novogrudok. At the time of the slaughter she was the oldest person in her town. Her husband, Dovid Berkovski had died 15 years earlier. He was a tailor in the township. He was a pious, honest Jew. He survived on what he earned from his work. His honesty and quiet disposition were inherited by his children. After her husband died, bobe Tzinke bought a plot next to her husband in the cemetery. She prepared her burial attire and waited, but was slaughtered by the Germans together with the Jewish population of Novogrudok. Though she was old, she managed to earn enough for her upkeep and did not have to rely on help from her children.

Bobe Tzinke was renowned in all the villages around Wselub as an extraordinary healer by pouring lead. If somebody fell ill and the doctors could not help him, he would be taken to bobe Tzinke. She poured hot lead into a basin of cold water over the head of the sick. The head was covered with a sheet. She did the pouring from three to seven times, whilst uttering certain incantations. The sick began to feel better and most did recover. Most of the sick suffered from melancholy and lost strength from their affliction. She had a few patients every day and this is how she earned a living. She always had enough money to spare for the poor. There were several poor families in Wselub which bobe Tzinke supported, without anybody knowing about it.

Bobe Tzinke was also a midwife and practiced it for many years. On occasions, when a doctor was called to attend a birth, bobe Tzinke was called also. She would spend a week with the mother and child. She had a long, beautiful girdle and after each birth she made a knot in the girdle. She asked that the girdle with the knots should be put around her after she died, so that the newly born children would be her reference to allow her an entry to heaven. The money which she earned as a midwife she gave to charity. She would gather donations of food from the wealthy households and distribute it to the needy on Thursdays. She went to the synagogue three times a day. Midweek she was the only woman who was representing her gender at the prayers.

Bobe Tzinke, with all other Jews of the township of Wselub, was taken by the Germans to Novogrudok, where she was killed and buried in the mass grave of the 4000 [more than 5000] victims in the Koshelevo [Skrydlevo] ditches.

Barukh Wolf (Tshutshelo)

Yoshke "the Klipe" (an odd man)

[Page 137]

The Public Bath

by A. Y.

Translated by O. Delatycki

The public bath was to be found at the corner of the Shul Heif (Synagogue Square) next to the Koidanov synagogue. This was the meeting place of all the Shul goers on Sabbath eve, and in mid-week, on appointed days, of all women of Novogrudok. The bath served as a club where all news and gossip were told and retold. I went there every Friday with my father. At the bath father would buy a broom [made up of twigs] for one kopek [the lowest denomination of Tsarist Russia currency]. He would take two water containers, one for each of us, and we would go in to the sweat room. In the corner of that room was a pile of hot stones. Each bather would pour cold water on the hot stones. As a result, a thick, choking steam would fill the room. Five rows of shelves were built into the walls of the bath. On the shelves lay those who were seeking a thorough steaming. I was able to endure only the heat on the lowest shelf. On higher shelves I would choke. My father would climb onto the second level. Only few would be able to endure the third level. There were however, four bathers who would climb fearlessly onto the top shelve. Who were they? They were Leibe Bodjung, the father of the well known Kandibe family, who lived in Pig's lane, Fishke Noske, the stone paver, who was given the name Noske because he had a flat nose, through which he would bellow as he spoke, Shachne the tandetnik [purveyor of second hand cheap goods] a small, rosy cheeked Jew, who would carry around during the week a mound of old clothing, which obscured him almost completely and Ele the fisherman, an ancient man, whose age nobody in town could remember. They were the uncrowned rulers of the bath. They would come to the bath on Thursday afternoons, when the oven in the bath would be lit and would go out on Fridays before dawn to pray. They had a corner at the entrance, where they would cool off between periods on the top shelf. They would sit on their water containers and indulge in an endless conversation. But when they would rise to go into the sweat chamber, all others would run away as if perused by a wild animal, nobody could endure the sweat chamber when the foursome entered. The steam and heat would issue from the chamber and cover the wash room with a dense mist and a hellish heat. Undeterred, the foursome would climb onto the fifth shelf, flog themselves with the brooms and shout in a loud voice, as if someone was about to kill them. This would last for a substantial time. After, they would slowly go down, go out from the sweat room, pour over themselves cold water and go to the outer room to cool off. They looked red, like boiled crabs. After a rest they would return to the sweat bath and on and on until the time for the blessing of the candles.

Once a month they would apply cupping glasses over cuts in their skin "to clear the blood". This "operation" was done in the entrance to the bath. Following the operation the entrance looked like an abattoir. The foursome would rest after the bath. They would return home to regain their strength. I was curious to find out how Fishke Noske had regained his strength after the cupping glasses treatment. He lived not far from our house. His wife was waiting for him with a home made brew of beer, a large plate of tzimes [stewed carrots] in which a large portion of fat mutton was to be seen. He ate all that was prepared for him and finished up with a samovar of boiling tea, which he drank by sucking the tea through small lumps of hard sugar. After such a repast he would have a snooze for a few hours.

On Friday night he would partake of a Sabbath meal. For most of the week he would live on black bread and sour milk, which he would buy at the market from a Jewish milkman from Skridleve. On Sabbath they ate meat and fish. On Friday his wife would buy from Ele the fisherman small fish, which were cheap. At the butcher she would buy cheaper cuts such as the lung, liver, tripe, flap, fat and a few meters of small intestine. She would also buy one or two cow's legs, which were used for making "fisnogie" [jellied meat]. From these raw materials she would make a number of dishes: large plates of fish balls, sweet and sour fish, she would clean the gut and stuff it with flour and fat, put it in to two large pots and take them to the baker for baking. She would also bake in a very large baking dish of a sweet kugl made of noodles and raisins. All that food was consumed on the Sabbath weekend.

[Page 138]

Schlos Gass – a distinct township

by Eliezer Berkovich

Translated from Yiddish by O. Delatycki

Following the First World War , life had returned to the normal state of most townships in Poland. There was a division of opinions in town concerning the merits of the rabbi, Reb Meir Abovich. A section of the congregation, including the slaughterers and butchers was not in favour of him, because of his piety and inclination to pass rigorous rulings. A strong opposition had been created and, as a result, they appointed a rabbi who suited their requirements and taste. He was Reb Meir Meirovich from Swencian (Swienciany, Svencionys). When he took over officially the position of the rabbi of the town a great dispute between the two rabbis began. Reb Meirovich settled in Schlos Gass [Castle Street]. The householders of Schlos Gass created a separate township with their own rabbi, because they considered that Reb Abovich lacked authority and bearing, as is befitting for a rabbi and a great scholar of the Torah, who had written several books. But to merely appoint a rabbi was not enough, so the congregation hired their own slaughterer and built a slaughter house in the yard of the synagogue. Having invited the rabbi they had to give him an income. Well, there were the fees from the slaughter house, fees from the sale of Sabbath candles and yeast for the Sabbath bread as well as other income, from weddings, circumcisions etc. And so it was all arranged. The street had a large synagogue, bigger than any one in any of the other streets (except, of course, for the Shul Heif), and with nice, clever Jews who had impressive faces that were bearded and had side locks. [The Schlos Gass Shul was in the third house from the corner of

Schlos Gass and the entrance to the Schlos (Zamok)] On Friday nights, the Jews would shed their weekday attire and dressed for Sabbath. Their appearance changed beyond recognition, they seemed like different people. The welfare of the neighbourhood depended on them. Everyone held their youngest by their hand and the older children followed their father to the synagogue to begin the Sabbath prayers. After the service, a number of paupers would be waiting at the door. The poor men were drifting from town to town. The congregants would each invite a needy person for a Sabbath meal.

I considered it appropriate to list the names of the people who lived in the street, beginning from the end of the street:

Avrom Ostashinski, timber merchant

Chaim Klitelnik, gardener and before Passover a baker of matzot (by contract)

Avrom Volfovich, farmer and (horse drawn) cab driver (to amend his income), a simple, honest Jew

Mordchai Movshovich, grain merchant

Shloime Movshovich, son of Mordchai, grain merchant, an intelligent, clever man, from whom, when in need, one would ask for advice

Shmuel Mikulicki a boiler maker and part time farmer to supplement his income, a man of many parts

Mordche Angelchik and his son Yankef, tailors (the family Angelchik is mentioned in the memoirs of Chaim Kravets)

Yankef Ratner, draper, a man of the Book

Avrom Moishe Bielski, baker

Gavriel Arievich, baker

Dov Lagatkier, shoemaker

? Shmulevich, grain merchant

Irme Shmulevich, son of above [captain of the Maccabi Jewish Football Club]

Meyer Aicher, an enlightened man with wide world views, a good man of the Holy Book, he was for many years the head elder of the synagogue and a grain merchant

Shmuel Eliezer Benzianovski, timber merchant

Avrom Rudnicki, owner of a soft drinks shop

Dov Berkovich, my father, shoemaker, we had a nickname [as, I suspect, did most people in town] of which we were not ashamed

Tzvi Hershl Itzkovich, farmer

Itzchok Leizer Moishe Sapotnicki, farmer and gardener

Chaim Maslovaty and his father, flour merchants

Chaikl Berkovski

Avrom Benzianovski, timber merchant

Alter Kamenetzki, a wise man, a man of the Book, timber merchant

Shloime Bruk, shoemaker

Velvel Kaplan, tin smith, did not participate in the life of the community

Jehuda Gershonovich, shoemaker, loved to be involved in the life in of the street and participated in the games the children played

Velvl Bloch, laundry owner, prayed with fervour and meaning

Boruch Velvl Volfovich, a shoemaker

Yehyda Peresetzki, an honest carrier, who was trusted to carry money and deliver goods from Grodno.

Those were my neighbours for a part of my existence. Alas, in 1941 their lives came to an end in a most brutal manner. Blessed be their memory.

Beginning of the Fortress Street

[Page 140]

by Miriam Lipchin Negrevitski

Translated from Yiddish by O. Delatycki

Yiddishe Gass

Many years have past since I saw last Yiddishe Gass [Jewish street]. There is nothing left of my beloved street. However, in my memory all is clear, as if I saw it yesterday. I lived in the Yiddishe Gass, there I grew up and everything matured with me, good and bad times, songs, dances, sadness and happiness, I experienced it all in my Yiddishe Gass. If you stood in the centre of the Market place, you could see all streets of the town. All the streets were descended from the Market place. Yiddishe Gass was the straightest. It was clean, was cobbled with big stones in the centre, and had paved walkways on both sides. Along the walkways were rows of young trees. The houses were mostly made of timber, only few were of brick. On both sides of Yiddishe Gass were many lanes. On the left, the lanes led to Valiker Gass. The first lane on the left was called Rabbi's lane, because there lived the rabbi. The second lane on the left was called Hegdish lane, because there stood the old hegdish (poorhouse). There lived the poor and the deranged of the town and district. Often dead people were brought there for burial. There you could see the destitute of the world. The third lane was called Pig's lane - it was not cobbled. In the summer there was always sand and dust in the air. For the rest of the year it was a large bog, which was created by the autumn rains. The bog would freeze in the winter. During the long dark nights, when only one light provided meagre illumination of the lane, one would need to know how to find one's way. If you did not know the way, you were likely to finish up in the bog, looking like a dirty pig. Further along was the Talmud Torah lane. In the evenings, classes were held there by Shokdey Melocho. Before my time another evening school was operating there. There, too, was no shortage of mud. Further still was the Jail lane, which led to the jail. Further down the street one could see the quarter for the public servants [kolonia urzednicza], followed by the station of the narrow gauge railway. Beyond the station, one could see in the distance the Skrydlewo forest. We used to go there in the summer to collect berries [it would not have occurred to anyone that within a few years 80% of the Jewish population of Novogrudok would be killed and buried in that forest]. In the Yiddishe Gass, opposite the Talmud Torah lane was the Jewish hospital, which was surrounded by a large orchard with all kinds of fruit. On the corner of the Yiddishe Gass and Talmud Torah lane was the Moshav Zkeinim [old people's home] where old people lived. We used to say that the angel of death did not like them. On the right side of Yiddishe Gass was the Shul Heif [Synagogue court], where the old and new synagogues were standing as well as 12 small prayer houses (klozes), the slaughter house for poultry and the bath house. I remember on a Friday evening, when a Jew dressed for the Sabbat would come from the Shul Heif to Yiddishe Gass and would give a sign to indicate that it is was time to close the shops and celebrate the Sabbath. At that moment a festive Sabbath joy would spread over the town. Everyone went to a synagogue to pray.

In Yiddishe Gass there was a house on the border of the Shul Heif. In the house was a 3 metres long kitchen, with windows that looked out onto the Shul Heif and in the middle of the kitchen was a big oven. The house belonged to the worker's union. In the kitchen was the worker's library. It was difficult to create it with little help. There were many collections organised for funds and money. In that kitchen a theatrical group was founded to support the worker's library. All problems concerning the working people were discussed in that kitchen. Many meetings of the workers' parties were conducted there. In that kitchen you could meet members of Bund, Communists, Frihit (freedom), Hachaluts Hatzair. Even the Polish police found its way there, though nobody invited them. We, the youth, gave it a name - the historical kitchen.

I could see it all in my Yiddishe Gass - in the summer evenings when the sun would shine until late, in the winter with bountiful snow, I liked to stroll in Yiddishe Gass. Coming back from work, from the cinema, from the theatre, I would get the feel of the Yiddishe Gass. If I were asked why I liked the Yiddishe Gass, I would answer: "because in this street the sun shines longer during the day and at night there is the moon". There were no tollhouses in the street, which would obscure the sky. I left my home at the end of 1930 to go to Eretz Isroel, when the first snow was falling on the cobblestones and on the roofs of the houses in the Yiddisher Gass.

Yiddisher Gas

[Page 141]

United Jewish Artisans Association

By Samuel Nikolayevski

Translated by O. Delatycki

The United Jewish Artisans Association occupied one of the leading places in the communal life of Novogrudok. The foundation of the Artisans and Small Business Bank helped substantially to improve the existence of those engaged in minor commerce and crafts. The bank helped support very many Jewish families. A separate commercial bank was also established, but that bank was supporting larger businesses. Artisans and small business people represented 80% of all enterprises in town. They were the customers of their bank and members of their associations. This is why the Artisans Association was of great importance in the Jewish life of the town. The Artisans Association was also well represented in the Polish municipal council and the Jewish kehila. The government authorities were aware of the influence of the Artisans Association.

I joined the Association as soon as I settled in Novogrudok and I participated in the activities of the Association until the last moment of its existence. I was a member of the board of management under the leadership of Yankef Lubchanski. The Artisans Association had looked after the interest of its members in a number of ways. It provided financial help and loans, it also assisted with legal and social problems.

A small factory that produced edible oil existed in Novogrudok. One night one of its workers was seriously injured. He was taken to a local doctor for medical treatment. The doctor's wife did not let him into the house under the pretext that the doctor was not at home. The injured man could not obtain help anywhere in town. He was taken to Vilno, but died of blood poisoning. The management of the Artisans Association had investigated the matter. It came to light that the doctor was at home at the time but he did not want to get up at night. The Association decided to summons the doctor to face an arbitration tribunal. I was appointed to act as the prosecutor in the hearing. I started by investigating the doctor's attitude towards poor patients. I discovered that on one occasion the doctor refused to attend to a pregnant woman, who was brought to the hospital and was in labour, unless he was paid in advance. The woman was left sitting on a bench outside of the hospital, where she gave birth to her child without any assistance. I found out also that a resident of the old people's home had fallen ill but the doctor refused to see him unless he was paid. This was sufficient proof for the arbitration tribunal. The doctor was made to pay a fine, but, more importantly, such medical transgressions did not occur again.

A committee was formed in the Association which supported poor tradesmen. There were families among the members which were not able to buy bread or chala for Sabbath, let alone potatoes or meat. The committee undertook to provide discretely the necessary commodities to the needy. Five members served on the committee: Yankef Lubchanski as the chairman, Samuel Nikolayevski as secretary, Leibe Muler, Notke Sucharski and Shloime Gershenowski. The committee was particularly busy before the holidays, and specially Passover. We had to supply matzos, potatoes and meat to the needy. The poor requiring help were arranged in three categories: 1/ those who required provision of flour and matzos as well as other products, 2/ those who required money for baking matzos 3/ those who required both 1 and 2. The means for the assistance were obtained from the members, charitable organisations and at times collections. The Artisans and Small Business Bank was also of assistance in providing loans. On one occasion I was sent to Grodno to buy a freight car of flour. This eased the situation and reduced the cost of the assistance program. The poor craftsman received the provisions cheaply or at no cost.

Alas, shortly before the war the Artisan Association was split into two factions: the majority remained members of the faction under the chairmanship of Yankef Lubchanski, the minority formed a group headed by Meme Gordievski and conducted their own affairs. Obviously, this did not improve the condition of the artisans. The split was caused by competition between the two groups and differences in the political views of the parties. The conflict lasted till the Soviets occupied Novogrudok, when all came to an end. These were the battles and the bubbly life of the people of Novogrudok till the Nazi animals have exterminated the life of the town for ever.

I would like to use this opportunity to commemorate the names of my family who shared the fate of the population of Novogrudok – my wife Chanka Fishman- Nikolayevski and our innocent four small children Leje, Dwoire, Gawriel and Rifka.

May G'd avenge the innocent blood.

Members of the Craftsmen Association

[Page 143]

The Professional Movement

by Eliyahu Berkovitch

Translated by O. Delatycki

In the year 1920, when Novogrudok became part of Poland, Jewish professional associations began forming in town. An association of shoemakers and an association of tailors were formed. The shoemaker association integrated all leather workers: shoemakers, makers of slippers, saddlers and all others in that field. In the tailors association were: tailors, hatters, milliners and employees in drapery shops. The associations started an intensive campaign to involve all workers engaged in those trades. An eight hour working day was introduced in the enterprises where the members of the association worked. The associations put an effort into enforcing the eight hour working day rule. The employment inspector of the Polish government helped with the implementation of the regulation.

Dramatic Circle Professional Society

After hours cultural activities were conducted such as lectures, literary evenings with the participation of members of the intelligentsia of the town including teachers and students who would participate in all events organised by the associations and made their contribution. The leather association was connected with the central association in

Warsaw. The association was infiltrated by communists. The textile association was connected to the central association in Warsaw which was allied to the Bund. The leather association was allowed to exist for a short time. Because of its link to the communist party the association was disbanded by the Polish authorities and their leaders were arrested. On the other hand, the textile association had become stronger and represented most of the textile workers. The cultural sub-committee had also increased its activities. They started setting up a library. Money was collected for that purpose by organising such events as flower sales, with the permission of the government. The money was used for the purchase of books. At the same time the workers dramatic actors circle was organised under the direction of Yoisef Israelit. Every two weeks there were theatrical performances. Later performances were arranged every Saturday night. The performances of the dramatic actors improved and the audiences were drawn from all levels of the population. They were successful and they made a profit. The money supported a number of institutions such as Shokgdey melocho, orphanage, workers library and other deserving institutions. At the same time, a reading room was set up where the whole Jewish press, dailies and weeklies, was on display. The Polish press was also available. The reading room was open from 7pm to 11pm and people would come to read the papers or play chess. Masked balls for Purim were run. It should be noted that our functions were frequented by the cities' intelligentsia, and that encouraged us to continue our work.

And this is how we lived – workers and intelligentsia working in harmony until the town was destroyed in the Holocaust. May their memory be implanted in our souls.

[Page144]

"TOZ" activities

by Majrim Ginzburg

Translated from Yiddish by O. Delatycki

"TOZ" stands for [in Polish] "Towarzystwo Ochrony Zdrowia", which translates as "Society for the Preservation of Health".

The name of the organization in Yiddish was "Society for the Preservation of Health of the Jewish people". This was a Jewish organisation with the head office in Warsaw, under the leadership of the highest Jewish medical authorities in Poland. About 10 years before the second World War , under the influence of the journal "Folks gezunt" [Health of the People] (a monthly popular medical journal), which was published by the head office of TOZ, several medical workers in Novogrudok had decided to establish a division of TOZ in town. Several persons founded a preliminary committee which undertook to attract members. The monthly membership fee was set at half to one zloty per month. After a number of people joined, a general meeting was called to initiate the organization. After the general discussion of the aims of the organisation, a committee of 7 persons was elected: Dr. Marmurshtein, dentist Shimon Kamieniecki, cantor Eliezer Rabinovich, Dove Eicher, Mrs Movshovich, Jankef Abovich and the author of this article [Majrim Ginzburg].

Doctors and nurses from the Jewish hospital

The elected committee started an energetic campaign.

The majority of the population of the town were small business men and tradesmen, who were hurried and overworked in search of a living. The care of health was largely neglected. Therefore, the committee decided that its first task was to awaken in the population an interest in the problems of health. It was decided to organise frequent meetings of a wide circle of people. At these meetings the problems of hygiene prophylactics were discussed in a popular form. The nature of micro organisms, how transferable diseases occur and how to prevent their incidence were explained. After the lectures questions were answered by the lecturers. It was also undertaken to increase the number of subscribers to the journal "Folks gezunt".

The second task was to open in Novogrudok a "drop of milk" station. The central organization of TOZ was approached to help out in this matter. They welcomed our initiative and provided help. Assistance was also sought from the American Novogrudok Help Committee. The Americans supported the project and contributed a significant sum of money. Due to the support from the above two sources it was possible for TOZ to extend the proposed projects. A "drop of milk" station was opened. The station had many functions. The Sister at the station, Miss Iveniecki, began visiting the houses of the poor population, particularly in the poor quarters of the town such as the Synagogue square, Rachelo and Zalatuche. Her duty was to instruct the women how to look after themselves and their families, particularly during pregnancy. The sucklings were brought to the Sister for a weekly examination and, if necessary, to the TOZ medical officer Dr Marmursztin. There was a file at TOZ for every child, in which the development of each child was documented, such as: weight, height, vaccinations that the child was given etc. Newly born children of needy families received assistance and food. In time new people were attracted to help with the work among them were Dr Kiwelewicz and the midwife Rive Szwarc. The organisation was becoming wider known in town. TOZ had taken its honourable place among older established and well known organizations such as the Beit Cholim, Moshav Skeinim, Shogdy Meloche and the orphanage. Annual general meetings of TOZ were conducted, when the management and the revision committee presented reports of their activities in the previous year. Members of the committees were elected. These meetings were of great interest to the members and were well attended.

Hospital Committee

Every summer the TOZ organised for the children of Novogrudok day programs. During the day the children spent time in fresh air under the supervision of experienced guides. At night the children slept in their home. During the day the children received three meals. The cost of the program varied with income: the better off parents paid the full price, others paid half the price and the poor paid a nominal amount. Often the management was able to collect sufficient money to pay fully for the poor children. Thus, for instance, Moshe Brojdo, a respectable founding citizen of Novogrudok, would contribute each summer a sum which would pay the fees of several children. He always insisted that his donations should remain anonymous. It was indeed a great satisfaction and pleasure to see the Jewish children happy, cheerful, sun tanned, doing gymnastics and dancing under the direction of the kindergarten teacher. Chasan Rabinovich, who was devoted to the institution, would spend much time with the children and teach them to sing traditional songs.

At a joint meeting of the TOZ management of Novogrudok, Baranovichi and Lida it was decided to create in the forest of Novojelnia a joint holiday home for the children of the above mentioned towns. Money was collected in the three towns. The population supported the initiative. The required money was readily made available. A splendid corner in the Novojelnia forest was secured. A suitable big building surrounded by a fence was erected. Many children from the three towns were given a chance to spend some time at the home and benefit from the fresh, healthy country air. The fees were structured in the same way as those for the day programs.

Members of the Hospital Committee

Children's outing in Novoyelna, fifteen miles from Novogrudok.

The holiday home in Novojelnia had become well known in the district, because of its fine management and good order. A very vigorous and devoted activity in founding and managing the home was displayed by members of the Baranovichi TOZ committee Dr Nachimovski and Mrs Dr Izakson.

An event related with the holiday home comes to mind. Alexander Harkavy, during his second visit to Novogrudok, was making a film for our American townsmen. To do so Harkavy hired a crew of two operators from Warsaw. It was decided to include in the film scenes from the holiday home. I intended to travel with him to Novojelnia. Before we went, the deputy Mayor of Novogrudok Ostashinski had suggested that on the way we should film the Novogrudok narrow gauge railway station. We arranged for the crew to make the film. We had no idea that it was prohibited by law to photograph railway stations. The station master had seen us filming and started to abuse us heatedly. We ignored him and went to Novojelnia. The station master informed the local police, who in turn phoned the police in Novojelnia to apprehend the "criminals". A few kilometres from Novojelnia a car full of policemen armed with rifles stopped us. We were taken to the Novojelnia police station. Luckily the policeman in charge knew me as a pharmacist from Novogrudok. Having spotted me the policeman was very surprised. I explained to him that the older gentleman in our group is a guest from America, a person of renown, who came to us to help our community. The other two were hired by the American gentleman to make a film of his visit. The policeman passed on this information to the police in Novogrudok. He was told to set us free and to cut of the portion of the film, which was made at the railway station. I was told to report to the police station in Novogrudok. After we had taken the film of the holiday home we returned to Novogrudok, where I went to the police station and I repeated my story. With that the matter was concluded.

In the spring of 1939 the committee of TOZ decided to buy a block of land and to put up a building in Novogrudok for the children who were enjoying the day programs. A delegation was sent to the Graf of Wsielub, one of the richest landowners, with the request for help with the project. The Graf promised to assist by supplying building materials, some free and some at a reduced cost.

[The Count of Wsielub O'Rourke stemmed from a long line of Irish nobles. His forebear, Lieutenant-General Count Joseph O'Rourke fought in the Russian army in the Napoleonic wars. In 1819 General O'Rourke retired and subsequently settled down in the Novogrudok region of the Minsk province. He was a prominent landowner in Byelorussia and held in his possession about 20,000 acres of land, including the small town of Wsielub and five villages. His grandson was known as a benevolent man, who treated fairly the Jews of Wsielub. He was somewhat eccentric and was known to wear a kilt, when inspecting his farm (see the articles on Wsielub in Pinkas Novogrudok on p.167, p.168, p.170)]

The war brought an end to all our plans.

The Home for the Aged in Navarudok Committee and Members

Aid for Jewish prisoners

by Aharon Rudnicki

Translated from Yiddish by O. Delatycki

There was an institution in Novogrudok which was called "Aid for the arrested". It was headed by my father OBM. The task of that body was not an easy one. Its main aim was to supply kosher food for the arrested Jews. It was not easy to obtain permission to do it. On a Sabbath and on festive days hot food was delivered to the prison. Before Passover new kosher dishes, matzos, wine and all that is required to celebrate Passover in a proper manner was provided. There was not always a minyan (ten adult Jews) in the prison. My father and I prayed in the prison on every festival. On occasions, persons picked at random were invited to make up a minyan. My father would serve as the guarantor for their good behaviour.

Jews on forced labor during World War I

Once an event occurred which could have had dire consequences. This is what happened. There was a holiday. We arrived to join, as usual, in the prayers. The warden provided a nice, separate room for the prayers. The prayers were conducted uneventfully in a nice Jewish manner. I should mention that my father and I were cohanim (descendents of the priests in the ancient temples). This is important to stress to make the rest of the story clear. Having finished the prayers we went to fetch the food. As he walked, my father felt pressure on his foot. Initially he did not pay any attention to it. After the meal, having returned home, my father decided to have a nap. As he took off his shoes a letter fell to the floor. In those days, to smuggle a letter from a prison was punishable by exile to Siberia. My father dressed in a hurry and returned to the prison. He rang the doorbell and was asked "who" – father answered "it is I". The door opened in an instant and the surprised warden asked him what happened. Father requested that the Jews be assembled for another prayer. The warden was surprised: "Haven't you just prayed?" he asked. None-the-less he ordered the prisoners to return to the room where the prayers were held. The prisoners reassembled. They were all frightened. Not knowing what happened they looked at each other and shrugged. Father began as follows: Dear Jews, today is a holy day and we all prayed. You should now confess who slipped a letter into my shoe. All prisoners were afraid and did not know what to say. All were swearing that they knew nothing about it. Father spoke to the prisoners emphatically: You all swear that you know nothing of the matter, yet one of you is not telling the truth. I will ask the Rabbi to come and he will make you swear on the bible. At that moment the warden opened the door and asked father to come out to see him. He said to father: "You passed the test. I put the latter in your shoe to test you and see if you are honest and trustworthy. As of now I have complete confidence in your honesty". Father returned to the prisoners and asked them to forgive him for suspecting one of them. The prisoners answered in one voice: "We forgive you and go in peace".

[Page 149]

Village Jews

by D. Cohen

Translated from Yiddish by O. Delatycki

Yoshe Horodechner (Horodetshner)

It could be because I was born in a village not far from Novogrudok, that my heart belongs to those Jews who lived in the villages surrounding the town, who cohabited and traded with the peasants, lived in harmony with them and frequently helped those in need, spoke their tongue – Belarusian. It was only on the Sabbath and holidays that they shed their everyday peasant clothing and became festive Jews. Those who lived in the vicinity of the town would walk there on Sabbath to pray. Those who lived too far would arrange a local minyan, would listen to the cantor, would be called up to read a portion of the Torah and for the duration of the holiday not hear an alien word. They would be certain to partake of a stiff drink, but would never get drunk. The mouthful of vodka would be followed by traditional Jewish festive delicacies and they ate morsels with gusto – eggs and onion, liver, jellied fish, meat, cholent, kugl (both typical delicacies of east European Jews) and in between bites they would wash down the fatty food with a stiff drink of vodka. It was no wonder that such a repast was followed by deep sleep. Thus passed the Sabbath or holiday and again one would return to everyday living, to trading with the farmers... and so on and on year after year. Children were born, they grew up together with the other village boys. And when the inevitable hour would arrive, they would not summons doctors, they would die and be buried among their own, facing the far yet near land of Israel.

Rivers of tears have been shed for the exterminated Jewish community of Novogrudok. An extra tear must be shed for the fallen dear, undemanding village Jews who perished with their sisters and brothers and were buried in the mass graves.

I would like to describe and immortalise the memory of a few village Jews, and through them the memory of all Jews who lived in villages around Novogrudok.

Joshe from Gorodechno

A large timber house is standing on a hill overlooking the Gordelovka forest. Next to it is a flour mill, a tavern and a small, low smithy which is issuing sparks and gathering around itself horses, wagons and sleighs. Reb Joshe sits in the tavern. I can still see him – tall, upright, looking like the lofty spreading tree which is shading one of the windows of the tavern. I don't know if he acquired the tavern as part of an inheritance, but he liked his tavern. He would meet all passers by with a cheery good morning or good evening, he would serve them a glass of vodka and a snack, but would never permit drunkenness in his tavern. He spoke to them in their tongue, but he kept himself at a distance. He would exchange with everyone a nice word, he would comment on political and social issues. He was very popular.

It was the time of the First World War . Novogrudok was only some 20 wiorsts (about 20 km) from the front line. The Germans, as was their habit, were requisitioning grain, eggs, poultry and horses. The farmers were anxious to learn of news from the front and naturally they would ask Joshe the innkeeper. As the night approached the farmers would assemble, tie the horses to the posts, take a hefty drink, sit with bulging eyes, with their ears wide open, ready to listen and to find out the news of the world and from the front. I was the one who supplied Joshe with the news and he demanded of me the names of the Russian generals and kept asking for more names. So I invented resounding Russian names, which were neither here nor there. I don't know if Joshe believed me and took the names I gave him to be real but for the customers he recited names with a particular aplomb: Ivan Petrovich, Nikolay Vasilievich came out of his mouth as terrific heroes, who attacked the foe fearlessly with their swords but, alas, at the end they had to retreat. The customers listened in awe, crossed themselves and asked for another drink and another story. Joshe smoothes his beard and smiles with pleasure.

I liked the tavern and the two daughters who played the guitar. They played longingly and romantically and looked up at the tree tops which were covered in hues of purple. They were a family of musicians. The son with the ringing name of Solomon had the feeling and taste of a performer and he became a music announcer in the young Tel Aviv in its early days. It was good news when I heard that Joshe the taverner was in Tel Aviv in Israel. I was immersed in memories, in romantic warm feelings and I can see him much older but still tall, His wide beard made him look handsome. He reminded me of a tall tree in Gorodeczno, but with its roots cut. He was missing his tavern and his customers and he returned to his home. He found his resting place in the treed cemetery in Novogrudok. In Israel he left a daughter with children and grandchildren.

Izik the blacksmith

I don't know why in my mind I associate Izik the blacksmith with winter, though I have seen him on occasions and had a chat with him in the summer. It could be that his black face was in strong contrast to the white winter world. I remember a Friday on a winter's day. I am walking to Slobodka. I pass the tavern and I am attracted to the warmth of the small house of the smith. The house is indeed pleasantly warm. Because of the inclement weather the smithy is closed. The wife of the smith stands in front of the blazing oven and is inserting a cholent in it. And the smith with his strapping son are engaged in an argument. The smith is glad of my arrival. He says to me: you are teacher so you will decide which of us is right, I or my son. I am impressed by that remark and I reply: "what is the problem?" I argue, said the smith, that we Jews are the chosen people and because of that we will all go to heaven and all gentiles will finish up in hell. "And what is your opinion" I asked the son. He replied: "I am arguing that the gentiles are not at fault that they were born gentiles, why do they deserve to go to hell?" Father gets irritated and shouts: "because the gentiles are like cattle and don't know anything". The son got agitated and screams: "and what about the scribe in the Volost' (shire), can't he read and write?" The smith was lost for a moment, thought and ran to the book case, took out the Chumash and opened it at the beginning and said in a quarrelsome tone to his son: "look at it and read it" Shamed and puzzled the son read: "at the beginning God made the Heaven and the earth". The face of the smith shone and he shouted: "you see, will the scribe of the Volost' be able to say that?" The son remained speechless; he inclined his head and said quietly: "it seems that you are right".

I heard lately that the son of the smith had become a strongman and was appearing in large towns, where he was showing his might.

Uri the flour miller

The events which will be related here happened before the first World War . I, a young boy, was captivated by the teachings of a Jewish revolutionary party, the Simovces. I found myself in the city of Proskurov. They were the days of political storms and the young sole could not understand the internal party fights, when the main enemy was the Tsar, who was sending everybody to jail or the hangman. Disappointed and defeated I was thinking of becoming independent of everybody, not to be dependent on daily handouts like pupils in the Yeshiva. I was contemplating to break out through the border and from there to America. At that time grandfather Uri came to see his daughter Luba, who was the wife of the head of the Yeshiva Reb Shmuel and to see his grandchildren. The grandfather had a surname which sounded like a name of someone from Frankfurt – Openheim. He was broad shouldered and had a fiery, wide beard, thick lips and good kind eyes. A rare Jew. He liked good company, a good measure of vodka, a fat morsel, but at the same time he did not forget the world hereafter. Two of his daughters married rabbis. The water mill, which he had in Slobodka, did not yield enough income for the third daughter to marry a rabbi. She, Ete, was capable, sturdy and she married a miller, who ran a mill in the village of Selatycz. The two rabbis, the older rabbi Eliezer, who was studying the cabbala and wanted to hasten salvation, and the other, rabbi Shmuel looked down on their uneducated brother-in-law Mordche, who, in turn, looked upon the rabbis as on squeezed out lemons. Grandpa Uri was always trying to make peace among them. Clever grandfather understood me, his grandson, who was looking for independence and offered me a job in the flour mill. The job was to keep tally of the grain which arrived and of the flour which was taken away. Grandpa determined the wages of 40 roubles a month for his 15 year old grandson. Grandpa also agreed for the grandson to eat with the other workers, as it would suit a revolutionary. I got to like my grandmother, with her three colourful names Dvoire Chaje Finkl. She knew that grandfather was sinning at times, but she was the guardian of peace in the house and she revered the famed head of the Musar Yeshiva, Reb Yoyzl as an idol. He would stay in their house in the hot summer months. Grandfather Uri, who was concerned about the better world beyond, built for Reb Yizyl a yehide shtibl, in the forest close to Novogrudok, where the pupils of the Yeshiva would reside in a detachment in the productive days of the month of Elul. It would seem that Reb Yoyzl had a good understanding of psychology because, not long after, he extracted me from the flour mill and readmitted me to the Yeshiva. I was missing Slobodka, my grandmother and particularly my grandfather. Two or three times a week, together with my older brother, who was also in the Yeshiva, we would visit Slobodka. We would greet grandfather and the farmers, who were quite workers, and we ate tasty bliny, which grandmother would prepare. Years later my older brother Yizchok Aizek took over the management of the flour mill in Slobodka. Grandfather Uri died suddenly having suffered a heart attack. He was missed by all: poor Jews as well as the poor farmers, who he treated like his children.

Meishe and Tamara

Not far from Novogrudok, crossing a dense forest one arrives at a small, rapid stream which drives the grinding stones of the flour mill of Gordelovka. The mill was leased by husband and wife, Meishe and Tamara. Meishe was an unremarkable man, but Tamara was a rare beauty. The young men of Novogrudok would gather in Gordelovka like bees on flowers. On Sabbath days in summer, people would come to cool off in the shallow, cold waters of the stream and delight in a drink of cold sour cream, black rye bread or a glass of fresh milk. It was likely that most of the family income came not from the flour mill but from Tamara's butter, sour cream and milk.

I remind myself that when in need I stayed in Gardelovka, and my pretty aunt Tamara was good to me, like a good mother. There must have been more than ten Jewish flour millers in the district and they contributed much to the community of Novogrudok. They donated holy ornaments as well as supported the town's poor. They would bring to town flour, potatoes and dairy products for the holidays and most of all for Passover.

The Jewish "land gentry"

All the flour mills belonged to Poles, who were leasing them to the Jews. I remember the family of Niankovski, who were leasing the Gorodechno land holding. The family behaved like land gentry. The owned horses and cows. One of the sons behaved like a Pole. He was riding a horse, spoke Polish and did not have Jewish friends. But the rest of the family behaved as Jews and in their house prayers were conducted each Sabbath and on holidays. Here the millers from the district would gather for prayers and have a generous kidush (something to drink and a snack after the prayers).

Avreml from Boyarsk

I was brought up with little Abraham, the son of Mordechi from Sielatych and my heart is fool of joy when I think of his name. I remember the days when he was a youth with poetic leanings, rich fantasies and his attachment to Henia, a renowned beauty, who later became his wife. His parents were opposed to the marriage, but Avreml took no notice and married his beloved. As a child and a grandchild of millers, he leased the flour mill in the village of Boyarsk and built his own life. The village was known to have a group of enlightened young farmers with secret connections to the Communists. The Jewish miller was friendly with them. The farmers used to say that in Avreml's house the table was always set so that a man in need could be taken straight to the table. On one occasion the leftist young farmers attacked and killed an informer. Arrests followed. Among the arrested was Avreml the miller. The Polish political police knew that Avreml did not participate in the murder, but they tortured Avreml to disclose the names of the guilty. To no avail. Avreml was silent. He suffered in jail and was determined not to be an informer. When he was released from jail, agents of the government put fire to the flour mill and Avreml, his wife, two beautiful daughters and a son went to live in Novogrudok. Here too Avreml led a nice life. When the Germans came, Avreml and his family were taken with all Jews to the Ghetto. He died in the Ghetto from sickness and hunger. Both daughters were killed by the Germans. His son escaped east ahead of the German invasion. Henia survived the invasion in the forests. After the war she met her son in a refugee camp. I was privileged to meet them on their arrival in Israel.

Where are you, dear, ordinary village Jews, hearty, strong children of the people ingrained in the live of the village and linked with our brethren in Novogrudok. Slain with the whole Novogrudok community, may their spilled blood never be forgotten. May their slaughter be remembered and revenged. May their memory be always with us.

[Page 152]

Benjamin Kotlover

by Wm. Uris

Translated from Yiddish by O. Delatycki

In the surroundings of Novogrudok there were numerous Jewish settlements, i.e. Jews who were leaseholders of land from the [Polish] landlords. Under the Tsarist regime Jews were not allowed to own land. Benjamin Movshovich was one of the lessees in the village of Kotlovo, about 14 viorst [about 15 km] from Novogrudok. Benjamin Kotlover was an interesting man, with an unusual character. He was strongly traditional and deeply religious, but he knew the fine points and was a maskil [follower of the Haskola – the enlightenment movement]. All his children, including his daughters, received both a traditional and secular education. He was a charitable man and always glad to see a visitor – no passer by who stopped at his house left without food or an empty pocket. Benjamin and his wife Simka made sure that they left in a happy frame of mind. Benjamin was a man with a warm Jewish heart. He bemoaned the troubles Jews were exposed to under the Tsar's anti-Semitic rule and was hoping to live to see a Jewish state in Israel. Benjamin was a close friend of my father Reb Yosef Jerusalimski (Yerushalmi) and a devoted friend of our family.

I had a particularly close bond with him. He would invite me often to the country. He was a strict disciplinarian, but I was allowed complete freedom in the country and I could do whatever I pleased, even to go horse riding. The good hearted Simka saw to it that I should eat well and drink plenty of milk.

The two Jewish families who lived in Kotlowo, Benjamin Movshovich and his partner Brine, were the only Jews in the village. Though their financial position was quite good, they suffered much due to anti-Semitic incidents and the Tsarist lawlessness. Brine and her children left for America and Benjamin moved with his family to Novogrudok.

Benjamin died when he was preparing to join his children in America. Only one daughter, Maryashe remained in Novogrudok. Among those killed by the German fascists in Novogrudok was Maryashe together with her husband and four children.

> [The above article is almost identical to the chapter on Benjamin Kotlover in Wm. Uris' 'Memoirs from before the First World War'. I included it for completeness. O.D.]

[Page 153]

Weekly papers in Novogrudok

by Yehoshua Yaffe

Translated from Yiddish by O. Delatycki

Two Navagrodker weekly newspapers: Navagrodker Life and Navagrodker Week

In 1933 a weekly newspaper named Novogrudker Leben (Novogrudok Life) was founded. The editor was Avrom Buselevich, the son of Moishe Dovid Buselevich, a Slonim chasid. On the editorial board were the lawyers Gumener and Ciechanowski, the teacher Solomon, who was the initiator and ardent supporter of the paper, and others. A third of the paper was taken up by advertisements, announcements and bereavements. They provided the main source of the newspaper's income. The newspaper was not connected to any party, it was mainly concerned with local problems such as the municipal council, the Jewish council (kehila), economic institutions and local schools. The newspaper published also historical articles about old Novogrudok and about events of the distant past. The newspaper was also in touch with emigrants, who contributed stories about old Novogrudok. One of the correspondents from Israel was Isroel Gurevich. The editorial board of the paper was also arranging memorial meetings to commemorate Jewish writers such as Mendele, Sholem Alechem and I.L. Peretz. The paper conducted open trials etc. The Novogrudker Leben made known its public opinion and took part in the economic, cultural and communal life of the Jewish population of Novogrudok. The newspaper continued publication up until the beginning of the Second World War .

In 1935 the newspaper Novogrudker Woch appeared, in opposition to the Novogrudker Leben,. Though it proclaimed itself to be an independent newspaper, unconnected to any party, it was an organ of the Revisionist party, which was opposing other Zionist organisations and the Histadrut.

[Page 154]

A Native of Novogrudok in the Herzlia Gymnasium

by Noach Yishayahu Avi-Amots

Translated from Hebrew by Aviva Kamil

Chaim Yaffe, the grandchild of the "gaon" Reb Gimpel Yaffe from Roznoy, was at the beginning of the twentieth century one of the revered and important people in Novogrudok. He was a gifted student and he knew Hebrew as well as general knowledge.

Chaim Yaffe had a large hardware shop and was considered to be affluent.

He had two handsome sons: Mordechai and Leibl. In order to give his sons a modern yet traditional education he engaged a teacher for them, Yishayau Tchernichovski, who was versed in the Torah and Hebrew as well as in secular subjects. Tchernichovski was known and respected in the town and the surrounding district.

The younger son, Leibl, had shown literary talent and at a very young age was composing beautiful poetry, which was published in "Haprachim" (the flowers) edited by Lerner, the known Rabbi and writer.

In the year 1907 Betzalel Yaffe from Grodno invited Y.Tchernichovski to teach pedagogical courses, which were conducted by the Society for the Dissemination of Knowledge in Grodno. One of the great pedagogues of the generation, Aharon ben-Moshe Kahanshtam was the head of that school.

Y.Tchernichovski wanted his talented student to be given the opportunity to undertake further studies in a high school that was renowned for its excellence. He approached Shmaryau Levin, who was one of the trustees of the Herzlia Gymnasium in Jaffa, and asked him to accept Leibl Yaffe as a non-paying pupil at that Gymnasium. The request was granted and Leibl moved to Jaffa to study at that school. Thus Yaffe's sons were the first in Novogrudok to speak fluently modern Hebrew.

Zeydl Bushelevits

by Ch. Leibovitch

Translated by O. Delatycki

Zeidel Buselevitch

Zeydl Bushelevits was born in Novogrudok to a prominent family. His father Moshe Dovid was a deeply religious man. Zeydl was given a traditional religious upbringing and general education. He obtained his matriculation at a gimnazjum [high school] in Vilno. At the high school he revealed his ability to write literary compositions. He was the editor of the student's newspaper. He also contributed articles to Vilno's daily newspapers. Having returned to Novogrudok, he became the organiser and actual editor of the newspaper 'Novogrudker Lebn' ['Novogrudok Life']. As a Zionist, he imbued the Zionist spirit into the 'Novogrudker Lebn'. He became involved with the Jewish intelligentsia and was devoted to the Jewish society. He was dedicated to the newspaper. He was an ardent student of the Yiddish language. He was very interested in photographs of Jewish subjects. He represented the finest traditions of Jewish Novogrudok. Zeydl liked Novogrudok with all its communal institutions, but his main devotion was to the 'Novogrudker Lebn'. It was a part of his being. He did not expect to get something from the paper, he did not use it to publish his literary works. He never published an article under his name. I don't know to this day if it was because of his diffidence or his intellectual pride. As a human being he distinguished himself by his modesty and heartiness. He was a true companion and friend. And just as he was true to others, he was true to himself. He never tried to appear to be greater than he was in the reality. He was one of the nicest types that lived in Novogrudok in the last decade before the war. After the war started 'Novogrudker Lebn' ceased publication. Zeydl Bushelevits was taken by the Germans with the second group, allegedly to work, but he was killed. It is unknown where his grave is. Let this modest contribution serve as a memorial to the editor of 'Novogrudker Lebn' Zeydl Bushelevits.

[Page 155]

Extinguishing the fire of hatred

by Noach Avni (Kamenietsky)

Translated from Yiddish by O. Delatycki

I can see it still in my minds eyes. At that time I was a young boy, a pupil of the Tarbut school. It is engraved in my memory and I cannot forget it, the first anti-Semitic event in Novogrudok that I was made aware of and the courageous, well organised resistance of the youth of the town. It was the time when the endec party [ND - national democrats - a right wing anti-Semitic party] was gaining influence. A leader of the endec party by the name of Chamiec, a virulent anti-Semite, was well known at the time. Wherever he would come underworld hooligans would appear and disturbances would follow. Jews were attacked and Jewish possessions were robbed or destroyed. This was Chamiec's main aim.

On a certain summer day Haman had appeared - "professor" Chamiec together with a bunch of hooligans had arrived. The mood in town was heavy and depressed. The local anti-Semites and a handful of hooligans were strutting about with their heads high. The curse "parszywy Zyd" (mangy Jew) was heard all around. There was a rumour that one of our boys was attacked, but he fought off the assailants. The day came when the "professor" had come out with a coterie and started pasting to the walls posters with anti-Semitic slogans, advertising a meeting which was to be held in the kasyno urzednicze [the club for public servants] on the top floor of the house of Lejzer Hirshl Shymon Izraelit in the Market Place. It was emphasised on the posters that all were invited except for Jews and dogs. Well, the troubles have started. The mood was heated. We, the schoolchildren, have decided to remove the posters quicker than they were put up. As I was swift on my feet, I put up a good show that day. I was busy for some hours and managed to remove many posters, until I was caught and led to the police station. I was given a beating, which I remember to this day. But, believe me, it was worth it, because I became well known. In time, the School Principal Korn defended me and other school friends for the same "crime".

But the most important part of the story will be told now. Who does not remember the Novogrudok fire brigade and the children of Motke: Moshe and Arke? There was no one who could climb on roofs faster. The fire brigade consisted of strong boys from Zalatucha and Rachelo with their leader Lejzer Izraelit and his adjutant Jankef Burshtain. On the Sunday, exactly at the time when the visiting anti-Semite was to give his speech - the fire alarm sounded. And it so happened that the fire was in the self same building where the meeting was taking place. Would you believe that our boys from the fire brigade have drenched the assembled with cold water. The heated mood of the forgathered, including the "professor", was cooled off. Some of our boys were beaten up, and yet they were proud that they dispersed a large crowd of rabid anti-Semites. The following week a court case has began. The accused were those who had provided the cold shower as well as those who had torn down the anti-Semitic posters. I was one of them. Our defendant was the splendid attorney Zeldowicz, who volunteered his services. He kept on calling the "professor" Cham-pause-miec [cham means in polish rude, uneducated from Ham the vulgar son of Noah] and used to feign each time a coughing spasm as the reason for the pause. The audience in the court room was laughing resoundingly, until the judge caught on and asked the lawyer to mend his pronunciation. The schoolchildren were defended by the school principal Korn, who spoke very well. As Korn was a Polish legionnaire who was wounded in the service of the country, his appearance made a big impression on the court and the public.

[Page 156]

Those We Remember

Edna Kagan OBM

by Baruch, Jakob and Meyer Kagan

Translated from Yiddish by O. Delatycki

From her childhood our mother was aware of Jewish cultural ideals. The first person who fostered that feeling was her father, Reb Benyomen OBM, our grandfather. He read to our boba Sheinke Yiddish and Hebrew newspapers and journals. Our grandfather was, clearly, a pious Jew, but he was also an enlightened person and subscribed to the newspapers "Hacfira", "Hamelits" as well as "Der frint" (The friend), which were published at the time in St Petersburg. When grandma was taking a rest from daily chores and even when she worked, grandfather read to her the most important items about the world and sometimes less weighty items. And on Sabbath eve and Sabbath he read to her Nochim Sokolow's essays. He read in a clear diction and tone. When he noticed that his daughter Yachnele (as he called our mother) was paying attention to her father's reading, he would put a stronger emphasis on his words. The readings created in mother a desire to read. Our mother was a good, pleasant reader. The father, Reb Benyomen, hired for his children in Kotlovo (a village 14 km from Novogrudok) good teachers. They thought his children general studies, Hebrew, and Chumash, and the boys Rashi and Gemorah. Grandfather invited children from neighboring villages to attend the lessons, to build up the numbers. No matter how busy he may have been he would supervise the learning and teaching of the pupils. As it turned out, our mother was a good pupil. Each time visitors came they were astonished by the knowledge of the children. Grandfather would display his daughter Yachnele as an example of a child with good abilities. Our mother came to the States in 1905, when she was 11 years old. Here she obtained her general schooling and her Yiddish education. Our grandfather, who was a respected resident of Novogrudok, sent his children to the States because of repeated attacks by hooligans on smaller Jewish communities. He was looking for a country where his children would have a better future.

In 1925 our mother began teaching Yiddish. She taught for 30 years. She was devoted to the cause of Yiddish education. Our father died when we were very young. Mother gave us a good Jewish education and instilled the respect for the Jewish traditions, for the Jewish people and for our national aspirations. Our mother new well and liked the Yiddish literature. She had an extraordinary feeling for, and understanding of, good poetry. She collected her favorite pieces. Her collection held hundreds of remarkable Yiddish songs. Our mother was also a busy writer, but she published little. She wrote episodes from her childhood, which showed the strong influence of her upbringing on her formative years. Our mother had a specific ideological attitude when she was speaking or writing in Yiddish. She had a liking of the Hebrew language. She believed that in time a world order would be established which would be built on the foundations of freedom and justice. From her earliest youth she had a strong feeling of tolerance for people who believed in ideals different to her own.

In all her doings there was order and a system. When she retired from her teaching carrier, she handed over to YVO (Jewish Institute of Knowledge) her collections of festive songs, national, social, and folk tunes, also games, tales for children, and short essays arranged according to subjects and festivals. In the last few years of her life she was busy helping the editors of Pinkas Novogrudok. She did the work with enthusiasm and a sense of responsibility. If our mother undertook something, she was certain to finish it. Her word was her bond. Her correspondence with her Novogrudok compatriots was a nice chapter of her social activities. Her correspondence in the last few years of her life with Dovid Cohen, writer and teacher, the editor of Pinkas Novogrudok, is of certain historical value. It reflects mother's honesty and devotion. She kept up the correspondence to the last letter, which she received a day before she died.

[Page 157]

Louie Zlotnik

by Chaim Leibovich

Translated by O. Delatycki

A tree fell... we lost a young and friendly companion. Louie was born and raised in Novogrudok in a poor household. He did not have an elementary education. At the age of thirteen he was apprenticed to a blacksmith. To recompense him, God gave him a good soul and a warm heart. Louie was a man of the people who spread warmth and love. A friendly atmosphere always surrounded him. He spread the eagerness for communal work. Louie migrated to the States in 1913. Shortly after his arrival he involved himself with enthusiasm in communal work, and became an organiser in the Branch 146 of the Workers Circle. He was also a member of the board of directors of the Workers Home for the Elderly. He participated in the activities of the United Jewish Appeal, the Histadrut, and bonds for Israel. Louie was not a man of many words. He always donated to worthy causes. Louie held for 8 years the position of the chairman of the Alexander Harkavy Aid Committee. He did all he could to help refugees in their need. He participated in establishing in Israel the Loan Found for the Jews of Novogrudok. Louie was a trustworthy friend of Israel. He loved the Jewish people with all their faults. There are no bad Jews, he used to say, but only Jews that had bad luck--one should show understanding for people who had bad luck, one should show sympathy, consideration, and extend help. And Louie did provide help to many friends. His heart and hand were always open for everyone.

Louie Zlotnik

With the death of Louie Zlotnik, the Alexander Harkavy Aid Committee, Branch 146 of the Workers Circle, and all Jews from Novogrudok in New York lost one of their most devoted members. His communal work, his friendly, affable conduct, and his open handed generosity have left an indelible mark. The Jews of Novogrudok will always remember with respect the modest and good hearted Louie Zlotnik.

Ilia Aronovich Gumener

by Ch. L.

Translated from Yiddish by O. Delatycki

He arrived in Novogrudok in 1925, and he worked as a lawyer. Gumener was one of the most outstanding individuals who participated in the communal activities in Novogrudok. He took part in many public affairs, and did not restrict himself by belonging to one organization. He was the head of a number of progressive societies and public institutions. He was a member of the city council of Novogrudok, as well as chairman of the committee of the orphanage. He was a member of the council of Shogday Melocho and the city library. He was a representative of the societies YAKAPA and ORT. He participated in the establishment of a furniture trade school at Shogday Melocho, where many youths were given an opportunity of becoming well qualified tradesman. He participated also in arranging evening classes for the working youth. And though Gumener stemmed from a russified family that spoke Russian at home, he had a great respect for, and love of, the Yiddish language, literature and culture. Gumener put a great effort into the foundation of a kindergarten and a Yiddish elementary school. He had to uphold the economic existence of the elementary school and fight its opponents from the right and left. Gumener was always a steadfast defender of the elementary school and the Yiddish tongue. Since his youth, he was a member of S"S and later Friland (full English name "Freeland League for Jewish Territorial Colonization"). He always taught how to fight for national and social liberation. He was constantly following his chosen path with youthful vigour. He never allowed side issues or personal interests to influence him and was staunchly following the ideas in which he believed.

Ilia Gumener with his wife and daughter were murdered by the Germans on the 9th of August 1942 in a slaughter in Dvorets.

[Page 158]

Shmuel Salomon

by Ch. L.

Translated from Yiddish by O. Delatycki

Shmuel Salomon was born in Vilno in 1896. From his early youth

Shmuel was displaying outstanding ability to learn. After he finished the Yiddish elementary school, he enrolled in the renowned Teachers Seminary, which he finished with distinction. The director of the Teachers Seminary sent him to Ekatarinoslav (now Dniepropetrovsk) to work as a teacher. He stayed there till the outbreak of the Russian revolution. He then returned to Vilno and was employed in the central administration of schools. His next appointment was to establish a Jewish elementary school in Danilevich, where he taught for 3 years. From there he was sent to Horodyshch and subsequently to Novogrudok. He was by than a well-experienced teacher with a love of the Yiddish language, and was teaching in the Yiddish elementary school and in the evening classes of Shogday Melocho. He displayed inordinate abilities to teach. Regardless of the difficult economic conditions, he did not give up his work. In that period Solomon was involved in a number of committees of institutions such as Shogday Melocho, TOZ, library etc. Shmuel had a liking for music. He organized a choir, and when the dramatic society would produce a new show, he would prepare songs and parodies on current events, both lyrics and melody. His parodies could be heard all over town. He was totally involved in the matter of schooling when the Jewish school changed from Fisher to Tarbut. At the change, he gave up education. He was very involved in the study of Jewish (Yiddish?) literature and took an active part in all Jewish cultural events. He was a lively promoter of the use of the Yiddish language and made certain that this tongue was not neglected. The main characteristic of Salomon was modesty. He never offended an opponent in a discussion. He was honored in the democratic circles. He was nominated by the democrats to the position of an alderman on the city council. In that capacity he responded to all problems under consideration. He was a good speaker and a correspondent for the "Navaredkier Lebn". When the war started, Shmuel Salomon tried to escape to Russia. Having almost made it to Minsk, he was forced to return. He was among the first 52 Jews who were executed without reason by the Germans in the marketplace. Their bodies were taken to the Jewish cemetery and buried in a pit. Thus died Salomon, the cheerful singer and friend. Died the gifted poet who recited his parody on a "buried little town". Alas, his parody became an appalling reality. Our town is now a cemetery. Who knows if even the cemetery exists. Who knows...

(We can answer the above question. In 1952 the Soviets allowed the tombstones of the Jewish cemetery to be carted away by the local populace and used as foundations. On the deserted hill goats are grazing.)

Attorney Eliyahu Gumener

Shmuel Salomon

[Page 159]

Itzchak Gurvich

by a Townsman

Translated from Yiddish by O. Delatycki

Yitzchak Gurevitz

Nobody could equal his devotion to the people who stemmed from Novogrudok. Where he obtained his information about Novogrudker, even of those living in distant Siberia, nobody knew. But the expression on his face gave him away – today he is in a festive mood – he has a new address. It is a hot summer's day and it is too hot to travel in the midday sun, let alone to walk in the sand. But Itzchak Gurvich is on the move, with his thick jacket under his arm, his face sweaty. His breathing is laboured, but the eyes are shiny. After a brief respite he exclaims "I found her, one of Limon's daughters', she is in the depth of Russia. He had already sent her a parcel. It is no wonder that all those who settled a long time ago in Eretz Israel, not to mention newcomers, considered him their envoyto Novogrudok. They were all asking for his advice. The newcomers knew no other address. Many spent the first night in Israel in his home. Itzchak Gurvich had a good nature so typical of many of our townsmen. Though he cast his roots deep in Israel, he lived to his last breath in Novogrudok. The help for a survivor from Novogrudok was his first aim. One of his greatest pleasures was to chat about Novogrudok. He is remembered with love and admiration by all who knew him. It is natural that the loan fund of the Novogrudok committee, which assisted people in need over the years, carries the name of Itzchak Gurvich. His memory will linger in our hearts.

Family Vager

by Chaim Leibovich

Translated from Yiddish by O. Delatycki

The family consisted of two sisters Chana and Nachama and a brother Mandl. Chana and Mandl were well educated and were considered to belong to the intelligentsia. Nachama, who was also well educated, clever and businesslike, was the provider for the family. She managed the family business, which was a shoe shop. She assumed the part of a mother in the family Vager. Mandl and particularly Chana were good teachers. Mandl, as far as I know, was an adherent to socialism. The pupils and teachers of the gymnasium respected them. Nachama was honest and good hearted and sought contacts with ordinary people. The people of the town looked with approval on the engagement of Nachama, not with a member of the intelligentsia, but to a man who was working in her trade and was also a gifted artist. The theatre was one of the few diversions available in the gloomy days of the German occupation (the author writes of the German occupation in the First World War). It was destined by fate that the family Vager left

Novogrudok and was spread to different parts of the world. Mandl went to Russia, where he worked as an engineer in Moscow. Chana lived in Vilno where she perished together with all of the Jewish community. Nachama found a new home in America. Nachama channeled all her efforts and love into the work of the Novogrudok Relief Committee. She conducted the correspondence with the Novogrudok committee in Israel. Her letters were filled with love and devotion to those who survived the Holocaust. Her work on the committee was her sacred duty. The death of Nachama was a great loss to the relief effort in America, and to all survivors from Novogrudok. May her memory remain with us forever.

[Page 160]

Grandmother Slept

by D.C. (In memory of the old woman Etl Goldberg.)

Translated from Hebrew by Aviva Kamil

Etl Goldberg more than 100 years old

When the great granddaughter heard her parents talk about the very old grandmother, who passed away, she said with a child's seriousness: "you are mistaken, the grandmother did not die; she is asleep". There was some truth in it, all those who knew her believed that grandmother would go on and on to live her clean and beautiful life, that she would continue to sit on the veranda on clear days, follow with a merciful and loving look the children of the street, who now and then would glance at her in amazement - such an old woman!

The old woman arrived in Eretz-Israel more then 30 years ago, and lived in the home of her only daughter. She was then 70 years old.

In her hometown Novogrudok in Byelorussia she was one of the striking figures on the Jewish street. Simplicity and grace, loyalty and devotion added to her charm. Here, in the new land, she found that the weather was different. She observed the robust way of life of her grandchildren, natives of that land, and their interest in current events. The new surroundings influenced her and added to the old women's personality. She also knew the secret of silence. The two worlds - past and present - became combined in her soul and she loved them both.

Her memories of the distant days were full of anecdotes and humour. She told the story of the Turkish prisoners of war, who passed through the town and asked for "ak mak" (bread). The Russians ordered to give them nothing, but she disobeyed and fed them. "And when was it?" asked the grandchildren. "It was then, a long time ago" she answered.

She remembered the event when the Rabbi of Novogrudok, Rabbi Yitzchak Alchanan, before departing to accept the rabbinical chair of Kovna, blessed her, as a little girl, wishing her a long life. When asked how old she was she would answer with a smile: "I did not learn accountancy."

A hundred years old and she did not listen to the doctor, who told her that it was permitted for her to eat something on Yom Kippur . "Are you promising me that I will reach the next Yom-Kippur?" she asked and added that "the One who helped me to go through all the other fasts, will help me to go through this one too." She had the good fortune to take part in the elections to the "Knesset" twice and considered it a great Mitzvah.

The years burdened her, her back was bent, her hearing had diminished and she complained that the Cantors of today could not reach the volume of the voices of cantors of the past. "I could hear the trill then, but I can not hear it now" she told us. She brought a special material from home and secretly prepared her last garment. She was not afraid of death, the fate of all that were born is to be buried. She was happy to be buried in the soil of Israel. (She would not have

"Chibut Kever" - beating in the grave - on the way from the Diaspora to Jerusalem or Israel?).

No wonder that her great granddaughter, who was much loved by her, could not accept her death. "Grandmother is asleep in her eternal sleep, our grandmother and mother", she told us.

[Page 161]

Alter Kaminiecki

by N. K.

Translated from Yiddish by Oskar Delatycki

Alter Kamenetsky

His father Elivahu Ber was a chazan (cantor) and shochet (ritual butcher) in Zetl. He was liked and valued by all. Many remember his original tunes. The son lived in Novogrudok and was a timber merchant. He was a respected business man, whilst at the same time he was immersed body and soul in communal work. He was a member of the Kehile (Jewish self-governing body), a member of the committee of Hakodesh hospital, of the Chevre Kadishe (burial society) and Mojshev Skeinim (old people's home). Almost all of his spare time was spent visiting old people. He scrutinized the cleanliness of the establishment and its inhabitants. He introduced a weekly "day of cleanliness". On that day the whole house [Mojshev Skeinim] was washed and cleaned. All old people had to bathe and clean all corners of the house. He was helping them in that task. He used to say in jest on such occasions "I cleaned out today a cart load of sins". He meant by it that he removed all rags, which the old people kept and treasured, though they were of no use to them.

He liked a joke and a wise saying. He had a knack of solving all problems playfully and with ease. He never offended anyone and was liked by all. He had no enemies. Because of these attributes he was called upon often to act as arbitrator if altercations between business men, neighbours or married couples occurred. He always found a way to a peaceful solution of problems without offending anyone. At home he was always cheerful and smiling and therefore harmony always prevailed. His wife Bejlke was good and handsome and she always met her husband with a smile. If she saw good humour on his face, which indicated that a good piece of work had been done, a good outcome had been reached, a worthwhile arbitration had been concluded, she would meet him with a witty remark "will they give you a pallet of wine for your troubles"?. He was doing his work unsparingly when it was necessary. When the new Tarbut school was being built he put a lot of energy into the project. He was supervising, providing materials of construction and resources as if the school was his private possession. If he saw an injustice he was ready to put up a bitter fight. For example - he was the adherent of the Lubch rabbi [see p.129 "The last of the rabbis" by Yehoshua Yaffe] he was devoted to him body and soul and fought for him with all his might. He was a constant supplicant in the Shloss gass shul. Reb Alter would not tolerate a wrong doing against a Jew or a gentile. All remember the story of the cow. One market day Reb Alter was seen leading a cow to the market. Everyone looked at him in wonder. They asked what he was doing with a cow? He told them "wait and see". He went to the market place and found a woman who was the wife of one of his workers. He told her: "take the cow, it's yours". He explained: "your husband works for me in the forest, I know that he spends his wages on liquor and let you and your children starve, so I started without him knowing it, to deduct every week a small part of his wages and saved up enough to buy the cow, here is the detailed account" he said, handing over to her the record, "take the cow home and feed your children". The farmers of the whole district repeated the story and esteemed his name.

Kaminiecki with thousands of others in the district was killed by the Germans on the eighteens day of Kislev Tov Shin Bet [8 December 1941].

[Page 162]

Shmuel Goldberg

by Luba Cohen

Translated from Hebrew by Aviva Kamil

I see it as my duty to add to the number of personalities in our town before and after W.W.1, the image of my father Reb Shmuel Goldberg of blessed memory, who died on Kaf in the month of Adar 1922. He was chosen as a bridegroom for my mother from the Yeshiva of Lubch, where he had qualified as a Rabbi, but he did not practice as one. He joined the business of my uncle Reb Leib Boruchovich, learned slaughtering and "Nikur" in Minsk and was the first to introduce ñNikurî to our town.

Like all men of Torah, he knew how to divide his time between Torah and daily contact with people. In the late hours of the night, after midnight, one could hear his pleasant voice as he was learning a page of the "Gmarah". He was also an enthusiastic Zionist and dreamt about going to Eretz-Israel. His daughter studied Hebrew and received a secular education. He subscribed to a Hebrew newspaper and distributed the "Shekel". My father was among the studious people of "Sha's" and taught "Gemarah" at the "Kloiz". Many members of the Kloiz were people revered in the community. I remember the dinners of "Sha's", which were held at our house and became a celebration to all. My father had a good voice and during the holidays he acted as the "Ba'al Musaf" and "Ba'al Hakriah Ve' Hatkiah" in the synagogue. I was at the time a young girl of 10, yet I accompanied my father to hear him sing in front of the ark. I can still hear his melodious voice when the days of Atonement come close.

Father was the treasurer of the societies "Gmilut Chesed" and "Maskil el Dal" (welfare societies), which were established, in their time, by a number of great people including Mr.Gatzov and Leib Harakavy. He was whole-heartedly devoted to this modest enterprise, which gave loans with no interest to the needy. These people would come to our house after Sabbath to either return loans or to borrow money for their small businesses at the market. They were given a cup of tea and spent some time in a social atmosphere, discussing daily affairs.

The elderly and strict "Mohel", Rabbi Danzig, kept an eye on talented men and trained my father to replace him. He was very gifted and his name as an expert "Mohel "became famous. On many Shabbats and Holidays he left his family and spent time in the villages for "Brit-Milah".

Because of all of father's duties, mother had to assist him in their business. In his later years, when he was terminally ill, he still went on serving the community and never expected any reward. Father passed away at the age of 60. He was liked and revered by all his friends and many turned to him for advice.

Mother was lucky enough to come to Erets-Israel and lived with her daughter's family. She grew very old and lived to see her grandchildren and great grand children. (See the article "Grandmother is asleep").

Those good Jews bequeathed to their children attributes, which helped them in their struggles in their new land.

The Jewish town and its good people were erased, but their memory will stay with us forever.

Yehudah Kaplinsky

Yehudah Kaplinsky

[Page 162]

Yehuda Kaplinski

By Luba Rudnicki

Translated from Yiddish by Oskar Delatycki

On sleepless nights, when the thoughts take one over the seas and fields to the far lands and return to one's birthplace, to our town Novogrudok, which not so long ago pulsated with the life of Jews. Now there are only ruins, empty as a desert. There is no one there. The stones in the ruins are crying and the voices of our brothers are emanating from the bloody earth. And among all the voices I can hear my father calling with his voice full of love and warmth.

The figure of my father stands before my eyes, his smile, his penetrating look full of wisdom. This is how he looked when he was alive. Since the early days of our childhood, as soon as we could comprehend, he implanted in us the love of knowledge and the love of Eretz Isroel. He was an active member of the Zionist organisation of Novogrudok. He mentioned frequently that if he had sons (he had three daughters) he would have wound up his possessions in Novogrudok and would have gone to Israel, but with young daughters this would be a difficult task.

Our house was a traditional Jewish home. It was a warm dwelling for everyone. Our mother a quite, reserved and noble soul met everyone with hearty friendship. Many of our friends who came to study in our high school, found in our house a warm home.

In our home we had a large Jewish library of the classics as well as many Hebrew books. In those days there was no Hebrew school in our town and we learnt Hebrew from the private teacher, Mr Auservitz. He was a bachelor from Korelich, very shy but very knowledgeable. In his quite, rasping voice he was finding for the children the sources of Hebrew literature. My father had a serious problem – where should his children continue their studies? At the time there was a Talmid Torah (which was not open to girls) and a Jewish primary school. The Polish primary school (powszechna) was not considered to be suitable. Due to his energy and strong will, and with the help of like minded supporters, the Tarbut school was started in 1923-24 (but see p.89, Hebrew Education in Novogrudok, By Moshe Steinberg-Sarig).

In the Tarbut school most subjects were taught in Hebrew, from arithmetic to geography. The first director of the Tarbut school was Korn and the teachers were Lidski, Pieresedski, Mrs Yorman, Gudsvirk, Chasn Rabinovich, who taught singing and the school doctor was Dr Marmurshtin. Later came the director Steinberg. Father had to conduct strong battles. The problems were created by the various political parties. But in time the opposition got used to the idea of the changes and they became resigned to it.

Large expenses were required to maintain the Tarbut school. The Tarbut School was situated in the upper story of Israelit's house. The City Council (magistrat) did not contribute to the upkeep of the school. The organisers had to find the means to maintain the school. This was the most difficult issue. In the beginning, the pupils came from middle class homes. It was not possible to charge high fees. There were also pupils who had to be assisted by providing them with books.

Father was not at a loss in those difficult times. He created a parent's committee of which he was the chairman. They tried to raise funds by different means: they brought to town the Chasn Sierota, as well as artists, lecturers etc. Thus the Tarbut School grew in size in time and became the centre of Zionist organisations and of the enlightened youth. But father did not rest. His dream was to build a new building to house the Tarbut school. His dream came to fruition. A splendid building with all facilities was erected with a large yard surrounding it. His joy was boundless. Even though father was very busy in his own business, he always had time for community affairs. He was a member of the merchant association, he was a member of the commission for rates. He was also respected in non-Jewish circles. His opinions were taken in consideration. He was the secretary of Chevra Kadisha (burial society) to his last day. Among other members of the Chevra Kadisha, it is worth mentioning Raphael Yoselevich the shoemaker, who was a fine, honest Jew, clever and good. And there was Leizer Izraelit the painter.

Father wanted us to be acquainted with a wide range of things. His cosy chats were full of good humour, wisdom and deep thoughts. I can hear his voice to this day. Those were the days when the big troubles were about to begin, when the German murderers have occupied Novogrudok and an order was given that Jews were to wear the yellow Star of David. I had sewn on the yellow patch to my father's jacket. My father burst into tears like a small child and said "my child I am proud to be a Jew, I believe and hope that you will survive the slaughters and that a new world will arise. Then you will frame the yellow patch and that will be the witness of our pains for generations to come."

May his memory be with us forever.

[Page 163]

My Mother and Sisters

by Luba Valkin

Translated from Hebrew by Aviva Kamil

With a heavy heart and a trembling hand I am trying to recreate some memories of my dear mother Beilka Simchovich and my two sisters Lea and Masha.

My mother became a widow at a young age. She had to provide for her three daughters by working as a linen seamstress.

She made an effort, using her meagre earnings, to give her daughters a good education. She always worked till late at night. My sister Lea graduated from the "Tarbut" school and was a teacher.

Despite her lack of means, mother took pity on the hungry boys who studied at the "Shulhoif" near our house. She came out smiling and shared with them the little she had.

My poor mother, she felt, when we said our goodbyes, that she would not see us again.

The cruel hand of the enemy put an end to her life and to the lives of my two sisters and all the dear community of our town Novogrudok.

I will never forget my dear ones.

[Page 164]

Hersh Ostashinski

By a townsman

Translated from Yiddish by Oskar Delatycki

Novogrudok was blessed with great rabbis, a large and famous Musar Yeshiva and with ordinary, hearty people. Novogrudok had also a goods and worldly intelligentsia, which was distinguished by its devotion to work for common causes. They had good habits, open hearts and pockets and had a broad Jewish and worldly secular education.

From far away my thoughts at times go to the family Ostashinski: he was known as father Hirsh and she as mother Rivka. Their shop in the Yiddish street, not far from the Market place, sold textiles. Yet it was unusual – a Jewish shop where there was no bargaining, where the prices were not raised and not lowered. Every customer knew that here he was treated fairly – the prices were firm and the measurements were accurate. Also the treatment of the customers, be it a Jew or a gentile, was courteous, and with grace. Hirsh Ostashinski was acknowledged by everybody in town. In the town council, where he was a councillor, and in all other communal organizations he was widely respected. He was never servile to high officials.

It was a pleasure to enter his shop or the home of the family Ostashinski, which was radiating with courtesy and goodwill.

Let these lines inscribe and commemorate the well regarded family Ostashinski. Let it also remind us of the surviving son of the family Avrom Ostashinski, who is a lecturer in the Department of Chemistry in Warsaw, and is in close contact with the Novogrudker in Israel.

[Page 164]

With the Coffin of Reb Yosef Yozl Horovich in Israel

Translated from Hebrew by Aviva Kamil

Reb Yosef Yozl was the founder of the "Musar Yeshiva" in Novogrudok. It was a special privilege for the students as well as the students of Reb Yosef Yozl's students, to accompany his coffin, which had been brought from Kiev U.S.S.R, more than 40 years after the Rabbi's death and to lay his bones to rest in Jerusalem, the capital of free and independent Israel. Reb Yosef Yozl did his best to establish Yeshivas along the length and breadth of Russia. These Yeshivas were considered to be the children of the mother Yeshiva in Novogrudok.

The Yeshivas were destroyed, Torah and Musar were uprooted and the Rabbi's bones were to be removed because the Kiev cemetery was to be demolished.

His followers performed a great "chesed" and much effort into bringing his bones to Israel.

Among those who accompanied the coffin were members of the committee of the Jews of Novogrudok in Israel and the editors of Pinkas Novogrudok, who dedicated a place of honour in the Pinkas to the memory of the Rabbi, the Yeshiva and the Musar movement.

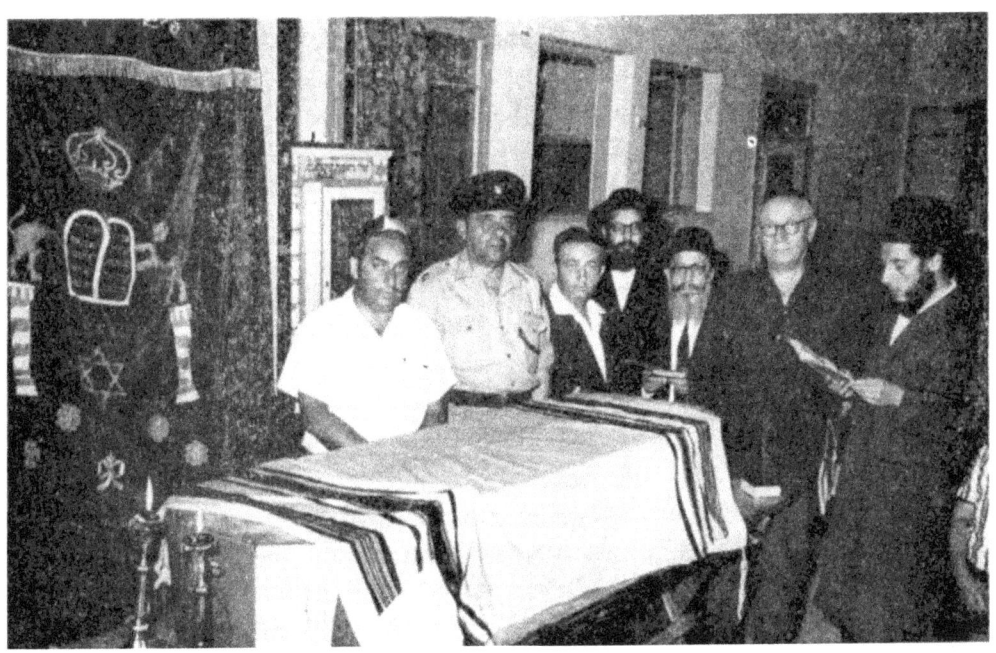

Rabbi Yosef Yozl's body in Tel-Aviv.

[Page 165]

The Surroundings

Karelich

by CH. T.

Translated from Hebrew by Aviva Kamil

Karelich, [the name in Polish is Korelicze], is a small town 21 kilometres from Novogrudok. In the period of the "Rzeczypospolita" Karelich was in the "wojewodztwo" (district) and powiat (sub-district) of Novogrudok. Most of the Polish wojewodztwo of Novogrudok was part of the Minsk gubrnia in the days of the rule of the Tsars of Russia. Karelich, which is known for its fertile soil, is situated on the river Ruta on the road to Slutsk, Nesviz and Mir, which is the main road to the heart of Lithuania and the kingdom of old Poland.

The landlords of Karelich, since the distant past, were the Grand Dukes of Lithuania, followed in turn by the Princes Czartoryskis, the house of Radziwills, then it was given as part of the dowry of Princess Stefania Radziwill, when she married a Prince of the House of Wittgenstein. Later the Putkamers and, after the first World War, Count Zoltowski were the landlords.

Important events in the history of Poland and Lithuania occurred in Karelich. It was fought for by many invaders. In 1395 Swidrygajlo with the help of the crusaders fought against GD Witold. In 1505 the Crimean Tatars devastated the town. And again in 1655 the Swedes occupied Karelich. Russian Tsar Pyotr the Great, in 1705, on the way from Grodno to Moscow, stayed in Karelich. In the following year the town was once more ruined by Swedes. The patriotic Polish "shliachta" gathered in Karelich in 1733 in an attempt to crown Stanislaw Leszczynski. As a direct result of the division of Poland in 1795, Karelich had become part of Russia until World War I. In 1812 Karelich was host, in turn, to the French, Polish and Russian troops. The Radziwills built a well known gobelin tapestries plant in Karelich.

The History of the Jewish Congregation until World War I

Because of the Holocaust not many documents were left from the early days of the Jewish community in Karelich

The oldest tombstones in the Jewish cemetery in Karelich were from the 18th century, according to a person of our generation, who visited Karelich on the eve of World War II.

There is some information that the Jews settled in the town much earlier. It would appear that initially they buried their dead in the cemetery of a neighbouring congregation, and in the 18th century they established their own cemetery. According to the census of 1765 there were 336 Jewish persons in the congregation, who paid "head tax". As head tax was paid by the adult population, we can deduce that of the order of a thousand Jews lived at the time in Karelich. According to the census of 1897, 1840 Jews were resident in Karelich (out of an overall population of 2259) (Evrejskaja Encyk.1X, 751).

During the Russian rule, the congregation did not have a formal status. Funds for the needs of the congregation were raised from the meat tax - "karabeika", which was collected by a Jew, who acted as a custom's official.

The Institutions of the Congregation

There were two synagogues and a "Kloiz" called "Chasidishe Shtibl" in town. One of the synagogues was called "old", because it was built in place of the "Alte-Shul", which burned down during the great fire of 1911. The previous "Alte-Shul" was built of timber in the middle of the 18th century.

The synagogue, which was built in place of the "Alte-Shul", was called "Beit-Midrash", because up until World War I "Yeshiva Bochers" (Torah students) studied there. During their time at the Yeshiva, they were invited to "eat days" (ie eat each day) in different homes. The "Beit-Midrash" was also a hostel for the students societies: "Ein-Yaakov", "Mishnayot" and "Tehilim reciters".

There were also in the town the "Chevrah Kadisha", "Linat Tsedek" (sleeping quarters for the needy) "Hachnasat-Kala", which arranged weddings for poor brides, and "lending cash boxes" for the needy. According to the information given by a person of our generation, the congregation took care of its poor and needy, so that they did not have to humiliate themselves by seeking alms from strangers.

Karelich was known for its famous Rabbis. This showed that the standard of learning of the Torah of the community was high. Among those who served as leading Rabbis until World War I were: Rabbi Mordchele also known as "der Oshmianer" (from Oshmiany), Rabbi Eliyahu Prochiner, Rabbi Eliyahu Baruch Kamai, who was the head of the Yeshivah in Mir and the "Gaon" Rabbi Avraham Itzchak Cohen from Plashnitz, who was called "The Eelui (genius) from Plashnitz" and was the Rabbis who came to town on the eve of World War I . The Rabbis were not paid a regular salary but made a living from duties on yeast and candles. Karelich was the birthplace of the poet and martyr Itzchak Katsenelson (1885-1942) and writer David Einhoren (1885-).

The History of the Town after World War I

During World War I , Karelich was a battlefield for the German army. The civilian population vacated the town and dispersed to surrounding towns, which were under German occupation. The town was completely destroyed. With the end of battles, in 1918, the refugees started to return to town. But many of the Jews who left, established themselves in their places of refuge and never returned to their birthplace. According to the Riga treaty of 1921, following the war in 1920 between the Poles and Bolsheviks, Karelich came under Polish rule. The Jewish community gradually began to rebuild again, and organise its public and spiritual life.

The first concern was the children's education. Two "cheders" were established followed by the school "Tarbut" (five classes). Jewish children went also to a Polish Primary school, and those with means continued their education in the government high school in neighbouring Novogrudok or in Vilna in the Hebrew Seminar for teachers or the high school "Tarbut". Social life in town was dynamic; the youth displayed a lively spirit.

All Zionist Youth movements were represented: "the Young Chalutz" "Chalutz", "Hashomer Hatsair" "Beitar", and the "Bund" (non Zionist).

The youth worked for the national funds: "J.N.F" "Keren Hayesod" "Keren Hachlutz" and the like. There was a big library with books in Yiddish and Hebrew, which had developed from a small children's library.

Karelich contributed greatly to pioneering and "Aliyah". From the beginning of the twenties there was an uninterrupted stream of men and women who went on "Aliyah" after years of working in "Hachsharah" in "Hachsharah" kibbutzim of "Hachalutz" or "Hashomer Hatsair".

The Economic Composition of the Jewish Community of Karelich

On the eve of World War II the community consisted of approximately 1300 people (from the overall population of 2000 residents). The Jews made a living as small shop owners, tradesmen (50 families app.), farmers [growing mainly cucumbers], orchardists, flour millers, "sacred items" (?), leasing fish ponds from Polish land owners etc.

There was one Jewish doctor (apart from the Christian doctor who served mainly the Christian population), a midwife and one pharmacy. The community had from the beginning of the twenties a bank, "Cooperativer arbeter un hantwerker bank" (the cooperative bank of workers and artisans). It served the community by providing loans at a low interest rate.

The Jews worked hard but found it difficult to make a living. With exception of a few families; most were supplementing their income with financial help from relatives overseas. The economic situation deteriorated, especially when the Polish colonists ("osadniki"), who served in the legion of Piltsudski, came to the district from other parts of Poland to settle as farmers. They initiated a wave of anti-semitism, and incited the Byelorussian village population (which lived with Jews peacefully for generations) to boycott Jewish shops. Some Jews from Karelich managed to migrate to Erets-Israel, just before the holocaust.

In June 1941, with the start of Hitler's offensive against the Soviet Union, the Germans invaded Byelorussia and the fate of the Karelich community was similar to the fate of the other Jewish communities that came under the cruel enemy rule. The Germans built a Ghetto in the town, drafted men for forced labour and slowly started the physical extermination of the Jewish population.

In February 1942 they started to transfer the Jews of Karelich to neighbouring Novogrudok, where a large Ghetto was built for the Jews of the district. Most Jews of Karelich together with their brethren from other towns surrounding Novogrudok were exterminated.

Only a few managed to save themselves by escaping to the forests of Naliboki and joining the partisans. They numbered no more then 20 souls.

That is how a remarkable Jewish community, which was like a gleaming pearl in the string of sacred communities in the Jewish Diaspora of Eastern Europe, was erased from under God's sky.

The Condition of the Remnants of the Karelich Community and What They Did to Perpetuate the Town's Memory

The remnants of the Karelich community are scattered all over the world: North America, South-America, Africa, and Soviet Russia. But most of them, about 100 in number, are privileged to live in Israel. The organisation of the Jews from Karelich in Israel was started by the initiative and dedication of Mr. Kalman Avrahami (Redrovich) ZL.

On Memorial Day, which was decided upon by the organisation to be kaf gimel-Kaf Dalet in the month of Av, all the people of Karelich from Kibbutzim, Kvutzot, Moshavim, Moshavot, from Jerusalem and Tel-Aviv, assemble in order to commemorate the memory of their murdered brothers and sisters.

The committee of the organisation consists of 9 members. They meet 3-4 times a year.

The committee members are: Chairman Michael Beigin, China Kaspi, Yaakov Abramovitch, Yaakov Pluzanski, Avraham Koznitch, Noach

Gershonovski, Mordechi Meirovitch, Rivka Reuveni, Yehuda Shapira. The address of the organisation is: Michael Beigin 13 Straus St. Jerusalem

The Activities of the Organisation

The committee keeps contact with all the members, including those outside Israel. It organises the annual Memorial Day. It built the Memorial on Har-Zion. The committee takes part in the meetings of "Yad-Vashem" in Jerusalem and the "Union of emigrant Jews from Poland" in Tel-Aviv. It conducted a review seeking information about the history of Karelich. It took part in the World Congress of Polish Jews, which assembled in Israel in January 1961. Plans for the future: To perpetuate the name of our town by publishing a book by using at least stencils. To plant an avenue in the "Forest of the Martyrs" to the memory of the Karelich martyrs. There is the thought of creating a fund for the needy ("Gmilut-Chesed") dedicated to Karelich.

To our regret our financial resources are scant and we are at a loss to know how we are going to bring about all these modest plans to fruition.

We hope that our brethren across the seas will stand by us with financial help, so that we will be able to erect a memorial worthy of the community of Karelich.

Sources:

> Personal memories of the writer, of the chairman of our committee-Mr. Michael Beigin, Chaim Kalmanovski and Lea Kaplan (kibbutz Givat-Chaim), Reb Pesach Kaplan (Karkur) Notes of Reb Mordechi Meirovitch who was born in Karelich, were saved on the day of the slaughter in the ghetto of Novogrudok and ultimately came to Israel.

[Page 167]

How I remember Selub (Wsielub)

by Y. Y.

Translated from Yiddish by O. Delatycki

My township Selub, where I was born, is situated 14 km from Novogrudok. For several hundred years, about 100 families lived there. The Jews of the town spread firm roots in the land and made a living from that land. Almost every household owned a piece of land. They worked on the land and lived off it. A Jew in Selub ate his own home-grown potatoes and his own bread from grain grown by him on his own land. He sowed and harvested his own food. Everybody had cattle and everybody had milk, cheese and butter. Almost everyone was a worker or a tradesman. Even business people and shopkeepers worked on the land in their spare time.

Selub was a small township with a small market place in the centre, where all shops were located. From the market place, four streets emanated, forming a cross. There was a small lane were the synagogue was situated. Selub had one synagogue and one pharmacy, one Jewish woman doctor, one timber merchant, one flour mill (which ran on water), four shops selling textiles, eight food shops, six haberdashery shops, two bakeries, a rabbi, a slaughterer, a melamed (religious teacher of the young) and two teachers, one hatter, two blacksmiths, four cobblers, ten tailors, two butchers, two cabmen and two wool combing factories.

It was a Zionist town. In anti-semitic Poland the youth did not have an economic future in a small town. In the 1920's after the First World War many young people emigrated to Venezuela and Argentina. Later the ideal of every youngster in Selub was to immigrate to Eretz Israel. Only those who left the town survived. The most prominent Jew in town was the Rabbi, Reb Nataniel Zarkain, a son of a Baranovich turner, who hid (the future marshal of Poland) Pilsudski. He was a quiet Rabbi who did not interfere in local affairs. He preached in the synagogue twice a year. He was not a great preacher. His wife managed the business, which was selling yeast. He sent his daughter Sorele to study in a Polish gymnasium, which was not readily acceptable by the rabbis.

Reb Kalman Yeshie Shmulevich was a Jew who knew well the Torah, but he did not want to be a rabbi. He was fluent in Shas, in the Agoda and Midrash. His son Josef was a brilliant student. They had a food shop which Reb Kalman's wife Fejge managed. Apart from Josif, they had three other children: Tuvie, Abe and Hinde Bejle.

Reb Yehuda Vigacki was one of the respected citizens. He was a tall, handsome Jew, fluent in his knowledge of the Torah, and had a fine tenor voice. He was the ritual slaughterer and also performed circumcisions. He was a student of religion and an intelligent Jew. He had intelligent and well brought up children.

Reb Eliezer Jona Halevi Movshovich was an honest, fine Jew who was a preacher. He travelled a lot on behalf of the Jerusalem Yeshiva Ethach Chaim. The house was run by his wife Shejne, who was a good pious woman who took on the duty of earning the income for the family.

Jona Movshovich preached religion and also Zionism. They had four children: two daughters, Zlata and Liba, and two sons, Zvi Hershl, a tailor, and the second son Yehuda, who was studying in the Yeshiva. The brothers Mate and Yessel leased the flour mill from a Polish landowner. They were good, hard working fellows, and with the help of their children they ran the mill. The nicest house in the market place belonged to the timber merchant Binchanski. His son Jankel was also active in communal affairs. The two textile shops were also in the town square. They belonged to the brothers Matke and Hershl. The third textile shop belonged to Gershon Berkovski. His son Leibl was a communal worker in town. He was the chairman of the Zionist organization; he was the organizer of all communal and cultural affairs, created a dramatic circle, created a Jewish library and represented the town in contacts with the government authorities. After he married he moved to Lida. During the German occupation Gitl Berkovski with her daughter Sonia were first hidden by farmers and later joined the Bielski partisans. They survived the war.

Selib was a town of tradesmen. The best tailor in town was Nojach Berkovski, who employed two apprentices. One of them, Sender, immigrated to Argentina, but came back and married a local girl. Nojach the tailor had three sons: Isroel, Jehuda and Josif. Chaim Eliahu Berkovski lived in the market place. His daughter Chana was in hiding during the war and lives now in Haifa. Nochim Berkovski was a tailor. His wife Henie learned tailoring from her husband, and together they made leather coats and textile jackets for the farmers. They also kept bees. The old tailor, Dovid Berkovski, roused the Jews for sliches [a prayer asking for forgiveness which is recited before the high holidays]. His sons Leizer Berl and Avrom Leib immigrated to Venezuela. They lived in Shul Heif Lane. If one walked through the lane, one would hear various melodies from Yoim naroim, which he converted to Zionist tunes and would mingle them with the sound of the sewing machines. There were also a few tailors in town who travelled and worked in the villages during the week, and for Sabbath they would return home. The same was true for the cobblers, Berl Leizerowski, Michl the cobbler, Dovid the cobbler, Hertzl Berkovski, Jashke the cobbler, and his son Chaim Eliyahu. He was a jolly one; he would jest and tell jokes. Among the settled inhabitants of the town were the shop owner Michl Gurvich, the family Shmulevich, and brothers Rubinski. All those families were Zionists. Their children went on hachshara and immigrated to Israel, where they are among the few survivors of the town. Selub was a small township but the Jews lived an intensive, communal, Zionist and cultural life. They were simple working people, good people immersed in the Jewish nation and the Jewish spirit. This is our memorial to them. They all perished on the 8 December 1941. May God avenge their blood.

[Page 168]

My Shtetl Selub

by Liba Shmulevits

Translated from Yiddish by O. Delatycki

As a misty memory stands before me, my shtetl Selub, with its few streets, the Jewish market square with the synagogue, the fine households around the market square. When I think of it now, I can see that we lost a nice, small, decent religious community. I remember how many chevres (groups, societies) such a shtetl had - chevre Shas, chevre Mishnaies, chevre Thilim, a chevre which studied every week a portion of Chumash. I am thinking, where did all those humans come from? It was really simple; it was their main interest in life, and children were educated to follow the way that was binding the people with God and *mides toives be adam lechaverim* (good deeds of man to man). This is why in those days there were no Jewish thieves, bandits and every one was *sameiach be chelko* (contented with his lot), his poor, primitive life.

In the market square, all buildings were Jewish. In the centre was the house of Jakov Brodner. He owned a textiles (Manchester) shop which had a high porch. He was rich, highly educated, and strictly religious; his children were well educated, and he owned a substantial library. He subscribed to several papers, including Hebrew ones, which he subscribed to with partners. Opposite him lived Reb Leib a householder, a wealthy Jew, nice, clean, a Jew who wore Tfilin. He had honest, nice, hard working children. All children who married were taken on as partners in the business, and it was a household of unity. They were devoted to each other and had respect for their elders. And they lived to an old age. Reb Sloyme Maker was a respectable citizen, who had a house in the market square, conducted a nice household, and rode in a horse driven carriage which was followed by a dog. He looked as if he was perpetually cross; however he had a good nature. He was always ready to help out, if help was required. Reb Kalman Yshayhu had a haberdashery shop and a house in the market square. He was a Jew who studied day and night. His wife Reize ran the shop. The customers had complete trust in them, and knew that they would not be misled. They had a daughter Feige Rochl who was well educated, enlightened, and was very clever. She married a gifted man and the chain of the faith continued. Moishe Itzchok of blessed memory was a learned Jew, very clever, always friendly, though he was always depressed, because his wife was constantly sick. The children had a religious upbringing and married students of the Yeshiva and continued the tradition. Reb Mendl the blacksmith, a fine, honest, religious man. He was always ready to help anybody in need. His wife Frume was a fine Jewish woman. In another part of the house lived his brother, Arche the cobbler. He was an honest, good Jew. In that house lived six families. In the market square lived Smuel Josl the tailor. I remember his wife particularly well because she, Slava, was making eiderdowns and I liked her work. Her husband was called "American", because he once lived in America. He was a learned man. He had a hotel, but struggled to make a living. His children were well educated. I think that one of their daughters lives in America.

In the middle of the market was a big cross. Many Christians were praying in front of it. All processions ended at the cross. This did not trouble the Jews. The whole week the Jews were concerned with worries of earning a livelihood, because there were very few affluent Jews. But on a Sabbath there were no poor people in town. On Sabbath in all houses, even in the lane, where poor people lived, there were on the table all varieties of meat, fish, and good cholent. The whole town was filled with the spirit of Sabbath. Delicacies – which are now unknown, but anyone of us would eat them gladly – included special dumplings, veal shanks etc. On Sabbath one ate enough to last the week, because meat was not served every weekday, particularly in the summer. Everything was cooked on the day it was eaten and the food was never smoked. I think of the women of those days, and I think that they must have been brave. They cooked and they baked in the one oven three separate times. First biscuits and challah, then they reheated the oven and cooked milk based products, then reheated the oven again and cooked cholent made of a variety of ingredients. They washed and ironed, brought up eight to ten children, did all their sewing, knitted socks for the winter, mended, baked bread, and plucked feathers in the winter evenings. On a Sabbath everyone would go for a walk on the hill. On Lubch street, some distance away, was a nice peaceful stream with yellow sand and small fish, which would disperse in fear of every passer by. One could find there a big stone to pummel the washing. Close to the bridge, nut-bearing trees grew densely. Further on was a place to bathe in the river, but the water was cold. Further along was the tall, nice hill with flowers on both sides. Next to it was the Count's orchard with the branches of the trees breaking under the weight of the fruit. In the orchard were flowers and alleyways and benches to sit on. This was a place to relax in and have pleasure. Some would walk into the pine forest, which was located one kilometre from the township. They would fetch food and spend the day there. The Selub Count was a handsome, good man. He was enormously rich and owned a lot of land, including the land the town was built on. His fees for the lease of the land were very modest. Jews had been leasing from him the flower mill for many generations. The last lessee was my grandfather Moishe Percig, a wealthy man. I remember that every Passover it was traditional to give the Count matzo and wine. The Count supported the poor of the town and gave enough wood to the synagogue to heat it through the winter. Even money for Passover for poor people was given by the Count. His end was tragic. When the Red Army came, he was arrested and taken through the town on a wagon used for carrying rubbish. The Jews of the township cried when they saw him. He was in the Novogrudok jail and was made to do demeaning work. He died in jail.

Members of "HeKhalutz" in Selib

[Page 170]

My Shtetl Selib

by Sara Shmulevich

Translated from Hebrew by Aviva Kamil

There was a small Jewish shtetl. It sounds today like a fairytale.

The Jews, the people of Gemarah, Jews of Tehilim, men of property, (Ba'alei-Batim) and tradesmen and the town disappeared and fell silent. Honest and innocent people, who worshiped God faithfully and believed whole heartedly in the coming of the Messiah. They died sanctifying God's name with the belief that "Netzach Israel Lo Yeshaker" (the people of Israel will tell the truth). And we, the few who stayed alive, remember them with respect and love. We will never, never forget them. We will never forget and never forgive what the Amalek of the twentieth century did to us!

Tsemach, The Coachman (A type from the shtetl Selub)

by Yehushua Yaffe

Translated from Yiddish by O. Delatycki

Tsemach the coachman was renown in the whole district of Novogrudok, regardless whether they did or did not travel with him from Novogrudok to Selub. They all knew him. When he was approaching Novogrudok from Peresike, you could hear people in Shloss Gass say "uwaga pan Tzemach jedzie" (take care, Mister Tzemach is approaching). He was of above average height, with sinking cheeks, a twisted nose, with large eyeglasses held in white frames, with bleached trousers and a mended jacket. With a short white whip in one hand he held the reins in the other as he was walking next to the cart and calling "Mister Tzemach is coming". The farmers knew him and gladly made space for him to pass. Tzemach's cart was arranged like a taxi - four seats in the back and three in front. The cart was filled with straw and covered by a peasant's overcoat. The back of the cart was raised higher than the front to allow the passengers to sit comfortably. Tzemach would help the passengers get onto and off the cart, particularly girls and young women. He would shout at them "you kids get quickly off the cart". The road from Novogrudok to Selub was not paved till just before the Second World War and Tzemach's cart struggled along the sandy road. His horse was not very strong or well fed. As they would come to a small elevation, Tzemach would jump off the cart and the passengers would follow and climb the rise on foot. If anyone failed to do so, they would get a tongue-lashing, and even the elderly women dismounted. That would cause Tzemach to shout even louder "who asked you to come down, it will take you half an hour to get up again". Tzemach had a great self-esteem and everyone had to travel with him. If they did not, he could stop them in the street in Novogrudok and would shout "you, young goat, don't you like riding with Tzemach? Wait till I tell everybody who you go around with at nights". That was enough. The young girl would beg her parents, aunties and uncles in Selub to travel only with Tzemach, else she might end up an old maid. Tzemach was also known to shout in the synagogue. If for any reason praying was interrupted or a quarrel would start in the synagogue Tzemach would shout louder then anyone. He often did not know why he was shouting, but if there was shouting, he would also shout. The only person who could silence him was Chaje, his wife. If she would poke out her head through the curtain of the women's section they would warn him "Tzemach, Chaje is watching". And that would silence him.

The other coachman in Selub was Judmem, who initially came to town to marry someone's daughter. His name was Shloyme. When he arrived in town to get married, they tried to cheat him out of the promised dowry. He started to shout "If you give me the dowry all will be well, if you won't I will do you a judmem and a memjud (which are initials of Russian swear words) and I will go back and leave the bride to you." The potential father and mother in law took fright of Judmem and counted out the promised dowry. Tzemach, however, was not frightened of Judmem, and prevented him from taking on passengers. Judmem had to wait till Tzemach's coach was full before taking on passengers. It took a time for Tzemach to get used to the idea that Judmam was also a coachman and had the right to carry passengers to Novogrudok. But the citizens of Selub travelled mainly with Tzemach.

Later a new calamity occurred. A bus started to travel between Selub and Novogrudok. The prosperous people of Selub were ashamed to travel by horse and cart. Later arrived more competition - a second bus. Almost everyone started to travel by bus and Tzemach lost most of his livelihood.

Later still, the Second World War started. The Soviets arrived, commerce stopped, and there was no reason to travel anywhere.

I saw Tzemach for the last time on Monday the 8th of December 1941. The Germans had amassed all the Jews in the district court at the end of Korelich Street. All the buildings were packed with Jews from everywhere. All the Jews from Selub were there. As the court buildings filled, up the Germans started hoarding Jews in the building that served as the wood store of the court. More than 500 people were packed into the store. The Germans started by selecting the people: who were to live and who to die. When the Germans came to the store one of them shouted: "typhus" and all Jews from Selub were led to the trucks to be taken to their death. Tzemach started arguing with the Germans - he wants to live, he is still young, he will work, but he must not be killed. He started to shout and was taken shouting to the death pits of Skrydlevo.

[Page 171]

Novoyelnie

by Chana Kamin (Kaplan)

Translated from Yiddish by O. Delatycki

Novoyelnie was a small township, a place that has left good and pleasant impressions not only in the memories of the Jews of Novoyelnie, but also in the recollections of many people of the district. Firstly, Novoyelnie was known for its railway station, the only contact between Novogrudok and the world. Novogrudok was joined with Novoyelnie by a narrow gauge rail line. The small train travelled so slowly, particularly in the winter snow, that it would have been quicker to walk. Sometimes the passengers would jump off the train, rub their hands with snow or throw snowballs at each other, run a bit to warm up and still manage to catch up with the train. The railway station in Novoyelnie was the centre point of the township. Here one would meet friends and relatives. Here one could conclude commercial transactions. In winter it was quiet in the township, interrupted only by hooting of the locomotives. The Jewish life in Novoyelnie was concentrated in the main street, where a few dozen Jewish families lived. They made their living by commerce. Once a week on a market day, the farmers from the neighboring villages would come to purchase things and to sell their produce. For the rest of the week, it was very quiet and the rabbi together with the chasan and several traders, with my father OBM among them, had time to pray and study after lunch. The young people were educated mainly in Novogrudok and would come home only during vacation time.

Next to the township was a large pine forest, which was deserted in the winter, but during spring it would wake up. Immediately after Passover the Jews of Novoyelnie started preparing for the vacations. Novoyelnie was a holiday place for the whole district. In the summer people from all neighbouring towns would come to Novoyelnie. The pine forest and the river would attract both young and old. Here the TOZ had its holiday home. There were pensions and houses for rent by families. The vacationers rested and amused themselves in Novoyelnie. They had a good time and could forget their daily worries. The forest was alive. Late into the night one could hear laughter and singing of the young people in the alleys of the forest. Each of us had happy memories of the pleasant times in the forest. The German assassins wiped out this life suddenly, and many near and dear ones were murdered.

[Page 172]

Our Sisters and Brothers in the USA

The Alexander Harkavy Novogrudok Relief Committee in the USA

by Yakov Maslow

Translated from Yiddish by O. Delatycki

An organization to help the people of Novogrudok began when the First World War was declared.

In 1915 a committee to render help was created in New York. The first money was raised by imposing a levy of $100 on each Novogrudok association.

There were no contacts with Novogrudok during the war. In due course the Joint Distribution Committee started accepting financial donations to be forwarded to the needy of the district. The first contribution of $500 was speedily sent out to Novogrudok. Five months later the second contribution of $550 was sent.

Receipts were obtained for the contributions. There were no further contacts with Novogrudok until the year 1919. There were occasional meetings of some members of the Relief Organization, but little was accomplished.

When the war was over, distressing letters arrived from Novogrudok in September 1919. The situation in town was pitiful. Novogrudok was ruined.

The Relief Committee called a mass meeting. Money was collected. The problem was to know how to deliver, as soon as possible, the collected money. It was decided to send a delegate and the honoured townsman Alexander Harkavy OBM was elected to undertake the journey.

In early 1920 Alexander Harkavy departed for Novogrudok, representing the townspeople as well as the surrounding townships, who participated in the collection of the aid money: Lubch, Karelich, Wsielub, Horodishch and other nearby townships.

Harkavy's news from Novogrudok was appalling – there was hunger in the whole of the Novogrudok district. The Novogrudok townspeople in New York have started a vigorous campaign to raise help for Novogrudok.

In 1921 a second delegate was sent – Max Jelen OBM. Mr Jelen took with him a substantial sum of money for the Novogrudok institutions. In addition, individual donations were sent to relatives. Jelen's report on his return was also depressing. The situation in Novogrudok was catastrophic. Help was needed to rebuild Novogrudok. The Novogrudok Relief committee started again to collect money for the town. Shortly afterwards a third delegation was sent to Novogrudok. This time two delegates went: Yankov Finman OBM of the Novogrudok committee and Yankov Maslow of the branch of the Worker's Circle. They were asked to familiarise themselves with the needs of individual institutions within the community.

The delegation left on the 22 February 1922. They arrived in Novogrudok a week before Passover. The money sent for individual families was immediately distributed. The money for the institutions was distributed next, following the instructions of the Novogrudok Relief Committee of New York.

After a thorough investigation it was decided that the people's kitchen should be closed down. Few people used that facility, but the cost of operating the kitchen was substantial. The Novogrudok Kehile (Jewish self-governing body) agreed with the decision and the building, which was housing the kitchen, was given to the orphanage. All other institutions were serving a useful function in town.

Having familiarized themselves with the poor condition that the town was in, after lengthy meetings and consultations with the representatives of all Novogrudok organizations, it was decided that the main function of the American organization should be to create a loan facility for all needy in Novogrudok. A considerable sum, which was collected for that purpose, was sent to the loan facility. Several institutions were also supported.

In the years of the great depression in the US the Relief Committee ceased to function for a time. After a time the Joint invited the Novogrudok institutions to a meeting. All Novogrudok associations were represented. Joint announced that all organisations in Novogrudok were about to cease operations. They suggested that the institutions should renew their activities and the Joint undertook to help by financing the revived activities. As a result, the Relief Committee in New York also renewed its activities. The Committee met in the Novogrudok synagogue, but only a few attended the meetings. Something had to be done to infuse more life into the Relief Committee. It was decided to add to the title of the Committee the name of Alexander Harkavy, which would add substance to the identity of the Relief. This is when the name 'The Alexander Harkavy Novogrudok Relief Committee' came into existence.

Work was started with new vigour and a considerable amount of money was collected. But not long after the Second World War began. Knowing that help would be required again in Novogrudok, we began gradually to build up our activities. After the war, we learned about the great disaster committed by the Germans. We lost most of our dear and beloved, 10,000 human beings. Only a handful survived.

We commenced the work of helping the survivors, wherever they were dispersed. We sent money, food, clothing and medications to a number of camps. We established contacts between the survivors with their families in the States. The Relief obtained affidavits and helped the families of the survivers to obtain affidavits so as to bring them to the US as soon as possible. The countrymen of Novogrudok did all they could. And now, when a considerable number of refugees are in America and have settled in, we started to help our fellow countrymen in Israel. We found out yet again that the best form of help was not charity, but the creation of a loan fund in Israel. Some money was already sent, more is being collected. We are certain that our countrymen from Novogrudok will yet again do their duty.

It is also important to note that at the same time, our Relief Committee was also contributing to other American institutions, such as the United Jewish Appeal, the Joint, United Service for New Americans, HIAS, trade union activities and other institutions.

Members of Navagrudker Alexander Harkavi Committee in America

[Page 174]

Novogrudok Progressive Branch 146

by B. Seltzer

Translated from Yiddish by O. Delatycki

Navagrudker activists in New York

The Novogrudok Progressive Branch 146 working circle was founded in 1907, but for a number of years prior to that the Novogrudok Progressive Association existed. Every conscientious Novogrudok fellow countryman who came to America, or more precisely, to New York, had joined that youth organisation. The main purpose in those days was to support the activities of the Bund in Novogrudok and to conduct communal and literary activities. At most meetings a lecture followed by a discussion took place. The speakers were: Alexander Harkavy, S. Yanovski, Emma Goldman, Dr A. Liber, Dr I. Kling and others. After our Novogrudok Association had joined the working circle our work increased and broadened. We became a branch of the large working circle organisation. At that time the working circle had tens of thousands of members and hundreds of branches. Most of the branches bore the names of the towns from which the members stemmed, eg. Vilno branch, Minsk branch, etc. We were installed as the Novogrudok Progressive Branch 146 working circle. The working circle with more than 70 thousand members was considered to be the equivalent of the Red Cross for the Jewish workers and people. It was the progressive force in the American Jewish community. The working circle took part in organising the Jewish unions. Each branch conducted its activities, however all activities had to be conducted in the spirit of the working circle. As an example, a strike breaker could not be a member of any branch of the working circle, a member of the working circle was not permitted to exploit any worker. The working circle had a sanatorium for members who suffered from tuberculoses. The circle opened progressive schools for children of the members. The working circle was part of the American workers movement, which provided assistance to Jews of Eastern Europe, helped in cases of sickness etc. The Novogrudok branch took an active part in all the above activities. It is impossible to enumerate all the activities of the Novogrudok Progressive Branch 146 in the 55 years of its existence. One thing is certain – it had never been a passive branch It participated in all the activities of the Alexander Harkavy Novogrudok Help Committee.

The current Aid Committee in America
Sitting from right: Zeltser, Kushnir, Maslov, Mrs. Mas and Mrs. Maslov
Standing from right: Mr. and Mrs. Bel, Mas, Mr. and Mrs. Alpershtein and Fridberg

To this day the secretary of our working branch, Jankef Korman is the treasurer of the Novogrudok Help Committee. L. Shnider, an important officer of the Branch, is an executive member of the Help Committee, as is the writer of this article, who is the chairman of the Branch 146 working circle and is the vice chairman of AHNHC. The high point of the activities of the working circle was in the 1930's. At that time the branch had almost 300 members. During the 55 years of our existence many of our members have passed away. At present not many new members are joining the branch. Very few of the post war newcomers have joined our working branch. Despite of that, the Novogrudok Progressive Branch 146 working circle is still one of the most active branches of the working circle.

[Page 176]

Yaakov Maslov

by L. Ch.

Translated from Yiddish by O. Delatycki

Festive welcome for Yakov Maslov and his wife in Tel Aviv

As we are issuing the Yizkor Book of Novogrudok, which is being printed at present, and which is to be a memorial to our beloved town of Novogrudok, and will illustrate its cultural communal Jewish life, its institutions and public activities, I was encouraged to write a few words about our beloved friend Maslov. Mr Yaakov Maslov is one of the most faithful and devoted members of the Alexander Harkavy Aid Fund Committee. He has participated in many activities that have been undertaken by the Novogrudok Aid Committee in the 45 years of its existence. The name Maslov will be always associated with the history of the communal life of Novogrudok and he will be considered a faithful and devoted friend to his fellow townsmen and the communal institutions.

Mr Maslov was born in Novogrudok. He obtained a Jewish education. When he was very young he went to Minsk, where he worked as a bookbinder. In Minsk he met and joined members of the workers party Bund. He began his revolutionary activities with great enthusiasm. He had a dream of a world of perpetual sunshine, of equality and brotherhood, a world, which would bring joy and liberty. He threw himself enthusiastically into the activities of the Bund movement. He worked for the party enthusiastically in a number of towns. He was detained and arrested by the Tsarist police and put in jail. He managed to get away and to migrate to America. Having come to America in 1906 he followed a path similar to that of many members of the Bund who came to America. In time he left the Bund and joined the Aid Fund for the Novogrudok fellow townsmen. He became a member of the group of founders (together with Alexander Harkavy) of the Novogrudok Aid Fund Committee. He was always in the front row of every aid activity in support of fellow townspeople. He loved and treasured the memory of Novogrudok and the institutions in that town, such as Shogdey Melocho, the orphanage, the library etc.

The name of Yaakov Maslov became well known in the interval between the wars. Maslov represented the Jews of Novogrudok in America. He was the person others turned to when help was needed. He devoted all efforts to help his fellow townsmen. For Maslov, Novogrudok was not only a geographic feature and a place of past experiences and of longings, a town where he spent his youth, for him Novogrudok was fixed in his soul and was an organic part of his being. This impelled him to be one of the most active members of the Relief. In 1922 Yaakov Maslov was sent by the Aid Fund Committee to Novogrudok to alleviate the needs of the poor population, who were impoverished during the First World War . Having come to Novogrudok Maslov realised that the form of help afford by the Relief Committee was not suitable any more. Maslov found a more appropriate way of helping the needy of Novogrudok. He created a loan facility, which would lend money to shopkeepers and tradesmen at a low interest rate. He also helped to reorganise the orphanage. It was decided that children on reaching 13 years of age, would be automatically transferred from the orphanage to Shogdey Melocho to learn a trade and, in time, to become independent. He helped to reorganise Shogdey Melocho, which, together with YEKAPA of Vilno, formed furniture workshops, where the pupils learned the trade. In addition, evening courses were conducted, where specifically Jewish and world problems were discussed.

In 1940 [1939?] the Second World War broke out. The Jewish communities of Europe were cut off and destroyed, as was the Jewish community of Novogrudok. Only a small number of Jews was saved in the forests in partisan groups and in hiding. The survivors did not want to remain among the graveyards of their families, where every stone reminded them of the horrible past. Almost all of them left in search of a haven. Initially they went to Poland, Germany, Austria and Italy. They lived in camps and searched the sky to see where the salvation may come from. A group of Jews from Novogrudok who were in Italy, contacted the Novogrudok Relief through Mr Maslov. They received a reply from Maslov within 10 days and from then on a close contact was established with the Relief committee. Mr Maslov wrote to the refugees every second day.

Navaredker committee in Argentina headed by Gutman

At that time Maslov formed many friendships with the newcomers. He always had the time and patients to answer every letter he received. The displaced persons received assistance every month from the committee. It was not just money and food, it was the feeling that there are friends on the other side of the ocean. The committee helped to establish contacts between the refugees and their relatives, which resulted often in obtaining visas to immigrate to America. Help was also given to those who went to Israel. A loan fund was established in Israel, which serves to this day as a source of financial help for the Novogrudok Jews in Israel. Yaakov Maslov participated in all the above activities.

Though Mr Maslov has been living in America for the past 55 years he has still retained European manners and the European outlook and he has made easy contacts with the newcomers. Maslov has the command of the Yiddish language and has contacts with Jewish institutions. Last year Maslov travelled to Israel, where he met the Novogrudker who live there. He was very well received. He took a keen interest in the living conditions of people in Israel. He returned full of enthusiasm and love for Israel. It should be mentioned that though Maslov is not young, he still preserves a warm feeling to everything connected with Novogrudok. He is always ready help with advice and deeds anyone who turned to him.

Novogrudok lies in ruins. The beloved town had vanished with all its organisations and institutions which Yaakov Maslov helped to establish. The orphanage, Shogdey Melocho, the library, which were supported by Maslov, have vanished.

But we will always remember the organisers in the Relief fund, who have given so generously of their time to help the people of Novogrudok in their time of need.

[Page 178]

Committee of Emigrants from Novogrudok in Israel

by Lyuba Rudnicki

Translated from Hebrew by Aviva Kamil

The first of the pioneers of our town arrived in Erets-Israel at the end of the XIX century. They kept in close contact with each other, but did not always have the possibility to meet. Conditions at work did not allow frequent meetings. But the news about the holocaust and the worry about the fate of their hometown brought them together. On the 19.12.1942 a few people from our hometown gathered in the home of Mr. Horovitch ZL, to discuss the need to help our brothers who were far from our land. They decided to call a general meeting of all the emigrants from Novogrudok.

A committee was elected and consisted of: Mr Yitschak Horovitch Z"L, Mr. Aharon Rudnicki, Mr. Israelit Z"L, Mrs. Rachel Fantal-Kitaevitch, Gershon Aicher and Mr Shlomo Kaminski. The secretary was Mrs. Yehudit Mirski Z"L.

Members of the committee and the editional board of the Pinkas commemorate the Martyrs

It was decided immediately to establish a fund to help the survivors of Novogrudok and surrounds. Among the resolutions was one suggested by Gershon Eicher, to impose a monthly tax on each member (donors to decide for themselves the amount to be donated). The committee members were made responsible for the collection of the tax in allotted areas. They contacted the Organisation of Polish Emigrants, the "Sochnut" and other institutions, which took care of refugees in Russia. Later, representatives from Lubtch and Karelitz, Mr Koznietski and Mr. Avraham Kaplan, joined the committee. .At that time the organisation was renamed "The Organisation of Emigrants from Novogrudok and Surrounds". The number of donors of personal tax grew, people wanted to extend their activity. The emphasis was on sending parcels to Russia.

In February 1943 the first consignment of parcels was sent to an address that was given to us. It was a commendable operation. Thanks to those parcels of food and clothing many families were saved from hunger and cold. The driving force behind the consignment of the parcels was Mr. Yitzchak Horovitch Z"L, who, despite his ill health, made an effort to provide a suitable parcel for every family and personally packed and mail them. Consignments were sent monthly. Mr. Horovitch's home became the centre of activity for the committee members. The overwhelming worry concerning the community in our hometown strengthened even more our emotional connection to Novogrudok. The first people who came during the war from our home town were those who arrived in 1943 with Anders's Army. We heard from them a little about the fate of our brethren, though they did not witness the horrific end that befell our dear relatives.

Commemoration of Navaredker Martyrs-18 Kislev, Tel Aviv

The late Yitskhak Hurvits and his wife with youngsters from Navaredok, soldiers in the Anders (Polish) army

The first survivors from hell arrived in 1945; they witnessed the first big slaughter in our town, on the day of Yod 'Heit of Kislev 1941 [8 December 1941?].

On the 22.11.1945 the people of Novogrudok and surrounds assembled for the first time for a memorial day to our martyrs who perished in the first slaughter. A memorial day was observed ever since. At the opening of the Memorial Day, a eulogy was said to the memory of Mrs. Yehudit Mirski, who was the dedicated secretary of the organisation. (She had died of typhoid). On that Memorial Day we heard for the first time from our member Lyuba Rudnicki, who witnessed the beastly murder of our martyrs, about the slaughter of approx. 5000 Jews from Novogrudok and surrounds.

(The Navaredker committee in Israel)

Sitting from right: Asher Gershon Meiri, Rachel Falkovitz, Liuba Rudnitsky, Aharon Rudnitsky.

Standing from right: Herzel Barukh, Yakov Rudnitsky, Noakh Avni and Yitskhak Volfovitz

More members joined the committee, which included: Yitzchak Berkovitch and Yitzchak Dzienciolski Daniel. The number of newcomers grew from year to year, as did the number of the needy. The committee started to lend money. The recipients took upon themselves to repay the loan. They paid by bill (cheque?) countersigned by guarantors.

The need for money grew and the committee turned to our brethren overseas. The first to reply were people from our hometown in the U.S.A. They sent a considerable amount of money to our committee, which was lent by the committee to the needy.

Following Mr. Yitzchak Horovitch's death the organisation decided to establish a loan fund in his name "The Welfare Fund of the Emigrants of Novogrudok, in memory of Yitzchak Horovitch Z"L

Since then the fund is considered a source of help to those who need it for a constructive or other vital purpose. First of all it helps the newcomers.

Apart from a few cases, the debits are repaid when due. But the committee is making an effort now to collect all the moneys owed to them.

On the memorial day of 1960 in the general assembly a decision was taken to publish a book to the memory of our hometown martyrs, who were murdered in World War II between the years 1939-1945.

In 1962 a memorial stone was erected to the memory of our martyrs in the holocaust cellar in Jerusalem.

> *The editors and the committee are making an effort to publish "Pinkas Novogrudok" on time.*

[Page 181]

About the Editorial Staff of the "Pinkas Novogrudok"

by the editorial staff of the Pinkas

Translated from Hebrew by Aviva Kamil

We don't know how various memorial books were written; we only can say that the editorial staff of the Pinkas excelled in its painstaking task of collecting articles, notes, poetry, and stories of the shattering descriptions of the Holocaust and the stories of heroism. We should stress that the editorial staff in Israel and the U.S.A worked in perfect harmony, with devotion and not for rewards. Of course we did not reach perfection. There are some flaws and we anticipate that we will receive complaints and criticism. But we believe that we did our utmost to make the Pinkas a worthy living testimony to our sanctified dead. It is with deep sorrow that we note the deaths of two members of the editorial staff: Dr. Yerushalmi, who edited the Pinkas and our faithful friend Edna Kagan. They passed away and did not have the joy to bless the end product.

Our prayer is that the Pinkas will be found in the dwellings of the people of our hometown, to read it and tell their children about the town, which was a home of Torah, of wisdom, and of Jewish life. All was exterminated at the hands of the most evil people - the cursed Nazis.

Hayim Noakh Leibovitz (USA)

Edna Kagan (USA)

(The editorial board of the Pinkas)

Sitting from right: The late Dr. Eliezer Yerushalmi, David Cohen, Dr. Aharon Mirski,

Standing from right: Shelomo Kamin, Yehoshua Yafe, Moshe Sarig (Shteinberg), Yakov Rudnitsky and Yakov Kivelevitz

We will remember our cherished people with awe, and we will carry in our hearts an eternal curse of their destroyers.

Let the Pinkas be a document and a testimony to the life of mothers and fathers, brothers and sisters and little children, who were killed in the Holocaust.

Blessed be their memory.

Poetry and Prose in Novogrudok

Supplication

by Aharon Mirski (written in 1948)

Translated from Hebrew by Aviva Kamil

Professor Aharon Mirsky

I came to plead for my people with my poem—this is my instrument, I have no other.
This is what my generation possesses, a generation that learned all sorts of harmonies
But forgot its ancestors' melodies.
Like a player who sold his harp and in exchange bought a whistle.

I know:
The "piyut"[1] of Reb Shimon Beb-Itzchak
Carries seventy violins within its folds.
Desires of his people were not expressed by words; they were drawn out with the melody.
The evenings of discourse[2] and the tunes of Torah
Like cymbals, accompanied his "piyutim"[1].

But my poem –its scale is a gentile scale, my ancestors didn't know its values,

Only rhyme beats in it, like "istar belagin"[3] and imperfect tune—its melodies;
Sighs in its lines; lamentation in its stanzas[4]; and the howling of the "shofar", his tongue.

Although you have chosen the attributes of "payatim"[5],
At the writing of my pen don't sneer,
Listen to my sighs, expressed in this poem
Like you listen to Reb Itschak Ben-Tsvi,
While his people spill their blood for you.

And if in my song there isn't a golden word like the forgiving word of the prophet,
But only the stuttering pleas, the moaning of the broken; that my delirious body is writing.
Because my people too, their blood was spilt; but they didn't know what for.

And here I'm standing on earth like in a valley fenced in on all sides,
And utter my songs like a consumptive cough, spitting blood.
Like a player in a trench, thus I'll blow my rhymes
And no-one will know that it's he.

"Payatim" narrated the story of creation, and bared their soul in a tale,
The discourse of ancestors; like the voices of cantors echoed in the "siddur" prayers.
A Jew in the synagogue wets with tears the pages of Yom-Kippur chapters.
And "shliach Tsibur"[6] his tune is a moan- a memory of the priest's splendour-
Pleading for the valley and its dwellers; let no creature be exterminated.
You were satisfied with the plea and the remembrance of your deed,
For every closed gate it will open.

If I'll write as "payatim" do, and my turbulent song will be accepted,
I'll imitate them with my story; like a child imitates the grownup, and his act is empty.
Through my song I'll please him, by my tale I'll coax him with a drained and a broken heart.

You created a world, and fragmented its borders to the number of Jewish Diasporas,
You stretched in it oceans and lined it with pathways and many wondering trails.
You divided the days with curtains of nights, black as slavery,
You stamped the nature of beasts into the nature of people; to eliminate the unfortunate and the frightened.

You sifted peoples with the sieve of selection and chose fathers, friends,
And their sons as unique, for you, among nations --that's how children read in the Torah,
like a foundation for a city so is Israel for the Gentiles so it is said in the books by the preachers.
My song lost its way; the end is a story which has no answer in learning:
How the shell still exists; this is an oblivious world; and Israel was lost in the ruins?

Strengthen my song against doubt or fear; I still have some words to rhyme,
I wish my story to pull like a river stream, let it not be stopped like a tale of an idiot.
In Egypt you sent love messengers to my ancestors-that's what the "midrash"[7] said.
And you let, like a singing hero, basking in its powers the fetters to take off their hands.
You ordered with the blood of lambs on their doors to mark redemption.
Now, I don't understand, the story is deep, and I present my question:
Here are the rest of my people, come to their houses; don't skip to the right or to the left.
Every house is splattered with blood, smeared and blushed with all hues of red.
And the angels of love did not come to the rescue.

I'll support my opinion gently, like Abraham who pleaded and again.
Lest you'll stain my story of the ancient account; which was broken in the middle of the song.
In an ancient desert you appeared to your followers, frustrated of Paran and Se'ir,
In the desert with my ancestors you set the bond like with a youth and a maiden.
You gave them the flame of faith but the reward they didn't get, only the decrees of cruel rulers.
Heaven and earth in their place, and terms from the beginning of creation:
If Israel won't accept the Torah, to chaos you'll return them.
I could not sustain to question thrice, am I to continue or to stop the song:
How could heaven and earth be still in place, while the Torah by the enemy was burnt,
Did God annul the terms?

"Payatim" told you historical memories, I can't tell those.

I haven't the eminence of "Payatim": at peace with religion, innocent and see no crooked ways.
My heart is bitter and bewildered, and at the beginning of the story it stumbles upon flaws, state of denial and shutting of eyes.
On any straight and smooth way it trips. And then I return ashamed like a climber who fell of a cliff.
I don't ask for greatness, I'll go back to my moaning, to moan to the beat of my scale,
I have got no song to ease my burden; I'll go back to my habitual eulogy
About my people who were lost.
As the custom, I'll climb up to my pulpit of dirt and lament my moral;
The moral is: God was bereaved of his people, compare to...there is no comparison.

There is no comparison to the moral; no dirge to the moral.
The mourner has no tears of fire to pour on the Diaspora that went up in flames.
The imagination of ordinary flesh and blood couldn't come close to grieve over their grave of fire.
The ear of a mere human couldn't hear the words that were told through the fire.
Commentary of Jonathan Be'uziel[8] carried by Rabbis, were hushed in the fire.
Silenced were the angels, the executers of prayers, from praying from within the furnace.
God's messengers singing went up with the "Ani Ma'amin"[9] of the inferno.
Seraphim will tremble from nearing Poland's graves, where fire eats fire.
As if on his own to their grave he'll direct them with the approaching of the carriage of fire.
And will revive them with the dew of fire.

It's known, the secret of wailing women, they finish their lamentation with a plea:
Let the dead plead for us in heaven and ask God to protect us here on earth.
I'll ask every wounded soul to plead with me and repeat my supplication:
To claim our right: To build tombstones to cry upon.
On the graves in Gentile Poland to build markers to my people,
Like road signs to comment on the ways of heaven:-
Answer us for the sake of longing Jews who were discarded on the dunghill.

Answer us for the sake of lovely communities that went up in the smoke of a furnace.
Answer us for the sake of pieces of soap which were sold around the nation.
Answer us for the sake of your people whom you judged, and no-one understands the judgment.
Answer my people, every way is right, please answer.

Now, when there are no Jews in Poland only tombstones and priests and icons.
Bring back the divine presence from Europe's Diaspora, what could she find there
In a vacant sky.
Pull out your spirit from its sky and earth, and let their sky fall lifeless.
Here is Jerusalem, her stones in blossom, in her air perfumed spikenards.
The maiden from the Song of Songs awaits her lover, like the vision "Acharit Hayamim[10]
And the remnant of my people who did not benefit from your goodness,
Forgive them when they ask for consolation and plead before your thirteen attributes[11].
God the king sits on the seat of mercy.

Footnotes

1. "piyut"+ "piyutim"-religious song(s)

2. Discourse in "beit-hamidrash"-place of religious learning

3. "Istar belagin"-making a rattling noise like a (roman) coin in an empty jar.(Aramaic).

4. Stanza – in Hebrew- Ba'it= House

5. Pa'yatim-writers of "Piyutim"

6. "Shliach-Tsibur"-Sa"Ts-a selected person from the congregation to lead the prayer.

7. Midrash - Homiletical.

8. Jonathan B'uziel- commentator of traditional law. Halacha.

9. "Ani Ma'amin"- "I believe…"-A prayer.

10. "be'acharit Ha'yamim"- The vision of the prophet Jeremiah. "In the end of days" chapter 49, verse 39.

11. Your thirteen attributes-The thirteen attributes of mercy (of God).

12. At that time there were several Jewish characters like Mojsze Harkavy, the erudite rabbi, who had written about Chassids in German and was introduced to the Austrian king, and also the big contractor Leizer Bruchovich de-Lion one of the three members of the Petersburg committee (footnote by the author).

[Page 186]

The Holy Ark Falls

by Chaim Grade

(final chapter of his epic poem "Moralisers" (*Musornikes*)[1]

Translated by Andrew Firestone

While still a young man, the poet and prose writer Chaim Grade published an epic poem "Moralisier" It portrayed the students of the Navaredok Yeshivah – their lives, inner conflicts, philosophy. This last chapter we give here appears to depict the impending destruction, in a vision already experienced by Grade as a youngster.[2] *by Grade as a youngster.*[2]

Quietly the trees bent over their curly crowns,
preparing for the Fall
like a congregation for self-sacrifice, for the glory of the Holy Name.
A small thin tree sighed deeply and began to cry,
as if from a dream the trees turned towards him:
"Be still, you will get used to it,
all of us got used to it."

Hidden in green leaves, a white glow-worm fevered,
spitting out its great net of trembling light
to enweb the broad trunks.
Chaim Vilner found himself in the midst of it all,
trembling with the rest of the Gardens.

The sky blue of the wind-swept paths ran out,
and like a weary gardener night slunk in,
touching the trees and binding
with shadows the branches, which trembled green and moist.
On far-off streets, the marketplace after the Sabbath
was shining now with firelight,
that found its way into the old Gardens.

Chaim Vilner was stunned to silence,
becoming more stunned, more silent every moment.
A sunny buzz trembled past him,
a golden buzz, as of a summer bee,
and died away like a sick bird in the branches.

The autumn wind started up a *Musor*[3] melody,
soft and pious, sobbing through the trees;
then the melody rose higher
until it turned into a growl.

Chaim Vilner remained silent
listening to his own silence.

To and fro the trees shook,
throwing their heads around like Musornikes at prayer,
a distant secret scream
was broken up by the thickets into quiet sounds
of suffering, agonies in the dark...

Chaim Vilner began to run,
wanting by running to overtake his own shadow.

The wind covered over the path
with heaps of rotting leaves,
and like a flock of birds there flapped around him
far-off holy songs.

The sounds imprisoned him.
He followed them as if enchanted.
The wind disquieted, perturbed him,
scattering tinkling sounds like autumn leaves on every side.
He ran through it,
what was near obscuring what was far,
the night extinguishing his steps...
he hurried, and the nearer that he came,
the freer and heartier sounded the roar;

Chaim Vilner ran towards the *shul*,[4] like one singed by fire
running to save his last barn.

The prayer house was in the back streets.
The crowd swayed like a sea cramped by the shore.
No lights were lit, all out after the Sabbath
but in the fast-formed, thick darkness
he could feel the ecstatic faces,
and swiftly touched his own –
cold, with sagging cheeks, a bad twitch around his lips;
and broken, he started towards the Ark to pray.

In the dark House of Study a sea was roaring,

and cries flamed forth like birds on fire,
wings beating fearfully at the walls
and the fire put out, falling right back
onto the outstretched praying hands.
The forest wailed, each tree with distinct voice,
and in that storm sounded the Rosh-Yeshiva's voice:
"Gentlemen, let us pray again now:
vouchsafe us a clean and honest heart, G-d!"
Came the echo, returning a hundred-fold:
"Gentlemen, let us pray again now:
vouchsafe us a clean and honest heart, G-d!"

Outcry. Through his entreaty everyone seeks for healing.

Now clapping: the Rosh Yeshiva hasn't strength to yell.
Everyone strives to quench his own crying out,

then the Rosh Yeshiva's words do away with all the wailing:
"Gentlemen,
to attain the Truth takes but one hour;
to retain it – calls for lifelong struggle!"
Chaim Vilner grasped the far-off meaning,
and gave a sigh like a house about to fall.
"Gentlemen,
if we can't cross over – then we must cross over!"
In the prayer house the tempest broke again.
By the door Chaim Vilner, isolated from all the crowd,
wept bitterly within himself in the darkness.

"Gentlemen,
in those bloody days of chaos in Russia I saw:
a man had pushed his way onto a crowded train,
they threw him out from that cramped space, from the moving train.
Entering is not enough,
you have to clamp on hard, clasp tightly,
sometimes in the midst of it you can be hurled out..."
Heads and fists start hammering on the walls

as the Rosh Yeshiva storms on:
"That greatest libertine, Reb Eliezer ben Dardia
buried his head between his knees, weeping on the ground
like an expelled angel and like a beast,
until Heaven did hear his plea at last.
So let us once more pray:
Our Father our King, tear up the bitter decree!"
and like earth pouring down a mountain to the valley
the calls poured out, of the sons
from Ukraine, Lithuania, Poland and Volynia.

No longer could the Rosh Yeshiva's words be heard,
his tearful voice turned sick and tender,
like a child just starting to sob...
A second voice poured out like hard and shiny steel,
until a red and thirsty voice drank them both up,
then sank itself into the darkness.
Now a cry flickered through,
as lightning marks a cloud with fire.
And like steam rising from the drenched earth,
the prayer rose up. It climbed right up the prayer house
up cliff stairs, cloud stairs, up and up...
and Chaim Vilner's whole body trembled,
like an autumn tree surrendering its last leaves.

Suddenly a deafening crash,
like eyes of cattle before the slaughter, the lights turned on
the night burst open like ice
the light dripped from the hanging lights, like blood from wounds.
Slowly the Holy Ark began to lean;
the old Ark full of Torahs, with its dusty carvings
with outstretched palms of priests above, slowly
it fell upon their heads, choking all cries.
Frightened bodies reached up high,
lifeless eyes stared fixedly at the silver Torah hangings,
the Holy Ark leaned over the spellbound crowd...

All at once a cry of help roared out, a call
that pierced them so they threw themselves into it –

feet stepping on heads, on necks and bodies –
to hold the Holy Ark aloft.
With faces twisted in fear, mouths hot from crying out,
but in their eyes blind trembling faith –

all pushed forwards, crawled and pushed -
the prayer house buzzed, like a besieged town at war:
"Our Father our King, take pity for the sake of them martyred for your Oneness."

Chaim Vilner lay trembling by the prayer house door,
struggling with himself, wanting to be with the rescuers, to save – and could not leave the threshold,
could not moan – his tongue froze at the root.
Suddenly the whole prayer house tore away from him,
the Holy Ark began to rise higher, higher, held tightly by the hands,
Chaim Vilner clamped his teeth into the floor
the walls swam past him, a deafening thunder moved further and further from him:

"Our Father our King, take not your holy spirit from us!" and Chaim Vilner remained – in a trench bewildered, blind in a forest at night, by an extinguished bonfire.

Vilna 1937

Footnotes

1. (all footnotes by translator): Musornikes was published in Vilna in 1939. Chaim Grade (1910 - 1982) had left Yeshivah life at 22y, to become a leading member of the Yung Vilna poets' group. A list of all his works can be found in http://shakti.trincoll.edu/~mendele/vol08/vol08.136

2. this paragraph appears in the Yizkor-Bukh; author unknown

3. see entry Musar in Wikipedia

4. in fact his Yiddish is *Beys-haMidrash*

[Page 188]

Mickiewicz and the Jews of Novogrudok

by Prof B. Marc, Warsaw

Translated from Yiddish by O. Delatycki

The writings of the greatest poet of the Polish people, Adam Mickiewicz, are associated with Novogrudok, with its country surrounds, with its plants, animals, landscapes and with the people of the region.

Not just in the early creations of the poet, in his ballads and romances, can one recognise Novogrudok and its environments with its splendid festive nature and the romantic legends, but also in his largest and best known work 'Pan Tadeusz' are the descriptions of nature, the colourful people, the traditions drawn from the deep impressions of his old Novogrudok home, which remained forever in the memory of the poet.

In Novogrudok and its vicinity, which was his birthplace, lived a population of a mixture of nationalities and religions: Polish Catholics, Orthodox Belorussians, Jews, Tatar Moslems, a few Germans and even a small group of Karaims. The farmers were Belorussian, and by borrowing from the Belorussian folklore Mickiewicz included in his poetic language and in his folk motives many Belorussian words and ideas. The average land owning class (szlachta), to which Mickiewicze's family belonged, stemmed from a mixture of Poles and Belorussians, however their culture was Polish and their religion Catholic. In the first half of the XIX century (Mickiewicz was born in 1798) the Jews of the Novogrudok district and of the whole of the Belorussian part of Poland assumed a significant economic and cultural position. They managed a significant share of the internal and external commerce. They also managed a significant proportion of the large land holdings [Jews were not allowed to own agricultural land in the Tsarist days and under the interwar Polish regime, but they were allowed to manage land holdings]. The trades in town were almost entirely Jewish. The communications and land transport were also in Jewish hands. A significant number of Jews lived in the villages. They were not only lease holders but also tradesmen such as black smiths, carpenters and similar, farmers and gardeners.

Thus a section of the Jews of the area served as middlemen between the small landowners and farmers and the world at large. They conducted business with Lithuania, Poland, Koenigsberg and Danzig and brought back not only various goods but also news, books, tidings of political and cultural events and information of impending changes. Other Jews introduced innovations in trades and agricultural production. The Jews were pioneers of new types of trades and also new cultural ideas. At the same time they were deeply religious and with their heart and soul tied to Judaism. Such Jews were mixtures of old fashioned Judaism with new worldliness. Due to contacts with foreign businessmen, German Jews and non-Jewish firms, and because of their travels to distant lands and due to contacts with enlightened local land owners, such Jews acquired knowledge of foreign languages allowing them to conduct worldly conversations, to be well dressed and have good manners. But, on the other side a Jew had to be true to his Jewishness, to his Jewish faith. And because he had to associate with Christians, his Jewish religious watchfulness had to be more acute. One of these types of Jews was a frequent visitor to the house of the parents of Mickiewicz as well as the houses of Mickiewicz's neighbours and friends. Mickiewicz mentioned him in his letters and in his recollections from his youth. Mickiewicz called him Rab Factice, who was a big merchant of cereals from the vicinity of Novogrudok. He bought from the local land owners wheat and corn and travelled widely. Mickiewicz remembered Factice's positive characteristics. This Jew remained in Mickiewicz's memory as the incorporation of life's best characteristics: knowledge, earnestness and honesty. Mickiewicz remembered him in his later years when he lived in Paris. He told one of his friends that in a certain sense the Jewish merchant from Novogrudok had become a prototype of the well known character Jankiel in Pan Tadeusz. The villager Jankiel, who appeared in Mickiewicz's epic as the incorporation of the ideal Polish patriot and folk singer (Jankiel's concert)[12].

A farmer in a village near Navaredak

Obviously, when a poet uses a live prototype for one of his fictional characters it is not a photo but a composition. The Jewish merchant from Novogrudok, who was a frequent visitor to the Mickiewicz's in Wiereszczaki, has contributed, without knowing it, to the picture of Jankiel. Yet he was only a part of the total. The rest of the description of Jankiel, Mickiewicz based on other Jewish characters that he knew and on his artistic inventions. The characteristic of Jankiel's honesty was 'borrowed' by Mickiewicz from the above mentioned Jewish merchant. The musical talent of Jankiel was drawn by the poet from other Jews of the region such as the numerous Jewish musicians, who were in those days the predominant performers of folkloric music. They played inspiringly not only at Jewish weddings but also at peasant and land owner's celebrations. The cymbals, on which Jankiel played out the tragic story of Poland, was a Jewish instrument. The Jewish klezmers played not only Jewish, but also Polish and Belarus melodies. The music was not only folk tunes but also music for dancing and among them tunes such as the famed Polonez, which were played on big occasions for the szlachta. The young Mickiewicz knew Jewish musicians and heard their soul music. He was impressed by the musicians who were uneducated but had a G-d given talent. Their musical ability was often handed down from father to son. In the first decade of the XIX century there were many Jewish musicians in the Novogrudok district. There was also another Jewish group in Novogrudok which Mickiewicz was familiar with in his youth – they were the Jewish coachmen. We mentioned previously that in the Poland of old, the communication and land transport was in Jewish hands. And if in Wielkopolska and Malopolska [literally Great Poland and Little Poland, the names of two ancient Polish regions] there were both Jewish and gentile coachmen, in the eastern regions, particularly Belarus, the land transport was almost exclusively in Jewish hands. The only means of land travel was by horse and cart. Transport between Novogrudok and the surrounding settlements was in the hands of Jewish coachmen. Few people, except for the large land owners, had their own means of transport. The average land owners, such as Adam's father, Mikołaj Mickiewicz used hired Jewish coachmen for longer trips. The coachmen conveyed passengers, goods, letters and news. They travelled long distances to Wilno and beyond. When the young student Mickiewicz travelled back home for the summer vacations from Wilno or Kowno, as well as from Zaosie to Novogrudok, he travelled in the coach of a Jewish coachman. The impression of those journeys remained for long in the poet's memory. He recollected years later in his letters, travels in shaking carriages and the long stories the Jewish coachmen told to pass the time. Some stories were legends of the region, others were stories about highway men and romantic tales about land lords and maidens that sometimes finished with murder caused by jealousy. The Jewish coachmen knew well the folks tales, both local and of the surrounding region. They told their stories in the language of the local country people. The young poet absorbed these stories as well as the fairy tales of his Belarus nurse and the stories of great adventures told by the local Tatars. All these stories found their way into Mickiewicz's ballads, which were very well received because of their genuine national flavour. They heralded the beginning of the romantic period in the Polish literature.

Mockiewicz was very impressed by the story told by a Jewish coachman about a band of robbers which attacked a merchant on the highway, but when the merchant told them that his children were waiting for him at home they became sentimental, broke down, thought of their own children and set the merchant free. It is obvious that the coachman spoke of a Jewish merchant, because Jews were moving most merchandise in the area. Mickiewicz combined a progressive world view with his deep religious feelings. He used a folk tale to compose the ballad 'Father's return', in which the Christian belief is emphasized. The ballad had arisen from the strong impression on the poet of a Jewish coachman's tale of the sudden metamorphosis to the good of the soul of hardened bandits.

There is no doubt that Mickiewicz was influenced strongly by Jews and the Jewish mystique. He believed in 'the historic mission of our older brother Israel'. He was looking in the Paris synagogues for allies in the battle to liberate the world, he had a dream of a Jewish legion, the image of Jankiel in Pan Tadeusz, all this is evidence of the seeds that were planted in the poet's soul during his youth in Novogrudok. The seeds grew in his long wanderings into big and beautiful flowers. It is true that the feeling and thoughts of Mickiewicz were very complex and often not clear and sometimes he wove plans of spreading among Jews the Christian mission. But on the whole he kept in his heart and mind the memories of his times in Novogrudok, in which the Jews occupied a touching and substantial place.

Svitezh-was described by Mitskewitz

The Polish literary researchers of the period between the wars did everything to cover up and erase the Jewish element in Mickiewicz's creations and to belittle the influence of the Jews and the Jewish folklore on the author of the ballads, romances and Pan Tadeusz. In the official biographies of Mickiewicz there appeared every one except Jews. Mickiewicz was accused of introducing the Jew Jankiel, who, according to the interwar literati, was an unreal invented romantic figure. In the official biographies of the Novogrudok period appeared all except Jews. The only one who emphasized the influence of Jews [on the creations of Mickiewicz] was the essayist Boy-Żeleński. But Żeleński did not write about the Novogrudok period, only about Paris, where Mickiewicz was involved in a romantic interlude with a Jewish woman, who may have been a convert. She may have introduced the mature author to mysticism.

At present, information is being introduced of the influence of the Jewish element of the Novogrudok period on Mickiewicz's life and creations, which is the truth. It is impossible to imagine the influence of the Novogrudok environment on Adam Mickiewicz without Jews and Jewish folk culture. On the other hand, Mickiewicz's contemporary Zygmunt Krasinski, a count who was remote from the people, was a convinced anti-Semite and a reactionary. Compared to him, Mickiewicz was closer to the people. As he searched for new ideas and new motives, he dug deep into the folklore, where the culture of the Jews of Novogrudok was strongly represented. Thus, if we view Mickiewicz, the greatest poet of the Polish nation, then one of the stimulants of his poetry was the Jewish element embodied in the Jews of Novogrudok at the beginning of the XIX century.

Adam Mitskewitz

[Page 191]

Adam Mickiewicz and his attitude to Jews

by S. L. Shnayderman

Translated from Yiddish by O. Delatycki

From Wilno to Paris

In the year of 1798, three years after the third and final division of Poland, Adam Mickiewicz was born in Novogrudok [in Zaosie in the district of Novogrudok]. His father Mikołaj was an impoverished land owner and lawyer. When Adam was born his father still owned agricultural land, but his income was derived mainly from his legal work. His important clients were the wealthier Jewish traders of Novogrudok. In the diaries of members of the Mickiewicz family there are notations which indicate that there were good relations between the former land holder and Polish patriot Mikołaj Mickiewicz and the Jews of Novogrudok. The diaries show also that of the five Mickiewicz children, four were delivered by a Jewish midwife Dawidòwka (Dowidiche). Only the youngest, Adam, was delivered by a Polish midwife Molodiecka. Dawidòwka was a frequent visitor to the house of the Mickiewicz's. All children called here 'boba'.

The early years of Mickiewicz's life were spent in an atmosphere of longing for the liberation of Poland and great hopes were placed in Napoleon Bonaparte. A Polish legion under the command of [Jan] Henryk Dambrowski, joined Napoleon's army and fought in all the battles in Europe. The poetic talent of Adam Mickiewicz developed quite early. He wrote songs when he was 10 years old. He was, however, criticized by his teachers, because they thought that his melodies were reflecting the tastes of the 'common people'. Of the early creations of Mickiewicz only one song had survived, which the twelve year old had written having been moved by the big fire of 1810, when almost all timber houses and the Jewish shops in the Novogrudok market place were burned to ashes.

At the age of 14, Mickiewicz witnessed the arrival in Novogrudok of Napoleon's army and the Dabrowski's legion. This memorable event, which remained in Mickiewicz's memory, was later described in Pan Tadeusz [his most famous poem, which described the lives of the Polish landowners in his native region]. There is no mention, however, in Mickiewicz's works of Jews he may have known or came in contact with in his youth. In Poland the poet had no contacts with Jews. It was not until Mickiewicz found himself in Paris, having travelled in Russia and Germany, that he became aware of the Jewish problem, which he acquired through his meetings at the house of the Rothschilds, where he was a frequent visitor at their literary salon, through his acquaintance with the French-Jewish statesman Adolph Kramie and his contacts with Heinrich Heine, though these were not entirely friendly. The poet discovered a lot about the situation of the Jews in Europe and specifically in Poland. It was curious that Mickiewicz's main source of information about Jews was from the chief medical officer of the French army Armond Levy. Levy was born a Christian but reverted later to Judaism. Mickiewicz travelled to Istanbul with Armond Levy to organise the Jewish [Polish] legion. It should be emphasised that the friendship with Armond Levy developed long after Pan Tadeusz was published. This is proof that Mickiewicz had a friendly attitude toward Jews before he developed friendships with Jews in exile. This does not alter the fact that Mickiewicz did not know the condition of Jews in Poland, and the Jew he depicted in his large poetic opus is the idealised portrait of an owner of an inn, who existed in the fantasy of Mickiewicz. Jankiel was a symbolic Jewish figure.

For the Polish Jews, the image of Mickiewicz remained as the friendliest of all the Polish cultural leaders over the hundreds of years of the Polish-Jewish historical interrelationship. Before Mickiewicz and after him there was no political or cultural personality who had shown that degree of sympathy to the Jewish nation as did Adam Mickiewicz. The Jew Jankiel in Pan Tadeusz is the first positive Jewish figure in Polish literature and the most idealized Jewish image which has ever been depicted by any Polish writer, including Eliza Orzeszkowa. Jankel is not, however, a prototype of a real Jewish inn keeper. It is a symbolic figure, which was put forward by Mickiewicz as a spokesman and an asserter of the conscience in the environment of the spoiled Polish landowners, who were drinking to excess, made merry and were always ready to fight to defend any real or imaginary slights to their honour. Whilst most other heroes in Pan Tadeusz are earthy characters, who are described with all their faults, paltry achievements, trifling ambitions and daily strife, the Jewish inn keeper on the other hand is portrayed as an ideal character, with no faults, an extraordinary musician, a masterful cymbals player in whose heart burns the love to his Polish home land. The Jewish inn keeper is put on the same level as the legendary Polish leader general Dambrowski, for whom Jankiel performed at a family wedding in the estate of Soplicowo, in Lithuania. Jankel bestowed on the general his Jewish blessing, he spoke of Lithuania as 'our Lithuania', which was waiting for liberation, as we Jews were waiting for the Messiah. Jankiel spoke in an elevated tone, not as an inn keeper, but as a Polish divine. Reading it, one cannot escape the feeling that through the mouth of Jankel spoke Mickiewicz. Jankiel's performance in Soplicowo was described as a superlative concert, a sort of a non-Jewish Song of Songs. The description of Jankiel's performance is the masterful chapter in Pan Tadeusz.

It is in the last, the twelfth chapter of Pan Tadeusz, which was named 'Let's love each other', an expression which in the independent Poland was used almost as a curse and was an attack on those who were promoting friendship between Poles and Jews. Adam Mickiewicz, however, meant seriously the expression 'Let's love each other' and he began the description of the inn keeper with the following lines:

Było cymbalistòw wielu,
Ale żaden z nich nie śmiał zagrać przy Jankielu
(Jankiel przez całą zimę nie wiedzieć gdzie bawił,
Teras się nagle z głównym sztabem wojska zjawił).
Wiedzą wszyscy, że mu na tym instrumencie ,
Nikt nie wyrówna w biegłości, w guście i talencie.
Proszą, ażeby zagrał, podają cymbały,
Żyd wzbrania się, powiada, że ręce zgrubiały,
Odwykł od grania, nie śmie i panów się wstydzi;
Kłaniając się umyka; gdy to Zosia widzi,
Podbiega in a białej podaje mu dłoni
Drążki, którymi zwykle mistrz we struny dzwoni;
Drugą rączką po siwej brodzie staraca głaska
I dygając: 'Jankielu', mòwi, 'jeśli łaska,
Wszak to me zaręczyny, zagrajże Jankielu,
Wszak nieraz przyrzekałeś grać na mym weselu!'
Jankiel nieźmiernie Zosię lubił, kiwnął brodą
Na znak że nie odmawia; więc go w środek wiodą,
Podają krzesło, usiadł, cymbały przynoszą,
Kładą mu na kolanach, on patrzy z rozkoszą
I z dumą; jak weteran w służbę powołany,
Gdy wnuki ciężki jego miecz ciągną ze ściany,
Dziad śmieje się choć miecza dawno nie miał w dłoni,
Lecz uczuł, ze dłoń jeszcze nie zawiedzie broni.

'Cymbalists there were many,
But none dared to play when Jankiel was present
(Jankiel was absent for the whole winter
Yet now suddenly returned with the headquarters of the army)
All knew that none could equal him in playing this instrument
There was none as good in fluency, taste or talent
They begged him to play and gave him the cymbals

The Jew was declining, said that his hands have coarsened

He bowed and tried to escape; when Zosia saw it,
She rushed in and in her hand were
Sticks, which the master uses to strike the cords

With her other hand she stroked the beard of the master
And said 'Jankiel, if you please, these are my nuptials
Remember, Jankiel, you promised to play at my wedding.'
Jankiel liked Zosia enormously, he gave a sign
To indicate that he concurs; they took him to the centre
Brought a chair, he sat, they brought the cymbals
They put it on his knees, he looked on with delight
And with pride; as a veteran recalled to service,
When his grandsons drag his heavy sword from the wall and
Grandpa smiles, though he long since did not have a sword in his hands,
He felt, that his hands will not let down his weapon.

Jankiel in Mickiewicz's Pan Tadeusz is neither a subservant Jew nor an ordinary klezmer at a landlord's celebration. The only description of inn keepers given in the Polish literature before and after Mickiewicz was that of money lenders, avid enemies of Poland, often accused also of diluting vodka with water. This was the only type of Jew that was mentioned in the Polish literature in the XVIII and XIX centuries. But Jankiel was the incorporation of the ideal and of the nicest. In this poetic figure Mickiewicz had incorporated all the good characteristics which he had seen in the Jewish people. Jankiel, who was endowed by Mickiewicz with the part of a rabbi's assistant in the neighbouring community (it is called in Polish 'podrabinek') is represented as the greatest connoisseur of Polish national music, as an outstanding performer of patriotic songs, which Jankiel played on his magic instrument, bringing to life happy and sad moments of Polish history.

Razem ze strun wiele
Buchnął dźwięk, jakby cała janczarska kapela
Ozwała się z dzwonkami, z zelami, z bębenki.
Brzmi Polonez Trzeciego Maja! – Skoczne dźwięki
Radością oddychają, radością słuch poją
Dziewki chcą tańczyć, chłopcy w miejscu nie dostoją-
Lecz starców myśli z dźwiękiem w przeszłość się uniosły,
W owe lata szczęśliwe, gdy senat i posły
Po dniu Trzeciego Maja w ratuszowej Sali
Zgodzonego z narodem króla fetowali;
Gdy przy tańcu śpiewano: 'Wiwat Król kochany!
Wiwat Sejm, wiwat Naród, wiwat wszystkie Stany!'
Mistrz coraz takty nagli i tony natęża,
A wtem puścił akord jak syk węża,
Jak zgrzyt żelaza po szkle – przejął wszystkich dreszczem
I wesołość pomięł przeczuciem złowieszczem.
Zasmuceni, strwożeni słuch zwątpili,
Czy instrument niestrojny? Czy się muzyk myli?
Nie mylił się mistrz taki! On umyślnie trąca

Wciąż tę zdradziecką strunę, melodyję zmącą,
Coraz głośniej targając akord rozdąsany,
Przeciwko zgrodzie tonòw skonfederowany;
Aż Klucznik pojął mistrza, zakrył, ręką lica
I krzyknął: 'Znam! Znam głos ten! To jest Targowica!'

Together from many strings
A tone, as if from a Turkish infantry band
Has issued with bells and drums
The tone of the Polonaise of the Third of May! Dancing tunes,
They spread joy, they fill your ears with gladness
The lasses long to dance, the lads can hardly wait –
But the memory of the elders turned to the past
To those happy years when the senators and the deputies

After the Third of May, in the town hall
The king, at one with the people, was feted;
And they sang as they danced: 'Long live the King,
The Parliament, the people and long live all estates!
The master started to increase the tempo and tone
And suddenly issued a cord like hissing of a snake

Like dragging a knife over glass – everyone cringed
And the gaiety had changed to a foreboding of evil
Saddened and confused the listeners were wondering:
Was the instrument out of tune? Was the musician erring?
No, the master is not at fault! He is deliberately playing
The wrong tune, he muddles the melody
He plays louder the wrong cord
Against confederated voices who were in agreement
And suddenly the Warden guessed it and covered his face
He shouted: 'I know that voice! It is Targowica!

Bringing forth the Jewish inn keeper as evidence, as the demanding voice which reminded the Polish nobility of the big evil of Targowica, was a rare and daring move. It stirred up certain elements of the Polish emigrants in France, where Pan Tadeusz first appeared in print.

Leading Polish literary critics of that era have accused Mickiewicz of having cheapened the purity of Polish poetry and of having sharply broken away from the classical tradition.

[The author of the above article had translated the two sections from the poem Pan Tadeusz into Yiddish verse. The English translation above is in prose for lack of talent by the translator.]

[Mickiewicz (1798-1855) was born in troubled times for Poland. Poland was occupied by Russia, Prussia and Austria in three stages: 1772, 1793 and 1795. In 1794 a small group of Polish nobility formed the Targowica confederation with the aim of assisting Russia in completing the partition. Targowica was cosidered by most Poles an act of betrayal.]

[Page 195]

The Preacher from Siberia

by Dr. S. Shabbat

Translated from Hebrew by Aviva Kamil

In the midst of the calamity that befell us on the 14th of June 1941, the Soviet regime arrested a multitude of people. On the first day of my arrival in the camp I saw a short fellow who was noticeable for his mild manners and apathetic reaction to the turmoil around us. We were desperate, depressed and stunned by the terrible blow, which we received - we lost our world in an hour and became slaves. The world darkened around us. We sat in a hut, which stank appallingly. We were humiliated and silent; our heads were bowed like those of mourners. From time to time the silence was punctuated by a moan, which filled the empty space. In between the moans a strange melody was heard, a tune that refused to blend in with the sound of the shocking moans. The tune expressed not only mourning and sorrow, but also a longing for a shiny future. The melody had risen and subsided in a moment. It was hard to imagine that within the sound of the moaning of hundreds of miserable people we could hear those tunes, which shook our souls and took us into a different world. At times we would think that those tunes sounded like a voice of a miserable or insane prisoner, but our astonishment grew when the moans grew weaker and the tunes grew stronger. After a few moments, one could distinguish some words in the melody. The words reminded me of some known verses that were heard during the festivity of "Simchat-Torah" and "Simchat Beit –Hashoevah" (water festival).

While still searching for the source of the melody, the tunes grew louder and suddenly I could distinguish the figure of the singer. It was the same short man that I noticed on my arrival. I shuddered; I could not understand why that apathetic person was suddenly singing. What was the "simchah" (celebration)? I could understand some of the words by then, "Do not fear a sudden scare and evil holocaust if it comes" hes sang with passion. While I set frozen to my sit trying to convince myself that I was not day dreaming, the melody grew louder, I walked a few steps forward and stood in front of the singer, who sat with his eyes closed and his arms moving in time with the tune. The impression was that the man was floating in another world unaware of the tragic situation he was in. He continued his singing until the head warden gave the order to get out for an inspection. Only then did the melody stop and the singer rose from his seat, straightened up and looked around him with amazement.

The people in the hut pushed each other towards the door, they were afraid of being late and being punished for it. While racing to the door I managed to have a look at the singer. He did not take any notice of the chaos around him, with slow steps, humming a melody ("mizmor") he moved towards the exit. I came outside but turned my eyes towards the door to see if he was coming out behind us. We stood in lines but he still did not appear. We were waiting for the officer to emerge, fearful for the singer. We believed that the Preacher would not escape a severe punishment this time. With the appearance of the head warden, the inspection started. There was a complete silence before the shouting that we had expected, because we could judge by the warden's expression the mood they were in. They will release their anger on the Fascists who resented their new situation. As a rule the inspection took a long time, the wardens did not manage to count the prisoners rapidly and accurately. The wardens could not match the number of prisoners each one arrived at. They became tense and nervous, counting us again and again. And we stood silently amused by their inability to count accurately. In the middle of all of this suddenly appeared the singer slowly walking towards us as if nothing concerned him.

His appearance angered the head warden who met him with abuse and curses and threats to skin him alive. But nothing had an effect on him. Our hero, who became a famous personality in our camp, continued to mumble "tehilim", loudly "God guards all his followers and exterminates evil People". That strange behaviour led the head warden to believe that the man was insane. He ordered him to stand at the end of the line. The man did it mumbling, his eyes turned towards heaven. The warden's patience came to an end. He shoved the singer and ordered him to return to the hut. But the singer did not move. The head warden shrugged his shoulders and left him. Our hero became the talk of the camp and every one told tall stories about him. The camp commander decided that this fellow "is still deep in religious thoughts" and it would not be easy to indoctrinate him.

After that event I would see him often, once in a "minyan" (at the beginning, praying was allowed three times a day) and many times in the queue for food in the kitchen. I noticed that even in the queue his behaviour was dignified, while others, hungry, were shoving and pushing for a scrap of prison food. As every one wanted to be the first in the queue to get the miserable meal, he stood peacefully mumbling his "tehilim", noticing no one.

To the chagrin of the "Goyim", he paid no attention to them. The Jewish prisoners tried to tell him not to behave like a mad man and embarrass his people. But he gestured with his hands and kept mumbling his prayer.

Once, someone turned to him and asked him: "Why do you stand like a "goilem"? There won't be any soup left, and you will suffer hunger more then anyone else!" Hearing this he blushed and he answered fuming, "What are you saying? Do you really think that I stand in this queue to get this Soviet "traifah" water? I swear on all that is dear to me that not one drop of this "traifah" will touch my mouth. And if you see me standing here to get another drop of soup, it is because I want to ease the suffering of a sick person who suffers severe hunger."

I used to meet him every evening loaded with kettles and bowls, running to the kitchen to get some extra soup for the sick. Once, during an evening, he approached me and asked me to join him in his activity so that I also would enjoy the "mitzvah" of taking care of the sick. These were his words: "These murderers deprived us of the possibility to fulfil the "613 mitzvoth" but God in his goodness gave us the privilege to fulfil the "mitzvah" of visiting the sick. This, in our present situation, is worth all the other" mitzvoth" put together, and I thank God who in his kindness gave me the privilege to fulfil this important "mitzvah".

Witnesses said that despite of him being sometimes very hungry, he never touched the portions of soup for the sick and was always in a hurry to bring the soup to them as early as possible. He made a name for himself with his distinct behaviour; even those who used to ridicule him changed their attitude and started to regard him with admiration and reverence, which a "tsadik" like he deserved.

The wardens, in one of their searches in the huts, found "tefilin" that somehow escaped the eyes off the wardens till then. They wrote in their record that it was a camouflaged radio. That confiscation touched our "tsadik". First, he tried to convince the wardens that it was a sacred item but to no avail. He heaved a sigh and said: "God has given and God has taken away, blessed be his name"

Next morning, before our departure to work, he rolled up his sleeve, as if he was ready to put on "tefilin", he raised his voice and said: "I am ready to perform the "mitzvah" of "tefilin", God, look from your seat in heaven and see that evil people have stolen the "tefilin" from me, God is witness of my great desire to perform this "mitzvah", consider my sorrow and see that I tried to fulfilled the "mitzvah" of wearing "tefilin".

From that day he kept looking for all kinds of "mitsvoths". With the change in the kitchen staff, the amount of extra soup for the sick was reduced. He looked around and saw the terrible despair that enveloped his own people, he started to console each one of us: "the blessed God will help". When things became even worse he started preaching to us, and this is what he said: "We are all the sons of our father Abraham who had the privilege to fulfil the "mitzvah" of "akedah" and stood the trial. Why cannot we have the privilege of being tested and stand this easy trial, which is nothing in comparison to the trial of our father Abraham. We should stand the trial, overcome our hunger and overlook troubles. If we will triumph and bless the bad as we bless the good, only then will we reach Abraham's level and will be deserving of the title "children of Abraham". He was often walking from hut to hut to cheer up his brethren the Jews, and to his credit it was said that he never criticised or even minded his miserable fellow-Jews lack of religiosity. In his preaching he related to the audience about miracles that happened to him when he was a student in the "Yeshiva" of Novogrudok, for instance, when they (the students) walked to the forest seeking solitude, God took care of their material needs and so on. The conditions in the camp went from bad to worse; every day brought new troubles. We deteriorated fast and were fed up with our life, but the "tsadik" continued with his hymns of thanks and outcry that we were privileged.

His confidence did not let him down. By the end of September 1941 all the Polish citizens were released and he was among them. He left us with cheerful words and tears in his eyes. On his departure from the camp's gates his tune could still be heard: "depart joyfully and return in peace".

I must say that the "tsadik's" departure left a strong impression on us, his words and tunes stayed in our hearts and were a source of consolation during the horrible times that lay ahead.

The preacher disappeared and we have not seen him since, but I am sure that he reached a safe place, a place where he could live a righteous life of a "tsadik". The Novogrudok preacher reaped what he had sown. It was said about him: "the life of a "tsadik" is his faith".

*

[Page 196]

My Home, poem

by Bertha Kling

Translated from Yiddish by O. Delatycki

Mother, nobody brought me up
Only your good eyes
The sight of which I carry in my mind
All my days

And your table, which I remember
With benches on both sides
And real black bread
Which was waiting for every guest

And the old bedstead
Which was there for every homeless
Just as if he came
To his own home

Water from a deep well
And always in the right place
Was a barrel with a ladle
And whoever was thirsty
Came there to drink water

Father, mother had so little
And gave so much
May G-d guide me in their ways

A Friday in Novogrudok

by Fruma Kamieniecki

Translated from Yiddish by O. Delatycki

It was five o'clock in the morning. The sky and the earth awakened from sleep, yawned and the first ray of light fell onto the tin-plate rooster. The rusty red tin-plate rooster, on the roof over the booth next to the water pump in the middle of the market place, rotated on one leg for many years. It was showing the citizens of Novogrudok from whence the wind blew. At that early hour, at the beginning of a calm Friday, the rooster was at rest. No one looked at it. It looked intently into the Yiddish street, but the town slept. The shadow of the rooster fell on the splendid white columns and the row of shops. They were built by Prince Radziwill opposite his beautiful palace*. Later the palace was known as Belin's house.

In the cellar of the house of Kiwelewicz, under Efron's linen store, one could hear a quite interchange between Shifre Isher and her partner Moshke the lame. 'We should not bring up the perch now, not yet' said Shifre 'let's take outside the basket of dace, tench and pikes'. The sons of Moshke took outside the table, the balance and weights. The plates on the balance were the colour of fish. Once a year, on Passover eve, the plates were thoroughly cleaned and their colour changed.

Josif Leipuner was the owner of the best restaurant in town, which was renowned for its wine list and the Italian chef. The restaurant was well known not only in the surrounding countryside among the landowners, but also in Warsaw among the top public servants, who travelled to Novogrudok for conferences. They knew that in Leipuner's restaurant they could find genuine Russian caviar, French foie gras, Dutch blue cheese (the mouldier the dearer), a good, tasty boeuf Stroganoff, a piquant entrée and cooked live red crabs and lobsters. But it was certain, that a good piece of Jewish gefilte fish was tastier than all those gourmet dishes.

Leipuner saw from his top floor window that Shifre and her partner were ready for business. He lit deliberately his pipe. He went down the steps and stopped for a moment on the Nevsky Prospect. It is doubtful if the Nevsky Prospect in St Petersburg looked similar, but that was the name given to our central square by a wag. It was possible that Leipuner suggested that name, because he was the author of all the better jokes in circulation.

As he approached the fish cellar, Leipuner could hear Shifre saying

'Moshkie, I am not going to change my mind, I am reserving the perch for Pernik'. Moshke looked up with his black eyes: 'What is it about Lejzer Pernik? A big deal!' It was not the problem of who would get the fish that riled him, but he was getting the impression that his partner was having the bigger say in running of the business and he found this offensive. Shifre was a tall, nice looking woman with a clever head, but he, Moshke would show her for once that he was a partner of equal standing. He leaned over a barrel as if he was going to take out a fish and whispered 'She, she thinks that she is the clever one, because her husband is a Gabay [president of a synagogue] in the Shloss street synagogue and sits next to the Rabbi at the East wall'. He decided that he had to take her down a peg or two. He dried his hands by rubbing them on his trousers, which were as shiny as leather. 'I can't hear what you are muttering about' said Shifre, 'but I can tell you that Pernik is still our best customer and comes always first and not later when we are busy'. Moshke wanted to get out from the cellar, but above him stood Shifre, nice, majestic and he forgot what he was going to say. 'Well, he muttered, I don't like it when a man in his 60's is following every command of his wife, like a small boy'. Shifre was about to answer him, when Leipuner arrived: 'Good morning Mr Leipuner'. Leipuner remained standing a little distance from the cellar as if to say; 'Who needs fish?' But he said 'I am on my morning walk', yet he knew that he would need that day a fair few fish: the Count Mirski had ordered the previous day fish Jewish style and that night there would be a ball in the casino. The guests would eat in his restaurant and he would need pike. However, he just said 'Good morning' and moved on past her. But she was not giving up: 'Mr Leipuner, I have today live carp, just look how frisky they are'. He obliged Shifre and glanced into the barrel. 'My guests are in luck', thought Leipuner, 'they will eat fresh fish tonight'. But aloud he said: 'No, today you don't have the fish I am looking for'. Shifre was perplexed "Do you need pike?' she asked. 'No, I need a perch'. As Shifre was contemplating what to do next, Moshke decided the issue, he appeared from the cellar with the perch in his hands. 'Mr Leipuner, you have not seen such a perch as this one. Just look at it'. 'How much does it weigh?' 'About 3 kilo' 'Will you weigh the fish?' said Leipuner. Moshke shouted to his son "Come and take it to the restaurant'. 'No', said Leipuner, 'I will fetch it on my way back'. He put down the fish next to the scale. 'Well, what do you think' Leipuner said as if in doubt 'should I take a few carp and pike too'. 'If you do, you will not regret it.' said Shifre with a smile, 'I will give you only the best'. Leipuner paid for the perch and the cost of the two baskets of fish, which the boys took to the restaurant, was put on his account.

Leipuner stood at Hershl Motkies shop and looked up Valiker Street, where he expected to see Pernik coming to get his fish. Leipuner enjoyed the thought of telling his boys Sima and Mitia how he had tricked Pernik.

The Valiker Street was still asleep. Mrs Blacher, a wealthy woman, half asleep, was out with a broom, shovel and a basket. Leipuner ignored her and walked past. Next came out Rafael the shoemaker. He was a good hearted man, who liked to do a good deed. He was always the first to help anyone in need. He was active in a number of institutions and had become the chairman of the Chevra Kadisha. He was also active at any time when a new rabbi was to be appointed. Rafael looked at the empty street, saw Leipuner and greeted him. In reply Leipuner pointed his pipe at Mrs Blacher, as if to say 'What do you think of her? Can she not afford to hire help?' Rafael understood the implied message. He replied by shaking his head.

Leipuner noticed Pernik from a distance. As Pernik approached, Leipuner took out the fish by the gills and said in an innocent voice 'A substantial fish, don't you think?'

The "Nievski"

The row of shops, or rad kromen in Yiddish, was in the centre of the market place. It was built opposite Radziwill's palace in 1833 to replace the Radziwill stables [date provided by Tamara Vershitskaya, director of the Novogrudok museum]. There were about 40 small shops in the row.
I recall a severe, late winter's night. I saw a meagre light from a shop in the row. I walked closer. In the shop, with few goods on the shelves, sat a woman huddled over a pot of smouldering charcoal. There were no customers and none was likely to come at that hour, but the need

must have been great. I have carried this picture in my mind *for all these years.*

The row of shops and the ex-Radziwill palace, as well as half of all other buildings surrounding the market place, were destroyed by German aircraft on Saturday the 28 June 1941 [this date was confirmed by Jack Kagan of London].

Special thanks to Mrs Charak for translating the names of the fish].

[Page 199]

The First Rosh Hashona of the Survivors of the Holocaust

by Chaim Leibovich

Translated from Yiddish by O. Delatycki

It was 1945.

The war had finished. We had been freed. The long awaited salvation had come. We, the small numbers of survivors of the Holocaust – partisans and others who were in hiding, came back to our place of birth, Novogrudok. We all rushed to our houses. Perhaps something, perhaps someone was saved. But we found only ruins and graves. Dejected, shamed we turned to our former neighbours, the Byelorussians. Have they seen anyone, any member of our family? We thought that after we had experienced such trouble and pain, our neighbour's conscience would be stirred and they would meet us in a friendly manner. But their faces were inscrutable and with a sly smile on their faces they asked 'are you still alive?' We found out also that our wish, which we had in the forests, that we would have a chance to witness punishment of those who participated in the demise of our families and plunder of our properties, turned out to be another unfulfilled wish. The authorities had warned us and hinted that we should keep quiet. All that was left to us was to remain silent, with our lips firmly pressed shut. Deep in our hearts, however, was a hatred which we throttled inside. We thought that one day we may come to a free country, among our fellow Jews, and then we would be able to tell it all for future generations to remember.

This is how we walked around the town and looked at the ruins. It was hard to believe that this was the place where an active Jewish community flourished. There was no sign left of the wonderful town. Oh, my beloved Novogrudok, brilliant dreams of my youth. So many memories, so many dreams had disappeared together with our dear ones. Over the years in the forest, I was troubled by the thought: how will I be able to see and survive the sight of the ruin of my home? Now I was dragging my feet through the centre of the town, the Market place, from which streets and lanes are branching out through the devastation. Ruins were everywhere. Glassless windows of Jewish homes were covered with boards or filled with rags. From the distance one could see the hill where the cemetery was. It was bare. The Byelorussians had dragged away the grave stones [they used them as foundation stones for a forest of new garages for their newly acquired cars]. We came to the synagogue square, a place were tens of houses of prayer stood. The place was bombed and burned by the Germans. No synagogues were left. The square was overgrown by grass. In amongst the grass a few yellow flowers could be seen. There were also a few bushes on the edge of the square. In the middle of the paddock stood the south wall of the big synagogue. The bombs could not destroy it. There was no footpath leading to the wall. Not so long ago there were houses of prayer there and from them one could hear the voices of youngsters learning the Gomorrah. Their voices were heard in the adjoining streets. We stood still as stones. [The current Belarus city management 'improved' things. The south wall of the big synagogue disappeared some time ago. The only structure in the square is now a large public lavatory block built in the centre of the Synagogue square. When last seen, ill smelling effluent was oozing from the lavatories. It could not have been an oversight, it is an ultimate insult to the memory of the dead.] The sun was spreading warmth. I looked at the sky and could not see the sun, only a yellow object, which threw shadows on the ruined walls. If only the walls could speak they could tell the stories of all the horrors that were committed here. We walked aimlessly, moving as if in a nightmare.

Slowly the sun set and the eve of Rosh Hashona came. Our instinct called us to go to pray in a synagogue. Our hearts were full of pain and we needed to unload it. We hoped that praying would make things more bearable. But there was no synagogue, not a single house of prayer remained. We found a house, which used to be a tavern where the farmers would drink on market days. The house was in ruins with the windows broken and the walls wet from seepage. On the floor were broken bottles and pieces of glass. We found a broken table and covered it with a cloth. That had to serve as the bimah. There was no Torah to be found, just one prayer book. Of a community of 16 thousand Jews, twenty eight of us were the only survivors, among them were a few people in Red army uniforms. [The Jewish population of Novogrudok was of the order of 6 thousand when the Germans arrived. There were a few hundred survivors.] The people in the house felt alienated and constrained. A few candles were lit and prayers began. The candles were flickering and swaying up and down. Shadows moved on the walls. It seemed as if they were the shadows of the dead, which rose in the air and twisted as if they were complaining that their cries were not heard by all Israel. We were standing around the table. Chanan, the shoemaker began praying. His voice kept failing and changing into crying. Suddenly tears began to roll. There was crying and whimpering. The crying reverberated in the empty tavern. At the table stood a Red army man, his head bowed. His eyes were in tears. He was a long way from home. He had received no letters from his family for the last two years. Who knew what fate befell them. A partisan was standing engrossed in his thoughts, his eyes were lowered, and he was looking into the prayer book. He looked at the letters in the book, but he saw the faces of his children. But that could not be possible. He had seen his children tossed, like animals into a black truck. Next to him stood a Jew who was saved by chance. His face was as yellow as wax. He still did not know how he survived and he could not understand why he had survived. Who needs him, he thought. He looked in to the prayer book, but he saw the pictures of the past. Whole families dressed for the festivity and in festive mood, fathers, grandfathers with their grand children were going to the synagogue to pray. And now-such a decline. The tears were blocking his throat. A young man stood alone on the side. His head was down and he was immersed in thoughts. He was in the forests for three years, he saw death before his eyes every day. He was waiting for the day of liberation. His heart was pounding. When he thought of the happy day of the end of the war he believed that life would improve. His bleeding wounds may heal. Peace had come. For some it brought happiness. But for him it was the beginning of new sufferings. Where should he go? Back to the gentile neighbours, who look at him as a ghost from another world? He could not imagine going back to the world of the gentiles who looked on with indifference at the bloody deeds of the German murderers and did not move a finger to stop the horrors. They may have even been pleased that the Germans were conducting the annihilation. He had to live in this world and start do rebuild his existence from the beginning. He could not look at the murderers who were moving free and unimpaired with their heads high.

This is how the few Jews were standing immersed in their thoughts.

Chanan, the shoemaker was reading from the prayer book and the others repeated each word after him. Outside was deep darkness. Only the candles flickered and danced spreading a wild light as if they were saying: you must go on living, don't be disappointed. We went off slowly to our ruined lodgings.

We all thought:

How should we live among the graves?
Where could we put down our weary heads?
What will tomorrow bring?
Where could we go, what could we do?

In those good days - a group of masters

[Page 201]

Three Kol Niddrie's

by Chaim Leibovich

Translated from Yiddish by O. Delatycki

The Novogrudok Ghetto 1942

The sky was dark and threatening over Novogrudok. The city was in ruins. The houses that were still standing looked as if they were in deep sorrow. The windows of the Jewish homes were covered up with boards. The Jews moved like shadows dressed in rags. No one thought how to live, they only thought how to survive. It was astonishing, it was hard to believe that the Germans were exterminating the Jews. 'The Jews are exaggerating', said the 'wise' men of Novogrudok, 'the Germans will not kill anyone without an adequate reason'. The Jewish children were huddling to their mothers. There was disquiet in the air. It was the eve of Yom Kippur and the Jews had to give an account of their consciences. The Jewish skeletons slid close to the walls on their way to the synagogue. The synagogue was filled with both young and old. The Jews kept as close to each other as a flock of sheep. It was stifling in the synagogue, there was no air to breathe. Outside there was a light breeze, the trees shook slightly and seemed to whisper: 'save yourselves, save yourselves'. A choked wailing and cry could be heard as they prayed the 'Tfile zakro'.

The Rabbi in a white kitl (linen robe) stood on the bima (dais). On both sides stood respected members of the synagogue holding the Seyfer Toyre (Scroll of the Law). The rabbi called out in a fervent voice: 'recite the Kol Nidre'. Hundreds of voices call out the plea: 'May the will of G-d be done, may the supplications of the Jews be granted, may good deeds be done, which will bring their pleas before throne of G-d, so that the harsh decree will be erased'. The Jews stood the whole night in front of the Holy Ark and prayed Thilim.

A few days later the Germans appeared in the streets and gathered a group Jews, put them up against the wall and for no reason shot all of them. The wives who came looking for their husbands were forced by the Germans to wash the blood of the stones. The children dug graves for their parents with their bare hands and buried them. In the evening they brought to the square where the Jews were killed a band and played music. Belarusian girls started to dance, there was joy and laughter, music and dancing spread over the square. The Jewish survivors hid in attics or cellars and prayed.

Kol Nidre in the forest in 1943

We were in the heart of a dense forest enclosed by marshes. We were surrounded by the Germans. The German murderers controlled the whole of Europe and where their boots stood there was death and murder. Yet they could not manage to exterminate a few surviving Jew, who hid in the dense forests. Jewish girls and boys, often the only surviving members of their families, had escaped to the forests to be able to take revenge. From time to time they would attack the German garrisons and their Russian collaborators, who robed Jewish possessions. German murderers surrounded the forests with the aim of exterminating the remaining Jews. They were not keen to enter the forests, where an enemy of the Nazis could hide behind every tree. The Jewish partisans built their dug-outs among the pine trees. It was the eve of Yom Kippur and the detachment was in a holiday mood. The commander had ordered that an early lunch should be eaten before the fast. As the evening approached, the woods were quiet, it smelt of autumn in the fields and forests. High pines stretched their tops to the sky. The sky was dark with thousands of stars spread all over. The stars were winking, as if they were saying: be strong, be of good heart. The partisans gathered around the fires, some with arms on their shoulders, and formed a half circle. The old butcher stood in the middle. All were prepared for Kol Nidre. There were no prayer books and yet we all wanted to pray. We wanted to cry our hearts out, we hoped that that would bring us some ease. The butcher started with a quiet voice: 'Kol Nidre ve esurai'... The partisans stood with their heads bowed. We repeated the prayer word for word. We were engrossed in our thoughts. In front of our eyes were the shadows of the departed. Hundreds of women and children in a tight squeeze, the old who tore at their hair at the last moments of their lives... It seemed that we could hear the shouting of the children as they were being smothered. I remembered the recent past, when whole families: fathers, mothers, grandmothers and grandfathers were going to pray Kol Nidre. Tears ran down our faces. The crying throttled our voices. The praying of Kol Nidre had finished. The butcher took a kritzes haderech (short cut) in the prayer. Kadish followed. We prayed for the whole nation that was taken to the slaughter.

Kol Nidre 1945, Rome Italy

At long last the salvation had arrived. People from the concentration camps were freed, the partisans left the forests. People went to their pre-war homes. Maybe, maybe somebody survived. All we found were ruins and graves. No one was left. We had lost everyone. Only graves and more graves. We were spoken to by the gentile neighbours, who asked with a smirk 'are you still with us?' We cursed the bloodied earth. We were lonely, broken. We walked away with sticks in our hands to roam over the roads of Europe. We jumped borders. Further and further from the unlucky places. We went where our eyes took us. We went into camps, we were given the name of 'Shaires ha plytim' (holocaust survivors). Some of us went to Italy, to Rome. It was Yom Kippur eve. The big synagogue was packed. It was the first Yom Kippur after Hitler's defeat. A strong light blinded our eyes. Among those praying were many soldiers in uniforms: English, American, soldiers of the Jewish brigade, partisans, concentration camp inmates, Italian Jews, the gathering of the clan. All came to pray Kol Nidre. An American soldier, Halperin from Brooklyn, stood and held a machsir (prayer book) in his hand and his lips whispered. A soldier from the Jewish brigade stood nearby. He followed the baal tfile word for word. Partisans and ex-prisoners of the katzets with numbers burned on their arms, the remainder of Germany. They were standing and thinking, sunk in their memories. The war finished the suffering of many, but for those who survived new suffering began. Where can we go, where can we rest our tired heads?

New York

At the entrance to the synagogue stood young boys. They were tall, a pleasure to look at. They were standing trouble free with the prayer books in their hands. The synagogue was filled with people, men, women, whole families. Grandfathers and grandmothers all nicely dressed. On their faces one could see joy. The synagogue was well lit. The Chasen and his assistants prayed Kol Nidre. People were listening in deep silence. I was standing in a corner. In my heart was also Kol Nidre. I was looking in the prayer book and saw shadows in front of my eyes. The letters were dancing. I was deep in thought – seventeen years after the big catastrophe, always on the move. It seemed that it was only yesterday. As through a fog I could see familiar faces. I was always in fear that in time I may forget the contours of the faces of my beloved. Thoughts were rolling through my mind. Yes, I am in the Jewish New York. I was looking for the shore of a safe country. Deep in my heart I had different thoughts. When I was in Italy I thought I was remembering and I thought that time would heal my wounds. I would start a new family, make peace with my fate, smooth my furrowed brow, tear out with roots the bitter memories. But it is difficult, very difficult to forget the tragic past. In the blunt, satiated present the heart is aching and the sole is troubled. I cannot find peace within myself. I don't know whether it is a longing for the past that will never come back, or whether it is a demand of the sole to come to a peace with the old/new homeland, of which I was always dreaming. Who knows who knows...?

> *[The assistance of Mr David Grynberg in translating the above article is acknowledged.]*

[Page 203]

Legends and Fables

The Path to Riches

A Chasidic Tale

by David Cohen

Translated from Yiddish by O. Delatycki

To the blessed memory of the Slonim Chassids of Novogrudok

All knew that Shleimele, the maker of candles, could have been a wealthy man, the wealth was in his hands, yet he remained a pauper. We will tell you now how that happened.

Who was he – Shleimele? Were there in fact three Shleimeles? – Shleimele from Volozyn, Shleimele from Byten and Shleimele Meilach from Novogrudok.

The old Rabbi (OBM) said: 'If the three Shleimeles would combine into one Shleimele the world could not bare such holiness. Every one of them is blessed with good deeds.'

We will refer this time to Shleimele Meilach, who was all heart.

And why was he called Meilach? We will tell you about it too.

Shleimele was the only maker of candles in the learned misnagdish[1] town of Novogrudok, which is positioned on a mountain and in the winter, when it is covered in deep snow, it is often called Siberia.

The little house of Shleimele stood quite separately at the bottom of the town. And next to it was the 'factory' of the candles. Shleimele got his sustenance from selling the candles and he considered his task to be holy work: he was making candles, which the Jewish mothers were blessing on the eve of the Sabbath. His candles had a special shine, a special holiness. The very pious women would not buy the candles in their small synagogues, but would go down on Friday mornings to Shleimele's tiny house, where he would take down from a narrow shelf in his factory a bundle of candles and pass it to them with his greasy fingers.

As it was said, Shleimele made his meagre living by selling candles. But Shleimele did not blame the Almighty for that, nor did his wife, a mother of five children, who suffered from swollen legs and poverty. They had to get by the whole week on bread and a watery krupnik, but always enjoyed sumptuous meals on the Sabbath. Shleimele was renowned for his pleated bread rolls which he baked for Shale-shudes [derived from Shlosh Seudos – three meals on a Sabbath, a detailed derivation is attached at the end of the article [2]. The Chassids maintained that those who desired to experience the taste of the food which the Jews ate in the desert after they left Egypt, should taste Sheimele's pleated bread rolls. Shleimele would carry the tasty rolls wrapped in a red kerchief on a Saturday evening, when the town's mesnagdim were assembled in the synagogues and the sad tunes of their prayers wafted in the air. At that time Sheimele, was dressed in his worn velvet coat and wide belt, his craggy face darkened from exposure to the fumes of the candle wax. He was elated and was murmuring a hearty Sabbath tune. It happened at times that Shleimele with his bread rolls would meet the old misnagdi[2] Rabbi, a great Goan, who was on his way to the Great Synagogue for Ma'ariv (The Evening Prayers). Shleimele bowed his head to the Holy Man and bade him 'Gut Shabes' [Good Sabbath]. The Rabbi muttered 'A Jew should study at that hour a paragraph of Mishne, recite some Tehillim (Psalms) and not conduct feasts'. Shleimele listened to the Rabbi and answered passionately 'We Chassids are engaged deeply in Shale-shudes'. The old Rabbi replied: 'Chassids, feasts, kapores [3] may a good Jew not know you'. He spat and went into the shul.

In the [Chassidic] shtibl [a small synagogue] a small group was sitting around a table covered with a table cloth. Shleimele blessed the twelve bread rolls. Each one received a portion of bread. All those assembled thought that Sabbath, which finished already in the Misnagidi synagogues, where the daily prayer of Ma'ariv was being read. And yet it was still being celebrated in the shtibl. The hearts were full of joy listening to the melody with the words of the holy Sabbath. Shleimele was repeating the words and over his craggy face ran hot tears for the love of Sabbath. This was how the Chassids farewelled the Sabbath when in the rest of the town the week had begun.

But the world was not standing still. New candles appeared in town – spruce, giving a special light and they did not spray wax. Shlemiel's income started to decline week by week. At the same time Shleimiele's wife gave birth to another child. She was bed ridden. It was a Friday during the winter, cold, wind and snow and the eruv [4] of the town was broken. The vergers were running all over town to announce that the eruv was broken. Shleimele did not know anything about it. On Saturday the frost was severe. But in the evening, as usual, Shleimele bundled up 12 bread rolls and went to the shtibl. The frost and wind were fearful. Shleimele met on the way the old Rabbi, who started to shout 'Thug, you are carrying [stuff] on a Sabbath, and the eruv is broken!' Shleimele lowered his head and said 'I did not know, Rabbi, that the eruv was broken'. 'Throw away the bread rolls' shouted the Rabbi. Shleimele answered 'Rabbi, without the bread rolls we will not complete the Shale-shudes'. The Rabbi, shaking from anger, shouted: 'I will forbid the sale of your candles'. And that is what the old Rabbi did. The old Rabbi's a ban of Shleimele's candles was announced in all synagogues. Hunger and cold prevailed in Shleimele's home. One winter night Shleimele's wife said: 'We are jeopardizing the life of our youngest. Let us bundle him up warmly, take him to town and attach a notice that it is a Jewish child.' Shleimele heard his wife's desperate plea and he thought 'Why can't I be a wealthy man?' As it happened, the old Rabbi was at that time a Chassid. Shleimele went to see the Rabbi and told him that he could not continue to be poverty stricken. The old Rabbi listened with a gloomy face and he said: 'It will not be difficult to make you a hero, but you will have to experience a big ordeal. Shleimele was frightened, but remembering his sick wife, the hungry children and the baby, he said: 'Rabbi, I will do anything to be wealthy'. "Good' said the Rabbi and took out of his purse a few coins. He gave them to Shleimele and said: 'Go and buy fresh bread, cheese and butter and go home. Put the food on the table and eat all the food by yourself. Did you hear me, by yourself, don't give anyone a crumb'. Shleimele listened and yet did not hear the Rabbi's words. He just knew one thing – he did not want to be a poor man. Shleimele did as he was told. He bought fresh bread, cheese and butter and went home. When the smell of food spread over the house, the hungry children came running and begging: 'Father, a piece of bread'. But he, Shleimele pushed them away, he washed and ate alone. It felt as if he was swallowing hot stones. He finished, listened to the crying of his wife and children as he left, a broken man. He went on shaky legs to the Rabbi. The Rabbi asked Shleimele: 'Shleimele, do you still want to be a rich man?' Sheimele shook and answered 'Rabbi, if the way to riches is paved with the tears of children, I don't want to be wealthy'. Shleimele remained a Chassid and a poor man.

[Page 205]

Belief in the Messiah

by David Cohen

Translated from Yiddish by O. Delatycki

To the blessed memory of my father, the rabbi and revered Avrom Eliezer Cohen and my mother Rashke, daughter of Ari Openheim, both buried in the demolished cemetery of Novogrudok.

The little township in Russia would not have been able to sustain their own rabbi, were it not for the Jewish miller from the village of Slbodka, close to Novogrudok in Belarus, who took it upon himself to support his son-in-law, a young dreamer, the rabbi. This miller, broad shouldered, with a fiery beard was a man of this world. He liked a glass of vodka and a fat morsel to follow, but he also gave a thought to the world to come. He found a student of a Yeshiva, an ardent scholar and very pious, who accepted the proposed match – they assured him that after the marriage he would be able to study without having to worry about his family's income. The young, dreaming yeshiva student was also attracted to the quite village, where he was sustained by his father-in-law. The village was lost in the fields, a noisy brook was turning the millstones, thick forests surrounded the fields and were extending all the way to the marshes of Polesie. The young man stemmed from a village which smelt of the marshes and, as a youngster, he breathed in the melancholy of the still, slimy waters. He absorbed the mythical stories of pursued souls, who float over the marshes and linger in hope of resurrection. When he was told by the miller that a separate small cottage would be built for him next to the mill, where he would be able to study in seclusion, he agreed to the match, without having seen the bride. Fortuitously, it turned out that the bride was very suitable for the bridegroom. The miller had three daughters, and because he did not have a male heir he was anxious for the daughters to have a thorough Jewish education. He brought to the village a teacher, who taught the daughters not only sidur but also various interpretations of it as well as comments on the Chumesh and holy books written in Yiddish. As the time passed, the middle daughter grew tall, had a pleasant face and light blue eyes. She was a good pupil and hearty readings and the beautiful biblical tales filled her soul. She suffered with mother Rachel, who dressed in black when she said farewell to her children who were banished from their homes. She, the dreamy middle daughter, was the favourite of their father, the miller.

Rabbi Avrom Eliezer Cohen

After the oldest daughter, a strong and lively girl, married a village boy, who also leased a mill in the vicinity, the middle daughter was happy that she was marrying a boy from a yeshiva. He was delicate, of middle height, with a light, pale face, nice dreamy eyes, and a round black beard with two wavy sideboards. The miller's daughter liked him as soon as she saw him.

They lived in the village with the miller for a number of years. Four children were born: two boys and two girls. Their father was happy that he had no need to be concerned with earning an income. He was immersed in learning. In the depth of the night he studied the Kabala. In his heart he had a deep longing for salvation (geula) by the Messiah. Walking in summer days in the nearby forest he saw himself as the one who would bring the Messiah.

In the mean time the miller was looking for a future for his son-in-law, the great man of religion. There was no chance of becoming a rabbi in a bigger town, because the son-in-law was removed from worldly city concerns. The miller looked for and found a small township in Russia, were the people did not hope to have a permanent rabbi, because they could not afford to sustain one. The income from selling candles and yeast would not buy water to cook porridge. The people of the township were happy that the miller had assured them that he would support the new rabbi.

The new rabbi arrived in the little township and settled in a small house. The people of the town became attached to their rabbi. They knew that the rabbi was engrossed in studying and they did not bother him with questions and with the settling of disputes. They were happy to see the rabbi in the synagogue and he, the rabbi, was the last to leave the synagogue. And here, in the sad small township, he became engrossed in the Kabala and he recognized that the solution to his salvation should be his withdrawal from all every day problems, to eat and sleep less, to cleanse himself and prepare for the day when he would be able to distance himself from the world. He should fast for forty days and then he would be prepared to approach salvation.

It was his secret – no one knew about it. And yet his wife felt that a calamity was approaching. She and the three older children tried to dissuade him from pursuing his dream. The only one who sided with his father was the youngest child, who was only eight years old. He believed and hoped that his father would bring the Messiah.

The wife of the rabbi had written a letter to her father, the miller, asking him to come and try to dissuade his son-in-law from his dreams and plans. When the miller arrived, he locked himself up with his son-in-law in his confined room, argued with him intensely and said that it was not his destiny to seek the final solution. But the rabbi explained that those who are seeking salvation for themselves should not seek the final solution, leaving the rest of the people in the wilderness, but those like he, the rabbi, must do it, because they strive to join all those who are looking for salvation for everyone. The rabbi managed to persuade his father-in-law that the deed he was contemplating was a command from above. And the miller, who was a man of the world as we know it, was persuaded by his so-in-law and promised him to build next to his mill, a hut [suka], which would stand separated and elevated 20 arshin [approx. 1.4m] from the ground, supported on four posts. The rabbi would sit in his hut and conduct his deliberations – no human or beast would see him. A separate exit for him would be arranged, which he would use to attend to his needs.

The miller tried to appease his daughter and the grandchildren, but the daughter would not listen to him. Her heart told her that a catastrophe was impending. But there was nothing she could do. Separated in his hut, the rabbi was sitting engrossed in his thoughts. Very early in the morning he would go, accompanied by his youngest son, to bathe in a cold wash room [mikva]. The boy would walk in the deep darkness, with the sky covered in stars, trembling, holding on to his father's hand. At times a star would split off, burst into a fire and fall into the depth. It would seem that not just the boy, but the early morning darkness was trembling, and in the darkness the voice of his father could be heard: 'splendid and pretty is the light of the world and my soul is lovesick for you' and father shed a tear. The boy sobbed and said: 'father, I am afraid'. The rabbi pressed the boy's head to himself without interrupting his prayer song till they reached the cold bath. He got undressed and dunked thirty six times. As they were walking back the day began to show its early light. A pale sky hung over the township. The rabbi was the first to arrive at the synagogue. The boy slipped quietly into his bed and his mother covered him with an eiderdown, whispering: 'my dear boy'.

The day came when the congregation discovered what the rabbi intended to do and they were proud of him. The whole township bid the rabbi farewell, who was moving for two summer months to the Belarus village, to the miller, where he intended to fast for forty days. And as the rabbi, the revered, sat in his isolation in his Jehuda's hut in the strong belief that a miracle would happen. Nobody knew what the outcome would be, but they were hopeful. The only one who was seen to be in deep sorrow, whispering a prayer, was his wife. In her heart she assumed that instead of a miracle a calamity would happen.

The fortieth day had arrived. The day was sunny and the fields were in bloom. The forest raised it's top to the hut, where sat in holy contemplation the rabbi, the revered. The miller, the children and the rabbi's wife changed into festive clothes. The farmers, who worked in the mill were crossing themselves in fear and were casting frightened looks at the hut, which was covered in sunlight. The miller with the help of the farmers attached the ladder, which was usually attached every evening to allow the rabbi to go down to attend to his needs and to receive a light meal, which could be consumed without a wash. All eyes, particularly those of the young boy, were looking up and their hearts were pounding. Milling was stopped. It was as quiet as on Yom Kippur.

The door of the hut opened and the rabbi appeared. His face was pale, his eyes were open wide, the hands above his head looked like two wings. Before anybody could react, the rabbi fell from his hut to the ground. As it transpired later, the rabbi had seen before him the image of the Messiah, but did not see the ladder. There was panic among the onlookers. The youngest son was not seen anywhere. It was the rabbi's wife, who took matters in her hands. She ordered the horses to be harnessed, the carriage well cushioned and the rabbi in a faint, accompanied by the family except for the youngest son, was taken to town to the Jewish hospital. Much later the youngest son, crying and sobbing, was found in the high grass of the fields. He kept asking: "Where is he, where is the Messiah?"

For many months the rabbi was on the verge of death. The Jewish doctors did all they could and in the end they were lucky. They told the family that it would be advisable to take the rabbi to Koenigsberg because he had a broken leg and a stomach illness. The small town was prepared to help. Expenses were raised and the rabbi with his wife went abroad. On taking his farewells, the rabbi put his hand on the lowered head of his youngest son and said: 'My child, one should not be disappointed of not having brought the Messiah, but it seems that one should find another way....'

The rabbi, sickly and limping, had returned with his wife from abroad. He did not agree to return as a rabbi to the small town in Russia. The miller found for him a rabbinical post in a small town in Volyn. But the heart of the rabbi was longing for the village, where after the sudden death of the miller, the mill was taken over by the older son of the rabbi, who was himself a qualified rabbi, but he wanted to live in the village and run the mill.

During the first World War the township in Volyn was substantially destroyed and the youngest daughter of the rabbi was frightened by the Cossacks, who broke into the township. She became sick and died. The rabbi and his wife returned to the older son, the miller. The miller supported the rabbi, who lived in Novogrudok. He did not want to practice as a rabbi, but the Jews of Novogrudok held him in great esteem. When the wife of the rabbi died, she was buried in the Novogrudok cemetery. The rabbi fell into a deep melancholy. He would say to his near ones 'that the happy time had come, because his youngest son had found the right way to the rightful solution – he went with the Chaluts movement to Eretz Israel'.

"The good hour had come" his pale lips whispered as his soul had expired.

[Page 207]

"We will do and obey"

A Legend

Translated from Hebrew by Aviva Kamil

In memory of the owners of flour mills around Novogrudok; ordinary Jews, dear and sincere people. Many of them were massacred by the Germans.

Chasidim and shopkeepers sat around the "shulchan" (table) on the eve of the festival of Shavuot, their eyes glued to the face of Rabbi "Sheyichye" (the blessing of the life), who was talking at length. They sang one melody after another and listened with reverence and excitement to a lesson from the Torah given by the holy man. The lesson was about two words 'Na'ase Ve'nishma' (we will do and obey). The Rabbi said: 'Na'ase' (we will do) is the main command. 'Nishma' (we will obey) comes easily, without an effort. In contrast 'Na'ase' (we will do) demands an endeavour to overcome the natural desire and inclination. Seeing the divine and receiving the Torah are the rewards of a Jew, who truly reached the state of 'Na'ase Ve'nishma'.

The people around the table were listening to every word of the Rabbi. Everyone felt that the Rabbi was talking to him alone. Listening to his voice, they were repeating the words to themselves: 'Na'ase Ve'nishma'.

It was a wonder that the Chasid, Uri the miller, a very simple Jew, chose of all the festivals to attend the festival of Shavuot, when only Torah people and scholars attended the Rabbi's lesson. He too stopped working, came to hear the Rabbi, sat at the table, listened to the melodies, drank 'Le'chaim', and when the time to study the Torah came, and only the Rabbi's words were heard, murmured slowly in the silence, tiredness overcame the miller; a relaxed feeling overtook his large body and despite all efforts he dozed off, his eyes shut, his head dropped and a loud snoring noise came out of his opened mouth. It startled the Chasidim, they stared at him angrily and the Chasid next to him pinched him hard. The pinch woke Uri who jumped out of his seat bewildered, his eyes moved from one angry face to another till they rested on the Rabbi's good and appeasing face who was whispering: 'some times even the sound of snoring rises up to heaven'. Then the Rabbi turned to Uri and said in his deep voice: 'Calm down Uri, tell us how the dispute between you and your rival concerning the leasing of the flour mill ended?' And Uri started to tell his story, first with a little stutter, and as he talked he gained confidence and said: 'The rival was a rich Jew who wanted to take over my lease of the mill. He knew how much I paid the 'poritz' (landlord) and offered him much more money. The landlord who leased the mill to me and to my father before me, invited me to his place and told me: 'I was offered a higher fee for the lease, could you match it?' I replied 'I could pay that much money only if I put up the fees for milling, but I know that the poor peasants could not afford it. Thus, unfortunately, I wont be able to pay a higher fee'. The 'poritz' heard this and said: 'You are indeed an honest Jew', and the lease stayed with me'. The Rabbi smiled and asked: 'And what happened to the rich Jew?' Uri sighed and said: 'I hope it won't happen to any of us. He lost his money and has nothing'. 'And what did you do?' asked the Tzodiac. Uri, blushing, answered stuttering: 'Without him knowing it, I took care of his needs for the Shavuot and Passover festivals'.

The Rabbi returned to his interrupted lesson and said: 'Na'ase' (we will do), 'when a Jew behaves like our Uri did, he makes up for other shortcomings and is rewarded by receiving the Torah.'

[Page 208]

An Ethrog for Succoth

by David Cohen

Translated from Yiddish by O. Delatycki

To the memory of the kind Avrom Jarmovski and his two daughters Sonie and Feigele, who were killed by the German beasts.

There was an excitement in town when Dvoire the flour miller's wife had arrived by horse and cart at the Rabbi's house. She shook off the flour from her dress, whilst the coachman Lukash carried in through the back door a bag of flour, potatoes and a clucking chicken. Dvoire entered by the front door, greeted profusely the rabbi and his wife, who thanked her for her gifts. The news spread in town that Dvoire, the flour miller's wife came to town to select an ethrog [5].

It was the morning after Yom Kippur. The Jews, tranquil after Yom Kippur, knew that the days between Yom Kippur and Succoth [five days] are days when neither meat nor milk was eaten, they were pareve days. After repenting their sins in the month of Elul [6] and the first [nine] Tishre [7] days, they wished to have a respite. In any case, it is likely that in the four days between Yom Kippur and Succoth the Jews would not have committed major sins. And it was not worth worrying about minutiae. This was generally known and appreciated, and this was the time to be mischievous, to laugh. And was it not a laugh that Dvoire, the flour miller's wife came to town to select an ethrog? So people were laughing and some were remembering when Dvoire was a young girl.

She was a lively child and a beauty. Gorgeous eyes. She was brought up in wealth. And who would have thought that of all marriage proposals – rabbinic students, learned young men, some potential rabbis - Dvoire would choose Arie the flour miller. Arie appealed with his valour and good looks. Not just village girls, but daughters of merchants in town carried a torch for him. In the summer days, when the people in town were sweating, young couples were cooling off in the evenings by swimming in the lake next to the mill, which Arie was leasing from a Polish landlady. Arie, in his miller's garb, his face clear, his eyes glowing. He was bursting with youthfulness. The girls were fascinated by his looks. They were trying to engage him in a conversation. But just then farmers appeared with wagons full of grain. Arie carried one bag after another. The country girls were also attracted by the looks of the miller and smiled displaying their white teeth. They come running to Arie and took the bags from his hands. The landlady, an old maid, was also fond of Arie. It was said that Arie had no time for women. The match between Arie and Dvoire was arranged by the Polish landlady of the mill. Her parents endeavoured to dissuade Dvoire from the proposed match. Arie, in their opinion, was too simple, not erudite in the finer points of knowledge. But to no avail. Arie and Dvoire became engaged and in time married.

It was well known that Arie was generous and he and his wife sent many gifts to the rabbi for the poor of the town before every holiday. Arie, though an observant Jew, was not concerned about the commandments. Dvoire, who held the keys to the mill house, was 'carrying the household', she provided vegetables for Shavuot, bought two seats [in the synagogue], for herself and Arie for the New Year and Yom Kipur, and at Passover she provided matzoth for the poor. And she travelled to town to select an ethrog and lulav and every one in town was laughing. 'A connoisseur of ethrogs – she had really gone too far – who does she think she is, the miller's wife. Does she think that an ethrog is a chicken?'. But that was not the view of the rabbi. He had a high opinion of Dvoire and looked forward to her coming to his house. He opened the box of ethrogs for her and let her do the choosing. And indeed she selected a beautiful ethrog. It had no blemishes and was light yellow in colour. And she did not dwell and took home the perfect ethrog. The town got used to it. Dvoire's charity was outstanding. During the First World War there was hunger in town and without the help of Dvoire and her husband things would have been desperate. The Germans had requisitioned the flour mill but employed Arie to run it. Dvoire managed to smuggle bags of flour to town. This saved many lives. The Germans had announced many restrictions. The town which was close to the front line was shut off from all sides. Even those who had permits to travel were risking their lives. The town was isolated, enveloped in fear as the holidays approached. New Year and Yom Kipur had gone by and with Succoth approaching what could be done without an ethrog and lulav? The rabbi was thin and ailing and dressed in rags and fear was seen in his eyes. Not long ago a respected Jew from the town bought a few eggs from a farmer. German cavalry men caught him, they tied him to a horse and dragged him behind the horse at full pace. No, one should not risk one's life to go afar for an ethrog. As the holiday approached, Jews put up succoth [small temporary dwellings where Jews lived for the duration of the festival]. But no ethrogs. The Jews asked the rabbi if under the circumstances they could use another fruit instead of an ethrog. The rabbi said sadly 'just as one cannot replace Israel with another land, no matter how splendid, one cannot use another fruit instead of an ethrog'. One must forget the enticing smell of the ethrog. Israel is far away. On the last day before Succoth people of the town were making preparations for the festival. And unexpectedly Dvoire, the miller's wife appeared. She was dishevelled and sweaty but her eyes shone. The rumour spread 'Dvoire brought an ethrog with 'four fringes' [8]. On the morning of Succoth all were gathered in the synagogue. The rabbi sent the ethrog and the lulav to the female section of the synagogue. The rabbi said that the first person to bless the ethrog should be Dvoire, because it was due to her that the town had a nice and kosher ethrog. In the deep quiet one could hear the voice of Dvoire 'asher kidishanu bemitzvotav vizivanu mivareyach al nitilat lulav' and the rabbi and all people said 'Amen".

[Page 209]

A "Din Torah" - a Jewish court

by David Cohen

Translated from Yiddish by O. Delatycki

To the holy memories of my sister Reichl, her husband Mojshe Szapiro and their daughter killed by the German savages in the township Alevsk.

It happened to a Lithuanian Jew, a Jew who was a brilliant scholar (Talmid Chochem). He was a Jew who had no grievance against anyone, not even G-d. He studied the holy books and his wife was the provider. As a result they had nothing, not even grits and water. But somehow they survived. As the years rolled by the oldest daughter was getting on in years. She was not bad looking, nor was she dumb, but they had no dowry. And young men, even tailors and shoemakers, expected a dowry. The wife complained to her husband: 'my whole life I have been carrying the burden of providing for the household and you just sat in the synagogue and studied. But I can not find a husband for my daughter and I don't want to wait till she will be grey.' 'What would you have me do?' asked her husband, the Talmid Chochem. 'Do what others like you have been doing – be on your way – go far from home and beg for help to marry the bride. Jews know it is a mitzvah (a meritorious deed) to help a bride. And with the help of the Almighty you will come back in good health and an adequate dowry'. And thus the husband, the Talmid Chochem, went on a long journey, far from home. And, as his wife predicted, the Jews opened to him their hearts and there wallets. Our Talmid Chochem collected a nice wad of money and began to head for home. He was at the time many miles away in the depth of Russia. The local Jews, former soldiers in (Tsar) Nicholas's army, vague in their knowledge of the Torah, but with hearts of gold and their Rabbi, not one of the greatest men of learning, wished him success in arranging the marriage of his daughter. The Rabbi gave him also a present for the bride. On the last evening before the departure our Talmid Chochem was happy. He took even a strong drink and drank to the health of the guests in the tavern he stayed in. He told them the story of his daughter, the bride, the dowry he had collected for her and of his wife whom he had not seen for a couple of years. He was talking and weeping from longing. He showed them the purse with the money and the gift of the Rabbi for the bride. The Talmid Chochem fell into a deep sleep and when he woke up in the morning the dowry money and the gift were gone. It was likely that one of the guests had stolen it in the night. The Talmid Chochem sat for hours immersed in sorrowful thoughts. He did not blame the thief, who knows, perhaps he too needed a dowry for his daughter. He blamed only the Almighty – how could he do such an injustice? He will call the Almighty to a Din Torah (a religious hearing of a dispute) in front of the local Rabbi, who gave him the present for the bride. He went to see the Rabbi, who had just finished a sumptuous meal and was very happy to see the Talmid Chochem. He said: 'I thought you were well on your way by now. What happened?' The Talmid Chochem gave a deep sigh and said 'You are the Rabbi here and I want you to be the judge in a Din Torah'. 'And who is the accused' asked the Rabbi. 'The Almighty' said the Talmid Chochem. 'What are you talking about – how can there be a Din Torah with the Almighty in front of me? You came from the country of great Rabbis and Geonim (Torah Geniuses). Go to them – they are better versed in matters concerning the Torah. They are holy man. In front of them you will argue your case against the Almighty.' 'No' replied the Talmid Chochem 'in front off them, the learned ones, I will not get a hearing, because they would be afraid, they fear the Almighty. Therefore they can not be the judges. But you, as I can see, are not particularly scared of the Almighty, hence you will be a fair judge in this argument.' The Rabbi was quite satisfied with this contention. After he heard the whole story, how the traveller wandered and suffered till he collected enough money for the dowry and how the money was stolen the Rabbi gave his verdict. 'You are right and therefore the Almighty said that his is the money and the gold and he should return the dowry'. The Rabbi went to see his Nicholas's soldiers and collected for the Talmid Chochem more money than he gathered previously. The Talmid Chochem was happy and said 'Well Rabbi you can see now – I was right that I chose you as the judge. You are not overwhelmed even facing the Almighty and your verdict was right.'

[Page 210]

Yitzchak "Yam-Suf"

by David Cohen

Translated from Hebrew by Aviva Kamil

To the memory of Itzi the Melamed, one of the Slonim Chasidim in Novogrudok

The Rabbi came for Sabbath, between Purim and Pesach, to visit his few fellow Chasidim in a town, which was populated predominantly by Mitnagdim. At the time of "shalosh se'u'dot" he was preaching the Torah devoutly, and was repeatedly telling his Chasidim that every Jew, if he so desired, would be rewarded by experiencing the sensation of the parting of the sea (the Yam-Suf). The man who will have this experience will be blessed.

Those words touched the heart of Itzchak the Melamed, and he was frequently thinking about that matter. Itzchak was the tallest man in town ("me'shichmo va'ma'alah"), but he was as modest as he was tall, kept lower then the moss on a wall and was kind hearted. He loved with all his heart the few pupils he taught. His pupils came from poor families. The better to do families, the Mitnagdim, shunned his cheder saying that he taught his pupils the Chasidic Torah instead of Moses' Torah. It was true. From morning till night one could hear Chasidic melodies rising from his hut. He said that studying the Torah by using melodies was a good method of learning. Some were melodies of gaiety and laughter and others were filled with sadness. The pupils were repeating their lessons in the Chumash and Talmud and learning their Torah whilst singing melodies.

The festival of Pesach was approaching, the air was full of the light of spring and the festive melodies could be heard drifting from the cheder of Itzchak the Melamed. This year, after hearing the words of the Rabbi about the parting of the Yam-Suf, the Melamed taught his pupils continuously by singing "be'tzet Israel me'Mits'raim" ("When Israel left Egypt", a sentence from the Bible). The song was like a marching song, as if the pupils were joining the people who were following Moses out of Egypt. When they reached the sentence "Hayam ra'ah ve'yanos, ha'Yarden yisov le'achor", the words were rushing like a waterfall. The voices of the pupils were intermingled with the voices of those who were baking Matzos. As the festival was approaching, a rumor went about that Itzchak the Melamed was going to part Yam-

Suf on the Seder night. The town went wild. Some laughed, others thought it a blasphemy. The Seder arrived and many were in a hurry to finish it, they sang "Chad-Gadya" in a hurry, and rushed to Itzchak the Melamed's hut. The Melamed was sitting like a king with his wife and five children around him, reading the Hagadah with great joy, one melody followed another, and all the Chasidim who were packed the room joined in the singing. When the clock struck midnight, Itzchak the tall and his eldest son got up and brought in a bathtub filled with water. The Melamed put on his shoulder a bag of Matzo Shmurah, stood erect in line with his wife and children, and when they reached the sentence "Daber el bnei - Israel va'isuh" he stepped into the bathtub filled with water. His wife and children followed him and so did the Chasidim. They sang loudly "Ha'yam ra'ah va'yanos". At that moment the Mitnagdim broke in and yelled at the Melamed: "Itzchak Yam-Suf, Itzchak Yam-Suf....."

When the Rabbi heard of what had happened at Itzchak the Melamed's home and the behavior of the Mitnagdim, he said of them: "they have eyes but can not see, if they would've been rewarded with sight, they would've seen sixty thousand people leaving Egypt, joyful for their deliverance..." From that day on the Melamed was called by the people of the town: "Itzchak Yam-Suf" and that was his name from one Pesach to the next.

Translator's Footnotes

1. Misnagidim/Mitnagedim (opponents) is the name of the opponents of the Chassidim. Originally the name arose from the bitter opposition to the Chassidic movement. Although they have some common characteristics, Misnagidim tend to have a pronounced scepticism and a severe criticism of credulity and authoritarianism. Elijah b. Solomon Zalman, the Gaon of Vilna (1720-1797), gave impetus to the rise of the Misnagidim, and that way of life became characteristic of Lithuanian Jewry. The majority of the Jewish population of Novogrudok was Misnagidi.

2. The Gomorrah in Meshes Shabbats 117 (Babylonian Talmud, Tractate

"Sabbath") tells us that the concept of Shlosh Seudos (compressed into Shale-shudes) is taken from the incident of the Mon (manna). It is a dispute between Tanaim (Sages) as to how to interpret the thrice read word "HaYom" whereby the required number of meals on Shabbat is derived. The Rabbonan (Rabbis) posit that the thrice mentioned word "HaYom" teaches that three meals during the entire Sabbath are required.

3. *Kapores Chickens:* Kapores means "atonement". On the morning before Yom Kippur, some Jews have the custom of swinging a chicken over their head three times and reciting a small prayer that essentially says, "any punishment I am deserving of because of my transgressions should be passed along, instead, to this bird."

The chicken is killed with a quick cut to the neck and windpipe, which causes it to die instantly. However, some continue moving reflexively and even run around for a while, before finally expiring. So, what we have here is Agent Emes saying "stop running around like a chicken with its head cut off."

NOTE: Some, more sensitive souls, who want to do the "kapores" custom without killing an animal, will substitute a dollar bill (or some other currency) for the chicken.

4. What is an Eruv?

The Torah prohibits carrying on Shabbat between a public domain and a private domain or for more than 4 cubits in a public domain.. However, the Torah permits carrying within an enclosed "private" area. Public domains are typically non-residential areas including streets, thoroughfares, plazas ("open areas"), highways, etc. Private domains are residential areas, and originally referred to an individuals home or apartments that were surrounded by a "wall" and can be deemed to be "closed off" from the surrounding public domains. The rabbis of the Talmud developed a means to render a larger area as a private domain by surrounding it. Such an enclosure is called an "*Eruv*", more specifically "*Eruv Chatzayrot*" or *Sheetufe M'vo'ot*. The Hebrew word "eruv" means to mix or join together; an *Eruv Chatzayrot* (henceforth just "Eruv") serves to integrate a number of private and public properties into one larger private domain. Consequently, individuals within an Eruv district are then permitted to move objects across the pre-Eruv public domain-private domain boundary.

5. Ethrog Citron

Medium to large sized bumpy yellow skinned citrus having a very acidic flavour. Primarily the skin is used, and the fruit plays a role in the Jewish Feast of the Tabernacles – Succoth.

6. Elul the month of repentance and personal reflection that culminates with Rosh HaShannah, Yom Kippur and the start of the new year

7. Yom Kippur or Day of Atonement is observed on the tenth day of the month of Tishre.

8. The *tzitzit* are fringes that appear on the four corners of the prayer shawl worn in the synagogue and by Traditionalists as part of their regular clothing beneath their outer garments. The prayer shawl is called a *tallit*. Therefore "an ethrog with 'four fringes'" may mean 'an ethrog covered by a tallit'.

[Page 211]

"Boze moyi"

A story of a Jewish miller

Translated from Hebrew by Oskar Delatycki

In blessed memory of my brother Izchok Izek (Kahn), his wife Beylke and their children Shoshana, Zvi and Arye, who were killed by the Nazis.

Izchok Izek (Kahn)

It all started in the distant past, before the first World War. The small village of Slobodka, not far from Novogrudok, consisted of a single street with small timber houses with thatched roofs. On the top of a hillock, just visible through the leafy trees, stood a small church with a cross on top. The church overlooked a small cemetery where the deceased hard working peasants were buried. In the valley flowed a stream which drove the flourmill. The mill belonged to a Polish noblewoman, who let it year in, year out to a Jewish miller. The house of the miller was perpetually shaken by the mill, to which it was connected. That day was a day of celebration at the millers. The oldest daughter, married to a learned man, gave birth to a boy and it was his bris.

Guests arrived from town, among them the rabbi and the mohel. Millers from near and far joined them for the big festivity. Next day, when the mother of the child was already up and about, a party for the farmers was arranged. All farmers from the surrounding villages, who were customers at the mill, were invited. The old pop [orthodox prist] joined them. He was broad backed with a smooth face, a broad nose, watery eyes, the long strands of hair coming down in ribbons. The pop, having drunk a considerable amount of vodka and eaten well too, demanded to see the newly born, so that all could see him. 'What, don't we have a right to see the child, didn't his mother grow up with our sons and daughters? Why can't we see her first child?' There was no avoiding it. The old miller came in with his daughter and the newly born on a large cushion. The old pop, with the heavy silver cross resting on his protruding stomach, stood and looked with his watery eyes at the newly born boy and suddenly he fell to the ground, he crossed himself and started to shout 'Boze moyi (my G-d), he looks like our Jesus'. When the farmers heard this, they fell to their knees, were genuflecting and murmuring 'Boze moyi, Jesus Christ'. And this is how a rumour started in the surrounding district that at their miller's a small Jesus was born. As the boy was growing up he was surrounded by love of the farmers. The miller was urging his son in law to obtain his rabbinical appointment and take the boy away. The boy was pleased that the farmers likened him to Jesus.

The time came and the boy together with his father the rabbi, and mother went far away to a small town in Russia. The boy, who was growing fast, was longing to go back to his birthplace and to the farmers. Even after he started studying in a yeshiva, he used to go for the holidays to his grandfather. He would meet the farmers, who were happy to see him, and the farmers' daughters met him with ardour and would kiss him and press him to their ample bosoms. He was growing up. He finished his studies in the yeshiva and obtained his rabbinical qualifications. At that stage he joined the revolutionary movement. He managed to avoid imprisonment and, when his grandfather died, he took over the running of the flourmill. The old Polish landlady was fond of him. But most of all he was liked by the ordinary farmers, and he reciprocated their feelings. On Pesach he distributed among the poor farmers white flour and visited their poor homes, where he partook of their hospitality.

After the First World War started the Germans occupied the village. All mills were taken over by the army, except for the mill of our young friend. A couple of old Landsturm soldiers sat in the mill, and though they did not believe that the Jew was Jesus they did appreciate the gifts such as white floor, good quality butter, kept cool in the stream, bread rolls made with eggs, and, with all this, a good piece of pork. Those gifts were sent each week to Germany and the old Landsturm soldiers made certain that the mill came to no harm.

After the Russian Revolution and the Brest-Litovsk peace treaty, the Germans left the village and the Bolsheviks arrived. One day an agitator with a sharp tongue came to the village. He assembled the farmers in the centre of the village and gave an 'enlightening' speech: 'Please tell me, comrade farmers, the land which is owned by the landlady, to whom should that land belong?' And they all answered 'It should belong to the State'. 'And the factories in towns – who should they belong to?' 'To the State' the farmers shouted. The young Jewish agitator continued with growing vigour 'And to whom should the watermill in your village belong?'. And the farmers threw their hats in the air and replyed in one voice: 'The mill did belong and should continue to belong to our Jesus'. 'What Jesus, who is he – where could he be?' the agitator stammered. And the farmers answered 'Jesus is our Jew'.

The mill was requisitioned by the government, but Jesus remained as the miller.

When the Poles came with their blown up manners and their hatred of Jews, the Jews began migrating to Erez Israel. The miller was considering migration, but he was strongly attached to his farmers. The farmers used to jest: 'If they will take us all to Palestine, our Jew will come with us'. The older sons of the miller went to Israel, but the miller with his wife and younger children remained in the village. The farmers maintained their friendship to the miller.

After the Second World War had begun, the Nazi beasts were ravishing the towns and villages of Poland. The mass murders started. The Germans encouraged the farmers to kill the Jews among them, but the farmers protected their miller. They all believed that somehow they would all survive the fearful times.

One day the village was surrounded by German soldiers. They went into the mill and brought out the Jewish miller, his wife and two children. The third child hid among the bags of flour and they could not find him.

All villagers were watching. Among them stood their young priest. When the miller appeared, his features white, covered in flour, his delicate face with the gold beard indeed reminded them of the pained face of Jesus. All farmers kneeled, genuflected and the young priest murmured: 'the cursed anti-Christs are tormenting our miller, may the Almighty's wrath be cast upon them'.

The German soldiers took the miller and his family to the Jewish mass grave. The farmers hoped that the youngest son of the miller, hidden among the sacks of flour, would be saved. But the Germans left a guard around the mill. The farmers thought that after night fall they may be able to smuggle out the boy and hide him.

Alas, when it started to get darker, the boy, thinking that the Germans had left, left the mill. The German soldiers caught him. The farmers begged the soldiers to release the youngster, but the Germans led the boy away and took him to the mass grave.

In the quiet of the night the farmers bemoaned the loss of the miller and his family. The young priest was crossing himself and murmuring: 'may G-d's wrath spread on all Germans and their children for all generations'.

[Page 213]

Letter from a mother

by Edna Kagan

Translated from Yiddish by O. Delatycki

My dear son,

When I read how the Germans had destroyed our nation, smothered the young and the old, men and women and the Jewish towns among them our Novogrudok, where my sister lived with her four children, her husband and our extended family, how they tossed young children, in front of their parents, into ovens, whilst the music played on, and how they treated young girls, perhaps among them my sister's Mariashke's three girls, how the Jews were forced to dig graves for themselves, I felt numb and faint. I thought that I could hear my sister calling to me: revenge, take revenge for me, for my children and my husband. And this is why your letter announcing your resolve to join the army had filled me with elation. I suddenly knew that I and my children will not live in a world which others have fought for. Therefore I say to you – go. Be not afraid. I know, my son, what you think of the war. I know what your feelings were when you saw a gun or a sword. But go and take revenge for all the innocent children, for all the Jews who died for one reason only – that they were Jews. Take the gun or sword in your hand and destroy the wild beasts which threaten to destroy you and your nearest. Be filled with vengeance and hatred. Do not rest till the enemy of the world is defeated. You have a dual duty – to your nation and to the world. All viciousness that was committed against all nations of the world is of concern to the world, but not the viciousness against one nation, our nation. It is because of this that I am certain that you are going to fulfil a holy mission with certainty in your heart. What else, my son, can I tell you, when the entire world is unsteady under our feet, when the animal replaces the man? I am crying, I shed tears, not for you, who are going to fight for a better world, but for those unhappy, innocent children who were removed from this world. What else can I tell you, my son? Go and luck be with you, go with the will for revenge in your heart, and may your weapon be light in your hand. Greet Zita, tell her that your mother blesses you. Tell her to look after herself.

Your mother.

I am taking my son to the draft board

I am taking my Meyer to the draft board. I remind myself of all I lived through. My feeling when I took him for the first time to kindergarten, he was dressed up, shiny. I remember when I took him for the first time to the Jewish school, when I told him of my hopes. I said to him: my son, you will grew up to be a proud Jew and a good human being. You will not bring shame to your town. But where have I taken him now? Is he going to learn how to defend his country and its freedom? He may, perish the thought, not survive. A mother is taking her child to be educated, to be cured, to be married. But now I am taking him to the draft board. There are many people around us: mothers, fathers, wives and brides. There is a strange quite around us. Mothers are buttoning up the jackets of their children. They look helpless. It is the first time that they stand on the edge of danger and they can do nothing to save the children from that danger. Names are called out, my son's name among them. Somebody is speaking to the new soldiers. Young wives are covered in tears. Now the soldiers are boarding the busses. I hear the name 'Pennsylvania station'. I am running to the station. The station is packed with people. I am looking for my son. Here stands a young man and he drinks milk. His mother wipes his lips. The son is embarrassed. He is a soldier, after all. I noticed my son. I run to him, but some one pushed me away. At least I stood next to him for a moment. Suddenly there was the sound of a whistle. The soldiers fell in in rows. They started to march towards the rail lines. I follow my son with my eyes. I can see only his head. Now his head has disappeared. I murmur a prayer 'God, take care of my son, save him from danger, save all sons, the two of mine among them'. The station emptied. What now? Where could I go? Home? Why home? There is no one at home. I thought suddenly 'there may be a letter from my son Boruch'. His letters sustain me.

The battle of the Seventh Army

Ah, the night of the retreat will always remain in my mind. It was just as well that my sister slept that night in my house. As a rule I avoided having guests in the evenings. If I was alone I could listen to the wireless and could follow without interruptions the movements of the Seventh Army. My Boruch is in the Seventh Army. I am aware of all the strategic moves and I could listen to the radio till the late hours. I don't know how I got there, but, as I was thinking, I found myself in a house between a forest and a river. There were many people in the house. People looked suspiciously at each other. I was sitting next to a door and I was very strained. It was quiet, just like after a storm. The Seventh Army had occupied the whole area. I felt as if I was there, at the battle. I was concentrating, perhaps my Boruch will come by. I was imagining how surprised he would be to see me: 'what are you doing here, mother" he would ask. A mother is everywhere. Suddenly I could hear running feet, shouting, thumping of artillery. Soldiers were running in all directions. Ah, God, ours were retreating and were pursued. There was shooting. Soldiers fell. The enemy soldiers came running with bayonets at the ready. There was much noise, cynical laughter. And now I could see my Boruch walking. He was bent and was limping. I started shouting 'my child, my son, your mother is here, I was waiting for you'. I opened my eyes, my sister was standing next to me with fear in her eyes. "What happened' she asked me 'did you have a bad dream'? 'What were you shouting about? Who did you call'? I replied 'wait a minute, Freidl, let me recover my breath, let me think, have I really seen Boruch, my son. They were pushed back. They pursued the enemy several hundred miles into Austria. And now, such a setback'. 'What are you talking about' said Freidl. 'You fell asleep and you dreamt all this. I am not surprised. You have been listening again and again to the same news bulletins. Come, go back to sleep'. 'How can it be a dream, if I could picture the place in detail, the surroundings. I can see even now all that happened. I can not forget it.' I was waiting with impatience for the morning news. The Seventh Army had a substantial setback. My son Boruch wrote to me that he could not conceive how I could have seen in detail the place where they were pushed back by the enemy.

The telegram

I was at the house of my sister Golda, a block from my house. It was Passover eve. There was a knock on the door. It was a man with a telegram in his hand. My sister was lost and started to shout: 'a telegram, who from?'. I was numb and could not speak. I was thinking: 'it must be my neighbour, she knew that I went to my sister and she sent him here'. The man who brought the telegram put us at ease. He said that it was a Passover greeting. My sister and I could breath again. The man said 'I just delivered a similar telegram to a house near by'. I turned to the man 'is the telegram addressed to Mrs K?'. 'Yes' said the man, 'that is the name. Don't worry, my friend, it is addressed to you, Mrs K.'. The man departed glad to have brought good news and happy with the generous tip. I was reassured because it was not bad news. For a while I remained at my sister's. On the way home I stopped at a shop to make some purchases. As I walked home with the parcels in my hands, I thought: 'my neighbour is right, she said – frighten me G-d, but don't punish me'. As I approached my house I saw a group of people. As soon as they saw me they dispersed. As I got closer I noticed that my neighbour walked away from his window. When I started to walk up the stairs, he came over and took my parcels. I could not understand the sudden concern. I thanked him and opened the door. He pushed me aside and indicated a yellow envelop. Suddenly it had all become clear to me. I said 'this is just a holiday greeting, I know all about it, my sister received a similar telegram'. The worried look on the face of my neighbour changed in an instant. "Why didn't you ring us, do you know how worried we were? Go and speak to my wife.' Ah G-d, we are all on an edge.

Wartime postman

I could see him approaching with a bundle of letters. For some it will bring a greeting of joy, for another dark despair. For me the postman was in the days of worries a conveyor of good news from my children. I did not receive post every morning. On such days I could see him pass by my letterbox in a hurry, as if he was the guilty one. But when he had letters for me he would ring the doorbell and say cheerfully 'letters for you and photos, not to worry, now you have much to read'. My neighbour upstairs thought of a different strategy: why wait for letters that don't arrive, it was better to go for a walk and find an unexpected letter in the letterbox when she returned. Sometimes I could hear the postman assuring a neighbour 'don't worry, I will have a letter for you in the afternoon, the boat was late and the sorters are still working'. The postman had aged lately. It was hard for him to witness so much pain. Sometime days and weeks would pass without a letter. I was frightened when the doorbell rang. I decided to wait outside for my destiny. Having positioned myself thus I saw on occasions the postman coming around the corner with a bundle of letters in his hand, a smile on his face, and he would shout 'I saw the letters for you at six o'clock this morning. I couldn't make up my mind – should I phone you or not. My heart told me to ring, but my head dictated otherwise, because I may give you a fright'. I realise only now that I don't know the name of the postman.

Uncle from Riverside drive

I was at my brother's house in Riverside drive. One could see cars rushing one after the other through the windows. From the 21 floor they looked like armies that move without stopping. My sons may be among them. The full moon was reflected in the Hudson river. Opposite electric lights were changing colours. You may wonder what I was doing there. My son was given a few days sick leave. In a few weeks time they will remove the plaster from his foot. He took the opportunity to visit his mother, brother and uncle. Uncle and his wife were eating their supper. After they will finish eating we will talk business. This was the reason for my son's visit. The brothers are talking. Mayer was amused: 'if one had to break his foot why not during the war, why break a foot after the war? See how much time you have lost. Five months in the hospital in Chicago. Was it not silly, don't you think uncle?' Boruch was philosophical about it. 'Who knows what is best? I could have been killed, it is all a matter of luck. On one occasion a few of us armed with rifles went out. We had to take care because of snipers. Suddenly there was a cry and parts of a body flew everywhere. He must have stepped on a mine. He was my best friend. It could have been me. I could have been the one in front. My friend was shot to pieces, I broke a leg, it all happened during the war. It is the after-effect. It is all due to the war.'

My sister-in-law asked me why I was so depressed. We finished the meal. Uncle helped his wife to clear the table. Boruch said: 'Uncle, I imagined that things would be quite different. I did not expect that I would come to you. But, in a few weeks I will be rid of my impairment' and he illustrated his words by lifting his foot in the plaster cast 'so I came to you because I have to think of my future. I have a wife and a child. So I came to hear what you have to offer'.

Uncle was rearranging the table. He stopped and asked: 'what do you intend to do, Boruch?' 'It is difficult to tell, uncle. I am young, but I have experienced a lot. My head is in a whirl. I have seen ruined towns, homeless, rootless people. Our people had been slaughtered. The enemy is still proud of their deeds. I hear that everything is very different. The people are different, the streets are different. This life looks alien to me. The change has been too sudden. There it was hunger, heartbreak, and here there is laughter and merriment. People are so free with their money. We gave our best lives for no reason. We were perpetually in danger. Here all was peaceful. It seems as if I am in an alien world'.

'You should realise that it will take time for you to adjust.' 'I need help'. 'For the time being, Boruch, you are a soldier' his uncle said 'when you will be demobilised we will look at the situation again. I may try to find a job for you in the Zionist organization. I know a lot of influential people in the movement, because I am a substantial contributor to the cause.' 'Uncle, I believe that I would not be able now to do communal work. I am not able to make speeches, encourage people, stir up people's interest. The job would involve tensions, meetings, agitation. And' lowering his head, 'I am not the same Boruch that I was 4 years ago. Now I need a steady job under supervision. Could you use me in one of your businesses and give me a chance to recover.' For a while the conversation came to a halt and then the boys said 'mother, let's go'. Uncle took his nephews and sister to the elevator. He waited till they got in and before the door closed he said 'I will see you later'.

On the way home

The brothers sat in the train and spoke to each other. I looked at my sons and I thought how different their letters to me were. Mayer's letters were short, laconic, just the news that was most important for his mother, that he is alive and healthy. Boruch's letters were filled with detailed information. He shared with his mother his moods, impressions and events. In one of his letters he wrote: 'Mother, I am now working with the military government. The work is important and interesting. Because I can converse in a few languages, I am attached to a prisoner of war camp. I was travelling today through a big town in a jeep and have seen thousands of German prisoners of war. I was glad to see that this is what happened to the herrenvolk. But suddenly I noticed a group of deformed, ill looking people dressed in rags. I drove nearer. I recognised them, they were Jews, who must have recently been saved from the gas chambers. I got out of the jeep, walked over to them and spoke to them in Yiddish. They started crying. Can you imagine, mother, such an event? Among thousands of German prisoners of war, I, an American Jewish soldier stood and cried with the saved Jews. They were 15 to 20 years old. They were old looking children. They started asking me questions that caused me pain: 'why were you silent in America?, why did you do nothing to save us?' 'I assured them that now we will do all we can for them. I had in my pocket a Yiddish newspaper and I gave it to them. They read it ravenously. Don't worry, mother. Our military command will look after them. And so will I.' The conductor called out the name of our railway station and we walked off deep in our thoughts.

Sleepless nights

My dead sister is demanding of me in my sleepless nights; 'revenge, take revenge for me, for my children for my husband'. She spoke to me day and night. I spoke to her in my sleepless nights: 'sister mine, we know how you must have suffered, they will pay for it, can you hear the march of our armies, they are going, they will come with anger and lust for revenge, my sons among them. You can be sure, sister, that righteousness must win through. Innocent blood will not be forgotten. Rivkele, my 19 year old niece you may have been somebody's bride, Blume and Henie with the dreamy eyes, Benyomin, my little nephew, with your shiny face and clever eyes. How could anybody harm them? Jankel, you are clever and fleet footed. But now I know that Jankel was shot when he brought meat to the Ghetto, that you, my sister, were shot on your bunk and nobody will tell me what happened to the children. Revenge won't bring you back to life. I am shattered, in pain and helpless, my sister. We are all victims in the indifferent world. Oh G-d, bring a flood, bring a fire like in Sodom and Gomorrah till the whole world of darkness will disappear forever.

[Page 217]

The Shloss-barg

[The Castle hill]

by Dr. Avraham Ostashinski

Translated from Yiddish by O. Delatycki

I remember it well – the Shloss-barg, and which Novogrudker does not, the old, peaceful and so familiar and dear Shloss-barg. We all grew up on its wide space and spent many a day on its surrounding hillocks. I can see it in front of my eyes – the two hills divided by a valley and connected later by a road which went past the house of Szimanowicz. The round amphitheatre on the big hill with its two towers – the bigger one on the east side provided a nice view of the surrounding country side. One could see the road to Korelicze. The fields, neatly divided into squares, stretched to the horizon. Close by was a small grove where we would go in the summer to gather nuts. Through the fields winds a footpath to Brecianka, where people would go to the water mill to drink at the miller's warm milk straight from the cow, or try a plate of cold yogurt with black bread and hard, cold butter. It was a great pleasure on a warm summer evening. A little further on was the road to Peresika and Litowka. Aha! Here comes Chaim the water carrier, with the good water from Peresika for making tea. Further, on the horizon we could see the forests past Grodno Street. Under the hill was a deeper valley where in the spring and autumn was a stretch of water, which would evaporate in the summer. A hillock divided the area under the hill from the Sapotnicki's garden, where cucumbers, cabbages and other vegetables grew. The second, smaller tower stood on the southwest corner. Below was a narrow stream and past it the old fara [parish church] with a red roof, Niankovski's farmhouse, Kowalski, Korelicze and Sieniezyc Streets buried in greenery.

The stream at the bottom of the palace hill

As children we loved the Shloss-barg. On the hill all was interesting and attractive. The brag never disappointed us. We had much joy on the barg on a Friday in summer, when we had classes only in the morning. For the rest of the day one could do whatever one pleased. If you so desired you could play 'chaverlach' ['friends'] on the big hill. You could conduct battles, take bets on who was going to run up and down the big hill fastest, toss stones and bricks from the bases of the towers or go for a stroll to the grove. Some of us would attempt scaling the towers, though this was not an easy task. Yet there were always those who were willing. Some of them scaled the walls high up to the embrasures. Later we discovered an underground tunnel. Stories were told that the tunnel was a passage to the fara church. Others were more imaginative and spoke of the tunnel extending to the town of Korelicze [22 km away!]. We would lie on our stomachs and crawl inside. The inside was narrow and low and very damp. It was not possible to move forward a meter, let alone to Korelicze. But what was missing in reality was provided by our imagination.

The "Kopietz" - memorial for the poet Adam Mitskewitz

In winter the hill was covered by a white, glistening layer of snow. It was a big achievement to crawl up the hill and to be immersed to the midriff in snow. Everyone wanted to mark the smooth layer of snow with his steps. The best was to ride down the hill on ones backside. The tiny lake at the bottom of the hill when frozen made an excellent surface for sliding on. In the late autumn, when the lake was covered by a thin layer of ice, an attempt to slide on it would finish up in a dunking in the cold water and a speedy retreat home.

The Shloss-barg was an attraction not only for the young. On Friday evenings and on Saturdays the hill was visited by many. After consuming an ice cream at Rudnicki's it was time for a stroll on the hill, sometimes with the whole family and at times as a couple. The benches provided an airy and romantic place for couples. The revolutionary youth in 1905 and the Zionists, the Shomer youths on the Hachshara, everyone would come to the Shloss-barg. Sometimes quite late, the old Efron, immersed in his thoughts, would rush by in a heated discussion with the meek teacher Mirski.

Basically unaltered, the hill was subjected to some changes. On the lower hill, close to the Shloss street, stood an old windmill and a decrepit house. During the First World War the Germans filled in a narrow section of the valley and formed a passage from the lower hill to the big hill. Later the Poles conducted an archaeological investigation and dug parts of the wall surrounding the top of the big hill. The soil from the walls was used to form a small mound on the lower hill. This mound was put up as a memorial to the native son, the famous Polish poet Mickiewicz. The memorial hill was small and reminded one of a knob on a forehead. Later flowers were grown on the lower Shloss. The fire brigade would march onto the Shloss on major holidays with a band and torches.

The palace in snow

At the entrance to the Shloss-barg was the house of Szimanowicz, the photographer. Everyone knew the tall man. He was a philosopher. Wearing dark glasses he would walk immersed in thoughts. He was having deep thoughts about the formation of the earth and liked to tell his marvelous stories. His two sons, particularly Senia, were the real keepers of the Shloss. The boys used to say that Senia is not afraid of anyone. At the entrance to the Shloss lived also Kaminiecki and Benzianowski, two wise Jews with large families and many boys, who together with Senia shared the domination of the Shloss. Further along lived Benjomen Chaim Gordon, in the street where the old windmill stood. Next to the windmill lived the pork butcher, who had business contacts with Jews and a bad son, who was connected to Polish extremists who were hostile to Jews. [During the war the pork butcher Jarmolowicz hid eight Jews and saved their lives].

The last time I visited the Shloss-barg was during the summer of 1946, on my way from Russia. The hill was still the same dear Shloss-barg, which had seen so much and experienced the destruction of the town and its population. The hill was empty and sad. It seemed that it was in mourning for the soul of the town, which had gone.

The ruins of the palace

[Page 220]

My hometown (a poem of a kind)

by Emanuel Efron

Translated from Yiddish by Aviva Kamil

a

Novogrudok, my precious town, I remember and treasure my dreams and memories of my beautiful and pleasant childhood which I spent there. A great town, you were like a mother to the Jewish people. You were very old, one of the forebears of the Jewish communities of Poland and Lithuania. Three nations fought for you - Lithuania, Poland and Byelorussia, they wanted to conquer you and call you their own. But above all you were Jewish. The Jews gave you your attractive and noble image, they developed you and gave you your true character. With a bittersweet sadness and an unfathomable sorrow I will write my memoires to present the greatness of our hometown to the people of Israel and of other countries of the world. Let my memories become a part of this memorial book.

The synagogue square

Above all things, I remember well your Great Synagogue. It looked superior to my eyes and distinguished itself among all the houses of prayer that I have seen in my life. The synagogue was very old, built like a castle and one had to come down seven wide stone steps to fulfill the saying: "From the deep I called to you, G-d". The bimah was wonderful as was the Holy Ark decorated with exquisite engravings. Remnants of your beautiful and colourful paintings, which withstood the test of time, could be seen on your convex ceiling. Many attempts to hide the paintings could not erase their traces. They were seen now and then from under the thick layers of lime and paint.

The great synagogue was like an upright giant in the centre of the Shulhoif, opposite it stood the great Beit-Midrash. The small klaizlach crowded around them, like pullets around a brooding hen, as if they wanted to draw warmth and find cover under the wings of the synagogue and the great Beit-Midrash. As I was writing about the synagogue, the image of Rabinovich appeared before me. He was our last town cantor, who enlightened us with his pure and sad prayers.

b

How could I forget the aromas emanating from the kitchen on a Sabbath and Jewish festivals? And the calm and confident walk of our fathers and grandfathers, returning from synagogue, relaxed and surrounded by an air of holiness, as if they absorbed the greatest pleasure on earth.

I remember the images of the leaders of our community. With their tidy beards and their high brows, in their Saturday best, wearing suits that were sometimes old but always clean and tidy. In the centre of this group stands the dear image of Avraham Shlomo Efron: all his life he was dedicated to the social needs of the community, to the poor, orphans and widows, but above all he was fired by the love for Zion and its great poets who heralded its redemption.

On the hot days of Tamuz and Av he would leave his family and his businesses and travel around the district's towns and villages to preach of Zion and collect donations for Keren-Hakayemet and Keren – Hayesod. He did all that voluntarily and he bore the cost of all this activity.

c

How could I forget your noble teachers who were fired by their love to Israel and Zion? The martyrs, the friendly Mirski and the noble Lidski were the most memorable among them.

I can hear still the singing of your cantors who imparted in me a love of music.

Valiker Street

d

In front of me pass pictures of my childhood, of the market square and 'the row of shops' (Rad-Kromen), which was a big building supported on all sides by round columns, with scores of Jewish shops on all four sites. Every Monday and Thursday the market was bustling with Russian and Polish peasants, noise and clatter all around, carts loaded with the best of farm products, grown in the fertile soil of Byelorussia. The Jewish dealers were buying the products from the farmers. As they were paid, the farmers would wrap the money in their handkerchiefs. Having sold their produce, they would buy goods in the many Jewish shops. They bought everything: half a kilo of sugar-cubes to sweeten a hot cup of tea on a Sunday or a holiday, a packet of Machorka tobacco, wooden clogs (lapties). The rich among them would buy a pair of polished high boots. The women were attracted to colourful materials with red, blue and yellow flowers.

The brides bought colourful scarves, which reminded me of orchards of apples, pears, plums and cherries in their spring blossom. I wandered around the market. I saw the poor women –villagers who sat on the footpath in front of the row of shops and sold red forest berries. They displayed big ceramic bowls full of berries and measuring glasses, 5 groshy (a coin of Polish currency, 100 groshy = 1 zloty) for a small glass and 10 groshy for a big one. The buyers were many, old and young. A few poor children glared from a distance with hungry, jealous eyes, salivating and waiting for someone to buy them this unaffordable treat. My mother would notice these children, she would buy a glassful or two of berries and gave it to them with her blessing: 'to your good health children'.

The management of the Civic Club

How can I forget the red-cheeked apples and pears, and, as autumn was approaching, slightly overripe and tasty apples, which were sold by farmers who shouted in praise of their produce. The cooked legumes and broad beans, displayed in the peddlers' baskets, were ladled out for the children, who ate them while still hot. Special food was also prepared in private homes for Shabbat, Brith-Mila or weddings, in which all the community took part. The food's delicious taste is still in my mouth. Never in my life did I eat such tasty and satisfying food.

e

In the evening the commotion in the market calmed down. The last of the peasants hastened to depart, urging on their horses with the whistles and cracking of their long whips. Here and there a policeman was gathering the drunks, who could not stand on their feet. The sun went down, stars appeared and a round smiling moon lit the market square. At that time the town's youths, all nicely dressed and neatly combed, came out to stroll around the footpath of the market square. The air was full of merriment of the young. People talked to each other about the day's events, about successful sales or purchases. On the notice board they read that Charlie Chaplin's film "The Gold Rush" was showing in the cinema of Ivanetski.

I liked to walk around the Shlosbarg, climb up the ruin of the old castle from the days of the Lithuanian prince Mindaug, who chose Novogrudok as his capital, and to look at the soft and beautiful landscape. There was green scenery all around, blessed with sunshine and water. From a distance I could see the Brichenke wood and the little lake, the water was shallow, but we liked to bathe in its cold and refreshing water. On the right side of the castle, down the hill, was the old Catholic church, wrapped in golden dust of a sunset and in old legends. Boys and girls, Jews and Christians played at the foot of the whitewashed walls. We all picked spring flowers-the blue cornflowers and the white daisies with their yellow centres.

Excursion of the "Maccabi" youngsters on bicycles

f

In the morning, in the grey-green light of Byelorussia, I would wander sometimes into the winding lanes of the town and Rachelo to watch the Jewish youths.

I saw them hurrying to their cheder, with their soft faces and sad eyes, their skin white and transparent; one could see the blue veins through their skin. Their faces were pale from lack of food and sleep, from the stuffy air in their small dwellings with the low ceilings.

Fearful but excited they hurried to cheder. There they would search unknowingly for the sun in the land of Kenaan. When perusing the holy book they would hear the rustle of the sheaves in the fields of

Kenaan and smell the Mediterranean sea, the river Jordan and the Kineret, the Carmel, Judea and Galilee mountains.

I pitied the elderly Jews, when watching them in the kloizim and in the big Beit-Midrash, sitting in pairs or foursomes, discussing a "special problem" that they encountered in Rashi or one of the Midrashim. Some of them would get hungry and would go home for a poor lunch of boiled potatoes with pickled herring or cucumber sauce, and probably a thin soup made of bones and barley. Meat and fish would be eaten only on Shabbat and holidays.

The 'Maccabi" Soccer Team

Among them was my dear grandfather Reb Avigdor Efron ZL. He was a Talmid Chacham (a person knowledgeable in Jewish studies) who was a wealthy man (gevir) before World War I, a leather merchant. After closing his shop he would go to the Todres kloiz and study a page of Gemarah and a chapter of Mishnayot.

During World War I the soldiers of the Teutonic race robbed him of every thing he owned. They took his goods and gave him a cheque for a thousand marks, which did not have any value at all. For many years the old man believed in his naivety, that he would get his money back. Only on his deathbed did he realise the evil of the deception. My grandfather lost his wealth. To survive he was forced to accept help from my father, who supported him generously. My father supported also my sister Yehudit, who became a widow a few years after her marriage. She had a little boy, Avremaleh, a gentle child who had a good brain and was studying the bible and the Talmud. The Germans murdered her and her son. Her second husband was taken to a labour camp and never returned. We don't know where he was buried.

I can see in front of my eyes the image of my uncle. He was one of the learned people in town, Reb Berl Rabinovich, the dayan (arbiter-rabbinical judge). He knew by heart all the sacred literature; he could name the page on which a certain problem was discussed. Like the Gaon of Vilna, he studied the Talmud all his life. He was unassuming and would not accept kavod (honour) and fame. He lived in sadness and poverty all his life. A few years after his marriage his wife died and during World War I , his son Meir, the eelui(excellent student), also died. My father ZL supported him and his family generously. The words of Ch.N.Bialik in his poem "The Meek of the World-let me share what's mine with you"- would apply to my uncle.

g

When I think about my childhood, I remember my childhood games: the games we played on the castle hill or in the yard of our home, the Tsaichanes (jacks, using the knuckle bones of calves). Special holiday games: during Pesach-games using nuts, during Hanukah-spinning tops, cards and a lottery. You could not compare all these to the heroic game at Lag-Baomer, the bow and arrows, the beginning of the military training of the children of Israel. Even on the Ninth of Av, the national mourning day, we showered each other with prickly thistle flowers that we picked in the Jewish cemetery. We also liked to play with the colourful eggs that the shkotzim [gentiles] were given for Easter. We played with all the lack of care and innocence of childhood. Even the Russian Cossacks, when they camped on the castle hill, came to play with us and persuaded us to bring them purple plums-Vengerkes - which grew down the hill. In exchange they filled our pockets with lollies and aromatic Halvah.

I can still smell the tang of the branches, when I helped my father to cover the Succah. He watched me to make sure that everything was done properly. Who would not remember the taste of the Kiddush in the Succah or the flavour of the food eaten there? Even in pouring rain we continued eating our meal. My father ZL had his afternoon nap there.

Vivid are the memories of the night of the Ninth of Av in the synagogue, when all the praying people, young and old, with their shoes off, sat weeping and lamenting the destruction of the temple and the nation. The eve and day of Simchat-Torah were light and bright. A Jew forgot all his worries and was given to pure joy. We all remember the Chasidic dance in the shtibl. Chasidim in our town were few but on Simchat Torah they were the most important participants. Their frivolity was the talk of the town.

I grew up and drew my learning and understanding of life from the stories of grandfather Mendele, stories and plays of Shalom-Aleichem, there was nothing like those to illustrate the love to the Jew as a human being and the love to a Jewish child; the poems and stories of Ch.N.Bialik, Tchernichovski and Zalman Shneor, the knights of our national poetry.

The volumes of "Hatkufah" commenced their publication after World War I ; the best and most beautiful of the world's literature was translated for us. We read the books, which appeared in the "Shtibl" publication, in suspense and with interest. Every new book in the library was a cause for celebration. We touched the cover lovingly as if it was a pair of new shoes that we were given for Pesach. Where are all the many volumes of Jean-Christophe by Romain Rolland? With great expectation we waited for every new volume to be translated. Does the Jewish youth of today have that anticipation?

h

When my mind is in turmoil, I find refuge in my workroom, which is also my bedroom, where I think about you, my town and the landscape of my motherland. If I have a restless night or dream strange and frightening dreams, my heart beats with longing. I smell a familiar smell, which "comes with the wind and reaches my quivering nostrils"- I smell the spices in the hot fish, Gefilte fish for Saturday, caught in the river Nieman. Some times I smell the aroma of my mother's jam, served with a glass of tea on the long wintry nights, or I feel in my mouth the taste of Purim sweets and other holiday delights, the taste of kreplach on the eve of Yom Kippur, the honey cookies, the ingberlach served to the guests on holidays.

i

A few national events are engraved in my memory.

Scene a

The Balfour declaration of 1917. A rumour spread through the town: England had declared that it would help the Jewish people to build their national home. A dream of 2000 years began to materialize. All the Jews of the town assembled in the big Beit-Midrash and on the Shoolhoif(one building could not contain the whole congregation). The blue and white flag was brought in first, and hung up beside the Holy Ark. The Rabbi took out the Torah and blessed shehechevanu; at that moment a sacred thrill went through the hearts of the assembled. The Rabbi talked about the importance of the day. My father ZL was animated with joy and excitement. The crowd listened intensely to the speakers and erupted with Hatikvah at the end of the speeches: " Our hope is not lost."

Scene b

The day the Mandate was entrusted to England by the League of Nations. That day was remembered by the Jews of Novogrudok with joy and confidence. From now on the Jews would have someone who would not only help them to return to their old homeland but also would guard the newcomers from the Arabs, who were incited by their nationalistic leaders.

That day was declared a national holiday in town. The shopkeepers and the tradesmen shut their businesses till noon, among them were members of the Bund and a few Communists. All assembled in the Shulhoif, both old and young: schools, youth-movements, Maccabi, Hashomer-Hatsair (at that time there were no other organisations in town). The band of the Fire Brigade played. It was the only wind instrument band in the town. All musicians were Jews, they were the pride of the Jewish community.

It is hard to describe that event. The atmosphere all around us seemed different. The restless, sad eyes of the sons of the Diaspora sparkled with new merriment, as if they were open anew, as if confidence filled their hearts and gave hope for a better future. From now on ancient Israel would be one of the nations and would exist again, like in the days of old...

After the speeches of the Rabbis and the Zionist leaders we went in a procession, with the band in the lead, marching to the market square, and we all sang. When we reached the building of the Polish government offices the starosta, the head of the sub-district, and the wojewoda, the head of the district, came out to welcome us. At the time the wojewoda of the Novogrudok district was Raczkiewicz, who was later president of Poland in exile during the World War II. He was an honest, altruistic and wise governor, a real liberal and liked by all the Jews of the town. During his days in office, no one, be it a Pole or Russian, dared to hurt Jews. Only a few people in Poland were like him. I remember the blessing he gave to the Jewish residents of the town and to Jews everywhere: "I wish you to obtain complete independence, like we have, and to be a free people in your old motherland". It was the first time in the history of Novogrudok that a governor blessed Jews sincerely and warmly. The Polish and Russian residents watched amazed, but applauded and congratulated their Jewish acquaintances.

The market square from the south side

Scene c

The time was the end of World War I .Summer of 1920.One Friday after sunset the Shabbat candles were lit in Jewish homes. Most of the Jews were in the synagogue when the rumour spread that the Red Army was about to enter the town. From a distance one could hear the music of the Cavalry band. A big crowd, especially the youth, boys and girls came out to welcome the new "redeemers". Few older people gave up their evening prayer (or perhaps they prayed at home earlier) and also joined the crowd. And I, a ten-year-old boy, was among them. The Red Army impressed us no end, especially the Cavalry "da zdrastvuvet rivolutsia, tovarishchi"(long live the revolution, comrades) they greeted us with enthusiasm. "We redeemed Great Russia from under the yoke of the despots and capitalists. We brought you peace, victory, bread and freedom". It is hard to describe the happiness of the crowd. Cries of Hurrah filled the air. Young hearts honestly believed in the new redemption and were full of enthusiasm. We sang with great feeling the International the Marseillaise and the Bund anthem. No one could guess that within a short time those "redeemers" would betray their principles and crush with arrogance everything dear and sacred to the human spirit including all that was sacred to the Jews, who contributed so much to the Russian Revolution! No one thought that in the new Russia Hebrew and Yiddish schools would not be allowed to exist, that Jewish theatres and newspapers, contacts with Jews abroad, all would be forbidden. It hurt to see all our hopes evaporate. As our national poet wrote "the wind carried them" and we were left alone with our suffering and frustration.

Scene d

They were the burning days of the month of Tamuz. They praised the French general Weygand and his divisions positioned on the Vistula. They came to help Poland and to halt the Soviets' advance into Europe. The Red Army retreated before the Polish Army. The market and streets were full of Red soldiers, tired, hungry and broken; they were desperate. Many of them were bandaged and their clothes were in tatters. They dragged their feet behind carts loaded with badly wounded soldiers. Among the injured were some with their entire heads bandaged. I could hear moans and quiet weeping. Their procession lasted for days. The remnants of their cannons and machineguns were towed slowly behind them. The flags were down and folded. That was the first and the last time I saw a military in retreat and I realized its significance. There were no words and no point to describe what happened spiritually to these soldiers who just a few weeks earlier believed in their absolute victory. Most of the onlookers, little I among them, cried. Some could not take it and went home.

A decision was taken by the committee of the Hebrew congregation and Tarbut school, to pick plums and apples in the neighbouring orchards and distribute them among the soldiers, who were hungry. I volunteered to be among the fruit pickers. With the fruit collected we walked from cart to cart and gave it to the soldiers. They looked at us with good and sad eyes and thanked us "spasibo dorogiye" (thank you, my dears), I will never forget those words.

j

I could bring up many more scenes and pictures, I could sing to you many songs of longing for my dear town Novogrudok. But a voice within me tells me to end.

After 35 years

On the 1st of May 1960 it was 35 years since I left you, the town of my birth and my childhood dreams. On a few occasions I came to visit the town, to see how my parents and the dear family, my friends and all those who built the town were getting on. I cannot deny it, I was glad to return to my town for a few months, to stroll in the sad but attractive streets, to look at the little wooden houses with their sloping roofs covered with shingles. I saw the town's poverty when many of the residents, young and old, had left to look for a home elsewhere in the world. A great number of them came to Eretz- Israel and put down roots there. This made me happy. When I was back in town I would climb up the Shlos-barg and would call out: 'be consoled my people and you - the great Jewish town- you will always have a vibrant

Jewish and national life, and you will continue to send many of your sons to Eretz-Israel to strengthen the hands of the builders of the third Temple'.

To my sorrow my prophecy did not come true.

The history sentenced you, my town, to be eliminated with the rest of the Jewish communities of Europe. But I promise you, my dear town, as you were a good mother to me, that I will never forget you.

[Page 229]

Shoah

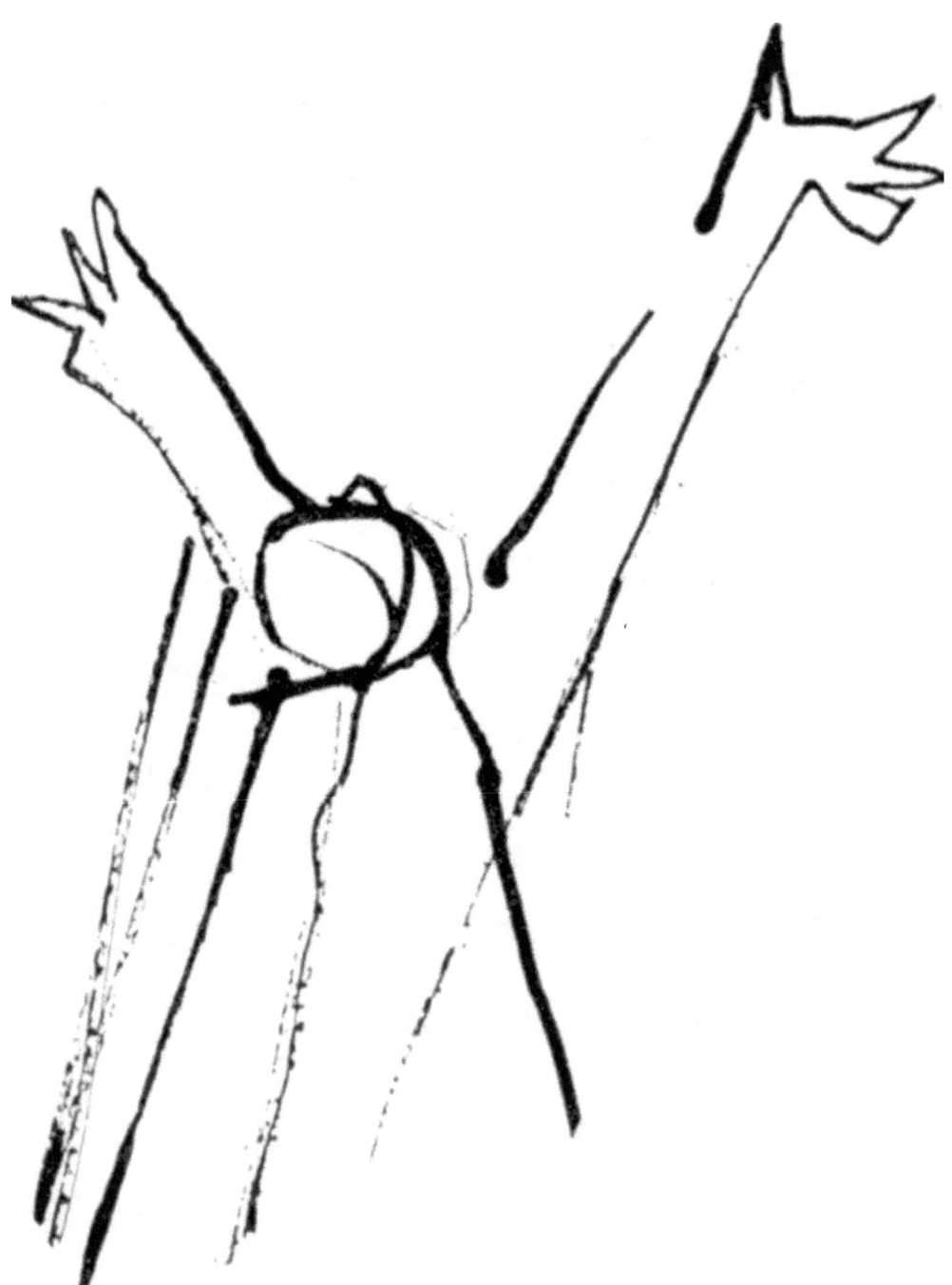

Holocaust

by A.Mirski

Translated from Hebrew by Aviva Kamil

I dread the terror of consolations which will arrive now, in the end.
And in front of my eyes, desecrate my catastrophe and destroy the depth of my mourning.
Consolations will come now; they should not lessen my agony, and expiate my anger,
The way consolations for the bereaved do.

Rip off the consolation of my soul, lest it'll scare away the grief,
My soul shouldn't be given cheering or compassion;
Let it stay angry in its grief to the end.

Bring agony to my heart till it'll be sated with bewildering destruction,
Till it'll suck out its rage like a leech; and sink in its sorrow, tranquil.

Only one wish I have in my heart, and let it be the last,
Let my devastation live forever and let it smolder in my soul all the days of my life.
Cursed is the one who clears my ruins, like the builder of Jericho, he will be cursed.
Like the mourners' temple, it will stay and residing in it will be the desecrated name.

[Page 230]

On the threshold of the shoah

By Yaakov Kivelevich

Translated from Hebrew by Aviva Kamil

It was Sunday morning, 22nd of June 1941. The town rose from its sleep expecting a day of rest after a week of work and worries. We, the youths, were just tasting the first feeling of the summer holidays after a year at school. Officers of the Red Army, family men and bachelors, as always on weekend leave, stayed in their private apartments in town, far from their units in the army camps.

We did not expect that day to be the first day of the Shoah.

In the early hours of the morning, before dawn, the murderous offensive of the Nazi German army against the Soviet Union started, without a declaration of war.

Our town was not attacked from the air as yet. A few planes could be seen at high altitude, but apart from a short raid on the army camp in the Skrydlevo forest, nothing happened. On the same day, we heard Molotov speak on the radio (he was at that time the Soviet foreign minister). He talked about the Nazi offensive, which only strengthened the impression that the Soviet government was not ready for war.

Imke and Yashke Kivelevitz

No one knew about the situation at the front or how close it was to our town. It was announced on the radio that cities in western Poland were bombed and that the German army invaded the western borders of the Soviet Union. The radio was broadcasting marches and encouraging appeals to the population almost non-stop, but, somehow, there was no unusual activity in the town and no signs of panic. Army officers who resided in town hurried to their units. Government officials of the Soviet administration, who came from Russia - "vostochniks" [meaning "people from the east" i.e. people who arrived from the east to the former territory of east Poland, invaded by the Soviets on the 17 September 1939], rushed between the different government and Party offices.

The Secretary of the party organisation of the city and the Recruiting Office issued an order to all those who were eligible for service in the army to assemble at the Cultural Centre, which was on the corner of Bazilianer Street.

The youths of military age, mainly Jews, were high school graduates, miscellaneous workers and tradesmen. With no clear instructions, they waited near the club and after a while dispersed. Young Jews walked around the market square and the old citadel (Shlos barg), their spirits high, not having the slightest idea about the coming Shoah. The adults were worried and cheerless. The Jewish refugees, who had come to Novogrudok from Nazi occupied Poland in 1939-40 were noticeably distressed. They comprehended the criminal character of the Nazi occupier and had seen the signs of Hitler's bestiality. We heard from those refugees of the horrors committed by the Germans and their aides, and we could assume that the Jews would not be allowed to live under the Nazis. But the massacre of millions, the genocide... no one could imagine that.

The first day of the war passed without any notable events. Housewives started to stockpile food and other necessities. Some officials took interest in the old shelters that were dug in the first days of the German-Polish war of 1939. The town was orderly. The public services were functioning as usual.

The night came. No lights were lit in the streets, the windows were covered with blinds. The town sunk into darkness. Now and then the movements of the militia and army interrupted the stillness of the night. Those who had a radio listened to Moscow or Minsk, but nothing that made sense was heard. The news was about fierce battles along an uncertain front and heavy bombing of unspecified cities and ports. No one knew what tomorrow would bring. Many could not sleep that night.

At the dawn of the 23rd of June, the second day of the war, the town's Jews hurried in the early morning to the main streets and the market square to hear the news. A change was noticed in the behaviour of the "vostochniks" and the soldiers of the Red Army. Their families assembled with all their possessions in a few places around the town, mainly around government and party offices, waiting to be evacuated. Scores of trucks loaded with women, children and private possessions were on their way to Minsk. This activity was accelerated towards noon, and it appeared that it was a complete evacuation of all the people who had arrived in Novogrudok with the conquering Soviets not long ago, among them Jewish families, many from East Byelorussian towns. Units of Russian soldiers on foot and in motor vehicles appeared from the direction of Lida (through Grodno street) and continued their journey east, to Minsk. A few army units marched in an orderly fashion with their weapons and equipment, but there were also scattered groups of soldiers, tired and dusty with no weapons and no commanders. It was obvious that the army was retreating after fierce battles and heavy bombing, the front was disintegrating. The sight of the defeated army was not encouraging.

The latest news on the radio was continuously interrupted and unclear. The situation was vague. There were messages about widespread operations of the German parachutists who landed behind the broken front lines in order to sabotage the roads, bridges and other means of communication and spread panic among the population. In the meantime the Germans advanced at great speed along the railway line Brest - Baranovich - Minsk, with no serious opposition.

The people of the Soviet administration could not explain the situation and could not advise the Jews what to do. It could be that, as a result of the chaos, the local government did not know what to do, or they had instructions not to encourage the local population to leave, so as not to flood the roads with refugees.

The last of the "vostochniks" were preparing to leave the town at any moment. They were looking for means of transport. I saw a number of Russian teachers who worked in various schools in town (among them women teachers who taught me in the Russian school). They left in a truck with their families, through Karelicher Street; they waved to me and called out "see you soon".

What a difference between today and yesterday. No high spirits and no confidence in a quick victory. All that evaporated and disappeared entirely with the approaching evening. The Jews were perplexed, fearful of what was to come.

The soldiers, the militia, and all the government and party officials were evacuated from the town. All the vehicles were confiscated for the evacuation of the "vostochniks" and their families. The volunteer firemen (mostly Jews) drove off in their fire fighting trucks. The town was left without the fire brigade at a time when fire caused by bombing could become a real threat.

In the morning and at noon a few German planes could be seen at high altitude above the town. But nothing happened. Echoes of explosions and shootings could be heard from afar, but no one knew what was happening.

We thought of the Jewish families, who were considered to be an undesirable element by the Soviets and were removed to Siberia. They were deported on the night of the 19/20 of June, taken by trucks to Novoyelnia and from there in a freight train to Siberia. Heads of families were separated and sent to a jail, deep in Russia. When it happened it shook all of us, but now it looked as if it was a salvation for those families. It was a pity that only a few were saved in that way from the claws of the Nazis.

Near the citadel (Shlos barg) was one of the meeting points for the evacuation of the " vostochniks". Crowded around the trucks were Russian women with their children, Party officials, chaos, no organisation, people forced themselves onto the trucks, hung to the sides of vehicles, pleaded with the drivers and beseeched them to take them east. Vehicles went on their way loaded to the brim. In the crowd I met my brother and many of my friends. We stood stunned and observed the happenings. No one told us, the town's Jews, if we should stay or leave and if we were to leave who would take us? Time was short, the hour urgent. For those who decided to leave, it was the last moment. What could the local Jews do? Officials and members of the Party, who were local people but were afraid to stay, found places on the trucks that were leaving and followed the "vostochniks"

I returned to the market place. It was bursting with people and all sorts of vehicles, I noticed young people, Jews among them, but only a few could find a place on the trucks, most of them rode bicycles or left on foot.

I met my friend, Yoshka Kopelman, near my home. My brother joined us and we examined the situation. After discussing things for a few moments we decided to leave the town. We ran home to take some supplies and to say good-bye.

My brother told our parents that we were leaving. They listened, understood and kept silent. There was tacit agreement, and also a feeling of inadequacy among all of us. Our parents were resigned and let us be responsible for our own fate.

We packed quickly some food and coats. Our parents gave us their wedding rings as if they knew that our separation was forever.

We said good-bye.... And left....

When we look back on the events of that day, we ask ourselves: why did so few (200) leave the town then, and why did so many, young and old, stay? It is not a simple question. One must remember that it is not so easy to leave a home at a time when the danger was not that obvious, as it became later. One of the reasons for the lack of information about the current situation was the fact that Novogrudok was positioned far from the main routes, the nearest railway line was in Novoyelnia (23 kilometres from our town). One could leave the town in a motor vehicle, bicycle, horse cart or on foot. Not many had a car or a horse, so one had to leave on foot. Many were forced to walk hundreds of kilometres to reach a distant railway station which had not been bombed. The railways west of Minsk (the lines Lida- to the east via Molodechno, and Baranovich-Minsk) were bombed. Some people maintained that there was nowhere to run, or that it was no use to wander along the roads in time of war with no shelter and no food. Many Jews were quite fatalistic. They kept on saying: "What will happen to the sons of Israel will happen to Reb Israel". But the sons of Israel in our town did not know about the extermination plans that the Nazi beast was preparing for them. Many remembered the Germans from World War I and thought that it would be possible to live with them.

My brother Yoshka Kopelman and myself were among the last to leave in the late hours of the evening. Mothers, fathers, friends and acquaintances stood in front of the building of the fire brigade. They accompanied those leaving with sad looks, pain and dread. Tears were in many eyes. Everything happened in devastating silence. No waving, no shaking of hands. In our hearts, as we walked down Karelicher Street, were some doubts and regrets: "wouldn't it be better to go back home to the family..." I will never know how we overcame our terrific urge to return home.

Along Karelicher Street loitered groups of young Poles. They ridiculed us, their comments were full of hate and venom. They enjoyed themselves. They did not have to wait long to put their blind hate into practice. The Germans gave them a lot of chances. We passed by the Mount Mendog and the Court Houses. The sunset could be seen through the trees and it illuminated the rooftops on the hill. As we moved on, the silhouettes slowly disappeared into the night. We could still see in front of our eyes the looks of our dear ones, who just a short time ago accompanied us on the start of our long journey.

Two kilometres out of town we met the teacher Solomon and his two sons returning slowly to the town. We were friends, but at that time they did not look at us and did not say a word. A short time later we met Abrasha Plozinski and Dr. Bergman (a surgeon who came to our town as a refugee), they were also returning home. An armed man wearing a Red Army uniform came out of the trees of Hardelovka forest. He asked us in Russian if the Germans are already in town. We told him that they were not and continued walking. A suspicion arose in us that he was one of the saboteurs the Germans parachute behind the front lines.

The traffic on the road was heavy, all sorts of army vehicles raced in the direction of Stolbts - Minsk. We tried now and then to stop a car and ask the drivers to take us with them, but to no avail. We walked at night at a brisk pace, taking notice of nothing, not even a familiar face; we did not want to lose precious time. At midnight we arrived in Karelich. The town was fast asleep. All was calm and relaxed as if there was no war in our world. At dawn we passed the town of Turets. Again we met groups from Novogrudok. We walked with them for a few kilometres until we realised that it was too dangerous because of raids by the German planes. A small group of three was not that noticeable and it was easier for it to find cover when it was needed. In the morning we saw from a distance the town of Mir. On the road signs of recent bombing could be seen, the ground was covered with holes, ditches and fragments of bombshells. We entered the town. The war was felt there. The streets were crowded. We met people from Novogrudok everywhere, in food shops and restaurants. There were a few who came the night before and slept in the town. We spoke with some fellows who just returned on their bicycles from Stolbts. They told us that Russian soldiers were stopping anyone who was trying to cross the old Polish-Soviet border and were sending them back. Many people from our town came to the conclusion that it was impossible to escape and turned back to Novogrudok. Others could not decide what to do and stayed for the time in Mir.

We were very tired after many hours of walking non-stop. We decided to take a nap in a small wood across the river near the bridge. We lay down in the shade of a few trees, close to the bridge. We were inexperienced, and did not know how dangerous it was. Within minutes we fell into a deep sleep. We woke up to the sound of terrific explosions. The earth trembled and dirt was thrown on and around us. Above us circled planes that shot at and bombed the bridge. All was covered in clouds of dust and smoke. We started to run as fast as we could up the hill and into the wood. We sprawled on the ground among the thick bushes and waited for the raid to end. From our high position we could see the town burning. When the planes left we returned to the road.

We had forgotten about our desire to have a nap, it was much more important to distance ourselves from the danger zone, there was no time to waste. On leaving Mir we met a few people from Novogrudok, among them: Solomon Zuk, Sema Shlobovski, Shimon Ostashinski and Moshe Niankovski and his son. They rode on a horse-drawn cart. In the afternoon we reached Stolbts. Getting closer to the big bridge on the river Neman we heard the echo of shots and the drone of planes. We found out quickly that the bridge was attacked non-stop by enemy planes. We had no choice, however, but to cross the long bridge. We crossed it in a quick sprint while hearing the drone of the planes above us. The town was in distress, the streets empty, we met a few militiamen who came from our town the day before. They advised us to hurry lest we would be too late. The hint was transparent, but before we left town we experienced more air raids, which forced us to run for cover. It looked as if the enemy planes did not leave Stolbts in peace even for a minute. Suddenly, while passing the last houses of the town, a German plane dived on us without making any noise, and showered us with bullets. The attack was so sudden that we could hardly understand what was happening. We jumped into a wheat field along the road, and flattened ourselves to the ground while blood-curdling whistles of bullets hit the ground around us. We lay without moving a limb; the plane passed above us and then gained altitude with a deafening boom. None of us expected the others to be alive after that amount of lead that was showered on us. To our luck no one was injured. Stunned and excited we looked at each other, what would have happened had one of us been killed or injured? We dusted ourselves down, tightened the straps of our kitbags and were again on the road. Near a big farm, a few kilometres out of Stolbts, we ate the last of our food. We did not know what was going to happen to us. We walked on the dusty and sandy road, our eyes sore from lack of sleep and from the exhaust fumes of the motor vehicles, which sped, forcing us off the road. We pleaded with the army drivers to take us but most of the time we did not even get a reaction. Walking became very difficult. The thick dust penetrated our throats and lungs, our shoes were full of dust, our legs were covered with bloody sores. Our eyes would not stay open. Our heads were as heavy as lead. We urged each other on and with the last of our strength we dragged our feet forwards.

Night fell, as we were advancing along the road through the thick forest, around us were Russian soldiers from different units retreating with no order or discipline. The torrent of people, motor vehicle of all descriptions, carts and horses were moving in one direction - to the east. As we moved on we saw some frightening figures; bearded ruffians wearing worn-out clothing, their gait heavy and their appearance proof of them having been in difficult circumstances. Clearly, they were criminals, who were released or had escaped from a prison, as the Germans were advancing. We felt that they were interested in our kitbags and clothing. It was a very dangerous situation; we understood the meaning of the prisoners' interest in us. Somehow, with the cover of darkness and the unrelenting flow of masses of people, we managed to evade our pursuers. We were aware of the danger of meeting German parachutists or saboteurs, who were everywhere, their task was to murder, destroy and spread fear and panic behind the lines.

Near one of the army trucks, which stopped for repairs, we engaged in a conversation a friendly Russian officer, who showed us his understanding and who was ready to give us a ride. He tried to explain to us that our effort was in vain, because as far as he knew the Germans cut off all the roads around Minsk. We listened to his advice but continued our journey with the hope that we would somehow succeed.

At about midnight we reached a railway crossing. It was a checkpoint on the old Polish border. Soldiers who were guarding it stopped us before the road barrier. We were ordered to identify ourselves. While explaining to the soldiers who we were, I noticed a pile of corpses in the ditch beside the railways. It was hard to see the faces of the dead in the dark, but judging by their clothes they were people from our part of the country. It could be that among the dead were people from our town. We felt we had to get away from the place as soon as possible. Later we found out that the army guard stopped scores of refugees like us from crossing the barrier, many people were concentrating in front of the barrier, and an enemy plane spotted them and gunned them down.

We walked all night at a quick pace. We knew we must not lose time. With the morning light we could see the horrors of war. The roadsides were strewn with broken and burnt cars, in and around them were corpses of men, women and children. It was the work of German pilots who did not overlook even a single refugee walking beside the road. Now and then we were forced to look for cover or hide in the fields when planes marked with black crosses appeared. They kept raiding the bloody road to Minsk.

Late in the morning we met Motke Movshovich on his bicycle. He brought us the bad news that a number of kilometres in front of us, the NKVD built a barrier and no one was permitted to cross it, except for "vostochniks" and army personnel. One had to have a document to prove that one was from the eastern parts of the country. We met hundreds of people who were returning, desperate and lost. We tried our luck but to no avail. We were ordered to return to the place we came from. We decided to circumvent the barrier through the forest and then return to the road, leaving the barrier behind us. But we were frustrated there too; the forest was swarming with armed soldiers, camouflaged and dug in. We knew that we should avoid endangering ourselves; the risk of being shot by the soldiers was too high. We set in a ditch not far from the barrier and waited for whatever may happen. We looked for a way out of the situation, one thought chasing another.

We were hoping to overcome the hurdle in front of us, but did not know how. We were afraid that the moment the Russian soldiers would leave the barrier it would be too late, the Germans would capture us. Hoping that, perhaps during the chaos created by an air raid it could be possible to sneak through without being noticed. Thirsty and hungry we sat waiting for developments. After a short time, a dozen German bombers appeared on their way to Minsk. The anti-aircraft guns, hidden in the forest, opened fire. Big pieces of metal from the bombs, which exploded in the air, sprayed us. We covered our heads with our kitbags for protection. Patches of white smoke and fire appeared around the planes in the sky above, but they continued to fly and disappeared behind the horizon. In the meantime a young

Russian soldier, from a defeated unit, who was looking for a new group to join, sat down beside us and told us, with the typical Russian openness, about a great battle at the old railway station near Baranovich, where the Red Army suffered heavy casualties, especially from air raids. "How could we fight when we could not raise our heads above the ground?" he complained. We understood that the German forces moved from the direction of Baranovich parallel to our route and there was no power that could stop them.

At noon we noticed that the guards at the barrier disappeared. Without losing a moment and at a fast pace we took the road towards the Negoreloye railway station. The heat and dust worsened our thirst and hunger. The kitbags were heavy and their straps cut into our flesh. Many of the walkers, and we among them, threw away some stuff in order to lighten the load. (Later, when the Russian winter came, we regretted the loss). In the late afternoon we arrived at the junction before the town of Negoreloye. Clouds of smoke covered the burning town. The railway line to Minsk was cut. The road we walked on till then led to Minsk, which lay 50 kilometres from the junction. A dirt road led to the right (south-east). It circumvented the town from the south. We did not know where to turn. The soldiers around us said that Minsk was bombed and burning and advised us to turn to another road. Most of the people from Novogrudok went, though, in the direction of Minsk and took side paths to go around the town before reaching it, in order to find a railway station that was still functioning. After a time we realised that the way we had chosen was safer but much longer.

The 25th of June drew to an end. Darkness fell. Huge flames were seen from the distance. It was Minsk drowning in a sea of flames and smoke. Around us small fires flickered -villages and small towns were burning, The Nazi planes did not spare them. The skies were red-grey; no star could be seen. Echoes of explosions were heard regularly. We watched the horrifying sight, our eyes red from lack of sleep and fatigue. Because of our weariness we did not feel our feet which were covered in sores, our heads were heavy, our senses dull. On that eternal walk we were overtaken by a strong longing for our homes and our dear ones, something inside us oppressed us terribly. Sometimes we stopped by a well, a creek or a puddle to draw water to quench our thirst. We did not dare to rest because whenever we sat or leaned on a tree sleep took over. Sometimes we fell asleep, as we were walking. We had no choice but to move forward, we knew that the enemy was following close behind us. In our mind was the persistent question: "would we be able to get away as far as possible from the battlefields to be saved from the enemy's claws?" We were still walking when the morning of the 26th of June arrived. We reached the small town Uzda, the first town behind the old border .The locals stared at us with suspicion. They saw that we were strangers, our appearance and strange dress was different from the usual dress of local citizens. Some people asked where we came from and who we were. They also asked us about the front and the German advances. We told them that we were evacuated from the front zone by the government. We did not say that we left on our own initiative; we did not want to be told that we were spreading panic and damaging the war effort. We tried as hard as we could not to stand out. It was long since we had some food; the hunger troubled us. With no other choice we stood in a queue for bread in one of the shops. We all bought a ration of bread and our mood improved. We entered a local restaurant that was still serving meals, and ate well. In one of the shops we bought a map of the district, so that we could find our way without asking too many questions, which was dangerous for us to do because of the constant suspicion of officials and the population. It stemmed from the fact that there were warnings about the activity of parachutists and saboteurs sent by the Germans. We stopped by one of the houses to ask for water. The owner, an old Jew, asked us in. We used the opportunity to look at the map to find the way to the railway station. Our clothes and behaviour made our host suspicious. Without saying a word he sneaked out of the house while we were still glued to the map, and called the police. We left the house and after a few steps we were suddenly surround by a dozen "militia men" with bayoneted rifles. They ordered us to go with them. When we reached the police station they put us in a locked room, despite our desperate attempts to explain to them who we were. They did not even want to have a look at our documents, as if we were spies. Our situation was bad. We heard that even if there was the slightest suspicion, no effort was made to find out the identity of the suspects. In the conditions that prevailed then, there was no hesitation in shooting the suspects, all was dependent on the whim of local security people. We tried to make it clear to them that we are Jews who were evacuated from our town and were trying to escape the enemy. We waved in front of them our passports; but the police officers did not take any notice of us. After a few hours and a change of guards, one officer eventually agreed to check our documents and listen to our explanation. After a thorough investigation they released us with a severe warning to leave the town immediately and not to loiter around. We did so and had no intention to get involved with the police again. We left Uzda without turning our heads. Suspicious looks followed us.

Leaving the town behind us, we stopped to discuss our plans in a small wood. It was clear that we had to be careful, and not only of the Germans. We read the map and found that we were walking on the road to Shatzek. It looked strange to us that neither in Uzda nor on the road did we meet people from Novogrudok. It worried us, "did we take the wrong route or miss the train?" we were asking ourselves. Some weeks later we found out that a few people from our town, who reached Negoreloye junction, turned to the other road which lead to Minsk. Some of them went through the bombed town and caught trains at other stations. Train loads still departed along that line to Orsha and Smolensk. Others took side roads around Minsk and arrived from the south to stations on the railway line to Bobruysk or Mogilev. Those who had cars, horses or bicycles continued on their way to the big cities, mainly Mogilev and Smolensk.

We continued walking. From bitter experience we learned not to enter villages or towns unnecessarily and not to ask locals or soldiers any questions.

Several times we saw soldiers and policemen arresting German parachutists and saboteurs. We noticed that the Germans wore Red Army or militia uniforms to try to deceive the Soviets. In the late afternoon we reached a crossroad on the road Minsk-Slutsk. A few kilometres further, on the left side of the road, we saw Red-Army units hectically digging themselves in. Cannons were pointing to the north. It was done at speed and in battle order. Orders and the rattle of weapons were heard. To our left on the far horizon a few tanks appeared, they looked like small tins. They crawled towards northeast, probably towards Minsk. It was hard to distinguish whose tanks they were. Behind our back we heard cannon shots. The units that just dug themselves in went into action. It was clear that we came upon a break in the front, through which the German armoured units advanced. The next day the Germans had occupied some positions behind Minsk and were attacking the important road to Moscow. Danger was everywhere. We raced on. At nightfall we entered a big forest. Darkness, the road was silent, no traffic. We felt the dread of loneliness and feebleness. We did not know the direction we were taking. Cannon shots echoed in the night. It seemed that somewhere behind us a cruel battle was fought accompanied by rockets and flares. The horizon was red. Before midnight we left the forest. In the darkness we came close to an isolated village. We stopped by a group of villagers. They noticed us and one man introduced himself as the chairman of the kolkhoz. He invited us to the village club to sleep till the morning. He did not hide from us the severity of the situation. He did not know how far the enemy advanced. We entered the club. A man was sitting by the phone trying in vain to contact someone. His monotonous voice added drama to the gloomy atmosphere of the club. Some people lay on the floor. We stretched ourselves in one corner to catch a short nap. Tired, in a few moments we were asleep. After a few hours I awoke in fright. I dreamt that the Germans occupied the village. I woke my brother and Yoshka and forcibly dragged them out on to the road. It was still night. We started walking, half asleep, our legs heavy. The dawn of the 27th of June arrived. The echoes of explosions were not heard any more. Silence. We felt the tension reducing slowly. A strange fatigue came upon us.

We passed by the small town called Shatzek. Caution and a desire to hurry prevented us from entering it. We sat for a few minutes by a well and watched with interest the movement to the east where the front was, of army vehicles loaded with supplies. It was something new for us-we were not used to see convoys going towards the front. It cheered us up a little, hungry and sweating we kept on walking. At noon we reached a small river. The weather was hot and oppressive, our clothes stuck to our bodies. The cool river water tempted us; we washed in the shallow water, roughly bandaged the sores on our feet and sat on the riverbank to read the map. A few Russian soldiers approached us suddenly and grabbed the map from our hands, saying that they needed it to investigate the surrounding. We tried to convince them that without the map we would lose our way and might fall into German hands, but that only aroused their suspicion. They examined us and said that they knew nothing about us, "and what were we doing here, anyway". As luck would have it, that incident ended without further repercussions and the soldiers left. It could have been for the best that they took our map; we might have lost our lives because of that piece of paper, our naiveté and our carelessness.

Now and then we reached junctions and did not know where to turn. Sometimes we tried to use our natural sense of direction. We seldom asked questions, so as not to awaken the suspicion of the local population and the security people. While we were still debating which route to take, a man dressed in a Russian shirt and boots, with a revolver, turned to us and asked us about our destination. He gave the impression of a party man responsible for security matters in the area. When we told him who we were and what we wanted he pointed to a road across some green fields and said that that was the easiest and shortest road for us. He had a fatherly attitude towards us; we shook the good man's hand and started to cross the fields. After half an hour we came to a well-made, straight road, which was not marked on our map. Was it not shown for security reasons?. After walking a few kilometres, we reached a land of endless swamps covered with rich vegetation. It was a flat plane with no settlements, divided by the strip of a narrow road, like a long bridge over the boggy swamps. If planes were to attack us then, we would be lost; it was impossible to step off the road. It seemed that the Nazi invader did not know about that road. We did not see dead people or destroyed vehicles. It was the quietest section of our long walk from Novogrudok. In early hours of the evening we reached the end of swamps. The landscape changed.

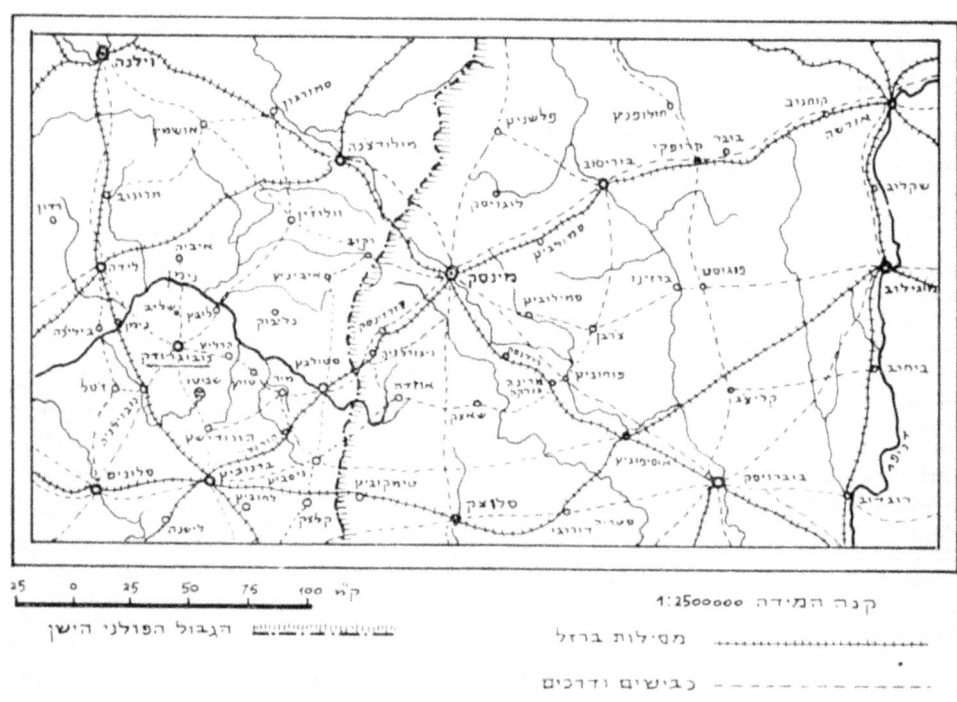

The way of wandering

Symbols of the map on the right: railway
roads
highways

Symbols of the left: the old Polish border

Distances in km.

We came to the town of Marina-Gorka, a few kilometres from Pukhovich. We remembered the name from the map and we knew that there was a railway station in that town. There we met our teacher from the Russian school, who taught us Byelorussian. His name was Zaloga. He was a "vostochnik" and a member of the party. We were glad to meet an acquaintance from our town, especially when we did not know what to expect in the town we were in. The teacher told us that he was in Novogrudok on the 24th of June and saw on the market square scores of dead people after an air raid. The streets of the town were deserted, no one was burying the dead. He escaped by car.

The news was worrying and depressing. We feared for the fate of our families. The teacher pointed out to us the water tower at the railway station and we went straight there. It was a big station. There was no sign of it being bombed. We noticed a freight train with scores of railroad cars and a smoking engine. The train was ready to depart. We tried to find out from the workers where that train was going, but we could not get a clear answer, or they did not want to tell us. We decided to climb into one of the carriages because it was obvious that the train was departing soon. With the last of our strength we climbed into a high carriage. We were exhausted and weak, all our limbs ached, we helped each other and the three of us managed somehow to crawl into the carriage when the train's wheels started to roll. We lay on the floor of the carriage without moving. Our hearts beat like hammers from the exertion and the excitement. Finally we were in the desired train, which was taking us to a safe shore! Our mental and physical strain was at its peak and at the same time at its end. Absolute fatigue and fogginess of the senses came over the three of us. Moving pictures of the events of the last days, like a dream, passed in front of my eyes. Eyes shut, the monotonous sound of the train's wheels and its rocking quickly put us to sleep. It was a deep and peaceful sleep after four nights of walking with a minimum of sleep and a tremendous physical effort. We woke up when the train stopped at Mogilev. To our surprise the sun was shining. We realised that we had travelled all night and passed the railway junction Osipovichi. We climbed down from the carriage and found out that it was a big station bustling with army men and civilians. We went into town to find some food. Walking with the kitbags on our backs, looking around for a restaurant we felt the stares of passers-by. Our clothes, again, betrayed us; did they think that we were saboteurs or Germans? Preparations for war were felt in the town. Long queues stretched in front of food shops. Russian fighter planes circled over the town as a defence against enemy bombers. We entered a big and splendid restaurant and ordered a meal. Our appearance awoke the curiosity of the diners, but no one bothered us. While eating we noticed one person looking at us with suspicion. The result was not long to come. The police was waiting for us on leaving the restaurant. The person who was watching us called them. He thought we were spies. This time, again, we had to convince the Russian security men that we were evacuated youths from the front in west Byelorussia and not German saboteurs. After a thorough investigation we were released. We returned to the railway station and knew that we had no choice but to go east as far as possible away from that dangerous zone. Without asking anyone, we entered a passenger car of the nearest train that was ready to depart. We chose some comfortable seats and after a short time were on our way. After a pleasant journey of a few hours the train stopped at a small, forlorn station. It was night and we had to find out where we were. Soldiers' voices were heard, they went from car to car. They wore battle-dress and were heavily armed. They arrested us, of course, and took us under heavy guard to the station building. We were brought to a lit room. In it sat a few officers around a table loaded with maps and communication devices. They investigated us at length, felt our kitbags in case we had some incriminating evidence. We explained to the officers that we were students from a Novogrudok school and we fled the Nazi army and only by mistake had boarded the train that brought us there. This time we were in real trouble, we were in the hands of a battle unit, its people under the circumstances could draw a conclusion which would be tragic for us. We went through some difficult moments but in the end our investigators were convinced and told us that the next train returns in the morning to Mogilev and we should be on it. We went outside and heaved a sigh of relief. There was absolute darkness, on the horizon, we could see sudden splashes of lights and we heard the echoes of explosions. We spent our night under the open sky and waited for the morning. Before dawn we boarded a train and at noon of the 28th of June we were back in Mogilev. All around the station zone one could see the signs of bombing, but the trains kept going after quick repairs of the rails. We met two fellows from Lida who told us that they were among the few who managed to escape the bombing of their town. They joined us in the evening when we caught the train that left Mogilev in the direction of Moscow.

The train sped over great Russia, we passed the towns of Roslavl and Kaluga, but were not permitted to enter Moscow. The militiamen took us off the train, checked our passports and told us to board another train, which circumvented the capital from the south. In that train we found a number of people from Novogrudok among them: Shmuel David Dzentsolski and Uri Yarmovski. We travelled together. Every one of us had a lot to tell. We were glad that our group grew bigger and we were not alone any more in a sea of strangers. At one of the stations we met Dr. Levin, the dentist from Novogrudok. I could hardly recognise him. The hard life on the road left its mark on him. He told me that at the start of the war he went on an errand to Minsk and could not return. He did try to reach his brother in Orsha.

We left behind us the towns: Penza, Kuybyshev, the Ural mountains, Chelyabinsk, till our train stopped at Kopeysk, a coal-mining town in the Urals. My brother, Yoshka Kopelman, Dzentsolski and I continued from the Urals to the south. We travelled days and nights through barren land till we arrived in Uzbekistan. We stayed a few days in Tashkent and then moved to Samarkand, our final destination. We decided to stay there, find work and wait and see what would happen.

People from our home town, who left Novogrudok like us were scattered all over Russia, reached remote Siberian towns and the planes of Central Asia. Some stayed in one place, some moved from town to town trying to make a living. Soon the Russian winter came and with it hunger and epidemics. To some of the fellows fate was cruel, because of the harsh conditions. They became sick and died in some lonely places and no one knew where they were buried. On occasions, it happened that people from Novogrudok met each other in remote places in Siberia and Central Asia looking for work, troubled by sickness and hunger.

We were worried and fearful about our families back home. We knew nothing about them in the first few months of the war, but we expected the worst. At the end of the winter of 1942 shocking stories were published in the newspapers. There was news about the horrors the Nazis committed in the conquered areas, the murder of Jews in the towns of Byelorussia and the Ukraine. The worry and dread turned into despair and sorrow, into passion for revenge and with it a horrific sense of inadequacy.

Months and years passed by, the horrific war continued to play havoc, spreading destruction and extermination. Many young men from Novogrudok were enlisted into the Red Army, fought the enemy and fell as heroes on the battlefields. Among them was Izek Boldo, whom I met in the autumn of 1941 in a kolkhoz near Samarkand. We met others.

A large part of our men departed Russia with the Polish army under general Anders and arrived in Erets-Israel [The number of Jewish men and Jewish families who were allowed to leave Russia with Anders' army was very small, much smaller than the proportion of Jews among the Polish population in the Soviet Union. Later Anders was severely criticised by Jews and others for his anti-Semitic behaviour]. Men from Novogrudok also served in the Polish Army, which was organised by the Soviets. Every man met his own fate. Most of them succeeded to reach Erets Israel after the war and strike roots there. But a few were not permitted to leave the Soviet Union and they are still there, dispersed in the vast country, lonely with no contact with the rest of their brethren (among them was Yoshka Kopelman). We heard nothing about scores of people whose traces disappeared in the wide expense of Russia, in the midst of war, hunger and epidemics. Their memory stayed with us, who had walked the bloody roads of Byelorussia with them. We share the memory of those who left but did not arrive.

Today, when we think about that fateful month of June of 1941 and the events of those days, the hurtful question comes up again: "Why did we depart, when the catastrophe was on our doorstep, without the other members of our families whom we could have saved?"

There are many answers but we should not look for justification - our dead forgave us...

We cannot escape the burning ache and deep grief in our hearts and the memory of our dear martyrs is living with us forever.

> *[Yaakov Kivelevich, who has written these memorable recollections, left the Soviet Union with Anders' army, fought in Africa, was severely wounded, practiced law in Erets Israel. He died a few years ago.]*

[Pages 237]

A sea of troubles

by Eliyau Berkovitz

Translated from Yiddish by O. Delatycki

A. Under the Soviets

On the 1st September 1939 the people of our town were overcome by unexpected bad news of the outbreak of the Second World War . There were immediate worrying consequences: mobilization into the Polish army – sons and husbands were leaving their homes and were taken to the frontline to fight the Nazi beast. The war was brief. The Polish army was defeated very quickly by the much larger, motorised army and superior air force of the Nazis.

Eliyahu Berkovitz

On the 17th of September the Polish forces left Novogrudok in haste and the town became ungoverned. Some said that the Germans were coming and that spread a fear. At 4 o'clock in the afternoon we heard the news that the Soviet army crossed the boarders and was advancing to the west. At 7 o'clock in the evening a loud noise was heard and the first powerful Russian tanks appeared in Korelicze street. They were met by the Jewish population with jubilation and flowers. It was announced by loudspeakers that the Polish population should not evacuate the town. No one will be harmed. People in the streets were in a festive mood. The Soviet forces were coming from all directions. Some soldiers picked up children for a ride on the tanks.

There were Jewish soldiers in the Soviet army who made themselves known to the local community. At 10 o'clock in the evening the loudspeakers announced that the town was governed by a military administration. A 10 pm curfew was in force and all civilians should go home. At 1 o'clock in the morning sounds of intensive shooting were heard. Everyone endeavoured to take cover. No one new what caused the shooting. A rumour spread next morning that some bullets broke window panes. Some soldiers told us that they were fighting the Poles, who were shooting from cover. The strong fire was concentrated in Kowalski Street, where the Catholic Church was. The resistance was suppressed by the morning. During that night the first Jewish victim fell – the older son of Aba Zamkowy was shot by the Poles.

Some days passed. Things returned to normal. Farmers were again coming to town. The shops resumed trading. A parity of the Polish zloty and the Soviet rouble was declared by the authorities. Thus both currencies were in circulation and trade was brisk. The Soviet soldiers were eager customers. They bought everything in sight. The merchants soon realised that it was a fool's game. In a few months time crippling taxes were imposed on all traders. However much the takings were they did not suffice to pay the taxes. The privately owned shops were shutting down. The state started to organise cooperatives of all kinds. The cooperatives employed the owners of the shops and artisans. Manufacturing plants were established such as a clothing factory, which employed all tailors. This was followed by a shoe factory and a furniture factory. Gradually life was changed to the Soviet style.

Thus life continued uneventfully till the beginning of 1941. At that time a mass deportation to Russia of a section of the Jewish population occurred. On one Friday morning packed carriages were seen. They were the possessions of Jews who were previously wealthy. [Several details of this are wrong]. On that Friday there was disquiet in town. The relatives and friends of the deported were bemoaning their loss. Life continued monotonously till the 22 June 1941 [two days of monotony, the event described in the previous sentence happened on the 20 June 1941] when the Germans attacked Russia.

The tunnel

One day a segment of the surviving Jews met and formed a plan to attack the guards of the Ghetto and run wherever they could. We managed to purchase and smuggle some arms into the Ghetto. We knew that we were all destined to be killed. We thought that if we ran a few might survive. We organised ourselves in fighting units. We were all able to fight and knew weapons. A date was set to carry out the attack. All was ready. As the time approached we noticed that the guards had been doubled in strength. We realized that our plans had been disclosed. We decided to investigate the leak and find the culprit. We had in the Ghetto a Dr Jakubovich, who now lives in Israel. He was injured in his leg. His brother was the chief of the Ghetto police. The brother knew of our plans and was prepared to escape from the Ghetto with the rest of us. We asked him what was to happen to his brother, since he would not be able to run. He answered that 230 people of the Ghetto could not sacrifice themselves for one, even if that person was his brother. He told us that he was in favour of the attack on the guards. The doctor's wife, who was a midwife and was doing her best to cure her husband, found out about our plans and opposed the plan to attack the guards. She was protesting and pleaded not to sacrifice her husband and to postpone the attack. The attack was postponed and this, in the end, turned out for the best.

We were looking for a solution and considering all possibilities. Perhaps, perhaps... A group of us got together with the chief of police Jakubovich. As a result of our discussions it was decided to dig an underground tunnel. It seemed a fantasy. But gradually the fantasy was changing to reality. We planned how to go about the job. When the plan was ready Berl Yoselevich and Jakubovich were put in charge. The work was started with great enthusiasm and strict secret, because we were continuously watched by the police on the outside and the foremen of the workshops, who were Russians. Fifty people were selected. They were young and, we hoped, they could keep the work confidential. Every day each man had to work a two hour shift in the shaft. The digging was started in the barn where some of us lived. One of the first problems to be solved was to dispose of the soil removed from the tunnel. As it happened a few buildings in the Ghetto were built under the one roof. Holes were made in the partitions under the roof to create a passage. Men were seated every few meters and the soil in small sacks was passed from one to the other and thus transported to the loft. The sacks were made by the tailors from rags. In time the loft was full. At that stage double walls were made and soil was deposited under the floors. The work proceeded in silence. Communication was in sign language. The most intensive work was done on Sundays, because it was officially a day of rest and the gentile personnel was not present. On Sunday the Ghetto was cleaned and the garbage removed. The opportunity was taken to mix the soil with the garbage and get rid of it. A number of technical problems had arisen. The walls of the tunnel had to be shored up to prevent them from collapsing. The carpenters prepared sections made of wood. The wood was stolen from the workshops, carried under coats, made up into panels and installed at night. Thus meter after meter, the tunnel was extended. Two to three metres were dug daily. The next problem was lack of air and darkness. Kerosene lamps were made, but they did not work for lack of air. Our tinkers, such as Niomke Portnoi and others, came to the rescue. They made up pipes in form of cones – wide at the bottom and small at the top, where they penetrated to the outside. This solved the problem of air supply. The men inside the tunnel worked naked because of humidity in the tunnel. It so happened that July was a wet month and it rained daily. Water entered the tunnel. A new job of removing the water had begun. We would empty it and new water would seep in. In time we overcame this problem too. The tunnel was 60 centimetres wide and 70 centimetres high and ran 2 meters under the surface. This made it possible for a person to crawl through the tunnel. At this stage the tunnel was 100 metres long and it became more and more laborious to remove the soil. We looked for a solution. A carpenter from Zetl by the name of Borecki came to the rescue. He made two platforms on wheels with timber rods for rails. He designed it very well. One carriage was moving forwards and the other backwards. The carriages were pulled by ropes made from rags. This innovation made the work much easier. One improvement led to another. Electric light was installed in the tunnel. We had no electricity in our rooms, but there was electricity in the workshops. Our electrician Gershon Michalovich had run a concealed connection through the loft. We smuggled in lamps and we had light in the tunnel. The work continued. In the beginning of September 1943 the tunnel was 250 metres long. News began to circulate that the Ghetto was going to be liquidated and the town would be made Judenrein [cleared of Jews]. We heard from our Belarus police that the Ghetto in Lida was liquidated and all Jews were taken to Majdanek. The police was pleased to convey to us such news. We decided to escape as soon as possible. The news about the tunnel was disclosed to everybody in the Ghetto and was received with enormous surprise. There were however some who had expressed doubt about the possibility of an escape. Some said that we would be trapped alive in the tunnel. Others thought that we should wait and see what the time would bring. We made every effort to convince everyone. We told them that if we do nothing we would be all killed. If we tried we might succeed. It was decided to conduct a secret ballot and we would follow the will of the majority. The result of the ballot was 165 votes for and 65 against. We decided to escape. The next problem was who should go first and who would be last. Everyone wanted to be first. We came to a decision that no one would be told where he was in the line. Everyone was given a piece of paper with the name of the person ahead of him. The small supply of arms was divided in two: half to those who would guard the exit the other half to those that would guard the entrance. In case of a hold up nobody would be allowed to enter the tunnel to give a chance to those inside to save themselves. It was decided that we would leave on Saturday night. The night turned out to be clear and everyone was held in readiness till one in the morning. It was decided to try again on the next day, Sunday. Everyone went quietly to their barracks. The men in charge knew that they could risk the delay because the Germans never conducted an 'action' on a Sunday. Next day was a clear sunny day, but this time there could not be further delays. The living dead in the Ghetto milled around in feverish excitement. As our luck would have it, at 5 o'clock in the afternoon dark rain clouds began covering the sky. Soon after the rain with thunder and lightening came down. We loosened deliberately the metal sheets on the roofs and the wind made them flap noisily. As soon as it was dark we were all in our appointed places. We slithered through the holes in the loft to the entrance to the tunnel.

Now I have to tell my story, because I did not escape through the tunnel and nobody knew that I remained in the Ghetto. I saw all that was happening in preparation to the escape. With me was my sister Chaje Sore Ludski. She had a heart disease. I knew that she would not be able to crawl 250 metres on all fours through the tunnel. She would only stop others, because nobody could pass her in the tunnel. I was looking for a solution and I believed that I had found one. I spoke to a Jew in our Ghetto by the name of Shmuel Kulachek, who stemmed from Iveniec. He too suffered from a heart disease. He had a 14 year old son. We discussed the situation. He told me that he had prepared a hiding place. He said that if I was in agreement, we could wait and after the escape we would decide what to do next. He took me to a loft and showed me what he had built. It was a double floor 50 centimetres high, covered on the outside with a high pile of smelly rubbish to discourage people approaching it. I liked his preparations and we started storing our provisions, water and blankets, to make it possible for us to survive in the hiding place for some time, if necessary. I included in the conspiracy my brother-in-law Zisl Raisin who was the husband of my younger sister Bejle, who was killed by the Germans on the 7 May 1943. When I explained to him our intensions, he answered that he left the planing to me and would do what I intended to. In the evening, when all departed to the tunnel we hid in our hiding place. There were five of us: my sister, I, Zisl Reisin and Kulachek with his son. At 8 o'clock the escape started with the agreed signal: Gershon Michalewicz the electrician short circuited the current to the projector. The projector was installed on the roof of the court house and illuminated the whole surroundings. We saw from our hiding place the projector blinking a few times on and off and than stopping for good. Our Gershon did well. From then on till about 9 o'clock there was total silence. It was calculated that the escape through the tunnel would take 20 minutes. We were certain, therefore, that the escape was successful. At 9 o'clock intensive shooting started in town. This lasted for about half an hour and then there was silence again. At 11 o'clock we heard more shooting and running by the

Belarus police all over the Ghetto. Of course they found no one. They must have been puzzled about the escape. I heard them shout in Russian: 'not a living soul'. There was a lot of activity and after a time they found the entrance to the tunnel. There they found a letter to the district commissar Traub, in which he was informed in a humorous way that the Jews had departed. The rest of the night was quiet. In the morning all the gentile supervisors arrived and were arrested. In the afternoon they dismantled and removed all the equipment in the workshops. For the next three days there were visitors to the entrance to the tunnel. Gentiles from everywhere came to look at the rarity and to see what people under threat were capable of. We, in our uncertain situation, were also glad that at least some Jews saved themselves. We stayed in hiding for eight days, till we felt that the guards were not there anymore. On Yom Kipur at 1 o'clock at night, in the rain, we decided to abandon our hiding place. We were aiming to go towards the forest in search of the partisans. I went out barefoot and shook intensely the barbwire. When there was no reaction we convinced ourselves that the guards were not there. We came down one by one. We went out through a hole which the police used to trade with the inmates. We were carrying my sister. We were aiming to get to the Sieniezyc forest. We got to the forest which was about 6 kilometres away. In the forest we felt more secure. It was beginning to get lighter. We saw in the distance two men with rifles. We thought that they may be policeman and we hid in the bushes. They shouted at us to come out and come over. To our joy we discovered that they were Dr Rosenbloom and his gentile superior. He was very glad to have met us. He told us about the escapees from the tunnel. He said that more then half were caught and killed by the Germans [Jack Kagan, who escaped through the tunnel {see his 'How I survived' on p.299 of Pinkas Novogrudok}, investigated after the war the number of survivors from the tunnel and found that more than 170, or 74%, of the escapees through the tunnel survived]. The rest joined various partisan formations, most of them joined Tuvie Beski's group. He was glad that some were saved. He advised that we should not join a small partisan group, because Jews may not be safe among gentile partisans. He said that they were not keen to help us, and if they meet a Jewish partisan alone they might behave like the Germans. He gave us information of how to find Bielski's group. It took us another 8 days to find Bielski, where we met our people from the Ghetto. We were well received by them. We were not alone at last. We found ourselves among Jews with arms in their hands. We were in the forest and free to fight the Germans. We were in the partisans for 10 months. Every now and then we experienced hunger, but we were alive. On the 22 June 1944 the Russian offensive against the Germans started. The Germans were running to the west faster than they came to the east. At the end of June 1944 Novogrudok and the district towns were free of the

Germans. [Novogrudok was liberated by the Russians on the 8th July 1944]. When the Russian army came we were in the forests. They have seen for themselves that there were partisans and their families in the forests. A day after liberation plans were made to return to our homes. But what homes? They found large mass graves. Some of us were mobilised to the regular Russian army. About 50 Jews out of 6000 remained in Novogrudok. Most of us could not live among the ruins. We made our way to Poland and from there to Israel.

[Pages 241]

Under the German Yoke

by Lyuba Rudnicki

Translated from Yiddish by O. Delatycki

Yiskor – remember for generations to come what the Germans did to us. Recall - pass on from one to another what is written here in blood. Yiskor - remember the beginning of the Soviet – German war. On Thursday the 18th of June 1941 [the correct date is the 19th of June 1941] there is an unquiet and fear in the air. There is a movement of horse carriages in town. We didn't know the meaning of this. There were various rumours. One said that the carriages were needed to transport grain (we had no big trucks in town), someone else thought that they would be needed to transport people, the third thought that they would be used to deport the very rich and send them to Siberia. In the depth of the night we were woken by the sounds of the horses and carts moving on the stone pavement. The night passed in tension.

In the morning we found out that overnight the Soviets transported 'the very rich, the exploiters' and the refugees [whilst who is 'very rich' or an 'exploiter' depend on the definition, there were no refugees from the German occupied part of Poland in the transport of the 19/20 June 1941], who were given paragraph 11 (this was a paragraph which was given to people who were not the inhabitants of Novogrudok and big businessmen [this is not correct]). Heads of the families were taken to jail. The other members of the families were told to take some belongings and were driven off in the carts. The next day was a day of sorrow, like on Tishe b'Av [ninth of the month of Av –a day of mourning – the day of destruction of the first and second Temples]. There were tears and lamentations by the members of the separated families. Children of the deported families who were married, were not deported. There were instances when a daughter of a family to be deported was allowed to remain, when a neighbour swore that the girl was his wife (for instance Ada Ziskind-Shapiro). She was in her mother's home. But Ben-Zion (Benche) Movshovich came and insisted that she was his wife. At the time it was thought that the worst thing that can happen was to be sent to Siberia. Next morning all those who were given paragraph 11 went to sleep in their neighbour's houses. I remember that my parents went to sleep in the house of Joselewicz, the son of Rafael the shoemaker, he was certain that he would be safe being a tradesman. Everyone was sure that the deportations had only started. It was a very long day. There was no escaping the deportation. It was difficult for a settled family to give up their possessions, which they had accumulated in a lifetime. They were certain that they were provided for for years to come. And suddenly all changed and was destroyed. In addition there was the separation of husbands and wives, break up of the family and the deportation to the distant Siberia. Could anything be worse? We did not realise then that the deportation was the only way of escaping from the hell that awaited us.

In that tension and grief two days have passed. On Sunday morning people went on with their business. There was an unusual quiet. As the saying goes - a quiet before the storm.

War!

In the streets were small clusters of people. There were rumours of a war. Somebody said that he listened on Saturday night to an English broadcast which claimed that Germany would attack Russia on the 24th of June. This was startling news. The deportation was forgotten. There was disquiet. In the evening the excitement had grown. Men were getting ready to leave their families. It was assumed that men alone were endangered during the war. They said that the Germans employed men to do heavy work. Women were not in any danger. And this was when the tragedy began. Men were parting from their parents, wives and children. They were heading for Minsk, to the east. Rumours were circulating that the army barracks in Skridlewo were attacked from the air. Four aircraft flew quite low. There were casualties. The panic was growing. People were looking for horse drawn carts, motorcars, bicycles, any form of transport to get away as quickly and as far as possible. My husband and I decided to go to Minsk. We took out our motorbikes and were ready to start. In the last moment I changed my mind. I thought: how can I leave behind my father and mother, my sister? Can I live without them? We became apathetic. We were resigned, we thought: what would happen to everybody would also happen to us. We remained. Perhaps it was our destiny to remain so that those of us who would survive would be able to tell what our eyes had seen. As it happened we were the only witnesses of the tragic end of our near and dear ones. We also witnessed the end of the town of Novogrudok. This is our story for all of those who were not with us so that they could read it and pass on the story to future generations. Perpetually the question arises – how was it possible and how could words convey the feelings of our suffering? Every word that was written came through blood and tears. But there is the urgent need to always remember what the Germans and their helpers did to us.

Remember. Sunday the 22nd of June 1941 the Soviet radio announced that the Germans attacked the Soviet Union. The broadcast urged all citizens to be calm, not to panic, the ultimate victory is certain.

But even on the first day of the war there was a big disorder at our places of work. The officials who came to Novogrudok from the east since September 1939, specifically directors of enterprises, left their posts and were looking for ways to escape. None of them were to be seen. In the morning of that day the sound of aircraft could be heard. We thought that they were Russian planes, but it turned out they were German. They flew past and vanished. The panic was increasing. Nobody knew what to do. Some started building shelters. The streets were filled with people who were escaping from the town in large numbers. Most were going in the direction of Korelicz or Sieniezyc. The Soviets were leaving with their families. On the next day many did not come to work. It was thought that in a bombardment one would be safer in a field or a forest. Some believed that the Soviet air force would put up a strong defence. But on Tuesday the 24th, at 10 o'clock in the morning 9 aircraft appeared in the sky. They lost height and started bombing. They were aiming at concentrations of the Russian army. The Russian headquarters were in the Zamkova [Castel] street in a new house which belonged before the war to Szloyme Mowszowicz. The first bomb destroyed that house. It was flattened like a house of cards. Other objectives were the hospital in Yiddish street and the row of shops in the centre of the Market place. Some houses on the corner off Korelicz street were also destroyed, as was the house of Leizerowski where my in-laws had their soda water shop. The bombardment lasted a few minutes. About 30 people were killed and many were injured. I was on the Castle hill during the bombardment. I was going to Brecianka. When the bombardment started I was lying flat without movement. When the aircraft left I found out that I was covered in soil. A bomb landed not far from me. The bombardment was entirely unexpected. Novogrudok had few strategic objects. Why were we bombed so early? Some people tried to explain it by the allegation that some soldiers discharged their hand guns at the planes. Since the first bombardment, people were escaping to the nearby villages of Brecianka, Hordzielowka, Litowka etc. At night we slept at home and early in the mornings we went to the villages. In town there was no administration or militia. It was surprising that any sort of order was maintained. There was no control and yet there were no reports of thefts or more serious crimes. On the surface there were no changes. Possibly the fear or the common danger restrained everyone. There was an abundance of rumours. Some said that the Russians were advancing, others said that the Germans had already occupied Minsk. We were isolated from the world. We were satisfied if a day passed without major disasters. We were of course extremely worried. It is the unknown that we feared. This is how a week passed till the frightful Saturday evening, the 28th of June. It was a calm day. The sun shone, the air was still. There was no sign of aircraft. People stared moving back to town. It was a Sabbath and everyone preferred to be home and not in a barn or just a paddock. The last few days were uneventful and quiet. As it got darker and the time approached 7 in the evening we heard suddenly a frightening noise of approaching aircraft. We were at that time in Brecianka and decided to remain there. The planes flew low over the town and disappeared. We just started to breathe again, when a mass of aircraft came from all directions and a bombardment began. The noise was appalling. High flames and black smoke rose everywhere. It lasted 15 minutes without a break. Looking at it from Brecianka we were certain that nobody survived and the town was a heap of rubble. The first survivors arrived after 10 at night. They ran over dead bodies and burning houses. The town was in ruins. Waliker Street till the house of the dentist Lewin was destroyed. Zalatuche was undamaged. Yiddish street till the houses of my uncles Kaplinski was gone. The quarters of the public servants were undamaged. In the Synagogue square only the walls of the big Synagogue and two walls of the cold Synagogue were standing above the rubble. Slonim Street on the side opposite to the Catholic Church and as far as the jail was damaged. The church was untouched. All of the shops in the row of shops in the centre of the Market place were in ruins. Schloss Street to the Synagogue was gone. The Town Hall and the Polish gymnasium (high school) on the left side of Korelicz street were in ruins. The right side of Korelicz street as well as Mickiewicz street till the house of Czyz in Sieniezyc street were completely wiped out. Only boulders remained. If one stood where the row of shops was in the Market square, one could see the gate of the Jewish cemetery with its ornate inscription on the façade. The gate was a gift to the town from Itzchok Gurwicz and his wife. On the left one could see the district court which became later the Ghetto. One could not believe that this was recently a blooming, bubbling, clean town, which was changed into a heap of stones. Only a minority of houses remained undamaged.

The bombardment resulted in 300 deaths and many injuries. Most of the casualties were Jewish, because the Jewish part of town suffered most. Very many were left without a roof over their head. For several days many people were not accounted for. After a few days the extent of the big catastrophe had become apparent if not believable. I was witness to the selfless, humane behaviour of the Jews of Novogrudok. People gave shelter to those who lost their homes and helped everyone in need, including strangers. They fed them and looked after them. One spurred on the other. They were sharing everything. To my mind the behaviour of the people in town was exemplary. I never knew that we had so many good-hearted people. I still think often of Novogrudok which in my memory is so dear to me and which I lost forever with all my nearest.

The first slaughter

In memory of my dear sister Raichel and my dear, unforgettable parents.

Monument on the mass grave in Litovke

Remember – on the 5th of December 1941 announcements appeared: all Jewish able bodied tradesmen with their families must be ready to relocate to a Ghetto and they would be permitted to take with them only luggage they were able to carry. The immediate question which had come to mind was: and what would happen to those who were not tradesmen? The word Ghetto had created a fear. People tried to rationalise. Some optimists said that in the Ghetto it may be possible to survive. It was known that a Ghetto was established in Warsaw at the beginning of 1940. What we could find out about it from the distance was not all bad. We knew that some refugees who came to Novogrudok in 1939 from the German occupied part of Poland had returned there of their own will. Some wrote that they were surviving in the Ghetto. Their main complaint was shortage of accommodation. Whilst we were worried about the Ghetto, none of us gave any thought to the future after the Ghetto. It was gruesome enough to think of being locked up in a limited space. But we had no alternative.

On Friday they made an announcement. We were ordered not to remain outside of our homes after 6 o'clock of that evening. If found in the street after 6 o'clock one would be shot. Those were the so called police hours. As to the reason for the restriction there were various rumours. One was that a large detachment of Gestapo was going to march past. Some assumed that Hitler may visit briefly Novogrudok. We were all naïve. There was also a rumour that in Horodyszcz there was a slaughter, where everyone without exception was killed. Same argued that the reason was that the people of Horodyszcz did not obey the orders of the Germans, but we in Novogrudok we were obeying the law and the German orders and we had nothing to fear. We were resigned to the idea of being confined in a Ghetto. We did not sleep that night. We were glad when daylight came. Since the early morning, Jews were seen trying to leave the town. Not many succeeded. Those caught were put in the Ghetto, where all others were hoarded. Two Ghettos were created. One was in the building of the district court the other in the First of May street in the building of the Catholic school. Everyone tried to be selected to go to the district court. The police and one member of the Judenrat were rounding up the people. None of us foresaw the great calamity that awaited us. Being herded into the Ghetto was tragic enough. We left our houses and surrounds that were built by generations of our forebears. Suddenly we did not have a home and could not imagine the conditions that we would be exposed to. Where would we sleep? We took what we could carry on our backs. We got to the district court. Entering into the yard was a frightening experience. Around the building stood SS men with sticks. They restricted our movement. Whoever came in could not come out. There were some Jews who had certificates from their places of work. Everyone who had such a certificate felt more secure, because he thought that he or she was considered to be a necessary worker. My sister Raichl had a special certificate. She was working for the head of staff. My father-in-law Avrom Rudnicki had also a special certificate - he was supplying soda water to the Germans. There were only a few who were so lucky. People were of course envious of those who had certificates. On entering the Ghetto the holders of the certificates and their families were put in a separate place. It was assumed that they were the most secure should anything untoward happen. Many did not want to think too hard. We had no option and we saw no reason why anything extraordinary should happen. We were good and obedient detainees. Everyone tried to choke the fear deep in their heart. The frost outside was severe, but they did not let us go inside. We were shrivelled up from the cold and were huddling close to each other. There was no free space. There were more than 5000 people in the yard. We were standing and waiting. What were we waiting for? When it got dark the doors to the district court were opened and we were pushed in like cattle into dirty, narrow rooms. There was no room to sit. We tried to make space for the old, sick women. The district court consisted of a few buildings. We were running from one building to another trying to find more space. Between the buildings in the centre was a space. We were tired and hungry. If someone brought food he could not extract it. There was no room to put down luggage. The night has nearly over. We were hoping for a better day. On Sunday morning we were told to go to work. The Judenrat was sending people to their usual places of work.

Those remaining were waiting for the return from work of the members of their families. The German soldiers who were guarding the doorways expressed their regrets for the lack of space. They promised that space would be created. When those who were at work started to return they told us that the Christians in town told them that huge pits were dug for us next to the army barracks in Skridlewo. Others argued that the pits were for the old people who were kept in the Catholic school. Those who correctly assessed the implications did not return to the Ghetto. They sought shelter with Christian acquittances. Others were hiding in the destroyed houses. Those who were in the court buildings had no choice. The buildings were well guarded and were surrounded by tall walls and barb wire fences. We turned to the Judenrat as our representatives, who were in touch with the authorities. Judenrat carried out all orders of the regime without fail. They told us that we were not in any danger. The head of the Judenrat was the lawyer Ciechanowski. Members of the Judenrat and their families were located in a separate building to which we had no access. Despite the assurances all were disoriented, panic stricken and frightened. At such times, when there is no visible path for salvation one can only try to switch off. One becomes atrophied, apathetic and just lets go. There were no alternatives. Even if one could escape - what about the family. Under those frightful conditions the night passed. This was a night that one wished would go on forever. We were huddled together. I see before me my dearest sister and parents. We were hugging each other without saying a word. What was there to say? Each one was trying to invent a trade that one could claim to have mastered. It was rumoured that tradesmen would be spared. I can still hear the voice of my cousin Noimele, who was four years old. Despite her youth she understood the essence of the events. She said to her mother: 'Mummy, don't worry about me, I can knit'. Nobody could sleep. Everybody was listening for the slightest noise. In the morning the Judenrat was trying to provide a meal. A kitchen had been set up in a separate building. Each one was given a plate of hot soup. It was cold outside. A fierce wind was blowing. Suddenly an order was given: 'Get inside the buildings'. Families were separated and were not allowed to reunite. A fear of death was hanging over all of us. At that stage a door opened. As people walked in there was a selection: one was sent to the right the other to the left. At that moment I was separated from my parents and my sister. I was pushed forward. I could not move left or right. Suddenly we were alone – I and my husband. A few other people were pushed into the room. They were followed by an SS man. He searched everyone. He took away from one person a watch, from another a chain and left shutting behind him the door. We could see through the cracks in the wall people being moved one way and the other. Where were they going? We could hear the sound of motor vehicles, crying of children.

Those who were sent to the left were taken by trucks to Skridlewo, where the pits were prepared. They were surrounded by Germans with machine guns. Between the two pits was a narrow path. They were made to get off the trucks and walk along the narrow path. They were shot at that point. The bodies fell into the pits. Some were killed others were injured and some were untouched. They fell on top of each other. This is how five thousand innocent lives were rubbed out. Fathers, mothers, small children. Innocent lives were terminated. I find it difficult to describe this scene. We heard of my in-laws Avrom and Rivka Rudnicki. As they were driven to the pits they saw a group of Jews who were working in the barracks, among them their son Mejer. They shouted: 'Tell our children to take vengeance'.

Was there anything we could do to avenge a bestial crime of that magnitude, after our nearest and dearest had been murdered so brutally? Can there be solace in vengeance? A few people managed to save their lives by jumping from the trucks. Among them were Sorke Nachimovski and Chaim Maslowaty from Zamkowa Street. His daughter was shot whilst she jumped from the truck. That day Sorke and Maslowaty were hiding in bushes. At night they managed to return to the court buildings, where they were smuggled in. All members of the Judenrat and their families had survived the slaughter. When I saw Sorke I cried hysterically. She was a smart woman. She told me that as soon as she was put into the truck she with her husband and their 12 year old son decided to jump. In the truck were German soldiers with machine guns. She waited for a suitable moment and jumped. Maslowaty and his daughter followed. The Germans opened a vicious fire which killed his daughter. Her husband and son were prevented from jumping. The woman had a tremendous will to live, despite her debilitating illness. Her main solace in life was her gifted 12 year old son. Even after she lost everyone and everything she had the drive to live. She reproached me for being apathetic. She used to tell me: 'We must survive to bear witness to what has been done to us. We must shout loud enough for the world to hear. We should demand that justice must be done. We must reveal what the cursed Nazis did to the civilized world and specifically to the Jews.' At that time we were naïve enough to think that people would listen.

No matter how difficult it is for me to write these lines, I will be true to my destiny, and describe the murder of our dearest. When the last group of workers returned to the Ghetto it became clear that none of our relatives and close friends survived. Everyone in the Ghetto was in deep mourning. Can one describe the feeling of having lost the closest for ever? We waited the whole night. Perhaps somebody would return. But in vain. A strong wind was blowing emitting tones that were in harmony with our feelings. As I write this story I can not comprehend how we could survive our losses. No one lost their mind, there were no heart attacks. And to this day I can not understand it. There must be a drive to survive that gave strength to overcome our indescribable losses.

As we were sitting in mourning, the head of staff came with some bread for my unforgettable sister Raichl. He came to help her. She was a great person. Alas, she perished with our parents. She did not want to be separated from them. I believe that she clung to them when she died. I still can hear her last words: 'I will not remain behind without my parents'.

In this, the first slaughter, 5000 Jews were killed. About 1000 Jews remained. They were transferred to the Ghetto in Peresike. But only some of them were destined to survive to a new life of suffering and pain.

[Page 246]

Outside of the Ghetto

By Lyuba Rudnicki

Translated from Hebrew by Aviva Kamil
To the memory of my brother in law Meir Rudnicki

May 1942. Life in the Novogrudok Ghetto is "as usual": every morning the Jews go to work outside the Ghetto under heavy guard. The ones who stay behind the Ghetto walls are waiting for their safe return, consumed by fear. Rumours started to circulate that there are partisans near Novogrudok and that their chief is someone by the name of Gromov. People are curious, but there is no concrete information. Somebody said that Gromov left a note in the barbershop, which read: "Gromov was here". Everyone wants to see or contact him. People would do anything to leave the Ghetto. Those who are still alive begin to comprehend that gradually all of us will be killed. But the Germans promised that the ones who were left alive are needed and nothing untoward will happen to them. Despite that, the aspiration of most of us is to get out of the Ghetto. Is it the influence of spring or plain common sense that guides everyone? The main question is "where can one hide?" They look for contacts among the villagers.

One bright morning we found out that a few people had left the Ghetto overnight. Those were: the smolarnik [tar maker] (I forgot his name), Ben-Zion (Benche), Movshovich, David Golvicki and Ada Ziskind-Shapiro.

They went to an acquaintance of the smolarnik, near the village of Shchorsy. But after two days the smolarnik and Golvicki returned and said that the guard near the Shchorsy Bridge detected them and opened fire. The two managed to escape, but Movshovich and Ada Ziskind-Shapiro were killed on the spot. That incident shook everybody. If anyone held any hope of escape, it disappeared. We realised that all is lost, there is no safe refuge, we are all hermetically shut off. In the meantime rumours went around that the second slaughter was about to take place. The murderers prepared themselves with all the thoroughness ("planmaessig") of the Germans. The rumours materialised. The terrible "day of judgment" arrived. It was the 7 August 42.

In the morning, as usual, people left under heavy guard to work. We, my husband and I, worked in the infirmary in the house of Mordechi Movshovich in the 3 rd of May Street. There was a lot of restlessness. Everyone was looking for a hiding place till the killings would end.

From the experience of the first slaughter we knew that those who managed to hide during the slaughter, returned unharmed to the Ghetto. The Judenrat prepared a list of all the tradesmen who will have to move to the building of the district court. Till now the Ghetto was only in Pereseka. Many made an effort to be among the lucky ones who were transferred to the second Ghetto. We wanted to move too. But we met with the stubborn reluctance of the Judenrat and the police, though the medical personnel, to which we belonged (my husband was a dentist and I was a nurse) were promised previously that they would be left alive. This time we did not trust them and found a hiding place in the cellar of the dentist Shimon Kaminiecki ZL (of blessed memory). It was a house next to the German police station. We entered into the jaws of the cruel beast in the hope that they wouldn't look for us there. "Who would think that someone would dare to hide there?" we asked ourselves. Fifteen people were concealed the cellar. We put a kitchen cupboard in front of the entrance door from the kitchen; we brought water and bread to the cellar and waited for the terrible storm to pass. At night we heard sirens above our heads. From the house next door, the police station, we heard cries of people, the sounds of beating, cursing, sobbing, moaning and from time to time shots. We set huddled close to each other, did not move, and waitedÉ hoping to survive, to let all the troubles pass. That was the strong desire within each of us. We did not know the time; light did not penetrate the cellar. By listening to the traffic we estimated that it was dawn. We were desperate. How could we find out if the slaughter had ended? Who would tell us when to come out? No one knew where we were. While we were thinking and whispering too each other, we heard the sound of steps from the other side of the cellar. The cellar under the house of the family Kaminiecki extended under the vacant apartment of Kushi Plazenski (who lives today in Israel). The entrance to that apartment was from the main thoroughfare, the market square, and only a thin wall separated our cellar from the abandoned and dilapidated apartment. We did not know about it at the time. There was no time to contemplate. The wall was pulled down and, as the light penetrated, policemen appeared, their guns at the ready; the order was given for us to come out. They pulled us out one by one; it was still dark inside. I managed to hide under a washing basin in the cellar. I curled up under it and lay quietly. Suddenly I heard screams from the police station. I thought: "they killed everyone". I wanted to go out, was there any value to my life alone? When facing death you don't know what to hold on to. One moment you have a strong will to overcome all and the next you are enveloped in such despair that you want to die without resistance.

Suddenly the basin was lifted, a policeman lit a match and recognised me. I knew him too, it was a Byelorussian policeman. I took off my gold watch, gave it to him and told him to go and save my husband, I promised him that if we will stay alive we will give him money. He agreed, covered me with the basin again and went out. From time to time policemen entered the cellar moved the basin and I moved with it. It was hard to say how long it took. I thought that a very long time passed. Suddenly I heard a familiar voice calling out: "Lyubinka, come out". I thought that it was a dream. It was my husband's voice - was it possible? Where was he? The call was repeated again and again. I came out and saw my husband without the yellow patch, with the police officer, they asked me to follow them. I was confused, where were they taking me, is it life or death? No, now I want to live, I must overcome all troubles in order to bear witness to all that happened to us. A sort of courage arose in me. I kept quiet. Erect I walked into the police station. An interrogation started; " why did I hide, do I know what is going to happen to me?" I don't remember my answers. But till today I can hear my cry: "I want to live, this is the right of every human beingÉ" The cry was not normalÉ it was a cry for life.

After I saw many acquaintances around me, one was sobbing the other was tearing his clothes in desperation, they wanted to know what I was askedÉ There were hundreds of people there. After a few hours nine people were taken out, among them, my husband and I. They led us under guard to the court house. We stayed alive thanks to the head of the Polish police. My husband treated his teeth and made a bridge for him. Later we found out that the policeman was in contact with the partisans. We don't know what happened to him.

In the Ghetto we met some members of our family: my brother in law Meir, who was saved by a miracle, my uncle Rafael Kaplinski with his wife. Their daughter Lea was killed in the slaughter. Some 800-900 Jews, broken and shattered, remained alive. We entered empty rooms. They smelt of mould. Still shaken, the survivors of Meztal (?) were brought in. They numbered approximately 250 people. From all sides stories were told about the slaughter. One said that he saw with his own eyes babies who were torn out of their mothers' hands by the brutal oppressors and had their heads smashed against the wall. Some told us about the way they were saved. Staying in the toilets in the yard saved many.

Soon came the order to divide the Ghetto. The courthouses were to house the tradesmen, and the professionals and those with no trade were to be moved to Peresika. Everyone tried to stay in a place they thought safe. People started to invent trades. Like everywhere else, friendship and family relations were useful, a talk with the "Judenrat" could help. I thought about one thing only: how to leave that "safe" place. That thought did not give me rest. We started to prepare an escape. Where could we escape to? And how? After the first slaughter, when I lost all my dear family, I was desperate and nothing interested me, but later after facing death a strong will to live overtook me.

At that stage we heard nothing about the partisans. I contacted a Christian woman by the name of Pargowicka. She lived 2 km. from the courthouse, in the village of Selco (Selec). She was an honest and God fearing woman. I trusted her. I told her everything and asked her for help. I was not mistaken; she did help me. She had relatives in the village of Khrapenevo near Iv'e. She heard that there were Russian soldiers in that area, who had not managed to escape and were hiding in the forests. Her readiness to help us was great. She believed that if she saved us, God would bring back her husband, who was taken prisoner by the Germans. She was left with 4 small children.

My husband, brother in law and I decided to break out of the Ghetto. One day Dr. Sasha Ziskind approached us. He was a good friend of ours, and asked if we would agree for him, his wife, Tamara Viner from Volkovisk and Dr. Mark Berkman [also spelled Bergman in another article], a surgeon from Warsaw, to join us. They did not know Mrs. Pargowicka. They learned about our plan from a friend of Mrs. Pargowicka. We agreed, of course, to let them join us, without doubt or hesitation. Leaving the Ghetto was a very risky undertaking. Getting out was, in itself, a very dangerous operation, and then there was the problem of surviving outside the Ghetto. But the idea of leaving the Ghetto was stronger then any doubts we had. We decided to do it. We decided to escape from the Ghetto on the 19 of August 42.

Our group consisted of 5 people: Dr. Berkman, who was then the head of the "Judenrat", Dr. Tamara Viner, Sasha stayed in the Ghetto because of ill health and was to join us in the winter, Meir Rudnicki, my dear brother in law and a school master, my husband Yaakov and I. We were to meet at the water well in Karelicher street, where people from the Ghetto, under heavy police guard, were allowed to draw water every evening.

On the appointed day we returned from our work in town in time when people from the Ghetto had arrived to fetch water. We stayed till dark in the barn of Benzlavski, a postman. We had to pass by the Ghetto, there was no other way, except walking through the fields, which was more conspicuous and, therefore, dangerous. We took off our yellow patches and walked on the road, singing, so as not to awake any suspicion. Our hearts thumping, we passed by the barbed wire fence of the Ghetto. It was an unusual courage that grows from desperation and the strong will to live.

We arrived safely to Mrs. Pargowicka's house. A guide was waiting to take us to Khrapenevo.

We left at midnight and walked a meandering route, circumventing the police station in Gorodelovka. While crossing the river at a shallow place [next to Selec there is a small river called Volovka] we realised that the light projectors of the Ghetto lit the surroundings. Crawling, we crossed a wide field and entered the forest. We felt safer there, but as our bad luck would have it, it was harvest time and Russian planes appeared and bombed the granaries. The bombing started fires, which lit a large area. Slowly we advanced towards the town of Vselub [about 14 km from Novogrudok]. We stayed in the forest without knowing exactly where we were. We thought we were in the depth of the forest and to our surprise we saw villagers going to the church in Vselub. Our guide went to the church too and told us to wait till the darkness of the night. [Another day must have passed since they left Selec at midnight]. Crawling we entered the forest, hid among the bushes and waited for it to get dark. Quietly we exchanged opinions: Tamara wanted to return to the Ghetto, we: my husband, brother in law and I, stood by our decision not to move back from there but to go forward, even if we were to meet the most horrible fate, but not to return to the Ghetto. It was a frightful time, we were crowded behind a bush with no food or water. Now and then we heard voices of Germans who went to and from Novogrudok. Hour after hour passed. Finally it was dark. The guide did not return. Doubts arose again: "He betrayed us, let's go back" one of us said "where are we going from here, who knows the road?", another said "we are in these unknown surroundings for the first time in our life". At 10 o'clock the guide returned. We walked all night along narrow tracks among bushes. Eventually, at dawn, we reached our destined place. [Khrapenevo lays some 25 km north of Novogrudok and about 4 km south of the river Neman. It is desolate country, full of swamps and isolated villages. The nearest town of any size, Iv'e, is 15 km away, on the other side of the Neman.]

It was a swamp and we had to sit there all day. Only at night were we allowed to sleep at the granary, which was at a distance of 200 meters. A new life started there. The main thing that was demanded of us was to sit in absolute silence, lest the shepherds near the swamp would detect us. The guide's sister, and her kind mother, supplied us with food. We did not hear about partisans yet. We were told that once Russian soldiers had been in the district, but they had left. It was a quiet area. Just an isolated house far from the road. A month passed by, the winter was approaching. We decided to dig a bunker (zemlianka) in the forest. The men went out at night, they tied a stick or a hoe to their shoulder, which looked in the dark like a rifle, to deter villagers, if they were to meet them. The women stayed put. The aim was to dig a bunker 2 meters deep, because my brother in law was very tall. They dug even deeper, till they reached water, which was a necessity, if we were to dwell in the bunker.

Once, early in the morning, we were fortunate to meet two Jewish fellows: one from Vselub and the other from Swencany, who lived at present in Vselub. They put us in contact with a few partisans who operated in the area. It was a small unit, altogether seven people. Their leader was an escaped Russian prisoner of war by the name of Anton. Our life changed. Our men went out for reprisal operations, they returned to their bunker, but did not tell their friends about the women in the bunker. Later, only in one operation, the women were involved.

At the beginning the operations were small, there was a shortage of weapons. Not everyone had a rifle, they only dreamt about rifles. The first big and important operation was to destroy the bridge [across the Neman] to Zboisk. All of us went out one night to fetch barrels of tar, which we took from a tar factory, located about six km from our shelter. We also got some kerosene, which we appropriated from a village. We set fire to the bridge. It burned for a few days. No one dared to reach it for fear of partisans. It was a audacious operation.

Our big enemy - the bridge - was eliminated and was not repaired at the time we were there. We felt safer and we moved around more freely. We were looking for weapons. The men ambushed some Germans, killed them and took their weapons. That is how they got their rifles. With the passing of time the men started to worry about the safety of the women ie myself and my friend Tamara Viner-Ziskind. The women did not take part in night operations, but were waiting, fearful, for the return of their men. It was necessary to obtain food. They crossed the Neman, went into villages, which were hostile to the partisans and took some food. That was how a small unit of partisans in the district of Ivia-Novogrudok was formed. [At that time, Belski was gathering the largest body of partisans, which, on liberation, numbered over 1200 Jews. Twelve months prior to liberation the Belski detachment settled in the wilderness of Naliboki, across the Neman, not far from Khrapenevo.]

We passed the days by telling stories about our lives. That is how I know about the life of Dr. Mark Berkman. His home town was Warsaw. He worked before the war as a surgeon at the hospital on Czysta Street, Warsaw. He was clever and intelligent, but had a hard character. He said himself that he would walk over dead bodies to achieve his aim. But we liked him, he had a good sense of humour and liked to tell stories. He reached Novogrudok from Lvov, whence he had escaped, after the Germans conquered Warsaw in 1939. Dr. Limon, who was then the manager of the hospital in Novogrudok, accepted him as a surgeon in the district hospital (Sejmikowy). He left a wife and a daughter in Warsaw. He was a brave man. After the second slaughter in Novogrudok he was elected the head of the "Judenrat".

My dear brother in law, Magister Meir Rudnicki, was born in Novogrudok. He finished high school in his town and then the faculty of history at the University of Vilno. When the Russians came he was the head master of a school near Slonim. He was an honest, quite and modest fellow, good hearted and unpretentious. He never liked people to talk about him or praise him. Always with a smile on his face, he used to say: "If we will get over all this, I will show you that I am not that shy!". Poor man, he did not survive. When he took the rifle for the first time, his hands trembled. It was said about him that he would never hurt a fly, and yet he had to become a fighter. The first operation was hard on him; he could not shoot from an ambush. But when he reminded himself who the people that he was shooting at were, he found courage and used his bullets.

We lived together. It was like one family, and we became close to each other despite of our differences. Dr. Berkman and my husband Yaakov (who finished dentistry at the university of Bordeaux, France) many times helped the villagers. The partisans did not have a permanent location. Everyone was hiding separately, waiting for the spring. The aim was to unite and create one fighting body. It was hard to do that in the winter because of the climate. At that time we did not hear about other Jewish partisans. We thought we were the only ones. The Russian partisans were doing their rounds in the villages and if someone was sick they came straight to us and asked Dr. Berkman to help. My husband always accompanied him. Once, when one of the partisans was wounded, my husband pulled out his tooth and made him a primitive prosthesis from a piece of wire. Contacts between us, the locals and the Christian partisans were firm. That friendship and trust brought a disaster upon us in the end. We believed that we were all in the same situation and we all had the same aims. We forgot about the ever-present anti-Semitism.

From time to time we sent messengers from the village to find out about the situation in the Ghetto. We received news that the conditions in the Ghetto had become more severe. Guarding was stricter, the food situation worsened. Dr. Sasha Ziskind was coming to join us. Sasha was born in 1915. He was a handsome boy and very talented, quiet and modest, always ready to help anyone in trouble. He finished his high school studies in Novogrudok and later finished medicine at the university of Vilno. During the Russian rule he worked as a G.P at the hospital in Novogrudok. His friends liked him. He and I went to school together from early childhood. He was a good and a loyal friend.

On the 5 of January 1943 he walked disguised as a villager on the way to our hiding place. A policeman from Vselub, who was once his patient, recognised him and turned him over to the Germans. They jailed him in the Novogrudok prison, put him through horrific torture and pressured him to reveal our hiding place. He died a martyr without uttering a word. I honour his memory. We heard the details of his imprisonment from the jail wardens.

On the same fatal day the Belski unit was attacked by the Germans and some escaped to the district of Khrapenevo. We waited for the arrival of Sasha. Looking around we came face to face with the Belskis. We never heard of Tuvia Belski before, but we accepted willingly his offer to join his unit in the spring. We had just said goodbye to each other and left the house when it was attacked. Everyone in it was killed and the house was burnt. It was half a km. from our bunker. We found out about the killings the next morning, when we went to Khrapenevo and found burning coal and smoke. [This episode is mentioned briefly in the article on p.359 "Novogrudok partisans who fell in action". According to that article, where no details were given, three Belski partisans: Hertzel Efroimski, Arie Volkin and Yitzchak Leibovich, as well as Tuvia Belski's wife and her brother Grisha were killed in that action. Khrapenevo was a tiny outpost, yet two Jewish tragedies occurred there.]

It was clear that we had to change our location. Too many partisans in the area were a threat to us. We just wanted the winter to pass, and waited for the spring to join a big and strong unit that would be able to stand up against the enemy that surrounded us.

The fatal day arrived, the day of the Red Army, the 23 rd of February. Early in the morning we heard knocking. Two Russian partisans asked my husband and Dr. Berkman to come to their dwelling, because a third partisan, Vania, had been injured during the night operation. Without any suspicion, they went with the partisans in their sledge. My brother in law Meir stayed with us. A few minutes later we heard machine gun shots. We knew it was bad news. Did the Germans attack them? We had no other thought.

Meir took his rifle and went to stand guard. Tamara and I followed him, though previously we, the women, did not show ourselves to the villagers in daytime.

My brother in law went further and suddenly we heard a horrific cry. They killed my brother, I thought. Tamara and I started to run away, but where to? Forest all around, the snow knee high and the legs did not move. We walked a few meters away from our bunker, when we heard the call of the two partisans, who only a short time ago took my husband and Dr. Berkman to the injured friend. I approached them first. With a pistol directed at my heart they ordered me to climb on the sledge, which stood, beside our bunker. I started to ask questions:

what were the shots? Where were my husband and his friend? Dr. Tamara, who was usually brave and cool, lost her head, could not utter a word and pulled me to the sledge. An unusual strength came over me, strength out of desperation. I started to ask about the fate of my husband, Dr. Berkman and my brother in law. One of them blurted out: "we killed everyone and we will kill you too, today is the Red Army day, we received an order to kill all Jews." I had a flicker of hope that one of the men was still alive, and it gave me the urge to go on questioning and talking. One thing was clear to me: if one of them is still alive, he will return early and if so, one must get rid of those murderers. Both were drunk, they smelt of spirits. Till today I cannot believe the coolness with which I manipulate them. Calm and relaxed I promised them that we would come to them, but only in the evening. I advised them to go home and sleep, rest for a while, and we would wait for them to come and pick us up. I explained to them that women cannot survive in the forest alone, and that we did not know the surroundings and wouldn't move without them. They accepted it, and told us to wait till the evening. I advised them that it was not good to see women among the partisans.

They left the bunker and we set out in the snow desperate, with no hope and not knowing what to do. We saw in the deep snow prints of man's boots. We got up and ran towards them. It was my husband, who was rushing to help us. He was stunned, tired and broken. His words were: "they killed Dr. Berkman, his head fell on my shoulder, where is my brother Meir? A miracle saved me, I managed to knock Sasha's hand (that was the partisan's name) and his revolver dropped to the ground, the second man was the driver of the sledge and had no weapon, Sasha (the partisan) took the machine gun, but I managed to jump into the forest, hung my coat on one of the trees, they shot at it thinking that it was IÉ In the meantime I returned to you, Where is my brother?" those were short, broken and terrible sentences. We told him the atrocious news that his brother was murdered. Hearing that made him deaf for a few days, only his lips movedÉ Our rifles stayed on the sledge with the murderers. Only one rifle with a broken barrel was left in the bunker. I picked it up and we started to walk away from the bunker. Where to go? It was a clear day. Broken, shattered and fatigued we walked, leaving behind brothers and friends, sacred corpses. We could not even bury them. We could not come close to them, lest we would also be killed. After a short time we heard deafening shots from the direction of the bunker. It seemed that the murderers regretted leaving us and came back to pick us up. Thanks to the dense forest we managed to escape. We remained very close to the bunker. We were afraid to walk during the day, for fear of being informed on. Enemies were all around us. Where could we go and what was going to happen? My husband was deaf and he did not talk!

The persistent question hounded us: where should we go? With nightfall my husband recovered a little, he was our only hope. He decided to go in the direction of Kostus Kozlowski, who was a friendly villager and a contact man of the Belskis. He lived far from us, we walked for a few days, with great fear, along winding tracks. We did not know the area and feared every stranger. We made a great effort not to be seen. Those were torturous and troubled days. It was our bad luck to reach Kozlowski a few hours after the Germans left his yard. Swiftly he led us and hid us in a small wood. The Germans, again, were attacking the Belskis, who were back in their old base. We could see from a distance the Germans retreating towards Novogrudok. After a few days we finally met the Belskis. There, a new chapter opened in our life.

I would like to add a few things. During all our time with the Belskis our first aim was to take revenge on the family of the policeman who caught Sasha Ziskind. My husband could not rest, the thought depressed him. He found out from the villagers where the policeman lived and took a few men with him to the policeman's house. It was a very dangerous operation. First, his house was close to the police station. Second, in order to reach the house one had to pass an area where Germans and policemen hung around. But that did not deter my husband. Finding that the policeman was not home, my husband killed with his own hands his mother, sister and everyone else who was in the house. They left a note to explain the murder and burnt the house down.

Dr. Rosenbloom was a good friend of Dr. Berkman. Hearing about the horrific murder of Dr. Berkman and my brother in law, he sought and found the two partisans and the family they stayed with who assisted them. He killed them all.

[Page 251]

The Days of Annihilation

In the Nazi hell

by Shmuel Openheim

Translated from Yiddish by O. Delatycki

The outbreak of the war between the Soviet Union and Germany on Sunday the 22 June 1941, was completely unexpected and caused confusion in the Jewish community of Novogrudok. Only next day, when the Soviet officials from the east began to evacuate in chaotic haste, the confusion turned to panic. It was becoming clear that our situation was shocking. We had to expect within the next few days the arrival of the Nazi beasts. We were told by the Jewish refugees from the west about the Nazi treatment of Jews, though we found it hard to believe that this could happen in our times.

Shmuel Openheim

To show our disbelief in the stories of the dreadful deeds, let me relate the following fact. In 1940, when a Nazi commission came to Brest to arrange the return of Polish citizens from western Poland, many Jewish refugees, who were living in Novogrudok, had registered their names to return to their homes, to the Nazi occupation. It was a miracle that the Soviets, instead of taking them to Brest, to the Germans, have conveyed them to the remote regions of Russia, and because of this most of them survived the war.

On the third day of the war the Germans bombed the town. Among the killed were Jews. A chaos ensued. No authority remained in town. The Soviets left in panic. A number of younger Jews had fled east. However, when they arrived in Stolbcy [on the 1939 Polish- Soviet border] they found that the 'westerners' [a common name for the inhabitants of the former eastern regions of Poland] were initially not allowed to proceed further. And when this restriction was removed it was too late, because the Germans occupied Minsk long before Novogrudok. Because of this, many who tried to escape returned home. Those who walked in the direction of Mogilev did manage to get through, but those who attempted to walk through Bobryusk could not get through, because the Germans had cut off the passage. They returned home.

The town was distraught, people were deserting their homes, and some went to the neighbouring villages. Some even camped in open fields. Lack of food had become an acute problem. Small groups of the defeated Red army were drifting through the town. Many soldiers had no arms, some were barefoot, hungry with their clothes in tatters. The Germans were expected at any time. On Saturday of the 28th of June the Germans bombed the town several times before noon. In the evening more planes arrived from all directions and began to incinerate the town. They were also shooting at the fleeing population, using machine guns. The town was burning all around. The casualties were light, because many people left their homes before the attack began. The German vandals proceeded in a pre-planned manner. They burned almost all of the Jewish quarters. The following streets: Yiddish, Synagogue square, Waliker, Rachelo, a section [half] of the Market place, Mickewicz, Sieniezyc, Korelicz, all Jewish houses but not the houses of the gentiles, who did not suffer any losses. After the fires all was still, there was nobody in sight, neither the Red army nor the Germans. The Jews started returning to the houses that had not burnt down. Five or six families moved into many houses. They sat in fear and hunger and waited for the dreadful 'guests'. On Thursday the 3rd of July the Germans arrived and immediately showed their intensions. They went into the Jewish homes and looted them. A dirty German soldier entered our house. I was sitting, because my leg was injured. He wanted to shoot me because I did not get up when he entered. On the third day after their arrival the Germans announced the first repression: all Jews aged 10 years or older had to wear a yellow patch 10 cm in diameter on both the front and back. Jews were not allowed to get out of their houses from 6 o'clock in the evening until the morning. All Jews without exception had to go to work. A city council was created headed by Smolski, a Pole, as well as a police force under the German command.

The mass grave of the murdered at the first massacre in the Skridleve forest

A Jewish group consisting of the lawyers Ciechanowski, Zeldowicz, Gumener, the pharmacist Meisze Lizerowski, the brothers Leizer and Meisze Izraelit, Shlojme Kabak, Momik Dobrin organised themselves into a Jewish committee. They did not know as yet the name Judenrat.

The Gestapo made their own arrangement. They demanded that on the 6th of July every member of the Judenrat should bring with him twenty Jews who would elect the new Judenrat, since the Judenrat had to be elected. As every member of the Judenrat wanted to be elected, they brought on the day their relatives and friends and more of them than was required. About two hundred Jews were assembled. A list was prepared by the murderers with all particulars, such as the occupation of each one. Later, all were locked up in a small house in the yard. The detained almost expired from heat, thirst and lack of space. Among the incarcerated was Vole Shapiro. Because he was tall and stout the Germans assumed that he was the leader of the Novogrudok Jews. They took him away and tortured him for the rest of the day. In the evening they brought out the rest of them and arranged them in a row. When they brought out Vole Shapiro he was unrecognisable and, clearly, he did not know where he was. Of the two hundred Jews they selected fifty. Most were professionals and merchants. The others were given a beating and sent home.

Those detained were taken next morning to a grove in Skrydlewo, near the barracks, and shot. The Germans told the Jews that the fifty were sent to work. And most believed the story.

Later some truck drivers, who were working for the Germans, told the Jews that they met Jews from Novogrudok at work in remote localities. They mentioned various names. Obviously, this was a deceit, planned to mislead the Jews. The relatives of the Jews that were taken away had begun sending food parcels with the drivers. The drivers made good use of the parcels. The Jews lived under the illusion that their relatives are still alive.

Continuously new restrictions were announced: Jews were not allowed to buy anything from the gentiles, there was be no communications between Jews and gentiles, Jews and gentiles must not greet each other, Jews were not allowed to walk on the footpath, they had to walk on the road, Jews were not allowed to travel by rail or bus, Jews were not allowed to change accommodation, all Jews 12 years of age or older had to present themselves for work, for all transgressions there was one punishment – death.

About two weeks later the murderers started a list and assembled again about fifty Jews, mostly the members of the intelligentsia including teachers and sent them, allegedly, to work. There were still many who believed the Germans, though farmers who lived close to the barracks, were telling that they had seen the Germans leading groups of Jews into the groves, they heard shooting, and then the Germans would return by themselves. Jews did not want to believe them.

On Saturday the 26th of July 1941 the Germans required the Judenrat to deliver 50 Jews. Members of the Judenrat soon assembled from places of work more than 70 Jews. The Germans lined up the Jews in the middle of the market place, surrounded the square with soldiers, selected 52 persons, among them the pharmacist Moishe Lizerowski, who was a member of the Judenrat, as well as Jehoshua Iwieniecki, who was nominated that morning to the Judenrat. The Jews were shot, ten persons at a time. The teacher Salomon tried to escape and was killed on the spot. In all 52 Jews were killed. The murderers left the bodies in the market square for 3 hours. The gentiles walked around the market square and looked at the dead Jews. Later 5 horse drawn carts were brought in and Jews were told to take the bodies to the Jewish cemetery and bury them.

As the bodies were being loaded on the carts, it was noticed that one body was moving. A Belarusian policeman shot him. Jewish women were told to wash the blood off the cobblestones, at the same time a band arrived and played.

This episode had a shattering effect on the Jewish population, because everyone could see the beastly events and the victims. It was made abundantly clear what the intensions of the occupiers were. Nobody believed now that the Jews who were taken away previously, were still alive. All were most depressed.

About one month later, also on a Sabbath, an einsatz unit arrived and demanded that the Judenrat provide 50 Jews. This was arranged and 50 Jews were assembled in the yard of the Judenrat. As well as the 50 Jews, the gestapo took with them several others who were in the yard, among them some members of the Judenrat. They were taken to the local jail and next morning were shot behind the barracks.

The gentiles took advantage of the situation. They reported to the police any Jew they did not fancy. This was sufficient to have the Jew arrested. No Jew came out alive from jail. The police would come to a house looking for somebody whose name had been given to them by an informer. Regardless whether the sought person was found, they would take all men who were in the house. They took all of them to jail. The police would also often detain men in the street and arrest them. They had also other tactics. The army and police would surround several streets, they would round up all Jews for the alleged purpose of checking documents. At the same time they would search the Jewish homes, rob them of anything they fancied and if they found anyone in the house, whether the person was sick or healthy, they would be taken to jail. The Jews lived in perpetual fear of death.

[Page 253]

The Slaughter in Horodyszcze

by Shmuel Openheim

Translated from Yiddish by O. Delatycki

In October [1941?], when the Jews of Novogrudok were droving cows to Baranowicze, this being one of the jobs the Jews were made to do, they passed through the town of Horodyszcze. There they had seen how the assassins were conducting the slaughter of the Jews of Horodyszcze. They assembled all the Jews in the market place, where they were loaded into trucks. They were taken a few kilometres out of town, where an excavation was prepared for them. There they were shot (see the description by Ch. Kravets p.263).

When the above news became known in Novogrudok, it caused considerable panic. It was expected that any day the Jews of Novogrudok would be subjected to the same fate. The beasts had another lie in store: they told us that the Jews of Horodyszcze had guns and were shooting at the Germans, but in Novogrudok this will never happen. Some Jews believed the story and lived with that illusion. The majority did not believe them. The Jews in the Ghetto had realised that being in the hands of the assassins they would never get out alive. Means were sought how to escape from the Nazi's hands. It was attempted to seek contacts with the partisans. The Judenrat and the camp police were doing all they could to prevent escapes from the Ghetto. If the police suspected that somebody was planning an escape, the suspect would be put into the cellar of the Judenrat, would be given a beating and would be left there. The police would take away in the evening the boots of those who were going to work outside the Ghetto and return them in the morning. The inmates were gradually getting used to the dog's life. The killers would appear at times in the evening and demand that the Jews give up all warm bedcovers, furs, winter coats and felt boots. The police would search the houses and remove these items. One day, when returned from work, we were met by the Nazis and the Belarusian police. They were searching every Jew at the gates of the Ghetto and everyone who wore boots had to take them off and walk away barefoot.

The Jews were of no account, as the following event shows. In the house of the Gebitskommisar [district commissioner] Traub water froze in the pipes. The Jews were made to light and maintain fires under the pipes to prevent water in the pipes to freeze. Once two boys were lighting fires in the middle of the night. After drinking and carousing at the head slayers, the revellers ran into boys, who were tending the fire. The Germans started shooting. One of the boys, who stemmed from Baranowicze, fell into the fire. The second, the son of Zejdl Kushner, was injured and though he too fell into the fire, he managed to crawl out and hide in a barn. Next morning they brought him into the Ghetto. He recovered, but was killed in the last slaughter.

Arke Nachimovski was working in the military barracks. He was delivering water from Skrydlevo using a horse driven container. On one occasion a friendly farmer gave him a bottle of milk. On arriving at the barracks the guards found the bottle of milk. They took him away and he was never seen again.

The son-in-law of Tiles was working in the barracks unloading trousers. Once he took a pair of trousers. Some time later he was sent back to the Ghetto.

Some time passed. The beasts were getting ready for another 'action' [mass extermination]. The Germans understood that the Judenrat was wise to their 'tricks' and that it would not be possible to persuade them to rely on them. They decided to liquidate the Judenrat. One evening they invited the Judenrat for a meeting under the pretext of making new work arrangements. One member of the Judenrat, Monie Zdzienciolski, was sick with a high temperature, but they sent a military policeman for him, under the pretext that without him no decisions could be made. As soon as the members of the Judenrat came in to the murderers' room, their death sentence was read, quoting various invented accusations and dispatched them to jail. Next morning they were all taken behind the barracks and shot. They were: the lawyer Ciechanowski [other sources have related that Ciechanowski refused to produce a list of persons to be executed and committed suicide], the brothers Lejzer and Mejszke Israelit, Momik Dobrin, Motl Niankowski, Shloimke Kabak, Shlojme Gershonowski and Munie Zdienciolski.

On the same evening the chief of staff of the district commissioner came and read a list of imaginary 'sins' committed by the Judenrat, which was the 'reason' for sentencing them to death. They also gave an order that by the next morning a new Judenrat must be formed. A new Judenrat was quickly established with Chaim Azikovich in charge.

At that time the Judenrat created workshops: fur coat makers, tailors, locksmiths, watchmakers, cobblers, saddlers, [knitters]. Some of them worked in the buildings of the district court. This was done in preparation for the arrangement that after the slaughter the Ghetto would be liquidated. Every day the workers went to and from work. At the same time the court buildings, except for the new, big building, were fenced off with several strands of barbwire. They also prepared large containers. The Jews understood that those were the preparations for a new slaughter, but they had no escape. A few young people left the Ghetto to establish contact with the partisans. The attempt failed. Benzion Mowszowicz and Eddi Rifkin were killed in that attempt. In anthers attempt, Mome Charny, Josl Osataszinski and others did get through but were killed in the forest. In the Naliboki wilderness a Jewish group attached to a partisan brigade was formed. The plan was to attack the Naliboki garrison, the Jewish group would be heading the attack and the other partisans were to follow. The Jews attacked, but the others did not follow and the entire Jewish partisan group fell [the story of the fight in Naliboki, which was told by eye witnesses was entirely different].

The German murderers were preparing the second slaughter. They installed a big projector on the Peresieke synagogue, which illuminated the whole Ghetto. The Jews were also getting ready. In all buildings underground bunkers were built and camouflaged. The bunkers saved many Jewish lives.

At that stage the Germans started bringing into the Ghetto Jews from the surrounding settlements such as Iveniets, Rubiszewicze, Naliboki (from the last one only adults). They were made to walk. The children were taken from their parents, who were told that the children would follow in horse carts. But all children were killed. They also brought to Novogrudok all Jews from Korelicz. They came in horse carts and were allowed to take some of their possessions. Some even brought wood for heating. They also brought with them their old, sick and paralysed. The Germans did everything to mislead the Jews (for descriptions of the events in the townships see the articles by Y. Yaffe).

The Ghetto became very cramped. All barns and store rooms were filled with Jews. The day of the slaughter came nearer. The murderers were making preparations in the open. They were even bargaining with the Judenrat about the number of Jewish lives. They have shown the Judenrat the list of Jews that would be spared and of those that would be destroyed. At the bottom of the list were all those incapable of work, the old and the sick. All children were to be eliminated. On the other hand, those who worked in the workshops and their wives were to remain alive. The Judenrat with their police and their office employees and workers would be safe, but under the condition that they would make certain that no one would escape from the Ghetto i.e. that nobody would avoid the slaughter.

On the 6th of August 1942, at the time the workers from the workshops were to go out to work, there was a feeling that they will not return. They demanded that their wives should come with them, otherwise they were not prepared to leave. The Judenrat made certain that they had the certificates for all the wives of the workers. They said that afterwards [meaning, presumably, after the slaughter] they would send the wives to join their husbands in the workshops in the court buildings. The Judenrat kept all the certificates the whole day. The police was watching them keenly in the Ghetto to make sure that no one should escape i.e. that no one's life would be saved. In the evening the Ghetto was surrounded by the German, Latvian and Estonian military. Shooting in the Ghetto could be heard. To move in the Ghetto was dangerous. At that stage the Judenrat decided to issue the certificates to the wives of the workshop workers, when it was impossible to leave the Ghetto or even to move from one house to another. Because of this most of the wives of the workshop workers were killed.

That day the German troops with the Belarus police went to Zetl to conduct there a slaughter. With the troops absent, a number of workers, who were working outside the Ghetto managed to infiltrate in the court buildings. Some of the workers managed to bring in their children into the court houses. They made no provisions for their wives because the Judenrat had certificates for them and assured everyone that the wives will be taken to the court buildings.

After work the tradesman were kept in the workshops. The court buildings were surrounded by Germans, Latvians and Estonians. Outside, the brown shirted murderers where everywhere. The Gebitskommissar noticed that there were children in the yard, who, according to the orders, were supposed to be exterminated. When the evening came and the wives did not arrive it became clear that the workers were told a lie. Nothing could be done. We lived through a night of grief and fear of death.

Many children and illegals were hiding in the big cellar of the court house. The doors were closed with heavy locks, but the children came in through the small windows. Those windows were camouflaged with pieces of timber.

On the next morning the 7th of August, early on that black Friday, the brown shirts heavily armed headed by the Gebitskommissar arrived in the court buildings. All the workers were lined up in the yard surrounded by the murderers and the search started for the children, who were hidden in the workshops, in the ceilings and elsewhere. They were dragging the children by their legs, like chicken, and throwing them into lorries. The crying of the children was awful, and we were forced to see it. When the parents broke ranks trying to beg the murderers for mercy they were met with guns and a threat to be shot. The luckless parents had to step back. One of the brown shirts came over to me and told me, because I was a locksmith, to open the locks to the doors to the cellar, where about 200 Jews were hidden, mostly children, among them two children of mine. I was surprised that my heart did not break at that moment. I can only assume that our life in abnormal conditions and constant fear of death had hardened us. I answered that the cellar was locked by a special lock which was impossible to open without a special key. A miracle happened – they actually believed me that the door could not be opened and therefore there was no one there. At the same time the slaughter in the Peresike Ghetto was conducted. Early in the morning the brown shirts together with the Judenrat and the Jewish police were conducting a hunt, going from house to house and searching in all places that could serve as a hiding place. They forced all Jews to go to the yard and lie with their faces down. Some Jews hid in places that were previously prepared. This helped a number to survive. The Judenrat, the office workers and the police were certain that they would survive the slaughter, because this was promised to them. For this reason they did not hide. The hangmen counted the victims and established that a number of people were missing, because they had escaped or were hidden in the Ghetto. The number of those available for the slaughter was not sufficient for them. They began to take everybody at hand, without exception, and put them in hermetically sealed buses, in which they induced a lethal gas. The victims were dead by the time they arrived at the previously prepared cavities in

Litovka. The murderers spared the chairman of the Judenrat Chaim Azikovich and the medical personnel, who were at the time in the Ghetto, and transferred them to the court buildings. All others perished, about 2500 Jews from Novogrudok, Karelich, Iveniec, Rubishevich and Naliboki. On Saturday morning some of the people that were hiding since Thursday started coming out, because they could not survive longer without air and water. Luckily that morning all the wild beasts in brown shirts had left the town. The gendarmes and the Belarus police conducted all Jews from Peresike to the court buildings and were well paid for that. However, the Jews who left the hiding places in the afternoon were taken to jail. The murderers have also conducted a selection of the Jews who were working in the military barracks. The Jews who were on their list were locked up in a barn and were well guarded by the Estonians. The remaining Jews were taken back to the Ghetto, where they perished together with the rest.

Three days after the action they brought back to the court houses the survivors from the barracks and from Zetl. The build up in the court buildings was indescribable. All had to fit into the old, small buildings, because the new court building was outside the fence. It was becoming obvious that only a part of the prisoners, probably the tradesmen, would remain in the court buildings. Everyone was trying to become a tradesman. Some believed that the tradesmen would survive. A few days later they assembled all Jews who were in the court houses in the yard. All were made to sit on the floor. The tradesmen remained in the yard. Some people, who still had gold, paid the Belarus manager and became tradesmen with the hope of remaining in the court houses.

All the others were sent to Peresike to the reduced Ghetto. About 500 Jews remained in the court houses and about the same number were in the Ghetto. The workshops were in the old court buildings. The workers lived in the smaller houses. The quarters were very congested. Three tiered beds were built. There was no room to sit or stand. One had to go straight from the door to the bed. The food consisted of a quarter kilo bread and a little soup per day. The place was closed. There were several rows of barbwire and a guard of Belarus police. There was no water in the court houses. Every morning, before work, the Belarus police led a party to fetch water from a pump. People were using the opportunity, while fetching water, to get some food from the gentiles in exchange for clothing. The food was hidden in the water barrels.

The Jews of Peresike were divided by the savages in closed groups. A guard would lead them to work and bring them back. They were in a somewhat better situation in regard to food, because they worked the whole day in town outside the Ghetto and could exchange whatever they had for food. The doctors were accommodated in a house in town next to the ambulatoriums [?] for the non-Jewish patients [the doctors were accommodated in the lower ground floor of the city hospital in Slonimska street] and were under supervision. With the doctors were a few pharmacists and young Leizerowski.

After a while, when they realised that they would be treated like all other Jews, the doctors escaped one night. They made their way outside the town, but they were caught and shot on the spot. [This is not true. Most doctors survived in the partisan groups etc.]

Some Jews who worked in the timber mill did not return to the Ghetto at the time of the second slaughter. They hid among the boards. A farmer informed the Germans. They were caught and killed.

At that time contact was made with the Bielski brothers from Stankiewicz, who were hiding in the forests near their village since the beginning of the German occupation. Everyone was certain that no Jews would be spared, no one would survive. The young and healthy people started to escape from the Ghetto to the Bielskis.

It was easier to escape from the Ghetto in Peresike, because they worked every day outside the Ghetto. It was also easier to escape at night because the Ghetto had a timber fence around it. It was possible to tear off a board from the fence and escape. To be able to escape from the Ghetto in the court houses it was necessary to transfer firstly to the Peresike Ghetto. There were many unsuccessful attempts to escape and many victims.

The life was unbearable. On one occasion, on an evening, several Polish youths, who were working for the Germans, started shooting at the court buildings. On that occasion we could not wait for the night to end. Some were afraid that the end had come.

A few months later there was another selection of Jews from the court houses that the Germans were not satisfied with. As a punishment they were transferred to Peresike. This was a sign that the Germans were preparing for the liquidation of the Peresike Ghetto. This, indeed, did happen. On the 4th of February 1943 the bandits conducted a slaughter at the Peresike Ghetto. No one, except for 2 or 3 people who hid in a bunker, remained alive. They took the victims to the place of the second slaughter and shot them.

In the court house, the head of the workshops and the boss over the Jews and their property, Reuter had thought of a new trick to mislead his Jews. He produced an alleged list of his better workers, who would receive each day an additional portion of bread. This was, however a trap to kill all the ordinary workers ,which occurred on the 7th of May

1943. On that day they lined up all Jews in the yard who were listed to be given additional rations of bread and sent them to a workshop to fetch the bread. The others were taken to a large hollow not far from the court house and shot. In that action 250 Jews were killed.

[Page 257]

The Fifty-Two Martyrs

By Yehuda Slutzki

Translated from Hebrew by Aviva Kamil

Yudl Slucki served as a fighter in the Bielski detachment. Mobilized in the Red army in July 1944, he fought bravely against the enemy. In 1946 he reached Palestine where he fought for the establishment of the State of Israel. He died in Tel Aviv in 1999.

It was Saturday the 26 of July 1941. In the morning there were frightening rumours circulating in town. We thought that it would be an opportune time to clean the streets. Jewish policemen went from house to house and urged us to assemble in the market square and told us that by doing so we would avoid a general slaughter. My father, David Slutzki Hey.yod.dalet (God will avenge his blood), prayed the Morning Prayer at the Breslin house of our neighbour. I hid in the garden of my friend Halperin, and my brother Mulik was at home. After we heard that we had to assemble in the market square we returned home and all three of us went their . When we reached the market we saw that it was full of people and was encircled by armed Germans. We understood immediately that we were facing a grave danger.

We were ordered to stand in lines along the market square. The Germans started the selection, sending people to either the right or to the left. Age was not the main consideration of the German selector when making his decision; it depended on his whim as to who would be sent to death and who would remain alive.

We were arranged in two groups. There was a rumour that we were to be taken to work somewhere, but soon enough we realised that this was a false rumour. The Germans ran around us like predatory animals and wildly screamed their orders. After the selection they separated 50 people, among them my father and brother, and stood them aside. I remained with those who stood on the other side of the market, close to those selected.

One of the Germans, apparently the commander, gave a 'speech', I did not understand him, I was stunned. His voice was that of a menacing animal.

At the end of the 'speech' the Germans took out ten people from the group of fifty, and positioned them opposite ten Germans and to the order of 'Feuer' they shot them. Then they took another ten. In that way they murdered all fifty. There were a few who tried to escape from the market place, among them I remember the teacher Solomon. The Germans, who stood in a chain around us shot him. The rest of us, who watched the atrocities, that terrible disaster, thought that our end was near, and that we also would go the same way as the others. But the Germans ordered us to go to the 'Judenrat' where we were given spades. Carts were brought to the market and we put our dead on them, brought them to the Jewish cemetery and buried them in a Brothers' grave.

I remember one detail: one of the fifty was still alive, he asked us to put him on top, he thought that he would be saved that way, but one of the Poles overheard him and attracted the attention of a German, who shot him again.

In the cemetery, we were terrified that the Germans would shoot us too following the burial. They 'only' beat us brutally, but did not kill us.

That black day came to a close at twilight. In the cemetery near the Brothers' grave I said good-bye forever to my father and brother without even saying 'Kadish' for fear of the Germans around us. Beaten, we returned from the cemetery. The martyrs' blood that was spilt on the ground was washed away by Jewish women, who were brought to the market place after the murders.

[Page 258]

The Slaughter

by Eshke Shor Levin

Translated from Yiddish by O. Delatycki

Those who survived the first slaughter did so each in his own way. I was at the time 15 years old. It was a Friday in December 1941. I was working in the court house grading potatoes. When I went home through the Shloss [Castel] Street, I noticed an announcement which said that Jews were prohibited to go beyond the town's limits. They must remain in their homes. I went home quickly and told my mother and my older brother Isroel about it. My father and younger brother Aron had not return as yet from work. My older brother had recently had a shocking experience. He, together with some young men, was sent to lead cows to Baranovichi. On the way they stopped in Horodyshch where he went to visit an uncle. On the way back he wanted to call in to see uncle again. Unfortunately almost all Jews of the town, except for a few, were dead. He returned to Novogrudok three days later. Isroel said to mother that as soon as father and the younger brother would come back, the three of them should escape to the village Stankevichi, where there lived an uncle and aunt with their family. When father and the brother came back the brothers dress warmly and departed. We promised to follow them. The brothers stopped in Ravniki to wait for us. Unfortunately, when we left the house two hours later we could not leave the town, because Belarus policemen were patrolling the outskirts of the town and we could not go further. My brothers waited for us until Saturday morning. At 5 o'clock they started on their way to Stankevichi, but two Belarus policemen stopped them and transferred them to the Germans. They were shot by the Germans and their bodies were thrown in a pit. The Germans shot also a passing dog and tossed him into the same pit. The older brother Isroel was 18 years old and Aron was 14. My father and I dug out their bones after the war and buried them in Israel. The rest of the family which included my two younger sisters, who were 6 and 10 years old, was taken to the court house. My mother, though she knew the likely outcome, urged each of us to look after ourselves and try to survive, so that at least some member of the family may remain alive and remember. Urged on by mother, I started to look for a way to save myself. My first thought was to pretend that I was dead, but I saw that they shot a girl from Baranovichi, and had loaded her dead body onto a truck, which was taking people to be shot. I changed my plan. I pleaded with them to let us live because father was a bookbinder. I was hoarse from my shouting, but nobody listened. I said to the family to let us try to delay our departure on the trucks.

Half an hour later the chief of staff arrived. He saved the furriers who had worked for him. At that moment I took on courage and walked over to the chief of staff. Acting like a child, I put my arms around him and asked him to let us live because my father was a bookbinder, and he would be useful. He answered that they could use father. I turned to my family and told them that they will let us live. A couple that stood close by me asked me to tell the Germans that they were my parents, because my parent would not hear me. They were probably right, but at that moment a miracle happened. The chief of staff said in a loud voice 'Bookbinder, come here!' A silence ensued. My father was totally disoriented with the change in events and came over without my mother and sisters. The man who was organising the slaughter noticed the confusion, came over and hit my father with the butt of his revolver. My father bled profusely. Having seen that, the chief of staff sent a German soldier to take us into the court building, where those who were left to live were assembled. On the way to the court building I tried to kiss the German who was leading us and I asked him to save my mother and the children, but with no result. A second German saw me and was shouting 'Rassenschande! You will be shot, you Jew'. This brought my hope to save the rest of my family to an end. We were taken to the door of the court house, where the Jews, seeing the condition of my father, were reluctant to let us in. Apart from us nobody from the court yard was saved. [But see the story of the furriers above. See also p.299 'How I survived'.]

[Page 259]

The First Slaughter

by Sima Yanos-Portnoy

Translated from Yiddish by O. Delatycki

It happened on the 5 December 1941 on a cold winter morning. The earth was covered with a white blanket of new snow. All men and women who were able to work assembled, as ever, at 6 AM, ready to go to their jobs in various parts of the town. The place of the assembly was next to the Judenrat, which was on Kabak's land (which was the surname of the owners). All those assembled had divided in groups and were waiting for their escort. Our escort was Mojshke Miller. We were working in the military barracks about 4 km from town. We walked to work on the highway singing, with no military or police accompanying us. Mojshke was leading us. But this time it was different. Kabak's land was surrounded by armed gendarmes with the rifles aimed at us. Every group of workers was conducted to their place of work by a guard of a few dozen Belorussian policemen and gendarmes. This is how we arrived in the barracks. In the court yard they divided us in groups. Each group was sent to their place of work. We were warned not to hang about the barracks and not to walk to buildings other than the one we were working in. The whole day there was a strange silence in the barracks, as a quiet before a storm. There was no usual singing heard from the building where men and women were working. Suddenly there was ringing of a bell, which interrupted the quiet. We were all waiting for it, because it announced our lunch. This time nobody walked to the room where we ate, we ran. Everybody assembled in the room except for Mojshke Miller, who was usually the first. Today he was missing, and that increased everybody's curiosity. We were anxious to know what was happening in town and in our homes. We did not have to wait long. The door opened and Mojshke, pale with his head down, appeared. The room was suddenly quiet. Everybody's eyes were turned in his direction. But Mojshke had nothing to say. He only knew that something was going on in the wood next to the barracks. The forest, which was usually quite, was filled with sounds of picks and axes felling the trees and digging the earth. Many men were working in the wood, but nobody knew of the purpose of their work. Mojshke told us that he saw several wagonloads of axes, picks and shovels on the way to the wood. He was looking for a possibility of contacting the people in town, but this was not possible. Suddenly we heard the marching of feet. We all ran to the windows. A group of Poles with shovels, axes and picks were marching to a song. The looked at us and smiled. Some even laughed loudly. As they passed our windows, some were making signs in the direction of the woods and were laughing. Others, however, were marching past with their heads down, as if they did not want to meet our eyes. Mojshke went out to speak to them. His aim was to find out something from an acquaintance. We remained in the room. There was silence in the room. Nobody thought of work. Everybody thought of the families at home. We were watching the door with impatience. Some minutes have passed. They felt like hours. Mojshke was back, but he had no news. He was told by the workers that they were preparing pits and they thought that they were for the prisoners in jail. A little time later a group of Jews and non-Jews surrounded by soldiers and Belorussian police marched past in the direction of the forest. Some time later some shooting was heard, followed by a silence. Soon after we heard the footsteps of the soldiers, who conducted the prisoners. One thought did not leave our mind – how is it possible that for such a small number of prisoners 150 diggers were required. Mojshke went away again. Though the lunch break had long since finished, nobody came to tell us to return to work. Shortly thereafter, Mojshke arrived and took me and two other girls to his room. He told us that only we could find out what is happening at home. He asked: are you ready to do it? We undertook the mission gladly, though we knew that escaping back to town would be very dangerous. To go to town in working hours was punishable by death. We started immediately. The snow in the fields was covered by a layer of ice and it was very slippery. Walking on the highway was much easier, but we preferred to walk in the field because it was much safer to do so. We were running on the ice. We fell frequently and our feet were bloodied. Often, to avoid something suspicious on the horizon, we had to crawl on our stomachs and hide behind a bush. As soon as we could we resumed walking. It was difficult to know how long it took us to get to Kabak's land. We came tired and sweaty to the Judenrat. As soon as we opened the door we were met by Kabak, one of the leaders of the community. He saw us running in the fields. Without asking what happened he met us with some Russian swear words. "Where did you come from? You were at work!" He shouted. And when I told him that we were sent by Mojshke Miller to tell them what we have heard and seen in the barracks, he slapped my face. He told me to be quiet and not to raise a panic. At that moment somebody arrived from town. When he saw us he exclaimed, "Why are you sitting here? Go and see what is happening in town. All the walls are covered in large posters. They are creating for us camps, but only for those able to work. And what will happen to the rest of us? It is also prohibited to leave our dwellings from 6 this evening till tomorrow morning." And added whilst sobbing "And anyone caught after hours will be shot".

All this happened on a Friday. The news made a great impression on Kabak. He asked us to get into the house, to sit down and rest. He went out and came back with some water. He mast have noticed that I was on the point of collapse. He left us and went to another room to retell all he heard. We did not have to wait long. The door opened and Mojshke Izraelit entered. He looked troubled by what he was told. He said to me: "Sima, I know you well and I can depend on you. You still have work to do. Each of you should go in the direction of your house. Tell everybody you pass what you told us. Don't overlook a single house. We were on our way before he finished speaking. The streets I walked through were empty. A copious snowfall covered everything in a white blanket. The first house I entered belonged to Mojshke Izraelit. His wife met me. I told here in a few words the horrible news and a ran further. The next house belonged to the family Shteinberg. As I entered I met Chane Shteinberg. She was feeding her two daughters. I repeated my story and asked her to contact the verger of the synagogue in which her family prayed. By the time a visited a few more houses it was very late. At home they were waiting for me anxiously. They were very worried. I told them everything, but it was too late to do anything. We could only stay at home and see what tomorrow would bring. There was a silence in the house. The Sabbath candles were providing the only pale illumination. Suddenly a wild cry penetrated the still of the night. Somebody was running outside of our window. Suddenly there was a shot followed by rapid steps. We jumped up from our seats as if were pursued by somebody. We opened the front door and ran outside, not thinking of the danger. We crossed the street and went to the house of our friends. They were frightened by our appearance. They told us to run quickly back to our home. We walked quietly back whilst looking around. After we got safely back, we heard again steps and shots. We locked the front door, returned to our seats and remained sitting as if mesmerised. We were awakened by a thump on the front door. My sister went to the door. We heard a command to open the door or else they will shoot. They spoke Polish. When we opened the door three Polish youths with rifles in their hands pushed their way in. They looked at our pale faces and the humble surroundings with ironic smirks and shouted "have you strangers here" and without waiting for a reply, screamed, "we will be back, and if we will find here strangers you will all be shot like dogs". One of them held a fur coat. He said with a smile "a Jew woman lost it while she tried to run away, pity that our bullets did not catch her". With those words they left the room. We locked the room. At that moment we were sized by a panic and we shook like a leaf. Every sound from the street made us fear that the Poles had returned. I don't know how long we were anxiously sitting that night. A knock on the door woke us up. A pale sun was shining through the windows. I opened the door. It was Gershonovski, a member of the Judenrat. He came in and behind him came two gendarmes. He set at the table, took out a long list and started reading. The two gendarmes stood by the door. He read a long tale. At the end he read out the names of my sister Nusia, her husband Shmuel and my brother Lon'ke. He told them to take food for three days and go to the buildings of the district court. When they asked what will happen to me he answered with a shout "she will remain here, in the house till they will come to fetch her". My sister and my brother-in-law began asking him to do something to make it possible for me to join them. He did not answer. My brother started speaking German to not create a suspicion of the gendarmes. But he did not budge. At that moment one of the gendarmes came over to him, pushed him aside, grabbed the list from him and added my name. "Dummer kerl" [silly man] he said to the member of the Judenrat, "she could (be assumed to) be your wife", he added, pointing at my brother. They left us and we started packing a few belongings. We took them and some food and left the house. It was a frosty morning, everything around us was white. The street was silent, one can only hear the creak of the shoes on the snow. Every now and then one could see some people with packages on their shoulders. We were living at the time in Peresike. The closer we got to the town the more people we saw in the streets. Some had packages on their shoulders, others pulled a packed sledge. Some even took a small table, others a folding bed. A dense pack of old and young women and children were moving to the district court buildings. The walking were surrounded by soldiers with helmets and rifles. Dozens of trucks followed the ill-treated Jews. Music was playing and photographers were taking photos right, left and center. One could hear crying of children and wheezing of old women. The walk continued without an end. It seemed that the notice specifying people able to work was overlooked. Everybody was in the long march, young and old, able-bodied and sick. Everybody concluded that to stay back meant death. Walking gave a hope of life. It took many hours till all arrived at the appointed place. There everything was filled to the brim. There was no room for the people who came, and definitely not for the packages that were dragged in. We were pushed one on top of the other. The cries of the children and the groans of the old were intermingled with the shouts of the German soldiers, who were trying to push everybody into the inadequate space. They were shouting, cursing, hitting and shooting. People were dying like flies. Suddenly a bang was heard and the dense crowd pressed forward. It would appear that a fence which was surrounding the ground was broken. By 10 o'clock at night all were in the buildings. Somehow families managed to keep together. Children tired out by the ordeal were asleep. Early on Sunday morning, when it was still dark, I was called to go to work in the barracks. Outside I saw groups which were ready to be taken away. After work, instead of taking us back to the court buildings to rejoin our families, we were divided into groups of women and men and taken to separate buildings. The doors were closed to prevent us leaving. It turned out that the SS man who was in charge of our working party made the arrangements to try and save us. Next day they told us that after work we would be taken back to the court buildings. But when we were not allowed to have, as usual, breakfast before work, we knew that something was wrong. We were very disturbed. Each of us had somebody in the court buildings, someone a wife with children, somebody else a brother, a sister, a mother, or a father. We were all disturbed and wanted to go back. Every hour seemed like a year. We moved aimlessly from room to room. We tried to think of a way to communicate with the men, to try to find out if there were news from town. About 12 o'clock, Jasha Leizerowski arrived. He told us that he and Mojshke Miller were looking for a way of contacting our superior Stabs lieutenant Reuter. But they were as yet unsuccessful. They contacted the head of the barracks. After a long discussion he promised to provide a military escort to take us to our families. Jasha left, but promised to return when he had news. We were sitting in a dark locked room till 6 o'clock at night without food. Only then were we taken under a strong guard back to the district court. On the way Mojshke told us that he had succeeded in contacting the head of the barracks. However, the head asked him to use his influence to keep us quiet and remain where we were until he would send for us. He could not explain why he was of the opinion that this would be better for us. When Moshke kept insisting, he shouted in the telephone "verfluchte Juden" and put down the receiver. It seemed that it was only now that he sent the military to take us back. We arrived at the yard of the court house at 8 in the evening. It was dark and peaceful all around. A faint light shone from some windows. There was a strong guard patrolling the surroundings of the buildings. The guard conducted each of us to the room were our families were. Having come into the room where my family was. I did not notice any changes. The room was stuffy and noisy. All sat on their bundles and argued loudly. All from the district court and the people who remained in town were assembled in the building of the Polish Nazaritanki school. All women and children were taken, even from the building of Judenrat, where their husbands were removed in the first days after the Germans arrived. The whole night we sat and talked about all we had heard. With the first light we were told that our troubles are only starting. It is difficult to describe what happened next. Old men were shaving their beards, women were painting their hair using coal and thir lips with red paint to try to look younger. There were battles to acquire a man, because of the rumour that single women would be first to be killed. But not every bachelor wanted a woman. The commotion continued till the morning. On Monday they led out every group separately, each family together into a big room. There was a commission of three people. The Gebiets kommissar Traub with his two deputies started the selection. Each person had to open their mouth to show their teeth. Each person had to state his occupation. At that point, Traub would indicate if the person was to go to the left or to the right, which is to die or to live. Those ordered to the left had to deposit all their possessions in a large box as they were leaving the room,. Our family was among the last. We stood the whole time at the window and saw all that occurred outside. Trucks were prepared. Each group as they appeared, was dragged like sacks to the truck. They unfortunate victims were abusing the murderers, shaking their fists and shouting "don't imagine that you will not pay for this". To us they shouted "you will live, take vengeance for us". At that moment I saw the wife of Krantz with her son and daughter and some other women. All of a sudden they started to dance on the trucks. They probably became deranged from fear. One truck after another was moving off. The selection continued till 4 in the afternoon. We went through the same procedure as the others, but somehow we remained alive. We sat till Tuesday morning, when they collected all men and took them to Peresike to prepare a camp for the survivors.

[Page 263]

Slaughters

by Chaim Kraviets

Translated from Yiddish by O. Delatycki

I worked in my trade for the Russians in the "Gospishchpromtorg" [State Food Industrial Commerce]. I was delivering meat from the slaughter house. When the Russians started retreating, everyone tried to snatch something. I kept the horse I used in my work and I left for my parent's home.

I said to my mother OBM "Mother, I will run away to Russia. Who wants to go with me?" My brother Hertzl replied "I am going with you." But my mother said "My children, it was a great hardship to bring you up, and now, in my old age I may have to depend on help from strangers. Chaimke, my son, don't punish me. If it will be our fate to die, lets die together." I obeyed my parents and I did not run away. I left the horse to have a feed in the field. I put a chain around its neck and fastened the chain to the ground. I said to my family "We will remain here. They say that the enemy is closing in on Minsk." Next morning I could see some people standing next to the horse. I ran over to them. To my astonishment, they were the murderous Germans. I came over and I told them that I have a family with a father and mother and I need the horse to nourish them. "Don't take it away. It is our sustenance." I begged them. "Are you a Jew?" they asked me. I said that I was. Without hesitation they gave me a beating. Now I knew how we stood. I wanted to get away, but they did not let me. They told me to untie the horse and come with them. They told me that they will give me in exchange another horse. They took me to the Cemetery lane. Their headquarters and transport offices were there. They were camping in a big orchard. They passed me on to another murderer. He said to me "Du verfluchter Jude. You wanted to have a war. I will show you what a war means". I thought "Here I am, I wanted a horse to help my parents and this will be my end. I will never see my family again." He put me to work. I had to pull by hand grass to feed the horses. I had no option and I started working. I pulled a bundle of grass and fed four horses. I was returning with the escort to pull more grass. When I returned with the new bundle, the first bundle was eaten. At that stage the Germans had shown their true face. One of them took a leather belt and started beating me. It felt as if my bones were made of rubber. They kept it up. One of them said to me: "You must work faster. When the last horse begins eating, the first horse must still have grass to eat." He hit me with his boot and shouted: "Work quicker". I was so severely beaten that I felt nothing. I was pulling the grass and they continued beating me all over my body. I heard somebody say: [in broken Polish/Russian] 'serves you right, you Jew". They were two Poles. The German asked me: "who are they?". Without hesitation I answered: "Jews". "Jews?" asked the German in astonishment, "come quickly here". The two argued that they were Poles. The German asked me: "what are they saying?" I had nothing to lose: 'they say that they would like to help me pull grass". They were made to do the work and received the same treatment as I. They kept saying "Not Jews, Poles." But the barbarian payed no attention and kept up the beating. As it happened, a German who spoke Polish was passing by. The Poles turned to him and told him that they were Poles and not Jews. The German told our escort to release the Poles and pay them for their work. I was barely able to stand on my feet. A German called Hans approached us. He said to my escort: "when you will finish with the Jew give him to me". By then it was two o'clock. I was in pain all over and hungry. The escort took me to Hans and said: "Here is the Jew". Hans showed me a black caldron and said to me: 'this must be polished clean". He sat himself next to a tree and started polishing his saddle. Two loaves of bread were laying on the tree. I asked him: "May I have a piece of bread?" At that moment his horses came to the tree and ate the bread. When he saw that, Hans cried: "My supper". He decided that he would shoot me. He put me up against a tree. I said to him "It is not my fault". I was lucky that I got off with a beating. I was sent with an escort to fetch water for washing the caldron. The water pump was at the cemetery. I had to go there and back several times, but he kept shouting that the caldron was dirty. The escort got tired walking me back and forth and said: "Go by yourself and make it quick". I went to the water well and from there I crawled into the bushes, having left the bucket at the well. In fear, I managed to escape home. I was unrecognisable, because I was black from the beating I received. I was filled with fear: I was afraid that they would come to fetch me, because they knew where they took me from. I had to hide. Next morning they came from the Judenrat to take us to work. Everyone had to return to his previous work and his name had to be entered on a list. I told them: "I am already on their list" and I showed them my body. They did not answer, gave a deep sigh and one said to the other "let's go". From then on I was careful.

In the forest

I heard that they were looking for people to work in the forest. I was glad to go to the forest because there I would not see the faces of the murderers and the workers would receive a bread ration. Kushe

Nochimovski and his son Hertzl worked with me. Kushe found it hard to split the timber and his son was a boy. I was helping them and they gave me some of their food ration. We worked together for a while.

The 100

One day after work I went to the Judenrat to get my ration of bread. Sholem Lubchanski appeared suddenly. He was out of breath. He said: "Do me a favour, we received an order that we should provide 100 persons for work and only 98 turned up. Come with me". I answered him: "How can you expect that from me. I have just returned from a day's work. Recruit those who did not work today". He did not answer, went into the Judenrat and said to the bookkeeper Pressman: "I can not find 2 persons". Pressman answered: "Come on, I will come with you. Now you have 99". Sholem said: "I am coming too".

They had to assemble in front of the jail in Slonim Street. When they came they counted 100 persons. The doors of the jail opened and the jailers pushed them into the jail using sticks. They were never heard of again.

After the war in 1945 I was in Lodz [a large town in Poland]. I met by a chance an ex policeman Gancik, who was at the time the chief of the jail. He told me the following: when he saw Sholem Lubchanski among the hundred he said to him: "How come you are here. This group will be shot tonight. You get out. I will let you out and you bring me somebody else as a replacement. It can be even the 'scarecrow" [the nickname of the feeble minded water carrier], but I have to have the right number. Lubchanski answered: "No, if that is my fate, I don't want anyone to replace me". (the policeman respected Lubchanski because he fought in the first World War in the Polish legions). At two o'clock in the morning a death squad arrived with machine guns and the prisoners were told to undress. When Lubchanski realized that Gancik told him the truth, he turned to him and asked him to save him. But Gancik told him that it was too late.

There were many such occurrences. The Germans would say that they were looking for workers, but they used to shoot all assembled. The unhappy families believed that their relative was sent somewhere to work. The wives used to talk. One wife would say that she heard that on the highway to Horodyszcz our people were working. The other heard of our people were working on the Korelichy highway. The wives would have parcels prepared to send to their husbands. But it was all in vain. Their husbands were shot on the first night after the arrest in the shrubs around Skrydlevo. The women waited for the time when they would share the fate of their husbands.

The slaughter in Horodyszcz

An order was given that the Jews must relinquish their cows. The first consignment of cows that was exacted from the Jews was taken to Baranowicz by several Jews including my brother Berl. A non-Jew was in charge. When they passed Horodyszcz they saw lorries taking Jews to be slaughtered. We had in Horodyszcz a big family: two sisters of my mother and cousins. My brother Berl had a chance to farewell the cousins, because, as they were led to the lorries, the road was blocked by the cows. They could see each other well. They only bowed their heads. They were told that they are being taken to work. As Berl was walking back from Baranowicz, he saw that most of the Jewish population was missing. Only a few Jews were held in the Ghetto. No one could get near them. When he returned to Novogrudok he told the parents that Horodyszcz was finished. Mother cried uncontrollably. She had in Horodyszcz a large family. My father said: "Let us all pray, some of us have gone earlier the others will follow later. You are crying for them. Who will cry for us?" My mother cried: "My sons wanted to go to Russia and I opposed it. It is my fault. If they had run away they would be safe. And now, because of me they will perish". I arrived in time to hear mother speak. When my mother saw me she kept on repeating that it was her fault that we did not escape. "My children, a fire from hell is burning around us. The murderers will finish us", she kept on repeating. I was very sad to hear the news and I tried to appease my parents.

Running cows to Baranowicz

I asked my brother Berl: 'tell me how you were treated on the way to Baranowicz, because tomorrow I am going to do it." He was trying to mollify me and told me that the work was not fearfully bad. In the morning I went with other Jews to Baranowicz, where we arrived safely. We saw there terrible things. Prisoners of war were led from work. On the side of the road women were standing with parcels in their hands. They cried "Our children are somewhere in the same situation. Maybe another mother will have pity on them". They were tossing parcels to the prisoners. The Germans were preventing them from doing so. If a prisoner stepped out of the ranks to catch a parcel he was punished or shot. The women who were tossing the parcels were also maltreated. At times the Germans shot at them. We saw it all. In that moment we were even more afraid. With luck we got to the railway station. Next to the station were big military barracks. Our foreman reported to the senior murderer that we brought a transport of cows. The German sent the prisoners of war to load the cattle into the rail trucks. The sight of the prisoners frightened us – they all looked like skeletons. They walked with difficulty. As they got to the cows they fell to their udders and sucked the milk. Their guards were pushing them away and beating them. They made them load the cows into the carriages. At that moment we had an opportunity to give the prisoners pieces of bread. We did it, though we knew that we had a long way to go back and not sufficient food for our journey.

We were told that we can now return home. We had to be careful on our way back to arrive safely. My family was very happy to see me back. I returned to my job in the forest. I was happy that I would not have to look at the faces of the murderers. And so some time passed.

The first slaughter

The murderers had decided to erase Novogrudok. One day a non-Jewish neighbour approached me. He was digging graves in Skridlewo. He said: 'they are going to kill you all. We are digging graves for the Jews. Many Gestapo soldiers had arrived". My wife OBM said "You run away. They will not touch women and children". This was the 16th day of Kislev. The snow was piled up high. The roads and fields were impassable. I thought that I would ask my parent's advice. As I approached, I noticed that in front of their house was a guard. I went in to the house of Itzchok Nochimovski (Factornik). He was a learned Jew, whose advice would be of value. I told him what was in store for us: they were digging graves and many murderers were arriving. He said: "My advice is to run". In his house were his two sons: Jankl with his wife and six children and Motke. Their father said: "Jankl, Motke, run." Jankl answered: "What will I do with my wife and children". "Run" answered Reb Itzchok "later will be to late". I returned home and said to my wife "Get dressed and we will run". "How can we run in the fields with a small child in the deep snow?" answered my wife, "you run, they are looking for men". There was no time to waste and I said farewell to my wife and one year old son and I ran. With me came my brother Berl and Reb Itzchok's Jankl and Motke.

The death of Reb Itschok Nochimovski and his daughter

As soon as we came onto the field and started to walk on the snow we were noticed by the guard, who started shooting at us. We were close to the house of Nochimovski. When he heard the shooting he came out to see if they were shooting at us. At that moment a German approached him and shot him. His daughter Sonia started to shout 'they are shooting at our father". As soon as she opened the door the German shot her to. Nobody else ventured outside.

Next day, it was a Sabbath, the Jewish population was herded in the court buildings and the bodies of Reb Itzchok Nochimovski and his daughter were left lying in front of the house.

We were hiding in the house of a farmer. His neighbour came in and told him that the bodies of Reb Itzchok Nochimovski and his daughter were left lying in the street. Their clothing had been stripped off them and the dogs were tearing their flash. We heard it all and we felt enraged.

The farmer told us that the Germans left a few Jews alive. My brother and I went back to Novogrudok. The sons of Reb Itzchok went to Zetl, because they knew by then what happened to the rest of their family. We wanted to go back home in case some member of our family survived. We did find our brother Hertzl and sister Peshe, who was married to Hershl Friberg. Before the slaughter we were a family of 5 sisters and 4 brothers. Alas, the sister and brother who we met after the first slaughter did not survive for long. They were killed in the second slaughter. When my brother Berl and I retuned to Novogrudok we decided to part. I told him that I would go on the highway and he should go through the fields. If something untoward should happen we should not be together. And that is what we did.

When I walked next to my father's house, I saw our non-Jewish neighbours removing contents of the house. The table was carried by a neighbour who I would have never suspected capable of doing so. My heart was racing with rage, but I could not do a thing. Later, when I was a partisan in the forests, I and my cousin Josef Borecki have evened the account with this neighbour. We left him alive, but he could not sit at the table ever again. We spared him so that he could tell everyone that one can not spill Jewish blood and remain unpunished.

Back in the Ghetto

In the Waliker street Jews were riding on German horses. With them was a supervisor. Michl Lejbovich took care of two horses. When he noticed me he said: "you can ride on one of the horses and you will be able to slip into the Ghetto". As we were riding he told me of horrible tragedies. I was siting on the horse stock-still. I entered the Ghetto with the other workers. I could not find a place to sleep. I went to the Jewish police to ask them where I could sleep. They told me that I could sleep anywhere I could find a space. I wanted to be close to my last sister, who, as it turned out, had only a short time to live. There were three levels of racks, but everyone was occupied. But there were very kind hearted people and they helped me. They were: Judl Lewin, Isrolik Jankelewicz, Jankl Angelewicz, his wife Chana and Zamkowy with his wife and son. They allowed me to put a bed in the kitchen. This was a very noble thing to do, because the kitchen was used in shifts through the night. I will never forget the goodness of Mrs Angelewicz and Mrs Zamkowy. The help given to me and my brother (who in the mean time also came into the Ghetto) can never be forgotten. Chana Angelewicz would give us a portion of her food. We were reluctant to accept it, because she too did not have food to spare, but she insisted. She told us: "Please don't worry. If you will be able to get some food you will share it with me. You came into the Ghetto with nothing." My sister Peshe had a six month old baby and I wanted to help her too. But I had nothing, I had not even a shirt to change, nor had my brother. Mrs Angelewicz said to us; "Don't be ashamed, take of at night your shirts and I will wash them." She would help every needy person. I implore you, remember for ever the names of Mrs Angelewicz and her husband. People would say to Angelewicz: "Look, Jankl, your wife does not look well, she does not sleep at night." But Jankl used to answer: "Never mind, if we will survive, the people will return the favour." He was never angry. If he would find a butt he would give it to us. He did not smoke. He told me how to obtain a shirt. "Dovid Tabakovski is sorting clothing left from the dead in Kowalski street at the nuns. Every day he is going with others to sort the clothing and if you will ask him he will arrange it." I followed Jankl's advice. I spoke to Dovid Tabakovski. I asked him: 'take me with you for two days, so that I will be able to take some undergarments for me and my brother." He replied: "Wait for me at the gate tomorrow morning, I will take you with me." Next morning I went with him. My first task was to change my underwear. When I had a look around I shuddered. Everywhere were parcels of the best clothing. People took with them their best possessions when they were leaving their homes, because they did not know that they were going to be exterminated. All this had to be sorted for the Germans. I went into a corner to change my underwear. As I was getting dressed I saw a German looking at me. He asked me: "What are you doing here Jude." I was scared to death and I answered that something fell into my boot and I was removing it. "Be quick about it verfluchter Jude" he muttered and he hit me in my face. I was glad that I got away with a small punishment. I went back to work. I was content that I had on me two sets of underwear for me and for my brother. I was looking for something else to take to use as a bed sheet. Rummaging among the clothing I found my fathers bag for his Tfiln. On the bag was father's name, surname and his date of birth. I froze. After that I did not need anything any more. I only took the Tfiln bag back with me to the Ghetto.

Smuggling meat into the Ghetto

I had to begin to think how to obtain food. Lebke Lis was a hero. He managed to trade in the Ghetto. He told me: "Why did you let yourself go? Come with me. I know of a farmer who has a cow, which he wants to sell." We got out of the Ghetto at night. We got to the farm, purchased the cow and slaughtered it on the spot. The farmer gave us his horse and cart to take the meat back to the Ghetto. When we got to the boundary of the Ghetto we started tossing the meat over the fence. We heard a call "Halt". Lis said to me "Let's run". I answered that if we run the policeman will shoot at us. "Let us stand still" I said. And he agreed. A policeman approached us and told us to raise our hands and asked us what we were carrying. We told him that we had a piece of meat. I started to appeal to his conscience. And with luck we got away with it. Naturally we had to pay for it, but we were happy to survive. We lived through a frightening moment, but if we did not risk it, people would die of starvation. This was not the only time we risked our necks.

Before the second slaughter

People were brought from Lubch, Karelicz, Iwieniec, Nalibok and some other towns. The luggage, which the Germans permitted the Jews to take, came on horse driven carts. When the people arrived at the Novogrudok Ghetto in Pereseka they were very depressed and afraid. They were exhausted from the trip. An order was given to collect the luggage from the carts, but the farmers decided on the way on a requisition. Everything that the farmers liked they kept. As I was passing by I heard a woman with two children begging a farmer: "please give it back to me, as you can see, this is all I have got". The farmer did not listen to her and hit her with the whip. The children were crying: "Mother, lets go". The same was happening on the next cart. My heart was aching. I thought "no matter what the consequences would be, I must speak to the man in charge". This is what I have done. He asked me where did it happened. I showed him the farmer. He walked over to him and gave him a beating. Seeing it, the other farmers stepped back from their carts and all possessions were recovered.

New punishments were devised. The Germans with the police were standing at the gates of the Ghetto and were waiting for the workers to return. They were looking for people wearing high boots. They took them to one side and told them to take off the boots. People were entreating: they will remain barefoot. In answer they were beaten. One man wearing boots, Jeshye Kevelevicz, was smart – he cut of the uppers. Later he laughed – "you should be wise to them". Having seen all the punishments I decided to flee.

First attempt to flee

Before fleeing I wanted to help the family Szwarc to escape – Aron, Ester, Lilie, Dine, because Mrs Szwarc saved me in the past. She gave me a hiding place when I needed one. I discussed frequently escape with Aron Szwarc. He told me that the only place to go was the Naliboki wilderness, he knew there every bush. But it was very difficult to get there and whoever tried was caught on the way. I thought of another way. I told Lilie Szwarc, their daughter, my plan. She told me that I would be caught. "Don't do it", she said. Regardless I persisted. Over the road from the Ghetto lived the farmer Ludski. He had a horse which he kept day and night in the paddock. I slipped out from the Ghetto at twelve o'clock at night and I got to the horse. The plan was to ride the horse for about 10 km to a farmer I knew and ask him if he would be prepared to hide us when I would come to him with a few people. Obviously, we would pay for it. I took the horse and led him by the chain. I was thinking that this is wrong, somebody will hear the clanging of the chain. Ludski, who slept near by, started to shout: 'thief, stop you Jew". I had to let the chain go and run. The reflector above the Ghetto was searching, and if I would be caught in the light I would be finished. The guard was standing on the road and he shouted "Arms up". I put up my arms and started to laugh. I don't know what made me laugh at that time. The German asked me "Why do you laugh?". I could not answer him in German. His assistant, the policeman, asked me. So I told him: "He is running around and shouting that I wanted to steal his horse. What do I need a horse for, when I can not feed myself?" 'so why do you laugh?" asked the German So I told him that I was in his paddock with a girl and I frightened him and he is shouting "Catch the thief". This was translated to the German. He was interested in the girl. The policeman was pressing my leg. I knew what he meant and I promised him a reward. Ludski was chastised by the German who told the policeman to look for the girl. He told me to return quickly to the Ghetto. It is difficult to describe my feelings at that moment. At the gate I left for the policeman enough money to buy a litre of schnapps.

Escape from the Ghetto

I could not sleep that night. Next morning people were going to work knowing that on Friday there would be another slaughter. I had a word with Aronczik Szwarc and I told him of my adventures overnight. He suggested that I should hide in the cellar of the damaged house of Czyz in Sieniezyc Street. He said that he and his family would join me. I did not like the suggestion and I told him that I would go to the cellar if I could not think of a better solution. And I started to think of a more secure place. I went in to the office of the Jewish police. The policeman in charge was Meier Kafelman. He was a butcher by trade and a good man. He was trying to help everyone in any way he could. I said to him: "Meierke can you advise me what is to be done?" He answered: "Why are you afraid, only old people and children will be slaughtered, but workers will not be affected." I said: "You believe them but I don't. I want to run. I hope that you will not prevent me doing so." "Don't be silly, run, if you must. The main thing is to avoid being caught. But I think that you are foolish to risk under these conditions." I parted with him saying that I prefered to be shot from the back, rather than the front. I don't want to witness it when the old people and the children will be loaded into trucks. No, I am leaving the Ghetto. On leaving the Ghetto I met Dr Bergner [also spelled Berkman and Bergman in other articles – see p.246 "Outside of the Ghetto" by Luba Rudnicki] and Mrs Dr Ziskind. They asked me where I was going. I told them: "Where my eyes will lead me". They were allowed to go outside of the Ghetto, because, as doctors, they had a permit. I decided to walk with them to the centre of the town. I parted from them when we reached the pharmacy of Leizerowski. Above the pharmacy lived a non-Jewish woman, an acquaintance of mine. She worked for me in the past. I went up to see if she could help me. But when I opened her door I was dumb founded – a policeman sat there. The woman winked at me and I did not lose my head. I asked her for some water and I told her that I came to the pharmacy for a prescription, but I have to wait for it. The policeman invited me to sit down and have a drink. I thanked him. I was happy that he did not arrest me. I started to walk to my home in Zalatuche, where many local people that I grew up with lived. Perhaps one of them would help me hide. But where ever I went I was told the same thing: "We are afraid". Now I was sorry that I did not go to work with my sister Peshe and my brother Hertzl, who went to work in the military barracks. They were deluded. They told them that the work in the barracks was for those who were able to do the work. They will survive. My brother in law Hershl Fridberg managed to arrange a transfer to the barracks with a great deal of difficulty. I remembered that in the Soviet days I was of considerable help to a christian woman. Perhaps she will be willing to help me now? Mrs Michalski lived in Kowalewski Street and going there I met Aronczik Szwarc's daughter. She was working in the convent. I asked her what her plans were. She told me that here father was going to fetch her. I went into the house of Mrs Michalski and asked her he she would hide me for a few days till after the slaughter. Naturally she was afraid. She told me that if they would catch me in her house she and her children would also die. I started to appeal to her conscience and reminded her of what I did for her. I said: "You can see that now my life is in your hands." She did have pity on me and told me to hide in the stable. She asked me to be careful, so that no one would notice me. She said that she would bring me some food. I asked her if she would permit me to hide a girl. She agreed, but urged me to make certain that nobody should see me. I went into the convent. I was happy. I said to Lilie Szwarc to come with me quickly because I had a hiding place. "No" she told me "I have to take my father with me, without him I am not going anywhere". I told her that I would go to meet her father because there was no time to waste. She agreed. I went and saw Szwarc running towards me. I told him of my proposition and he took both my hands and said "My G-d guide you." He told me that he was going to hide in Seniezyc St in the cellar of a destroyed house. He said that if we will survive we should meet in the cellar and he ran off, because his wife and young daughter Dina were in the Ghetto. Somebody informed on them. They were taken back to the Ghetto and they shared the fate of all others. I went back, happy that Szwarc permitted me to take his daughter with me. When I told her that I had father's permission to take her to the stable, she came with me. We got into the stable without being seen. On Thursday night Mrs Michalski came into the stable and brought us food. She said that the Ghetto was surrounded. It was permitted to get into the Ghetto, but whoever would attempt to get out would be shot. She also told us that Moishe Izraelit's wife was outside the Ghetto and was looking for somewhere to hide. She was prepared to pay handsomely for a shelter, but nobody was prepared to help. She was shot in the street. Her corpse was stripped of everything. A lot of gold was sawn into her garments. Next morning Mrs Michalski brought the news that the people in the Ghetto were lying on the ground, were being raised ten at a time and loaded into trucks. The trucks were taking them in the direction of Litovka. Lunchtime she came to tell us that all was finished. In the evening she told us that the shooting had stopped. If a Jew is caught he is taken to the jail. She repeated the news on Saturday morning: they were catching Jews and taking them to the jail. I thought of staying for another few days before leaving. Suddenly, at 11 in the morning two young shepherds walked into the stable and started playing. Suddenly they decided to climb up onto the hay stack, were we where hiding. I told Lilie that they would see us, but I had a solution. I would throttle them. It would not be difficult. But Lilie did not let me do so. She said no, there was too much dying. The boys were nearly at the top of the ladder. I asked them if they had seen me go into the stable. They said that they did not. I did it to make sure that Mrs Michalski would not be accused of hiding us. We all entered the house. When she saw us she was very frightened. She was afraid that the shepherds would know that she was hiding us. But I put her mind at rest. I said: 'they saw me enter the stable without your permission". Mrs Michalski started crying and whimpering "Oh, you are going to your death, why don't you leave your watches with me". Lilie Szwarc took off her watch and gave it to her. But I did not give her mine. I told her "Perhaps my watch will still be of use to me". Before we left I asked Mrs Michalski not to let the shepherds go too soon. We removed the yellow patches and we went outside the town in the direction of Horodyszcz. Not far along the way there was a young forest and bushes. We saw from the distance that a policeman was going into the bushes with a girl. I thought that that would be our end. I said to Lilie: "Now you have to help me or we will be finished". I gave her my pocket knife and said: Hold it in your hand. If the policeman will stop us and tell us to go with him we will obey him. But we will not go far, I will attack him and I will manage to overcome him. And you stick the knife into him wherever you can". Lilie saw that that was our last chance. But the girl was our saviour. She kept kissing the policeman and asking him to leave us alone. He let us go.

We were happy. We did not go into the bushes but found another way, to try and mislead the policeman. When we were out of sight of the policeman we got back to the bushes and made our way to Nachodka, where a Jewess who converted to Christianity lived. Her name was Manie Firkes. I knew her well because she used to come to town before Pesach to work in a matzo factory. When her husband saw me he said: "You had better go, because I expect that any day they will take away my wife and the children. They are killing all descendents of Jews even to the tenth generation". We did not know that he was hiding Arie the carpenter's brother in the bushes. We stayed till the evening. Ostaszinski came and we began feeling better. Ostaszinski said: "I have a dress of my wife's. Perhaps we should go to another farmer and he may hide us for my wife's dress". We realised than that he had lost his mind. Then he said: "No. How can I give up my wife's dress when that is the only one she has. No, I must leave you and take my wife's dress back to her". And he did go off to look for his wife and his son.

I went to a friendly farmer's wife who kept us for more than three months. In that time we suffered hunger and cold and a lot of fear. But we were restless. We were anxious to find out who among us survived. We sent the farmers wife to the Ghetto in the court house. The farmers were allowed go to the Ghetto on market days and order goods to be made for them. She returned and brought us the news that from the family Szwarc nobody survived. From my family, brother Berl was alive. He was working in the saw-mill. On the next occasion she went to the saw-mill with a letter. That night he came to me in the loft and we were together again. My brother was not with me long and he went to Bielski. I heard no more from him. After three months a sister of the woman who kept us was arrested. The woman who kept us came to us in a panic and said that we must run, because any time now we would be arrested. We had very little. All the gold rubbles, except for a 20 rubble piece, we had given to our hostess. In the evening I was thinking of leaving. The land lady asked me if I wanted to meet another Jewish person and his son. Indeed I did. "Who is it?" I asked. "He is the son in law of Garkave" she told me. I was very glad. It was my cousin. When we met we cried with excitement. We went out of the house and went together till we came to a fork in the road. My cousin said to us "Go in good health in one direction and I will go in another". We realised only then that a single person can hide more successfully than several people. Lilie was crying bitterly. "As you can see. Just one cousin and in such a moment we must part". I tried to calm her down and explain the reason for the parting. I found farmers that I knew and we hid in one place one night in another for two nights. And thus we moved about for a considerable time.

The first reprisal

Ivanke, Firke's husband said that if some time should pass and they would not take away his wife and children, we could come back. We could stay for a time. Lilie Szwarc said that she had not the strength left to run around, to wander. "Let us go to the converted woman for a period of time." I did not feel like going back there, but I had no alternative. We arrived back at the converted woman's and I told her husband an untruth that we were sent to him by the otryad [detachment, meaning probably Bielski's group] for a rest cure. We knew that he was poor. We would give him money for bread and a good overcoat. He agreed. I still had a 20 rubble gold coin, one 5 rubble coin and gold worth 15 rubbles. I thought "What will happen now? I have to exchange the 15 rubble gold for three 5 rubble pieces to remain flexible. I gave him the 15 rubble's worth of gold for him to exchange. As soon as I gave him the money I was sorry, because I knew him of old as not an honest man. But, so be it. If we trusted him with our lives we must trust him with our money. I said to Lilie Szwarc "You will see, he will not return today. He will come back tomorrow and will say that he lost the money". This is what happened. He came back next day, with his hat missing, bloodied and he said to me "Kill me, because I don't have your money". I felt like killing him, but Lilie would not let me. She said "Let's run away from the thief. I am afraid that he betrayed us to the Germans". I said: "Ivanke, you know what you have done. You took away the cane from a blind man. This was my last possession. What are we to do? And perhaps you told the Germans that you have Jews at home." He answered that he did not remember. He drank with policemen. Perhaps he said something about Jews. There was no time. I had to run away, because there was danger in his house. But before I went I told him "Remember Ivan, you shod a Jew in lapti [crude peasant's sandals]. But you made a big mistake – a Jew does not wear lapti. Tell me Vanka, which is a safe way for me to flee?" "I don't know" he answered, "go were your sense dictates". "Ivan, tell me, where is the police waiting for me, so that I can go another way". But all he would say was "go whichever way you like". We did not wait long and left his house. We knew that behind every bush a policeman may be waiting for us. And even if we survive, we had nothing to sustain us. With G-d's help we managed to get through untouched. We went to a farmer where we stayed for three months. One day Jews from the Bielski detachment arrived, among them my brother. They said that they came to see how I was getting on. I told them the story about Ivanke. Isrolik Jankelevicz, the commander of the group said: "Let us go to him and we will teach him how to behave". And all fellows said: "Good, we will deal with him". In the group were a number of men from Novogrudok – Michl Leibovicz, brothers Polanski and others. We went to Ivanke and they gave me a gun. We got to Ivanke. "Open up" we shouted. "Who is it" he asked. "Open quickly" we answered "or your house will be burned". Ivanke opened the door in fear and he spoke to me in a subdued tone. 'take my cow or a pig or both". But I did not need anything because if you are armed you can take anything without money. The boys shouted at him "Get dressed quickly we will teach you to steal money". I told them: "Don't shout" and I said to Ivanke: "You did no harm to anyone only to yourself. Wake up your children and say goodbye to them". He was begging us: "I did worse things in my life and they did not shoot me." We did not let him speak too long. 'say goodbye to your children and your wife" we told him. He said to his wife: "You are of their blood, ask them not to shoot me. How will you manage with small children?". And he said to his children: "Your father's life is in the hands of Chaim. Ask him to let your father live, because you still need him". But there was not much time left, because we could move in the night, but were restricted during the day. We said to him briefly "Ivanke, say goodbye to your family. You have deserved your end with your deeds". You can imagine the tragedy of that moment. He was certain that he was going to die. We said to the children: "Extinguish the light and stay inside because we will shoot if you don't obey". We went out into the street and I asked Ivanke: "Where should we shoot you, if in the bushes, let's go to the bushes." When we got to the bushes I said to him: "Do you think that Jews are killers? Do we shoot people for money? Never. Go home and tell your children that Jews don't kill for money". "Now tell us who in the village robbed Jewish goods". Isroel Jankelewicz had written down all addresses which Vanka gave us. When he finished Jankelewicz said: "Go home and be a father to your children and a husband to your wife". Ivanke did not believe that we were letting him go. He said: "I know that as soon as I turn around you will shoot me in the back". "Go home and find out who was robbing Jewish goods." And Ivanke went. His children were very happy.

A short time later Lilie and I were partisans in the forest. I was sent frequently to fetch food. We called it a task (zadanie). I had no problems with that. I would go first to Ivanke, who would point out to us everyone who was robbing the Jews. He also helped to find meat and other food. He would benefit too. We would always leave something for his family.

Lilie Szwarc became my wife and we have two children, a boy and a girl.

[Page 272]

Under the German whip

by Sula Rubin-Wolozynski

Translated from Yiddish by O. Delatycki

Initially my work was to sweep the grass in the destroyed, burned streets of the town, which was under the German whip. My parents still worked in their profession as dentists. My sister worked in the hospital. After a while, I obtained a job at the German cemetery. I anticipated at all times that we would be ultimately killed. My one thought was to escape and not to wait in the Ghetto. Alas, my parents did not understand me and thought that I lived in a dream, under the influence of the romantic writers. They accused me of thinking that a fly can fight an elephant. In the summer [7 August] of 1942 the second slaughter took place. I managed to take my sister with me to work at the cemetery. We were taken from the cemetery to the military barracks where they sorted us into two groups: one to live and the other to die. One group was standing close to a forest the other next the buildings. I soon realised that we, who were close to the forest, would be killed. I took my sister by the hand and we ran to those who were standing close to the buildings, disregarding the Germans who were shooting at us. And we survived. At the barracks we were kept in stables for three days without food or water. There we were subjected to all sorts of physical and moral degradations. In the end they chased us through the streets to the buildings of the district court, where we found our parents. We were the only family which, so far, had survived. In the court house I decided not to go to work but to escape to the forest to Bielski, and later bring my parents and sister. I knew of Bielski from the partisans, who returned to the Ghetto and from the posters in town, which promised a large sum of money for Bielski's head. The only way of escape from the Ghetto was by way of the water pump, where we were led in small groups, guarded by the Belarusian police, to fetch water. My friend Jarke Tiles and I agreed to tear off the yellow patches, wait for the time when the two policemen were busy trading with the Jews and slip out. We went unnoticed through the gardens to Brichinke and from there onto the Wsielub highway to Litowka.

Some one informed on us and we were caught not far from the Litowka forest. They flogged us with whips and took us to the town's police station, which was manned by Belarusians and a few Poles. In charge was a local man by the name of Gonsior, who was a client of my parents. He asked me where I was going and did I want to stay at the police station or be taken to the German gendarmes. I answered that I was looking for food and I would like to be transferred to the gendarmes. I just could not look at the policemen among who were my fellow pupils from the gymnasium [Polish high school] and I did not want to give them the pleasure of shooting me. They took us to the command post. It is difficult for me to describe my feelings. My throat was dry and constricted with fear. But I tried to think that perhaps this time I would remain alive. I was not a hero, but my friend and I decided not to cry and not to beg to be spared. The main thing was not to change our story that we going to find food. We had to make sure that we did not mention the name Bielski or the names of our gentile contacts. We wanted to maintain a certain pride and not be in despair. I was troubled by the thought that my parents and sister knew what happened to me and knew how I felt, but they could not help us. After a delay we were transferred to the gendarmerie. We were fortunate, Meister Wolf, who had the reputation of being a fair man, was in charge. Usually Miller, a known Jew hater, led the gendarmerie. Meister Wolf asked my friend to wait outside. He asked me to sit down and spoke to me at length. He was a rotund, older German with pink cheeks and blue eyes. I wondered how a German murderer could have such a pleasant face. He told me that he believed that we were going to buy some food and we did not know where the partisans were. He told me in confidence that he had a Jewish wife and a son in England. He knew my mother during the First World War . It was a real piece of luck to meet him in our circumstances. He promised that we would be unharmed, but he had to work out a plan so that the others would not know about it. He had to send us first to jail. After a day or two, when a truck would be taking prisoners from the jail to be shot behind the barracks, we would be on the list of those to be shot. But on the way we would be taken of the truck and conducted back to the court house. As I was going out he asked me with a smile: 'Did you really go for food? Don't worry, you will survive the war. Will you spare my life if you catch me somewhere when you will be a partisan? Don't answer and don't deny it but think about it. Life is like a wheel: today it is you and tomorrow it could be me'. The old, smart German knew where we were going. They took us to the jail and put us in a small room with some dirty straw on the floor. We were frightened, hungry and doomed to die, because we could not believe a German. I told Jarke what the German promised me. We cuddled each other and waited. A face appeared in the small window in the door and my name was called. It was my friend Avreml Iwiniecki, who was arrested some time ago for Rassen Schande [race disgrace], because he visited his gentile girl friend. He was caught and arrested. He brought us bread and water and wished us luck. On the second day they assembled us in a group to be taken for execution. Around us were people in a state a fear. We too did not believe that we may be saved. And yet we thought that perhaps... At that moment the adjutant of Meister Wolf, named Boyd, appeared. He called out our names. I took Jarke for her hand and we both went out the gate. He led us to the court house. I opened the door of our barrack and saw my parents and sister. Suddenly the barrack was filled with laughter, shouting and questions. I noticed that in my absence my mother's black hair had turned to grey. My father too looked older. As I looked at them I thought that I could not stay there. It was better to die than to have an existence like that: to sit and wait for the end in a barn with forty bunks. A short time after my return they counted us and sorted us in the yard behind the court house. I was afraid of that procedure and I hid under the bunk in a small hole. My sister told me that the gate in the fence surrounding us could be opened, because they had made a duplicate key. I begged her to escape with me, but she refused, because she worked as a cleaner in the police station next to the court house and if she disappeared our parents would be shot. She did not want to risk it. It was late in 1942. There was no time to lose. I did not see my father, but my mother did not want me to go. I just left the barn, waited till the policeman walked away from the gate and I left. I crossed the street and got to the small forest opposite the court, on the way to Gardielovka. I could hear the voices of the Jews and the Germans in the yard of the court. The snow creaked underfoot. After I reached the forest I decided to wait till dark and than go to Litovka to the house of the gentile who served as the contact with the partisans. Sitting in the forest I noticed shadows of people under a tree. To my joy they were four people from the court house, who left in the same manner as I did. I was more encouraged, it was better to be in company than alone. This time I got to Bielski. Three days later I joined the partisans. This was the start of a new phase in my life which lasted till the autumn [early July] of 1944. My parents were killed in May 1943 in the last mass murder of the Jews from the court house. My sister Rita left the Ghetto through the tunnel in September [26th] but she did not get to me and I don't know to this day what happened to her.

[Page 274]

They Burned the Town

by Yehoshua Yaffe

Translated from Yiddish by O. Delatycki

Twenty eighth of June 1941. The Russians escaped and the Germans had not arrived yet. Every day German planes were flying in and throwing bombs. Many people were running out of the town into the fields of corn, the small wood in Brecianka or into the barns of the Jewish villagers in Rawinka and Lachowicz. Through the town passed streams of evacuees and Russian soldiers, sweaty, dirty and sad with grey, hungry faces. They faced the Germans and barely managed to escape alive. They were trying to get away as far as possible from the front, as far as possible from danger and death.

Novogrudok: part of the market place - December 1941

In the barn of Ele the Black, on the way to Peresike, 18 Jews were concealed. They were lying in family groups, one next to another on the spread out straw and were listening for the sound of aircraft. They suddenly heard the rev of a motor. They all quickly returned to the barn and crawled into the straw, lying in deathly fear, hoping that a bomb would not hit the barn and kill everybody. Some of those who tried to escape to Russia returned to Novogrudok. They were not allowed to cross the 1939 Soviet-Polish border and hence they came back. The roads were strewn with thousands of corpses, overturned cars and carts with dead horses. Over all of this flew German aircraft, threw bombs and shot from above. There was no alternative, there was no salvation, one had to expect anything. There was a rumour circulating among the non-Jewish population that the Germans would arrive on Saturday and whoever would not be at home would not be allowed to return. This prompted us to leave the barn on Friday night and go home. The streets were empty. The doors to some houses were open, in other houses doors were nailed down. Inside were people who were waiting for tomorrow. They wondered what new trials the new day would bring. The night passed quietly and on the next day there was only one air attack. We went back to the barn.

The day was hot, the sun was as intense as in the middle of Tamuz. The air was sultry in the choking tightness. We were afraid to go out onto the street. Vehicles were travelling in all directions through the town. The sound of the aeroplanes grew louder. In large units they flew down closer to the ground, like crows, and started to bomb the town, as if they were in a race to destroy what the Jews had built in hundreds of years. The bombardment continued for a couple of hours. The fire bombs ignited the timber houses. The whole of Novogrudok was one burning blaze. It was impossible to walk close to the burning streets. The flames were spreading like fiery tongs. The choking smell spread for many kilometres. The night began, but there was no night. Mighty flames rose to the darkened night sky and painted the darkness. It looked as if the sky was burning and enveloping the earth in a red blanket. The tin sheets on the roofs were bending and crinkling in the heat. As soon as it was dark, the aeroplanes flew away. The streets were filled again with endless columns of Soviet soldiers going east. We were returning home to see if anything could be saved. We walked in the fields between Grodno and Slonim Streets. We came to the Synagogue square. The roof in the Old Synagogue had a large hole in it. Sections of the wall were broken off and strewn on the ground. The Big Synagogue was burning from all sides. The fire was rising from the inside of the building fed by the prayer books that were moulding in the bookshelves on the wall. Alter the verger would air the books in the summer by spreading them on the grass. Now the fire consumed the books and the mould and converted them to black ash.

The Shoemakers Synagogue was burning from the back. My father called for people to help extinguish the fire. We found tin buckets and poured water on the walls. But it was no use. The fire had too strong a hold. We just managed to extract a few scrolls. We ran to our house to try and save some clothing and food.

Next morning I was walking through the burnt out streets. The brick houses disintegrated to their foundations, and from the timber houses only chimneys remained. They were standing upright on piles of rubble. On the roads burned bodies of people were lying, who were killed by fragments of bombs. Not far from the row of shops, near the old manège [a square used as a bus terminal] was lying the body of the kosher butcher from Lubcz and the wind was blowing the hair of his beard. It was the only part of his dead body that moved. Next to him lay his prayer shovel. Near by lay the body of a farmer clutching a bundle of leggings. He died scavenging the contents of the clothing factory. On the other side of the row of shops lay the body of a Soviet officer with a torn stomach. He was hurrying people from the market square and was killed whilst doing so. Anna, a farming woman from Slichovichi, who was a cleaner in Jewish homes, was robbing them during the bombardment. Now she was lying dead in Grodno Street next to the Orthodox Church. Jewish clothing and candle sticks were strewn around her. The old Rudski, who was always collecting bits of wood, corks, bottles and rusty iron, would not leave his house and see it burn. He was carrying water trying to extinguish the fire. But the fire was fierce and Rudski burned with his house. Ginienski, the hardware merchant, was trying to extract his savings from a pile of wood. His daughter ran to help him, having left her 2 year old child with her husband. Both father and daughter perished. A few months later, during the first slaughter, I saw her husband, Shabtai Nachimovski, with his daughter in his arms, on a truck which was taking them to their death in Skrydlewo.

Next morning, standing in the centre of the town in the market place one could see the houses next to the railway station, the mosque with the glittering half moon at the end of Waliker Street, the ornate gate to the Jewish cemetery with the large words לנצ המות בלע, the Rachelo and Sieniezyc Street were completely wiped out. The Polish church was left untouched. The Synagogue square was a burned heap with the four walls of the big synagogue protruding through the rubble. They were the sad remains of all the burned synagogues, which for hundreds of years were the source of spirit and enlightenment of the Jewish soul. Two thirds of the town was wiped out. In the few remaining streets four thousand [this figure is almost certainly a substantial underestimate] members of the Jewish community were bundled in.

The first days under the Germans

Novogrudok was burned-out. Thousands of people lost the roofs over their heads. All was gone with the fire: clothing, furniture, kitchen equipment. The worst was the loss of the stored food. Many were left without bread in the morning after the fire. They worried about the loss of food and thought of what tomorrow may bring. The Soviets closed down the synagogues and the shops in town. They established a large shop selling grains and flour. The store was hit by bombs. The doors were shut by chains and locks, but the sacks of flour fell on the footpath through the burst walls. This was an opportunity for the bereft people of the town to put away some flour. Jankef the coachman was delivering for years sacks of flour from Brojdo's warehouse to the shops. He was used to handling 80 kilo sacks. He grabbed a sack of flour under his arm, like a child lifting a toy, and took it to his wife and three children. The family found shelter after the bombing in Harkavy's synagogue. He left the sack with his family and went to fetch another. Other people followed his example. They came from all directions. Jews returning from their morning prayers stashed away their prayer books and carried sacks of flour to their families. People were helping each other to lift sacks on their shoulders. Others were apprehensive and did not take the flour. Women whose husbands went east were helping each other: two or three were carrying a sack together. On the way they were resting on the staircases of the preserved houses. With the backs bent, twisting in all directions, they carried the sacks home. Some dragged the sack on the footpath, pushed it, groaned and sweated till they brought it home. The weak could not make it and fell under the burden. Even ten year old children were attempting to move the sacks of flour. If they succeeded they were showing off their strength. Suddenly there was a sound of approaching vehicles. This caused a panic. People were running away from the streets and the market place. Everybody thought that the Germans were coming. Some were hiding the sacks of flour under stairways and hiding themselves behind the sacks. But they worried unnecessarily. The troupes passing through town were the stragglers of the Red Army, who, tired out and blackened, were making their way east. The Jews waited for the column of trucks to pass and started shifting the flour again. It was not always that simple. On the third day of the war a bomb fell next to the railway station and landed in the military food store. Talia, a strong and solid Belarus, who worked in Zilberman's printing works, loaded sacks of sugar onto a carriage and intended to drag it home. He was stopped by a Russian officer who asked him who allowed him to rob Soviet goods. Talia answered 'The Germans are coming and they would take everything'. The officer replied 'The Germans would not defeat us and you would not rob our property. We sacrifice our blood to combat the Fascists.' He shot him on the spot and left him lying in the street. Elsewhere a member of the NKVD found, in the shoe factory, a farmer from the nearby village of Pucewicze, who had crammed leather uppers of shoes in a sack. He was shot and the black uppers turned red.

Everyone was looking for a place to stay. Some went to their friends or acquaintances. Families moved into kitchens, in barns and in lean-to's where wood was kept. Even those who lived in one room found a place for those whose homes had burned down. Everyone saw the Jewish misfortune. They were also helping each other with food and clothing and tried to console the despairing.

Two days later the first German vehicles came into town. The Jews were hiding in their homes. There were among them a few curious ones who wanted to see how a German looks, those heroes who thought that they would conquer the world. Through the streets travelled the self assured Germans, with strong, elongated faces. They looked down on everyone. They did not react to the welcoming greetings of the non-Jews, who came out to meet them. Like devils they rushed through the town and disappeared back along the Slonim highway.

On the 3rd of July Novogrudok was occupied by the German army. The Polish population re-established the police, and by supporting the Germans they wanted to be accepted by them. They were later bitterly disappointed.

The German soldiers were bored in the ruined town. They were looking for some entertainment. In among the burnt out streets a German came across an elderly Jew with a white beard. The German stopped the Jew in the middle of the street and started pulling at strands of his beard. A group of the locals stood opposite and laughed. The German sadist was satisfied, he managed to gain acceptance by the local population with his bestiality. He went further and met a Jewish woman with a child in her arms. He kicked the woman in the stomach with his heavy soldier's boot. The woman and child fell blooded to the ground.

There was no bread in town. Next morning there was a queue in front of a bakery. In the queue were both Jews and gentiles. A German soldier was passing by. He expelled all Jews from the queue and gave them a beating. The gentiles were supportive of the event. They would eat the bread and the Jews would go without. A second soldier arrived. He interceded on behalf of the Jews and told the shopkeeper to sell them bread. 'One cannot live without bread' he argued. But by the time the Jews rejoined the queue bread was sold out. In the city store there were cucumbers for sale. There were no Germans about. The shopkeeper decided that he would not sell to Jews. And the gentile customers saw to it that Jews would not enter the shop. Jews disappeared from the streets. When they saw a German they would vanish if they could. But the Germans would come from nowhere with sticks in their hands or rubber whip and would beat every Jew they came across. The Germans started to catch Jews to force them to work. They would drag them from their homes. The Germans would also search Jewish homes for gold and other valuables. They took also clothing and underwear and sent it to Germany. There was a shortage of wood for cooking. Late in the afternoon I went to the row of shops in the centre of the market place and removed a door from one of the shops. Two of us carried it home. The sun was setting. The last rays were colouring the sky. The new head of the police force appeared from nowhere. We showed him with sign language that we were carrying the door to the German command post. He let us go. We brought the door to the back door of the command post and leaned it against the fence. After it became dark and no one was allowed to be outside, we crept to the back of the command post and took the door into our home. With the help of everyone, the door was demolished into pieces of timber. We hid the pieces under the beds. We had enough firewood for a week.

Later farmers began to appear in town. They came with their carts and left them in the side streets. They were not allowed to trade with Jews. But they would sneak into Jewish homes through the back doors, pretend to borrow a pail to fetch water for their horses and in the mean time exchange a pood [about 16 kilo] of flour for a cushion or a kilo of butter for a pair of shoes. The Jews were selling their last possessions for food. They sold their bed linen, their clothing. They could never wear it under the Germans, but if they would survive they would get new clothing. In the mean time the farmers acquired the best items.

Tormented and murdered

On the 3rd of July 1941 the Germans occupied Novogrudok. Three days later they selected some members of the Jewish intelligentsia – religious, cultural and public figures - and killed them. The German policy was to eliminate likely leaders of an uprising. The military commandant announced that all Jews of the town must gather in front of the command post to elect a Judenrat [Jewish committee]. There were not many Jews who wanted to work with the Germans. Some pre-war communal workers may have thought it their duty to participate. They were the first to be massacred. The majority of the Jews were hiding in their homes and tried to avoid going out. The police went from house to house forcing people to go to the command post. They assembled forcibly a few hundred men. This is when their hell on earth started. First they were packed into one room. They were very cramped. But this too did not last long. Every few minutes another person was removed from the room. No one returned. The Germans had with them a Pole who knew everyone and it was on his say so that people were sorted to either live or die. The interrogation was short: name and surname, occupation. Those selected to work were placed left, the rest to the right. Those on the right were led outside. They were divided into groups of ten. Each group was attached to a Gestapo functionary. Each Jew was given two buckets of water, which they had to carry to the third floor, whilst they were beaten on the way with rubber truncheons. Each one who brought to the top less than half a bucket of water was handed over to a second German, who took the victim to a room to polish the German's shoes. The Jew was polishing and the German was lashing out over the body of the victim with a rubber truncheon till the Jew fainted. The body was dragged outside and thrown into a truck.

The other group of Jews was lined up in the yard and water was poured over them from the top floor of the building. When the water was emptied the buckets were thrown on the terrified Jews. An order came: 'anyone injured, stand aside, but quick'. Anyone who was slow in following the orders was told to fill the buckets with water and run upstairs. Two Germans stood at the water well and were beating everyone who was drawing water. The Jews were pushing each other at the well, each wanted to get to water as soon as possible and get out from under the lashings. Some Jews spilled water, others fell. The Germans kept up the punishment, had drawn blood and were laughing. And again, anyone who spilled more than half a bucket of water was sent to polish boots. In the end the whole group of beaten and bloodied bodies were thrown into the trucks, together with those who were put their previously. The truck was not full. The commandant came over and ordered to put ten more Jews in the truck. Two Germans went into the room where the Jews selected to work were kept and grabbed more Jews, accompanied by savage beating and wild shouting. The commandant approached the truck again and said that the truck was too full and they would all suffocate. He ordered to remove half of the Jews and shoot them on the spot so that the rest would have more space The Germans started shooting in the air. The Jews were jumping out of the truck. They pushed each other and were running around the yard. The yard was fenced in. At the fences stood Germans who kept the Jews off the fences. The Jews were running from one end of the yard to the other and were met with beatings and laughter. They were ordered by the commandant to stand in a row. The Germans were beating anyone who was slow. An order was given: 'those whose initial of their surname was A to K must lie down facing the ground, from K to S with the face up, from S to the last must stand on all fours'. They were lying in that position for about ten minutes till a second truck arrived. All Jews were packed into the two trucks. The trucks drove off. Nobody saw any of them again.

Later they took to the remaining Jews who were detained. They were told to clean the building, to wash the floors and the walls, scratch off all the pictures on the wall. They were told to work fast and were encouraged by beatings. But at least they remained alive. They were allowed to go home weary and bloodied. They returned to their wives and children who were glad to see them. The bereaved families of those who had not returned were in mourning and nobody could help them, because all were overwhelmed with their own troubles and every day brought new anxieties and disasters.

The front line was moving further east towards Moscow. The command had gone and was replaced by a new one. The Judenrat proposed by the Jews was accepted by the Germans. The Judenrat had to provide workers for the German army and for the town council. Wearing of yellow patches by Jews was made compulsory. A Jew was not allowed to walk on the footpath, or have any commercial dealings with gentiles. Jews were anxious to go to work because hunger was acute. Those who worked were given by the army a cooked meal of sorts. They could also exchange at work items of clothing for food. One gradually became used if not immune to the insults by the gentiles, to the beating by the Germans and the police and to the work. Jews were made to clear the debris of the burned houses. Many worked in the German military barracks others worked in town.

Enforced labour

At eight o'clock in the morning the gentile supervisors would pick up the workers from the Judenrat. A German feldwebel [sergeant] would arrange the workers in rows and hand them over to the supervisors. This arrangement continued for more than a week. The Judenrat had to meet other demands, such as to furnish quarters for the Germans, provide bedding, crockery etc. Some members of the Judenrat tried to rationalize the demands. The accountant Landau argued that in the First World War the Jews were also made to work. He concluded that the Jews were a proved and tested nation. They suffered and can get used to suffering. 'We would also get used to the Germans' he concluded. 'And what happened to the missing people?' asked the lawyer Zeldowicz, who was the chairman of the Judenrat. 'The judges used to rummage in the criminal code before sentencing a man. This time more than seventy people disappeared and there is no word of them'. 'And who knows if after the first disappearance others would not follow' somebody else added. The conversation in the Judenrat was interrupted by the German feldwebel, who told them in confusion that this morning the commandant would be present at the departure to work. 'We are very pleased, Herr feldwebel' said Landau 'let the commandant see for himself that the Jews are ready to help the Germans win the war against the Bolsheviks'. 'We don't need the Jewish help. Why did only few workers turn up? Let all Jews go immediately to work'. He left the Judenrat banging the door. 'The Germans are cooking up something' said the chairman 'the commandant is coming himself'. 'What can we do?' said Dobrin 'we must provide more workers, otherwise things may turn out badly'. 'Workers, workers' said the brothers Israelit and left with a few other members of the Judenrat to chase Jews to work. The commandant lined up all Jews in a row and kept the Judenrat separately. He spoke briefly 'The German army is at the gates of Moscow. Jews must work for the German army. If they would, their lives would be spared. We need also the Jewish intelligentsia to work. I would separate the intelligentsia from the workers.' He approached the members of the Judenrat. He asked the chairman of Judenrat 'what is your profession?' 'I am a lawyer'. 'Yes, this is good. You would defend the interest of the Jews in the German Reich'. He put him on his left. 'And your profession?' he asked Landau. 'I am a bookkeeper'. 'That we definitely need. You would provide statistics of the work of the Jews'. And he put him next to the chairman. 'And your professions?' he asked the brothers Israelit. 'Merchants' they replied. 'We don't need swindlers in the German Reich' and he put them to the right. In this manner the commandant went through all those standing in the yard. Teachers, bookkeepers, lawyers and all other professionals he sent to the left and the others he distributed among the supervisors. At the same time other Germans were going to all the Jewish homes and arrested all members of the Jewish intelligentsia. They have even taken the teachers of the Cheders [Jewish religious primary schools]. They were removed to an unknown destination. The gentiles were spreading various rumours: that those taken away were seen not far from Baranowicze, others said close to Minsk. Some wives have gone to look for them and they too disappeared. A few weeks later alarming rumours came from the small towns. All Jews from the township of Rekov were burned alive in the town's synagogue. In Ancewicze and Horodyszcze all Jews were killed. I tried to contact farmers I knew. They were afraid to let a Jew into the house. They were told by the Germans that anyone hiding a Jew would be shot with his whole family. I had no alternative but to go to work. We worked for the town's council. We were sorting various implements and materials for various workshops. Our store also supplied the Judenrat with everything they required. One Friday a messenger from the Judenrat came and asked for 25 brooms for the commandant's office. We found out from the messenger that new Germans had arrived and ordered from Judenrat 40 silk eiderdowns with covers, forty tables, ten wardrobes and 15 pairs of boots. They had to supply also sixty workers with 25 brooms. We became very depressed. Why do the new Germans require 60 workers? We were wondering if it may be a preparation for a new slaughter. We thought about it and asked the Polish supervisor to try and find out what this was all about. He returned and told us that the Gestapo had arrived and there was a need for caution. He suggested that we should remain overnight in the store and lock the doors. But what about the parents and my wife at home? I went to see my brother who was working in the food supply department. My brother was about to go to us. The chief of the food supply department was fond of my brother. He fed him and gave him food to take home. He regretted that my brother was a Jew. Before I came he asked my brother if he had men in his family. 'I have two brothers' my brother answered. 'Where are your brothers' the German asked. He was visibly concerned. 'They work in the town's supply store' my brother answered. 'They must come to me to fetch water' the German said. We started to carry buckets of water from the pump in the market square to the food supply office. We poured the water into a bath tub, emptied the tub and began filling it again. In the mean time the Judenrut tried to locate workers. They took workers from other enterprises and transferred them to the Germans. Niankowski came over and told us to leave the buckets. My brother called the German and Niankowski disappeared. In the yard of the Judenrat some workers arrived, but quickly left. There was too much commotion in the Judenrat. Everyone thought that from the anticipated work nobody would return. The Judenrat succeeded in rounding up 40 workers and taking them to the Germans. The head of the Gestapo took the workers to the jail and told the Germans to go to town and catch Jews. The Judenrat decided to hide. Several workers had returned home from work and did not know of the events. They were caught by the Germans and taken to the jail.

We were the only Jews in the market place and we continued to drag the buckets of water. Suddenly the chief of the food supply office came running and told us: 'Enough water, go and hide'. He took us home and we hid in the cellar. Children were running around in the streets. They were stopping Jews and imploring them: 'Jews go to work, otherwise our fathers will be shot'. Apparently the Germans announced that if the required number of workers would not be available the Jews in jail would be shot. But everyone knew that when the right number of workers would be found they too would be shot. The required number was not found and those arrested were not seen again. To the list of women who lost their husbands another 60 names were added.

This was the last of the series actions when the Germans took out the Jews behind the barracks and shot them. They would say that the men were sent to work. Later the Germans became more blood thirsty.

We harvest potatoes

The land which belonged to large landowners was taken over by the state under the Soviets. The Soviets escaped and left a large field of potatoes. The land belonged in the past, in the Polish days, to the landowner Truniewski. The potatoes had to be harvested and the Judenrat was told to supply the workforce to do it. Over a hundred Jews, in the majority women, came to harvest the potatoes. Each worker would arrive with a large bag which was taken home filled with potatoes. In addition, each worker was supposed to be given a pood of potatoes for every day's work. Nobody was too keen to work and ways were found to do little. The Polish supervisors were also not concerned if the job took another week or more to finish. There was no shortage of Jewish labour and the Poles were paid by the day. The days were cooler and it was pleasant to be in the fields. Our supervisor Walowski, a young Belarus, was a communist before the war. He had compassion for the Jews. He saw to it that nobody would work too hard and that everyone should have potatoes to take home. 'You need it more than the Germans' he told us with a smile, 'but you must be cautious'. One morning before work started, he gathered all the Jews and gave a brief summary of the political situation as he saw it. 'The Jews don't suffer alone, but all people who want to live free and honest lives are suppressed. Those who would survive would see the defeat of all the fascist murderers. But one must be cautious.' Once when some Jews were sitting idle he told those that worked to join them and he called a lunch break. Suddenly the Germans arrived. This time we got away with a fright. Walowski would load a pood of potatoes in a bag and carry it for the elderly Jews who lived in town. He would leave the bag in one of the Jewish homes and the Jews would distribute the potatoes among themselves. After a time Walowski was caught and the Germans arrested him.

We were sitting in the field, far from the town and our thoughts left one no peace. The families were left in town in the hands of the Germans, who robbed and beat up everybody. If a person was caught he disappeared. Nobody ever returned.

This situation did not continue for long. The road was jammed with trucks loaded with heavy boxes of arms. Not far from us one truck overturned. The driver was killed and some boxes were strewn in all directions. The movement on the road stopped and the German soldiers suddenly saw before them Jews. A German came over and ordered that all Jews must go to the overturned truck. There he separated the men from the women, counted them several times whilst beating them in the process. The Jews were told to turn upright the overturned truck. We tried, but without success. The truck was buried in the ground. They lined up the Jews and removed from the line-up every fifth man. Fourteen men were separated. They were made to lie down with their face down. The others were sent off to try again to upturn the truck. When they had not succeeded again, three soldiers started beating severely the fourteen lying on the ground. Twenty more men were made to lie on the ground and given a severe beating. Next all other men were made to lie on the ground and those that were previously beaten were made to upturn the truck. The truck remained overturned. After all Jews were severely beaten and some women had blood running from them the Germans permitted the Jews to unload the truck. When unloaded, it was possible to upturn the truck and reload the boxes. The Jews were made to lie down again and the Germans fired automatic weapons over them. The whole incident lasted for three hours. After the Germans departed the Jews were made to return to dig potatoes.

Forced labour

The District Commissariat was in the building which, in the Polish days, was the wojewodztwo [district – pre-war Poland was divided in 16 wojewodztwos]. In the adjacent houses lived the German high echelon officials. The houses of the Germans were surrounded by burnt out ruins of brick houses – all houses in Slonim street and the Synagogue square and most houses in the Yiddish and Waliker streets were in ruins. At that time the first partisans made bold attacks on the Germans. The Germans were concerned that the partisans might infiltrate among the ruins, close to their homes and attack them. The Germans ordered that the burnt out ruins of the houses should be demolished. They made the Judenrat responsible for that job.

This job started in the middle of winter, when the frost was severe. Snow was spreading and the cold penetrated the bodies. Everyone was reluctant to do this work, because they had become used to the work they were doing. This work was heavy. The walls had to be broken up with heavy crowbars. The bricks were held together with mortar for hundreds of years and they would not come apart with ease. A few dozen workers were standing, looking out for the Germans. Nobody was keen to do this work. It was bitterly cold. Everyone was hungry. And the member of the Judenrat was shouting and swearing. This did not help. He started begging us to do some work. He reasoned that if the Germans would come and see that no work was done they would punish the workers. But this did not help matters. At that point a German was noticed. Everyone grabbed the crow bars. The walls were attacked and holes appeared. Bricks and sections of walls were flying in the air.

A farmer with a white bag in his hand was passing by. He stopped not far from the Jewish workers. He had a piece of butter and wanted in exchange a pair of galoshes. The Jews were amused. Some of them wore galoshes to work on the previous days hoping to exchange them for food, but there were no takers. The gentiles were looking for textiles for a suit or a dress. And today, when they had with them fabrics, the gentile wanted galoshes. A few Jews approached the farmer. The first pair of galoshes he was shown was not to his liking. Two more Jews came with their galoshes. At that moment a German appeared from nowhere. He wanted to arrest all three Jews. He accused them of neglecting their work and trading with farmers. The Jews started to plea with him, asking him not to take them to jail, where they would surely be shot. The German demanded gold. But the Jews did not have gold. They said that they had long ago sold any gold they had. He answered that he would take watches, money, anything of value that they had. The member of the Judenrat went to the workers and asked them to surrender anything of value . 'We must save three Jews from death' he told them. When the German saw that the Jews gave them everything they had, he took a stick and started beating them. Than he told them to start working and left.

Schmitt, the German director of works, came over leading a big dog. He was not interested if the Jews were working or not. He has one aim - to beat Jews. He was running around hitting anyone who was handy with a rubber truncheon. Other Germans also took an interest in the work. Every so often somebody would come over to see whether the Jews were working. Each one of them wanted to show his importance. They were shouting, cursing, beating the workers and shooting into the air. We were used to it and we learned not to be afraid, like an old horse that got used to the whip. This was one of the worst places to work in. Nobody wanted to work there. The Judenrat, to encourage people to work there, gave them double rations of bread, which helped to recruit the required number of workers.

Novogrudok was a small town. Water was drawn from the wells. There was no running water in the houses. The Germans decided to install water mains in the German colony and to have running water in their houses. Trenches were dug and pipelines were installed. It was winter. The soil was frozen. The work was hard. The work had to be completed quickly because it was inconvenient for the German hausfraus to fetch water from the wells. The Jews were required to work around the clock. They were told to dig without interruption. People were hungry in the Ghetto and some volunteered to work at night. They received a three fold ration of bread. At night it was possible to snooze at times. Most Germans were asleep. On one particular night only three Jews were working in a certain section. It was a very cold night. The furrier was scheduled to work that night, but his 17 year old son replaced him. In another household a man replaced his brother. He meant to replace him for a night's work. In fact he died instead of his brother. It was one o'clock at night. The strong wind was blowing the snow from the frozen earth. Most houses were immersed in darkness. Most people were fast asleep. The three Jewish workers were standing in the long, narrow trench and were trying to warm their frozen hands. They rubbed their fingers, which were needled by the frost. They were in town for the first time since the Jews were hoarded into the Ghetto. A German policeman was standing nearby. He was responsible for the security of the town. He was casting hostile looks in the direction of the Jews. The Jews had not heard in a long time spontaneous laughter of happy people. In the Ghetto everyone was gloomy and disconsolate. But here, in the trench they could hear laughter from the house of the District Commissar. They were amusing themselves and were happy that they conquered the world. Those were drunken voices. And suddenly there was a shout like that of a wild beast: 'Come here, Jews!' Three Germans were standing on the steps of the veranda. At first the Jews thought that perhaps they might be given leftovers to eat. This did happen at times. After a meal, the scraps were sometimes given to the Jews, as to dogs. The Jews came out of the trench toward the open door. The district commissar took out his revolver and shot the three of them. The laughter continued unabated. The corpses were thrown into the trench onto the fire. Zejdl, the son of the ferrier, survived. He had a small injury to his hand. Having been injured he lost consciousness, but the fire brought him back to his senses. He crawled away from the fire and removed the two dead bodies. He remained in the trench and kept rubbing his frozen hands. Later he crawled into a ruin of a house and waited their till daylight. A fresh white snow covered the surrounds and the shrunken dead bodies. Strong winds were blowing the snow over the surfaces. The telephone wires were shaking. Ten workers had come to replace those who worked overnight. They were surprised that there was no fire in the trench and the three workers had disappeared. They jumped into the trench and found the dead bodies of their friends. Shortly after, the son of the ferrier came out of the ruins and told them what had happened. There was nothing they could do and they had no one to speak to. They could not start working till the district commissar would wake up and give permission to bury the bodies. I went with the other workers to the Jewish cemetery to bury the dead. We brought the bodies on a peasant's sleigh. I looked around and saw the grave stones. Some were very old. All was deathly quiet. On the nearby mound was an old burial stone with a barely readable inscription. One could decipher that here lay buried an old Jewish man from the Novogrudok of old, who lived his unremarkable live. If somebody would come here many years later and ask who was buried in the new grave, he would be told that all Jews were killed in a mass slaughter, but those two were shot and burned for no reason at all by a German murderer. And they were the last to be buried in this cemetery. The man guilty of the murder was in charge of the whole district. He had no reason for killing the Jews, who did not do anything wrong. He was thirsting for Jewish blood. He could not go to sleep without it. The burned bodies were buried. Somebody recited the Kaddish. And the world was silent. The sun was covered by grey clouds. The wind blew stronger. And the earth was covered with clear, white snow.

The Germans were looting

The Jews were confined to the Ghetto. Villagers moved in to their houses. The Germans took the furniture. They were sending it to Germany. The Jews were made to sort and carry the furniture. Farmers' carts were moving from house to house. Jews were carrying from their own homes wardrobes, beds, buffets, tables and chairs and were taking them to the tall building of the former Polish court for sorting. Room after room was filled with various wardrobes sorted by size, colour and the variety of timber it was made of. In another room were wardrobes with mirrors, two door, three door, with or without cornices. Similarly, beds, tables and chairs, buffets and bedside tables were sorted. The Jewish group engaged in sorting the furniture consisted of one hundred men. In charge was Rauter, a crazy, wild animal, who walked around with a rubber truncheon in his hand and would hit anyone who was handy. He lined up in the court yard the hundred Jews and began counting. When he would count to ten he would hit the Jew before him, and on and on till he counted to a hundred. Ten workers with one carpenter attached to them were sent to the fourth floor. The next group of ten and a carpenter he sent onto another floor and so on. The last forty Jews were to remain on the staircase to carry the furniture from one floor to another. When Rauter was present one had to work quickly else the truncheon went into action. Workers were running from one floor to the next with a wide wardrobe. Rauter was behind them with his truncheon. After about an hour he would go away and return after lunch. Whilst Rauter was gone the workers rummaged among the clothing and household goods that were robbed from the Jewish homes, to find something that they could exchange with a farmer for food. As soon as Rauter returned, everyone would resume moving furniture. Up the stairs and down the stairs. At one time Rauter sent everybody to the fourth floor, where a few dozen wardrobes were stored. He told the workers to bring them down to the yard. Each wardrobe was to be carried by four workers. They started moving the wardrobes down the stairs. It was difficult to manoeuvre the wardrobes over the banisters. One wardrobe got stuck on the stairs and would not move. Rauter started shouting and hitting the workers. The wardrobe slid from the hands of the workers and slid down the steps. The stairs were strewn with broken wardrobes and injured workers trapped under the wardrobes. The workers started freeing those injured from under the wardrobes. Rauter assembled all the workers in the yard. He counted them to make sure that a hundred were present. He put to one side those injured. He was aiming to have them flogged for breaking the German furniture. At that moment a big truck arrived. Three of the nicest wardrobes were loaded on and the truck together with Rauter departed. He needed three wardrobes but ordered forty to be taken down the stairs. Rauter was not present when the Jews left for the Ghetto. The Jews used the occasion to take bundles of cloth to exchange for food and they broke out pieces of wood from the busted wardrobes to use for fires in the Ghetto.

Chopping ice

At the end of Grodno street was a small lake. They called it Szumski's river, because the owner of the house near by was named Szumski. During the New Year celebrations Jews used it for Tashlich. But in those days I was not praying very attentively. I looked at the big willow trees, the tall lake grasses that grew out of the lake and the shrubs on the shore. Many varied birds warbled in the trees. The frogs croaked in the swamp. And by the time I stopped listening and looking all around me, Tashlich was recited. I would join the elders walking back to town. It was not safe for a Jewish boy to wander alone outside the town. Before the war, at the end of winter, farmers brought on sleighs into town large blocks of ice from Szulski's river for the soda water makers and restaurants. That year ice blocks were not produced, because there were no shops and no restaurants in town and no one was buying ice. The farmers from near by villages moved to town and lived in Jewish houses and acquired many Jews possessions. They were not interested in producing blocks of ice. The Judenrat was told to send five Jewish workers to cut blocks of ice from Szulski's river. They need ice in the German hospital. Five of us went. The winter was still cold and there was severe frost in March. We went onto the ice. We took off our gloves. Our fingers began to freeze. We took our tools and started hammering the thick layer of ice. We made no impression on the ice. I did not know how to do the job. But we learned in a hurry. We went closer to the shore, where the ice was thinner and we all started to hit the ice in the same place with mattocks. And the ice gave way. The block of ice floated on the water. One of us ran to retrieve the block and fell into the river. We pulled him out quickly. He was soaked right through and was shivering. Frozen lumps of ice were hanging from him. The German did not allow him to get into a house – he should stay and see how lumps of ice should be recovered. Shortly after, with G-ds help, the German fell into the icy water. When we got him out he was covered in ice. We took the German and the Jew into a house near by. The farmer's wife busied herself drying the wet clothes. The German was furious and as soon as his clothing was dry he went outside and took out his wrath on us. We were all wet from sweat and water. We loaded the lumps of ice onto the farmer's sleighs. We looked back on the episode. We thought that we had become quite skilled in chopping and removing lumps of ice. We went back to the Ghetto in our frozen garments. All five of us became sick and had a high temperature. We spent several days in bed.

The Russian supervisors

Many Soviet soldiers were cut off and were trapped in the occupied districts. Many managed to dress like farmers and were working in the villages and towns. Some of them worked for the Germans. Some became supervisors of Jewish workers. They were at times worse than the Germans. They were beating us and were forcing us to work hard so as to please their German masters. But the Germans, regardless, considered them as enemies. When the Soviet army started to push back the German armies, the Germans started arresting the vostochniks [men from the east], as they were commonly called. In the middle of February many lorries loaded with the vostochniks drove through the town and came back empty. Initially the Germans packed them into the jail. Later they were taken straight to the military barracks. They were shot not far from the mass grave of the Jews [5100 Jews were killed there on the 8 December 1941] and thrown into one mass grave. Among those were some vostochniks who supervised Jews. They tried to please their German masters by mistreating Jews, and yet their destiny was determined. It was their time to perish. Not all were caught. They were used to deceiving death. They went into the forests and organised the first partisan formations in the district. In the Ghetto they were reasoning that if the Germans were prepared to kill all Russians, they would have no compunctions in killing Jews. The Jews assumed that the Ghetto would be soon wiped out. Every movement of the Germans was followed closely and a new slaughter was expected at any time. The Jews who considered themselves needed by the Germans were those with a trade. In the first slaughter, the Germans refrained from killing tradesmen. The Judenrat endeavoured to organise new workshops where tradesmen would be employed. Groups of tailors, shoemakers, saddlers, carpenters and other trades were formed. People were leaving their previous employment and were endeavouring to become tradesmen. A tailor would put a needle in his brother's hand and call him a tailor. A shoemaker sat his brother-in-law in front of a last and got him to form a shoe. Some became tradesmen through the Judenrat. For money their name was added to the list of tradesmen and they were sent to work in the workshops. The people in the workshops were also Jews and they had pity of the new 'apprentices'. They taught them the trade, to be able to work when the German supervisor visited the workshop. I did not have patronage which would allow me to join officially a workshop. I decided to become a tanner. The only tannery in town, which belonged to Maslowaty, was nationalized by the Soviets. Later it belonged to the Germans. I gave Maslowaty a table clock for the Polish supervisor of the tannery. For this I received a worker's certificate (Arbeitsschein) as a helper (Gehilfe) in the tannery.

The ground bark

During the first few days I was preparing bark in the yard. I dried it in the sun in the daytime and I took it into the store at night. Later I was allowed to work in the lime processing area. We washed the raw hides in a big bath filled with water. We were emptying the bath and filling it with fresh water. Later we placed the skins in a lime bath one over the other. I learned the art of neutralizing the lime treated hides using water cooked with the bark that I dried in the sun and ground. The hides were hung out to dry. The last process was to tan the hides. The work was hard and smelly. One was always wet and dirty. But one presumed that one's work was important to the Germans. Leather was for them a critical commodity. It was assumed that in the case of a slaughter we would be allowed to remain alive. In time we established an accommodation with the Polish supervisor. He was a rabid anti-Semite, but permitted the Polish black marketeers to trade with us, because his cut earned him more than his pay from the Germans. In the tannery we felt secure. We worked in a warm house. As a rule Germans did not come to the tannery. On rare occasions when a German came he was handing out cigarettes. We were, after all, skilled workers. The man in charge was Rauter, who was in charge of all workshops. He assured us that as long as he would be in the Novogrudok Ghetto the workers of the tannery would be safe. But once we had a misadventure. As a routine, the Polish supervisor was accepting from his acquaintances hides for tanning. He was not allowed to do this. Once a farmer brought two hides for tanning. The Pole was not there. Maslowaty accepted the hides on behalf of the Polish supervisor. The chief of the police found out about it. He assumed that the Jews were trading with German property. The supervisor did not admit to his responsibility for the event. As it was usual at the time, all the Jewish workers of the tannery were destined to die. The Commandant did not want to intervene. His reaction was that all tanners should be shot. We went that night back to the Ghetto and thought that we would die due to this cruel injustice. I did not tell the family, but I went to the Judenrat. 'We can do nothing about it' they told us 'this is a matter involving only 9 Jews. The rest of the Ghetto is not endangered. Each of you must try to save himself as best he can'. We decided that we must not run from the Ghetto, because this would put everybody in danger. We resolved to wait and hope for a salvation. Next day we went to work in the usual way. All nine of us were their. We were, of course, depressed and did not talk to each other. At nine o'clock we saw Rauter with his dog and the Commandant of the police with about twenty armed policemen. We were all standing frozen and the Pole was as white as the wall. We were all still and ready for the worst. In the past we had gone through many frightening moments and we learned to live always close to death. The animals burst into the tannery and ejected everybody outside. Rauter spoke briefly: 'We hate Jews, we hate even more Jewish swindlers, but if you would work honourably you would remain alive. I would shoot you today, but I need your production. Next time you will all be dead.' The policemen stood in two rows. We had to pass between them. Every policeman hit us with his truncheon or a butt of his rifle. We were severely beaten. But we returned to the tannery and we started working. The Polish supervisor had become friendlier from then on. He did not believe that we would not betray him. He told us that he did not want to take any of our money in the future. In the second slaughter he did what he could to keep us alive.

When we returned home my wife was very upset with me. How could I keep such an event secret? I explained to her that if I told her what was happening I would not be able to get up and go to, what I thought would be, a certain death.

[Page 287]

The Great Destruction

A. How 300 Jews saved themselves

by Chaim Leibovitz

Translated by O. Delatycki

On the 7th of February 1943 the third slaughter took place, which destroyed the communities of Novogrudok, Korelicz., Lubcze, Wsielub, Najsztat and Zetl. From approximately 12,000 people 550 Jews remained. The German head of the district solemnly assured at a specially arranged meeting that the surviving Jews, who were useful would outlive the war. An official government order was issued confirming this. The surviving shadows of human beings were locked up in the district court buildings, where workshops were set up. Sleeping bunks which allowed 60 cm per person were provided. Bread mixed with straw was baked. The ration was 100 grams per person. A thin soup, black in colour was provided. It was made of water and potato peels. To make sure that the survivors would not escape from their quarters, the buildings of the district court were surrounded by a fence made of barb wire. Outside of that fence a tall second fence made of boards was erected. On top of that fence was more barb wire. Outside, next to the road leading to the farms, trenches were dug. The trenches were to prevent an attack from the partisans. At the fence a watch tower with a projector was erected and machine guns were mounted. Eighty policemen kept watch. The Jews were made collectively responsible for the behaviour of each one. This meant that if one Jew offended in any way all Jews would be punished. They were also told that if one Jew would escape from the Ghetto, all Jews would be shot.

Helpless and resigned, the survivors looked on the fires of the burning Ghetto [This refers to the 'second' Ghetto in Peresike, where, apart of some survivors from Novogrudok, the Jews from surrounding towns and villages were interred after the first slaughter. During the first slaughter 85% of the Jews of Novogrudok were killed]. Some of the onlookers had in that Ghetto members of their families, friends and acquittances. It was horrible to contemplate that many of those confined in the Ghetto were convinced that they would be spared by the Germans. They believed it, because the commandant of the Ghetto promised this to them. Their hopes vanished in death and fire. Only now, in the district court, had the Jews come to the conclusion that the German promises were worthless. They now knew that they, the few remaining Jews, would meet with the same end. In silence, with their heads bowed, the Jews in the district court went to sleep on the hard boards. In the morning a meeting was called of former members of Poalei Zion and Bund. The purpose of the meeting was to look for ways of escaping from the claws of the murdering Nazis. The meeting was chaired by Dr I. Cohen, a member of the Central Committee of Poalei Zion in Poland. He spoke with pathos and stressed that our lives must not be sacrificed cheaply, we should aim to take a head for every head killed by the Germans. He continued 'It is disgraceful to die like our misled brothers and sisters died. It is an insult to live such a shameful life. There is only one way left – a worthy death. We must attack the Germans with any means available – using knifes, stones, with teeth and nails. And only than will we be united with the souls of the fallen'.

As a result of the meeting it was decided to prepare an armed uprising. To cut the wires, conduct the Jews from the Ghetto to the forest some 15 kilometres from town, and join the partisans who were located there. The organization of the uprising was on military lines. The membership was drawn from young captives, who were united in one desire. The fighters were divided in groups of five: four combatants and a leader of the group. The headquarters of the operation was at the infirmary where Dr Cohen and Dr Jakubowski had their office. The recruited members were called to the headquarters, where they swore at a burning candle that:

1. They will obey all orders

2. They will not betray any secrets of the movement even if they will be tortured to death

3. They will revenge for the spilled Jewish blood

4. They will not be captured alive by the Germans, and if they will have to die, it must be a worthy death

5. If they should betray the movement they will be punished by a dishonourable death

The plan of the uprising was worked out in detail. Dr Cohen was nominated the head of the uprising. The attack will be made from all four corners of the Ghetto. The leaders of the four groups, who will attack the Germans were: Jankef Nevachovich, Berl Yoselevich, Avrom Rakovski and Mandri.

Korzuchovski together with a group would throw hand grenades at the watch house and destroy it. Orlanski with a group would cut the telephone wires. Czernichowski with a group would cut the wire fences. The more skilled tradesmen would lead the Jews through the wire. Initially most of the people in the Ghetto knew little of the conspiracy. As time passed the situation in the Ghetto got worse. The Jews were counted twice a day. Frequently shots were fired into the windows of the Ghetto. The committee was preparing the uprising. Arms were purchased. This was easier said than done. Arms were purchased for substantial sums from the policemen who were guarding the Ghetto. Non-the-less five rifles, six revolvers and four hand grenades were obtained. The uprising movement was growing in strength. To the surprise of those preparing the uprising, a resistance to the uprising was building up in the Ghetto. Some were arguing that the Germans would not be able to manage without the input of the tradesmen from the Ghetto. Others were arguing that they were not prepared to take their own lives. They did not mind how they would die. God gave them their life and only God could take their lives, they argued. The committee, however, was continuing with their preparations. The blacksmiths were making knives, metal rods with sharp ends, cutters for the wire fences and telephone wires. The preparations continued for two months. The uprising was planned for the 15 April 1943. The order was given for the units to be ready. The young people were thirsting for revenge. On the Sunday night, when, as was the custom, the guards were drunk, the members of the uprising opened the main gate using copied keys. The arms were taken from the hiding place. All were waiting, as arranged, for the first shot, which was a signal to attack the guard. Suddenly, a Mrs Burshtein, whose son was sitting in jail, came out shouting and calling the guard. The members of the uprising have removed the woman. But it was too late. The policemen started to run inside, but they found no one. The members of the uprising moved back inside the Ghetto. A member of the committee told the guard that the woman was deranged. The door was closed and the uprising failed. It should be mentioned that Mrs Burshtein was the mother of Moishe Burshtein, who was at one time one of the managers of the works office in the Ghetto. He was a young man 24 years old and naïve, he was made a member of the Judenrat (works office). In the beginning he collaborated with the Germans and believed them. The systematic slaughters and his disappointment in the German assurances sobered him up and he joined the organisation of the fighters, where he took an active part. It is not known who informed the Germans that Moishe Burshtein was connected with a fighting group. He was arrested without any explanation. The German Gestapo tortured him in order to obtain information about the resistance movement. But he did not disclose anything. He managed to smuggle out a letter written with his blood on his shirt. He wrote 'I am waiting for my death. I am in great pain. I will not betray you.'. He died a martyr's death. After the failed uprising there were several attempts to rekindle the fire of resistance. But the enthusiasm for the uprising had waned. The enthusiasm to bare the breast to a bullet and to become a martyr for the cause had gone. Dr Cohen had resigned from the leadership of the fighting group. The organisation of the fighting group had not been abolished. All fighters were concentrated around the group of furriers. They moved to the same block and consolidated the fighting unit.

The Ghetto lived under tension. In the evenings all were dressed, wore their rucksacks and were ready to attack the gates of the Ghetto. There was fear and panic in the Ghetto. A slaughter was expected at any moment.

At that stage the commissar Reuter appeared and declared that he was satisfied with the behaviour of the remaining Jews. He praised in particular the tailors and shoemakers. He ordered that the tradesmen should be divided into categories: those highly qualified should be given a ration of 200 grams of bread a day, those less qualified – 100 grams. The gentile director accompanied Reuter on a tour of inspection of the workshops and pointed out to him the well qualified workers. About 80% of all employed were considered to be highly qualified. Among those were people that the director knew and those whom the director wanted to oblige. The rest were considered to be 2nd category workers. It was ordered that the highly qualified tradesmen should eat in a separate room to the rest of the workers. This selection caused aggravation among the Jews. They felt that something evil was to happen. The extra bread had a taste of death. Those selected would have gladly forgone the extra ration, but they were made to eat in a separate room, where the bread was allocated.

This change caused, as was usual, various comments. Some, who spoke to the Germans, were told that the better workers would be sent to Germany to work there in factories. Those that were not selected would be left in Novogrudek and would work for the local population. Most of the people in the Ghetto saw in the selection a new ploy by the Germans. They saw it as a measure of misleading the Jews prior to a slaughter. There was panic among those that were considered by the Germans to be less qualified. They were collecting money for the gentile supervisor, hoping that he may persuade Reuter to reconsider them as better qualified. They were also looking for places to hide during the selection. They lifted the floorboards under the bunks and tried to find hiding places, should they be needed. This went on for five weeks. Gradually the excitement subsided. Everyone got his allocated portion of bread, which he ate while standing in the cue for soup.

On the 7th of May at 5 o'clock in the morning the Ghetto was awakened. Commissar Reuter came to check that no workers were missing and to make a list of the workers of the 2nd category, with the object of increasing their bread ration. The workers who were promised by the gentile supervisor that he would endeavour to have them all transferred to the 1st category, have gone out without hesitation onto the yard and arranged themselves according to their trade and category. The better qualified workers stood separate from those less qualified. Commissar Reuter read from a list. He removed deliberately his gloves, lit a cigarette, smiled knowingly, looked around, took out his watch, removed from his pocket a pencil and started writing on a piece of paper. He ordered that the workers of the 1st category should be given on the spot their portions of food. As soon as the better qualified workers entered their canteen, Belarus policemen appeared from behind the fences. They were called crows, because they wore black uniforms. With them, in green uniforms, were heavily armed Latvians. They surrounded the workers who remained in the yard. The workers realised that they had been tricked. They started to shout, cry and try to run, but the Germans opened fire and killed 3 people. The others were beaten with butts and forced on the ground with their faces down. They selected 298 persons, who were led out of the gate and made to lie face down on the ground. They were forced to completely undress and were taken, ten at a time to prepared trenches, where they were shot. The trenches were dug 400 metres from the Ghetto. This may have been done deliberately, to make certain that those who were left in the Ghetto could see the slaughter. Those that were led to their death were shouting, singing, waving their arms to take leave of their friends. Some women put up a resistance. They were severely beaten and dragged by their hair to the trenches.

Some managed to escape from the trench, but the machine gun fire put an end to their lives. It was all finished within half an hour. Our Belarus neighbours willingly covered up the trenches. All that was left was a small elevation where the trench was. Farmers with their horses and carts were trailing slowly and indifferently to market, past the place where a short time ago the slaughter occurred. The morning sun shone on their round, well fed faces, as if to imply that they could travel undisturbed, they were not in any danger.

The slaughter had a shocking effect on all those who remained alive in the Ghetto. The dead were with us. We could see clearly from the yard of the Ghetto the mound over the trench. The members of the organisation were moving around silently with their heads bowed. Ahead of us lay long, sleepless nights and joyless days. During the day we were waiting for the night. And at night we were praying for the light of the next day. The members of the organisation started to plan anew an uprising against the Germans. It was decided to post a guard in the day time on the loft, with the order to raise an alarm should the Germans surround the Ghetto. It was decided that if the Germans should approach, a group of fighters armed with hand grenades should meet them at the gate. It was also decided that each time there was a head count in the yard, the members of the organisation should come to the yard with hand grenades in their pockets. About that time it had become known from the concealed radios that there was an uprising of Jews in Warsaw, which resulted in the liquidation of the Jewish population of Warsaw (the committee had a secret radio receiver in the Ghetto, only the members of the committee knew of its existence) . From the same source news was received of great defeats which the Germans suffered at the front and the bombardment of the German towns. The Germans started to hint that the Jews would be transported to a safer place. One German, a certain Zellinger, who played the role of a friend of the Jews, let it be known that the remaining Jews would be treated better, because the attitude of the German government to the Jews had changed for the better. The members of the committee were bitterly disappointed with the past events and were not deceived by any overtures. In the mean time news arrived that all Jews of Lida Ghetto were liquidated. It was ordered that all members of the group must be on guard.. The members of the committee gathered and discussed the possibility of an attack on the Germans on this day. At the same time Jews who did not want to leave the Ghetto met to discuss the situation and decided to hinder the efforts of the fighters. They decided to stay in the Ghetto as long as possible. Their argument was that they did not want to commit suicide, because an attack on the Germans would be unsuccessfully. On the other hand, if the Jews would remain in the Ghetto, their may be an opportunity to save one's life. One must have faith. One of the group who decided to stay told us in confidence that Ing. Kaltenhauer had assured him that the remaining Jews would be allowed to live till after the war and after that they would be sent to Madagascar, where the Jews would live among themselves. It was also possible that the Germans would lose the war and would be expelled and the Jews, miraculously, would be left alive. It was also contemplated that the American Jews would succeed to persuade their government to exchange the German prisoners of war, which they were holding, for Jews from the Ghettos.

And finally G-d gives and G-d takes. Nobody is at liberty to take away the gift that G-d gave him – his life. And to discourage the members who favoured an uprising, they sent a delegation to the uprising committee suggesting a plan to build a tunnel leading outside the Ghetto, and then get out to the forest.

The committee had stopped for a few days the activities of the conspiracy. At that time, within three days the project to dig a tunnel was approved. Berl Yoselevich was appointed technical manager of the project. The structural supervisor was Dworecki.

It was decided to build a tunnel 70cm wide and 70 cm high. The work proceeded at a fast rate, but the digging was very hard, because only one man could work at the face of the tunnel and he had to dig in a lying position. The soil was dragged out in bags. The ropes for dragging of the bags were made from shirts. The bags were moved to the lofts by a conveyor line of sixty men. When the lofts were filled, the soil was put into the water well. This created a shortage of water in the Ghetto. The Germans, who did not know the reason for the shortage, supplied water in barrels for the Jews. At that stage the Germans ordered that the water wall should be cleaned. The Jews dug the soil from the well and added to it the sand dug from the tunnel. The Germans were petitioned to give permission to dig new toilets, so as to maintain cleanliness in the Ghetto. The permission was given. The Jews dug trenches for the new toilets and added to it the soil from the tunnel. Within two months a tunnel 110 metres long was dug. The tunnel led to a field outside the Ghetto. A meeting was called to discuss the evacuation of the Ghetto. However, those Jews who were previously opposed to attacking the Germans were now opposed to leaving the Ghetto through the tunnel. They were in favour of digging a longer tunnel. There were others who also wanted a longer trunnel, but would not be used. Their idea was that when the Germans would come to take the Jews from the Ghetto every one would hide in the tunnel. It was decided to continue digging the tunnel to a total length of 220 metres. At that stage heavy rains began to fall. The soil above the tunnel began to crumble. Cracks appeared in the walls of the tunnel. There was a danger that the whole tunnel would collapse. It was decided to line the walls of the tunnel with boards. For that job, boards used were those delivered to the Ghetto for making furniture. When the Germans came to collect the furniture they found that the boards had disappeared. The Germans suspected that the Jews used the boards for heating the interior of the Ghetto buildings. The Germans came and flogged the carpenters from the furniture workshop. Being in a playful mood, they hanged a carpenter named Shaffer. Mrs Hodl Samsonovich from Wsielub came over and cut the rope, thus saving Shafer. Shafer escaped and was hiding. (He is now in Israel). Samsonovich also escaped punishment.

The work in the tunnel continued with a great energy. The tunnel was 280 metres long when it was finished. Holes were made in the ceiling of the tunnel to allow air to enter. Electric light was installed. The tunnel led to a wheat field. The mood in the Ghetto improved. The news of the German defeats at the front was also encouraging. A meeting of all the Jews in the Ghetto was held in the carpenter workshop. Members of the committee spoke and suggested that all should leave the Ghetto by the tunnel. There were a number of people who opposed the proposal. It was then proposed that all Jews should express their view in a secret ballot. The result of the ballot was that 65% voted for getting out through the tunnel. In view of that result, the committee selected an evacuation group which was empowered to force all Jews to leave the Ghetto. A group of armed persons was established, which was ordered to see to it that all Jews would leave the Ghetto. The committee had accepted the following rule about the order of evacuation: first those between 17 and 35 years would leave, secondly the intelligentsia, thirdly the workers who actively participated in building of the tunnel and last would go all others in order decided upon by the committee. The evacuation committee was working intensively. Every Jew was given a number indicating the order in which he had to leave. The punishment for not obeying the orders of the committee was flogging to death. All Jews were given a number with exception of three: Dr Jakubowski with his wife and the convert Mendelson, A Jew from Vienna who worked in the office of the Germans. Dr Jakubowski, who was previously a member of the fighting organisation, was wounded in his leg by the Germans when they were shooting at random into the Ghetto. Because of the wound he could not walk. His wife threatened that she would inform the Germans if there would be an attempt to escape.

There was a meeting of the united committee, chaired by Dr Cohen. Salek Jakubowski, Dr Jakubowski's brother was also present. Salek Jakubowski was in the lead as he was the head of the Ghetto police and was totally devoted to the committee organisation. When the problem of his brother and sister-in-law came up, Jakubowski expressed his opinion that the only way the people of the Ghetto could leave undisturbed was to kill his brother, sister-in-law and Mendelson. It was decided that an hour before the escape the members of the committee would kill the three. The people who would do the deed were appointed. In the last minute some members of the committee decided to try to speak with Jakubowski. Jakubowski was taken to the place were the tunnel was dug. He was taken inside. Behind them came a member carrying a bag and a rope to throttle him if he should not agree to escape through the tunnel. Luckily Dr Jakubowski and his wife agreed to get out through the tunnel providing he would be allowed out first and that he would be carried for the first 100 metres after leaving the tunnel. Mendelson was locked up in his office and was killed later.

The last preparations for the escape were made. There were some difficulties regarding the projector, which illuminated an area of several kilometres. Shutting down the projector by causing a short circuit would arouse suspicion by the guards. The projector was disabled by reducing the current. This meant that the light shone bleakly no further than a few metres around the projector. The committee published for the people of the Ghetto a leaflet about the escape. Our aim was to gain liberty, and if in the process we would die, this would be G-d's will. A leaflet was also printed urging the Byelorussians to escape to the forests, because the Germans had lost the war and the day of liberation was nigh.

On the 26th of September on a rainy dark evening, when the guard was engaged in getting drunk, all Jews went through the openings in the ceilings to the entry to the tunnel. At 9pm all were standing in an order arranged by the committee. At the entrance to the tunnel stood the members of the fighting unit with revolvers and whips in their hands. They let everyone into the tunnel in the order set out on the list. One hundred and forty persons were allowed to go into the tunnel. At exactly 10pm the exit was opened. Within 3 minutes all Jews were out. The last were the members of the fighting organisation. In all 323 Jews got out, which was almost the entire population of the Ghetto. A few 'clever' people hid in the Ghetto. They assumed that all those that went through the tunnel would be caught, and in a few days they would leave. Those that stayed behind were caught the next day. [Not quite so. See eg p.237. A sea of trouble.]

It was arranged that after leaving the tunnel, the Jews would crawl to the shrubs. But, as soon as the Jews got out and felt free they became disoriented and started to run. Also, the last to leave forgot to extinguish the light at the entrance to the tunnel. This drew the attention of the guard. They thought initially that the partisans came to free the people of the Ghetto. They opened a hefty fire. The German military and the gendarmes, having heard the shooting in the Ghetto, started shooting using machine guns and lit the area with projectors and rockets.

Next morning the chase started. Germans in tanks and motorcars began looking for Jews. The Jews ran in all directions. Some, in confusion, ran into the town. Forty four Jews were caught in town. They were tortured. Some had their eyes removed. All were burned in a barn. Some were killed in the fields and bushes. Almost all members of the fighting organisation were slain. Dr Jankef Cohen, the leader of the uprising, Berl Joselewicz, technical leader of the construction of the tunnel, Jankef Newachowicz, deputy leader of the uprising group, died on leaving the tunnel. Salek Jakubowski carried his brother 200 metres before being killed by a bullet. His brother lives in Poland. The fighters Kozuchowski, Czernichowski, Orlanski and another 5 fighters, found three days after the escape a partisan unit led by Victor. They were asked to surrender their weapons. They had two weapons. The fighters refused to surrender their arms. They said that only death would make them part with their weapons. They were killed by the partisans. The commander Avrom Rakowski found a gentile partisan group where he had excelled in his fight against the Germans. He was highly decorated by the Soviet government. He was killed in the fight for Berlin. About 143 men joined various partisan groups and survived the war. They fought the Byelorussians, who collaborated with the Germans. A number of them took part in the war and were killed on the approaches to Berlin. Some made their way to Israel and fought for the liberation of the country. Some died fighting in the Negev.

Their names will be remembered for generations. We will remember the heroes Berl Joselewicz, Avrom Rakowski, Dr Cohen and other heroes of the Novogrudok Ghetto.

[Page 293]

B. The last Passover

by Chaim Leibovitz

Translated by O. Delatycki

It was 1943. Spring was early. In March the sun created some warmth and brought the expectation of the arrival of spring. But the Jews of the Novogrudok Ghetto, in perpetual fear of death, were not warmed by the sun. It was the eve of Passover. The snow had melted. Here and there rivulets of water were flowing. The aroma of the fields and forests sneaked in to the Ghetto through the fences and bars. The Ghetto was enmeshed in sadness. The 550 Jews in the Ghetto were holding on to their lives by the skin of their teeth. They were the last of the 18 thousand Jews of Novogrudok [6 thousand Jews lived in Novogrudok at the beginning of the war]. They were the last of those who were segregated tens of times by the Germans and allowed to live. They were considered to be qualified tradesmen, who were of service to the Germans. They were assured that they would survive because the Germans needed them. They were told that when the war will end, they will be sent to Madagascar where they will be able to continue to live as Jews. The Ghetto was like a fortress, it was locked up, and one could not come in or get out. The Jews were checked twice a day. A collective responsibility was imposed. There was extensive hunger. People were moving like shadows. Every day another shadow was missing. Some one was buried in the yard next to the building. In the corners next to the workshops groups of people were arguing. There were rumours going around that the Ghetto would be liquidated any day. The Jews were distressed. They didn't want to believe it. Was it possible that the Germans would kill the tradesmen? We heard on the radio hidden in the Ghetto that there was an uprising in the Warsaw Ghetto. As we were isolated from the world around us we wondered whether that could be true. Could it be that after very many tortures and killings the Jews were capable of launching a fight against the well armed murderers? We could not believe it. But then again we found in our souls a quiet hope – perhaps, perhaps...

The youths were assembling separately. They still had hope. We gathered in a corner. Dr Kagan from Baranovich said that such an existence made no sense, here we could expect only extinction. A slaughter could be felt in the air. One solution was preferable – to attack the Germans and die as heroes. The assembled quietened down. Nobody uttered a word. One could hear only the branches swaying softly. They seemed to be saying 'save yourselves'. Disappointed, we dispersed slowly each to his own corner. Though death was nearly upon us, though disappointed not knowing what tomorrow would bring, the Jews were preparing themselves for the Passover feast. There was no way we could bake matzos. Instead of matzo, we toasted on the fire the 100 grams daily ration of black bread which contained straw. The women grated the skins of the potatoes and made dumplings and we were ready for the Passover. The evening was approaching. The rooms in the Ghetto were packed with people. It was difficult to breathe. Old Gertzovski, the brush maker from Zetl, crawled onto the fourth tier of the bunks. He was joined by another six Jews. They conducted the Passover service. He recited the Haggadah and was heard in the quite. The others repeated every word after him. There were no children left to ask the kashes (questions). Various memories were passing through our heads. We were thinking of the years gone by, the Passover feasts we had been to when whole families were sitting together at the festive tables, fathers, mothers and children, well dressed and jolly. In the Ghetto were mostly skeletons, single members of families, walking shadows. Someone started weeping. The crying spread.

In haste we recited the Haggadah. The words were said monotonously 'Next year in Jerusalem'. Could it happen? Could there be a miracle and someone would survive? Who knows what tomorrow would bring. Who knows?

Quietly the Jews slid down from the bunks and in mourning each went to his corner. They wrapped themselves in rags and tried to sleep, because tomorrow at five o'clock in the morning they had to be ready for the daily inspection. On the bunks among the women was a girl from Warsaw, Linka Landau. The Germans did not kill her because of her good looks. She was tall, slim and gracious with a smooth thin face. She had big black eyes and long lashes and black hair. A veritable Jewish beauty. She sat with the other women on the bunk and sang a sad song:

In a hamlet not too far
In a small house on a side
From a small window
A Jewish child looked out

His mother brought him here
Wrapped late at night
She kissed him cried and wept
And spoke her last parting words

Around were mothers from whose hands their children had been torn away. They started weeping uncontrollably.

On the bunks opposite men were lying and reciting quietly the Haggadah.

[Page 294]

C. Three who were burned to death

by Chaim Leibovitz

as told by Chana Kirshner

Translated by O. Delatycki

This happened in 1942

A year had passed since the German boot had smashed Byelorussia and the wild beasts have murdered many Jews. In the middle of December an order was issued by the District Commissar Traub to send six workers to him to install water pipes to his palace. It was stressed that the work must be done promptly. The Jews sent six workers, three for the day shift and three for the night shift. H. Gershovich, Florent from Baranovichi and Chanan Kirshner were working on the night shift. The Jews were trying their best, but the work was difficult because the soil was frozen. To keep warm they lit a small fire. They were tearing lumps of soil using axes and spades. The District Commissar Traub would go out from time to time from his palace to see if the Jews were working. He warned that if the job would not be completed in time he would shoot 100 Jews. He was smiling whilst looking on how the Jews were working diligently.

It was midnight on the eve of the New Year. Traub went out of the palace, approached the Jews and told them to stand in line. He took out a notebook and asked their names. He had written down their names and told them that tomorrow they would not work there anymore. He hit them with his whip and ordered them to shout three times 'Ich bin ein varfluchter Jude' [I am a cursed Jew]. The Jews complied. Then he told them to shout 'Heil Hitler'. 'Louder!' he shouted, 'Louder still!' The Jews were shouting with all their might. Next he took out his revolver and shot them all. He shot Gershovich first. Next he shot Florent. And as he was going to shoot Kirshner, Kirshner ducked trying to escape, but he was hit by a bullet and fell unconscious. Traub grabbed the Jews for their legs and dragged them to the fire. He stacked them on top of each other with Floret at the bottom and Kirshner on top. He covered them with branches. The branches were catching the fire slowly. Traub stood by smoking a pipe. From time to time he pushed the branches with his foot. However Chanan Kirshner was not dead. The bullet hit him in his buttock and he fainted from pain and fear. When he came to he felt a dreadful noise in his head and heat in his body. He was dressed in a sheepskin jacket. He felt with his hand the hair of his friend. He opened slowly an eye and saw the face of the murderer Traub. He closed his eye and feigned death. He began to feel strong pain in his side. He felt that his fur coat was smouldering. He was lying without movement. Traub stood by his victims and from time to time pushed their bodies with his boot. Then he spat and slowly went back home. Kirshner was lying holding his breath. The minutes moved slowly, like an infinity. He lifted his head slowly. All was quiet and covered in snow. The only sound was that of the steps of a policeman, who walked back and forth in front of Traub's door. Kirshner felt that his fur coat was burning on him. He decided to wait no longer. He got up and ran in the direction of the fence. The policeman heard the steps and shouted for Kirshner to stop. Kirshner took off his fur and threw himself in the snow. The policeman mistook the fur for the man and shot in the direction of the fur. Kirshner, using all his strength, jumped the fence. He crawled on all fours to the other group of Jews who were working in the horse stable for the Gestapo murderer Hose. Kirshner got into the stable with his last strength and fainted. The workers threw water over him and brought him back to consciousness. They hid him in a corner of the stable, covered in straw. In the morning, after other workers replaced the night shift, they returned to the Ghetto and told Kirshner's parents what had happened. The Judenrat sent a horse and cart with workers under the pretext of cleaning the yard. They brought Kirshner back in the cart, covered with straw. They took him to the ambulatory where he was given medical help. A day later the Chief of Staff Wolfmayer came to the Ghetto and inquired about Kirshner. It is not known how Wolfmayer found out about Kirshner. He visited Kirshner and he told the doctors to take good care of him. He asked Kirshner what had happened and how he saved himself. He said: 'Jude du hast dein Leben gerettet, but you will parish anyway'. Since than, any time the Chief of Staff would come into the Ghetto he would inquire after Kirshner. After 90 days Kirshner was feeling much better, though he limped slightly. But it was not destined for Kirshner to survive. He died from a bullet wound shortly after he got out of the tunnel.

It is not known to this day why the Chief of Staff was so interested in the fate of Kirshner, because he was the organizer of all the slaughters. Is it possible that he had a human feeling? Or did he want to see Kirshner healed so that he could shoot him in good health. Who knows what he had in mind.

> [On p.274 in the article 'They burned the town', Yehoshua Yaffe described an incident which is similar, yet in a number of details different from the above narrative. It is probable that the two articles described the same event. It is difficult to know which version is the correct one.]

[Page 296]

D. Escape through the tunnel

by Chaim Leibovitz

Translated by O. Delatycki

On the 26 of September at 10pm, as I get out of the Ghetto through the tunnel crawling on my stomach, a strong rain is cutting my face. A light wind carries the smell of the field and forest. It is very dark, gloomy and one cannot see even a meter in front of the face. I find myself on the wet grass, with no strength left in me and yet I am drunk with the surprise. I take a deep breath and feel strength pumping into my limbs. A rush of warmth circulates through my body. I am saved, I am saved. Now the Germans can not torture me any more. If I will be killed, I will die as a human being. My dream had become a reality, I may die now as a free man the other side of the barb wire. Suddenly a hurricane of gun fire opens up. Machine guns are shooting from all sides. Projectors are illuminating the countryside and the wet sky. I have only one thought – to run. I find it difficult to drag my legs. They feel as if they belong to someone else. I run however, spurned on by an internal compulsion. Without design, without an aim I fall into a hole with water above my knees. I am trying to pull myself out of the morass, but I feel powerless. The shooting is more intense, more frequent and closer. The bullets fly with a whistle above my head. Near by shadows are moving. The shadows are people. Who are they? I hear a whisper. It is Rybak, the teacher and his wife. They help me out of the bog. They hold me under my arms and we are running together. But my feet are not obeying me. They drag. Rybak and his wife drag me about 100 steps, when I fall and drag them down with me. I am begging them to leave me and save themselves. But they continue to drag me. In the end they leave me and disappear in the darkness. The sky begins to get lighter by the minute. Rockets cross the sky. My sight begins to darken. Suddenly everything before my eyes begins to jump, vibrate in the air and tumble in a prism of colours. Large wheels are turning, blue, green, red rainbows. Suddenly I feel a mild sensation in my limbs. I don't know how long I was lying half conscious. Drops of rain wake me. Where am I? I must run, but run where? Is there anywhere one can run? The Germens are everywhere. I feel my head. My hat is gone. My thoughts are pursuing me. I am saved, they will never take me alive. Not far, just over the hillock my family is buried. I may join them shortly. I take out a sharp knife which I made in the Ghetto. It will be useful. I get up and walk slowly. Suddenly it seems to me that I hear some voices. I bend down closer to the ground. They appear to speak Yiddish. I walk in the direction of the voices and begin to shout: Yidden! [Jews]. A few people approach me. I recognise some of them: Rybak and his wife, Mazurkiewicz, a Jew from Poland and Chanan, the cobbler from Makrec. We are happy to have met. It started to get lighter. We look around and we can see that we are close to the military barracks in Skridlewo. German soldiers are housed in the barracks.

Gradually an autumn day is beginning to evolve. We hide in low shrubbery. We divide up into two groups. The day is getting rapidly lighter. We can see herdsmen and cows. They graze close by. We can see farmers travelling in horse drawn carriages. Shma Isroel, whispers Chanan the cobbler, shma Isroel, save the Jewish folk from an evil eye. The heart is pounding fast. Lorry loads of German soldiers are passing by so close that it seems that we could reach them with our outstretched arms. We are lying flat, holding our breath. The day stretches endlessly. We long for the darkness. May G'd give a salvation - prays Rybak. Thus we are lying in fear until it begins to darken. After darkness falls we crawl over to the other side of the highway in the direction of the forest. We begin to feel hungry. But where can we get food? We decide to find the nearest farmer's house and ask for food. We walk in the darkness a mile when we see a small isolated house. We move slowly to the door and knock on the window. 'Who is it' asks a hoarse voice. 'Give us some bread' we reply. 'We have no bread' answers the farmer. 'Have pity on us sufferers' pleads Chanan the cobbler. A window opens and a hand throws out a thin slice of bread. We take it and go around the corner were the bread is quickly swallowed. We begin to feel more hungry than before. We decide to return to the farmer to ask him where other houses are where we could find some food. We creep silently to the house and knock on the window. 'What do you want again' asked the farmer. "You gave us too little bread" we reply. 'I have no more, the Germans took all I had' the farmer replied. 'Show us were other farmers live?' we ask the farmer. 'I don't know, go away from here, you punished by G'd Jews' answered the farmer. We take out the knives we had made in the Ghetto. Mazurkiewicz takes out a revolver made of timber and points it at the farmer through the window. As soon as the farmer sees the revolver, the farmer begins to talk in a silky voice and is begging 'My little fathers [a Belarusian turn of phrase indicating the will to compromise] why are you shouting?'. 'Give us bread' we shouted. 'Don't shout' he answered 'I will ask my wife, she may have something for you'. After a few minutes the farmer brings two large loaves of bread, weighing about 20 pounds. We take the bread and walk away. We stretch out on the wet field and begin tearing lumps of bread. In a few minutes we finish the bread. We drink some water from a puddle and fall into a deep sleep on the wet grass.

This is how we spent the first 24 hours of freedom.

[Page 297]

E. The heroic death of Berl Yoselevich

by Chaim Leibovitz

Translated from Yiddish by O. Delatycki

Twenty years ago Berl Yoselevich died heroically. He led to freedom 330 Jews [elsewhere it was claimed that 230 Jews were at that time in the Ghetto, see eg. 'p.237. A sea of troubles'. A figure of 250 was also mentioned elsewhere.] through a tunnel, which was dug from the Novogrudok Ghetto on his initiative. Berl Yoselevich was one of the heroes of the Ghetto. He led a battle against the Germans, he encouraged the Jews of the Ghetto, he urged them to break out from the bondage of the German bandits and he led them to freedom.

The Jews, the remnants of four slaughters, were held in a locked up Ghetto and were guarded by 80 armed policemen. It was impossible to break out from the chain of the armed German and Belarus crows (they were called crows because they wore black uniforms). A collective responsibility was imposed on the people of the Ghetto. There was acute hunger in the Ghetto. Many inmates were swollen from hunger. The food ration was 100 grams of heavy dark broad made of grains mixed with straw. A bowl of dirty water, with a few pieces of potato peel swimming on the surface, was given for lunch. Shadows wrapped in rags with wooden clogs on their feet were moving through the Ghetto. People were dying every day. They were buried in their rags in a house next to the workshops. The graves looked like garden beds in the autumn after the harvest. Various rumours circulated in the Ghetto. The youths were congregating in groups in the yard and whispered to each other. Everyone expected a slaughter at any time. Some were saying that the Jews would be taken to Germany to work. The survivors were going around with bowed heads. They knew well what the future was likely to hold in store for them.

At that difficult time, when the situation seemed hopeless, Berl Yoselevich became prominent. He was moved to act by the dormant feelings of the national consciousness. He became the leader of the Novogrudok Jews.

Berl Yoselevich was born in Novogrudok in 1904 to a family of respectable tradesmen. His father Rafael was a member of the management committee of Shogdai Meloche and a gabi in the Chevre Kadishe. Berl had a traditional Jewish education. For 2 years Berl and I were pupils at the cheder Menaker. Berl was a studious and able schoolchild.

In 1918 Berl started learning photography. This became his occupation. In 1924 he was called up for army service in Slonim. Berl was a protagonist of Hashomer Hatzair. But his main involvement was with the sporting club Maccabi.

Berl did not have the appearance of a brave man, he had daring, courage and fearlessness. He was always the first to do things and was a good organiser.

When the Germans occupied Novogrudok, Berl worked, as all Jews did, for the Germans. He lost all his family during the three slaughters. When he and the handful of survivors were locked in the court house, he and some young friends were planning an uprising against the Germans. But the attempt fell through. It was obvious that the remaining Jews were certain to perish. Berl assembled a group of 10 people. He told them that remaining in the Ghetto was senseless, it would spell perdition. There was only one solution: to build a tunnel and get out. And if they must perish, let it be in a fight. The assembled elected Berl to be in charge of the project to build a tunnel.

Berl started to organise the work. He assembled a group of reliable young men. As the work began, all those in the Ghetto who were able to work were drawn into the task force. It was decided that anyone who would betray the secret would be killed.

The building of the tunnel took till September. The tunnel was 220 metres long [elsewhere the length was quoted at 250 metres] under the corn fields. It was decided to get out on the 26 of September. Berl ordered that in the workshops all sowing machines should be dismantled to make them useless. A leaflet was printed in which the Belarus police was urged to drop their guns and go to the forests, because Germany was certain to lose the war. On Sunday the 26 September, when the Germans were getting drunk, all Jews crawled through the cellars to the entrance of the tunnel. Within half an hour all were arranged in a row in the order which the committee had previously decided. Berl was standing at the entrance with the prepared list. In the prearranged order one after another crawled into the tunnel. Next to him were the members of the committee, who were making certain that all orders were obeyed.

Everyone entered the tunnel in the prescribed order. By 10 o'clock all Jews left the tunnel. The last to leave were the members of the committee and Berl. In all, 332 Jews had got out through the tunnel. The majority did not want to go, but they went nevertheless, except for a few 'wise guys' who, unbeknown to everybody else, hid in the Ghetto. They thought that all those who went out would be caught and those who remained would get out a few days later and would survive. The 'wise guys' were caught the next morning. [As far as it is known, 6 people decided not to go out with the others through the tunnel. The story of five of them is described in detail in 'p.237. A sea of troubles.' All five stayed in hiding for 8 days after the escape through the tunnel. All survived. There was also a single person, who hid separately. He stayed back till the next day. He walked out of the Ghetto unhindered. He told his story after the war in Germany.]

According to the arrangement those escaping from the tunnel were supposed to crawl half a kilometre from the outlet of the tunnel, to a shrubbery. But when the people left the tunnel they became disoriented and started running. The members of the committee overlooked turning out the light in the barn at the entrance to the tunnel. The movement and the light drew the attention of the guards. The guards thought that the partisans had come to liberate the Ghetto. They started intensive shooting from automatic rifles, turned on the search lights and fired rockets. The members of the committee could not stop the Jews, who were milling in a panic, and had forgotten to run to the forest, which was 4 kilometres from the town.

The brothers Orlanski and Chernichovski, who were armed, were killed after they got to the forests and met a gentile partisan group. The commander of the group Victor asked them to surrender their weapons. Orlanski refused to part with his gun. They were shot on Victor's orders.

Berl Yoselevich, the organiser of digging of the tunnel, was killed in a forest not far from the village of Horodechno about 4 kilometres from Novogrudok, having fallen into the hands of the Germans on the 27th of September 1943. The name of Berl, his fighting spirit and courage remain in the memory of the Jews of Novogrudok. His memory, as one of the heroes who sacrificed his life for the Jewish people, will be preserved in our memory.

He will be remembered forever among the heroes of the Jewish people.

[Page 299]

How I Survived

By Idl Kagan

Translated from Yiddish by O. Delatycki

Thank you, my feet (feet of mine?), frozen, bloody, you kept creeping and crawling and you saved me from death. When the war broke out I was barely 12 years old. My early religious education was acquired from the melamed (teacher) Menaker, and was similar to the education of many other children in Novogrudok. Later I was enrolled in Tarbut. But our generation was not destined to study at length because of the outbreak of the war. A few days later, our town was bombarded and our house was destroyed. We moved to the house of [uncle Israel OD] Delatycki, behind the fire station. Four families occupied that house: two brothers Kagan, Sosnowski and Sucharski. We were uneasy, but for the time we were not short of basic necessities. I was working. My job was to remove bricks and stones from the destroyed houses. This continued until the first slaughter, in which members of our family, Moshe Kagan with his wife and son were killed. It was not ordained for my dear uncle Moshe to survive. During the selection process [of those who should die and who, for the time, would be spared] an SS man came running looking for Moshe Kagan to remove him from the group selected to die, because uncle did not finish making the saddle for his riding horse. But he arrived too late; uncle was already taken to the mass graves. But his son was miraculously saved. During the selection a German called out: "who is a motor mechanic?" Berl Kagan, standing among those selected to die, shouted without hesitation: "I and my friend are mechanics". And for the time he saved himself and his friend Openhiem.

After the slaughter, I continued working with my father as a saddler, and, somehow, we were surviving. My circumstances changed for the worse when I was transferred to the army barracks. The barracks were some distance away, the food was sparse, and I suffered continuous beating from the sadist Makash. He selected me in particular, and I was subject to more assaults than the others. One morning, suddenly, a mob of SS men with machine guns appeared. They selected 50 workers and I was among them. They took us a little distance aside and lined us up to be shot. I turned my head so as not to see the barrel of the machine gun. I felt paralyzed in expectation of the inevitable death. Any second the end would come. But the SS man would not allow me the pleasure of not seeing myself being killed. He came over and hit me with his white glove telling me to turn and face the machine gun. Suddenly a temporary reprieve arrived. A German came running and ordered the postponement of the shooting. It appeared that the reason for the execution was that two boys were found to be smuggling food. They overpowered the German who caught them, and ran away. But at the last moment the Germans decided that in view of the eminent mass slaughter they may as well wait. The approach of massacre was palpable. We were instinctively aware of the smell of death. Too many Jews were brought from the neighboring towns. All available houses were packed solid with people. The over-crowding was life threatening. At that time it was easy to escape from the Ghetto. Why didn't people escape, though everyone expected a slaughter? I could not understand it while I was young. But now I can comprehend their motives. The instinctive desire for families to stay together, the fear of the forests and of the peasants, who were catching and slaughtering Jews, were the reasons for remaining together in the Ghetto. I succeeded somehow to get out of the barracks and to be transferred to the workshops, where I worked with my father. The second slaughter of the Jews in Novogrudok took place in August 1942. I am shuddering every time I think of the horror of it. I remember the selection of children. I did everything to look bigger. I wore father's jacket; I tried to walk on the tips of my toes to look taller. I was successful--I stayed alive. My father, mother and sister also survived. We managed to postpone the death sentence. After the second slaughter, the escapes started. All youngsters were seen whispering to each other and at night they would vanish. A contact with the partisans in the forest had been established and the youth in the Ghetto was getting ready to flee. Ishie Openhiem came from the forest to the Ghetto and chose a group of young men. Among them was my cousin Berl Kagan. At the time of the escape, I was given the task of watching the movements of the guards. The escape was successful. I was looking with envy at the older boys who could escape to fight and take revenge. After Berl Kagan escaped, I was restless in the Ghetto. The nights were sleepless. I was contemplating how to break out as soon as possible. I did not need to convince my parents. Father prepared a pair of good felt boots for me and blessed me with the wish that at least one member of the family might survive. The day had come. It was December 1942. We left through the gate in broad daylight. It was a nice, frosty day. We tore off the yellow patches. We looked at the free world, which was not meant for us. We stole through the town. My heart ceased to panic, knowing that we left the walls of the Ghetto. We stopped to rest in a clump of trees not far from the town, to wait for nightfall. We planned to get to the dogcatcher, where the partisans would fetch us. [Bobrowski, the dogcatcher used his isolated house as a meeting point of the escapees from the Ghetto with the partisans. He was ultimately caught and killed by the Germans. The sole survivor of the family, his daughter, is cared for by the author of this article. OD]. For safety we chose an indirect path via the lake in Brecianka, which pre-war was a popular spot for bathing. As we were crossing the lake, the thin ice broke and some of us fell in. The felt boots absorbed a lot of water. My feet became very heavy. It was very cold. But the desire to live urged me on. I was trying to get to the dogcatcher's house and the thought that the partisans, and Berl among them, would be waiting for me, gave me courage. We made it with difficulties. Alas, it turned out that the partisans had been and left. My situation was tragic beyond belief. My feet were hurting unbearably. They were frozen. I felt that I was loosing my feet. I had to return to the Ghetto. But how could I manage it with my felt boots wet and ice amassed all around them. I looked like a clown walking on high stilts. I could not walk far. The daylight was breaking. It was 6 o'clock. I dragged myself to the road. I was in luck. A farmer on a sledge, with his head wrapped up to protect him from the cold, came by. I slid surreptitiously onto the back of the sledge. He took me to the Korelich Street in town and continued on in the direction of the Court [the Ghetto was in the building complex of the Polish District Court]. I slid off the sledge and found myself among a group, who was out on the daily chore of fetching water from a well for the Ghetto. They surrounded me and let me crawl slowly with the last bit of strength back behind the wall of the Ghetto. They started to take off the felt boots by cutting them into small bits. It was all one piece of ice glued firmly to the skin. With a lot of effort my black frozen toes were freed of ice. They had to be removed by an operation as soon as possible. An operation could only be performed in the Ghetto with a sharp knife. One was held strongly whilst the toes were being cut. You were not allowed to cry out, so as not to attract the attention of the guards. Removing of the toes was not the enough, since the bones were also affected and further cutting was necessary. When the cutting was finished I was left on the slab in great pain. I did not know when my pains would stop. But my greatest enemy were the bed bugs. The plague was frightful. My feet were wrapped in rags and the bugs could penetrate them easily. They were attacking my wounds and biting them fiercely. I could not stand it and I had to scratch the wounds thus opening them. In February Ishie Openhiem came again to the Ghetto and took out my cousin Sheindl Zubarski and her friend Sosnowski. Going through the town they met a Polish girl they went to school with. She denounced them and they were shot. At that time the Ghetto in the Court Buildings was more securely fenced in and guarded. Escape was made impossible. By May 1943 my feet began to heal; my young body was aiding the recovery. I was beginning to move slowly on crutches. I was thinking again of escaping. I envied Pesach Abramovich. He also had his feet frozen during our attempted escape, but his injuries were less severe. He was running around, using his crutches. I kept thinking "when will I be able to run like this?". On the

7 of May 1943 I was lying as usual on my slab watching the daily roll call in the centre of the Ghetto, where the head count was conducted and the meagre ration of bread was distributed. I did not go to the roll call because I was unable to do so. Suddenly a horrible event unfolded. SS men surrounded the people in the queue and start beating them mercilessly with sticks. I could not watch the scene and buried my head in the cushion. I was thinking fast. I believed that this was the end of the Ghetto – a slaughter. I started to hide instinctively. I arranged the cushions such that the bed looked empty. I could hear machine gun shots – this was the end of our existence. Many thoughts went through my mind. I was not afraid to die, but, if I would be injured in a beating, I would be unable to move. And how would I survive if everyone else would die? But the desire to survive was strong. I buried myself deeper among the cushions. Policemen appeared. They were looking for things to rob. They found mostly rags and threw them on my slab, providing me with a better cover. Hours passed, each one seemed like a year. Suddenly I could hear steps. My dear father appeared in my hiding place. I survived. My father told me that my mother and my sister were lost in the slaughter. We were irreconcilable. There was nothing to hope for. The only question was – when would our end come? Few Jews remained in the Ghetto. Escape was impossible. A desperate plan was conceived – to force our way through a gate and escape. The organisers were proposing to use hand grenades. The night and time for the break out was set. As we waited, the mood in the Ghetto was tense. But what could I do without feet? My father came to see me. He looked terrible – skin and bone. He spoke to me warmly "Idl, my son, I prepared two ropes. When all will escape the two of us will hang ourselves from the rafters. You know, I am sure, that to fall in the hands of the SS will be a lot worse". I can see still his penetrating look and hear his sombre tone. I said "Father, you did not think of yourself, you decided to remain with me to the last minute". As it is known, the plan of the uprising was abandoned and changed. It was decided to dig a tunnel and the work began. One morning my father came to see me, his expression was gloomy. He said, "they are sending me to work in the Koldychevo camp". At the time the Judenrat was reduced to one man. He was selecting the crew to be sent off. Father told me that he begged and implored him, explaining that he had to look after me and feed me – to no avail. The man had no compassion or pity. My father parted from me...forever. He fell while escaping from Koldychevo. I was left on my own and my grief and distress was great. But I was not deserted by all. Efraim Selubski looked after me and brought me a piece of bread. By August 1943 I was beginning to move more freely but I still had to use crutches. The work on the tunnel was nearing completion and the time for the escape was approaching. But I was still moving with difficulty. Would I be able to break out? At last the dark night of the

flight arrived. Peisach Abramovich and I were the last to crawl through the tunnel. We waited many hours. We moved swiftly. We approached the exit. It was very dark outside. The sentry sensed something and began to shoot without pause. Peisach and I clung together. We followed the same route we took on our previous escape, via Brecianka, bypassing the town. That saved us. The Germans had taken the shortest route in pursuit of the escapees. We ran the whole night. We forgot our feet. At daylight we hid in some trees. Only now did I feel the pain in my bleeding feet. We were also very hungry. At nightfall we approached an isolated farm house, holding an empty holster of a revolver, and asked for bread and milk. In this manner we crawled for six days. We were hungry and wet, our feet were bleeding. As we ambled on we saw a horse drawn wagon. We hid in the grass behind a tree and tried to see who the people in the wagon were. We could not believe our eyes. They were partisans. A fellow I knew sat in the wagon. We burst into tears. I found out from an acquaintance that my cousin Berl Kagan was alive. We were taken to the unit of Belski. Berl Kagan came that evening. We were very happy. The two of us were the only survivors of our large family. When my cousin saw the condition of my feet he decided that he must remain with me. He left the Ordzonikidze fighting unit and returned to the Belski unit. It was not easy to live with me. At that time there were constant raids. We had to run from one place of concealment to the next. We would find out where everyone was going and we would drag ourselves behind them. When we rejoined our group, we found out that in the meantime the Germans had attacked the group and killed a few Jews. Our aching feet turned out to be yet again our salvation. This happened several times during the raids. We dragged ourselves to the new place, we came late, and we avoided death. After a while we decided to go to the Nalibok wilderness, where Belski's family group was located. After a week's travel at a snail's pace we arrived in the forest. There I met Notke Suborski, my uncle Sucharski and many others. Berl Kagan went on foraging expeditions. In the meantime we remained in the forest without a place to sleep in. It was very cold. Later we managed to find a deserted dugout. Luckily Peisach looked after the supply of food, because I could not walk. When Berl returned he brought fat and bread. This was the life! We ate our fill. I slept well and my feet were healing fast. I became less dependent on others. I threw away my crutches. I became an ordinary being. From that time and until the liberation there was no shortage of food. Berl looked after me. The liberation came and the survivors returned to Novogrudok. And soon we had to face the problems of adjusting to everyday life. I was 15 years old. What does one do, what does one live on? How does one build a new life without a family? The loneliness was depressing. But life came up with a solution for the hardened people. There was a strong feeling of having to escape from the mass graves, from the cursed land, where we were massacred and robbed. I decided to leave. I passed along the well-used route through Germany. I suffered through a succession of operations on my feet. My longing for a home was overwhelming. My cousin in England had invited me to join her in the hope that it would become my home. So I went to England and started rebuilding my life.

[Page 302]

The Ghetto in Peresike

by Frume Gulkovitz-Berger

Translated from Yiddish by O. Delatycki

1941-1942-1943

May 1942. A nice spring day. The sun was smiling on everyone, except us Jews. We were forgotten by nature. Over our heads hung heavy lead clouds. We were standing in rows of four in the Korelicz market square. I was standing in the first row with my three sisters. Our father was standing behind us. His legs were swollen. At that time our mother was already dead. She was flogged by the Nazis and died from the wounds inflicted by them. I will never forget it. We were guarded rigorously by the Nazi police, as if we were the worst criminals in the world. We started to walk. We were wondering how far we had to go to get to our grave.

In the evening we arrived in Novogrudok. We were weary, thirsty and hungry. They horded us, like animals, into barns in the Ghetto.

Here we were faced with new troubles, which were indescribable. They sent us to do hard work. The conditions were inhuman. Men were turned into beasts. Our sufferings were greater than those endured by the Jews of Novogrudok, because we did not know anyone. At that time they gathered in the Novogrudok Ghetto all Jews from the surrounding townships such as Nalibok, Iviniec, Lubcz, Karelicz, Delatycz, Naisztot [could not find it] and any other place wherever there was a Jew in a village. A Jewish policeman from the Ghetto had flogged me because I wanted to go to work with a group from Novogrudok. I wanted to go with them because perhaps someone would have pity on me and throw me a piece of bread. On another occasion a policeman caught me entering the Ghetto with a piece of cheese hidden under my dress. I was arrested and put in the lock-up. Such episodes were considered to be trifling.

The second slaughter

One could feel in the air that something was being prepared. The Judenrat had increased the number of policemen guarding the Ghetto to make sure that no Jew would escape. They made sure that the Germans would have the required quota of victims. When my brother Benzion tried to escape to the forest with a group of others, they took away his boots and made every effort to prevent him from leaving the Ghetto.

On Thursday morning the 6th of August 1942, we were walking towards the gate to go to work. We had a feeling that any day they would surround the Ghetto. My niece, a six year old girl, was asking me to take her with me. I agreed and I was successful. The policeman at the gate turned a blind eye. It seemed that there was a little more ease at work. But only a fool rejoices without reason, a minute before death things are easier. Suddenly there was panic. We started to run. No one knew where to run. We heard that the Ghetto was surrounded. My brother's wife and I ran to the military barracks, because many ran in that direction. My sister vanished. In the barracks we passed a selection: some to the right to live, others to the left to die. Those who were selected to die [which included the author of this article] were marched back to the Peresike Ghetto. It was getting dark and the Ghetto was surrounded by Nazis. I went into our barn. My father was standing next to his bunk, shrouded in his Talles and praying Tihilim. I could not comprehend how could a bullet kill such an honest and pious Jew? At that time my sisters were already hidden in an attic. Jehudit, my sister-in-law pulled my arm 'Come, let us go and seek a spot to hide'. I was completely mummified. We left the barn. Where can we find a hole to hide in? We were strangers here. The earth would not open for us to hide. We walked past a few dead bodies. I recognised one of them, a girl from Karelicz, Mirke Jelen. She had the courage to spit into the face of a German. We walked next to the big lavatory, which stood in the middle of the Ghetto. Without a minutes hesitation we chose it as our hiding place. We descended into the filth, which reached to my breasts. Two other women were already there: Ester Menaker and Masza Rabinowicz. We each went into separate corner, so that in case someone should look in he might see only one of us. The night passed without any disturbances. Very early next morning on Friday the 7 August (24th day of the month of Av) we heard the sounds of motor vehicles. The murderers arrived for their victims. I can hear the crying of the children to this day: father, mother where are you, why did you leave us? The children were locked up in the automobiles. The sound of the vehicles had subsided. Next we heard shooting followed by an eerie silence. Four thousand lives had been wiped out. We could hear music in the Ghetto. A loud Nazi voice was heard to say that a sacred job had been accomplished, but the job had to be finished and the Jews in hiding must be found. We heard suddenly human steps and barking of dogs. When the dogs barked it was a clear indication that Jews had been found. They started shooting at us. The first bullet hit Ester Menaker. She did not even make a sound. A bullet tore my dress and grazed slightly my right hand. They probably did not see the other two who were on the other side of the ditch. I heard the murderers speaking to each other: 'if they are still alive they will die there anyway'. They went off to look for other hiding places. We remained in the lavatory for six days without food or drink. Worms were eating our live bodies. Every time someone entered the lavatory our hearts stopped beating. My heart has not fully recovered to this day. On the sixth day they brought back the surviving Jews from the military barracks. Among them was my brother Benzion. The Ghetto was reduced in size and we found ourselves outside the Ghetto. When my brother found out about us he dragged us out of the ditch. It was then that we realised the magnitude of the destruction. Only few of us were still alive. We began to escape from the Ghetto in small groups. My brother was among the first to run. Soon he came back and took us away together with another 25 people. We became partisans. We fought the Nazis for two and a half years and survived to see the liberation as proud Jews.

The mass grave of the murdered at the second massacre in Litovke

[Page 304]

Chapters from the Holocaust

A. Escaping from the slaughter

by Y. Yaffe

Translated from Yiddish by O. Delatycki

Meilach was an American. Under the Germans he worked in the workshops as a locksmith. It was better than working as an unskilled labourer and having to go to a different place every day. In the workshop they established a modus vivendi with the supervisor, he did not make unreasonable demands on the workers. Germans with truncheons never turned up at the workshops. If a German did arrive by mistake, he was usually polite and offered a cigarette. They were not being paid for their work. Meilach was looking for a way to earn some money. He was searching in the fields and was looking for burnt out sawing machines. He would soak them for a few days in kerosene and then take them apart. He would clean the parts. He would reassemble the machine and it would work again. He would repaint the machine and attach to it the burned out legs. When it was ready, he would look for a customer to buy the machine. He would usually find a farmer who would give him a poud of flour and some butter for the machine.

That was enough to feed Meilach for a short period of time and gave him an opportunity to look after work, for other means to earn some money. He was asked once to go to a woman's house behind the Shloss [Castle] mound to repair a sawing machine. He told the woman that he would need to take the machine apart, clean it and make some new parts. But the woman did not agree to pay the price he asked and said that it was not worthwhile to repair the machine. Meilach thought that he should take the job and rely on the woman to pay him, because there was no food at home. He told her that whatever she would pay would be acceptable. Meilach took apart the machine in the woman's house and started repairing it. He took some parts with him to the workshop. He came back every evening to the woman's house. After a few hours work she would give him bread, milk and a piece of butter to take home. The Belarus people, who lived in town were poor before the war. But under the Germans they became rich. They robbed the Soviet stores and exchanged with farmers the goods for food. In time the woman developed a liking for Meilach. She was sorry that he suffered as a Jew. He was a good tradesman, she told him, and he had to work for nothing. And also he was not certain whether he would remain alive. Meilach was a young and handsome man and the young woman started to flirt with him. The machine had been long since repaired, but Meilach continued coming to the woman and she would give him something to eat. When strong rumours started that a slaughter was approaching, Meilach was thinking that he must find a place to hide. He decided to go to the woman. He was in luck. On the way nobody stopped him and there were no strangers at the woman's house. She was initially bewildered. Hiding of a Jew was punished by the Germans with death. He did not say a word, but looked at her attentively. She took him for his hand and led him inside. She said to him 'never mind, for a good deed it is sometimes worth to die, you do not deserve to be killed, you did no harm to anyone. If it will be possible I will save you '. She took him in and held him close. 'I got to like you for your calm, for your black eyes and white teeth, it was just as well that my husband was not home, I could not have you here otherwise'. The night came. The town was as quiet as if dead. At times shots could be heard. The woman came in and told him to be very careful, to lie down and not move. Under the house were rooms, where people lived. Every step would be suspected. The time moved on. In the morning she came in and told him to go to the barn through the house. This way he would not be seen. He got out of the house but could not get into the barn, because a woman was drawing water from the well nearby. When she left, he crawled into the barn and closed the door. He went up onto the loft and waited for the woman to come. The door opened. A man entered the barn. He had an axe and started splitting logs of wood. He could not see Meilach on the loft. The time went on but the man kept splitting wood. Meilach was very cold. His toes were frozen. He was also hungry, he had had nothing to eat since the day before. He was also anxious to know what was happening in town. The man stacked up the split wood and left the barn. After that the woman he stayed with came in with some bread and warm food. She stayed with him while he ate. She made up for him a place to sleep in the corner of the barn inside a big heap of hay. She gave him also a warm sheep skin fur coat. She left the barn. She went out to find out what happened to the Jews of the town. When she returned she told him that the Jews were being crammed into a Ghetto. But a Polish policeman had told her that the Jews would not stay there. Some would go to another Ghetto, but most would go to the pits which were dug for them in the Koshelevo forest. The survivors would be put in a Ghetto in Peresieka.

The woman left the barn and Meilach buried himself in the hay stack. He stretched his legs and covered them with the fur. The quiet was interrupted by the wailing of the Jewish women being led to the Ghetto. Nobody listened to their woes. The streets were empty, people were occupied with their own affairs. The Germans were preparing the slaughter, the Jews were led to the slaughter, and the town's gentile population was getting ready to rob the Jewish homes.

The sky was cloudy, the wind was blowing fiercely and was twisting the snow in whirlers. His thoughts were all muddled. He saw in his mind one group of people which was going to destroy the other.

Meilach began to work out what was happening and was thinking about his next move. It was not a solution, he thought, to remain in a barn close to the centre of the town. The Germans would search and would find him. Also he wanted to be among the other Jews. He spoke to the woman and told her that he would go to the court house, which was where all Jews were taken.

The court house was surrounded by German gendarmes. They did not allow anyone to come in or to get out. Meilach did not know how he got inside. He was certain that he was going voluntarily to his death. In the yard stood the Jews, each one next to his bundle. The Germans were shouting, cursing and hurrying the Jews from one side of the yard to the other. The guards were armed with machine guns. They were laughing at the sight of the disoriented Jews who were running in all directions. 'This is not the behaviour of living people' thought Meilach 'the Germans look upon us as if we were dead, and one can not hurt a corpse. It is allowed to mistreat them and abuse them. Their life must be made unbearable, so they would not think again of escaping, to get away as far as they could to escape death, but they would long for death. There would be no opposition.' He was running from one end of the yard to the other. Everywhere were armed gendarmes who kept them at a distance. He took off his watch and gave it to a gendarme. The gendarme moved aside and Meilach moved to the other side of the house and freedom. The sky was getting darker. As the night approached, the sun appeared briefly. Meilach walked briskly alone through the empty streets. He had to behave in a way which would not attract any suspicion. The gendarmes who were patrolling the empty streets did not stop him. When it was completely dark he reached the house of the woman. The door was opened by her husband, who asked him what he wanted in an unfriendly tone. But the woman got to the door and took him inside. There was a sharp exchange of words between husband and wife. The man was saying that he would not harbour a Jew, because he would not risk his life. If the Jew would not leave he would call the Germans. The woman said that she would not hand over anyone to be killed. They must find a way to take the Jew to the outskirts of the town, where he would have to look after himself. The husband agreed to that. He was certain that the guards placed around the town would catch the Jew. The woman took upon herself to lead him out of town. The husband was opposed to the idea and told his wife that she would be shot together with the

Jew. 'Let them shoot' said his wife 'I will not let them murder him in front of my eyes. I would not have it on my conscience that I handed him over to be killed. The man came to hide in my house. You can lead him out of the town, you know the police' she told her husband. 'If you go with him they will let you pass'. The husband spoke to a police patrol near the house and came back puffed up. He did not like the idea of letting a Jew escape, but he found it difficult to oppose his wife. 'You can go' he told Meilach 'the policeman would look the other way'. But his wife did not agree and said that the Jew may be killed on the outskirts by another patrol. She went with Meilach and saw to it that he was well on the way out of town. On the 7th of December after the first cold winter night Meilach was free and moving. The night was dark and cloudy, the sky filled with wet snow which was hanging low like heavy lead. Strong winds were shredding the fresh snow, which covered the ice bound earth. Meilach, who was dressed in light clothing, felt the wind blowing and penetrating his whole body. Barking of dogs could be heard from the distance. Occasional shots were fired in the surrounded town.

Meilach met no one on the way. He did not know where he was going. No farmer would let him into his house. He had to be certain that he would not be seen by anyone. He had to hide but had no place to conceal himself . He was hungry, but had no food. He was cold but could not find a warm shelter. He kept going into the night but did not know where he was going. Why did he escape from his executioners? Why continue this punishment? He would not be able to escape his death. And yet his frozen feet kept moving in the snow, his eyes were searching the empty night and his brain stopped thinking. Let it be what must be. If he would be caught and handed over to the Germans his suffering would stop. But somewhere inside the desire to live was hoping for a miracle. He walked on and on. He avoided villages, where the hamlets were sunk in deep sleep. He went into a small forest of tall trees with bowed branches shaking in the wind. He sat down to rest on a stump of a tree. He took off his boots and rubbed his feet with snow to create some warmth. He put his boots on again. He got up and started to bang his hands against his coat to improve circulation. He felt warmer and intended to continue his journey. Suddenly he heard two quiet voices talking. He held his breath. Having listened intently he recognised the voices of two Jewish people – Leizer the dispatch agent and his wife. They must have escaped from the slaughter and were looking for a place to hide. When he got close to them the woman started shouting loudly. It reverberated in the forest. Leizer told Meilach that they were close to Walewke, 18 kilometres from Novogrudok. He and his wife were looking for a hiding place at a familiar farmer's house. The farmer used to supply them with milk for the cheese factory. Leizer would not take Meilach to that farmer, because the farmer might get scared and refuse to hide any of them. Leizer and his wife went to the farmer who lived close to the forest. Meilach followed them at a distance. On the edge of the forest in an empty field stood a lone house. Meilach watched Leizer and his wife, who were walking towards the house, to see what was going to happen. If the farmer will hide them, Meilach thought, he may be able to join them later. The farmer may let him in for fear that Meilach may denounce him. The night was dark, the wind was bending thin trees and shaking their branches. It was getting colder. He stood at the edge of the forest. He saw a dog running out of the house and barking loudly. A lamp was lit inside the house. Next Meilach heard the loud voice of the farmer. He told the couple that he would not hide Jews, he did not want to risk his life and the lives of his family. The Germans would shoot them all if they would find Jews in his house. Leizer asked him if he remembered the times when the farmer was in need, when Leizer lent him money to build a house, when his cow died Leizer helped him to buy a cow and many more times when the farmer was in need over a period of tens of years. Leizer's wife started to cry and asked the farmer were could they go in the big frost. She was bemoaning their fate and saying that they should not have left the town, but died with everyone else. But the farmer did not budge. He said that he would give them anything, but not risk his life. The farmer's wife gave them a loaf of bread, a jug of milk and a peasant's overcoat. They went back to the forest.

The night was slowly getting lighter. The snow in the forest caught a glimpse of light. The wanderers were looking in vain for a place to hide. Even here death was not far from them. Here among the trees the nature was cruel to them. They were tired and depressed. They broke pieces of bread with their frozen fingers and drank some cold milk. They were less hungry but felt more tired. Their feet were hurting. It was hard to keep their eyes open for lack of sleep. Their bones were aching. They moved deeper into the dense forest, where the wind was not as fierce. They cleared an area of snow, spread the farmer's overcoat and lay down to rest. It started to get lighter. Golden beams of light penetrated the forest. The darkness gradually disappeared. The threesome was restless. They were perused by dark thoughts. The woman dozed off. She dreamed of wolves among the trees. They were hungry and their eyes were burning. They smelt the human breath and they got nearer stealthily. One wolf tore off a human leg, but it did not hurt, because the leg was frozen. Shooting could be heard. The German hunters were running and shooting the wolves and they stumbled onto the sleeping Jews. They started hitting them with their rifle buts. Blood was running from their heads. Meilach was shot in the stomach. They were dragged through the snow. The three of them were tossed onto a truck. They were brought to a big pit full of dead bloodied bodies piled up one on top of the other. The Germans tossed them into the pit. They were among the dead but they felt nothing and suffer nothing. But it was frightening to be dead and covered with earth. Suddenly the woman woke up with a frightful shout and started looking for her wounds. She was feeling frightened and her leg was cold. She was told to be quiet. The farmers were cutting trees in the forest and they might spot them. The woman was shaken by the terrible dream and was swallowing here tears. The forest was filled with noises. The horses were neighing, the sleighs were squeaking, the axes were splitting timber and saws were issuing a mournful sound as they were cutting the timber. The nature was free, the horses were moving freely. Only the three unfortunate Jews had to conceal themselves among the snow covered branches so as not to be discovered, because they were destined to die. The short winter day was dragging on endlessly till it began coming to an end. The last of the farmers had loaded and tied the timber on the sleighs and speedily left the forest. Only one farmer remained. He was still fussing over his load. When all others left, he turned to the forest and the hidden Jews. He gave some food to the hungry Jews. He told them that he spotted them earlier in the day, but did not approach them when the others were there. He suggested that they should follow his sleigh from a distance and he would take them to his home. He asked them to be careful, to make sure that no one would see them. They entered a small farmer's house with low grey walls and a water stained ceiling. On one side stood an old, peeling couch, a slanting table with two long benches on either side. A few white chickens and a brown cockerel were walking on the earthen floor. On the other side of the house, separated by thin boards were a few goats and sheep. Next to the animals were heaped some cereals and grass. The farmer's wife with clogs on her feet, a shrivelled face and bleached dress was busy at the stove. Her husband told here to warm up the house, because they were freezing the whole day in the forest. His wife put in the oven a big pot of potatoes and prepared food for the guests. She served it at the table in a big wooden bowl. Everyone was given a earthenware plate of sour milk to eat with the potatoes. After the meal the farmer brought in a big bundle of straw which he spread on the floor and covered with a dark blanket. The three Jews went to sleep on that bed. They felt warm and well. They were sheltered from the wind and the snow. They were not running away from the Germans. And they slept soundly. In the morning the farmer moved them to a cellar behind the barn, where potatoes where stored. He lifted a large lid and they crawled under it into a small pit. There was no air in the pit and it was hard to breathe. There was a heavy smell of rotting potatoes. It was dark. A few rays of light could be seen through a few cracks. It was not possible to stand, because the pit was shallow. One could only sit or lie. But they were protected by thick earthen walls. They did not feel the cold of the winter. The wind did not blow and the snow did not fall on them. They got used in time to the rotten smell. They were lying most of the time and were waiting for the horror to pass. The farmer's wife brought food during the day: a big bowl of soup, one spoon, and three lumps of black rye bread. The bowl of soup and the spoon was passed on from one to the other. When the bowl was empty it was put to one side and they sat and looked into the dark. In the evenings they came into the farmer's house and breathed deeply. They enjoyed the fresh air and the warmth of the low farmer's house. In the morning their new hideout was ready for them. In the barn, behind a large mound of hay the farmer built a small room underground. Above it he built a platform, which was covered with hay. A small window in the back wall of the barn gave them a view to the outside. They could see through that window the winding road to Baranovichi. Above the platform was a large board, which they could use to walk on. On that level was also a cage for geese with grains and grass inside cage, as well as bowls of water. At night the three of them returned to the house. They would warm up and enjoy some fresh air. In their quarters they had a stock of rusks and water. At night they ate cooked food. Early in the morning they would wash and return to the barn. The farmer would lock the barn and they would not be able to get out. Some days went by. The generosity of the farmer came to an end. He was arguing that the slaughter had finished. The remaining Jews were in the Ghetto. Why don't they go back to the Ghetto? He was a poor farmer and he could not keep them. His land yielded barely enough bread and potatoes for the two of them for the year. He had no money to feed three extra persons. The Jews understood that the farmer was not obliged to sustain them at his expense. It was a great gesture on his part to have saved them and kept them for a time. Leizer took out the paper money he had on him and gave it to the farmer. He told the farmer that he did not have more money on him, but he had some more hidden in town. If need be they could go to town and get it. And so their life continued. The farmer supplied any amount of bread that was required and sometimes a piece of butter. In the evening they ate a meal of lamb's meat. They got used to the confinement and they hoped to survive in that way the war.

Once the air in their hiding place had become unusually hard to breath. They were waiting for the night to be able to get out into the fresh air. But they were not released that night. It was getting dark and the farmer did not open the door for them. They were trying to figure out what had happened. Were there visitors in the house? Why did the farmer not tell them? Maybe somebody found out about them? Maybe the farmer was arrested and they would die of hunger and thirst. They could not open the door by themselves. They could not see anything through the window. They were lying in the darkness and thought of their sad situation. They were hungry and thirsty. They had to do their physical needs on the spot and the air became unbearably heavy. They looked for a solution but could not find one. The night seemed to last for ever. They were reclining in the darkness without speaking. Towards the morning they fell asleep. In the morning the farmer was chopping wood. The farmer passed to them through the window a large loaf of breads and a jar of milk. He whispered to them that the Germans had come and were staying in the other barn. He collected the chopped wood and went into his house. They saw from the window that a German soldier in a green uniform was walking up and down the road with a machine gun. They could hear the neighing of many horses and the sound of a mouth organ. They escaped from the Germans and the Germans came to them. Death was hunting them to every corner of the earth. They could hear the barking of German dogs. The dogs would smell the humans and they would be found. The farmer would die too because of them. They were suffering in the underground, in the stale air, in the darkness. But outside life was running normally as if nothing had happened. The guard on the highway was changing every few hours. The noises from the barn were the same: neighing of horses and the banging of the German boots. They were confined underground and listened with greater heart beats to every noise. It was dark again. And again the door to their hiding place remained closed. They were confined underground for two days and two nights. They longed to breathe a lung full of fresh air. It was difficult to breathe. They became more and more hungry. Their heads were aching. They were continuously thinking but did not come up with anything. They fell asleep again. A night passed in tiredness and pain. More hunger and thirst. The farmer had not been near them. They knew that the Germans were still there. Who knows when they would go away. And when they would leave it would be too late. They would expire from hunger and thirst. Their hiding place would be their grave. They had swollen faces and extended stomachs. They could not move. They were suffering from acute dehydration. Their eyes were looking into the darkness of the cellar and they were waiting for their death as a release from their suffering. Only on the fourth day did the farmer open the door and told them to get out into the fresh air. They could not move. The farmer thought that they were afraid of the Germans. He told them that the Germans had gone. But they still did not move. The farmer got down to them in their pit. He was repulsed by a strong disgusting smell. He came out. When the farmer got used to the smell he removed first the bucket of slops. After that he carried out the three Jews, one at a time. The Jewish woman fainted in the fresh air. She came to with difficulty. They were sick for several days. They could not seek medical help of course. But they gradually recovered and went back underground to hide from the Germans. The farmer was afraid of hiding them any longer. This was because an event occurred which shook the farmer. Before the war in the house of Shimie the barber in Korelich Street served a village girl, who was a nursery maid to his newly born daughter, named Chana. The girl had become very attached to the child. After the village girl got married and moved back to her village she used to visit the child a few times a year. When the woman heard about the slaughters of the Jews she came to town and took Chanelle with her. Chana spoke Russian well and had blond hair and blue eyes. Nobody would know that Maruska was a Jewish girl. They lived in an isolated farm and the child had a chance to survive the war. At one time a group of Germans came and stayed in the farm. The Germans played with Maruska and gave her lollies. Maruska was told to speak only Russian. One day the Germans drank in excess and started boasting of their murders of the Jews. To prove it they had pockets full of photos, which they showed each other. One of them told his story that in Novogrudok a barber jumped on him and wanted to cut his throat. He killed the barber and took a photo of his body, which he showed them. Maruska saw the photo and started crying and calling her father's name in Yiddish. The Germans killed her and the family that kept her. They burned their house. This had become well known and the farmer told Meilach and Leibl that he was afraid to keep them any longer. The farmer took the three of them to Novogrudok where they were smuggled into the Ghetto in Peresike.

[Page 310]

Chapters from the Holocaust (cont'd)

B. The second slaughter

by Y. Yaffe

Translated from Yiddish by O. Delatycki

The Ghetto was divided into twelve blocks. Each of the twelve members of the Judenrat was responsible for his block. In the evenings a member of the Judenrat would come to his block, call everyone outside and check to see whether anyone was missing. He warned us that if anyone was absent everyone in the block would be held responsible. Everyone would be shot if someone escaped.

There were among us people that honestly believed that if one would work and remain in the Ghetto he would be spared and, therefore, they were on the lookout for people who were getting ready to escape to the partisans. They would report such people to the Judenrat. And immediately camp policemen would come and take away the suspects boots or put him into the lock-up for the night.

All roads were leading to the slaughter. In the Ghetto was a big empty space. 'You can grow there cabbages for winter' said the German Stadtsleiter [city leader] to the Judenrat. 'Who is expecting to survive to the winter?' replied searchingly one member of the Judenrat. 'Of course you will live if you will be loyal and work well' assured the Stadtsleiter. Next day the Jewish workers dug the soil and sowed the cabbages for winter. The sun warmed the growing leaves, which were getting greener. In front of the lean, despairing faces of the Ghetto Jews green leaves of hope were growing under the blue sky. They seem to say: 'you will live, you will survive'. One day the leiter came to the Ghetto and stood next to the green, growing cabbages and said 'Dumme Juden [silly Jews], they hope to be here in the winter' and he laughed.

They began to remove Jews from their places of work. The skilled tradesmen were supposed to be given new certificates. But those who were unskilled did not receive the certificates. This meant that they were no longer required, that they had no right to remain alive.

People began to approach members of the Judenrat and non-Jewish supervisors. They tried to gain acknowledgement as qualified tradesmen and to get a work certificate. Every day more workers were relieved of their duties. Previously there was a shortage of workers. Previously the Judenrat was looking for an excuse to explain the shortage of workers. But at that time many people without work were circulating in the Ghetto.

The first of August 1942

The qualified tradesmen, who previously worked in various German institutions, were transferred to the German military barracks. The others continued working, doing the same jobs as before. It was assumed that the tradesmen were engaged in doing urgent skilled work for the army. It turned out that they were doing unskilled work. A few times per day they were subjected to a check and they were asked their age, their trade, and the number of years they had worked in their trade.

Next day all those that were sent back from the barracks were given other work. Their names were inscribed on a list. They were told that they would be engaged as permanent workers in the barracks.

The monument on the mass grave - Litovke

Suddenly there was panic in the Ghetto. The Gebiets commissar was driven past in his car. People were hiding in their dwellings. Small children were hidden out of sight. But the commissar did not enter the Ghetto. He went off and half an hour later he returned to town. People tried to explain his secret mission, but no one guessed that he went to Litowka, 3 km out of town, where he decided on a spot for the burial of the victims of the second slaughter in the sandy ditches.

The fourth of August

Six hundred Estonians arrived at the military barracks. They travelled in light family cars, cleanly dressed with well fed faces. They were not front line soldiers. Why did they come to Novogrudok? They refused to speak to Jews. They were ill-tempered, bad men. They were unapproachable and looked down on everyone.

The fifth of August

The slaughter was about to take place. The Judenrat stopped denying that the slaughter was imminent. Yet they prevented people escaping from the Ghetto. They were controlling the sleeping quarters. People were running inside the Ghetto this way and that and were seeking advice. The Judenrat maintained that they knew nothing. They were waiting for Daniel, who did not return from the Gebiets commissariat. The last group of workers returned to the Ghetto. The parcels they brought with them were not searched. The policemen were busy trying to find places to hide their families. Late in the evening Daniel returned to the Ghetto. He held in his hands the yellow certificates, which would be distributed to the workers in the morning before they were to leave for work. He was tired and in a bad mood. He was busy the whole day sorting out from the lists, according to German procedure, the names of Jews who would be spared. He did not care about the others. In the German Gebiets commissariat, behind closed doors, a game was played with Jewish lives treated as pawns. The Germans relied on Daniel to do the sorting. They trusted him to be the signatory on the certificates which would grant, for a time, the right to live. He did not sign any additional certificates. He was afraid that people would run away and there would not be the required number of victims. He kept back, just in case, more than 200 certificates for the wives of the tradesmen, who were supposed to be allowed to live. In the event he did not issue those certificates in time. The wives were slaughtered. The night came. The black sky covered the last red swaths of the sunset. A silence fell over the Ghetto, as if the martyrs got used to being dead. Many were standing on the threshold of oblivion, of death, yet, somehow, they became indifferent to it. The slaughter was expected for months. And now it had finally come. The night had snuggled the Ghetto into a deep sleep. The last night before the slaughter.

The sixth of August

Jewish policemen separated one group of workers from the other. Those that were working in the military barracks went first. Those who were working in the workshops were given yellow work certificates. The rest was kept in the Ghetto. There was a heavy feeling in one's heart. I was saying farewell to the eight months I had spent in the Ghetto, to my life, to all my years. We, the remaining two brothers of my family, were separated: one went to the military barracks the other to the printing shop.

My wife and our nine month old child remained in the Ghetto. The child would certainly be killed. My wife should receive a workers certificate and should be transferred to the tradesmen's Ghetto. I was certain of that arrangement. We had to go to work and I could not remain in the Ghetto any longer. I ran for the last time into the barrack. I saw the smiling eyes of my child. I was aware that I saw them for the last time. I felt helpless, a father that could not save his child. The Germans decided that the child must die and there was nothing I could do to prevent it. I did not take leave of my wife, because I thought that we would see each other after work.

A few hours passed. Suddenly a disquiet spread in the town. The Germans, the police and the Estonians went to the township of Zetl, where they participated in the slaughter. The Jewish police was given an order not to allow anyone to leave the Ghetto. They took up positions, with rubber truncheons in their hands, along the fence of the Ghetto and cut off the exit of the women and children, who wanted to join their husbands and fathers.

The atmosphere in the Ghetto had become tense. The police were hitting the women and losing control of the situation. A group of gendarmes was stationed not far from the Ghetto. They kept guard on the roof of the Peresike synagogue, which was the highest point. The guard saw the disturbance in the Ghetto. The gendarmes moved in and surrounded the Ghetto. They shot anyone who attempted to escape.

In town a few hundred Jews were milling around not knowing where to go. Some of them went to the new workshops, where there was a big cellar. They gave some money to the foreman of the workshop who let in about 50 workers to the cellar and blocked the door. At 12 o'clock the Polish supervisor told us that we had to wait in the workshops till they would come to take us back to the Ghetto.

Jewish workers were going back to the Ghetto. They were released from work earlier. We told them not to go to the Ghetto, which was surrounded by German gendarmes. "Where should we go?' they asked "we will die anyway, we have nowhere to hide'. They walked slowly away from us. I looked at them and I wondered. People were prepared to die as if it was natural. At the same time people were running around the town as if they were poisoned mice. Some slipped into a cellar of a ruined house. They disguised the entrance. They sat there for a few hours and went off to look for another hiding place.

In the evening a group of about twenty policemen had come into our tannery. They surrounded us with rifles at the ready. We were led outside under guard. They led us through the empty streets. At the door of the workshops they checked our certificates and they allowed us to go inside. The night was a nightmare. We looked at the sky, which hung threateningly over us. We sat in the darkness and tried not to think. I lay on the bare concrete, with my head resting on the concrete wall and was asking myself: 'Am I alone? Where are my brothers? Where are my wife and my child? What do they think of now? How long will I suffer? How many slaughters will I survive? How many times will death threaten me? Will I have to witness the total destruction of the Novogrudok Ghetto? Will I continue to live on the verge of life and death?' I thought that I would rather be among the dead and feel nothing. I looked at the black sky and the heavy clouds which were moving slowly through the darkness. My thoughts were obsessed with one subject - death. The morning woke me from my short sleep. Someone stepped on my foot and I woke up. I assumed a strange pose, sitting on my feet and thinking hard. I was looking at the day. Why did the sun rise? For the Germans to see the people they were shooting? For us to see and feel our destruction? I looked unseeingly at things around me. I looked and I saw nothing. We walked around the workshops and kept asking each other whether they heard anything. We did not want to hear the answer. We did not want to know that the Ghetto was dead.

Hours have gone by. We tried to tell ourselves that it all was a wild dream. We were trying to escape from our thoughts. We wanted to push away from us the thought that our dear ones were dead. That we were now alone. But one cannot escape reality. Seventeen Jews were brought alive from the Ghetto into the workshop. Three and a half thousand were dead.

In the workshops

The Germans who brought the 17 people from the Ghetto stood by the doors and turned us out into the yard. We thought that they would check our certificates, to find out if there were among the tradesmen escapees from the Ghetto. It turned out that they intended to organise a search for small children. On the previous day some fathers smuggled their small children into the workshops. They were hidden in the cellars under mounds of felt boots and leather coats. With all men standing in the yard the Germans dragged the children from the cellars and threw them onto the truck. The fathers were standing helpless and were trying to hold back their cries of anguish. The Germans found over thirty children and they took them and put them over the dead bodies of the martyrs from the Ghetto.

The seventeen people from the Ghetto told us the gruesome stories of the death of the Ghetto. Chaim Ajzykowicz, the chairman of the Judenrat, told us that all the people were removed from the Ghetto onto the street. Man and women were separated. The children were taken straight onto trucks and driven to the ditches. All Jews had to lie on the ground with the faces down. Over every third Jew stood an Estonian with a gun and beat them and kicked them with his feet.

Trucks came. They were loaded full of people, who were taken to the ditches. At the gate the Germans made Bursztyn, from the employment office, stand and witness the gruesome execution. They told him that he has to tell the Jews from the workshops what he had seen. It took five hours for all the Jews to be transported to the ditches. At one stage the chief of the German hospital appeared in the Ghetto. He suddenly realised that the Jewish doctors and pharmacist would be killed in the Ghetto and he came to save them. He took them to a separate house and told them to wait till the end of the slaughter. At the end, he brought them to the workshops. He also brought the chairman of the Judenrat, who he presented as a doctor. But all the other members of the Judenrat and the police perished. It did not help them that they were the ones who did not allow anyone to leave the Ghetto. During the slaughter they forced all Jews to go out onto the street. The Germans promised to save them, but they did not keep their word.

The policeman Altered der game (that was his nickname) was determined to survive no matter what. He found Jews hidden in the cellars. He even found and expelled his wife and children from a bunker. e even HThe chief of the Gestapo promised to keep him alive. 'You are a brave man' he told him. 'Now come with me and you will see how it is done'. He took him to the ditches in his car, but Alterke did not come back.

Chan and the shoemaker were going to the workshops, where he could have been safe, but he did not want to survive without his wife and children and he went back to the Ghetto. But he could not find his family. The Germans took ten people from the Ghetto to the ditches to help to drag the dead bodies. Chanan went with them. When they came to the ditches the site was so terrible that Chanan jumped in alive onto the ditch with the dead bodies and waited for a German bullet. And yet he survived.

Above the field with the ditches was the highway. This was where the trucks unloaded the Jews. They were told to undress and crawl on all fours to a ditch. Some did not want to undress, particularly the women. Some were beaten to death. The others had to crawl over the dead bodies. Most were shot before they got to the ditch. A group of Jews was given the job of dragging the dead to the ditches to make room for other victims. The clothes of the dead were gathered and loaded onto trucks. The clothing was taken to a store where the Germans looked for gold and jewellery in amongst the garments.

When the massacre was finished all participants, about a thousand of them, gathered in the empty Ghetto. They drank vodka, ate food and had a feast. An orchestra was attached to the group and played for them. The Jews who were hidden in the undiscovered bunkers in the

Ghetto heard the music.

More than a thousand Jews worked in the military barracks, of whom more than half were to be massacred. The man who was going to do the selection was a certain Moscalov, who was the supervisor of the barracks. He spoke politely to every Jew and promised to put him down on the list of the living. Naturally he was going to do it for some consideration.

In the evening the Estonians arrived back after the slaughter in Zetl. All Jews were made to stand on the parade ground. Moscalov took out a list and started calling out names. Those selected stood in a separate group. There was a distance of 100 metres between the groups. One group was designated to live for the present and the other one to die. In one group was a father in the other his children, who were selected to die. Two brothers were in different groups. Initially they thought that perhaps there would be changes. After all Moscalov was paid. But Moscalov made fools of them. More then 500 were selected to die. Some from the group that was designated to die tried to run to the other group. The Estonians opened fire and those selected to live were removed from the ground. Those destined to die were confused and started running in the direction of the Estonians, who opened fire. The Jews wound their hands around the guns, they put their arms around the necks of the Estonians, one was scratching and throttling an Estonian even after he was dead. There were about 100 dead strewn on the ground. The others were taken to the Ghetto.

Those that were selected to remain alive were locked up in stables. The door was closed and those inside were immersed in complete darkness. The small windows provided no view. During the night one could see before the minds eye pictures of the frightful happenings of the day: how one left the family behind in the Ghetto and went to work, one hoped to save one's life, the sorting to the left and to the right, the parting of those who were allowed for the time to live and those who had to die, the blood flowing on the hard ground, blood of children, of parents, of friends. One could see, but one was not allowed to move or make a sound. One could see the bandits who were shooting, but one had to stand as if one's hands were tied. One could not attack the murderers and tear them to pieces, because of the urge to remain alive. One submitted to the murderers and was led by them to a stable. One had a wild urge to avenge the evils. The thoughts were compelling, but the body was welded to the spot. There was no talk, because everyone was ashamed of himself. There was no peace, and the stronger one confined the pain within, the more it hurt and the greater was the fear of tomorrow. Nobody wanted to be killed, but the feeling was that one would be killed. These thoughts were destroying one.

The people in the stables were waiting for the morning. They were mummified. They felt the pain in every particle of their bodies. The body was aching. The night was endless. They had to lie sleepless and listen to the monotonous whistling of the guard. The morning arrived cold and bleak. A grey light penetrated through small windows and we could see each other. This gave one an idea of how one looked himself: black and emaciated.

The stable was locked. There was no access to a lavatory. A corner of the stable was used for that purpose. We had to tolerate the frightful stench for almost 3 days and nights. We were not fed. Even water was not supplied. In the beginning we kept quiet. We did not want to speak to the Estonian guards. In time we could not stand it any longer. We stood at the small windows and begged for water. The Estonians demanded gold. Some people still had wedding rings on their fingers. They took them off and gave them to the Estonians, who brought a few buckets of water. We drank the water from the buckets in turn. The Estonians looked through the small windows and laughed. Later they demanded watches for water. They took the watches, but gave no water. They just looked in and laughed. We were lying thirsty, hungry and weak. We were afraid to think of what may follow. We were sorry that we were still alive. It was obvious that the Germans were trying to kill us by denying us food and water. We were going to expire in the stinking stable.

But we were wrong. On the third day the door of the stable was opened and the Jews were taken to the workshop Ghetto. There were assembled all the Jews that had survived. They were 1240 of us.

The Ghetto of Peresike

Two days after the second slaughter the Germans had plans ready for the third slaughter. They formed two Ghettos: one for the tradesmen, for Jews that were working in the workshops, where they also lived and a Ghetto in Peresike for Jews who were working in town. It was clear that the Germans would slaughter next the Jews from the Ghetto in Peresike, and those who worked in the workshop would be spared for a time.

After the second slaughter 550 people were selected and taken under guard to the Peresike Ghetto. The people who remained in the workshops took their final farewells from us. We had been looked upon as if we belonged to another world. If they could remain alive a little longer the war may end. On the other hand we were those who were about to die. We were walking surrounded by Germans and policemen. From a ruin a man appeared with his eyes showing fear, his face yellow, his cheeks cadaverous. It was obvious that the man had not eaten or drunk for several days. He ran alongside us and wanted to join us. The Germans noticed him and shot him. They left him lying on the ground with blood spreading around him. We went on and I thought: the Jew was hiding for the last four days. He lived in fear but was hoping to save himself. But death was waiting for him. We walked on past the remains of ruined houses. We noticed a Jewish boy who slid around a corner. He wanted to approach us. We were in a panic. They were sure to shoot him. We began waving at him, indicating that he should hide. He did not see us. A German raised his hand and the column stopped. There was dead silence. The German and the boy looked at each other. Not a word was spoken. The boy stood in front of the German like an offending child in front of his teacher. It lasted a second but it seemed an eternity. 'Weiter gehen' shouted the German and the boy went with us into the Ghetto. Why did the German shoot one Jew and spared the other? I thought that that was not clear even to the German. It just happened. In the first instance the murderer had a blood lust and in the second instance the lust was satisfied. A little later a policeman came leading a Jewish woman with a small child in her hands. A German shot with his revolver the child in the woman's arms. The woman fell with a frightful cry and the child, all covered in blood, slid out of her hands. The child remained on the road and the mother walked on with the rest of us.

We came to the fence of the Ghetto which was made of long boards of various colours and looked like an army made up of various people. The fence surrounded the houses where the Jews were kept and separated the Jews from the rest of the world. The fence hid some people. Those who were guarding them were united in their will to rob and murder. They were aiming to spread their might into the world around them.

We walked into the Ghetto through a small door in the large fence. A woman was lying dead in a door of a house. She was found in a hiding place and was shot on the spot. Close by a few more bodies were lying. They too were hiding in bunkers. I went into a house. The air was heavy with stench. Three men died in a hole under the house. They were too frightened to leave their hiding place and died there. Each of us went to the house he had previously lived in. All was in great confusion. The doors and windows were open, clothing was spread about. Everything signalled death. The houses were empty. Some died where they lived. We sat on the hard bunks and bemoaned those fallen.

The Ghetto was reduced in size to half. The fence was shifted and the Ghetto was now reduced to twelve houses. The houses outside the fence were empty. They smelt of death. All was empty. Inside the Ghetto a few people were moving about aimlessly. No one bothered to clean up, to arrange things. Autumn spread its rainy gloom. The air was full of moisture and clouds. The dark sky had swallowed the sun and its warmth. The earth was immersed in mud. A swampy spread, which would never dry out again.

At the mass grave in Litovke

With the first light the Jews were driven to work. The Germans did not look upon the Jews as people who would live much longer, but as tired out horses, which were about to die and every last drop of strength must be forced out of them. The Germans had become used to flogging Jews for no reason. They just lowered the stick and broke somebody's hand. Most Jews were depressed and defeated but in some a feeling of resistance awoke, to oppose the tormentors. We were standing on the threshold of annihilation so some developed a desire to escape. They hoped to save their lives by escaping from the Ghetto to the forests where they could fight the Germans.

Some were prepared to go any length to postpone their death. There was also the desire for revenge for the killing of many. The last survivors of the Ghetto would take their revenge. Some had a desire to became a partisan and have a weapon. They would travel and attack German convoys. They were debating among themselves and some escaped from the Ghetto. There was no Judenrat in the Ghetto. The Ghetto was eliminated for all practical purposes. It was changed into a work depot. There was one Jewish policeman and three members of the Judenrat in the camp. They did not exert any authority and did not attempt to flog the inmates. They knew that when the Jews would be killed they would die with them. The members of the Judenrat did not interfere if anyone decided to escape to the forest or to keep arms. They were helpless, confused people, who were on the margin of death. They were hoping that the partisans would take revenge for the spilled blood. The Germans had power over everything.

Baretsky-from the few Jewish survivors at the mass grave

Rosh Hashanah [New Year] fell on a Sunday and therefore there was no work. We assembled in the houses and many prayed. They were the last prayers of the last survivors which were about to die. Some remembered the past and compared it to the present in astonishment of how things had changed in such a short time. The past had vanished together with the future. The tree was torn together with the roots. Only few branches held few leaves. People were summing up their existence on the last Rosh Hashanah of their lives.

But even that was interrupted – there was no time to rest, no time to think about one self. One had to be always in fear of death. The Germans entered the Ghetto and ordered the Jews to assemble on the square. A Belarusian woman, carrying a loaf of bread, walked past the Ghetto. A Jew jumped the fence and approached the woman. The Germans arrived suddenly and found the Jew outside the Ghetto. Such a transgression was punished by death. The Germans took the Jew back into the Ghetto and tied him to a tree. After, they took him with them and he was never seen again. The Jews were lined up. They were all there, no one was missing. The Jews were made to march past a young man, who looked every Jew in the eye. He pointed at a 15 year old boy, who was removed from the line. The Germans took him with them and left the Ghetto.

The 15 year old boy tried to save himself. He escaped from the Ghetto and was wandering in forests and byways. He knocked on doors of farmers asking for bread. In this manner he survived a few weeks. He slept in the fields, behind trees. When he heard that some Jews survived the slaughter he returned to the Ghetto. In one of the houses where the Jewish boy came asking for bread, lived the young man who recognised him in the line up. He was treated well in the house of the young man. They fed him and allowed him to sleep the night. They had pity on him. Some time later the boy took a watch from a friend in the Ghetto and went back to the farmer who treated him well to exchange it for bread. He returned to the Ghetto. The farmer told the Germans about the young man and came to the Ghetto to identify him.

The only way to survive was to escape to the forests. Several men had gone to the forests and they let it be known that they were safe. Some came back to the Ghetto and took with them their friends. This was done surreptitiously to avoid a mass escape, which would put everyone in danger. Others wanted to go to the forest but they did not know how to find the partisans. A few did escape by themselves and managed to find the partisans.

Preparations were made by a larger group led by the Charnes of an escape to the Lipichanski wilderness. One night they made the escape and a group of others followed them. A fight began among the escapees. A German patrol arrived and started shooting. Some managed to run back to the Ghetto, others managed to escape. Yoel Lis with his wife were shot behind the Ghetto. The Belarusian neighbours had stripped the bodies naked and removed their gold teeth. The Germans did not allow their bodies to be buried for four days. We thought that the Germans would slaughter all survivors of the Ghetto. But the Germans had their own plans and the escape did not cause them to change them.

When the number of the escapees reached 100, the Germans replaced them with the same number of Jews from the tradesmen's Ghetto. They were mainly older and weaker people.

The family Gafkin consisted of 7 people. Before the first slaughter they found a hiding place. In the second slaughter the mother of the family with three children were killed. The father with a 17 year old daughter and a 15 year old son remained alive. Father escaped to the forest and told the children that he would rescue them as soon as possible. The time of hunger and pain dragged on. The boy and girl worked for the Germans. They were frequently flogged. In the Ghetto they were lonely. No one took them under his wing. They decided to go in search of their father. After the first snow fell they escaped one night and went off. They did not know the way. They hoped to get to Sluchovich, three kilometres from town, to a farmer who was an acquaintance of their mother. The farmer received them well and promised to hide them for a few weeks till he would find out where their father was. The children were happy. They gave the farmer the small amount of money which they had on them and went to sleep. They were awakened by the German policemen, who the farmer brought from town. They were taken back to town and put in a cellar in the jail. Four days later they were hung.

Because there were many escapes, the Germans put a strong guard around the fence. They were patrolling day and night. Not far from the Ghetto, in the highest house in the area, the Germans posted some gendarmes. At night a reflector lit the Ghetto and the surrounds. They shot, using a machine gun, at every suspicious movement.

> *[The difficult story finishes abruptly in the Pinkas.*
> *We know of no reason.]*

[Page 319]

C. The final wandering

by Y. Yaffe

Translated from Yiddish by O. Delatycki

Regardless of the fact that all were depressed and subdued, the Jews of Karelicz, Lubcz, Iweniec and Derewnoe were preparing for the happy holiday of Shavuot. Though the Germans had taken the cows which belonged to the Jews, the wives managed to obtain cheese from the gentile neighbours and they fried bliny (pancakes). After all, Shavuot is supposed to be a happy holiday. For a moment a long forgotten spark of hope arose in the depressed hearts. Perhaps in time conditions would change and it would be possible to celebrate happy Jewish holidays. No matter how difficult the situation was, the Jews were hoping that things would change for the better. Little children were gathering flowers in the meadows. The parents cleaned as best they could, the dresses they wore – the festive garments were either taken away by the Germans or were long since exchanged for bread. The under garments were washed and dried. All was ready for the holiday. But they were also prepared for wandering, the last wandering before death. The order came suddenly and was short: within two hours all Jews from the townships were to be ready to walk to the Novogrudok Ghetto. One was allowed to take the clothing that one was wearing. There was great panic and crying. Some did not believe that they would be taken to the Ghetto. They thought that it was a lie, that they were being led to their death. Some escaped into the forest and took their fate in their own hands. Parents were searching for their children. Others were anxious to seek advice from their friends. People were packing bags with their belongings and tying the bags to their bodies in preparation for the expulsion. They were leaving their houses with the bags on their backs. Some looked back at their houses and recalled the years of work they had put into their upkeep. They thought of all the memories that were connected with their houses, which they were now leaving forever. Outside of the townships the Jews were surrounded by a number of armed policeman, led by a few Germans. The next order was: children under the age of 12 would be taken to a home for children, which would be established next to a monastery. The policemen moved in swiftly among the Jews and forcibly took the children. Mothers were crying, children held on to their parents. But the devils have done their work. Parents had to part from their future. Children were removed from the arms of their parents. The roots were destroyed. And they, the lone people, would have to perish in isolation. The Jews left their township and a day later all the children were killed. Before leaving, all parcels were checked by the Germans and all better items were taken away from them. The Jews looked in silence at the homes they were leaving. They lived and worked in the towns for hundreds of years. They developed and grew in prosperity. And suddenly they were separated from their homes and their mode of live. They walked on sandy roads, through wide fields to an unknown future. They were aware that they were going to their death. They would have to suffer for a few months on this earth, but they would finish up in a mass grave.

Early flowers appeared in the fields. The trees were covered in leaves. The sun was warming the earth. But humans were succumbing from pain and heart ache, from the difficult road and the heavy load on there backs. The policemen did not permit them to stop for a rest. They were beating them with rubber whips. They told the Jews to drop their parcels and accelerate the pace. People were hurried and they were losing their strength. One of them stopped and was unable to go further. He was resigned to face the worst. A policeman came over and shot him. He was left lying on the road. They were hastened. The Germans allowed 4 hours to get from Iweniec to Lubcz. In Lubcz the local Jews were assembled and made to join the others on the track to the Novogrudok Ghetto. All had to be done in the manner proscribed by the Germans. One township had to join the next in the race to perdition. The Jewish population of Lubcz, a little fewer than 2000 in number, was divided into two groups: the younger group of more than 600 men was sent to work on the roads. After all other Jews were expelled from Lubcz, the road workers were transferred to the village of Berovich. They were housed in a big barn. They lived there for a few days. Later the barn was surrounded by Germans with automatic pistols and all Jews were shot*. The rest of the Jewish population of Lubcz was led to Novogrudok. The group of walkers was enlarged and the walkers intermingled. They were interested in finding out from each other how they were expelled from their homes. Towards the end of the day the policemen got tired of urging on the Jews on and the rate of progress slowed down. They were even permitted to sit and rest a few times. They passed several villages. The local population came out of their houses and expressed their sympathy to the expelled Jews. Some dared to give the Jews a loaf of bread. When the policemen did not object, the whole village came out with gifts of food. All this happened without interruption to the walk. It started to get dark. They approached an estate of a land owner. The Jews were put into the barns. The Jews laid down on the bare floor and slept. This was the night of Shavuot, when in the night the sky opens up and angels come down and shed a light on the Jews who conducted midnight prayers and received the Torah. Now the Jews were banished from their townships. Their synagogues were closed. The Torah was torn and ravaged. All night the Jews rolled from one side to the other on the hard ground. They thought of the disturbed holy day. They regretted their disturbed life, they looked on to the dark skies for an answer, but they found no answer. The world was deaf and dumb to their sufferings. The sky was covered in a cloud like armour to make sure that the tragedy of the Jews would not be seen or heard. Next morning they were awakened early and were made to walk again with the same brutality as the day before. Those lagging behind were flogged and cursed using the crudest words. Finally they arrived at the Ghetto. The gate to the Ghetto divided the policemen from the Jews.

The policemen remained in the free world and the Jews were locked up in the Ghetto. They lost their freedom forever. They were fatigued, broken people, dusty and dry, weary and apprehensive. They dragged from their backs their parcels and lay down on the bunks. They rested their weary bodies on the parcels and looked around them at the Novogrudok Ghetto Jews, who were used to living in the Ghetto. In my mind I compared them to the Jews who were banished to Babylon and sat on the bank of the river longing for Zion. The Jews from the small towns never expected that they would be expelled from their homes, locked up in a Ghetto and ultimately killed. There was no room for the newly arrived in the houses of the Ghetto and the Germans ordered that they should move into the barns, where the farmers kept their horses. 'Won't the Jews freeze in the barns in the winter' the members of the Judenrat asked the Germans. 'It is summer now, in the winter you won't need the barns' they were told. They were implying that in the winter the people in the barns would not be alive. In the mean time the newcomers were trying to make some arrangements in the barn. The first night was spent sleeping in their clothing on their parcels. Next day boards were delivered to the Ghetto. The Jews made up double bunks and each one had a corner where he could sleep. Numbers were given to each location in the barn. If one was looking for someone in the barn he could find him if he knew the persons 'address'. Gradually people got used to the work and to the life in the Ghetto. One could do with 120 gram bread, to queuing up for a litre of thin soup and be prepared every day to die in a slaughter. And the more one was oppressed the more one wanted to live. Some wanted to believe that they would survive all the dangers and repressions and would live as free human beings. There was also a keen interest in the political news. The news from the fronts reached the Ghetto and the Jews were delighted to interpret them in a manner which would favour them. They believed that the Germans would be defeated and they would be liberated. In reality threats to the existence of the Ghetto were approaching. The second slaughter came.

Nochim from Karelicz was among those who were against escaping to the forests. Why suffer in the forest, be exposed to cold and want, to be in a constant fear of death. Either way no one would survive the Germans. It was easier to die in the Ghetto. He was among the first who went to work for the Germans. He worked devotedly. 'One must obey German orders, we cannot help it, they have the strength.' One early morning he jumped over the Ghetto fence, went into a near by garden and stole a head of cabbage. A policeman saw him and asked him why he was on the wrong side of the Ghetto wall. Nochim pointed at the cabbage, which he held in his hands. 'Get over the fence back into the Ghetto' the policeman ordered. When Nochim was on the fence with one leg in the Ghetto the policeman shot him and his dead body fell into the Ghetto. The policemen gathered and laughed. For them it was a matter of little consequence to shoot a Jew, as if it was a hare. The Ghetto was immersed in mourning and depression. Snow began to fall. The cutting winds of the late autumn were blowing. The life in the Ghetto became harder by the day. It was difficult at work. In the Ghetto hospital were workers with broken hands and feet and injured bodies. The Ghetto was fastidiously guarded making an escape difficult. The workers were taken to and from work by an armed guard. And where could one run? The partisans were not coming any more to rescue people. All were depressed and despondent. They looked and behaved like people much older than their age. They were waiting every day for death. They behaved like people suffering from tuberculosis, who spat out the last bit of saliva together with their lungs. Some were waiting for their death as a salvation. The severe winter penetrated the bodies. Their boots were in tatters and they could not be repaired. Their clothing that was torn when cutting timber, clearing snow and carrying bags and timber could not be replaced. The wind blew through the holes onto the bloodied bodies and wounds caused by German whips and sticks. The food was bad and getting worse. There were days when the Germans did not issue bread. On some days the Jews were not allowed to bring water from the well outside the Ghetto. On such days soup could not be cooked. But flogging was never spared at work and after work. Whenever a German met a Jew he had to flog him for no reason at all. The time of the slaughter was approaching and the Germans wanted to display their sadism. Soon there would be no Jews and they would have no one to flog and kill.

The time of the slaughter had arrived.

The third slaughter
The 4th of February 1943

Early in the morning when it was still very dark, the ditch in Great Brecianka was ready to receive the remaining 500 Jews from the Peresike Ghetto. The whole road from the Ghetto to the ditch, a distance of less than 2 kilometres, was lined with armed policemen and Germans. In the yard of the Ghetto the group of workers was lined up, just as they were doing every day, to make it look as if they were going to work. If someone was missing they went to fetch him. The Germans did not shout, but were patiently waiting till the whole brigade was counted accurately and walked to the other side of the fence. There tens of armed policemen took over. They surrounded the workers and instead of leading them to the town to work they took them in the opposite direction to the ditch. A few minutes later a second group left the gates of the Ghetto. They had no idea what was happening. When they realised that this was their last walk it was too late to attempt to escape. Some attempted to run. They were shot and remained lying where they fell: black stains in the white snow. Later the farmers collected the bodies and took them to the ditches. The last group of workers in the Ghetto realised that the Jews were being taken out of town. Forty people hid in a bunker in the Ghetto bake house. The Germans looked for the missing people. They searched scrupulously the 12 houses and pushed their bayonets into the earth. They discovered the bunker. Before full daylight all people of the Ghetto were dead. A few who managed to escape were turned over to the Germans by farmers. Only two people saved themselves. They joined the partisans in the forest.

> *The current information (July 2005) is that the slaughter of the road workers from Lubch (Lyubcha) occurred at Malyie Vorob'evichi of the Ostashino Soviet, a village on the east side of the river Ossa, 10km due south of the township of Delyatichi. According to Botvinnik, in "Monuments of Genocide', 635 people were killed on the 8 August 1942 i.e. a day after the second slaughter in Novogrudok (information supplied by Tamara Vershitskaya, director of the Novogrudok museum). These figures are in broad agreement with those quoted in the above article. After the war the Soviets erected a monument on the site, on which the number of killed was stated to be 950 and the date 8 August 1942. A new monument was erected in May 2005, due to the generosity of a friend from Novogrudok. On it the number of killed is stated to be 635, but the date of the execution is given as 3 July 1943.*

[Page 322]

D. The tradesmen's Ghetto

by Y. Yaffe

Translated from Yiddish by O. Delatycki

The workshops were housed in two large brick buildings. All surviving Jews in the Ghetto were tradesmen. The farriers were 'on top of the heap'. The Germans had penetrated deep into Russia and winter was approaching. The German army urgently needed fur coats. They feared that they would freeze in the blizzards without them. A few dozen Jews set to work and were pulling thick threads through the eyes of the large needles and attached one piece of fur to another, they shaped pieces of fur to form sleeves, attached pockets and collars. And the heap of fur coats grew by the day. A German truck took them to the front line. The Germans were satisfied and the Jews hoped that because of the need for fur coats they may survive the war. The shoemakers made felt boots, hard, compacted felt boots with thick leather soles. Their fingers ached from pushing needles through the thick leather. But they thought that their suffering was necessary to save their lives. And there was another benefit, every now and then they were able to trade in a leather sole for bread. In another room worked the skilled tailors. Their customers were slim, erect Germans with well pressed, brown trousers and highly polished boots. They wore well fitting jackets made of good quality textiles. They were well fed and had smiling faces. The customers were all members of the SS. Suits were made for them from textiles stolen from Jews and were made by the best, yet unpaid, Jewish tailors in the Ghetto. The shoemakers worked also for the population of the town and for the farmers. The best shoemakers made lacquered shoes and chevron boots for the German women. The German women with their upturned noses and silly eyes, the upstarts, the servant girls, who suddenly had become wealthy, were showing off their importance in front of the Jewish tradesmen. Having learned their behaviour from their men, they abused and often beat up the Jewish shoemakers when the shoes did not meet with their approval. The saddlers made saddles for the German horsemen. They were producing belts from hard, twisted leather. They formed the seats of the saddles and decorated the edges with nickel, which shone and showed up the horse and the Junker riders, when they went riding in the evening, after a day's torture and killing of innocent people. Carpenters and clickers, furriers and tailors, knitters and corsetieres all were locked up and were likely to die. The machinery was issuing monotonous sounds and the people became also monotonous. They worked all day and they thought that each day may be their last. The Ghetto was surrounded by a high fence of barbwire and on the other side policemen walked up and down. They were watching the Jews and made certain that no gentile would make any contact with them. The Ghetto was locked up. The Jews worked there and lived there. This filled them with fear, because it made an escape impossible. All the captors had to do was to surround the Ghetto and shoot everyone. One hope was that the war would finish with a German defeat, but they feared that the Germans would kill them in the last minute. Perhaps, they thought, the war would continue, and a miracle would happen. The Jews of the Ghetto were busy every day. The process of working, of creating, occupied their minds. As it would be expected of experienced tradesmen, they endeavoured to produce good quality work. Evenings were occupied with looking for food. There was business going on in the Ghetto. The policemen, whose job it was to see to it that the Ghetto was isolated, had business dealings with the inmates of the Ghetto. One could buy near neigh everything, if one had the means. But the cost was high. As a result, some were well supplied and others where hungry. Some had become apathetic and spent their free time playing cards in a secluded corner. A few were engrossed in chess and looked for a way of defeating their opponent. Most of the people were circulating in search of news, any news. Everywhere there were people standing around and talking. The main concern was, naturally, how to survive the Ghetto. When the Jews were taken to work outside the Ghetto and could move around more freely, they did not think of escaping. They thought that when they would hear of an approaching slaughter they would escape without difficulty. In the tradesmen's Ghetto the conditions altered. The Ghetto was surrounded day and night by policemen. A group was being organised for the purpose of escaping to the forest. Among them were a few who had been previously partisans in the Lipichaskaya wilderness. They returned to extract friends from the Zetl Ghetto and were trapped during the slaughter. Some survived and were transferred with other survivors to the Novogrudok Ghetto. They could not get used to the life in the Ghetto, to sit in a cage and wait for their death. They longed to return to the forest, to the freedom. They arranged an escape three days after the second slaughter. Tevel Leibovich, a partisan from Novogrudok, had a brother in the tradesmen's Ghetto. He managed to smuggle into the Ghetto. He had a gun and two grenades. His aim was to free his brother. In the evening the mall in the Ghetto was jam-packed with people. At that hour the last gentiles were leaving the Ghetto fence taking with them the items they had exchanged for food. The policemen smoked and chatted amongst themselves. They were satisfied with events of the day. They managed to make a lot of money by trading with the Jews. The go betweens took a rest after a busy day. They sold to their customers all the food they smuggled in and they were enjoying the fresh air. The ordinary folk walked hither and thither and spoke of nothing in particular. Suddenly all stopped and people whispered to each other. A partisan penetrated into the Ghetto. He got in under the barbwire, with a revolver in his hand. He looked searchingly at everyone in the square and disappeared behind the first door. Those that knew him spoke to him, the others looked on. Everyone looked at him and every word he said was passed on from one to another. He came to fetch his brother, but his brother was afraid to leave. 'I would be also be afraid to go' declared a curly tailor of leather pelts, who had in his lapel a big needle with a thick thread attached, to let everybody know that he was a tailor of pelts. 'I am afraid of going to the woods, but if I had a brother, a partisan with a revolver and grenades, who would come to fetch me, I would immediately leave the Ghetto'. Having spoken, he took out the needle and stuck it in his other lapel. But the brother did not seek advice from the tailor. Everyone was curious to know details of the event. 'I am not the Tevel you used to know' the partisan said to his brother 'if you will come with me, all will be well, but if not, I will shoot you here'. The brother had become apprehensive and agreed to leave the Ghetto. In the mean time others approached the partisan and asked him to take them out of the Ghetto. Each had his reasons for asking the favour – one was a friend of his fathers, the other went to cheder with the partisan, yet another helped the brother of the partisan in need. It was important to get ready in a hurry. They had to leave before sunrise. The partisan did not intend to spend the night in the Ghetto. The night was quiet. The dark sky spread over the Ghetto. The people sat in the houses. The police guards were huddled in a corner and spoke to a few Jewish girls to pass the time. At the same time about 20 people had, one after the other, bent the wires of the fence and left the Ghetto. They went in single file with the partisan in front holding his revolver. The others followed and became more encouraged as they went. The people in the Ghetto were convinced that the escapees were caught and shot. If anyone else attempted to escape he would meet with the same fate, they argued. But they did not have to speculate for long. The partisan returned to the Ghetto and told them that all who escaped settled in the forest. Some had already participated in the struggle with the Germans and all were well. He took with him a second group from the Ghetto and disappeared with them in the darkness of the night. A few other parties left. They too got away in the same way as the others. They slid out silently under the wires. The Jewish girls would deliberately chat with the policemen to distract their attention.

At the ruined Navaredok - a group of survived Jews

they were humans escaping from the Ghetto. The Jewish escapees pressed their shrunken bodies to the earth, to make themselves less visible as they slide under the wires and crawled over the field like nocturnal animals. The sky had become lighter and threw a bland, matt light on the dark bodies, which were crawling on the dark earth. The grass under them was rustling, and, slight as the sound was, it was heard in the still night. A car appeared from nowhere and cast a strong light on the escaping Jews on the field. The police shot a few rounds in the direction of the Jews. There was a shout. The car moved on and it was dark again. The escapees took quickly the injured Jew into a house. The policemen who went to look for the injured were distracted by a crying woman, who pretended that she was hurt by her husband. After that incident the police guarded the Ghetto with greater intensity. Escapes through the Ghetto fence came to an end. The gate to the Ghetto was always locked. The policeman in charge of the shift kept the key to the gate. One evening someone approached the policeman and offered him a watch for sale. The policeman put the bundle of keys on the bench and picked up the watch to inspect it. Berger the locksmith came over and took a wax image of the key to the gate. The policeman returned to the gate and Berger made a key to fit the lock in the gate. Next day a group of 11 men was keeping close to the gate by walking next to it back and forth. They chatted with the policeman and waited for a suitable moment. Mendl was the comedian of the Ghetto. He knew how to entertain people: he would perform tricks, walk on his hands, dance on one hand, pretend that he was blowing smoke from his eyes and he could roll around on the floor like a ball. As he was performing the carpenters would laugh and the laughter could be heard in the street. The policemen were curious to find out the reason for the laughter and they came into the workshop. The policeman who held the keys was among them. This was the opportunity for a group of Jews, including the locksmith, to get out of the Ghetto and lock the gate. At the head count in the evening 11 people were missing. No one knew where they were. Guarding of the people in the Ghetto had become stricter and it was practically impossible to escape. To add to the difficulties of escape winter arrived. No one could imagine how it would be possible to survive in the forests during the winter. Most gave up the thought. A few 13 and 14 year old boys, however, managed to get out from the Ghetto, strayed in the deep snow in the fields, knocked on the doors of a few farm houses, but no one let them in. They met a few Jewish partisans, who told them to go back to the Ghetto and bring their friends with them. They came back with frozen feet and gave up hope of saving themselves by running away from the Ghetto. The policemen became stricter, they did not allow access to the farmers who brought food for sale. The supervisors have become more demanding. They cursed them and beat them at work. They were not allowed to go outside the dormitories at night under the threat of being shot. Lighting of fires in the dormitories was prohibited. All of these were known signs that a slaughter was about to take place. The younger captives in the Ghetto were eager to escape. They knew that they would die so why not cut the barbwire and attack the policemen. Some might succeed and be saved. But the women were frightened and said that they were opposed to actions that would lead to a certain death. Some of those that would stay in the Ghetto may survive, they argued. But those that would take suicidal measures were certain to die. The arguments raged for a few weeks. In the mean time they watched each other. The members of the Judenrat took advice from a number of inmates, having selected the more prominent people. It was decided that each person had the right to attempt to save his or her life, provided that in doing so the lives of others would not be endangered. An uprising in the Ghetto would lead to certain death of all. Of all suggestions the plan to dig of a tunnel had become the preferred option. This would allow all people to escape in the night. The workshops were in a house facing the street. The living quarters were in a barn, which used to be as a wood shed. Three levels of bunks were built into the walls. Two people slept on each bunk. Outside of the barbwire fence there were fields. There were no houses. They started to dig the tunnel in the living quarters. The tunnel was to extend under the nearby field. The whole Ghetto, under the leadership of the Judenrat, participated in the work. The Judenrat previously opposed escapes from the Ghetto, but they realised that now they were likely to be killed with the others. The only remaining alternative was to escape to the forests.

February 1943

The Jews of the tradesmen's Ghetto were deeply shocked by the news that all Jews of the Peresike Ghetto had been killed. They realized that now their turn had come. This knowledge had urged them on to build the tunnel faster. On a certain clear night the full moon had risen in the sky. It spread its light onto the fields, onto the barbwire, leaving dark shadows on the fields. The policemen had moved away from the Ghetto wires and a human shadow slid inside. The Jews of the Ghetto led the arrival inside and hid him for the night. Next morning a truck delivered a load of boards to the carpenter shop. Waldrich the supervisor looked for people to unload the boards and ran into the new Jew. He ordered the Jew to work, but he refused and hid in the sleeping quarters. The Judenrat involved themselves in trying to resolve the problem. They offered Waldrich money to silence him. But Waldrich insisted that the unaccounted for Jew must give himself up. Next day he threatened that he would report the matter to the Germans. Later Waldrich spoke no more of the matter. The Judenrat was astonished that he did not ask for money to keep silent. They began to suspect that the new arrival was a spy. He was too busy moving about everywhere including the area where the tunnel was being built. He tried to go to places where he was told not to go. The suspicion had increased when during an inspection by the Gestapo he did not attempt to hide, as if he did not fear the Gestapo. He behaved as if had found out enough and was waiting for the Gestapo to arrest him so that he could pass on the information. Despite of all appearances, the Judenrat endevoured to save the stranger's life and locked him up in a cellar. When they brought him food, he insisted that somebody else should try it first to make sure that it was not poisoned. This was taken to be the best proof that he was guilty. In reality nobody thought of poisoning him. They asked him why he was snooping about everywhere and was behaving as if he wanted the Gestapo to arrest him. They searched his belongings and found nothing. They opened up the straw mattress on his bed and found pieces of paper with German writing on them: about the living conditions in the Ghetto, about the commercial dealings with the Ghetto police. They asked him why he became a German spy. He answered that he was taken to be slaughtered, they showed him the open ditch and said: 'you will die in two minutes unless you agree to be our agent in the tradesmen's Ghetto. When that Ghetto will be liquidated you will be transferred to the Ghetto in Wilno and the Warsaw Ghetto and you will be kept alive'. He agreed to collaborate with the Germans. But he could not remain alive in the Ghetto. He was killed by the Jews and was buried there. The Germans demanded from the Judenrat that the Jew who had smuggled into the Ghetto should be surrendered to them. The Judenrat answered that the man was not allowed to enter the Ghetto. He came in through the barbwire and, it seems, he left through the wire fence. It was suggested that the Germans should ask the Ghetto police, who guard the Ghetto day and night. That was the end of the matter. The Germans killed Burshtein, a young, capable youth, who negotiated with the Germans on various matters. He was the only one who was not killed during the slaughter in the Peresike Ghetto[1]

. Suddenly they came and arrested him. They tried to find out from him secrets from the Ghetto. Why was the stranger murdered? Why do the Jews buy arms? But he remained silent. After the liberation the following writing on the wall was found: 'I suffer, but I keep quiet. I will be killed, but I will say nothing'. Burshtin was arrested with Ruve Shabakovski, who was a locksmith. He worked in the army camp, where he stole arms and brought them to the Ghetto. They searched him and found a revolver. He was kept in the prison for a time, where he was shot later and buried in the prison yard.

The fourth slaughter

The 500 Jews in the tradesmen's Ghetto were divided into two groups. Better tradesmen were given an additional ration of 100 grams of bread. Early in the morning the Jews were made to stand in a line with the better tradesmen separated from the others. They were given their ration of bread and all went to work in the workshops. On the 7 of April[2]

the night skies began to light up slowly as if wakening from a heavy sleep. In the cool of the early morning people half asleep got up from their warm bunks, put on their clothes and hurried outside. There Reuter of the Gestapo was waiting. He was unperturbed and deliberate. His eyes were lit with a cynical smile. He was happy that he managed to deceive the Jews. He was running around the square with the rubber whip in his hand and was shouting at those who were late. The better tradesmen were standing in a separate row. He read out their names from a list and sent them to the workshops. He ordered the others to remain in the square. He left the Ghetto in his car. The policemen in a frenzy surrounded the Jews. The commotion was fearful. The Jews were running in all directions. Some managed to get through the barbwire and to get into the workshops. The policemen ran through the sleeping quarters and dragged out a few people, who were hiding and the whole group of 350[3]

persons was led out of the Ghetto. They were taken a few hundred metres from the Ghetto, on the other side of the road, where there was a big ditch left from a clay excavation. The police shot them their. Those who were left in the Ghetto could see through the windows the execution of their children, wives and mothers. Two people could not bear it and committed suicide. This was the last stage of the German annihilation. They did not bother to take the Jews out of town. They did not bring their einsatzgruppe [unit whose only duty was mass executions] to kill Jews, the local police, which was made up of local Belarusians, had learnt how to do it. Along the road, right next to the ditch, farmers travelled, workers went to their jobs and the police did nothing to hide their crime. It was done in town for everyone to see.[4]

Footnotes

1. There were two people from Peresike according to the above article, counting the spy for the Germans. There must have been others, though few in number, who escaped and survived with the partisans.

2. The date of the fourth slaughter given in the above article is wrong. It took place on the 7 May 1943.

3. A difficulty arose in trying to translate the expression 'drit-

halbun hundert' [see below] used to describe the number of those killed in the fourth slaughter. Several opinions were sought. The prevailing opinion was that this expression meant 350. If this is correct, a contradiction has arisen. On the memorial gravestone erected on the mass grave of those killed in the fourth slaughter the number of killed is given as 250. The number of Jews in the tradesmen's Ghetto before the fourth slaughter is generally assumed to have been 500. The number of Jews in the Ghetto after the fourth slaughter was given by various sources as 250 to about 300 [see eg. the article on p.287 'How 300 Jews saved themselves']. Those were the Jews who escaped from the Ghetto through the tunnel. After the war Jack Kagan took a count of the post-war survivors who escaped through the tunnel. He came up with the figure of more than 170 [including himself]. A number of people died in attempting to escape and later under various other circumstances.

4. It may be of interest to compare the above description of the fourth slaughter with that in the article on p.287 'How 300 Jews saved themselves'.

[Page 327]

E. The tar and pitch factory in the village of Karnyshi

by Y. Yaffe

Translated from Yiddish by O. Delatycki

In the village of Karnyshi, 7 kilometres from Novogrudok, lived just one Jewish family, the Wiszniewski's. They had a pitch factory. Night and day the oven was burning as they were extracting pitch and turpentine from the tree stumps. Boba Bejle Reine was particularly active. She was a spirited woman. Apart from the factory, which they managed, they also leased the pitch factories near Ivie and the villages of Berdivki, Yaryn, Stanievicz and Martsivil. She educated her male children and grandchildren in the Yeshiva and sent the girls to the gimnasjum [Polish high school]. Her daughters Tzipe and Leje she married off to Rabbis: Reb Mojsze Lipa Brodna, who was a Rabbi in Tnievo, next to Pinsk and Reb Mendl Erlich, who was a Rabbi in Latvia. Itzchok Ber Wiszniewski, the son of Bejle Reine, was learned in religious subjects. He always carried with him a chapter of Techile min Movel. He studied a 'page Gemorah' with an'eiver oirach' a man of learning who spent a night in their house. The family was at peace with their gentile neighbours. The farmers were proud of the Jewish family, who lived among them. Some of the farmers worked in the pitch factory and helped with working the land.

Itzchok Ber was 72 years old when the Germans came to Karnyshi to take the Jewish family to the slaughter in Novogrudok. He told his children to run and hide in the woods. He said that he was old and was not able to save himself. The children ran and Reb Itzchok Ber went alone to Novogrudok. He asked the German policeman to take him to the lavatory. There he hung himself, using his belt. This was the only suicide in the December 1941 slaughter. The other members of the Wiszniewski family saved themselves. Initially they were hiding in the forest and later they came to the Ghetto in Novogrudok and were working in the army barracks. The Ghetto was never at peace. The talk was always about the next slaughter. In the summer of 1942 the Germans abolished the Ghettos of Lubch, Delatych and Korelich and brought all Jews from those towns to Novogrudok[1]. At that stage a group of six people was formed: Benzion Movshovich, Ada Ziskind, Judl Ostashinski, two Jews from Karelich and Mojshe Wiszniewski, who undertook to lead the group to the Nalibok wilderness. They obtained arms and they contacted a partisan group in the forest. Behind Shchors they blundered on to a unit of policemen. Four escapees managed to elude them. Wiszniewski with another escapee got to a Russian partisan group in the Nalibok wilderness. The Russian partisans have disarmed them and accused them of being German spies. With great difficulty and daring they managed to escape from the Russian partisans.

The district court-at Karelitch Street, center of the ghetto-entrance to the tunnel

At the time of the second slaughter in August 1942 all other surviving Wiszniewskis were in the Ghetto. Since a slaughter was expected, the Wiszniewskis dug a bunker under the house they stayed in the Ghetto. The men worked in the military barracks and the Germans selected them to remain alive. The Polish supervisor in the barracks asked Nachama Wiszniewski to help him prepare a list of the Jewish workers, both of those that were selected to live and those who will die. She refused, which meant that she chose to die. She left the barracks and went to the Ghetto. On the way she met someone and asked him if there were news and should she escape. He told her that she should go to the Ghetto, because nothing was going to happen. He was the one who prepared the lists for the Germans and he new that all those who will be in the Ghetto will be killed. When both of them returned to the Ghetto the man's mother shouted at him that he should not allow anyone to escape from the Ghetto, because there required quota will not be fulfilled and they (meaning mother and son) will be killed too. At the same time Mirl Wiszniewski was wrestling with a policeman who tried to prevent her from getting under the fence and escaping. He asked her if she had gold. Instead he got a ringing smack on the face. Before the policeman recovered, Mirl was on the other side of the fence. She escaped to the forest of Karnyshi. There she met her brother Mojshe, who got there from the Nalibok wilderness.

The second slaughter

All those that were in the (Peresike) Ghetto were led to die and buried in the ditches in Litovka. The bunker which the Wiszniewskis made, was full of people who were hoping to save their lives. Breathing in the bunker was difficult and a number left the bunker. Among those who got out was an asthma sufferer, who betrayed the rest, so that no one would survive.

In the Ghetto were Germans who were searching for Jews in hiding. Shoshe Golde, the 54 year old mother of the Wiszniewskis, went out of the bunker. Before she left she said goodbye to her children. It was difficult to breath in the bunker. Thirst and hunger were acute. But the Germans were still in the Ghetto. Somebody died in the bunker. They took him out at night and left him in the Ghetto. Fania Wiszniewski left the bunker, found another hiding place, covered herself in torn regs and did not move. The Germans were coming and going but they did not see her. The Germans found the bunker. They opened the hatch and ordered everybody out. Those that got out were killed. Rosa and Nachama Wiszniewski pressed themselves into the darkest corner of the bunker in remained. After the slaughter 1200 Jews from the surroundings of Novogrudok remained alive, but not for long. The Germans declared that sooner or later they will kill all Jews, as Hitler ordered. The surviving Wiszniewskis went back to the forest and were hiding. They were hiding not only from the Germans but also from policemen, the farmers and partisans. Only a few farmers, who supplied them with food at night, knew that they were hiding in the forest. On one occasion, when they returned to the bunker they were hiding in they found it destroyed by the Germans, who found out where they were hiding. They built in the winter another bunker and spent there another winter. Later partisans came more often to see them, because there were more of them in the forests. When ten Bielski partisans were killed, Mojshe Wiszniewski served as a guide. He led a group of 25 partisans to the house of Belous. The partisans took revenge for the spilled Jewish blood. Before the liberation they joined the unit of Ordzonikidze, where they saw the coming of the Soviets.

After the liberation Aba Wiszniewski was killed on the Baltic front.

Footnotes

1. The roundup in the summer of 1942 involved a number of other towns, see eg. p. 302

The Ghetto in Peresike' in which it is said: 'they gathered in the Novogrudok Ghetto all Jews from the surrounding townships such as Nalibok, Iviniec, Lubch, Karelicz, Delatych, Naisztot and any other place wherever there was a Jew in a village'. In Lubch about a quarter of the population was taken away for road work and slaughtered at Malyie Vorob'evichi. According to Botvinnik, in "Monuments of Genocide', 635 people were killed on the 8 August 1942 i.e. a day after the second slaughter in Novogrudok.

Surviving the Holocaust with the Russian Jewish Partisans

by Jack Kagan

[This section was not part of the original Yizkor Book]

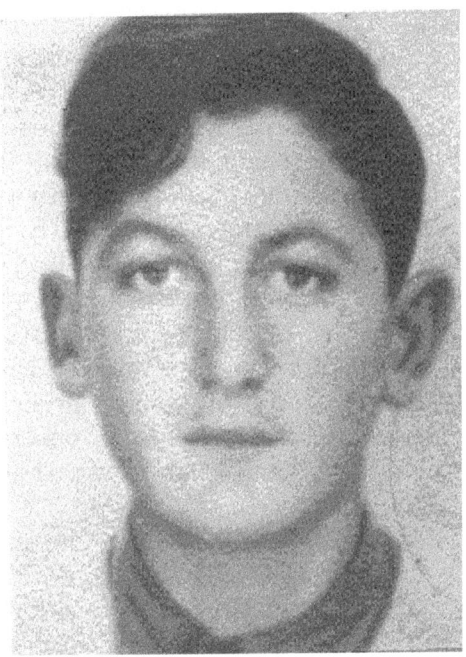

Jack (Idel) Kagan

"Thank you, my feet, frozen, bloody, you kept creeping and crawling and you saved me from death."

Jack (Idel) Kagan
 I was born in 1929 in Novogrodok to a unique family. Two brothers married two sisters and harmony reigned in our house! Although we had two houses, we lived in one. Everything was done together; the most important thing in life was family. My father Yankel was a businessman. My mother, Dvore, was a businesswoman who looked after our two shops, where we sold the saddles and sandals produced in our workshops. I had a sister, Nachama, two years older than myself.
 We were a middle-class family; we did not want for anything. More than 6,000 Jews, just over 50% of the town's population, lived in pre-war Novogrudok. Jews were always repressed. Many of the restrictions imposed on them in Tsarist Russia were retained by the Polish regime. The situation worsened after the death in 1935 of the Polish dictator Pilsudski.

Jews lived in the centre of the town, and most of the shops and workshops belonged to them; they formed the majority of the trades and professions. Jewish community life was centred around synagogues and guilds. There were many Jewish institutions - hospital, Hebrew school, kindergarten, trade schools, a number of political parties and organizations – Zionist and others, an orphanage, TOZ (Jewish Health Organization for children), a Jewish theatre, a library, a Jewish bank, Yiddish newspapers and more. In the light of the prevailing poverty and repression by the authorities those achievements were remarkable.

All that changed when the war broke out on the first day of September 1939. We were very worried of the likelihood of a German occupation. But on the afternoon of 17 September Soviet tanks came roaring down the street. Some Jews cried with joy, because we all feared the Germans. Our lives changed. We had to close down our shops and workshops, as private enterprise was not permitted. The synagogues were closed, the use of Hebrew outside the house was banned. All Jewish institutions were not allowed to continue. Our lives changed completely. There were repressions, arrests and deportations of all kinds of people, sometimes for no apparent reason. Thinking back of it now, I realize that the Russians wanted to destroy our rich Jewish traditions and culture.

On 22 June 1941 the war between Germany and the Soviet Union broke out. By the following day the whole Russian army was in retreat. We knew that we would suffer under the Germans; we expected labour camps and imprisonment, but never imagined that they would endeavour to liquidate all of us. I remember the discussion between my father and my uncle. 'There is no point in running. We are used to work. They won't kill us!' And so we stayed.

On 24 June 1941 the town was bombed. Four days later, planes flew overhead and dropped incendiary bombs. Most of the town was burnt down. Large numbers of people lost their lives. We, the Kagan family, lost everything. I was left with a pair of short trousers and a shirt. We found an empty house and moved in with about eight other families.

The Germans entered Novogrudok on 4 July 1941 and immediately started enforcing anti-Jewish laws. Yellow stars had to be worn on the front and back of our clothes, Jews were not allowed to walk on the pavement, and everyone from the age of twelve to sixty had to report for work. My father and uncle were working as saddle-makers. My mother, aunt, I and many others worked at clearing up the bombed streets. We were issued food cards for 300 grams {10.5 ounces} of bread and potatoes per day. Jews lost their rights as citizens, which meant that if someone wanted to rob a Jew (and many did), there was no point in complaining to the authorities, because a Jew had no protection.

We did not have to wait long for the beginning of the destruction of the Jewish nation. The following events were described in blood curdling testimonials of witnesses. On the 6 July 1941 the Germans started a series of tortures and murders of groups of Jews in the jail and in Skrydlevo. Some of those detained were allegedly taken to work, but had never been seen again. Most of those selected were professionals and merchants. It is estimated that 150-200 people from Novogrudok were killed in that period.

Early in July 1941 the Germans brought 105 Jewish men from Karelich and shot them in the killing fields of Skrydlevo.

On Saturday 26 July 1941, some Jewish men were rounded up by the local police and taken to the Market Square, where a group of SS men were waiting. I was near the Market Square at the time, and hid behind the ruins of a burned-out house. I heard shots being fired and an orchestra playing music. I waited there for quite a while and when I reached home I heard the awful news that the SS had selected fifty-two men and shot them. Jewish women were ordered to wash the blood off the cobblestones.

On Friday, 5 December 1941, posters appeared stating that as from six o'clock on that evening no Jews were permitted to leave the town, and that the next morning all Jews must assemble at the courthouse. They could only take with them whatever they could carry. Saturday was a bitterly cold day, -20 degrees centigrade. All 6,500 Jews assembled in the yard of the courthouse. We waited all day in the cold. Late in the afternoon, they opened the doors and there was just about enough room for us all to stand inside. We did not sleep that night.

We were locked up there all Saturday and Sunday. On Sunday, the Wehrmacht (the German army) arrived and took a party of about 100 men to build a fence around twenty-eight houses in the suburb of Peresika. They were creating a ghetto. Early on Monday morning, 8 December 1941, lorries arrived with the SS and local police. We had to form a line. Families had to stay together. The head of the family had to approach the SS man, and two questions were asked: 'Profession?' and 'How many children?' The SS man, just signalled with his gloved hand - right or left: life or death. My uncle went first with his family. 'Profession?' 'Saddle-maker.' 'How many children?' 'Two children'. The SS man signalled to the left. My father followed: Saddle-maker; two children, signalled to the right. In all 5,100 people were selected to go to the left and were taken to the village of Skridlevo. They were beaten up on entering the forest, and ordered to lie face down on the ground in groups of fifty. From there, again in groups of fifty, they had to hand over all their valuables, undress in the bitterly cold weather, and were driven into freshly dug pits where they were shot. That day we lost my uncle Moshe and aunt Shoshke, their younger son Leizerke, and Berele from Karelich. My cousin Berl survived by a miracle. It was an appalling blow to us all. The remaining 1,500 of us were taken to Peresika, where the ghetto had been formed. It was very small. We built bunks, about 60 centimetres (approximately two feet) wide per person. If you would turn over in the night, you would wake up the nine other people who slept in your row.

It was an 'open' ghetto, which meant we had to go out to work. My father worked as a saddler, and my mother stitched fur gloves for the German army. I worked in the Russian army barracks, along with about 250 men. The work was hard, and I had to walk four kilometres to work{two and a half miles}. I was barely thirteen years old - I believe I was the youngest worker in the barracks. After a while I was transferred to a better job - carting stones in a wheel-barrow. This work was also very difficult, and I received plenty of beatings, too.

Various regulations were being issued daily against the Jewish population. From the beginning of May 1942, Jews from the surrounding towns and villages were brought to Novogrudok. Altogether the ghetto held about 6,500 people, making it incredibly overcrowded. It is difficult to describe the misery of that time. People walked around aimlessly, knowing that they were sentenced to death, but not knowing when the execution would take place. Yet there was nowhere to run.

One day at the beginning of July, we arrived for work as usual. At lunchtime, I drifted away from the workplace, as I had done every day, to search for cigarette ends or pieces of bread, which the German soldiers might have thrown out. Suddenly, from nowhere, a German soldier jumped at me, shouting 'Raus, raus du verfluchter Jude!' (Out, out, you cursed Jew). He hit me with his rifle butt and pushed me into the middle of the barrack's square, together with about fifty other people.

The SS troops surrounding our group shouted insults at us and made us line up in a single row. Within a few minutes a machine gun was assembled. I thought that they were going to shoot us, and my legs felt like jelly. They kept us there for a long time but, eventually, a high-ranking SS officer arrived. He did not say anything, but just released us and we went back to work. After that, I went to work with my father to learn the craft of saddle-making Father was friendly with the foreman, who had given permission for me to come.

On 7 August 1942 we arrived at work as usual, and immediately we were surrounded by the police and the SS. There were about 500 of us, men and women. At the same time the SS also surrounded the ghetto and the barracks. They then took everyone from the ghetto to Litovka, which was one kilometre {about a third of a mile}away, to mass graves, which had been prepared in advance. They killed everybody from the ghetto; including my relatives from Karelich and my old grandmother. On that day, 4,500 men, women and children were killed in Litovka.

On the same evening everyone from the workshops had to line up for inspection. I stood next to my father, dressed in his jacket and long trousers in an attempt to look older. The Nazi chief passed and did not say anything, but all the children who were hidden in the loft and basement were found and thrown out of the windows. Then they were taken by a lorry to Litovka where they were killed. After the slaughter, the ghetto in Peresika contained 500 Jews and in the Courthouse there were 500 skilled tradesmen, I was one of the youngest amongst them. Of our family, my mother, father, sister, cousin Berl and myself were the only survivors.

We were kept locked up for a number of days without food or water. Then a van was driven into the Courthouse yard, where we were assembled, and loaves of bread were thrown at us. The Germans took pleasure in seeing us struggle to get hold of a piece of bread. Then the camp commandant told us that we were the lucky ones: we would remain alive because the Reich needed us, but we would have to work hard. We were issued numbers which we had to stitch on to the back of our clothes. Mine was number 334.

Now we no longer lived in a ghetto, but in a work camp. The camp was enclosed by two circles of barbed wire with a timber fence on the outside. Towers with searchlights and machine guns were installed. The camp had no water facilities, so every day a number of workers had to fetch drinking water from a nearby water pump. This was our only contact with the outside world.

After the second massacre, young people began to escape. There would be a lot of whispering, then they would disappear at night. At that time, we heard for the first time of a Jewish partisan group organised by the Bielski brothers. Contact had been established with them. The Bielski brothers gave us hope. They provided a place to run to. I knew the youngest brother, Archik Bielski very well, as we had gone to the same school and were in the same class. The four Bielski brothers had refused to submit to the German terror and had gone into hiding in the forest. They were joined by people from the Novogrudok ghetto. Thus the Bielski brigade was formed. Once it became known in the ghetto that there was a place to run to, people began to take the chance and escaped.

By the end of October 1942 the Bielski group consisted of more than 300 people. I started to prepare myself to escape and join them. Getting out of the camp was still quite easy; the danger was that in winter you could freeze to death. Then there was the problem of food, and the fact that the outside world was unfriendly. People were ready to sell you to the Germans or give you away just for the sake of it.

I became friendly with the Jewish warehouseman in charge of the store of felt boots. He had lost a son of my age and therefore wanted me to succeed in my escape. He risked his life and gave me a pair of the most beautiful, hard felt boots. I told my parents that I planned to escape and they gave me their blessing.

On 22 December 1942, the gates were opened to let in lorries to unload raw material for the workshops. It was very cold. I put on my special felt boots, loosened the yellow star and number, and then tore them off when I got nearer to the gates. There were no guards to be seen and I walked through the gates without looking back. I crossed the highway and went on to the small forest where a few people were already waiting. By the afternoon there were fourteen of us.

We waited until dark and then started to skirt around the town because a rendezvous had been arranged with the partisans at midnight. The going was very difficult because of the waist-deep soft snow. We had to cover approximately eight kilometres {five miles}. We reached the little river Bretyanka and had to cross it. We felt the ice under the snow, but suddenly the ice cracked and most of us fell in the water. I was the worst off; my felt boots immediately absorbed the water and snow started sticking to them. Each step became more and more difficult.

We all reached the place for the rendezvous but we were too late. The partisans had not waited, but we knew they were due to come back three nights later. We were advised to stay in the small forest for the next three days. After a while I just wanted to sleep. I started to dream but I realized immediately that if I fell asleep now it would be for ever. I fought hard with myself and made a decision that I must return to the camp, otherwise I would freeze to death. I crawled to the road and put my life in the hands of fate. I was fortunate. A peasant passed by in his sleigh and he did not notice me when I climbed on to the back of it. When we got near the camp I just jumped off and started walking towards the water pump. I knew that in a few hours' time the first party would come to fetch water. I waited in the bitter cold and eventually they came. The guards were wrapped up from head to toe and they could not see anything.

I moved forwards and was noticed by one of the carriers. He must have immediately told the others, as I found myself suddenly in the middle of the group. Before I knew what was happening I was back in my room. My father tried to take off my boots but it was impossible - a file and sharp knife had to be used. My toes on both feet were black with frostbite. There was no doctor to help and no medicine, there was nothing we could do. After a few days the flesh started to rot, and my toes had to be amputated. Now I felt sure that I had signed my own death certificate - I was in the camp, but I unable to walk. The strain on my parents and sister was unbearable: if I could not work, I did not receive any food ration, which meant a decrease in rations for the rest of the family.

We had a hidden radio in the camp. On the fourth of February the person that had listened to the radio shouted out: we are going to survive! The Germans had a great disaster in Stalingrad. They lost a whole 6th army.

We were trying to hearten ourselves. We thought that as we were stitching fur coats and fur boots for the army, they must keep us alive. Later on the same day we heard that the ghetto in Pieresika was liquidated.

Gradually I started to feel better, but a new enemy had arrived - bugs, millions of them. They made my life a misery. Because of the dirty conditions, lice and bugs reigned. They got under the so-called bandages and into my wounds. I had to scratch, and with the slightest scratch the wounds would bleed again.

In April 1943 there was a new announcement that specialist workers, including my father, would receive extra food rations. On 7 May 1943, my window was open and I watched the workers going, as usual, to get their extra rations of food. Suddenly I saw local and foreign police running about, hitting out with their rifles. My mother came to the window to reassure me. I was sure she had come to say goodbye. I could no longer stand hearing the shouting and seeing the beatings. I turned towards the wall, covered myself, put my fingers in my ears and lay quietly, crying my heart out.

Suddenly I heard guards coming into the room. They had killed everyone and were now coming to rob us, but we did not have anything they could steal. They grabbed some items of clothing took some belongings and threw them on the top bunk, and so covered me even more. How long I lay there I do not know, but soon I heard crying and realized the workers had been sent back, my father among them. All the others, including my mother, sister and aunt, had been taken just outside the camp and killed.

After this massacre, food was cut down to 125 grams {just over four ounces} of bread, mixed with straw, and a bowl of soup a day - a slow starvation diet. It was impossible for me to get used to the hunger. I was not occupied, and the days passed very slowly, lying there just waiting twenty-four hours for the next slice of bread.

An escape committee was formed, because we were now certain that nobody would be left alive, the war against the Jews was more important to them than the war against the Russians. The first plan was to wait for a dark night, throw hand grenades into the guardroom and escape. Some would definitely reach the forest, but what about me? I could not run and could not let myself be taken alive. In desperation my father prepared two nooses. As soon as we would hear the first explosion we would hang ourselves. However after about a week, this plan was dropped and a new one devised: to dig a tunnel 100 metres {328 feet} long to the other side of the barbed wire, into a field of growing wheat. The plan was worked out by Berl Yoselevitz. The work had to start immediately. The aim was to dig two meters per day. Digging actually started in the 2nd week in May. A works committee was formed and they met in the room where I lay on the top bunk. I couldn't walk. They used to meet three-four times a week to discuss the progress. Two permanent members of the committee lived in my room: Notke Sucharski and Ruvke Shabakovski. It is difficult to know how many members served on the committee; people were called in as they were needed. The word tunnel changed the whole atmosphere in the camp. It was not a secret, everyone but Mr. Mendelson (more about him later) knew about it. For me it was a Godsend. I felt that maybe I will recover in time and participate in the escape. For people that believed in the escape it gave a hope for salvation. People that did not want to escape did not have to make up their minds on the spot. It was decided to start digging in the stable. It was the furthest building from the guards and least occupied. I can't be certain, but I believe that in the stable was an earthen floor. Notke Sucharski and Lionke Portnoy promised to make available the necessary tools within a week and to keep them in perfect condition. The lower bunk was hinged to the wall, for quick access. A 2 m deep vertical shaft was dug. Sosnovski the tailor was called in and told to collect blankets and to make 60 bags, each 40 cm x 50 cm in size. A joiner was called in and asked to cut a trap door from the stable to the loft of the next building. Salek Jacubovitz, the policeman, was responsible for the selection of diggers and for finding extra food for them. It was established that the tunnel should be 65 cm x 70cm in cross-section. The soil was to be stored on either side of the loft. There was a builder in the camp. I can't remember his name. He was later sent to Koldichevo. He was responsible for storage of the dug out earth and to make sure that the loft would not cave in under the weight of the earth. After two weeks it was realized that it would be impossible to maintain the rate of two meters per day. The lamp in the tunnel did not burn properly. It was difficult for people to sit inside the tunnel and to pass on the bags filled with soil.

We had no electric light in the living quarters. Rukovski, the best electrician in the camp, was called in and told to look for an active electric cable and to provide electric light in the tunnel. After a few days he reported that he found the mains cable and he could do it.

Skolnik, the carpenter from Karelich, was called in and told to make as quickly as possible a platform on wheels 50 cm x 50 cm in size. They asked my father to stitch up two reins each 50 m long. They had to be strong and have rings at the ends. It was like magic, everything materialized under such difficult conditions. Skolnik built the platform in pieces to be able to smuggle them out from the joiners workshop.

I think that within three week electricity was provided inside the tunnel. The platform was functioning, but not good enough. Earth was spilling over and the platform was hitting the walls.

Skolnik was called in again, this time to produce four panels, 50 cm x 50 cm x 50 cm in size, fitted to the sides of the platform. Two of the panels were hinged, for quick loading and unloading of the soil. Wider wheels and guiding rails for the wheels were made, so that the platform would move in a straight line and not hit the walls. The request was enormous. It meant making and stealing four one meter rails a day to extend the rails. Whoever was caught stealing German property would be hung. Skolnik was caught carrying a piece of wood about six months previously; and he was hung by the arms. He survived.

The aim was to pull out 9 to 10 trolleys of earth a day and move the soil in the night. In the shaft at the entrance to the tunnel a space for two people was made. They passed on the bags of soil. From the entrance to the tunnel sixty or seventy people sat in a row and passed to each other the bags that were emptied at the other end on both sides of the loft. Nobody complained. From the entrance to the tunnel to the barbed wire fence was 40 m. On a Sunday morning at the end of June Lionke Portnoy installed an air pipe to let air into the tunnel. At the same time a test was made to measure the depth and the position of the tunnel. This was not a simple exercise, he needed to push through a two meter rod from a 65 cm cavity. Lionke brought with him 4 sticks. They had to be assembled into one. The top one was painted white so that it should be easily seen. At the same time Joselevitz went up on the loft and took out some tiles to be able to see the direction the tunnel took. Everything was perfect.

At the beginning of July 1943, my father came to me during the working day, took some belongings, and said goodbye. He told me that they were sending him and another ten specialists for a short while to a different camp. It was a very sad day for me, the parting was so quick. To this day I can see him with his small packet in his hands, putting on a brave face, saying he would see me soon, knowing very well that this was goodbye for ever. He was killed in an escape from Koldichevo in February 1944.

His job to look after the reins was given over to Efroim Sielubski, who made a good job of it.

When I began to feel better, I started to test my strength. After six months of lying still, I felt pins and needles and pain when I lowered my legs. I was very weak, but I was also tremendously determined. I was still only fourteen years old and life was hard for me. I could more or less get around on crutches, but I was just like a skeleton. I had to live completely on charity, for someone to give me a slice of bread and some 'soup water'. I started to participate in building the tunnel. Every evening I sat on the loft in line and passed on the small bags.

The digging of the tunnel progressed well. The escape plan was put in motion. Rukovski, the electrician, managed to make a switch board so that he could control the two large searchlights. To the end the Germans could not find out the reason the searchlights were not functioning properly. The escape was planned for the second week in August. The wheat outside the camp was the best camouflage.

Then one day in August the Germans brought a tractor into the field and cut the wheat. We were afraid that the tunnel would collapse under the weight of the tractor but luckily it held. However, we were left with a problem. Escape was impossible into an open field.

Had we escaped early August as planned, none of us would have survived. The Germans made a plan to liquidate the partisans in the Novogrudok-Ivenietz area. They named the operation "Herman". They assembled in Novogrudok and the surrounding villages 52,000 soldiers and police. The troupes consisted of: the 1st Infantry SS brigade under Nazi major-general Curt von Gottberg, 2nd infantry SS regiment, 30th police regiment, 4 separate SS-Sondercommando units led by SS lieutenant-colonel Oscar Dirlewanger, a group of three separate SS battalions under Kerner, the 15th, 57th, 116th and 118th Ukrainian battalions, a Latvian battalion, a gendarmerie group under Kraikenborn, police from towns and villages in the area of the operation, and special commandos of general Kube.

Their intention was to surround the vast forest, to push the partisans to the centre and liquidate them.

The Bielski partisans survived the German net. It was a miracle. Among the partisan fighters were also the old and the very young, the sick and the lame. They were there because Bielski vowed that he would accept every Jew who came to him. They survived the round up because they knew the wilderness in which they lived and because of their determination to survive Hitler and his Reich. In the end they did not lose in the German round up a single person. Would they have not survived, the Jews from Novogrudok, having escaped the Ghetto, would have had nowhere to shelter. Those interested in this incredible story can read more about it in the article by the historian Samuel Amarant 'The partisans' company of Tuvia Belski' on page 333 of the Yizkor (Memorial) book of Novogrudok. The internet address of the book is:

http://www.jewishgen.org/yizkor/Novogrudok/Novogrudok.html.

The committee met and decided to dig further to the end of the ridge, in excess of 150 metres more. Nobody can imagine how much earth accumulates from such a project. First the loft was filled, then double walls were built and filled. We had to hide any incriminating evidence. Sunday was the sanitary day in the camp. We had to make sure that outside the buildings all was clean. New toilets had to be built and that gave us an opportunity to dispose of earth from the tunnel.

At the end of August there were further problems: rain was seeping through and earth was falling from the roof of the tunnel. Timber had to be stolen and some bunks destroyed to make supports to prevent the tunnel from collapsing.

In the middle of September a meeting was called, and a vote taken. There were still some people who said it was better to die in the camp than to run, but the majority preferred escape so a list was drawn up. Mr Ytzhak Rosenhouse put together a list of the inmates and gave it to the committee to decide on the order people would go out through the tunnel. The only name which was left off was that of Mr. Mendelson. Mr. Mendelson was a convert from Vienna and he was not trusted. He lived separately and knew nothing about the tunnel. He was left behind. On the 27th of September he was arrested and later shot in prison.

The first to go through the tunnel would be the tunnel diggers, followed by five armed men, and then followed all fit persons. I would be among the last, along with my friend Pesach, who had also lost some toes. I had to make a trial run to see whether I was capable of making the distance. It went perfectly well. I was walking already without sticks.

On 19 September 1943 another meeting was called, and we were notified that the tunnel would be completed in the following week. So started the longest week in my life, but I was not afraid. People were saying goodbye to each other and exchanging tips about the route and the best way to go. It was thought that if we all went our separate ways, we would stand a better chance of survival.

The day arrived on the 26 September 1943, our chosen day of escape. We assembled in the rooms of the front building, There were about 10 rooms in the front building. Orders were given for some people to go up to the loft. This was a test. The committee was afraid that if 250 people would go up onto the loft at the same time the ceiling might collapse.

The night was dark and stormy. It was made to order. The searchlights had been cut off and some of the nails removed from the zinc roof in the stable, to make them rattle a lot in the wind. The leaders did not let anybody into the tunnel till they had broken through to the surface, to make sure that there would be enough air for the first 120 people to go into the tunnel. Only then did they go into the tunnel. The rest went up onto the loft and formed a line which moved slowly forward towards the stable. The first group that went in to the tunnel sat there for about ten to fifteen minutes until the hole was enlarged. Than the line started to move forward. But we had not allowed for the effect of the light in the tunnel. When people came out at the other end, the sudden darkness after the brightness in the tunnel disorientated them and they ran towards the camp, whereupon the guards opened fire. Although the searchlights were cut off, the guards could still see movement in the dark, and probably thought partisans had come to liberate the camp.

When I came out of the tunnel I could see the whole field alive with flying bullets. I saw figures in the dark running towards the forest, and was certain that in the morning the Germans would search that area. So Pesach and I stuck together. We planned to skirt around the town and wait on the other side. The fields had recently been ploughed, so walking was difficult. We took the same route I had taken on my first escape and crossed the same river.

Dawn started to break. We lay behind a bush and stayed there all day, about two kilometres {just over a mile}from town. As soon as darkness fell, we got up and went to the nearest house and asked for food. A man gave us a loaf of the most delicious bread and some milk. We walked for five nights in the same direction. It rained for some of this time, and I was afraid to take off my tattered shoes. Around the hole that had developed in one of them, I could see dried blood. On the morning of 1 October 1943, we set down to rest after a night's walk when we saw a group of people with horses and a cart. We hid ourselves, but then we heard them speaking Yiddish and I recognized one of the partisans.

They were fighters returning from a mission. We were very lucky to have met them: it is impossible to calculate the odds of going into that forest, without really knowing the way, and reaching the people we were searching for.

The partisans took us to their base, where I was reunited with my cousin Berl. We laughed and cried at the same time. I had reached the Ordzhonikidze detachment of the Kirov brigade. This was the name of the former Bielski fighting group of 180 men and women. Not long afterwards Berl decided that we should join the family group of the Kalinin detachment, better known as the Bielski detachment, so that we could stay together. He got permission for us to transfer, and we left the fighting group.

It was only a short journey on foot to the Kalinin group, whose commander was Tuvia Bielski. It was strange to see so many Jews in one place, quite unafraid, although we were close to German police stations.

A reconnaissance group arrived and told Bielski that the Germans and local police were on the move. That meant immediate evacuation of the camp. It could not have happened at a worse time for me as my wounds were just beginning to heal. We moved out slowly in the middle of the day, in a large convoy. The danger was great because we had to cross several major roads. Berl decided that he and I should leave the convoy, because if shooting took place, I would not be able to run. He found out the route the convoy was taking, and we left on our own.

Berl knew the way and we walked slowly. We met the group on the following day and heard that shots had been exchanged with the local police. We had something to eat and moved on again to the next meeting place. I got used to sleeping in the forest without fear. We continued moving for the next few days until we reached the base in the huge Naliboki forest. We arrived late and I was very tired. I took the outer rags off my feet with difficulty, than I took off my sweater and wrapped it around my feet. I covered myself with an overcoat and fell into an exhausted sleep. I woke up early in the morning. The pain in my feet was almost unbearable.

The Bielski base in the forest developed into a little town with a bakery, a sausage-maker, shoe workshops, tailoring and engineering workshops and, later, a tannery. Partisans from all over the region used to come to get their guns, shoes and uniforms repaired there, and would exchange flour for bread and cows for sausages. I did all sorts of work in the camp.

In the forest the Jewish partisans had another enemy - the 'White' Poles. Their slogan was, 'Poland without Jews and Communists' and many Jews who managed to escape from the ghettos were killed by them. The Bielski group took an active part in fighting the enemy and in committing various acts of sabotage, which included blowing up bridges and cutting down telegraph poles. Over a period of six months in 1944, the Bielski fighters stopped the German trains for a total of fifty-one hours, which was a great achievement.

At four o'clock in the morning on 22 June 1944, exactly three years after the Nazis started the terrible war against Russia, the Red army began its great offensive on the Byelorussian front. On 3 July Minsk was liberated. We could hear, when lying on the ground, the sound of artillery. We prepared for a fight with the German army, as we knew their retreat would be through the forests. Sure enough, one morning a large retreating group of Germans broke through our reinforcements. Unfortunately, nine of our partisans were killed.

On the following day we heard that the Russian army was in Novogrudok. We were pleased that the nightmare was over, but each one of us felt terribly sad. We all knew what we would find in Novogrudok. It was a destroyed town without Jews, without the friends and neighbours we had known before the war. And yet we had no where else to go. It was decided that we would all return to Novogrodek. Bielski requested that everybody should march out of the forest in an organized body and so it was done. I walked without difficulty the 100 kilometres {62 miles} or more to the town. Thanks to the Bielski brothers, 1,230 Jews arrived in a suburb on 16 July 1944. Although we were free, nobody talked or laughed or sang. We were all sad.

Long columns of German prisoners of war were led through the streets of Novogrodek. They were a scruffy lot, no longer the victorious army. I saw a high-ranking officer wearing a fine pair of boots, marching with his men.

I called the Russian guard and asked his permission to remove the boots. The soldier smiled and said with full approval 'Please help yourself!'. I caught up with the officer and spoke to him in Yiddish, which is similar to German. I wanted him to know that I was a Jew. I told him to stop and remove his boots, saying they were too good for him. Then the Russian soldier approached and gave the officer a push with his rifle, whereupon he sat down and pulled off his boots. I wore them for a long time after that. In fact, I was still wearing them when I eventually arrived in England in 1947.

When I first came to England, I found a job as a cutter in a handbag factory. Then after fifteen months, I started my own company, Princelet Handbags, followed by another company, Hi-speed Plastics. After that, I started up a number of other successful enterprises. In time I met Barbara Steinfeld, fell in love with her, and we were married in 1955. We have two sons, Michael Leon and Jeffrey David, and one daughter, Deborah Judith. Between them we now have ten grandchildren.

I eventually settled down to a normal life, but I can never forget the past. I regret missing out on my youth and educational opportunities. But I continue my study of the resistance movement in the Holocaust and I do speak to groups about the role of the remarkable Bielski brothers. To me they are among the greatest Jewish heroes

Over the past fifty years I have given many talks to children, to university students and to the general public, Jewish and not Jewish. Always the same question comes up: how was it possible to dig for more than 4 months and not be discovered.

I tell them of the reasons for the success of the tunnel project:
1. It was due to the consolidated effort of the Jews of the Ghetto and a great deal of ingenuity. There were numerous differences in the opinions on how to proceed, there were even threats of disclosure, but in the end most were united in the effort to complete the tunnel.
2. We were very careful. We were always on the look out. 2 people were always on guard and Rukovski installed a warning bell. The dug soil was moved only at night.
3. The Jewish tradesmen made certain that the work in the workshops was not neglected and that the output did not drop. There was no reason for the Polish and Belarus foremen to suspect that another activity was going on.
4. The sanitary conditions in the Ghetto were appalling and the smell was atrocious. There was a lack of everything, including water. This was one of the reasons that the Germans kept, as much as possible, away from the Ghetto.

And most importantly WE WERE LUCKY.

The Labour Camp and the escape route.

This photograph was taken of a model in the Imperial War Museum, London.

Key to the model.
1. Living quarters.
2. Workshops.
3. Police station.
4. Police station, watch tower and searchlight.
5. Machine-gun towers,
6. Two rows of barbed wire.
7. Wooden fence to prevent prisoners seeing the outside world.
8. Toilets.
9. Graveyard.
10. Gates.
11. Tunnel.
12. Main road to Minsk.
13. Tunnel exit.

In the camp, Yitzhak Rosenhouse had kept a list of the inmates. His list was used as the escape list. Part of it is shown here.

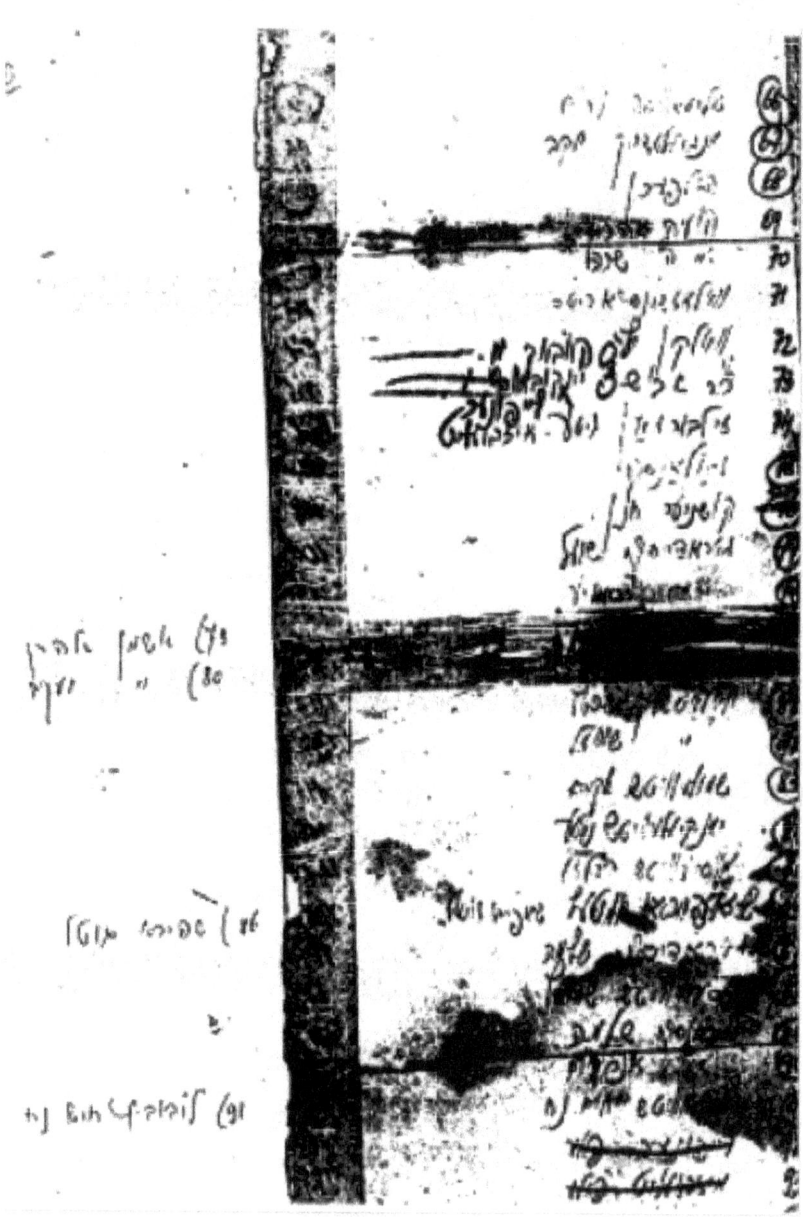

Photographs of some of the escapees from the Labour Camp.

30 Yitzhak Rosenhouse
    Creator of the escape list
    Bielski Brigade. Died in Israel

Notke Sucharski. Joined the Bielski Detachment. He died after Liberation.

Issac Yarmovski. He jointed the Bieslki Detachment. He later lived in Israel.

Yakov Shepsman. He joined a Soviet partisan Detachment. He died in Britain.

Lionke Portnoy.
Bielski Detachment.
Died in Israel

Chaim Ostashinski.
Bielski Detachment.
Died in Israel.

Elia Berkovitz.
Bielski Detachment.
Died in Israel

  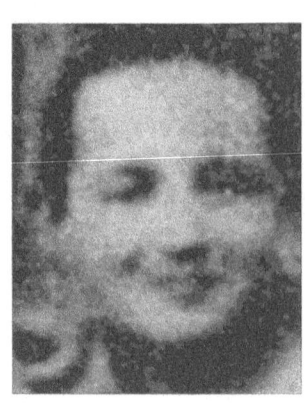

Zeidl Kushner
Bielski Detachment
Died in the United States.

Avram Chertok
Soviet Partisan Detachment.
Died in France.

Chonia Kushner
Killed during the Escape.

Shaul Gorodinski
Bielski Detachment.
Died in Israel.

Rita Volozhinska
Killed during the
Escape.

Moshe Niegnievicki
Bielski Detachment.
Lives in Israel.

Chaim Liebovitz
Bielski Detachment.
Died in the United States.

Yacov Oshman
Bielski Detachment.
Died in Israel.

Sonia Oshman
Bielski Detachment.
Lives in the United States.

 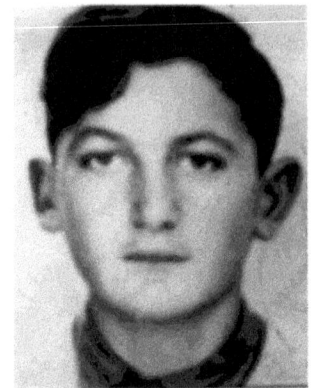 

Raya Kushner	Jack Kagan	Efraim Okonski
Bielski Detachment.	Bielski Detachment.	Soviet Partisan
Died in the United States.	Lives in Britain.	Lives in the United States.

Had we not escaped on 26 September 1943, the Germans would have killed us within a week. They wanted to liquidate the Lida ghetto before us, as the German documents indicate. The ghetto of Lida was destroyed between 17 and 19 September 1943.

[End of section that was not in the original Yizkor Book]

The Latest Kaddish

by Zelig Limon

Translated by Oskar Delatycki

I recall my folk, my shtetl
Novogrudok, my own nook
I remember Lubch and Zetl
See your mournful, silent look

You've gone, vanished all
Dear friends of my youth
Like fields of flowers toll
Crushed by enemy boots

Your grave, I look for, can not find
Lets say Kaddish – tell me when
Graves, anniversaries – I search my mind
The candle burns without an end

In Brichinke's green fields
Flowers bloom as before
The wind from Skridlewo brings
Quiet moans of pains of yore

Trees cry, flowers yammer
Woe is us, woebegone
Souls of children clamor,
Where have they all gone?

It's not the morning dew nor rain
It's our blood spilled
Blood of victims, blood of slain
Drenched from our killed

Isgadal, mothers, fathers
Veiskadash, sisters, brothers
Our people – strong and brave
Now holds its land safe

Believe, it's very near,
Our Kaddish, which is greatest
In the name we're holding dear
Our Kaddish, soon, the latest

Translation:

We will not forgive and not forget

Remember the dates of the commemoration days (Yartsait) -
of the murdered martyrs of Novogrudek and surroundings:

1) 18 Kislev   5702 - 8.12.1941
2) 24 Av   5703 - 7.8.1942
3) 29. Shevat 5703 - 4.2.1943
4) 2. Iyar.   5703 - 7.5.1943

1] Novogrudek Selib and surroundings
2] Novogrudek, Selib, Karelitch, Lubatch, Ivinietz, Rubiezievitz, Nalibok
3] Working camp in ghetto Peresieke
4] The workshops ("sand")

[Page 330]

No Yahrzeit (Memorial) Candle

(a poem)

by Nechama Layzerovski

Translated from Yiddish by O. Delatycki

I could not light for you
A Yahrzeit candle
I could not go to your grave
Where only the wind
Had blown shards
Of your last cry ---

My heart is now your monument
Harder than the granite stone
Your name is written there in burning letters

You will light my path
Till my dying day ---

As I am the last
to remain
The last cinder from the flame
The flame that brought woes
And oppression
To me and my extended kin.

[Page 330]

Where is my home?

(a poem)

by Miriam Ninkovski-Berkovich

Translated by O. Delatycki

Today is a holiday, skies full of joy
Spring has come, bringing jolly tunes
The forest animals have woken from sleep
The air is filled with songs of the birds

The birds are full of joy
They fly back home from the south
Back home to our small town
Where the castle tower awaits.

The sun is smiling and joyous
It warms and is kind
The birds are calling me:
Come to your mother

Fly home with us
It's time to go home

But where is my home?
Who has robbed me of it
Where were you, G-d
When the murderers dragged all to death

In a fierce frost, naked children
Who had not lived yet
Blameless children, small children…
I have no place to go
I can not fly with you

Nobody is waiting for me
All was burnt by the enemy in the frightful days
When my happiness had slipped away as a dream
Lonesome and abandoned am I today

Where is G-d, G-d of revenge

Wake up and hear my cry
Take revenge on the murderers, pacify my heart
Blood for blood will soften my pain.

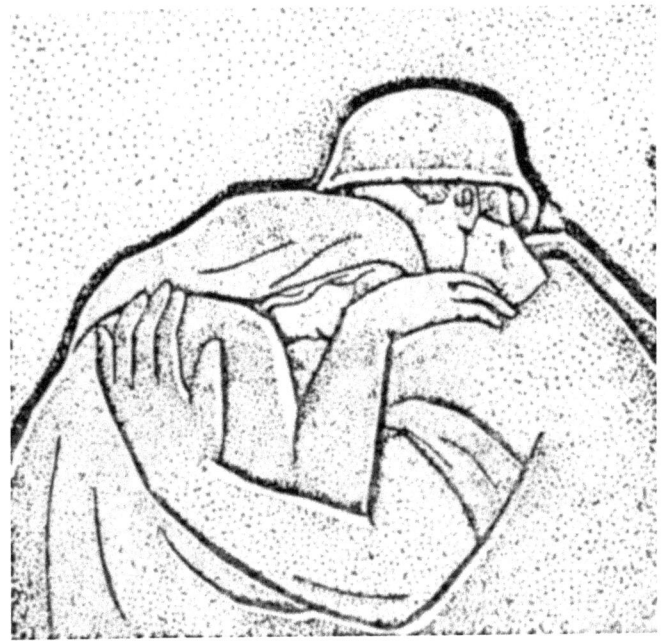

[Page 333]

And the Bravery

The Partisans of Tuvia Belski

by Dr. Shmuel Amarant

Translated from Hebrew by Aviva Kamil

Tuvia Bielsky commander of the Jewish partizans battalion

Map of the Bielski Otriad in Nalibocka Forest During the Last Phase of its Existence (Fall 1943 - Summer 1944)

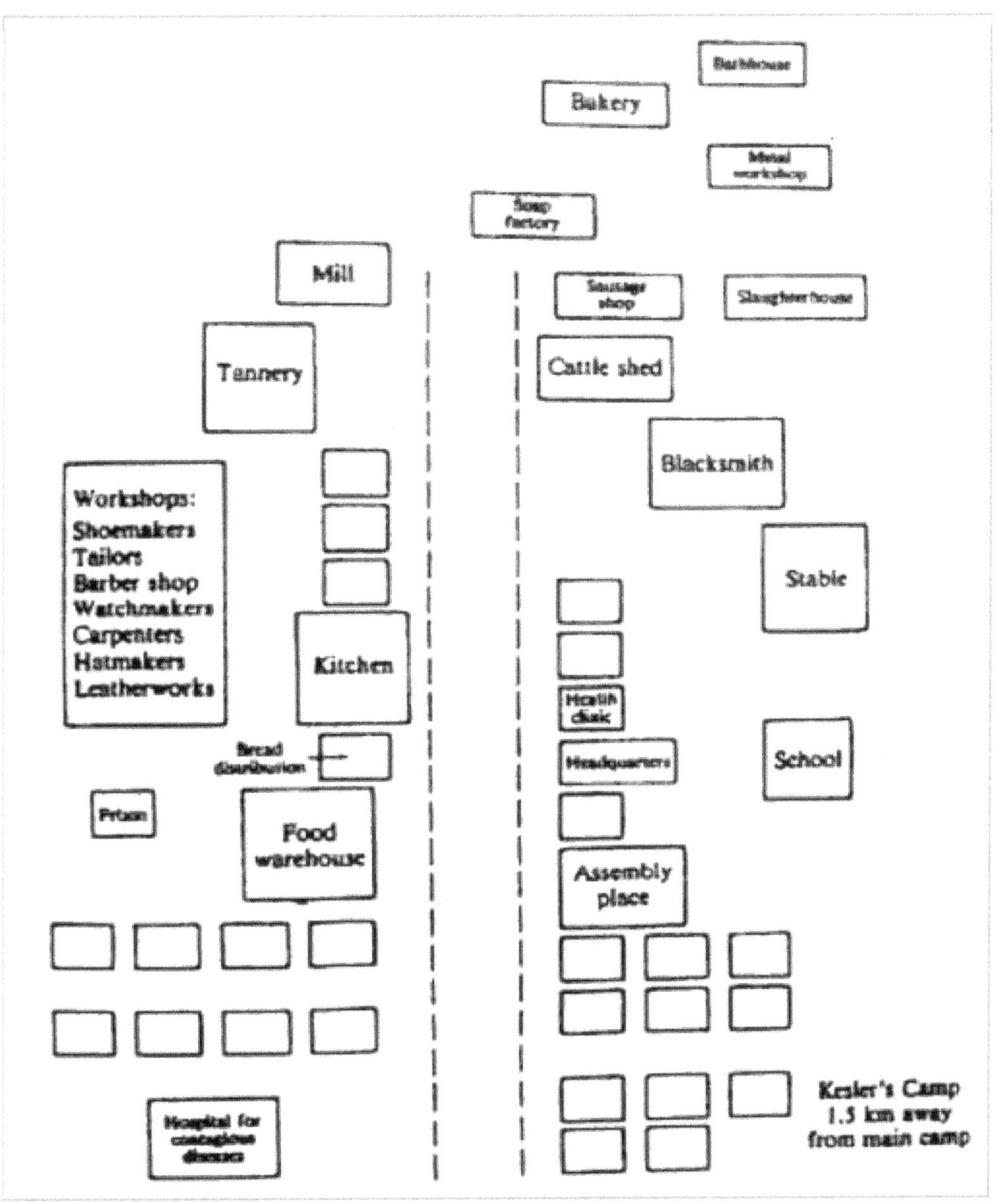

Unidentified structures are living quarters; all other structures are identified by the particular function each served.

This map is based on information provided by Chaja Bielski

Map donated by Jack Kagan

Dr. Shmuel Amarant, historian with the Bielski group.

The Belski partisans in the forests of west Byelorussia provided a refuge to people who escaped from the ghettos and working camps, to small family groups, which escaped to the country side and wandered without cover and protection from constant danger, to the Jewish partisans who suffered from anti-Semitism in the Russian partizanka [partisan movement] or were expelled by the Russians because of anti-Semitism, which was usually disguised under all sorts of pretexts and often they were made to leave without weapons or an alternate hiding place. [The Polish partisans would murder any Jew on sight, let alone accept him in their partisan units. Horrific stories of the misdeeds of the Polish partisans have been told. Some people maintain that in our district the Poles killed more Jewish partisans than the Germans.]

The unit's core developed in stages within the Belski family; slowly it grew with every new arrival of escapees from the camps and ghettos. Every wave of people fleeing to the forests brought with them their own way of life and influenced the life of the growing group of partisans. The history of that family camp, the largest in the Jewish partisan movement [anywhere], reflects the evolvement of family camps within the Jewish partisan movement, the process of unification on one hand and the trend towards division and disintegration on the other; the dependence of those camps on the conditions of the general partisan movement, their aspirations and achievements.

The Belski family escaped from their village of Stankiewiczi, near Novogudok, at the beginning of 1942. They wandered in the forests of Buszkowicz(?). Little groups of relatives and friends from the Ghetto of Novogrudok began to join them during the spring and summer of 1942. The people armed themselves and started to take revenge on murderous peasants and German collaborators. They contacted a group of Russian partisans under the command of Viktor Panchenko and together they carried out daring raids in the Novogrudok district.

From the beginning there were different opinions as to how the group should operate, many of its members [mainly women] tended to favor isolation, they wanted to take advantage of their good relations with the farmers around them and hide in the depth of the forests until the day of liberation. The fact that the family group turned into a huge unit was due to the personal influence of Tuvia Belski who was chosen as the leader of the partisans.

T. Belski was from the beginning bent on absorbing all Jewish escapees. The struggle to decide how the partisans should act lasted a long time, especially in times of danger. When the shortage of supplies was severe, there was a desire by some, particularly those who carried arms, to divide the camp and separate it into closed units, thus taking advantage of having weapons and having connections with the local population, and to leave the rest of the people, who had no weapons or fighting skills. "Why do we have to take care of these "malbushim"? – that is how they called the unarmed people – "we will get rid of them and take care of ourselves" maintained the ones who sought separation.

T. Belski held a different opinion; he exhibited a statesman like responsibility, and an understanding of the hour's needs. He accepted any Jew who came to join him, with or without a weapon, with or without fighting skills. He said again and again" I wish that thousands of Jews would join us, we will absorb them all". Disintegration of partisan units was very common at the beginning of the partizanka [1942] when there was no central authority and every group of partisans was an independent unit. If not for Tuvia Belski his partisans too would have been divided into tiny groups, each looking for hiding places in the depths of the forests. Belski maintained his line of action and his personal intervention saved the unity of the partisans and the lives of hundreds of its members. In the primitive conditions of the forest, at the beginning of the partizanka, when selfish tendencies were common, Tuvia Belski's stand deserves high commendation and praise.

In the winter of 1942-43, because of the increased danger and difficulty in supplying the camp, the unit was forced to divide into five groups, which settled in different locations in the district of Novogrudok. Some tried, together with their families and relatives, to separate themselves and abandon the unarmed people. Belski assembled his partisans and ordered that no Jew would be left alone in the forest. The Jews of Novogrudok and surrounds were the first to join the unit. Belski's messengers started to smuggle groups of Jews from the ghetto of Novogrudok, using prepared lists of names. Later the Jews of Iviah abandoned the Ghetto and joined the partisans, when they learned that they were going to be removed from the town. The remnants of the Dworec population, the bulk of whom was slaughtered in December 1942, also joined the Belski's partisans. Their camp was a refuge to small groups of Jews from Novogrudok and Dworec, which tried initially to survive independently, but, having encountered the murderous behavior of the Russian partisans, they were forced to look for protection of the Belski partisans. The commanders of the Russian partisans also started to press little family groups and forced them to join Belski's unit.

In the spring of 1943 the Jews of Lida started to arrive. Initially they tried to join the Russian partisan group "Iskara" on the banks of the Neman, but met with an anti-Semitic attitude, were disarmed and sent off to the Belski's partisans. These Jews formed the connecting link between the forest and the Lida Ghetto and hundreds of people from Lida began to arrive at the bases of the Belski partisans, in the forests of the Novogrudok district, Stara Huta and other locations. Groups of Jewish partisans from the Russian units also joined the Belski camp. They came, for example, from the "Arlianski" partisans, from the Lipiczanska wilderness, the "First of May" partisan unit, and others. The arrivals resented the anti-Semitic atmosphere that prevailed in the Russian units and left them of their own will, carrying their arms with them. They wanted to fight together with the Belski partisans, among Jews. The unit thrived and on the eve of the " Big Hunt" ["Oblawa"] of July 1943 it reached more then 700 souls.

At the time of the "Big Hunt", in July-August 1943, the divisive opinions were heard again. The units, which moved at that time to the forests of Naliboki, were forced to split into many small groups, which wandered in the area, trying to survive in those troubled days. Often the armed groups drove off the unarmed partisans and even threatened them with their weapons. There was no lack of display of extreme selfishness, which bordered on cruelty.

After the "Big Hunt", in September 1943, in the forests of Volsov(?), the commander of the "Kirov" brigade, captain Snichin(?), [Belski's partisans were under his command] decided to separate the fighting men from the non-fighting [family members].

From then on the armed people formed the fighting brigade called "Ordzonikidze" under the Soviet command [captain Lishanko(?)]. Tuvia Belski was appointed commander of the family unit and they camped in the old forests of Naliboki. All the groups that wandered in that area were ordered by the district partisan staff under the command of Platon (General Chernyshev) [who arrived from the U. S. S. R] to concentrate in the family camp. The reluctant were threatened with severe penalties.

At the end of summer 1943 a process of concentration started, the small groups united in large family groups. Small groups of the former Belski units and escapees also joined the new unit.

The Lida Ghetto was eliminated on the 18th of September 1943, a fighting group of partisans from Lida joined the Belski partisans in the forests of Volsov(?). At the same time a base for a large family unit was organized in the forests of Naliboki. Its core was a group of 40 people under the command of Israel Kesler. He never abandoned it. The base was established in the heart of the wilderness, about 7 km from Naliboki, within a dense forest of birches and pine trees. Many small groups started to join them, those who were with the fighting partisans and those who were just wandering and looking for a refuge in a large Jewish partisan group.

Kesler organized the base and took care of the supply for the future camp. He collected potatoes, which remained in the abandoned villages that were burned and destroyed by the Germans at the time of the "Hunt", prepared storage to preserve the products in the coming winter.

The Command of the district under General Platon-Chernyshev ordered that the camp from then on will become an independent unit under the Commander of the Lida District. Belski was appointed the commander of the unit.

One branch of the unit was an armed platoon under the command of Asael Belski. Their task was to protect and supply the camp. We will describe in few words Asael. He was seen often everywhere in the camp, riding on his horse and inspecting every corner. He was daring and devoted to his duties. His simplicity and honesty were reflected in his blue eyes and striking looks. His face was handsome, smiling and open. He was friendly, loved by his companions and people under his command. After the return of the Soviets, Asael was conscripted into the Red Army and died soon on the Prussian front.

The elimination of the Ghettos and working camps in Byelorussia was completed. The last of the escapees from the Ghettos and concentration camps found shelter in Belski's unit. Small groups of Jews from the forests of Krinicy(?) near Stolpcy and of Jews from Mir who were hiding in the forests of Zlushin, near their town, joined the Belski unit.

Jews from the labor camp of Koldichewo arrived – 100 people. On the way they met partisans from a Cherkaz unit who cruelly taunted and robbed them.

In October 1943, 150 people arrived from the labor camp of Novogudok, which was located in the buildings of the district court.

They managed to escape through an underground tunnel, which they had dug.

The Jews from Novogudok were the initial group of the Belski unit. The camp grew month by month, and in the winter of 1944 there were 1230 people in the unit. The Naliboki base of the camp had developed in the months from September 1943 until the liberation in July 1944 into an excellently organized camp. The stability of its existence in the last 10 months made it look like a settlement, the atmosphere of a Jewish town was evident, a community in which the population was the last remains of dozens of towns and villages which were razed to the ground. I will describe the life in that settlement.

A look through Belski's camp

The camp was located in the heart of the Nelibok wilderness, around it were hundreds of square km. of old forests and marshes. The whole area was "Partisan Country", a territory under the Soviet rule surrounded by the Nazi enemy. All that large area was under the control of the partisan commands, which were growing, ruling and directing all that was happening in that area. On the edge of the forests, on the banks of the Neman were strong partisan groups like: "Iskara", "Mitkobatshes (?)" who supervised the movement and carefully examined all comings and goings. Platoons of partisans from different units periodically left the wilderness raided the villages and fringes of towns [where German soldiers camped] and confiscated food and clothing for the people in the forest, right under the nose of the enemy.

Group of Jewish Partizans

Only in times of the "Hunt", when the Germans employed full divisions and dared to penetrate the wilderness with cannons, tanks and planes, only then the partisan units retreated into the dense forests looking for hiding places until the end of the "Hunt". And then the " Partisan Country" returned to normality.

In the autumn of 1943, after the "Hunt", the Soviet control of the Naliboki wilderness grew stronger. Hundreds joined the partisan groups: Byelorussian and Ukrainian policemen who realized that they backed the wrong side and were in a hurry to join the "partisanka" to atone for their collaboration with the bitter enemy, residents of villages and towns who did not want to be sent as forced laborers to Germany. Jews – escapees from the Ghettos and the working camps -, all those people looked for a haven in the ancient forests. The roads to Belski's camp were winding and rough; all comers were forced to walk dozens of km., were bogged down in the swamps, which could be crossed only on tracks covered by planks. The Germans destroyed all the Byelorussian villages, even the smallest of settlements {chutor} at the time of the "Hunt" when part of the population was sent to Germany as forced labor and the rest were ruthlessly eliminated on the spot. Often the person approaching Belski's camp stumbled upon ruins of towns and settlements [Naliboki, chutors and villages], destroyed peasants' huts appeared in front of him, charred chimneys', partly burnt fences, corpses of decomposed farm animals strewn around, stench in the air, frightened cats meowing amidst the destruction. For many months, the people from the Belski camp went into those settlements, to the ruins of Naliboki and Derevna, which were close by [7-10 km.], to collect anything that could be of use. In September 1943 the camp people still went out every day in carts, dug the fields, collected potatoes in sacks, loaded them and brought them to the camouflaged stores, to be kept for the winter months. We brought from Naliboki and Derevna parts of buildings, which could be used, such as: complete windows, heaters, boilers, barrels and kitchen utensils, which were strewn among the ruins.

In the beginning, people lived in huts built out of pine tree branches. Little groups or single people built provisional shelters ("succah", plural "succot") They spread soft branches on the ground, covered them with blankets and peasants' fur coats. From a distance the "succot" looked like kennels. In the autumn nights people who slept in them were drenched to the bone and were forced to get out, shivering in their wet clothes, and dry themselves in front of bonfires.

Snow started to fall and often when we went out of the "succah" in the morning the whiteness and sparkle of it surprised us. The commanders started the project of building larger huts. The work followed the design by Ribinski (Building Manager), and he was appointed to supervise the project. It was the duty of every person to take part in the work. To begin with the foundations were dug, rectangles to the depth of 80-100 cm. Next tree trunks from the forest were planted in the foundations. The trunks were held tightly together with barbed wire, the spaces between the logs were filled with moss. The roofs of the huts were made of rough timber planks, topped with soil and camouflaged with branches of trees.

At the entrance to the hut there was a door followed inside by a couple of steps. It was dark in the hut and it took a while to get used to the thin light filtering through the open door and a tiny window in the opposite wall. You could see wooden benches covered with straw along both sides of the wall. Forty people slept in each hut side by side. In the middle of the hut stood a small iron stove. It was looted from one of the abandoned villages.

The huts were erected in two long rows, both sides of the "main street". Every hut had a number and even a nickname, depending on the origin of its dwellers or their trade. For example, hut number 11 was called "intelligentsia", there lived the camp doctor Dr. H., a woman dentist from Pinsk, the lawyer Volkovyski from Baranowicze and a few other professional people. The "main street" was the main traffic route; it was always alive with people and all sorts of goings on. Partisans, women and men, strolled in the street in their typical "uniforms" partly peasant's garb, partly military, a strange combination of peasant's furs. The boots were made out of a light yellow leather, which was a product of the camp. Army hats, Russian and German or peasant's fur hats and weapons gathered from different sources. Friends met on the" main street", as did groups of guests who frequented the camp.

The hierarchy of the partisan society

The onlooker who watched the traffic at twilight time, could distinguish easily the rank and social importance of the person. That ranking was established in the camp, and was understood by everyone. Even there, in the heart of the forest, the order was the same, social status played its part. And it drew them closer or kept them apart, bred arrogance and envy, gossip and bitterness. The commanders and their relatives were the elite, they galloped on their horses wearing leather coats, breeches and a parabelum pistol in their belt, that clothing represented a high social status – many were happy to demonstrate the advantage they had in that social hierarchy and to show that they belonged to the elite of the partisans. The scouts – who also belonged to the elite – riding on their horses, their wives – young partisans – also did the same, riding their horses, wearing breeches and a pistol in their belt. They behaved like salon ladies showing off their jewellery. Their image reflected an arrogant self-assurance and personal success. Those people had a kitchen just for themselves, good food, which made them feel even more special.

Of lower status were members of the two fighting platoons, they were the defense force, took part in battles and were responsible for obtaining the supplies. Their status symbol was the rifle, always on their shoulder, from which they never parted. Their clothing was of lesser quality, gathered from wherever they could put their hands on. They also felt important and behaved that way. They looked with disregard upon the "Malbushim" &150; the unarmed people. They were tall, strong fellows, most of them sons of the low class families from the towns and villages &150; small timber merchants, peddlers, coachmen and tradesmen, their education minimal, but because of that they were close to the forest and adapted quickly to the conditions.

Among the "malbushim" too, there were different levels and status: tradesmen in the food industry, especially the essential ones like bakery, sausages making etc. enjoyed a better position to those whose trades were not as useful in the camp. At the bottom were the real "Malbushim", they were employed in a number of service tasks that changed from time to time: kitchen work, tree cutting and transporting, guarding the horses and cows and so on. They were the lowest class, the "amcho" of the camp. They were recognized immediately among the people on the "main street". The onlooker would know them by their untidy appearance, torn and patched clothes, thin and pale faces, and slow and heavy movements.

All those differences were obvious in negotiations, conversations, establishing relations and in mutual understanding.

Keeping warm

German planes were often flying over on reconnaissance, looking for partisans, but the huts in the dense forest were camouflaged with tree branches and were hard to detect from the distance.

At night in the rainy season, the floor of the huts became a sticky swamp and the cold dampness caused rheumatic pain in many of the dwellers. Many complained about pains in their leg and arm joints, especially at night. Frequently problems arose when people had to relieve themselves in the cold night. They walked like drunks, stumbled against the benches, where other partisans slept, and it was a nightmare to many. But eventually we became immune to it.

It was forbidden to light stoves or a bonfire during the day for fear of the German planes discovering the camp. During the day, unoccupied people prepared wood for the fire. In the winter they went out in groups to the forest close to their huts to select dried birch trees (suchostoj). They cut them down, sawed them into short pieces and brought them to the huts where they split them. In the evenings they lit the iron stove (kufah), which stood in the center of the hut. It became red hot and the hut dwellers huddled around it enjoying the warmth. Sometimes water was boiled on the stove for laundering an only shirt or for a wash. Some of the people, who sat close to the stove, held pine bark soaked with resin to rekindle the dying fire. Some held splits of pine tree which were used as candles in the long evenings, their dim light leaped onto the faces of groups of men and women who sat around, pale, weather beaten faces, their thinness accentuating the stubble of their beards. They sat and entertained themselves by singing lively songs or by telling adventurous partisan or prewar stories, in a special partisan style. Nightmarish memories of the holocaust were never mentioned on those occasions. An intimate family atmosphere enveloped the sitters around the stove. Sometimes the commander was visiting the huts, going from hut to hut, taking part in their conversations.

In the winter months small groups started to build for themselves huts in higher and drier places. The first builders were I and my wife and two young, intelligent couples. We all decided to build ourselves a more comfortable place. After receiving permission from the commander we started to build our hut a little further from the "main street" on a higher spot. We went especially to the destroyed town of Naliboki and brought from there a big window with the windowpanes intact, a door and an iron stove. We made three separate benches, a table in the center and chairs out of stumps. The window let through a pleasant bright light. The air was dry and fresh – a crowded clump of birches, like a green wall, was seen through the window. It felt like "home", it looked to us like a splendid villa. We were proud of it. The camp's people arrived to feed their eyes on that miracle of "architecture" and praised its comfort. In Naliboki we also found a small tin vessel, in which we could bath. In the forest it was a valued treasure. We dug a well near the hut and had water, dirty, but still it enabled us to wash every day. What a good life!!!! In the same vessel we laundered our clothes and boiled potatoes…it was a wonder utensil for universal use.

Many followed us, a small neighborhood of small family huts appeared on the slopes of the hill above the "main street" – the "villas" of the camp.

In our neighborhood lived the camp "Komissar" Shemyatoviec with his young wife and father in law. He belonged to one of the Russian fighting partisan groups in the area, but when the chief of staff demanded that he should be separated from his family and they should be transferred to the family camp, he preferred to come with them and join our partisans. He was a true Russian, a middle aged man, 50 years or more, with a big Kozak moustache, an angry expression on his face, broad shouldered and with heavy, bear like movements. His influence in the camp was not felt much. Shemyatoviec met his wife in a group of Jews who wandered in the forest near his partisan camp. He gave her and her father shelter and protection in his partisan hut. It was not a union made in heaven. She was 18 years old, dark, tall, pale faced with a Jewish prettiness, and there was never a smile on her face. Her father was the same age as his son in law, bearded and religious. We often saw him through his hut's window, wrapped in "talit" and "tefilin", praying. In the evenings he went to the tannery, which was used as a place to pray in. Was that religious Jew happy with his Russian son in law, with whom he was forced to stay day and night? Was he suffering because his daughter was forced to be a wife to that man? – No one could tell. There were many couples like that in the forest. The time and the hard forest life brought together many strange unions that would not be conceived in normal times. One of the couples who lived in our hut was like that: He was a middle aged crude butcher, she was a widow who lost her husband and sons and went with the butcher because of his physical strength and his work in the sausage factory. All that made her life comfortable. Joining together as couples was premeditated. It is surprising, that in a short time after such traumatic family experiences which those people went through, they were in a hurry to start new family relationships and make themselves forget the past.

We have made a detour to the "villa" neighborhood, now we will come back to the "main street". In the central street we have arrived to the hut of Tuvia Belski, the camp commander. Family huts of his relatives and friends were close by: his brother Asael Belski, the Boldo family, Dzienciolski and others. The elite of the camp met often there, and spent time together. Next to the commander's hut was the surgery, where Dr. H received daily the waiting sick. The dentist, a Jewish woman from Pinsk who turned up in our partisan camp, was also working there. To relieve the partisan's toothache, she was forced to use ordinary pincers, because of the lack of instruments. There were nurses to assist them. Further on at the end of the street, was the camp's common kitchen. Potato soup was cooked daily in a huge blackened boiler. A deep ditch was dug under the boiler, flames burst out of the smoking fire under it. A few boys, who worked in the kitchen, were splitting tree stumps and throwing them into the fire when it was necessary. The soup was usually thin and poor; it was a miracle if you managed to find some bones in it, which were sent from the sausage factory.

Sometimes, in times of "plenty", you could get some potatoes boiled in their jackets. The commanders and their relatives and friends had food prepared in a separate kitchen, which was across the street. There was a great difference between the quality and the nutritional value of the food from the two kitchens. That fact stirred up a lot of jealousy and anger, especially among the armed people, who demanded better food. In front of the common kitchen were long queues of people with eating utensils in their hands. The people standing in the queue were pushing each other in order to get the first serves which were thicker. Many quarrels started because of it. The daily portions of bread were distributed at the same time.

Seldom, like on the 1st of May, pieces of sausage were given

Those social differences influenced the way people ate. The partisans, who went on "farm" operations, left for themselves [whether it was permitted or not] products, which they cooked in their huts. The common kitchen was confined gradually to serving only the lower "classes" of the camp, the "malboshim", who had to make do with the thin portions given to them. At a short distance from the huge kitchen a bakery was built with a big oven, typical of that area, it was equipped with all the tools that could be found in the villages around, near the oven stood a primitive flour mill, where two horses circled around pulling heavy mill stones which milled flour. During the winter the bakery was nice and warm. On the holiday of the 7th of November revolution, after the parade in the open air, in the square decorated with flags, the commanders met at the bakery, and enjoyed drinking brandy out of a barrel that was brought for the holiday from somewhere.

The late Asa'el Bielsky - commander of the combatant unit - falled in battle against the Nazis

Further on there was the bathhouse. The partisans were proud of that essential establishment; guests visiting the camp were lead to it and admired its excellent arrangements. Decisions were made on "bathing duty". Dwellers of the huts bathed in a certain order from the early hours of the morning. There was also a room for disinfecting clothes. That arrangement was vital and very helpful, because the third Egyptian curse was very troubling to all. And in spite of the on going struggle with it, it came again with greater force to trouble the dwellers of the crowded huts.

An honorable place among the projects took the sausage-making factory, which was in a hut near by. On one of the forays a meat-mincer was found and a separate structure for smoking the sausages was built. Partisans from the neighboring units brought cattle in exchange of sausages.

In the same area was also a soap factory. Soap was made from discarded cow's milk and ashes and resembled a dark brown dough. There was not much of it, but it enabled the people to have a good wash and, now and then, launder their clothes.

Outside the "main street" there was a fenced in area for the herd of cows owned by the camp. They grazed there and their number reached at times up to 60 head. From the cow paddock the horses of the camp could be seen in the distance grazing in the forest, fenced in by empty peasants' carts, a few boys tending to the horses.

In the winter in the chilly nights, packs of wolves roamed around filling the air with their incessant howling, like crowds of women yelling desperately. Often, when the wolves drew closer, and their shining eyes could be seen in the dark, the guard was forced to shoot in the air to frighten them off.

Further out there was a muddy swamp with dense bushes and reeds. The incessant croaking of frogs always filled the air. We will go on and progress further along the main street because we have not as yet visited the nerve center of the camp. In the big square, on one side was the center of command and on the other were workshops. In the command room you could find the commander T. Belski, his brother Asael, the commander of the fighting platoons, sitting there were: Malbin who was the chief of staff, Gordon, second in command, Pesach Fridberg from Novogudok, the storeman and Volkovyski, a lawyer from Baranovichi who was the head of the" special unit". In the commander's room, the operations were planned, fighting units departed from there as well as units on missions to gather food from the farms. Every day management was concentrated in that room. There was the court, which dealt with cases of discipline in the unit; sentences were handed down with the help of Volkovyski, the lawyer.

The camp prison was in a special hut.

Workshops

The workshops were located in a wide and roomy hut. The sounds of work were heard from afar, the pounding of the sledgehammers and the digging machines, the hammering, the sawing of wood and the wild laughter and animated conversations, spiced with the partisan's slang.

The workshops were an organized project, which deserved praise. Dozens of craftsmen, divided according to their craft, were sitting in that all enveloping hut, with a raised ceiling, and an appearance of a factory . Big windows let in a lot of light, more then enough for the various workshops in every corner of the hut. Big stoves warmed the place. It looked as if you found yourself in a workshop of ages ago, in which hundreds of workers made a communal effort to put together things from the beginning to the end of a production cycle. The individual workshops were separated by timber partitions and in each of them worked several craftsmen. Not all crafts were concentrated in the central building. A few production facilities were scattered all over the camp. Because of security or hygiene requirements they had to be located at some distance from the camp.

All production lines were interconnected with each other. All the materials supplied by nature were utilized to the maximum. In the forest in "Robinzonda", in the heart of the wilderness much creative imagination was invested and lots of fruitful inventiveness.

The carpenters made huge barrels for the tanners to soak the skins of the slaughtered animals; they made shelves for the storeroom, lasts for the cobblers and wooden soles for the sandals.

The tanners, a few of them were from the Koldichevo camp, erected a tannery in a remote place. They supplied leather to the shoemakers, and a few weeks after the production started one could see in the camp partisans wearing boots locally made. Raw, they stood out in their light-yellow color.

The saddlers made harnesses and saddles for the horses and belts for the partisans. The shoemakers were always loaded with work, because the people, who arrived at the camp, came with barely a cover on their body and with torn shoes after their long ordeals. There were always long queues of people wanting shoes. Some clients from other partisan groups came too, and they paid the shoemakers with some other essential products. Often that was reason enough to favor one client from another. Gifts and products were brought from the "farm operations". Some girls received their boots quickly, because their friends who came back from their expedition, bestowed on the shoemaker a suitable gift. At the shoemaker's workshop were about a dozen craftsmen, stooping, sewing new shoes and patching old ones, making sandals with wooden or rubber soles [from tyres].

Opposite them worked the tailors, they were also kept very busy by the demands of hundreds of partisans, whose clothing was worn out and often needed patching. The tailors also received orders from other partisan units. Often the partisans received arms and cattle for their tailoring services.

Nightshirts made from coarse peasant cloth were also made in the clothing workshop. The partisans brought that material from the villages of the area. Most of the partisans were forced to wear that nightshirt for a long time without changing. No wonder that the shirt, in spite of the disinfecting room in the bathhouse, hurt and tortured the body. In the spring months of 1944 Soviet planes started to drop weapons into the wilderness. The parachutes were made of an excellent fine silk. It was used for making shirts and nightshirts. Great was the partisan's pleasure when he was awarded a shirt made out of fine silk of a light beige color!

Milliners and watchmakers were in great demand too

You could get a hair cut and a shave, given by the three barbers who worked near the workshops. Their instruments were blunt and ruthlessly scratched the skin, but the partisans had no other choice but to use their service. They were distracted by yarning whilst being shaved, which made them forget their pain. Partisans, when not fighting on missions , were using the chance to come to the barbershop to have a chat, to gossip about businesses in the camp, to listen to news from the front and to joke. The conversations were in the typical partisan style, Yiddish spiced with Russian expressions, mostly crude jokes. The girls tried to compete and outdo the men with their unbridled expressions.

At a little distance from the workshops was the smithy, there the blacksmiths shoed not only the camp's horses but the horses of a number of other partisan units in the area. One could hear the beating of the blacksmiths' hammers from afar. In a separate building worked the mechanics who repaired arms. They were putting together new weapons, using old parts, cleaning and repairing old arms. The stock of the fighting units increased, more rifles and machine guns became available. The mechanics also served other partisans in the area and were rewarded by more arms, which the clients left in the camp.

In the spring the economic situation of the camp improved. New lines of production were initiated, the allocating of chores and tasks became more efficient, and almost everyone in the camp was employed and productive.

Hundreds of people were involved in hectic activities and made an effort to forget their loneliness, the loss of their loved ones and all the traumatic experiences that they went through only a short time ago. Being productive helped the partisans to adapt to the forest's conditions and was a blessing to hundreds of partisans.

Sometimes the camp sent its own experts to fulfill important tasks in other units, like printers that published papers for the partisans in Russian and Byelorussian. Those workshops saved hundreds of people from the enemy's jaws and generally raised the moral in the "land of the partisans". They contributed to fortifying the battle against the Nazi conqueror. The non-military workshops fulfilled partisan missions that cannot be ignored and their efforts were part of the struggle of the partisan movement as a whole.

Health problems in Belski's camp in the forests of Naliboki

Belski's camp contained hundreds of people who in the prewar days would require continuous medical treatment, some would have been hospitalized or would be buried in the cemetery. But in a partisan forest, apparently, this did not follow. One would think that the harsh life and physical abuse in the ghettoes, the wandering without a roof over their heads, with no place to lie down and no protection from the elements, the unhygienic food and lack of nutritious meals would have destroyed the strongest of men. But what wonder, in Belski's camp almost no one died. As far as I can remember the typhus plague killed only one person, a young partisan died and was buried in the camp. If not for the Germans and their allies there was almost no need for a cemetery in the forest. The angel of death took a holiday and let the few escapees from the ghettoes and the concentration camps to bear their partisan's lot and hope for the end of the war. Old people, women and children wandered for weeks in the swampy forests, escaping from the ghettoes and camps or during the "hunts". The sun was assaulting them during the day and dampness tormented them at night, when they permitted themselves a short nap on the soggy ground while their stomachs shrunk because of hunger, and yet, in spite of all that, no one among them lagged behind because of fatigue. Feverish people were forced out of their sick bed and had to flee during the "hunt"; they were dragging themselves as best they knew how and usually the sickness was forgotten and somehow they survived.

When we escaped from the Lida ghetto, a deep, pussy wound developed on my wife's left leg. The leg had swollen and it looked like it was blood poisoning. Excruciating pain prevented her from walking, but how could we stop, when the ground was burning under our feet?

Who could dream of medical help whilst fleeing? It looked like the chasers were all around us! My wife continued walking, hopping on one foot, and did so for dozens of km., while every muscle in her body was crying because of the pain. As we made our way at night through slush and muddy clay, she was forced to walk with both legs deep in mud and filthy cold water. As it happened the mud cured the wound. The swelling diminished and the wound started to heal.

Pregnant women or those who just gave birth left their hospital beds to find refuge in the depth of the forest. They all walked without showing any signs of fatigue that anyone would notice, while fleeing the horrific enemy.

I remember one woman, a young, lonely widow whose husband perished in Lida. Grieving and looking for consolation she had a short love affair with a partisan. As a result, she, like many other women partisans, turned to Dr. H, the camp doctor. [we still lived then in our temporary "succot", and were digging, in groups, the foundations for our new huts]. Dr. H took the woman out of a group of diggers, went with her to one of the [then] uncompleted huts, he asked my wife for help. My wife was holding the patient; the operation was done quickly, the woman, lay on the bench, did not heave a sigh. After a short while the woman came out, pale and shaky on her legs and joined the group of diggers as if nothing had happened.

The bespectacled medical doctor Dr. H, always smiling, very thin, his clothes in tatters; with his case, which contained his instruments and medicines, was fulfilling his task faithfully, he was known as an expert in those discreet operations. Women partisans arrived from the most distant units for that operation and usually left after a few hours, relieved of their burden. Dr. H's wife, a qualified nurse, helped him with those "humanitarian" operations; for his services the doctor received different products: pork fat, flour, etc which were an unimaginable treasure in the forest. From the partisans who went out on "farm operations", the doctor asked for products and from people with means—gold coins. Gossip circulated in the camp that the bag, full of gold coins around the doctor's neck, was swelling.

The Belski's camp partisans who could not pay had the operation for free. He was polite and forever ready for his task. One could meet him in the morning hours, in his surgery, a hut, on the "main street", near the commander Belski's hut. There he received his patients who waited in a queue, helping him were a few qualified nurses like his wife and Chana Rivak from Novogudok. The groups of partisans who were hunting in the area for supplies were ordered to look for medicines. Farmers who acted as contact men ("sviznoi"), obtained medicines, which were ordered in the towns, and delivered them to the partisans. But there was always a shortage, even of the basic of medicines, in the forest.

In the afternoon the doctor made "home visits" hurrying from hut to hut to treat bed-ridden patients, then every day he went to the isolated "hospital" [one and a half km. from the camp] in a wagon pulled by a "skeleton" of a horse.

The doctor resided in hut number 11 [which was called the "intelligentsia hut" and housed 40 people]. I was his nearest neighbor, he did not sustain his personal hygiene nor the hygiene of his children. He did not take advantage of the washing facilities, which were available, even in the forest, he was shabbily dressed, and I almost never saw him wash. When we brought our thin meals to our hut from the general kitchen, we often found some filth that was revolting, but the doctor, in all seriousness of an expert convinced us that there might be some vital ingredients in those revolting pieces, to strengthen our bodies. " There is no need to get over anxious!" he would say. He spiced his talk with a few scientific terms, and eventually we were forced to swallow the food. The typhus plague was recurring every year in the partisans' units, it spread in the Belski's camp after the partisans of the Zukov brigade left the food for us.

The commanders of the Zukov brigade, which was leaving the forests of Naliboki to move to a distant place, permitted the Belski's camp people to collect whatever was left after the departing brigade. In exchange we had to take care of their wounded, their sick and a number of women who they could do without. Kitchen utensils were brought from the Zukov camp, parts of weaponry, food products, horses, cows, clothing like: peasants furs, trousers and boots.

A short time after the typhus plague erupted, we connected it to the gifts from the Zukov brigade. There were a few cases of typhus in that brigade and with the clothing came lice that brought that contagious disease. It was playing havoc in our camp. Every day, many times a day, the wagon was busy taking feverish people to the "hospital". Rivak Shlomo, who was a teacher in Novogudouk, was responsible for transferring the sick to Dr. H's hut, the pace was hectic, the hospital huts were crammed, the overcrowding started to worry the commanders. In the hospital worked a qualified nurse from Minsk, devoted to her profession, the wife of the director and theatre actor from Minsk, Shtesnovitz (?), who was one of the partisans.

There was a shortage of the simplest of drugs in the hospital. We cured the sick with a diet and boiled water, their only drink. As usual we drunk filthy water from the shallow wells we dug near the huts to a depth of a few tens of cm.

The multitude of the dangerously sick people did not have any other medicine, but in spite of the extent of the disease most of the sick were cured. And Rivak's wagon started to take the convalescing people back to the camp. They were weak, skeletal, a dreadful sight. They were given a cup of milk a day and satisfying meals at lunch and dinner. Those meals came from the commander's special kitchen

The quarrels, the personal frictions and the tension were more acute than usual in the crowded huts, but there behavior would be considered normal under the circumstances. There was only one mentally ill person in the camp. A 17 years old boy, Yankl, was insane. German soldiers, in the ghetto, hit his head hard with their rifle butts; and his behavior was the result of that. Lonely, neglected boy, in torn clothes, his coat's sleeve torn to the shoulder, was wandering about the camp without aim; craziness was reflected in his eyes. "Yankele- why don't you mend your sleeve?" we would ask. He would answer sharply " I want to shake you out of my sleeve, how can I do it if it is sewn?". During the heavy bombardments when everything was collapsing around, Yankele would stroll in the camp, no one could convince him to hide. "Yankele go to sleep!" they called after him," How much can I sleep? Where do you get such a long sleep?" he answered, and went on wandering.

The daily life in our hut was like in a madhouse. And there was no room to escape to real madness, people then preferred to escape to health, to strengthen their bodies, to use their vitality, whatever they had, to continue the struggle. With hyper activity, sometimes-aimless activity, they tried to distract their mind from the terror of their life. Sleep in the camp was mostly restless. People got out of bed a lot to urinate, especially during the rainy season, when the earth in the hut was wet. The atmosphere in the hut at night was always restive, often people tripped over each other in the dark. People did not have nightmares. It could be that this is a wrong generalization, but that was the case with most of my relatives, they dreamt a lot about food. One of our neighbors, Sonya, a lively girl who lived in our hut with her mother, used to relate in the morning her culinary dreams. "I dreamt at night about a plate full of gefilte fish and you, Mum, grabbed it from under my nose. Why did you do it Mum?" asked the girl. The listeners implored the girl to continue her description of that gefilte fish plate and the rest of the delicacies she dreamt about.

When the Red Army liberated us and we left the camp, the "hospital" was vacated too. The wounded were put on wagons, which followed the partisans who walked, to the hospital in Novogudok.

The children in the camp

There were in the camp a few dozen children, they used to assemble at central places in the camp and watch the happenings. They were near the commander's room when units departed for operations, and when the partisans returned from their missions. They followed guests from other partisan units, who visited our camp. They were at every corner, wandered between the huts, and never took an eye off the happenings. Wearing odd bits of clothing, in all strange combinations, they looked like lost creatures from a different world. They came to the heart of the wilderness (great forest) on their parents' shoulders. They were carried like that for days, when fleeing the Germans, from the ghetto, or during the" hunt" when drifting in the boggy swamps. I remember a small girl in our group of Lida Jews, which slowly meandered toward the Naliboki camp in the forest. October's cold rains, the misty nights, which we spent on the damp ground, weakened the girl, she was feverish her parents could hardly carry her; she was slowly deteriorating in front of our eyes. One evening, at twilight, her father managed to catch with his hat a wild pigeon that stood near by. He killed it and cooked it for his daughter. She felt better and in time returned back to good health. With time all the children grew stronger, they got used to the forest and could withstand the hardship of life there. I think that no child died in Belski's camp. During typhus plagues, the children suffered too, but recovered quickly in spite the horrible conditions. There was one boy, about 15 years of age, Y. Epstein, tall, skinny and fragile. He came to the forest with his older sister without their parents. He was visiting me often, craving for knowledge, alert and asking many questions. He was a terrific listener. He caught typhus and we were fearful that his sickly body would not withstand the disease.

After a few weeks he returned from the "hospital", a skeleton, but soon he started to develop, and symptoms of tuberculosis that he had before, disappeared as well. He grew taller and became a handsome, broad shouldered fellow only to be killed by the retreating German soldiers in June 1944. We buried him with 8 other victims, before we left the camp in the wilderness. I do remember one incident when a boy died, but it only confirms the fact that the forest strengthened the children and gave them the powers to withstand hardship.

A young couple P. from Mir settled in one of the huts. They had a few weeks old baby, who gave a lot of trouble at night. It is a wonder how those parents managed to reach the depth of the forest! One autumn morning the mother screamed that the baby was not breathing. The camp's doctor decided that he was suffocated by his mother body while sleeping; the result of crowdedness. The parents cried for many days and were inconsolable for a long time.

Other children grew without parent's supervision. They peeped into every corner of the camp and it looked as if they were studying the residents and knew all their comings and goings. They adopted the coarse partisan's language and loved to spice their talk with loud curses, like the best of the partisans, who kept the Russian heritage going. They knew all that happened in the huts and gossiped like the adults.

Older boys were recruited for farm work; some guarded the herd of cows and horses and helped the people responsible for the cowshed and stables. They took the cows to graze, and helped in the kitchen. Some of them found occupation in the workshops and became apprentices. A few children learned carpentry and shoe making. Coming out of the forest they could boast that they would be able to make a living because they learned a trade in the "partisanka".

A few boys aged between 13 and 14, maintained a contact between the Lida ghetto and the forest. A few times they smuggled Jews from the ghetto to the forest and did not fear the most dangerous operations.

The children assembled in the morning, after the first milking of the cows, with tins ("manashka") in their hands, near the cowshed in order to get their daily portion of milk. The leftovers were given sometimes to women, to old people and the frail. The children tried to compensate the severe deficit of nourishment in their diet, by collecting, in the winter, in the frozen swamps, under the snow, red berries (brusnika) that grew on tiny bushes. Groups of children were scattered around the camp looking for the red berries that peeped through the snow on a sunny day. Their happy voices rang in the forest. In the summer the children filled their tins with black berries or raspberries and brought that gift of the forest to their parents. Some times when the hunger troubled them, the adults too, joined the children and collected mushrooms and sorrel (shchavel). They cut with a knife the birch tree bark and collected the oozing juices into their utensils. They cooked the swamp berries in the juice. The result was a thin, sweet and sour compote with a sharp smell of medicine that was reviving souls. Those juices, so the doctor said, immunized our bodies and the nutrients in them added something to the portions of thin potato soup that most of the people ate twice a day, noon and evening. For an observer, watching those people move among the forest's growth with their children, it would have seemed like families on a holiday. But the camp people paid no attention to the charm of the forest, which they lived in for many months. Many of us were led to the slaughter in the forests, and watched the selections, which were conducted in front of the dug graves. Often one heard a partisan say: "If I will manage to get out of these forests, I will never look at them again. Every forest brings back to me the horrific memories, the crying of the slaughtered and the smells of forests mixed with the sharp smell of the victims' blood".

Confronting the neglect among the camp's children, the leadership decided to create for them a learning environment, like a school. Tens of children congregated every day and spent time together in a special hut, under the supervision of the woman partisan, Tsesya. They went with her for excursions, they did gymnastics, played team games; they were taught songs and sung along. The preparations for festivities were one of the important operations of that group. For Purim, the children made masks for parents and other adults. In the afternoon all assembled to watch the performance on a specially prepared stage on a higher ground, in the big hut of the workshops. It was a winters day, wind and whirlpool of snow; we watched the children sing and recite in Yiddish or in Russian. The children were dressed up for the holiday in white shirts and red ties. They were doing gymnastics; they danced, with the beauty of innocence on their faces and bodies. With tears in their eyes the audience followed the performance. Old, hidden memories came back, memories that were blunted by the harsh reality of the partisans. The wounds of the bereaved parents started to bleed again. By being hectically active they tried to forget their sorrow. But with the performance, all their lost love ones reappeared. Suddenly, after a dance of a pretty group, the Politruk A. Shlachtovic stood up and started to shout in Yiddish: "Where are my children? Revenge! Revenge!" His freckled red face became even redder under his red mop of hair. He drew out his pistol and shot a few shots in the air. And again he cried: revenge, revenge! Repeating many times his crying and groaning, he left the hut shaky on his legs like a drunk. The audience sat glued to their seats, they lowered their heads and a stifled weeping was heard.

It was as if the cruel reality burst through the dark wooden walls of the workshops. The beloved children carried their velvet heads high, innocent eyes looked at us; the echo of childish gaiety turned into a terrible cry and lamentation; and every thing went down in horrific and endless flames.

The people lifted themselves off their seats, drying their eyes and as if shy sneaked out of the roomy hut, which was enveloped in winter twilight shadows.

In the heart of the last of the escapees, the remnants of the settlements, nightmarish images appeared again, the dark chasm of the cruel reality with all its terrifying experiences, opened wide in front of them. A deep feeling of loneliness, as for no reason at all, fell on everything. It was carried to the chill and dampness of the fog, to the howling of the wind through the dense, dark forest, which stood like a wall around the camp. It penetrated the dark huts with the shadows of the people coming back from the concert. That evening, most of the huts sunk into a deep, depressing silence.

Waiting for the liberation

Time passed, the snow thawed, the birches started to put on green leaves, the air was perfumed with aromas of the forest and above the top of the trees a soft spring sun was shining. The expectation of a change grew daily. Every evening many people congregated in the square near the commander's hut eager for encouraging news. Scouts or guests from the partisan units who had a wireless, brought us news from the front and messages from the chief of staff of the Red Army. Connection by air with Moscow was improving all the time. More frequently, Soviet planes landed on the airport in the wilderness. Often guests from the front visited us. The partisans of our unit, under the command of I. Belski, guarded for a number of weeks the airport in the wilderness near Poldoruzshka.

The scope of the partisan attacks on communication lines grew to a great extent. During the nights, thousands of partisans raided the railways over a huge area and sabotaged them, bombing trains and cutting the enemy's movement for long periods. Echoes of explosions were heard at night from all directions; the partisans called those operations-"concerts".

The towns and villages were filled with Ukrainian collaborators (Kuban' Cossacks?) who were brought, with the retreating German Army, from Russia. They were stationed in the Byelorussian villages. There were many clashes with them, and supply of provisions for the camp was hard to obtain.

Sometimes we received Soviet newspapers, which were parachuted from planes, with other supplies. We read them eagerly, trying to draw our own conclusions.

Occasionally, some German papers fell into the hands of the partisans out on operations; we read them too, compared them and were trying to read between the lines.

The Partisan's Chief of staff issued papers in Russian and Byelorussian. These were distributed in the area among the local population and the partisans. They were printed in the forest on tiny pages of a dark yellow color with crammed printed letters.[*]

So, we had some good information and we could assemble the partisans together for political lectures and comments. In the evenings the partisans turned into brilliant war commentators. Arguments were going forever, about the significance of this event or other. And especially, what we had to expect when the front would reach us and the German Army penetrated the wilderness.

The German front collapsed and the Red Army advanced. Names of liberated places became more and more familiar, the Red Army already penetrated Polesie and Vohlyn, and liberated Pinsk and Rovno. Ferocious battles were going on during April near Ternopol. The 1st of May festivities in 1944 were accompanied by encouraging messages from the front, which was advancing towards us, bringing liberation. The celebration of the 1st of May that year was a very festive occasion. In the afternoon the camp's people congregated in the square in front of the commander's hut, red flags were out, the huts were decorated. It was a brilliant day, the spring sky was high and peaceful, about 1200 people stood in the wide square, on three sides were the fighting units, the scouts and the mounted units, their horses nicely decorated, and the armed platoons headed by their commanders. On the fourth side stood, in military order, the unarmed people.

In the center of the square stood the commanders, headed by T. Belski. He read to us the message of the Red Army chief of staff. It said that the war effort succeeded and after fierce battles over many weeks Tarnopol was conquered and the enemy had retreated in panic. Applause and shouting interrupted his words. After that the commander gave a short speech: "Shortly we will take the war to the Nazi beast's den in Germany and there we will exterminate him. The partisans took their part in the struggle against the cruel enemy. The front is coming close fast, we can expect days of hard tests, and we must be ready for them. Victory is looking us in the face".

What a joy it was, to hear those words! Every one was excited. The rule of evil was collapsing, the day we hoped for, the day of payback and revenge was approaching. That hope strengthened most of the people; it gave meaning to their sufferings, meaning to the worst of their moments. But there was a hidden anxiety that everyone had but no one talked about "What will face us when we will return to our places? We, the last of our people, the remnants! How will we continue?"

In the meantime we were pulled by waves of general enthusiasm. We danced till late that night and sang under the moonlight.

In June 1944 the Soviets broke the front near Vitbesk and advanced fast towards Minsk. The German Army retreated in panic from wide areas of East Byelorussia.

Many German divisions were surrounded near Minsk. At night, from a distance one could hear the sounds of muffled thunder and constant hum, which came with the wind. They sounded to us as a charming melody. We sat long at night, on the grass in front of our huts, waiting for the signs of the storm, which will bring our redemption. Excitement and tension in the camp grew stronger every day, with the echoes from the front, which grew lauder.

Scattered groups of German soldiers, who tried to escape from the

Soviet encirclement, started to appear in the area. Instructions came to be on guard. The great hour we waited for was coming. The armed platoons of Belski's partisans operated against the German soldiers who wandered in the forest. The partisans lay in ambush on roads and tracks that crossed the wilderness and eliminated many German units. Our armed units also clashed a few times with German groups. No prisoners were taken; they were all killed on the spot. Two of our members were wounded in battle, one of them had to be taken to hospital.

Tasks changed, the partisans were hunting the Germans and the Germans tried to sneak out. The mood of the partisans was elated. Our armed units enjoyed the activity. Every evening they returned all flushed and excited with new stories about their encounters in the forest. They tasted the taste of revenge. The Germans were like hunted animals, hungry and shaky on their legs, their desperate resistance weakened. How poor and miserable looked the remnants of the army which wanted to conquer the world!

Four German prisoners were brought in front of the camp's commanders. Three were young and the fourth who was older, was crying. Two of them said that they were Communists and blame the others of being Nazis. Only one kept his "identity", cursed the Jews and threatened them too. They were executed in the camp in front of all. Bursts of anger and revenge took hold of the people; it was so overwhelming that I prefer not to describe them.

The partisan's chief of staff was calling repeatedly to be ready. It was not known how events would develop; the front could shift to our side and it was possible that the Germans would penetrate the forests and employ all their power in battle. We had to be on guard.

In our camp we prepared for evacuation at any moment, night or day. There were trial evacuations to train the people for a fast planned departure. (within a few minutes).

Detailed instructions were given, new locations in the forest for each unit, were decided upon, tasks were allotted. We lived in an atmosphere of constant tension. Rumors chased rumors, one contradicting the other. We swung between desperation and encouragement. Alternately, we saw in our imagination the Red Army saving us, or the Germans attacking us. Since the big "hunt" in July 1943, we gained experience and were ready to repeat it when necessary and find cover in the wide swamps of the forest.

Once, in the early hours of the morning, we were awaken by shots from the central square. We could hear clearly German voices, loud orders, screams and curses. Bullets whistled above our heads! We ran out of the hut and hid in the undergrowth, the bullets' whistled continuously. We ran down to the swamp and lay down between the dense reeds. Terror took hold of us without knowing what happened. After a while there was silence. And then we found out that a group of 100 German soldiers was marching through the forest and surprised our people. Our armed partisans were away and guarding of the camp was forgotten, we were open to attack. That was how the Germans could get into a few huts on their way, surprising people in their sleep. They wounded seriously the deputy commander Gordon, who slept on his bench. They threw a hand grenade into one of the common huts and shot a few people on their way. But they had to retreat quickly. The partisans in the area heard the shots and came around. The Germans had left the camp but got into battle with the partisans who chased and eliminated them. That sudden raid by the Germans on our camp cost us nine lives, among them was Gordon who was wounded in the stomach and died after a few hours of terrible suffering, Epstein, a 16 year old boy, Patzovski, Ostshinski and others, were among the last victims in the wilderness.

After an hour a scout unit of the Red Army passed by the camp. All the camp people went towards them, they encircled the dusty and sweaty figures, hugged them, shook their hands, kissed them: "Welcome, comrades redeemers".

The soldiers continued their mission and we returned to the camp - liberated!

Nothing was left for us to do in that camp but to bury our dead. On the hill behind the "main street" we dug a common grave, the commander delivered a short eulogy, and a salvo of gunshots ended the sad ceremony.

With heavy steps, our heads down, we went to spend our last night in the huts. It was a restless night. I sat in front of the door, unable to shut an eye. In the darkness I recognized the tall figure of the man, who walked slowly, it was the theatre director and actor of the state theatre, Shternovitz (?), a Russian, who was transferred to us after his partisan unit dispensed with its entire group of non-fighting men. "Going home comrade?" he asked me "very soon we will be back at our places and will start a new"! "You, comrade, are going home" I answered him "it might be a destroyed home, but a home that you will be able to rebuild. We have got nowhere to return to. Nothing remained of our homes! We will go to our home towns, but only to say goodbye." We talked a lot that night!

In the early hours of the next morning, we vacated the camp. An order was given to destroy the huts, so that White partisans won't be able to use them. We smashed the windows, destroyed the doors and benches, filled in the wells, and buried the tools; for a short time the sound of wrecking and breaking was heard in the camp.

Afterwards an order was given at the Commander's square, to take only the things we could carry on our backs. Only two wagons for the wounded, followed the marching people. There was a long way ahead of us, fraught with unexpected dangers, and we had to be on alert! The commander, riding on his horse, scanned the marching people. One of the members of our partisan unit, P. did not follow the instruction and pushed a cart loaded with personal items. He was shot on the spot in front of his wife and small child who sat in the cart. The woman screamed a desperate scream, which shattered all of us. It was a very tragic end. The camp that was established to save Jewish life from the hands of the Nazis ended its existence with the murder of a Jew and the destruction of a Jewish family. The suffering woman cried for days and her screams accompanied us all the way. We marched traumatized through the forest, the corpses of German soldiers in their uniforms and of animals were scattered among the tall trees.

We passed the Kremin Lake, its blue water seen between the tree trunks, and continued to walk into dense forests.

The summer heat was oppressive, we walked tired and sweating, bluish mist started to envelope the forest undergrowth, which became denser. A smell of smoke reached us, the forests were burning. The battles that were fought there caused fires and they spread very quickly. Huge areas went up in flames, clouds of bluish-gray smoke filled the air, it was choking us and made our eyes water. We could see the silhouettes of burning trees; the fire licked the bushes, climbed up the trees and spread into the horizon. We marched in a landscape of flames, in the depth of the forest, a small distance from the sea of fire.

We reached the Neman canal, the fire stopped there. We camped under the sky. We marched like that for a few days. Leaving the wilderness we came to a busy road and marched through the village Shchorsy, the residents came out of their huts, looking with surprise in their eyes: So many Jews! So many Jews!

At the beginning we marched in a military fashion with the armed units in front of us and behind us. Later, people dispersed, walking in groups slowly in the heat of the day.

We advanced with heavy hearts, as we came closer to areas that were once Jewish. The extent of our catastrophe became clearer. It looked as if flames, which left a wasteland, surrounded our life, and we entered that wasteland.

On the horizon we could see the houses of Novogrudouk. We slept outside the town, in a farmhouse with a big yard and threshing floors around. We stretched ourselves on the chaff, exhausted from the long march. Afterwards we toured the town. The people from Novogudok, who were members of Belski's unit, brought us to the places where the ghettos were.

We stood in the places which were extermination sites, near graves of thousands of ghetto victims. The people of Novogrudok brought up memories, they walked, mourning in their own town, and so did we.

That was how all of us would return to our destroyed homes! That was the welcome that every Jew could expect on his return to the ruins of his community. We walked around the houses; in what was once a ghetto. Christians were living there, strange apathetic eyes were staring at us through the windows. Those were our inheritors; the Jewish settlement was completely erased! Hundreds of German prisoners were concentrated in a fenced yard. Through the fence we stared at those figures; a short time ago they brought with them murder and extermination; now they had dimmed eyes, and they were lying on the ground weak and impotent!

So the day passed. In the evening, after the walk around the town, the partisans assembled on the mountain slope of the ancient castle for a liberation celebration. Thousands of partisans from all the wilderness crowded the wide square, the flag of victory went up, and the ruins of the castle were lit with a searchlight. The speakers, partisans' commanders and officers of the Red Army stood on a stage, at the foot of the castle wall. The partisans raised the flag of the liberator, the Red Army. The Army delegates praised the partisan's struggle that hit the Nazi conqueror in its back, helping in their defeat.

The partisans last assembly was on the day after, at the farmyard that we stayed in. We stood in a rectangle, the commander gave a short speech and every one received a Partisan Certificate!

We parted with warm handshakes and went to the center of the town. We had to go back to our prewar location; the saga of the forest came to its end!

*

The story of the partisan's newspaper in the forests deserves mentioning. Eliyahu Damesk from Lida, who reached the partisans in 1943, had the idea of building a printing plant in the wilderness, to inform the partisans and the general population of the district. Damesk returned to the Lida ghetto and with the help of the partisans from the Russian unit "Iskara", which camped on the banks of the Neman, he brought the entire printing house of Shapira (also a member of the Belski's partisans).They brought it in cases in a farmer's wagon, a trusted man of the partisans, to the "Iskara" camp. The operation lasted 18 days. Damesk moved to the Lipiczanski wilderness following the instructions of General Platon, the chief of the partisans in that area. There, near the "Lenin Brigade" they built the printing house. The first partisan's paper in the area was published there, its name was "Krasnoe Znamia" (the red flag). It was issued three times a week. Afterwards, the printing house was moved to the forests of Slonim and to the team of printers were added some parachutists who came from the front.

The newspaper deeply influenced the local population and encouraged it, especially on the eve of recruitment to German labor camps, to abandon their villages and join the partisans in the forests.

Zusia Bielsky commander of the scouts in the partizans battalion

Lilka and Tuvia Bielski - Photo not in original Yizkor Book
(Photo courtesy of Yad Vashem)

Archik Bielski - Photo not in original Yizkor Book

Sonia and Zush Bielski - Photo not in original Yizkor Book
(Photo courtesy of Yad Vashem)

Asoel and Chaya Bielski - Photo not in original Yizkor Book
(Photo courtesy of Yad Vashem)

[Page 346]

Jewish Revenge

A. Fight of the Jewish partisans

by Chaim Leibovitch

Translated from Yiddish by O. Delatycki

Yudl Levin and Ya'akov Abramovitz as partisans

The days of torment began at the time when the German beasts on their march into Russia had occupied the district of Novogrudok. This was the beginning of fearful times of torture and slaughter of the Jews. Under the pretext of making Jews work, they were taken, killed and thrown into prepared trenches. In those horrible times some courageous young men had torn off their yellow patches, shaken off their resignation and doubts acquired in the Ghetto and joined the fight for their lives against the German murderers and their agents. It was not an even fight between the small, badly armed handful against a much stronger enemy. But those brave young men were taking revenge, and paid in a like manner for the spilt Jewish blood. One of the group, which participated in these actions was the Jewish detachment Kalinin under the command of the heroic leader Tuvie Belski and his brother Asoel, who died fighting in Koenigsberg. In the forests, the Bielski detachment was feared by the German murderers and their partners. Bielski brought fire and death to all of those who participated in killing Jews.

Of special importance is the revenge taken on the Belaus family. It was March 1943. The Bielski detachment was stationed for several weeks in a dense forest, taking a rest after weeks of moving from village to village to escape the persecution of the Germans and their collaborators - the village farmers, who helped in the hunt of the small number of survived escapees from the death trenches. The commandant Tuvie sent 10 Jewish partisans led by Avrom Polanski to obtain food for the detachment. The collection of provisions was done as follows: in the evening an armed group would leave the detachment, they would enter a village late at night, put up sentries on both sides of the village, they would then enter the houses of the farmers demanding provisions. The farmers would give them everything they asked for. The partisans would return in the night back to the base. The Bielski detachment was a family group, which consisted mainly of people unable to carry arms including women, children, old people, the injured and sick. The food supply presented difficulties, because only 30% of the members of the detachment carried arms. When Polanski's group gathered the required food, the time came to return to base. They were, however, very tired and frozen after the long night's journey through the forest. They were close to the village of Dobropolye, not far from Novogrudok. In Novogrudok was a large German garrison, which was pursuing the partisans. They decided to spend the night in the house of the family Belaus, who they considered to be reliable and who had a reputation for being honest. They brought with them the carriages containing food. The family received the partisans well. They were served vodka and tasty morsels. The Jews were cold and tired. Belaus made up bunks for them and they fell asleep. The partisans put up sentries and were untroubled.

When Belaus felt that he was not observed he sent his son to town to tell the Germans that 10 Jews were asleep in his house. In less than an hour a strong detachment of police and gendarmes arrived. They surrounded the house, killed the sentries and entered the house and killed 9 Jews. Only Avrom Polanski managed to hide in a chicken coup. When the Germans left, Polanski came out from the coup and spoke to Belaus. He told Belaus that his deed would not be forgotten. He did not finish speaking when Belaus's son arrived with an axe and split Polanski's head. Belaus buried the dead not far from his house and assumed that the neighbours did not see the events. To make sure that they would get away with their crime, the family moved to Novogrudok for a few weeks. There was disquiet in Bielski's detachment. Ten partisans had disappeared without trace. Scouts were dispatched to all surrounding villages, but they came back having not discovered anything. By a chance, a group of partisans contacted the family Wiszniewski, who was hiding in a dense forest in a bunker. The Wiszniewskis obtained food from farmers in neighbouring villages. One of those farmers told Wiszniewski all the particulars of the murder by the Belaus family. The information came from a neighbour of Belaus, who saw the events. Bielski sent partisans to speak to the farmer and to get all details. When the details of the events had become known in the partisan detachment, all were most upset. It was particularly upsetting that the family Belaus, which was considered friendly and reliable could betray them. The partisans could not feel safe anywhere among the Belarusians. The commander called for a general meeting. He told of the particulars of the gruesome event. He said that the perpetrators of this event could not be left unpunished. One had to take revenge. The family Belaus had to be liquidated, so that other farmers would know that collaborators with the Germans would not be left unpunished. The house of the guilty had to be destroyed. 'Who will take revenge?' asked the commandant. All hands were raised. The commandant selected 25 partisans and named Eschiel as the leader of the group. He told them to wipe out the family Belaus. Eschiel was liked by all partisans for his goodness and devotion. He supervised the preparations for the mission. As the night approached everyone was ready. A few carriages were prepared and the partisans were on their way. It was a quiet night. They travelled through the forests among tall pine trees. There was a freshness of early spring in the air. After a journey of a few hours they arrived at a crossroad. They stopped, unharnessed the horses and hid them behind the bushes. They arranged themselves in a single line. They were led by Wiszniewski and Eschiel along country lanes and byways. They arrived to a point 400 metres from the Belaus house. They were given an order to lie down flat on the ground. It was quiet. They were tense in anticipation of the action. As they waited they thought of their past, of all those who had been killed – families, friends, loved ones.

They craved revenge for the spilt blood. Thus past 10 minutes, which felt like hours. Eschiel ordered them to rise. He divided the detachment into three groups. One group was positioned along the road to cut off the exit from the house, the second group surrounded the house to make sure that nobody could escape from the house. At the entrance the experienced partisan Balda was stationed. Eschiel with his assistants Jankelewicz, Friedberg and the scouts Bencion Gilkowicz, Pszenica, Kotlar, Michele, Kemplowski, Nachimowski broke into the house of Belaus, where the family of 14 people lived. Belaus and his sons tried to snatch the rifles from the partisans. There was an intense struggle. Belaus grabbed the barrels of Jankelewicz's and Friedberg's guns and tussled with them. Eschiel run in and killed Belaus. He told the others to lie along the wall and he executed them. Michele, who lost two brothers in the Belaus deceit, did the rest. Eschiel ordered that the house of the treacherous family should be burned down, he fulfilled the revenge and made sure that nothing was taken from the house.

Lazar Malbin -Chief of staff of the partisan(battalion) and Moshe Reznik a scout

Michele found in the jacket of Belaus a letter from the Gebitscommissar (district commissar) Traub, in which he thanked Belaus for his noble deed. As a sign of Traub's gratitude he exempted him from taxes and gave him 50 German marks. He added that all neighbours should follow the example of Belaus and help to eradicate all Jews.

The house, the barns and the grain stores of Belaus were burned to the ground. The partisans retreated, but on the way they burned a house of another farmer in the village of Brecianka, close to Novogrudok. Having finished their mission, the partisans returned to their base. Next day posters were displayed in the district, describing the events of the previous night and warning the population that acts of collaboration with the Germans would be punished in a similar manner.

From that day on fear and terror had befallen the population of the Novogrudok district. All those who had in mind to inform the Germans were scared off. They were shown that there is a power, which would punish collaborators, and that those who spill Jewish blood would be dealt with.

A group of Bielski fighters in the Naliboki forest, 1943

[Page 349]

B. The Jewish Hero

Translated from Yiddish by O. Delatycki

When I met in the big Nalibok forests, the young Jewish lieutenant with a big crop of hair and black burning eyes, my heart swelled with pride. I could not believe my eyes. I had just escaped from the Ghetto through the tunnel, which we had dug in Novogrudok. I got away from the building of the district court were I was destined to die after a life of misery. And suddenly such wealth! In the large forests and wide fields moved freely young Jewish men, armed with rifles, brave men and among them a Jewish lieutenant with a machine gun and grenades hanging from his belt who had been sent from Moscow. Naturally, I was interested in him. One day he told me his story. His name was Dovid and he was born in a village not far from Pinsk. He was a carpenter by trade. He was educated until the age of 13 in a Cheder [Jewish religious primary school]. After that he was apprenticed to learn a trade. There he met members of a leftist organisation, which he joined. He was arrested several times. When the war started he was mobilised into the Red army. He was sent by the army to Moscow to study espionage and diversion. After six months at the school he was transferred behind the front line to the Novogrudok district to direct acts of diversion organise partisan groups and conduct espionage. After he arrived in the occupied area he saw mass executions and the annihilation on the whole Jewish population. His national conscience was reawakened. He concentrated all his efforts to save Jews. He helped remove Jews from Ghettos. He visited frequently the Bielski formation. He organised a diversion unit. He encouraged the Jewish partisans and argued that Jews should serve as an example of courage for the Russians. The Jews must destroy the legend of Jewish fearfulness. The Jews must be the first in a battle. The Jews must take revenge for the spilled blood.

As he was a commandant of Russian partisans he always went first. He served as an example for the gentiles, who valued him for his readiness to sacrifice all. He succeeded in derailing 23 echelons. Dozens of Germans died in the echelons. The Germans put a high price on Dovid's head, but they did not succeed in catching him. He spread fear and death among the peasants and German collaborators who participated in the extermination of Jews. After the war finished the government bestowed on Dovid the highest decorations and a high government post. Dovid intended to remain in the Soviet Union, for which he fought and risked his life. But other events occurred which caused him to leave his homeland. After the bloody war the residues of the Jewish population could not remain on the ruins of their lives, where every stone reminded them of their losses. They left the towns where they were born and were educated and went without an aim away from home. And with them went Dovid. When I came in my wanderings to Trofaiach refugee camp in Austria I went to the club of the partisans. There I found the former lieutenant with the black crop of hair among the partisans. On a certain evening Dovid with a group of partisans had disarmed and bound all members of the police unit in Trofaiach and released a group of partisans who were arrested by the Austrian police for crossing the boarder illegally. This is how David had immersed himself completely with his bubbling temperament into the activities of 'Bricha' [an organisations for, if need be illegal, emigration] with the aim of forcing open a way for the Jewish refugees to their home in Israel. The partisan refugees didn't require visas and did not recognise boarders in their desire to find a new home.

[Page 350]

C. Commander Shmatovich

by Chaim Leibovitch

Translated from Yiddish by O. Delatycki

Ivan Vasilevitch Shmatovich, a Byelorussian, was born in Minsk. A broad-shouldered man with a pair of bright eyes and a warm smile under his large eyebrows, Shmatovich was the political commissar of the Belsky Unit. Before the Russian Revolution, he was a railway worker in Minsk. Afterwards, he was appointed secretary of the Minsk railway workers union, and became a member of the Communist Party in Minsk.

In 1941, when the Nazi hordes attacked the Soviet Union and reached the gates of Moscow, Ivan Vasilevitch joined the Red Army as a volunteer. He was sent to study in a school of saboteurs. When he finished the schooling, he was sent to the forests of the Novogrudok region and was ordered to set up partisan groups to fight the Germans.

While travelling through the towns with large Jewish populations, he saw how the entire Jewish nation was being destroyed. This left a very strong impression on him, and he decided to help the Jews. He sought every opportunity to uproot anti-Semitism among the partisans, and he was able to save many Jews, among them Tzirl and Hanya

Berkovitch from Karelich, the Kozlovsky family from Ivya, Leah Dinerstein, and others. He saved many solitary Jews who wandered in forests and swamps, and he punished the peasants who mistreated them.

Later the command of the partisan movement of Byelorussia appointed him a political commissar to the Belsky unit, which consisted of 1,200 Jews. He was pleased that he now would have the opportunity to be of help to more Jews. As the commissar of the unit, he took an active part in all the important problems of the unit, and participated in the unit's battles.

The commissar was the only gentile among 1,200 Jews and he was friendly to all of them. He was a member of the unit, and was called by some the gentile Jew! When the Red Army liberated Novogrudok, Belsky divided up the unit: some partisans went to the front to fight the Germans as soldiers of the Red Army, and others remained and worked for the government. Commissar Shmatovich was appointed to the position of a director of the Lida railway network, and lived among the Jews. He met frequently with the Jewish partisans.

The Jews, however, did not want to remain in the towns where their homes had been destroyed. The Jewish fighters, who returned from the front and the forests wounded and mutilated, did not want to live any longer among graves, and could not adjust in those places. They felt uncomfortable in the cities of the dead, and could not rest. Thus many of them fled from their hometowns without any possessions, without roots and with no goals, and set off for wherever their eyes took them. This is how most remaining Jews left the district.

Ivan Vasilevitch, however, remained in his position. His face showed his distress, and he missed his friends with whom he lived through hard times in the forests and in the swamps. He now sat alone in the dark nights in his room and pondered. He could not figure out what had prompted the partisans to leave their hometowns, where some of them attempted to resettle after the war, and to go off to parts unknown with no aims. He could not anticipate or imagine that soon they would enjoy more rights than those they had in the country where they shed their blood. So Ivan sat alone every evening absorbed in his thoughts, and longing for his friends, the partisans. Where are you now, dear Ivan Vasilevitch Shmatovich? Where are you?

> [Dr. Amarant in p.333 "The Partisans of Tuvia Belski" mentioned also Shmatovich, whom he called Shemyatoviec. He painted, however, a different picture of the "Komisar". As many years have passed, it is difficult to know which the true image is. The reader is advised to read both descriptions and make up his own mind.]

Pesach Friedberg: Quartermaster   **Lazar Malbin: Chief of Staff in the Bielski detachment**

[Not in original Yizkor Book]

[Page 351]

Memories

by Reyzl Volkin

Translated from Yiddish by O. Delatycki

I remember the day before the second slaughter when I came into the Ghetto. Everyone in the Ghetto was expecting the slaughter. I was trembling all over. I was covered in a cold sweat. Despite of it I remained active. I had only one thing in mind: to take revenge for my parents, sister and brothers. The projectors were spreading light in the Ghetto. Disregarding it, at about midnight I tore off a board from the fence and slid out on my stomach from the Ghetto. I ran away over fields. The whole day I hid in the bushes of the Wselub forest. I lay burrowed in the earth like a mole. I lost the will to live. I was prepared to commit suicide. But the instinct to live had forced me to continue. I had no food and no money. Day and night I hid in stables, one night next to a sheep, another night in a bunker in a barn. I was emaciated from hunger. I did not look like a human. Just two large black eyes stared from my face. My body and hair was infested with lice. The smell of my body was indescribable. With great difficulty I finally reached our friend Tuvia Bielski. The situation in the forest was not easy, because we had no weapons to fight the enemy. My clothes were in tatters and I was almost bare. They sent me with a few other unattached persons like me to the Lipichaskaya wilderness. However, shortly after we had arrived there the big round-up began [this refers probably to the Operation Hermann from the second half of July 1943 to early August 1943].

Navaredker Jewish survivors beside the mass grave

We were stranded without water. Bullets and grenades were flying all around us. The three injured boys that were with me were panicking and crying. I tried to pacify them, because I was afraid that the noise would be heard by the Germans. When it had become possible to move I went looking for food in deserted dugouts. But I found nothing, not even water. At one stage I lost my way and was wandering from one big forest to another for eight days. I was nearing the end of my endurance. Suddenly I heard voices. I found two young boys. One used to live in the synagogue square and was called Chaimke and the second was Mejerke (he lives now in Israel). I put my arms around them and told them 'my dear children, we will die here, let us move into the forest, perhaps we will meet someone'. The boys did not desert me. We lived on berries. After a time we smelt something. We went in the direction of the smell prepared to surrender and, if need be, die. But we found two Jewish partisans with a loaf of bread and some water. I can not describe our joy. The partisans started a fire and we began to relax a bit. One of the partisans was the son of Naftali Grinkowski. I don't remember the name of the other. They did not desert us. We all got back to the Bielski group. In the group they knew nothing about our dangerous adventures. I remained with the Bielski group and shared its fate. Of the three injured boys two recovered: one is called Elimelach Zamko from Novogrudok the other Notke from Belice, who is now in Canada. They kissed me and thanked me for what I had done for them. But I did not expect to be thanked. I would have been glad to help more people to survive. In the forest we were divided into groups. I was placed in the Chaim Abramit's dugout. We got on well with each other and we fulfilled all duties. A friend of mine from Wsielub, Meshke Reznik had become ill with typhus. All were afraid of catching the disease and left the dugout. I remained with the sick friend and kept changing wet rags on his head to help reduce the temperature. I did everything I could for him when all others escaped. With great difficulty I persuaded those in charge to bring a doctor from another group. The doctor came and told us that the patient was very ill. The patient and I were transferred to a half finished dugout. We had no water or bread. I can not describe my sufferings. I stood nights next to the bed of the patient and changed his rag soaked in iced water. I took off my leather jacket and covered him. Next to us was a dugout of the Aloshke group. I remember the frosty mornings and the trees covered in snow. I remember going barefoot to their dugout and begging for a bit of soup or water. I was thinking: why do we suffer for such a long time? At one time I heard steps over our head. I told the sick: 'Meishkele they are coming to shoot us'. But they were the partisans from my group who remembered my fate and brought a good friend whose name was Chaim Charny. We were so happy we all started to cry. Our voices reached the sky.. I and Chaim dug a well, because nobody would give us water. As we were digging, the dugout, with the patient and Chaim inside, collapsed. Luckily I was outside. I ran immediately to the dugout of Aloshke and I was shouting: 'save my two brothers'. All came to help us and both survived. After all our troubles, after being separated from the world and human beings, the dugouts of the partisans near to us were attacked. We, in our underground dugout did not hear anything. A few days later we heard footsteps and voices shouting 'is anybody still alive?' We appeared and were taken for a few days to an isolated farm. I was asked what was wrong with the patient. I told them that he was injured by a horse. I made certain that nothing else was said. After a time we were told that we must be prepared for an attack. They took me and the patient away to the big forest where we built a new dugout. Everything was quite and peaceful in the forest. We had a chance to recover somewhat. We were moved from one forest to another. I lived in a small hut with Gitl and the daughter of Fania Berkovski. One morning they came and told me: 'the commandant wants to see you'. He said to me 'dear Reizl there is an unattached partisan and there is no one that could help him.' I answered 'if help is needed I am ready'. We were isolated deeper in the forest. The partisan suffered from typhus of the stomach. He was perpetually covered in sweat. I undressed the patient and I tried to wipe him. I cried whilst I was doing it. Though I did all I could I did not save his life. The man stemmed from Eyshishki or Vasilishok. Two of his cousins are alive. One is called Archik and I don't remember the name of the other. Despite of all the troubles, I remained in reasonable health in the forests. I was isolated from everyone except for the trees and wild animals. I was the only member of my family who remained alive. I extend my personal thanks for my life to our friend Bielski.

[Page 353]

Jewish Partisan Intelligence

by Moshe Reznick

Translated from Yiddish by O. Delatycki

In 1942, after my whole family was slaughtered, I escaped to the forest and joined a detachment of partisans under the command of Bielski. I was assigned to the group Red Reconnaissance. After several trials by fire I was given as a reward a pistol, a short rifle and I was made leader of a group of scouts. Our Jewish detachment was the first organised partisan force in our district and was the first to conduct diversionary actions against the German army. This caused considerable astonishment in all surrounding towns. The Germans offered a prize of 10,000 marks for anyone who would capture Bielski dead or alive. The detachment made it its aim, by the order of commander Bielski, to take revenge on the local farmers if one member of their family was a policeman or helped the Germans to conduct a slaughter, if he robbed or murdered. And seeking revenge we would find the guilty anywhere, even in a concealed hole. As the Russian partisan movement had become better organised, it was decided to reorganise our detachment. A part of the detachment: the elderly, family men and the unarmed were sent to the rear, with

Bielski as the commander. The young who were in a physical condition to carry arms and fight were attached to a Russian unit. The detachment would be commanded by Jews. Zisl Bielski was nominated commander of the Jewish reconnaissance and I became the commander of a platoon of scouts. The new detachment was given the new name of Ordzonikidze. Because of the special tasks of my investigations, I endeavoured to win the confidence and friendship of the local villagers by helping them, whenever help was needed, such as lending them horses for field work, distribution of food and protecting them from irresponsible partisans. We made, in time, real good friends, who risked their lives to bring us important news from town.

The reconnaissance of our detachment was praised by the gentile partisans because of our high morals and bravery. My reports were valued by the staff of the brigade. When the Red army returned to our district the whole unit was incorporated into the army. I was the only survivor. All others fell fighting the enemy.

After the war I left Russia and came to Poland, where I met H. Spiter, now the mayor of Rishon Le Zion, Yitzhak Zukerman – Antek, Mojshe Kaganovich, Boruch Levin and Bronshtein. We formed one command of PCH (Partisan Chaluts), which organised the departure of partisans to Israel.

[Page 354]

Jewish Bravery

by Yehoshua Yofe

Translated from Yiddish by O. Delatycki

A. The first Jewish partisans

Isrolik from Iveniec was 18 years old. His father sold soap, combs and sewing thread in exchange for rags to the villagers around Iveniec. Isrolik often accompanied his father and he knew the area well. Isrolik spoke to a few lads from Novogrudok. He told them that his township was surrounded by forests. The village houses stood in the forests. The Germans never came there. There were no made roads in the vicinity. The peasants were friendly toward the Jews and were hostile to the Germans, who were aiming to conquer the world. In the forests there were already Russian partisans. They travelled on the roads, attacking the passing Germans and disappearing into the forest. 'Why sit in the Ghetto and wait for death? Why should I be afraid of the Germans, let the Germans be afraid of me.' Isroilik spoke like that and the young people from Novogrudok listened to him. The conversations were conducted in secrecy. The Judenrat would put them in the lock-up if they knew of the discussions. And how does one part with one's parents? Mothers were wailing: 'How would you survive in the forests? Animals will devour you. You will die of starvation'. Someone had overheard the conversations, mothers told others in secret of the discussions and the whole Ghetto was saying that the partisans were intending to go into the forests. The Judenrat found out about this. The Jewish policemen were sent to the houses in the Ghetto to take away and keep overnight the boots of the young men. They were suspected of wanting to escape into the forests. That put a stop to the conversations about going to the forest. The mothers told the neighbours that the boys had recanted. They did not know the way to the forests. They feared that would be caught on the way. They did not have arms. The Judenrad did not take away boots anymore. One night young men were moving about in the Ghetto till late. They were going from one house to another. Some twenty odd boys moved behind Srulek's barn and all quietened down. The Ghetto was tired from the travails of the day and slept. The policemen that were supposed to be guarding the Ghetto gathered in a corner, smoked and spoke of putting behind the long, tedious night. The dark skies spread over the Ghetto. In the darkness shadows of men, one after the other, moved stealthily to the fence of the Ghetto. A board in the fence was eased off in the daytime. The boys slid through the opening and out of the Ghetto. They took out a few revolvers from their pockets. This gave them courage. They knew that if they met the enemy they would be able to defend themselves. During the entire night they met no one. These were times of trouble and everyone preferred to stay at home during the night. They walked through forests and fields. They passed houses immersed in sleep. They rested in the bushes and continued on their way. When they were hungry they knocked on the door of a farm. One of them entered with the pistol in his hand, the others remained at the door. The farmer gave them bread, butter and a jug of milk and they went on. Going along the way on which the Germans led the Jews of Iveniec to the Novogrudok Ghetto, the group reached the appointed place in the forest. There they sat under the big trees on the soft grass. During the day the sun warmed them. They were in a forest which stretched for miles. Here they were free, not restricted by fences, without fear of death. They were surrounded by friendly nature, which awakened their suppressed feelings and induced hope.

They met Russian partisans who taught them how to avoid German patrols, the art of partisan fighting and attacking German positions.

The partisans sharpened in them the desire of revenge. A partisan must be fearless, not to be afraid of the enemy and to be prepared to die. The main aim was to kill the German fascists and their supporters. Each of the twenty odd partisans was made to suffer by the Germans. Many members of their families had been killed in a most brutal manner. The survivors were locked up in the Novogrudok Ghetto and were waiting for their death.

The boys in the forest were eager to avenge the wrong doings. They were waiting at the roads for German vehicles and destroyed them. They had seen their murderers bleed and were happy. But this was not sufficient. They were planning, together with the Russian partisans, to attack the German police post in Naliboki. The murderers of the Jews from the townships were stationed there and the partisans were eager to revenge their deaths. The policemen were barricaded in the local church. The township was occupied by the partisans, but they could not get into the church. The partisans attacked from two sides – the Russians from one side and the Jews from the other. They were shooting at the policemen from the trenches. Suddenly the policemen stopped shooting, as if they had run out of bullets. The partisans were told to attack and get into the church. The Jewish boys were waiting for this. They aimed to capture the policemen alive, capture them and ask them why they were killing local Jews, who were in the past their neighbours and friends. Suddenly they heard the sound of approaching trucks, which were driven at great speed. The trucks arrived in Naliboki and the Germans started shooting. The bullets rained down on the partisans, who left the trenches and were about to enter the church. They did not realise that the Russian partisans escaped from the township and had left them behind. The policemen in the church suddenly started firing. And than the shooting stopped. The Germans announced through a megaphone: 'lay down your arms and we will not kill you, we will take you back to the Novogrudok Ghetto'. The Germans were certain that the Jews would surrender. They did not believe that Ghetto Jews were able to fight. They must be frightened and would give up the fight. But the Jews had other ideas, though they saw death approaching. They escaped from the Ghetto to avoid death. To go back to the Ghetto to be killed there did not make sense. It was better to die fighting. It was better to see some Germans die. They started to shoot at the enemy. Some German trucks were destroyed. The Jews continued shooting. They were shooting, were silenced and silently they died. Their enemy was manyfold. The partisans ran out of ammunition and died knowing that they did not surrender. The story of the fight had become known among the partisans: some twenty Jews have opposed hundreds of Germans and they did not surrender. They fought to the last- the fight for freedom and justice.

[Page 356]

B. The partisans avoid slaughter

by Yehoshua Yaffe

Translated from Yiddish by O. Delatycki

In the district of Novogrudek were a number of towns, among them: Karelicz, Lubcz, Delatycz, Iwieniec, Nalibok [Naliboki in Polish] and Cyryn. The Jews in the townships were exposed from the beginning of the German occupation to maltreatment by their non-Jewish neighbours. The neighbours took their cows, robbed their belongings and the Jews became paupers. When there was nothing left to rob they were left in peace. The Germans did not come to the townships and the local hooligans kept clear. However, in 1942, the Germans ordered the liquidation of Jews from the small towns of the Novogrudok district. Four vehicles of Germans and policemen led by high ranking Gestapo officers travelled to the townships. They assembled about 100 Jews in Nalibok. They demanded that the Jews surrender their gold and other valuables. Then all Jews were shot. According to the plan of the Germans, they were supposed to shoot on the same day the Jews of Jeremiche, Derewnia, Korelicz and Lubcz.

The partisan group Stalinec was positioned close to Nalibok in the nearby forests. They wore peasant cloth. They found out that there was a slaughter in the township. They did not have the numbers and the arms to attack the town. The group numbered a few tens of partisans. They prepared an ambush along the way out of town.

On the nicest day of the summer, when the sun was spreading its golden rays on the freshly green fields of early shoots, when the trees spread their waving branches, the earth received the warm bodies of bloodied victims. The Germen murderers were drunk from alcohol and blood. They were filled with joy because they satisfied their blood thirsty appetites. They had no notion that they would pay for their deeds with their blood. They went cheerfully on their way. The shouting and singing of wild men who were ready to demolish the world could be heard from afar in the forest. The partisans, who were hiding from the wild men in the forests, listened to their shouting. Their job was to fight the murderers. When they did not fight they vanished into the forests and hid living in tents, like the ancient people before they knew how to build houses. Their hearts were full of enmity to the violators of human lives. They declared a holy war against those who ejected them from their homes, slaughtered their families and robbed their possessions. Living in the forest they imbued the rustling of the branches and the grass and the croaking of frogs in the muddy marshes.

Suddenly the wild laughter filled the quiet forest. The bloody shouting penetrated their hiding places. In their memories they heard the voices of those smothered to death: 'Take vengeance for the murders, take vengeance for the spilled blood!' The partisans hid in the bushes and readied their weapons. They shot into the vehicles and the bullets hit the confused Germans. The vehicles stopped and the surviving Germans showed no opposition. They said that they were going to take the Jews from the other small towns. The partisans took from the Germans the goods they had robbed and released three Jewish who were taken by force by the Germans. All Germans were shot. The forest was quite again. One could only hear the voices of the departing partisans, who were carrying with them the arms they had captured. They were glad to have won the battle with the 'invincible' foe, who begged them to let them live.

The attack by the partisans was not mentioned by the Germans in Novogrudok. The Germans did not proceed with their plans to kill the Jews in the small towns. They brought the Jews to Novogrudok and killed them in the second slaughter ten weeks later.

> *[Difficulties have been encountered regarding the above article. The author states that the Jews of Naliboki were killed on the spot 10 weeks prior to the second slaughter which occurred on the 7 August 1942. We can find elsewhere no evidence of this event.*
>
> *Mention was made by several authors of the presence of Jews from Naliboki in the Peresike Ghetto prior to the second slaughter (see for instance p. 302 'The Ghetto in Peresike' by Frume Gulkovitz-Berger: 'At that time they gathered in the Novogrudok Ghetto all Jews from the surrounding townships such as Nalibok, Iviniec, Lubcz, Karelicz, Delatycz, Naisztot (?) and any other place wherever there was a Jew in a village.').*
>
> *There was an incursion in Naliboki of the Soviet "Stalin" brigade on the night of 8/9 May 1943, long after the Jews of the town were dead.]*

[Page 357]

Four graves of our fathers

by Miriam Ninkovski

Translated from Hebrew by Aviva Kamil

There are four mass graves around the edge of our town-- brothers' graves. Trees, bushes, wild flowers and grass grow, fed by the blood of the martyrs, who were murdered in all possible manners. You would think that the martyrs finally found their rest in the mass graves. But no, the killers, who, together with the Nazis, murdered the innocents, still come, dig and rob the graves, throw out the bones with no feeling of guilt or remorse.

All that is left today of our blood-brothers are the graves. The town, with which we were bound with all our hearts, the town that was the source of many of our precious memories, has changed its look: the market place with its row of shops in the middle, the spine of the Jewish life in town and the source of our livelihood, changed its face; ruins remain, the shops are empty. Flowers are growing in the square. There is a flowerbed, with Lenin's statue on the centre. [Since this story was written the row of shops - rad kromen - was removed. So was Lenin's statue. Only the name of the square was kept, it is still called the Lenin square]. Quiet at the market, no rush, no dash, no more Jews with worried faces, and fear in their eyes. The market awakens only two days a year for parades: the First day of May and the Seventh of November. Then a big crowd is assembled in front of the leader's statue. You seek in the throng familiar, dear faces, warm eyes of brother, sister, mother, father, but in vain. Strange eyes look at you, apathetic, hard, full of hate and derision. The synagogue square (shul-hoif), its low houses, a place of Jewish poverty, the noise of the children in the "cheders", the Jews wearing "kapotes" and long beards, Yeshiva students, their faces pale and the fear of God in their eyes. Where are they all? The ruin of the great synagogue stands as a memorial to them all. [This too was removed. On the ground, emptied of every scrap of the Jewish past, a public lavatory was erected.]

Rachelow, where the tradesmen and the shop keepers lived, that big trench that in autumn and spring became a bog and you endangered your life going down or climbing out of there. It is no more. It is now a field. There is no remainder of Rachelow. It was erased from the face of the town.

Only one place in Novogrudok did not change its face. It was a place loved by the youths. The most popular place for Saturday stroll - the

Shloss barg (Citadel Hill). It is still standing there today, observes the town, and listens to the strange language of the new inhabitants. The ruins guard every ancient engraving cut on its walls. There are now new engravings in a new language, but the old walls keep their silence. [The remains of the towers on the Shloss barg have been allowed to deteriorate markedly further and are in danger of total collapse. They may be beyond repair.]

This is our town today, a town that was a stepmother to us in days of troubles and in the holocaust. We have got no place in it today. That is why I am happy that I left it and came to Israel. Today when I look here at the people from my hometown, the few who escaped the claws of the Nazis, my heart overflows with pride and joy. Most of us did not dream in our small town to achieve all that we did achieve in our free land. I see our people, the citizens of Israel, as a large oak tree branching out, a tree that stood at the crossroads, beaten by blizzards and storms, which tried to grow, but could not. Its leaves were torn, its branches broken; it was ripped out of the Diaspora. But it sprouts now new roots in its own land. It did not despair and it is still fighting for its right to exist on our land, the motherland, for generations to come. Strong be the hands of our sons - the builders.

[Page 357]

People of Novogrudok After Liberation

by Yehoshua Yaffe

Translated from Yiddish by O. Delatycki

Less than a year passed since the last Jews had escaped from the Ghetto through the tunnel. Most joined the partisans in the forests. There were a few Jews in the Novogrudok prison. At the last moment, just before the Germans ran away, they killed the prisoners. The Russian army had expelled the Germans from the occupied lands. Novogrudok was rid of the German bandits.

We, the Jewish partisans entered the town as victors. We should have been happy that we had at last got rid of the enemy. But we were desolate. We came back to a house of death. We were not met by friends. Most of them were long since dead. In the first days after liberation we saw ruins and mass graves. We looked at the soil that held so many young lives consumed with their past and their future. We walked in empty streets. On both sides were foundations of houses concealed by grass. Those were the ruins of the houses of those whose lives were cut off for eternity.

Gentiles, who were unconcerned about the slaughters, occupied the Jewish homes that were' still standing. They became rich having acquired Jewish possessions. They met us, the survivors, some with grief, but most with hostility. Some were afraid that our goods and chattels, which they had robbed, maybe taken from them.

We moved as shadows that came from the world beyond and we were grieving every night and day. Our wounds reopened. In front of our eyes we kept seeing the pictures of torture and death. I spent hours sitting on a stone of the old synagogue in thoughts and contemplation of the past: of the cheder and school, of stories that were told about the old synagogue in the days of our great grand fathers. The Germans tore chunks from the old synagogue building, but they did not demolish it. It was still there with its walls torn apart. One could still see words on the bleaching walls. Over all this there was emptiness. There were the sad memories of death and fear, of destroyed houses, small children torn to pieces, of crying, of hoarse shouting, dishevelled women and depressed men, who kept hoping to survive. A nightmare of thought, a vortex of memories and one did not remember that in the end the enemy was defeated. The world of the enemies survived, but ours vanished forever.

Five of us, all orphans, moved into an empty house in Shloss gus. The hinges of the doors were broken, all windows were missing and we were all sad. We had no table, chair or bed to lie on. We lay down on the floor and slept the night.

Early in the morning, a girl walked by and looked in through the non-existent window. 'Are you Jewish?' she asked, speaking Polish. She came inside and started to cry uncontrollably. She said that she had not met a Jew for the past two years. They thought that she was Polish and this was how she survived. Where were her parents, her family? They must be dead, she told us. She did not know where they were buried. She stemmed from Volkovysk. She ran away during a slaughter and came to Novogrudok. She knew that she must hide her past. She told them that she was Polish and that her father was a high-ranking officer. Because of this she was escaping from the Germans. She arrived in the village of Sunchicy, three kilometres from Novogrudok, where she worked for an old Polish farming woman. They gave her documents and she stayed in that village for the rest of the war. Her friends were Polish girls and she went with them to church. She had to get used to their way of living.

The sun came up and it had been warm. The light shone into our room, as if it was listening to the story of the girl. She had a horrible experience, not unlike the story of the Moranos in Spain in the middle ages. Every night she had to pray to God with a cross in her hands. Every Sunday she had to pray in church. She had to walk through the ruins of the town, where Jews once lived. But there were no Jews left. She was thinking of her future. What will become of her? Will she be separated for ever from the Jewish nation? Will she have to hide her Jewish roots for good? After the liberation she returned to Judaism. She felt lonely and isolated, but glad that she had taken of the mask off her face.

A few weeks later some Novogrudok Jews came back from Russia. They were soldiers from the Russian army and they wanted to return home, but they found a house of death, all were dead and the township was in ruins.

There were several people who were in the same situation as us. We decided to join together and consider what to do next. We all came to the same conclusion: to leave the cursed land, to part from the ruined town, to leave behind the mass graves of the two slaughters and go to the land of Israel. We looked for the last time at the place that had been Novogrudok. We said goodbye to the past, to the story of the Jewish demise and mourning and we went on our last journey to Israel.

Tears on the mass grave.....

[Page 359]

Novogrudok partisans who fell in action

by Dr. S. Openhaim

Translated from Hebrew by Aviva Kamil

Hertzel son of Shalom Efroimski

Finished the "Tarbut" school in Novogrudok. Was a member of a pioneering youth movement. Worked as an apprentice in a bicycles repair workshop. He was known as a courageous fighter who went on dangerous missions. Hertzel was close to the commander Tuvia Belski. He fell in the village Khrapenevo in December 1942 at the age of 18.

Arie (Laibke) Volkin

Son of Sara Volkin (who was a milliner). Finished "Tarbut" school in Novogrudok. One of the best and bravest in the forest. Despite his young age, he became a fighter. Fell in Khrapenevo in December 1942. He was 18 years of age.

Yitzchak son of Natke Leibovich

Worked as a barber in town. His father was a horse trader and they knew the countryside well. Was one of the brave and daring fighters in the forest. Fell in Khrapenevo in December 1942. He was 23 years old.

The three partisans, mentioned above, were in a house of one of the villagers at Khrapenevo near Iviya, with Tuvia Belski's wife and her brother Grisha. In a sudden attack the Germans murdered all except for Arie Volkin, who was taken alive, tortured by the Nazis, but did not betray his friends. [This episode is described briefly in the article "Outside the Ghetto" by Luba Rudnicki on p.246.]

Aba Volfovich

From the village Rabniki near Novogrudok. He was on a mission (zadacha in Russian) transporting supplies from a train. Was ambushed and killed in December 1942. Was 30 years old.

The brothers Avraham and Reuven sons of Faivele Eliyahu Polonski

They were horse traders and knew well the surrounding country and the peasants. Were among the bravest in the unit. They fell together in March 1943 in the village of Dobro-Polia (?) near Novogrudok. Avraham was 22 and Reuven 18 years old.

Yehoshua Ostashinski

Finished school and worked as a tailor in town. Was a cousin of the brothers Polonskis and fell with them in Dobro-Polia in March 1943. Was 19 years old.

Eliezer, son of Yoel Chaitovich the paver (brukirer).

Finished school in town, was in the "Betar" movement and worked as a barber. Fell In Dobro-Polia In March 1943 with the brothers Polonski and Ostashinski.

The four fighters, mentioned above, stayed overnight, after an action in Dobro-Polia with a villager, whom Polonskis knew. The partisans felt secure, because the house stood outside of the village. When the partisans fell asleep, the villager sent his son to Novogrudok, who returned with the Germans. They murdered the partisans. Avraham Polonski managed to hide during the attack. When he came out after the Germans departed, he asked the villager why he did it. The villager killed him with an axe.

David Zilberman

The owner of a printing press in Novogrudok. Fell in May 1943, when he was ambushed. He was 50 years old.

Zvi Zilberman, his son.

Worked with his father in the printing house, was a unit commander and an instructor. Fell with his father in May 1943. Was 26 years old.

Moshe son of Mordechi Berkovich

Finished the "Tarbut" school. Was in the pioneering youth movement. Worked in a workshop repairing bicycles. Among the bravest in the unit. Relative of Tuvia Belski. Fell with the Zilbermans in May 1943, Was 18 years old.

Those three partisans, together with the second son of David Zilberman, Yosef and Michael Kvak, were returning from a mission to see a villager, whose son was a policeman serving the Germans. The son promised that he will take Mrs Zilberman out of the Ghetto. On their way back, the three partisans were ambushed and murdered. Yosef Zilberman and Michael Kvak escaped and returned to base. [David's daughter, Malke Zilberman, who was at the time in another partisan group, told a slightly different story. However, there is agreement on the number of partisans who participated and died in this action.]

Movshovich

Finished school and worked with his father on the land. Fell at the beginning of 1944, when he was standing guard near a house in a village, where a few partisans slept. A villager's son (who was a partisan in a Russian unit) attacked him from the back and murdered him with an axe. He wanted Movshovich's rifle. Movshovich was 18 years old.

Zvi son of Natke Leibovich

He was a brother of Itzchak Leibovich, who, as was described above, was killed in the village of Kapinyeva. Zvi was a courageous partisan. He fell on the day of the liberation [8 July 1944?]. He was 20 years old.

Mark Epstein

Son of the " Feldsher" (assistant physician). Fell on the same day. Was 17 years old.

Sara Gershonovski (Sarale the Shneiderke)

Fell on the same day. Was 48 years old.

Those three partisans fell on the day of liberation, an hour before the Red Army arrived. A group of Germans came upon the partisans' camp in their flight from the Soviet army. There was a battle and 10 partisans were killed. The other seven partisans were not from Novogrudok.

Zvi Plotnik

Worked as a brick layer (moierer). Worked most of the time for the villagers outside Novogrudok. Was in the forest with his son Yerachmiel. After liberation he was enlisted into the Red Army and fell at the front. He was 35 years old.

Yerachmiel Plotnik

Came to Israel in 1946. Was in Kibbutz Ramat-Hakovesh. Fell there in 1947. Circumstances unknown.

David, son of Shmaya Bruk

His father was a barber. He finished "Tarbut" school, was in a youth movement, and was a good partisan. After the liberation he joined the Red Army and fell at the front. He was 19 years old.

Yehoshua Menaker

The son of Alter Menaker (the Cheder teacher), he was killed in battle withGerman soldiers near Huta in the beginning of 1943. He was a brave machine gunner.

Asael Belski

Brother of the commander of the partisan unit, Tuvia Belski. He was in charge of a unit, which protected the camp and secured supplies for the camp. He was among the first to carry out the most dangerous operations, nothing stood in his way. After liberation was enlisted in the Red Army and fell at the front. He was 35 years old.

Michael, son of Shlomo Zamkovy

Studied in the Polish high school in Novogrudok. In the forest he was a brave and daring partisan. After liberation worked in Lida as a clerk for the Soviets. Fell when he was working in one of the villages outside Lida, killed by the Poles. He was 20 years old.

Yishiayhu (Shaike) son of Nisl Zamkovy

Studied at the Polish high school in Novogrudok. Was a good partisan. After liberation was enlisted into the Red Army and fell at the front. He was 21 years old.

Zalman Troitski
Son in law of Avremke Izraelit

Had a grocery store in the market square. Was in the forest with his 14 years old son. After liberation was enlisted into the Red Army and fell at the front. Was 35 years old.

Natan (Natke) Sucharski

He was a plumber [blecher] and had a workshop. He was active in the trade union movement. After liberation returned to Novogrudok. Died after an operation. He was 48 years old.

Mordechi (Meme) son of Israel Cherny

Finished school. Was in the pioneering youth movement. Was among the first to leave the Ghetto. He was in a unit of Jewish partisans. Fell at the beginning of 1942 while fighting German guards in the town of Naliboki.Ben-Zion son of Avraham (Avremke) Movshovich

Was a student and among the firsts to leave the Ghetto. Was ambushed by Germans on the road to Naliboki at the beginning of 1942.

Ada daughter of David Ziskind

Was the wife of Dr. Yosef Shapiro, fell with Ben-Zion Movshovich

Yehuda son of Avraham Ostashinski

Was among the firsts to leave the Ghetto. Fell in Lipichanski forest.

Avraham (Avremke) son of Itzchak Yaakov Rakovski

Finished "Tarbut" school in Novogrudok. Was active in Hashomer-Hatsair movement. Worked as an electrician. Was in the Ghetto in the court building. He operated an underground radio, which supplied news from the outside world. He was one of those who organised the digging of the tunnel, through which 300 (250?) Jews escaped from the court building. He found himself in a non-Jewish partisans' group and excelled in his courage. After liberation he was enlisted into the Red Army and fell on the at the front. His sister, who survived the war, received on his behalf a medal, which was conferred on him by the Red Army.

Zvi (Hershele) Gurevich

He belonged to the movement "Fraihait". He was a tailor. He left the Ghetto through the tunnel. He joined a non-Jewish partisans' group. After the liberation he was conscripted to the Red Army and fell at the front.

Yosef Razevski

He was a tailor and escaped from the Ghetto through the tunnel. He joined a non-Jewish partisans' group. He fell in a battle with the fleeing Germans.

> *[There are 39 dead listed above, of which 17 were partisans from Novogrudok, who were killed by the Germans (often betrayed by villagers) or were killed by villagers. Seven partisans were killed in the Red army, after the liberation. One partisan is listed as killed by the Poles after liberation. It is hard to know how comprehensive the above list is. It is known that the Poles were responsible for a number of deaths of Jewish partisans. For instance, on the night of the 17 of December 1943 a Stolpce unit of the AK has killed 12 Jewish partisans of the Zorin detachment. It is not known if any of them were from Novogrudok. One thing is certain - the partisan movement, particularly that of Belski, saved many lives.]*

[Page 361]

Such were the Jewish partisans

by Y. Yaffe

Translated from Hebrew by Aviva Kamil

Asael Belski

Before the Holocaust, Asael and all the Belski family lived in the village of Stankiewicze [Polish spelling]. Belski's partisan unit was created mainly due to the efforts of Asael. He thought that it was his obligation to evade the Germans. His village was isolated. Germans did not intrude often and it was possible to hide in the adjacent forest, if they did appear.

Asael knew well the roads and trails that connected the villages. All peasants in the area knew him well, because they used to come to mill their grain in Belskis' flourmill in Stankiewicze. He had to leave school and work in the flourmill from an early age, because of his father's ill health. He was a quiet modest man, loved work and was ready to help anyone. His good character stood him in good stead in troubled times. At first he hid on his own, close to the village of Stankiewicze. His brothers joined him later. Before the first slaughter in Novogrudok, he assembled all his family, approximately 15 people, and hid them in the homes of friendly peasants.

Next the Belskis joined a group of Russian partisans lead by Victor [Panchenko?], to fight the Germans. In the meantime Tuvia, their oldest brother, arrived from the Lida Ghetto; he was tall and broad shouldered, full of initiative, courage and a warm Jewish heart. He accepted the task of the leader of the partisans'. Tuvia was the commander and Asael his loyal helper. He carried out any undertaking with devotion and precision. He took part in scouting, fighting and negotiating [with the Russian partisans]. He was the commander of the punishment unit and, in dangerous conditions, completed perfectly his assignments.

Everyone loved Asael and put their trust in him. They were glad to participate in battles under his command. It was a pleasure to scout with him or just to be with him. He was a loyal and pleasant friend. By the end of the summer of 1942 the first groups from the Novogrudok Ghetto joined the Belskis. Everyone feared the Germans. Jews, who were roaming in the country, were captured by Christians and delivered to the Germans. The art of being a partisan was not familiar as yet. Asael and his group fought bravely. They also took revenge on

Christians who betrayed Jews to the Germans. As this became known the peasants did not dare to assault Jews any more and even helped them to find their way to the forest.

In November 1942 the Belskis with Victor's Russian partisans ambushed Germans on the Novoyelna-Novogrudok road. Asael was the commander of the Jewish unit. Scores of Germans were killed and many weapons were captured on that occasion. The weapons were used to equip the fighters from the Novogrudok Ghetto.

There was a second battle in November under Asael's command at the railway station Naziki on the Neman-Lida line [station Naziki could not be found on the map. There is a station Yacuki on the Novoyelnia-Nemen line]. It was a fierce battle with the Germans, who were dug-in in a bunker that guarded the station. It ended successfully.

The third action involved setting fire to granaries, where grain destined for Germany was stored. All of these operations created a favourable reputation of the Jewish partisans and helped other Jews to be accepted in Russian partisan units.

The fighters and non-fighters all loved Asael; he befriended the fighters and was like one of them. But he was also a friend of the non-fighters. He noticed the good qualities in every person. "We would not always be like Gipsies in the forest", he said, "after liberation every one will return to his profession or trade and will be successful, even if he was not a fighting partisan". He was the first in a battle and the first to aid the injured. "There is no need to fear death, we will die anyway". sooner or later. Our aim is to fight the Germans and their collaborators, who hate us. We have to avenge our brethren's blood. I am not interested in tomorrow". he said.

He was glad to go on an operation to punish a Belorussian family, for betraying to the Germans Jewish partisans, who were visiting their house. He killed them with his own hands. "Jewish blood is not cheap". he shouted and set fire to them and their house. He used to remind himself of that punishment operation to calm his aching heart.

Asael was a brave loved man, who always went out and returned from actions with his partisans safe and sound. He survived the forest, joined the Russian Army and fell in the war against the Germans in a foreign land. Blessed be his memory.

Arie Volkin

Arie came to the forest at the age of 18. He was a child when his father died. The obligation of providing for the family fell on his mother, who was too busy to take good care of him. She was a milliner. He received his education at the Polish State School and studied Jewish subjects with private teachers. The prophets and their visions did not attract him. I was his teacher for half a year. I taught him Isaiah and Yecheskel. We were reading the phrase about the end of days when the lamb and the wolf will live in peace together. He erupted "It will never happen, the goyim hate us to death". Every day he had to wrestle with non-Jewish children at school, and among them he learned that you have to fight back. He got beaten, but he could give a good beating too and the Christian children knew not to mock him with their call "zyd", like they called other Jewish children. When the Germans came, he worked in their camp. The German soldiers liked him, he was a good worker, cleaned the horses and the stables. They let him clean their weapons, take them apart and put them together again; this knowledge helped him in the forest. While working with the Germans he saw death every day. Every day people were shot and he got used to that. It was a familiar occurrence for him to see how scores of people were buried in ditches. After the second slaughter in Novogrudok, he escaped from the Ghetto. He was searching till he found Belski's camp. He was a good partisan and had no fear. On occasions he went back to town and entered the Ghetto, right under the noses of the Germans. He was successful in accomplishing all sorts of missions.

In the ambush that the Belski's and Victor's partisans set on the Germans in the forest of Koshelevo, he fought like a lion, killed a German and took his sub-machine gun, which he used as his own weapon.

He was a scout and the first in every action, until the bitter morning in December 1942, when a few hundred policemen surrounded the "chutor" Khrapenevo and opened with machine gun fire on a dozen Jewish partisans, who slept there [according to another account there were 3 Jewish partisans in the "chutor": Efroimski, Leibovich and Volkin, as well as Belski's wife and her brother Grisha. Belski, in his recollections, considered the event a major setback and mentioned more victims]. The fight was fierce with no hope of survival. Arie Volkin, shooting through the window, used his sub machine gun to the last bullet and was wounded.

He was the only one to be taken alive by the Germans; they brought him to the Novogrudok jail, tortured him but he did not utter a word, he knew a lot but said nothing. He endured tortures for a few weeks and when they realised that they would not be able to extract anything from him they hanged him in the Novogrudok jail. God will avenge his blood.

Eliyahu Yavnovich

Was born in 1908 in the Nasvich farm, 10 km out of Novogrudok. He completed primary school and later learned to repair sewing machines at Meme Gorodynski in Novogrudok and worked at the "Singer" company in Lida. In the summer of 1942, he was brought by the Germans from Lubch to the Ghetto in Peresike, he survived the slaughter of August 1942 and immediately after escaped to join Belski's unit.

Eliyahu was an educated man with an inherent intelligence. He was self-taught, read a great deal and studied at night after a day of hard and strenuous work. Eliyahu was well mannered and a pleasure to talk to. He had a vast general knowledge; and was among the few who brought some culture and knowledge to the forest.

As a mechanic, he was among those who repaired and cleaned the weapons of the unit. He was a capable partisan with a military knowledge and became a group leader after the division of Belski's camp into two, when the unit "Ordzonikidze" was established.

As a leader of his group, he was meticulous in supervising their duties such as: guarding, scouting and fighting.

He was serious and devoted, and was liked by his men. He insisted on order and discipline and fought for equality in the group. He was always ready to help. He was a good fighter and a good friend. With his help many left the Lida Ghetto. He instructed them and cheered them up in times of danger or crisis.

On the fatal day, he went with another partisan for a special operation in the village of Zeshirialnik, a group of policemen appeared in the village. When they heard about the partisans they surrounded the house and sprayed it with bullets from automatic guns. There was no hope of surviving. Eliyahu was wounded in his leg and could not escape. He came out of the house and hurled a hand grenade. He was killed but during the explosion the second partisan managed to escape to the near by forest. After his death he was awarded by the units' commanders a bravery medal and was promoted to a higher rank. God will avenge his blood.

Eliyahu Ostashinski

Eliyahu Ostashinski was born near Selib. He married Rachel Berman, the daughter of the blacksmith. The blacksmith was known for his strength. Eliyahu was a blacksmith too. He served before the war in the Polish Army and was promoted to sergeant. He was among the few in Belski's unit who had proper military training and a rank. He had many acquaintances among the peasants and it made his escape from the Ghetto easier. He joined Belski's unit together with his wife. He became an instructor of the partisans and was a unit leader. He put a lot of work into the training of partisans, from the use of a rifle to battle exercises. He took part with his men in fighting the enemy and in scouting operations.

His unit brought food supplies to the camp. During all his time in the forest he was busy, planning and organising operations, carrying them out with success. Quiet, polite and loved by all of the people in the camp and those in the fighting units. Two days before we left the forest, a few hundred retreating Germans, who were fleeing from the Russians, came near the camp, they overcame the guard and entered the camp. [Some other sources maintain that in the euphoria of the impending liberation the camp was not guarded, resulting in 9 or 10 deaths.] Eliyahu Ostashinski organised the defence and with a small group of fighters fought the Germans, it was a short face-to-face battle and he was killed. God will avenge his blood

The brothers Zuchovitski

Moshe Zuchovitski was born in 1922 and his brother Nisan was born in 1924. Their father Aharon was a "S.T.M." [?] writer and had a small grocery store, their mother was a dressmaker. The children received a traditional religious and national education. The influence of their education on them was noticeable in the forest.

They were quiet, decent, helpful fellows and were liked by all.

Moshe Zuchovitski was a brave partisan and an excellent fighter. He felt bitterness and hatred towards the Goyim who helped to kill and rob their Jewish neighbours, and was full of hate of Germans. Only one thing motivated him – revenge. He did not fear for his own young life, took part in the hardest of the battles, and went to the most dangerous places to take revenge on the Germans. He took part in many operations in the Belski unit and later in the group "Ordzonikidze". After liberation he joined the Russian Army with his brother Nisan. Both fell on [the] German soil. God will avenge their blood.

Chayemke Bloch

Chayemke Bloch was born in 1930 in Novogrudok. His father was a shoemaker. He studied at the "Tarbut" school. The Germans separated him from his family, sent his parents to death and he was left solitary and lost but with a strong will to live. He survived the second slaughter [too]. He heard talk about people who were escaping the Ghetto; about something happening outside, he followed the actions of the underground in the Ghetto. Watching someone escaping the

Ghetto he followed by running after him. He hid for three days, when he returned to the Ghetto he found out that all his relatives were killed. He was starving and pleaded with his acquaintances and strangers for food, he wanted to live. There were people who helped him, gave him a piece of bread and comforted him, as he was one of them.

There was no safety in the Ghetto. Many knew that their days were numbered. In a week, in a month they will also be killed.

People escaped to the forest, they hoped to survive there, Chayemke was among them, and he was 12 years old, the only child among the partisans.

In the forest they took pity on him [too], befriended him, washed his clothes, gave him food and he obeyed everyone. He used to say that at home he was a good boy too, and helped his mother and father, and the partisans loved him. We moved from forest to forest, we walked at night, sometimes 50 km and more and Chayemke with us. He was alert and not tired, carried water, cut wood, lit the fire and helped anyone who asked him for help. He was a partisans' helper, their apprentice, cleaning their rifles. He wanted to stand on guard and hold a rifle, hoping that he would grow up to be a good partisan and even take revenge on the Germans. He went through a difficult winter in the forest, but later in the summer it was easier. He was given a job to be one of the keepers of the horses. One morning, at dawn, when we were in the forest of Yasnyeva near the Neman, the Germans attacked the camp from a few directions with hundreds of policemen. Chayemke was killed. We escaped from the forest, and when we met again on the other bank of the Neman for a head count, Chayemke was not with us. He was left dead in the forest of Yasnyeva, and his desire for revenge was not fulfilled. God will avenge his blood.

Shlomo Stoler (Keidrel)

Shlomo Stoler was born in 1926 in the town Korelichi near Novogrudok. His father was a hawker, he went from village to village selling haberdashery and kitchen utensils to the peasants. Though Shlomo was a very talented boy, he had studied very little. He finished only a few classes of the Polish Primary School. At a young age he left school to help his father provide for his big family. Together they went from village to village during the week and before Saturday they returned to their poor family in the small town with their profit.

In July 1942 the Germans brought the Jews of Korelichi to the Ghetto of Novogrudok. Most were killed there in August 1942. Only a few escaped, among them Shlomo Stoler and his brothers. For months they were roaming the villages around their town, he knew the area and the peasants knew him and took pity on him. They let him sleep in their granaries, and in the morning they gave him a loaf of bread and a bottle of milk and sent him on his way. So he roamed till winter. Almost no Jews were left in the area, and the peasants were afraid of the Germans or did not want to hide a Jew. Then he found out about the Belski units. But unfortunately the Belski's camp was divided into many groups and these groups were hiding in different places and it was difficult to find them. When an acquaintance brought him together with his cousin to the Yankelevich group, Yankelevitch rejected him. I stood guard then and heard their conversation. "Why are you so stubborn" he asked "you have got a house underground, my father had a nicer house then you and they still drove him out of his house and killed him, who knows if soon someone will drive you out of your hut". The boy did not know that it was a prophesy, after a month the Germans raided our huts in the middle of the day, and we all escaped.

Shlomo Stoler was accepted by the Abramovich group where he had an uncle. From the first day you could see that he was a devoted and energetic fellow, used to hardship, to cold and complicated situations. He matured and became a courageous and disciplined partisan. He revealed all his skills when we were in the Pushcha Naliboki and all the area was full of Russian partisans. There were 1100 Jews in Belski's camp and it was hard to provide for all of them. He was the leader of a group of 20 people, they roamed the Korelichi area and took from under the Germans noses grain and meat to the camp.

I went with him a few times and saw how well he operated. He was a very modest and practical person; he knew that everything should be endured until the time when the Jews would be able to come out of the forest. After the liberation he reached Italy and was in the camps for a couple of years. With the outbreak of the Israeli War of Independence, he heard the "old man's" (Ben-Gurion) call, he came on a boat to Israel and immediately joined the army. He fell at Latrun, as our state was established. Blessed be his memory.

Yaakov Slutski

Yaakov was born in 1914 in Korelichi. His father was a farmer, he had cattle but his main occupation was growing cucumbers. Yaakov studied in a Polish school. A private teacher taught him Yiddish and Hebrew. When he grew up he learned mechanics and became a mechanic in the flourmill in town. He loved reading and solitude, talked little and thought deeply. With the elimination of the Ghetto in Korelichi he was brought to the Peresike Ghetto. At the beginning of 1943 he escaped to the forest and joined the Belski's camp. He was a good partisan, tall, broad shouldered, and healthy and loved to work.

He never avoided an action, the hardest of missions were given to him. Though he had no weapon he always came along, never afraid, possibly apathetic towards life, as he said. His aim was to get his own weapon. Once at a peasant's farm he found a dismantled rifle with no butt, he borrowed some tools from another peasant and made a butt, he never worked in carpentry before and said: "My rifle is not beautiful – but it shoots". It was his till he moved to a Russian partisan's unit and there he received a sub-machine gun and a pistol. He helped a lot with the building of the bunkers in the forest and the organising of the camps when we moved from place to place.

He was a bachelor forlorn and lonely. He had no one from his family. He befriended lonely people like him, and helped the weak that could not go to the villages to fend for themselves and therefore their situation was worse. Eventually he became disillusioned with the inequality in Belski's camp. It started when the Lida people arrived in the forest, and silver and gold were to be found in the hands of forest people and the commanders. He befriended Nachman Kirzner the son of the milliner Shmerl Kirzner from Novogrudok. He was a student at the Warsaw Conservatorium, and he also disliked the arrangements in the camp. When people came from the group of Alexander Nyevski to ask who wanted to move to their camp they were the first to volunteer.

Yaakov Slutski became a professional saboteur. He made the bombs, mined the roads and the railways and was known as the best in the battalion. On the fatal night he went with three other partisans to mine the railway. Due to human error they detonated the bomb too early and all of them were killed. He was known among the partisans as a brave Jewish fighter, partisan and a courageous and efficient saboteur. God will avenge his blood.

[Page 364]

My brother Meir

by Yaakov Rudnicki

Translated from Yiddish by O. Delatycki

Meir was born in 1912 in Novogrudok. Even as a youngster he was distinguished by his modesty, goodness and niceness. He was a quite boy, easygoing and good hearted. As a pupil in the gimnazjum [Polish high school] he taught children from poor families without expecting payment. In 1939 he graduated from the faculty of history of the university of Wilno. After the Soviets arrived he was made director of a school in the Slonim district. In August 1942 we escaped from the [Novogrudok] Ghetto and were looking for a hideout in the depth of a forest. We met partisans who were in the process of setting up a unit. The main problem was to obtain arms. A Jewish partisan gave us our first rifle. Meier was standing guard with the rifle when an enemy bullet killed him. I dug his grave in the village of Khrapenevo, not far from the river Neman. I put a big bolder on his grave. From Israel my thoughts turn to the distant grave of my brother Meir. Honour his memory.

[A much more detailed story of the escape from the Ghetto and the events in Khrapenevo is given on p.246 'Outside of the Ghetto' by Lyuba Rudnicki.]

[Page 365]

To the memory of my father
Asael Bielski, z"l

by his daughter, Asaelah

Translated from Hebrew by Aviva Kamil

A

You live with us wherever we go,
Whatever and wherever we think, you are with us.
I did not have the privilege of meeting you because
You were the first with ideas and the first for action:

The first in loving the forest and life of freedom,
To live, and to fight readily the enemy with clear eyes,
Not to be led like a lamb to the slaughter.

B

And when the mob rioted, saturated with hatred, and thirst for blood,
You rose as a father to the elderly, to women and children,
You collected the weak and those lagging behind,
Guided your stooped and sore brothers and sisters.
Paved the way through the thicket of ancient forests
And eternal swamps.
Led them on the road to life and freedom.

C

You loved every human,
Extended your hand to all who asked for it,
Found a cheering word for the distressed and dejected,
Shared your last piece of bread with the hungry,
Therefore you were loved by all, near and far,
Therefore those who knew you will never forget you.
Therefore you are always with us.

D

You were the first in danger and battle.
A model to all who followed you.
Every action, every deed was a mission to you.
Confident, you stepped towards the last battle,
And fell, with pride in your people.
You fell and rose in the memory of your friends.

Your past hometown community,
And your people.
Let your name be among all the names of the heroes
From Jehonathan and Shaul to Bilski Asael.

[Page 366]

How does Novogrudok look now?

by a townsman

Translated from Yiddish by O. Delatycki

A few days ago a met an old acquaintance of mine, who had returned recently from Novogrudok where he had been visiting a friend. I was, naturally, curious to find out about the current state of my home town. I showered my friend with questions about the town and the surrounds. My questions concentrated on three topics: how does Novogrudok look now, what are the present living conditions, and how are the few Jewish survivors in town.

Novogrudok had changed considerably in the 17-18 years since the war [1962-63], my friend began, not just has the town changed, but also the surrounds. The district [oblast'] administration was moved to Baranovichi [this occurred in 1939], a town which had since grown considerably. Novogrudok remained the centre of the sub-district [rayon] (the polish name was powiat). The population had increased (I was told) and numbers now 20,000 inhabitants. This is due to the big influx from the villages. There are big market days on Sundays in the square of Korelich Street, just past the mound of Mendog. They are not, however, the markets as we knew them in the past. There are few horse driven wagons, mostly lorries, and one can not see the old time typical peasant in lapti [slippers woven from sapwood of the pine tree]. You should know, he adds, that the surrounding country-side changed considerably, there are almost no private farms left. All farmers work in kolkhozes.

This is how the new, alien town looks, unlike the old Jewish Novogrudok. The town was destroyed and the new town changed its face and not just metaphorically but in reality. You remember, my friend said, that the centre of the town was destroyed and now looks different. The market place is empty. The long row of shops [rad kromen] no longer exists. The water pump is also gone. It used to produce a characteristic scraping noise in the summer and there was an ice rink around it in the winter, making it a challenge to walk over it with a bucket of water without spilling it. Today it is a big square filled with fir trees. The area where the Mickiewicz Street used to be, all the way to the Sienizyc and Korelicz Streets and Racewle [Rachelo] is a big park in the middle of which is the restored house of the poet Mickiewicz, which is now a museum where visitors come, mainly from all parts of Belarus. On the side of the market place which did not burn down, there are two department stores: one in the house which used to belong to Kiwelewicz and the other in the group of houses between where the pharmacy of Leizerowski used to be and the corner of Grodno Street. The town is growing on the peripheries. There is growth on Slonim Street in the direction of Skrydlewo, also in the space between Slonim and Grodno Streets, down Bazylianski Street in the direction of Pereseka. The famed Yiddish Street was almost completely burnt out. After the war a few houses were rebuilt. The synagogue square is dead. The walls of the ruined great synagogue are reaching to the sky. It is a symbol of the eradicated Jewish life.

The Jewish community in Novogrudok number at present 80 to 90 persons. They are mostly newcomers from other towns who work as officials. Of the original Jewish population 20-30 people remain in town. Dr Gordon, Pinczuk 'the ginger watchmaker', a colourful person from before the war and from the younger generation Eilowicz and a young Wolkin. Nobody is interested in creating a communal Jewish life. They are occupied with their own work. Nobody is concerned with the state of the Jewish cemetery, where many of the grave stones have been removed and used for building materials. The city administration is considering using part of the area of the cemetery for other purposes.

At the mass grave of those killed by the fascists, which is in Pereseka, on the way to Litowka, there is a small grave stone, actually a stone taken from the Jewish cemetery. Another mass grave in Skrydlewo is overgrown and is difficult to get to. And that is all, my friend finished.

It is painful and sad when one looks at the Novogrudok of today and remembers the past. Life goes on in the usual way, the Zamok [castle] stands as before with its old walls, and young, alien children play on the mound, laughing and shouting. Busses filled with people drive past, hammers are beating in the new factories and the trees are waving merrily in the city park. But lonely and forlorn stand the walls of the ancient synagogue, a painful monument to the 400 year old Jewish settlement, a community of famous rabbis, pious students, communal workers and simple, hardworking Litwaks with good souls.

The site of Synagogue Square, photographed in 1991
[Not in original Yizkor Book]

The Jewish cemetery in 1991. All the tombstones had been taken away by the local Soviet authorities in 1958 to build nearby garages and pavements.
[Not in original Yizkor Book]

Members of the Alexander Harkavy committee in the United States, 1960
[Not in original Yizkor Book]

Supporters and members of the Novogrudok Committee, New York, 1960
[Not in original Yizkor Book]

Novogrudok Help committee in Israel 1960
[Not in original Yizkor Book]

Front row from left; Aharon Rudnicki, Luba Rudnicki, Rachel Frankfovitz, Gershon Michl Meiri (Aicher)

Second row from left: Volfovitz Yitchak, Noah Kamen, Yaakov Runicki, Hercl Bruk.

Displaced Persons camp, Fohrenwald, Germany.
A reunion of Novogrudok survivors in 1945.
[Not in original Yizkor Book]

Displaced Persons camp, Fohrenwald, Germany.
A second reunion of survivors, 1946.
[Not in original Yizkor Book]

The Fohrenwald reunion, 1946
[Not in original Yizkor Book]

[Page 367]

The Conclusion

by the editors of Pinkas Novogrudok

Translated from Hebrew by Aviva Kamil

With the conclusion of the Pinkas we regrettably attest that we did not present all that Novogrudok gave to our fathers, their fathers and to us. The town was for hundreds of years a refuge and a home for Jews, who knew the Torah, education and a simple life.

We are grateful to all, among them the dear elderly people, who put pen to paper to write about the town and preserve for eternity its past: its Rabbis, its scholars, the Chasidim and Mitnagdim and above all the majority of the community, the ordinary Jewish working people, the tradesmen and labourers.

But, mainly, the Pinkas was written to tell about the floods of tears and blood in the chapters on the Holocaust and of the heroism of our people. Be blessed you the survivors from the valley of death, you who joined us to tell about your horrific experiences in those horrific days, the years of extermination, and the displays of heroism inside the Ghettos and above all in the forests with the partisans.

We thank all, in Israel and the Diaspora, who contributed to these precious memories of cherished mothers, fathers and children of Israel who were erased from the face of the earth by murderous hands.

Blessing to all, among them the Relief Organization in the name of Alexander Harakavy in the U.S.A, which contributed part of its resources towards the publication of the Pinkas.

We say farewell to you, friends, in Israel, the U.S.A and everywhere else in the hope that you will appreciate our effort. The editors, who faithfully prepared the material, edited it and arranged it for printing, were few, and we ask the forgiveness of the very many of whom we did not know of because of lack of information, and, therefore, their names and life-stories are not included in this book.

On behalf of all of you we express our thanks to the workers of Achdut Print in Tel-Aviv who made an effort to make the Pinkas worthy of its name.

And, again, we remember the splendid personality, Edna Kagan, who faithfully and generously helped with the preparation of the Pinkas but did not live to see its completion. Her soul is bound in the pages of the Pinkas.

We remember also Dr.Eliezer Yerushalmi, who was the main editor at the beginning of the composition of the Pinkas and died an untimely death never to see its completion.

Let the Pinkas be a testimony, a document and a brotherly covenant to all Jews of Novogrudok and the surrounds.

And let this covenant last for years to come.

And last: very recently we received from a faithful friend the following dreadful description: Novogrudok today, the gentile (Goyshe) town, blossoms. What about the Jews? 90 are left. And the mass graves? Weeds cover them. So, we will repeat and say to ourselves and to our descendants' -Yzkor! (Remember).

The Editors of Pinkas Novogrudok

> *[At the time the Pinkas was translated - 2003 - the condition of Novogrudok could not be described as blossoming. Other, far less favourable, words come to mind. In 1999, out of the 6000 Jews, who lived in town pre World War II, there were 3 Jews who were born in Novogrudok and less than a total of 30 Jews in all. There is one improvement - the four mass graves have memorials erected and the surrounds are well kept, due to the generosity of Jack Kagan of London. The murderers succeeded - Jewish Novogrudok is no more.]*

[Page 371]
The Blood Bond with the Land of Israel

To Those Who Fell for Their country

Ozer Gorodiski

by Dr. S. Openhaim

Translated from Hebrew by Aviva Kamil

He was born in Novogrudok and fell in the defence of Jerusalem.

Among the figures of the emancipation movement we must mention the 'Father' of 'Hachalutz Hatzair' in Novogrudok- Ozer Gorodiski. He dedicated all his energy to that movement. He started his activity in 'Hachalutz' and 'Poalei-Zion' and, to develop the activities of 'Hachalutz' further, he established in Novogrudok 'Hachalutz-Hatzair'.

In the movement he was an exemplary pioneer. During the day he was busy at his trade as a mechanic and his free time was dedicated to the movement. He organised the staff of Madrichim. Because of his efforts members were sent to the Seminar of 'Hachalutz-Hatzair', he fostered neighbourly relations with the surrounding towns and spread the word of the movement there. Many of the youth were sent to Israel and cast deep roots there.

I remember the meeting of the members of 'Hachalutz-Hatzir' of Novogrudok and Wselub, which took place mid-way between the two towns. The subject of the meeting was the discussion of the book 'Kidush-Hashem' (martyrdom) by Shalom Ash. The two branches prepared themselves well and it was a special experience.

Another example is worth mentioning: It was decided to establish a library in our branch. The members enrolled to do odd jobs in their free time and the money earned was donated to the library. Many books were acquired in this way. Who could count the activities that were guided by the 'Madrich', the father, the friend Ozer Gorodiski? We established a drama circle together with all the youth movements in town and performed the play 'Masadah' by Yitzchak Lamdan. It was a tremendous success, so much so that after the 'Hachsharah' we were invited to Novogrudok for a second performance. He was active in collecting money for the 'Blue Box' etc. I met Ozer Gorodinski on the 'Hachsharah' in Lida, Nieman and Bialystok; he also distinguished himself there by being a devoted, active member of the committee. He visited the 'Hachshara' branches that were established in the surrounding towns. When 'Aliyah' was stopped, he urged the members to be patient and prepare more people for 'Aliyah', when it would be re-established.

When he arrived in Eretz-Israel in 1933, he could not adapt to the social life. He started a family and was occupied with taking care of it. He moved from one place to the other: from the kibbutz to Tel-Aviv, from Tel-Aviv to Rechovot, where he worked as a guard at the railway station. During the riots of 1936-9 he moved with his family to Jerusalem. And during the War of Independence he fell in the defence of Jerusalem.

All those who knew him intimately considered him a humane and altruistic man. He fulfilled his duty to the last and fell in the defence of his country.

Yekutiel Solchinski (Kushi)

(from the booklet published to his memory by Kibbutz Na'an in a year after his death)

by Bilha Dalet in the month of Iyar, Taf, Shin, Tet (1949)

Translated from Hebrew by Aviva Kamil

Kushi was born in Novogrudok, son to a working family with many children. His mother died when he was a child and since then he helped his father in his work, till he decided that his future was in Eretz-Israel. He went through the Hachsharah in all its stages. He moved from one Hachsharah to the next until he reached Kibbutz Augustow. He stayed there for many years, because he did not have money for 'Aliyah'. Finally he obtained a certificate.

I won't forget our journey and how devoted he was to his friends, carrying luggage for one or taking care of food for another. That was his character; he wanted to help everyone with things big and small. We came to Na'an as a group. For many of us it was difficult to adjust to work in the Kibbutz, but Kushi immediately found his place in the carpentry workshop. And wherever he was, he carried responsibility above expectations. After a few years he decided to change his job and became a driver. To do that, he had to leave the Kibbutz for a short time. When he returned to Na'an he started a family and built his home there. But again he became involved in disagreements with the Kibbutz and left. When the British Army surrounded Kibbutz Na'an and most of its members were arrested and put behind barbwire, Kushi was among the first to rush to help them. After a few weeks he began to feel that the kibbutz was his place and he returned to Na'an. He started to rebuild his house and was happy in the fold of his growing family. He was a devoted father and took a good care of his own. He was aglow with happiness. When the days of the battles arrived, and death was waiting on the roads, he was going his way as usual. I remember him coming to the packing shed to say good-bye without telling us where he was going. And we did not feel in our hearts that we wouldn't see him again in our midst.

[Page 372]

With Kushi in his Last Days

by Shlomoleh Shwartz

Translated from Hebrew by Aviva Kamil

It was by chance that we met each other, Kushi and I.

We met for the first time in a truck in a convoy to Jerusalem and later for 6 weeks in Kfar-Etzion, until it fell to the enemy. On one of these days, on a Saturday, I drove a truck loaded with sacks of flour to Jerusalem. On the Sunday I returned to Tel-Aviv to load the truck again, but I did not have a second driver with me to go to Jerusalem. Kushi was in Tel-Aviv then and it was suggested in the 'movement' office that he would escort me, until a new driver could be found.

In the morning we left Rechovot. The journey from the Moshavah (Rechovot) to the road Masmia-Latrun lasted 12 hours. After we passed Ekron the convoy became bogged down in mud and Kushi walked home (to Na'an) and brought a tractor to help extract the trucks. At home he saw his daughter Shlomit for the last time and told her that he was going to Jerusalem and would be back in a few days. Who knew then that he would not see his loved ones and Na'an again! Hours passed as we were extracting the bogged vehicles. In the meantime a convoy on its way back from Jerusalem passed us, and the people said that the road was quiet, they had no problems and no one attacked them. At 7 o'clock in the evening we were ready to continue, but we still waited for another half hour. We were told that a unit of the Palmach in an armoured vehicle left Kiryat-Anavim and was travelling towards us to check the road. When they came the convoy started to move.

We arrived at Sha'ar-Hagai when it was dark. Of course we drove with no lights, the convoy progressed slowly.

Before we left Rechovot, Israel Galili wanted to join us to arrange some money matters for Na'an in Jerusalem. We convinced him not to go because we did not know when we would be able to return. He explained to Kushi what the issue was and asked him to arrange things for him in Jerusalem. That night at 11 o'clock we arrived in Jerusalem with no trouble. All the vehicles that were loaded with 'Tnuvah' products (farm products) were unloaded at night and in the morning they returned to Tel-Aviv. Our vehicles were loaded with flour and were detained for a day in Jerusalem. The next day, a Wednesday, a convoy to Jerusalem was heavily attacked. Eleven vehicles were damaged and were left on the road. It was only on the Thursday night that the convoy managed to open the road to get through to Jerusalem. In the meantime we stayed behind and waited for a returning convoy.

We were told to return to Tel-Aviv on Friday with the convoy that had come the previous day. We assembled, as ordered, at 6 o'clock in the morning near the Hospital Wolach. Kushi had managed to arrange all of the business that Israel Galili asked him to do.

We waited for two hours that morning and suddenly an order was given to go to the Shenler building. The atmosphere in the town was tense, and there was fear of what was coming. We heard exchanges of fire all night.

When we came to the Shenler building we were told to load supplies for Kfar-Etzion. One convoy, which had left the previous week, did not succeed in opening the road. (The enemy knew about this convoy and that was why it had failed). This time they decided to travel secretly.

It was not that simple. Many drivers were not happy to go. Many were members of Kibbutzim, had jobs to do in their Kibbutz and they could not decide on their own initiative what was the best thing to do. There were also problems with the city drivers. After much negotiation it was decided to go. On the eve of Sabbath, till mid-night, they were loading the trucks. That evening a festive meal was given to the people of the convoy. We were 50 drivers in all. Half of us were farmers. At 3 o'clock in the morning a bus collected us from the hotels, but we still did not depart. The preparations took 5 hours. We started to move at 8 o'clock. It was a huge convoy, scores of trucks, armoured vehicles and buses. 120 tons of supplies were loaded. With us went the Palmach armoured units and members of 'Chish'(Cheil-Sadeh, Haganah), who were going to replace the students from Jerusalem at Kfar-Etzion. We arrived without incidence to 'Gush-Etzion' (the Etzion-Bloc consisted of 5 settlements). They were ready for us at the Centre and they unloaded the supplies with speed. It did not take more then 20 minutes. The parking area was spacious and the trucks filled the whole area. Everything was unloaded onto the ground and carts went back and forth to bring the supplies for the settlements. When the unloading ended, a few trucks, and we among them, were instructed to take a load back. We loaded three mules onto our truck, the second truck took a bull and the third one took a plane with no wings. We stayed in the Gush (Etzion Bloc) for no more then an hour and a half. Because Kushi and I were busy loading, we were among the last in the returning convoy. When we were ready to move, reconnaissance planes informed us that the enemy had blocked the road in many places. When we departed the enemy opened fire on the convoy. We were together all the time, Kushi and I. He was in a quiet mood, ready, caring and doing all he had to do.

At the head of the convoy was the bulldozer. When we came to the first roadblock, which was cleared, we saw an upturned vehicle in the ditch beside the road. We did not see the drivers. (I found out later that they had been taken out of the vehicle). We advanced slowly and stopped from time to time until a new roadblock was cleared. All the time we were being shot at from ambushes along the road.

We had reached Nebi-Daniel when an accident occurred. The bulldozer broke down and we stopped. Kushi was sitting beside me. One of his jobs was to look around and observe what was happening. He was guarding the shutter. He shut it and opened it in order to see the road.

We had only a small gun for our defence and we were ready to jump out instantly if the truck would be put out of action. We remained at Nebi-Daniel for an hour and a half until the middle-link(?) together with the commanders turned back and went from vehicle to vehicle ordering all to turn back and return to the Gush. We managed to turn around with the help of a sidetrack. Kushi directed me, so that I would not skid into the ditch. We advanced towards the armoured cars that waited for us and continued to move to the direction of the Gush. Again, we encountered a roadblock that the Arabs, in the meantime, had managed to build. We were ordered to cross the roadblock. At the beginning of the journey we were the last in the convoy, on turning back we were among the first. There was no choice, we started to drive over the piles of stones with our truck and with great effort we managed to cross it. Barbwire was caught in the wheels and tore the brake cables. The truck continued and the wires were striking the bottom the truck. It sounded like a machine gun. But we knew only one thing: we must break the roadblocks and continue our journey. Somehow we reached the Gush. We were fortunate that the tyres were intact and so was the truck, thanks to the armour which was installed in Na'an.

While still driving, we opened for an instant the back shutter and saw that the mules were bleeding and dying. When we were out of danger we started to check our truck. Kushi lay under the truck and tried to pull out the barbwire off the wheels. At Kfar Etzion we sat by the wireless, and heard with dread the broadcasts about the fate of the people who did not manage to return with us. Only 5 trucks and 4 armoured cars managed to return. All the others were stuck, they could not move on nor could they return. For 28 hours they fought the enemy and the mob that was called in from the surrounding area. In Kfar Etzion they asked us whether we wanted to stay or to go on to Revadim. We told them that we wanted to stay. The mountain weather was harsh. Heavy fog covered everything. The rain came down and we were sick at heart. Kushi sent a note to his home with one of the pilots, I think it was Pinyeleh. He told them that we were all right, that we were back in the Gush. He did not forget to inform Na'an that the truck was also OK. He also brought a cheque for 750 Israeli Lirot that was given to him in the 'Sochnut' for Israel Galili. During the next day the Palmach commander came to the Gush (by air of course) and cheered us up. He promised that he would do everything to break the roadblocks in the next few days. But after a few days the situation worsened and we knew that the road was closed and there was no possibility to pass through. Kushi and I made a habit of climbing onto the roof every morning when the weather was fine to observe the surrounds and mainly Na'an, which was so close and yet so far. We could distinguish the clamps of trees in the valley, the houses of Na'an and the silo that looked like a white finger. Days went by and we were still under siege. In the meantime the sky cleared. We decided to work. It felt like being at the front. Sometimes there were barrages of shooting but no raids. We, the drivers and other Kibbutz members who were stuck there, discussed our situation with the commander of the Gush. The only chance was to get out by air. He told us that the queue for getting out was long and the wounded were the most important, but because our right of return to our Kibbutz was recognised, every third person that went out would be a driver. But that did not happen too quickly. The situation in the country and in the Gush worsened. The order was to sabotage Arab roads as a counter act. Apparently some of the British soldiers who were about were hit by 'Haganah' mines. They decided to penalise the Gush and opened cannon fire on the monastery that was in our hands. It was more or less quiet in Kfar-Etzion. Only an exchange of fire was heard now and then.

The situation continued till the end of April. Communication by air grew. The 'Primusim' (Piper planes) that arrived managed to take back four Kibbutz drivers. We were 8 drivers in all and had a raffle to decide on the order of leaving. Kushi was the fifth on the list and he was next to leave, I was among the last. But attacks started again and they were heavier and departures stopped.

On the 4th of May, in the early hours of the morning, the British and the Legion (Jordanian army) opened an attack on the monastery and the observation point, and they captured them.

In the afternoon a disaster occurred, a shell hit the tent were the Palmach unit had assembled, ready to attempt to take the monastery again. Six members were killed and six were seriously wounded. Four of us, Kushi amongst us, took stretchers to carry the wounded to the hospital. The path, which was 500 meters from camp, was difficult, tiring and open to enemy fire. Now and then we had to run for cover with the stretchers. We brought a wounded man - it was Arie Berman, who was in 'Hachsharah' in Na'an - to the hospital. During the attack all the patients were taken out of the hospital and were put down on stretchers in the communication trenches.

On the same night a scout was sent to the monastery and came back with the information that no one was there. We retook it and fortified ourselves again.

With that heavy attack with so many wounded, our attempt of departure was abandoned. We were healthy and needed for defence and work. We went to work on the airfield. Mainly the Palmach put in a great effort to establish the airfield. It was known that the fate of the Gush depended greatly on the airfield because the only contact with the rest of the country was by air. This was necessary for arms, for people to join battle or sometimes to be brought out urgently.

Kushi did any and every type of work, he befriended many Palmach people and local members. He was alert and his spirit did not falter. I could feel that he won the appreciation of the people around him. He managed to get a straw-hat, grew a moustache and was recognised from afar. In the evenings we sat together telling each other stories. Kushi talked a lot about his past, about the farm he had before returning to Na'an, about his family and children. He sat for hours writing letters home, I do not know if all of them reached their destination.

On the 12th of May, Wednesday morning, we were woken up at dawn to the sound of shooting. We lived near the command post and always knew what was happening. After an hour we had heard that the Legion had taken back, after a heavy battle, the observation post called 'Ukaf-Hamuchtar'.

Two units of P.L.M, (Haganah) with their commander wanted to reach the observation post but did not succeed. The field was under heavy enemy fire; they found cover among the rocks but could not retreat either. The Gush commander also advanced with his units towards the monastery in an effort to help the people who were fighting there. At 10 o'clock in the morning the monastery fell. The Gush commander was killed, part of the people managed to retreat to Kfar-Etzion and to Masuot and many were killed. Then the bombardment of Kfar-Etzion started.

That morning I was with Kushi until 9 o'clock. We stayed near the commanding room and waited for instructions. At 9 a.m. a shell fell near-by. It shattered the window panes, we rushed out and saw a wounded local man. We took him to the hospital, a distance of 200 meters. The patients were again carried on stretchers out of the hospital to the trenches.

When I came back from the hospital I saw Kushi but did not see Ernest from Giv'at Brener, who was with us all the time. I found a temporary cover in the trench; the firing did not stop. I felt shells falling near-by I jumped out of the trench into the commanding-room, I found out that the telephone wires were torn and communication to the positions around were stopped. I was sent to one position to find out what they needed, came out, crawling and sprinting from house to house and from tree to tree and reached the house near that position, shouting to them the instructions that were given to me. On my way back I met Ernest and he told me that he and Kushi were being sent to deliver messages. We did not have more to do and wanted to enter the shelter. The shelter had two entrances, one from the house and one from the outside; we could not get into the house because it was completely blocked. We were told to go around the house. When jumping through the window to reach the other entrance, a shell exploded and we were both injured. In the shelter we received first aid.

In the shelter I met Kushi who had returned from his work. I was wounded and talking was difficult. He was concerned about me, but waited with expectation for the next action. Evening fell, the commander came down the shelter and asked all the healthy ones to take weapons and follow him. It seemed that people were needed to take the place of those in the defence positions who grew tired and needed some rest. Kushi was given a rifle, checked it and gave me a good-bye look, then left. I did not see him again.

In the evening the fire subsided. I went up to my room and found there the Palmach people sitting and resting on the floor. They were ready for a counter attack the same night. I remember well the girl who was with them, Rachel Viner; she gave all of them chocolate. Later she also found her death in Kfar-Etzion. Those were the fighters that Kushi and his friends replaced in the defence positions.

At mid-night a unit arrived from Masuot and after inspecting the road it was decided to move the hospital with its workers and injured to Masuot, it was safer there. All were assembled and moved in convoy after convoy. The transfer lasted 4 hours. They walked silently in the dark; the sick were carried on stretchers, the guards in the front and at the back. The Legion sat on 'Mishlat Harusim' (observation post), We passed very close to them. This was necessary if we wanted to avoid the shelling. At a distance of 500 meters we saw the Legion's soldiers with their armoury sitting around small fires to keep themselves warm.

On the following day, Thursday the 13th of May, Kfar-Etzion fell. Kushi was there. The enemy captured most of the people. Miraculously 4 people escaped. We in Masuot knew that it was the last battle. We saw flames rising from the burning village and feared for the fate of the people there. Later we heard that one member got out of there. We could not talk to him, because he was seriously wounded.

Only when we were taken from the Gush to the police station in Chevron, did I see among the group of women prisoners' one girl who was on the last day in Kfar Etzion and she saw Kushi. I shouted to her: 'What happened to Kushi?' She did not answer only moved her hand in a despairing gesture, I understood.

I became a prisoner, and in my heart was the memory of a friend that on the last day was separated from me by fate.

[Page 374]

Reuven Openheim

by his father Shmuel Openheim

Translated from Hebrew by Aviva Kamil

Reuven Openheim was born on the 20th of September 1927. Fell in the battle of Latrun on kaf'alef in the month of Iyar, year Taf Shin 'Chet - 30. 5.1948

In his childhood he already exhibited his special character. When he reached the age of six he decided to go to school, but the school accepted only students from the age of seven. He did not despair and went to school day after day with his brother, who was a year and a half older. He was leaving home with him in the morning, staying around in the school corridor and after school returning home with his brother. This lasted for approximately two month until the school principal admitted him. He caught up with the pupils in a short time, though the others were older and started earlier.

He was very active during the elections to the Zionist Congress. He distributed propaganda material, facts, figures and so on.

Of course he was a great supporter of number 5 - the League of Eretz Israel Haovedet (the workers of the land of Israel). When the German-Russian war started he was 14 years of age, life worsened day-by-day, even wise adults lost their senses, but he calmly, went from place to place, listened to adults talking, heard the news, returned home and calmed his family down He went on doing what had to be done to ease the suffering. He started, almost without tools, to build a hand- pulled cart; he felt that it would be needed. When the Germans ordered the Jews to leave their homes within a few hours and take only what could be taken by hand, we appreciated the cart that he built.

During the night of the second slaughter, in August 1942, all the Jews in the Pereshike Ghetto were arrested, and no one was allowed to leave. Reuven worked then for the Germans outside the Ghetto preparing wood for the kitchen and carrying water from the well. He sneaked into the Ghetto through the fence, took his four year old sister out and hid her in the wood store where he worked. In the evening he brought her with him to the Court House, sneaked through the wire fence and together they hid in the cellar till the end of the slaughter.

After the slaughter everyone understood that we had no chance to stay alive. Any one who could, tried to sneak out of the Ghetto and escape to the forest, especially the young. Among them was his older brother. After 2 months, his older brother returned from the forest to the work camp in the Court building, in order to pick up people and smuggle them into the forest. He managed to bring out about 30 people, among them his brother Reuven. After a week, Reuven entered the Ghetto with the water carriers (people who carried water to the Ghetto from an outside well), they asked him for the reason of his return, and he told them that a rumour was heard outside the ghetto that the Germans were going to kill the rest of the Jews of Novogrudok. He therefore came to save his parents and little sister, to take them out of the Court House and smuggle them into the forest. It took him many days and weeks to convince his parents to get out of the Ghetto. They could not believe that it was possible to live in the forest in the cold winter with a little girl. He took out his mother, his sister and a few other young people; they were the first to get out when suddenly a German guard appeared. His father was left inside. He brought that group of people to a peasant who was in contact with the partisans, left them there and went again the next morning into the Ghetto with the water carriers to take out his father, but there was no possibility to get out. He waited for a week and the chance arrived, he brought out his father with another 30 people. It was January and it was a very cold winter. We walked, only at night, through the fields and streams. People fell through the thin ice into the river, they managed to get out but their feet were frozen and so were Reuven's feet. Afterwards a story was circulating about him in the forest: When he went back to bring his parents out, he went with partisans who were on an operation mission. On the way he fell asleep and dropped off the sled, when back at base they noticed his absence. He slept for a while in the snow, got up and came together with peasants who drove to the market place in Novogrudok. During his stay in the forest he was suffering, for a long time, with his feet, but regardless of all that he fulfilled all the tasks that befitted his age. He was sick with typhus in the forest, there was no hospital and not basic living conditions but he overcame that too.

After the liberation in July 1944, he returned with his family to Novogrudok. From there he and his brother were the first go to Poland. They settled in the town Chelm.

After a time he returned to Novogrudok, crossing the border on top of a military train that went from Poland to Russia. Once more he came to take his parents out of Russia to Poland. Reuven waited for about 2 months until it was possible to transfer his parents to Poland. Coming with his parents to Chelm, he urged them to leave Poland. He told them that there was no place for Jews in Poland. In the meantime he fell ill with typhus and it took him 2 months to partially recover. He did not wait to be completely cured. Still weak, he joined his family and left Poland with the "Brichah" (escape) to Salzburg in Austria. They stayed there for a few days and moved to the Foehrenwald camp in Germany. There he started High School studies in the morning and in the afternoon he was trained as turner and fitter in the Technical school "Ort". All this time he urged his parents to find a way to reach Eretz-Israel. He, as a young man, could go to Eretz-Israel by "Aliyah B" (illegal migration), but the parents with their little daughter could not take travel that way and he did not want to be separated from his family. In July 1947 he left Germany with his family and in September 1947 they arrived in Eretz-Israel and were transferred to "Beit-Haolim" (the house for immigrants) in Bat-Galim, Haifa.

After the 29th of November 1947, when riots started, Reuven was among the first to heed the call for volunteers, but first he did all he could to find a permanent place for his parents, which involved a lot of running around and some times even risk to his life on the roads. He found a home for his parents in Kiryat-Chaim near Haifa and two days later he joined the army. During all his time in the Army he visited home only once, for a day, on Passover 1948. It was the last time he saw his family.

He fell in the battle of Latrun on (Kaf'Alef in the month of Iyar Taf Shin'Chet) 30th of May 1948, It is not known till today where he was buried.

His tombstone is in the section for the Unknown Soldiers in the Military Cemetery on the "memorial mountain" in Jerusalem, among all those soldiers whose burial places were never found.

> *[As I was working on this translation, I realised that a few days ago Jack Kagan of London had written that, after 52 years, the remains of Reuven Openheim were found and identified at Latrun. The coincidence was incredible. I was overwhelmed. OD]*

An article in the Jerusalem Post of 24 April, 2001 says:

"The body of Pvt. Reuven Oppenheim, killed at Latrun during the War of Independence, has been located by the IDF.

Oppenheim, a Polish Holocaust survivor who immigrated in 1947 was killed on May 30, 1948 while evacuating casualties during the battle for Laturn. He was not identified and buried as an "unknown" in the temporary mass grave at Na'an. Later he was interred at the Nahala Yitzhak Military Cemetery.

The head of the IDF unit for locating MIAs, Maj. Gen. Yehuda Segev said that Oppenheim's body was identified beyond all doubt on the basis of Testimony and documentation.

[This not was not part of the original Yizkor Book, JK]

[Page 376]

Eliezer Kriner

by a friend

Translated from Hebrew by Aviva Kamil

He was called 'Kusha' or 'Kushi', son of Arie and Rivkah from Novogrudok. He was born on the 15 March 1928 in Tel-Aviv and grew up in a traditional home. He attended a boy's school, a commercial school and studied for two and a half years at a law and commerce school in Tel-Aviv. He worked for a lawyer.

His teachers, appreciating his talents, encouraged him to study. He scrutinised every problem thoroughly and in depth and it looked as if he was having fun. He did not study hard for his matriculation exams. He was always ready to help others with their studies and was ready with good advice. He was sociable, able, lively and amusing.

At the age of 14 he joined the Gad'Na (youth units of the Haganah) He put his energy into Hadracha and Chag'am (guide in the youth movement). He attended a course for squad-commanders and at the end of his studies in the Gymnasium joined the 'Notrim' (Jewish guards). He enrolled in an Officers course in Ruchama and was under the command of the 'Notrim' station in Tel-Chaim. His friends and his subordinates liked him. He helped them all he could.

With the declaration of the partition by the United-Nation, he took part in the battles in Abu-Kalbar, Selma, Yazur and Manshia and was noted for his courage. In Yazur he broke into the enemy lines with his attacking unit, without covering fire. He became an instructor in a squad-commanders course in Saronah. He completed a lieutenant's course and served in the 53rd battalion of 'Chativat-Giv'ati'. He went with his people on several missions, such as escorting convoys, scouting, sabotage and mine planting. He took part in the battles of Gat, Nitzanim, Falujah and others. 'I have no right to take care of my own survival only' he used to say. On 21.4.1948 with his platoon he broke into Beit-Daras for the purpose of diverting the enemy from Nitzanim, which was under heavy attack. At the end of the battle he went to look for one of his people and was injured in his leg. When he was carried to an armoured car he was injured twice again by the British, who had appeared in the meantime.

Eliezer Kriner

He was taken to the Hadassah Hospital in Tel-Aviv and suffered for three and a half months. Despite all that his morale was high and he was planning for the future. His friends admired him.

He died on the Rosh Chodesh Av Taf Shin'Chet 5.8.1948

Luka Shapiro

by a friend

Translated from Hebrew by Aviva Kamil

Luka Shapiro

I remember you, my dear Luka, from your childhood. You were a strong, brave boy. You were an example of courage and power. You loved sport, your body was fit and tough. On the coldest days in winter, we saw you wearing shorts and your knees were bare. You were among the first in town to join Maccabbi and Hashomer-Hatzair. You were coach of sports and drills. At the festivities of Lag Baomer you marched at the head of the movement's procession, proud and energetic. You were a true friend, always ready to help others. With the outbreak of the World War II, when the Red Army occupied Novogrudok, you were deported with others to Siberia. You were a prisoner in a concentration camp. You were deeply worried about your lonely parents, from whom you heard nothing. After the agreement between Sikorski, the head of the Polish ?migr? government in London and Stalin, many Polish citizens were released, you were one of them. You enlisted in the Polish Army. One day we met in Eretz-Israel, you were a corporal in the Polish Army, devoted and ready for battle, to fight and take revenge on the Germans, to fight to the victory. Once on a clear day you came to say good-bye to me: "I am leaving the country" you said "I am going to fight the Germans, though it is not easy for me to leave this land".

You died in a battle in Italy [Monte Cassino]. You fell serving in a foreign army, in a foreign land.

Blessed be your memory.

[Page 377]

A List

We will remember the Names of the Martyrs of Novogrudok, its vicinity and Karelich

Translated by Oskar Delatycki

As I am approaching the end of the long and difficult task of editing and translating "Pinkas Navaredok" I must confess that, would I have realised the magnitude and the difficulty of the task, I may not have had the courage to undertake it. I will not list the numerous problems, the endless hours.

The final job, which I dreaded most, was translating and compiling the list of the Jewish martyrs of Novogrudok and Karelich. I would not have been able to accomplish this job without the invaluable help of David Grynberg.

There are, without doubt, many and varied errors in the names listed. This is inevitable. Worse still, many names of individuals and families are missing in the lists, perhaps to be forgotten for ever. I will attempt to make an estimate of the size of the loss.

I think that it is important to review the events leading up to the almost total annihilation of the Jewish population of Novogrudok and the surrounding district.

What follows next is based on information supplied by Jack Kagan.

Novogrudok was bombed heavily by the Germans on Saturday 28 June 1941 with some loss of life and a great loss of homes by fire. The Germans occupied Novogrudok on Friday 4 July 1941.

The Germans lost no time in making clear their intentions. The following events were described in blood curdling testimonials of witnesses. On the 6 July 1941 the Germans started a series of tortures and murders of groups of Jews in the jail and in Skrydlevo. Some of those detained were allegedly taken to work, but had never been seen again. Most of those selected were professionals and merchants. It is estimated that 150-200 people from Novogrudok were killed in that period.

Early in July 1941 the Germans brought 105 Jewish men from Karelich and shot them in the killing fields of Skrydlevo.

On the 26 of July 1941, the Jews were assembled in the market square, 52 were picked out at random and shot on the spot, while a German military band was playing Strauss.

There were four mass slaughters:

The warning of the first slaughter came on Friday the 5 December 1941, when the Jews were ordered not to go back to work from Saturday the 6th of December. Very early in the morning of the 6th of December 1941 all Jews of Novogrudok were ordered to assemble, some in the Court House others in the Convent of the sisters of Nazareth. Most Jews, disregarding the order, went to the Court House. On that day Jews from the surrounding villages and the town of Wsielub were brought to Novogrudok. On the 8th December the Germans arranged a selection process at the Court House. At least 5100 were selected to die and were murdered on the same day by the Germans, assisted by Lithuanian and Belarusian police, at Skrydlevo. The killed included all Jews who were in the convent, as well as most villagers and the Jews from Wsielub. About 300 Jews were shot whilst trying to escape. About 1100 to 1300 Jews survived.

The Ghetto in Novogrudok was formed on the 10 December 41 in the suburb of Pereseka. On that day the surviving Jews were transferred from the Court House to the Ghetto.

A memorial for 5100 victims was erected on the site of the first slaughter in Skrydlevo.

In about March 1942 the tradesmen from the Ghetto and their equipment from various workshops in town were moved to the Court House, which had become a labour camp. In charge was a German sadist by the name of Reuter. Reuter had two hobbies: to thrash mercilessly Jews at any time without any reason and to mislead the Jews when a slaughter was approaching

Most of the Jews killed in the second slaughter were brought to Novogrudok from the towns and villages in the district in May/June 1942 and put into the Ghetto in Pereseka.

In the process of assembling the Jews from the district many Jews were killed in the townships they lived in or on the way to Novogrudok. The Jews of Lubch were made to walk 25km to Novogrudok. On leaving Lubch, children were taken away from their parents. The parents were told that the children will be taken to a crèche. The children were shot later that day.

On the 7 August 1942 the second large massacre took place, when Jews from the Ghetto were shot in Litovka, about 1.5 kilometres from the Ghetto, by Estonian policemen and buried next to the Pereseka – Litovka road.

The local people did not know the number that arrived from the surrounding towns and therefore could not estimate how many were killed in the second slaughter. At present the best guess is 4000.

On the 4th of February 1943 the third massacre took place. All remaining Jews from the Pereseka Ghetto were murdered and buried in a mass grave next to the victims of the second massacre. About 500 Jews were slaughtered. The Pereseka Ghetto was closed.

The conditions prevailing in Novogrudok at the time the monument for the two slaughters was being made did not allow for careful estimation nor for hesitation. It is written on that monument that 5500 were killed in the two slaughters. The actual number is 4500-5000.

The three slaughters in Novogrudok were executed under the command of Waldemar Amelung, a German from Riga, who disappeared after the war. The slaughters were ordered by the Gebietskommissar Wilhelm Traub, who was the slayer of the Jews of Novogrudok for the duration of the occupation.

After the war three monuments were erected close to the small village of Kot'ki. The monuments were put up on the graves of 10,000 (another source gives the figure of 7870) Jews of the Dvorec Ghetto, killed on the 28 December 1942 (13 December 1942). 51 Jews were retained in the Dvorec Ghetto and were killed and buried there shortly after. These are sites of a major slaughter.

The Ghetto in Dvorec was set up in spring 1942 and contained the entire Jewish population of 400. This number was rapidly increased by the arrival of Jews from the Ghettos of Ivenec, Rubezevichi, Derevnoe, Naliboki, Volmy, Kamen', Lubchi, Molchad', Korelichi, Dyatlovo as well as from a few large Polish towns.

Most of the prisoners worked on removing gravel from a field at the village of Vasevichi, where the soviets started building in 1941 a military aerodrome. The gravel was used for the maintenance of the Lida to Baranovichi railway line.

In 2004 the bodies of the 51 Jews buried in the centre of Dvorec were exhumed and reburied in the Jewish cemetery in Dyatlovo.

On the 7th May 1943 a group from the Court House, reported variously to number 250, 300 or 350, was shot by the Belarusian police and buried off Karelich St (now Minsk St.) in Hordzielovka, within sight of the Court House. The victims were mostly women from the Court House labour camp.

A memorial to 250 victims was erected on the site in Hardzielovka.

The memorials in Skrydlevo, Pereseka and Hardzielovka were erected by Jack Kagan.

Apart of the killings described above, Jews were being killed singly and in groups almost daily by the Germans and their henchmen in the Ghetto, in the labour camp, in jail, in the barracks and elsewhere during the German occupation. It is not possible to assess accurately the number of victims in those murders.

We estimate that more than 10,000 Jews, most from Novogrudok and the surrounding district, were killed in Novogrudok. The exact number or a close approximation will never be known.

The last surviving 250 captives constructed in the Court House labour camp a 250 metre long tunnel and escaped through it on the 26 September 1943. About 80 were killed while escaping. Most of the others survived the war in the Bielski partisan group.

About 700 Jews of Novogrudok survived the war. Almost 400 Jews survived in the Bielski partisans, of them more than 170 came from the Ghetto through the tunnel. Without the safe shelter in the Bielski partisans the heroic construction of the tunnel would have saved very few lives. About 300 Jews from Novogrudok returned from Russia after the war. Of those most escaped from Novogrudok ahead of the German army. Most of the others were arrested or deported by the Soviets. On the night of the 19/20 June 1941 (two days before the start of the German-Soviet war) about a hundred Novogrudok Jews were deported or arrested as part of the 4th mass deportation. About 10% of them died in the Soviet Union during the war.

In the 1950's the Soviets permitted and encouraged the local population to vandalise the Jewish cemetery in Novogrudok. The memorials were removed and were used as foundations, for road repair etc. The fence and the ornate gate were removed. With the help of the Novogrudok committee in Israel and Jack Kagan the fence was repaired and a monument was erected. Further restoration is planned.

At the beginning of the war Novogrudok had a population of 10,000, of which 6000 were Jews. In 1999 there were 30 Jews in Novogrudok.

In the Pinkas Navaredok are lists of Jews that were living in Novogrudok and Karelich at the beginning of the war and were killed by the Germans.

The list of the Jews of Novogrudok killed by the Germans contains about 2400 names or 40% of the Jews of Novogrudok that were killed. The list of the Jews of Karelich has about 850 names or about 65% of the Karelich Jews that were killed.

Names of the Martyrs of Novogrudok, it's vicinity and Karelich

A

ABOWICZ	Rebecn
ABOWICZ	Jakow, son, family
ABRAMOWICZ	Szrage
ABRAMOWICZ	Ciwia
ABRAMOWICZ	Henia
ABRAMOWICZ	Aron
ABRAMOWICZ	Dinka
ABRAMOWICZ	Sara, child
ABRAMOWICZ	Eliezer
ABRAMOWICZ	Szeina
ABRAMOWICZ	Jakob
ABRAMOWICZ	Szlomo
ABRAMOWICZ	Fruma
ABRAMOWICZ	Szmuel
ABRAMOWICZ	Rachel
ABRAMOWICZ	Benjamin
ABRAMOWICZ	Faiwl (Szraga)
ABRAMOWICZ	Pesia
ABRAMOWICZ	Jehoszua
ABRAMOWICZ	Ester
ABRAMOWICZ	Batia
ABRAMOWICZ	Sara
ABRAMOWICZ	Szlomo
ABRAMOWICZ	Nioma
ABRAMOWICZ	Mula
ABRAMOWSKI	Zalmon
ABRAMOWSKI	Malka
ABRAMOWSKI	Izchak
ABRAMOWSKI	Zelda, 3 daughters
AJZIKOWICKI	Awraham
AJZIKOWICKI	Munia
AIZIKOWICZ	Jakow
AIZIKOWICZ	Rochl
AIZIKOWICZ	Izchak
AIZIKOWICZ	Rywka Lea
AIZIKOWICZ	Chaim
AIZIKOWICZ	(SZWARC)
AIZIKOWICZ	Royze, 2 children
ALPERSZTEIN	Rysza
ALPERSZTEIN	Szlomo
ALPERSZTEIN	Joel
ALPERSZTEIN	Efraim
ALPERSZTEIN	Sender
ALPERSZTEIN	Batia
ALPERSZTEIN	Rysza
ALPERSZTEIN	Szlomo
ALPERSZTEIN	Joel
ALPERSZTEIN	Efraim
ALPERSZTEIN	Sender
ALPERSZTEIN	Batia
ANGELCZIK	Szlomo
ANGELCZIK	Leja
ANGELCZIK	Szolim
ANGELCZIK	Jakow
ANGELCZIK	Chana
ANGELCZIK	Cyla
ARANOWICZ	Lejzer
ARANOWICZ	Sara
ARANOWICZ	Awram Aron
ARJEWICZ	Chajka
ARJEWICZ	Rywka

ARONOWICZ	Mordechai	BELSKI	Jakow
ARONOWICZ	Jakow	BELSKI	Ida
ARONOWICZ	Arie	BELSKI	Jankel
ARONOWSKI	Osne	BERKOWICZ	Chaim Cwi
ARONOWSKI	Izchak	BERKOWICZ	Lea
ARONOWSKI	Aron	BERKOWICZ	Cipora
AZROWICZ	Nisan	BERKOWICZ	Elijahu
AZROWICZ	(OPENHEIM) Chaja, child	BERKOWICZ	Gdale
B		BERKOWICZ	Judes nee GINIENSKI
BACZYNSKI	Abraham	BERKOWICZ	Motl
BACZYNSKI	Ester	BERKOWICZ	Lea
BACZYNSKI	Szolim	BERKOWICZ	child
BACZYNSKI	(OSTASZINSKI) Minia, sons & daughters	BERKOWICZ	Mejer
		BERKOWICZ	Leiba
BACZYNSKI	Rywka, daughter	BERKOWICZ	Leib
BACZYNSKI	Szlomo	BERKOWICZ	Golda, 5 children
BAKAR	Josif	BERKOWICZ	Izchak, 1 child
BAKAR	Dwora	BERKOWICZ	Gerszon
BAKAR	Moisze	BERKOWICZ	Rochl Lea
BAKAR	Nachum	BERKOWICZ	Nechama
BAKSZT	Alter	BERKOWICZ	Chaszele
BAKSZT	Rywka	BERKOWICZ	Perele
BAKSZT	Feiga	BERKOWICZ	Dweirele
BAKSZT	Hadasa	BERKOWICZ	Aizik
BAKSZT	Szlomo	BERKOWICZ	Lipche (his wife)
BAKSZT	Jochevet	BERKOWICZ	Dveirele
BAKSZT	Jezl	BERKOWICZ	Feniele
BAUMSZTEIN	Bela	BERKOWICZ	Josef
BEKOLCZUK	Chaja Mirjam	BERKOWICZ	Hinda
BELSKI	Eszel	BERKOWICZ	Bejla
BELSKI	David	BERKOWICZ	Batia and her children
BELSKI	Bela	BERKOWICZ	Rachel
BELSKI	Abraham	BERKOWICZ	Lejbe

BERKOWICZ	Rochl	BOROWSKI	
BERKOWICZ	Chana Chawa nee SLONIMSKI	BOKATOWICZ	Stasek
		BOKATOWICH	Tonia
BERKOWICZ	Zlota	BOKATOWICH	Moisze
BERKOWICZ	Jehudit	BORTSKI	Sara
BERKOWICZ	Motl	BORTSKI	Akiva
BERKOWICZ	Sima	BLOCH	Welwl
BERKOWICZ	Avraham	BLOCH	Szolim
BERKOWICZ	Moisze	BLOCH	Chaja
BERKOWICZ	Arie	BLOCH	Chaim
BERMAN	Ruwen	BLOCH	Berta, 2 children
BERMAN	Rywka	BLOCH	Szolim, family
BERMAN	Abraham	BLOCH	Jehuda
BERMAN	Szifra	BLOCH	Sorke di sznajderkie, children
BERMAN	Sara		
BERMAN	Minia		
BERMAN	Gerszon	BOGATIN	Jakow
BERMAN	Majer	BOGATIN	and family
BERMAN	Sonia	BORECKI	Moishe
BERMAN	Sara	BORECKI	Josze
BERMAN	Henia	BORECKI	Mina
BERMAN	Itzchak	BORECKI	Fajwl
BERMAN	Bejla	BORECKI	Chaim Zelik
BIGUN	Luba	BORECKI	Ruwe
BIGUN	Eliyahu	BOROWSKI	(IZRAELIT) Szejna
BIGUN	Cirl	BOLDO	Alter
BITENSKI	Jehoszua	BOLDO	wife, 3 children
BITENSKI	Merke	BOLDO	Jakow Dawid
BITENSKI	Fejge Etl	BOLDO	wife
BITENSKI	(JARMOWSKI) Etel	BOLDO	Izchak
		BOLDO	Jakow
BITENSKI	Israel	BOLDO	Jankel
BITENSKI	Izchak	BOLSZOWICZ	Zeidl
BLECH	Hinda	BORKOWSKI	Gitl
BOKATOWICZ	Chana nee	BORKOWSKI	Gerszon

BORKOWSKI	Dowid	BORTSKI	Kalman
BORKOWSKI	Eliezer Dowid	BORTSKI	Lea
BORKOWSKI	Dina	BORTSKI	Chaja
BORKOWSKI	Noach	BOSEL	Jehuda
BORKOWSKI	Fruma	BOSEL	Lea
BORKOWSKI	Israel	BOSEL	Abraham
BORKOWSKI	Jehuda	BOSEL	Minia
BORKOWSKI	Benjamin Josef	BOSEL	Sonia
BORKOWSKI	Natan	BOSEL	Fytl
BORKOWSKI	Henia	BOTWINIK	Jehoszua
BORKOWSKI	Szmuel	BOTWINIK	Sara
BORKOWSKI	Chaja	BOTWINIK	Lewik
BORKOWSKI	Aharon	BOTWINIK	Brochke
BORKOWSKI	Etke	BRESLERMAN	Szrage
BORKOWSKI	Abram Leib	BRESLERMAN	Mayre
BOROWSKI	Josl	BRESLERMAN	Akiva
BOROWSKI	Raisl nee CHIMESZ	BRESLERMAN	Malke
BOROWSKI	Elie	BROLNICKI	Chana
BOROWSKI	Ciwja	BROLNICKI	Diva
BOROWSKI	Sara	BROLNICKI	Dow
BOROWSKI	Chana	BROLNICKI	Ruwen
BOROWSKI	Masza	BROLNICKI	Chasza Minia
BORSKI	Mordchaj	BROLNICKI	Rochl
BORSKI	Izchak	BROLNICKI	Chaim
BORSKI	Jehuda	BRUDNE	Moisze Lopa
BORSKI	Matisjahu	BRUK	Eliezer
BORSKI	Aharon	BRUK	Marysia
BORSKI	Devora	BRUK	Pesia
BORSZTEIN	Zelda	BRUK	Rysel
BORSZTEIN	Moisze	BRUK	Hilel
BORSZTEIN	Dasia	BRUK	Brocha
BORSZTEIN	Sara Osna	BRUK	Boruch
BORSZTEIN	Joina	BRUK	Elka
BORTSKI	Liba	BRUK	Michla

BRUK	Baruch	CIECHANOWSKI	Luba
BRUK	Itchak	CIECHANOWSKI	Herszl solicitor
BRUK	Chemie	CIECHANOWSKI	Herszl's wife
BRUK	Dovid	CIECHANOWSKI	Klara daughter
BRUK	Szlojme (der szuster)	CIMERINSKI	Jente
		CIMERINSKI	Beile
BRUK	Izchak	CIMERMAN	Dowid
BRUK	Finkl	CIMERMAN	Elijahu
BRUK	Zlate	CIMERMAN	Cywja
BRUK	Brocha	CUKERNIK	Chaim
BRUK	Benjamin	CYITLIN	Mola
BRUK	Fruma	CYITLIN	Mola's sister
BRUK	Mordechi	CYMERMAN	Keila
BRUK	Zelig	CYMERMAN	Rywka
BRUK	Moisze	CYMERMAN	Rywka's husband
BRUK	Szmaje	CYMERMAN	Rywka's child
BRUK	Dovid	CYMERMAN	Etl
BRUK	Rochl	CYMERMAN	Etl's husband
BRUK	Lea	CYMERMAN	Etl's 2 children
BRUK	Josef	CYRINSKI	Jehoszua
BRUK	Szifra	CYRINSKI	Jehoszua's wife
BRUK	Cyla	CYRINSKI	Zlata
BRUK	Rochl	CYRINSKI	Zlata's husband
BROYDO	Bejlke	CYRINSKI	Malka
BUSZEL	Zisl	CYRINSKI	Malka's children
BUSZEL	Broche	CYRINSKI	Masza
BUSZEL	Mosze	CYRINSKI	Masza's husband
BUSZEL	Wiktor	CYRINSKI	Masza's children
C		CZERTOK	Hosze
CHAJETOWICZ	Joel	CZERTOK	Mere
CHAJETOWICZ	Eliezer	CZERTOK	Pesie
CHESLY	Sara Eidla	CZERTOK	Chane
CHESLY	Gawriel	CZERTOK	Reizl
CHURGIN	Sonia	CZERTOK	Leike
CHURGIN	Josef solicitor		

CZERTOK	Joszke	DOBRIN	Jehoszua
CZERTOK	Cime	DOBRIN	Chawa
CZERTOK	Rywke	DOBRIN	Gitl
CZERTOK	Mojsze	DOBRIN	Mordchai
CZERTOK	Bejla	DOBRIN	(ZAMKOWY) Sara
CZERTOK	Bejla's 3 daughters	DOBRIN	Rafi
CZORNY	Herszl	DOBRIN	Rafi's son
CZORNY	Chana	DOBRIN	Dawid
CZORNY	Israel	DOBRIN	Czerne
CZORNY	Elka	DOBRIN	Josif
CZORNY	Noach	DOBRIN	Freidl
CZORNY	Moma	DODOWICZ	Lacki Fajwel
CZORNY	Izchak	DODOWICZ	Ariel
CZORNY	Chaim	DODOWICZ	Izchak
CZORNY	Jakow's 2 children	DODOWSKI	Moisze
CZYZ	Sara	DODOWSKI	Gita
CZYZ	Josef	DONIC	Sara
CZYZ	Fryda	DOROGOW	Abraham
CZYZ	Mosze Ahron	DOROGOW	Szeine
CZYZ	Jakow	DOROGOW	Naftali
D		DOROGOW	Beile
DAWIDOW	Kalman	DOROGOW	Feigl
DAWIDOW	Sara	DRINSKI	Jenta
DAWIDOW	Lea	DULSIN	Misza
DAWIDOW	Eliezer	DULSIN	Misza's wife, sons
DAWIDOW	Rachel	DULSIN	Eda
DAWIDOWSKI	Berl	DULSIN	Rachel
DELATYCKI	Eliyahu	DULSIN	Dawid
DELATYCKI	Chaja	DWORECKI	lawyer
DELATYCKI	Israel	DWORECKI	Sonia, 2 children
DELATYCKI	Israel's wife	DWORECKI	Henia
DELATYCKI	Israel's child	DWORECKI	Dow
DOBRIN	Moisze	DZIENCIOLSKI	Bejla
DOBRIN	Szmuel	DZIENCIOLSKI	Sonia

DZIENCIOLSKI	Moisze	EICHER	Majer
DZIENCIOLSKI	Malka	EICHER	Israel
DZIENCIOLSKI	Perl	EICHER	Szolem
DZIENCIOLSKI	Sara	EICHER	Michoel
DZIENCIOLSKI	Lea	EICHER	Ciwia
DZIENCIOLSKI	Jeszjahu	EICHER	Josef
DZIENCIOLSKI	Joel	EICHER	Zipora
DZIENCIOLSKI	Szmuel	EICHER	Szaul
DZIENCIOLSKI	Idl	EICHER	Nachama
DZIENCIOLSKI	Aizik	EICHER	Dewora
DZIENCIOLSKI	Etl	EICHER	Szifra
DZIENCIOLSKI	Beila	EICHER	Dowa
DZIENCIOLSKI	Mina	EPSZTEIN	Josef
DZIENCIOLSKI	Leib	EPSZTEIN	Slawa, children
DZIENCIOLSKI	Mendl	EPSZTEIN	Borys doctor
DZIENCIOLSKI	Rochl	EPSZTEIN	Riwka
DZIENCIOLSKI	Chonon	EPSZTEIN	Sara
DZIENCIOLSKI	Hirszl	EPSZTEIN	Herc
DZIENCIOLSKI	Sara	EPSZTEIN	Kreine
DZIENCIOLSKI	Wolf	EPSZTEIN	Chana Sara
DZIENCIOLSKI	Risza, 2 children	EPSZTEIN	Lejba
E		EPSZTEIN	Henia
EFRAIMSKI	Herzl	EPSZTEIN	Rachel
EFRON	Szlomo	EPSZTEIN	Riwka
EFRON	Rasza	EPSZTAIN	Josef
EFRON	Benjamin	EPSZTAIN	Josef
EFRON	Josef	EPSZTAIN	Josef
EFRON	Gerszon	EPSZTAIN	Rachel
EFRON	Sara	ERLICH	Sara Rochl
EFRON	Jona	ERLICH	Dowid
EFRON	Dow	ERLICH	Zwi
EHERLICH	Mendl	ERLICH	Miriam
EHERLICH	Zipa	ERLICH	Suzan
EHERLICH	Chaja	F	

FEIGENBERG		GINSKI	Malka
FEIGENBERG'S	family	GINSKI	Jakow
FUKS	Herszl	GINSKI	Feiga
FUKS	Rochl (SZMULEWICZ)	GINSKI	Szepsl
		GINSKI	Joszke
FURMAN	Motl	GINSKI	Chaja, 2 children
FURMAN	Czerna	GINSKI	Chana
FURMAN	Kalman	GINSKI	Chana's husband, children
FURMAN	Mosze		
G		GINZBURG	Ester
GARCEWSKI	Boruch	GINZBURG	Szimszon
GELER	Zorach	GINZBURG	Baruch
GELER	Yenta	GOLDIN	Ben Aharon
GENIKOW	Solomon	GOLDIN	Ita
GENIKOW	Solomon's wife	GOLDIN	Sonia
GERCOWICZ	Jakow	GOLDIN	Mordechai
GERCOWICZ	Chaja Gitl	GOLDIN	Israel
GERCOWICZ	Fejga	GOLDSZMID	Shlomo
GERCOWICZ	Matla	GOLDSZMID	Lea
GERCOWICZ	Meilach	GOLDSZMID	Israel
GERSZONOWICZ	Sonia	GOLDSZMID	Sara, 2 children
GERSZONOWICZ	Chana	GOLOWICKI	Szmuel
GERSZONOWICZ	Liza	GOLOWICKI	Rochl Lea
GERSZONOWICZ	Dora	GOLOWICKI	Zew
GERSZONOWICZ	Chaja	GOLOWICKI	Pesach
GERSZONOWICZ	Mara Rachel	GOLOWICKI	Mordchai
GERSZONOWICZ	Rachel	GOLOWICKI	Sara
GERSZONOWICZ	Szifra	GOLOWICKI	Dewora
GERSZONOWICZ	Jehuda	GOLOWICKI	Feiga
GERSZONOWICZ	Michoel	GOLOWICKI	Rywka
GERSZONOWICZ	Taiba	GOLOWICKI	Iche
GIMOLSKI	Arje	GOLKOWICZ	Zelig
GINSKI	Icik	GOLKOWICZ	Nochimke
GINSKI	Hirszl	GOLKOWICZ	Simke
GINSKI	Bejla	GOLKOWICZ	Golde

GOLKOWICZ	Miriam	GORSZTEIN	Jerachamiel
GOLKOWICZ	Dowid	GOTFRID	Nachum
GOLUB	Boris	GOTFRID	Chana
GOLUB	Boris's wife	GOTFRID	Jehudit
GOLUB	Borislate, children	GOTFRID	Nochim
GONCEWICZ	Zelig	GOTFRID	Chana
GONCEWICZ	Dvorka	GOTFRID	Jehudit
GONCEWICZ	Jehuda	GOTLIB	Henach
GONCEWICZ	Luba	GUMENER	Elijahu
GONCEWICZ	Izchak	GUMENER	Rachel
GONCEWICZ	Moisze Dovid	GUMENER	Havat (daughter)
GORCOWSKI	Dow	GURCOWSKI	Henia
GORCOWSKI	Fejgl	GUREWICZ	Josef
GORCOWSKI	Zwi	GUREWICZ	Brajna Fejga
GORCOWSKI	Sara	GUREWICZ	Nechama
GORCOWSKI	Brina	GUREWICZ	Chasia
GORCOWSKI	Leibl	GUREWICZ	Gitl
GORCOWSKI	Rochl	GUREWICZ	Oszer
GORDIN	Rafael Nachum	GUREWICZ	Mira
GORDIN	Brocha	GUREWICZ	child of Oszer&Mira
GORDIN	Chana	GUREWICZ	and 5 children
GORDIN	Sara	GUREWICZ	Szolim
GORDON	Dow	GUREWICZ	Zwi
GORDON	Risze	GUREWICZ	Hodl
GORDON	Izchak	GUREWICZ	Wiszniewski Bluma
GORDON	Hinda	GUREWICZ	Chana Gitl
GORDON	Aizik	GURSZTEIN	Lea
GORDON	Lule	GURSZTEIN	Jerachmiel
GORDON	Chaszke (KAPLINSKI)	GURSZTEIN	Chaim
GORODINSKI	Abram Meme	GURSZTEIN	Tanchum
GORODINSKI	Tamara	GURSZTEIN	Lea
GORODINSKI	Szlomo	GUSKIND	Cirl, children
GORODINSKI	Chonon (Chonie)	GUSKIND	Ester
GORODINSKI	Fenia	GUSKIND	Josef

GUSKIND	Sima	ISAKOW	Chaim
GUSKIND	Israel	ISAKOW	Lejzerl
H		ISAKOW	Sara
HALPERIN	Bejla	IWINIECKI	Izak
HALPERIN	Pnina	IWINIECKI	Chaja
HARKAWY	Lea	IWINIECKI	Abraham, sons
HARKAWY	Dow	IWINIECKI	Berl
HARKAWY	Israel	IWINIECKI	Isroel
HARKAWY	Jehuda	IWINIECKI	Brocha
HARKAWY	Berl	IWINIECKI	Diszka
HARKAWY	Israel	IWINIECKI	Czerna
HARKAWY	Jehuda	IWINIECKI	Israel
HARKAVY	Motik	IWINIECKI	Szlomo
HARKAVY	Motik's wife	IWINIECKI	Jeszayahu
HARKAVY	Motik's children	IWINIECKI	Rachel
HELFAND	& family	IWINIECKI	Abraham
HOROWICZ	Leib	IWINIECKI	Berl
HOROWICZ	Hinda	IWINIECKI	Chana
HOROWICZ	Chaim	IWINIECKI	Ciwia
HOROWICZ	Szlomo	IWIENIECKI	Branke
I		IZIKOWICKI	Menachem
ICKOWICZ	Kalman	IZIKOWICKI	Zlata
ICKOWICZ	Mara	IZIKOWICKI	Isroel
ICKOWICZ	Chana	IZRAELIT	Perec
ICKOWICZ	Izchak Leib	IZRAELIT	Pola
ICKOWICZ	Elijahu	IZRAELIT	Meiszke Herszl-Szimen's
ICKOWICZ	Sara		
ICKOWICZ	Herszl Cwi (Machne Drole)	IZRAELIT	Fania, daughter & son
ICKOWICZ	Rywka	IZRAELIT	Mina
ICKOWICZ	Mina	IZRAELIT	Mosze
ICKOWICZ	Cyrl	IZAELIT	Leib
ICKOWICZ	Jehuda	IZAELIT	Malka
ISAKOW	Malke	IZAELIT	Chasia
ISAKOW	Jona	IZAELIT	Mirjam

IZRAELIT	Mosze	JANKELEWICZ	Pia
IZRAELIT	Fenia	JANKELEWICZ	Pia's children
IZRAELIT	Bela	JANKELEWICZ	Szmarjahu
IZRAELIT	Szmuel	JANKELEWICZ	Sara
IZRAELIT	Josif	JANKELEWICZ	Sara's children
IZRAELIT	Feigl	JANKELEWICZ	Aharon
IZRAELIT	Jeruchem	JANKELEWICZ	Hania
IZRAELIT	China	JANKELEWICZ	Hania's children
IZRAELIT	Beila	JANKELEWICZ	Chaim
IZRAELIT	Pola	JANKELEWICZ	Chaim's wife
IZRAELIT	Jakow	JANKELEWICZ	Chaim's children
IZRAELIT	Ester	JANKELEWICZ	Gela (SOKOLOWSKI)
IZRAELIT	Mosze		
IZRAELIT	Szmuel	JANKOWSKI	Mira
IZRAELIT	Gronia, 2 children	JARMOWSKI	Ahron Zwi
IZRAELIT	Sonia	JARMOWSKI	Abram
IZRAELIT	Luba	JARMOWSKI	Szajna Sora
IZRAELIT	Abraham	JARMOWSKI	Fania
IZRAELIT	Szmuel	JARMOWSKI	Jehuda
IZRAELIT	Feigl	JARMOWSKI	Izchok
IZRAELIT	Szlomo	JARMOWSKI	Chaim
IZRAELIT	Israel	JARMOWSKI	Menachem
IZRAELIT	Abraham	JARMOWSKI	Majer
IZRAELIT	Josif	JARMOWSKI	Aba
J		JARMOWSKI	Gerszon
JAFFE	Abram	JARMOWSKI	Ita
JAFFE	Riwka Leja	JARMOWSKI	Jehoszua
JAFFE	Dewora	JARMOWSKI	Henia Genia
JAFFE	Jakow	JARMOWSKI	Chana
JAFFE	Cipora	JARMOWSKI	Moisze
JAFFE	Dow	JARMOWSKI	Rachel
JAFFE	Szimszon	JARMOWSKI	Efraim
JANKELEWICZ	Rywka	JARMOWSKI	Reizl
JANKELEWICZ	Eliezer	JARMOWSKI	Szimszon
		JARMOWSKI	Abram

JARMOWSKI	Feigl	JUDELEWICZ	Bela
JARMOWSKI	Sonia	JUDELEWICZ	Perla
JARMOWSKI	Roze	JUDELEWICZ	Jehudit
JASILINSKI	Zacharje	**K**	
JASILINSKI	Dina	KABAK	Szlomo
JAWNOWICZ	Nachum	KABAK	Szlomo's wife
JAWNOWICZ	Towa	KABAK	Szlomo's child
JAWNOWICZ	Ruwen	KABAK	Michoel
JAWNOWICZ	Rywka	KABAK	Nisan
JAWNOWICZ	Eliyahu	KABAK	Ita
JAWNOWICZ	Pesach	KABAK	Mira
JAWNOWICZ	Ita	KABAK	child (4 years old)
JAWNOWICZ	Elka	KABAK	Minia
JAWNOWICZ	Malka	KABAK	Dewora
JAWNOWICZ	Lea	KAC	Nechama
JAWNOWICZ	Ahron	KAC	Majer
JAWNOWICZ	Marsza (from Slobodka)	KAC	Jehudit
		KAC	Jehoszua
JEDIDOWICZ	Jeszajahu	KAGAN	Sender
JEDIDOWICZ	Jeszajahu's wife (DAWIDOWSKI)	KAGAN	Izchak Leib
JEDIDOWICZ	Jehudit the widow	KAGAN	Irsze
JEDIDOWICZ	Jehudit's children	KAGAN	Mejsze
JEWELEWICZ	Chaim Berl solicitor	KAGAN	Szoszke
JOSELEWICZ	Sare Idls	KAGAN	Leizer
JOSELEWICZ	Gronia	KAGAN	Jankl
JOSELOWSKI	Welwl	KAGAN	Dwora
JOSELOWSKI	Rode	KAGAN	Nechama
JOSELOWSKI	Szmuel David	KAGAN	Noach
JOSELOWSKI	Szlomo and family	KAGAN	Batja
JOSELOWSKI	Hajne and family	KAGAN	Batja's daughter
JOSELOWSKI	Batie	KAGANOWICZ	Ahron Dovid
JOSELOWSKI	Ester	KALICKI	Szabati
JUDELEWICZ	Simcha	KALICKI	Chaja Sara
JUDELEWICZ	Aron	KALICKI	Mirjam

KALICKI	Izchok	KANTOROWICZ	Rywka
KALICKI	Lejbe Szmuel	KANTOROWICZ	Mosze
KALICKI	Chasia	KANTOROWICZ	Ruwen
KALICKI	Pesia	KANTOROWICZ	Rejzele
KALICKI	Mirjam	KANTOROWICZ	Rejzele's 4 children
KALICKI	Leiba	KAPLAN	Gitl
KALICKI	Rachel	KAPLAN	Mosze
KALMANOWICZ	Boruch	KAPLAN	Welwl (butcher)
KALMANOWICZ	Adela	KAPLAN	Malka
KALMANOWICZ	Chana	KAPLAN	Alter
KALMANOWICZ	Luba	KAPLAN	Szolem
KALMANOWICZ	Malka	KAPLAN	Dwosze
KAMIENIECKI	Rafael	KAPLAN	Dwosze's 3 children
KAMIENIECKI	Bejla	KAPLINSKI	Jehuda
KAMIENIECKI	Masze	KAPLINSKI	Risza
KAMIENIECKI	Chaim	KAPLINSKI	Raja
KAMIENIECKI	Efraim	KAPLINSKI	Zelig
KAMIENIECKI	Rachel	KAPLINSKI	Luba
KAMIENIECKI	Cwi	KAPLINSKI	Hanna
KAMIENIECKI	Chana	KAPLINSKI	Samuel
KAMIENIECKI	Szimon dentist	KAPLINSKI	Rywka
KAMIENIECKI	Menucha dentist	KAPLINSKI	Luba
KAMIENIECKI	Jakow doctor	KAPLINSKI	Ajzik
KANTOROWICZ	Jakow Berl	KAPLINSKI	Leibl of Nowojelnia
KANTOROWICZ	Fania (CZERTOK)	KAPLINSKI	Roza his wife
KANTOROWICZ	Fania's daughter	KAPLINSKI	Asia
KANTOROWICZ	Chana	KAPLINSKI	Luba
KANTOROWICZ	Fruma	KAPLINSKI	Luba
KANTOROWICZ	Oszer	KAPLINSKI	Sonia
KANTOROWICZ	Izchak	KAPLINSKI	Szlomke
KANTOROWICZ	Welwl	KAPLINSKI	Rafael
KANTOROWICZ	Chana Sara	KAPLINSKI	Rachel
KANTOROWICZ	Oszer	KAPLINSKI	Pole
KANTOROWICZ	Szlomo	KAPLINSKI	Lea (MANISZEWICZ)

KAPLINSKI	Jekutiel (Kusze)	KITAJEWICZ	Mirjam
KAPLINSKI	Bluma	KITAJEWICZ	Gerszon
KAPLINSKI	Miriam (Mimka)	KITAJEWICZ	no name given
KAPLINSKI	Dowid	KITAJEWICZ	wife
KAPLINSKI	Sima	KITAJEWICZ	daughter
KAPLINSKI	Zew	KIWELEWICZ	Berl
KAPLINSKI	Benjamin	KIWELEWICZ	Mania
KAPLINSKI	Zila (CHODOSZ)	KIWELEWICZ	Frume
KAPLINSKI	Hilel	KIWELEWICZ	Mordchaj (Motl)
KAPUSZCZEWSKI	Chaim	KIWELEWICZ	Chasia
KAPUSZCZEWSKI	Malka	KLINICKI	Abram
KAPUSZCZEWSKI	Berl	KLINICKI	Abram's wife
KAPUSZCZEWSKI	Nechama	KLINICKI	Abram
KAPUSZOWSKI	Szmuel		Abram's wife
KAPUSZOWSKI	Jehudit	KLINICKI	(names given twice in different sections of the list)
KARAJINSKI	Ruwen		
KARAJINSKI	Ciwja	KLINICKI	Abram's child
KASMAJEWICZ	Josef	KLITNIK	Chaim
KASMAJEWICZ	Jenta	KLITNIK	Jeszajahu
KASMAJEWICZ	Jehudit	KLUBOK	Lena (KITAJEWICZ)
KASMAJEWICZ	Ester		
KASMAJEWICZ	Oszer	KODELMAN	Kalman
KASMAJEWICZ	Gita	KOHN	Izchak Ajzik
KAZAN	Szlomo	KOHN	Bejke
KAZAN	Majer	KOHN	Szoszana
KIRZNER	Szmerl	KOHN	Arie
KIRZNER	Feigl	KOHN	Zwi
KIRZNER	Perl	KOHN	Berl
KIRZNER	Freidl	KOHN	Lea
KIRZNER	Motl	KOHN	Dawid
KIRZNER	Rochele	KOLDICKI	Sara (GINIENSKI)
KIRZNER	Awremele	KORMAN	Joel
KIRZNER	Frejdl	KORMAN	Mosze
KITAJEWICZ	Rochl Lea	KORMAN	Szmuel

KORMAN	Silwa	KRULEWIECKI	Jakow
KOSZELEWSKI	Josef	KRULEWIECKI	Sima
KOSZELEWSKI	Chajka	KUPELMAN	Rywka
KOWENSKI	Josef Mejer	KUPELMAN	Meyer
KOWENSKI	Lea	KUPELMAN	Fajwl
KOWENSKI	Mula	KUPELMAN	Rywka
KOWENSKI	Silwa	KUPELMAN	Minia
KOWENSKI	Kuba	KUPELMAN	Czerne Braine
KOWENSKI	Luba	KUSZCZYNSKI	Abram
KOWENSKI	Rywka (BRUK)	KUSZCZYNSKI	Gitl
KOWENSKI	Szulamit (BRUK)	KUSZCZYNSKI	Benjomin
KOWENSKI	Szymszon	KUSZCZYNSKI	Leibl
KOWENSKI	Hinda	KUSZCZYNSKI	Chaja
KOWNER	sisters	KUSZCZYNSKI	Efaim
KRAWIEC	Daniel	KUSZCZYNSKI	Gerszon
KRAWIEC	Freidl	KUSZCZYNSKI	Jehudit
KRAWIEC	Bezalel	KUSZCZYNSKI	Gdaliahu
KRAWIEC	Keila	KUSZCZYNSKI	Bronia
KRAWIEC	Josef	KUSZCZYNSKI	Rochl
KRAWIEC	Sara	KUSZCZYNSKI	Chaja
KRAWIEC	Zlata	KUSZCZYNSKI	Moira
KRAWIEC	Rywka	KUSZCZYNSKI	Zalmon
KRAWIEC	Dwosza	KUSZCZYNSKI	Luba
KRAWIEC	Pesza	KUSZCZYNSKI	Benjomin
KRAWIEC	Lea	**L**	
KRAWIEC	Hercl	LAGATKER	Benjamin
KRAWIEC	Mosze	LAGATKER	Mosze
KRAWIEC	Bejla	LAGATKER	Rywka
KRAWIEC	Ida	LAGATKER	Szmuel
KRIMER	Eliezer grandson of Lucki, captain Izraeli army, fell in the war of independence	LAGATKER	Lea
		LAGATKER	Josef
		LAGATKER	Leibke
		LAGOCKI	Berek
KRULEWIECKI	(maznik-grease maker)	LAGOCKI	Chaya Lea

LAGOCKI	Josef	LEIZAEROWSKI	Leizer
LAGOCKI	Lea	LEIZAEROWSKI	Sara
LAGOCKI	Leibl	LEIZAEROWSKI	Breina
LAGOCKI	Simcha	LEIZAEROWSKI	Mosze
LAGOCKI	Reizl	LEIZAEROWSKI	Szmuel
LAGOCKI	Szmuel	LEIZAEROWSKI	Wlf
LAZOWSKI	Szlomo	LEIZAEROWSKI	Chana
LAZOWSKI	Batia	LEW	Mirka
LAZOWSKI	Szolem Izchak	LEW	Monos
LAZOWSKI	Josef (Josl)	LEW	Hadasa
LAZOWSKI	Genia	LEWIN	Mirl
LAZOWSKI	Mordechai	LEWIN	Berchik
LAZOWSKI	Szejne Reizl	LEWIN	Reizl
LAZOWSKI	Batia	LEWIN	Dina
LAZOWSKI	Awiwa	LEWIN	Adek
LEIBOWICZ	Izchak	LEWIN	Arie
LEIBOWICZ	Cwi	LEWIN	Gitl
LEIBOWICZ	Szlomo	LEWIN	Sonia
LEIBOWICZ	Szlomo's wife	LEWIN	Izak Mier
LEIKIN	Binyamin teacher	LEWIN	Dow
LEIKIN	Binyamin's wife	LEWIN	Chava
LEIZAEROWSKI	Chaim	LEWIN	Dwora
LEIZAEROWSKI	Joszke	LEWIN	Szoszana
LEIZAEROWSKI	Mosze	LEWIN	Cyla
LEIZAEROWSKI	Etka	LEWIT	Chaim
LEIZAEROWSKI	Dina	LEWIT	Chaim's wife
LEIZAEROWSKI	Jehoszua	LEWIT	Rywka
LEIZAEROWSKI	Sonia	LEWIT	Sonia
LEIZAEROWSKI	Chana	LIDSKI	Szmuel the teacher
LEIZAEROWSKI	Leizer	LIDSKI	Eszke
LEIZAEROWSKI	Dow	LIDSKI	Klubok Doszke
LEIZAEROWSKI	Taibe	LIMON	Rochl
LEIZAEROWSKI	Rywke	LIMON	Cyrl
LEIZAEROWSKI	Rywke's child Leizer	LIMON	Jehoszua (OWSIEJ)

LIMON	Eske	LISOWSKI	Abram
LIMON	Jehudele	LISOWSKI	Sara
LIPKIN	Dwora	LISZINSKI	Berl
LIPKIN	Jeszajahu	LISZINSKI	Sara
LIPKIN	Cyla	LITMAN	Eidle
LIPKIN	Chaim	LITMAN	Rachel
LIPKIN	Elka	LITMAN	Szmajahu
LIPKIN	Josif	LITOWSKI	Mordechai
LIPKIN	Zahawa	LITOWSKI	Zelig
LIPKIN	Chanan	LITOWSKI	Abram
LIPKIN	Jafa	LITOWSKI	Jechiel
LIPKIN	Chawa	LITOWSKI	Sonia (nee KAPLINSKI)
LIPKIN	Chana		
LIPKIN	Mordechai	LITOWSKI	Lejzer
LIPKIN	Mirjam	LITOWSKI	Chana
LIS	Chaim	LITOWSKI	Eliezer
LIS	Roza	LITOWSKI	Doszka
LIS	Roza's 2 daughters	LITOWSKI	Ahron
LIS	Josef	LITOWSKI	Ahron's wife
LIS	Joel	LITOWSKI	Ahron's child
LIS	Simche	LITOWSKI	Miriam
LIS	Sara	LITOWSKI	Nina
LIS	Mirele	LITOWSKI	Luba
LIS	Dawid	LITOWSKI	Iza
LIS	Lea	LITWIN	Jehuda
LIS	Sonia	LITWIN	Gita
LIS	Cwi	LITWIN	Sonia
LIS	Hercl	LITWIN	Szmerl
LIS	Szejne	LUBACKI	Rachel
LIS	Dowid	LUBACZANSKI	Jakow
LIS	Jakow	LUBACZANSKI	Chana
LIS	Rywke	LUBACZANSKI	Gitl
LIS	Chaja Minia	LUBACZANSKI	Cila
LIS	Michael	LUBACZANSKI	Masza
		LUBACZANSKI	Izchak

LUBACZANSKI	Israel	MANISZEWICZ	Borke
LUBACZANSKI	Gitl	MANISZEWICZ	Batia (nee GERSZONOWSKI)
LUBACZANSKI	Feigl		
LUBACZANSKI	Jachne	MANISZEWICZ	Batia's children
LUBACZANSKI	Kalman	MANISZEWICZ	Dowid
LUBACZANSKI	Aizik	MANISZEWICZ	Dowid's wife
LUBACZANSKI	Azik's wife	MANISZEWICZ	Cyla
LUBACZANSKI	Aizik's child	MANISZEWICZ	Moszke
LUCKI	Izchak	MARMURSZTEIN	Jakow Doctor
LUCKI	Dowid	MARMURSZTEIN	Gitl
LUCKI	Jona	MARMURSZTEIN	Rima
LUCKI	Szlomo	MASKIL	Chana
LUCKI	Duba	MASKIL	Ahron
LUCKI	Duba's 2 children	MASKIL	Fajwl
LUDSKI	Alter	MASKIL	Feigl
LUSZANSKI	Berl	MASKIL	Rywka
LUSZANSKI	wife	MASKIL	Bejla
LUSZANSKI	two children	MASKIL	Rachel
M		MASLOWATY	Chaim
MAGID	Joszke	MASLOWATY	Cipa
MAGID	Jerachamiel	MASLOWATY	Dow
MAGID	Jerachamiel's wife	MASLOWATY	Cipora
MAKIL	Feigl	MASLOWATY	Mulik
MALACHOWSKI	Duba	MASLOWATY	Israel
MALACHOWSKI	Jakow	MASLOWATY	Rywka
MALUSZICKI	Dwora	MASLOWATY	Mirjam
MALUSZICKI	Itzchak	MASLOWATY	Szlomo
MALUSZICKI	Sara	MASLOWATY	Chana
MANDELBAUM	Chajka	MASLOWATY	Ruwen
MANDELBAUM	Cypora	MASLOWATY	Rejzl
MANDELBAUM	Herc	MASLOWATY	Aharon
MANDELBAUM	Ester	MASLOWATY	Welwl
MANISZEWICZ	Bejla	MASLOWATY	Szjne Riwke
MANISZEWICZ	Chaja doctor	MASLOWATY	Gawrijel
		MASLOWSKI	Mordechai

MASLOWSKI	Gitl	MIRSKI	Jehoszua Izchak
MASLOWSKI	Chaja	MIRSKI	Sara Rywka
MASLOWSKI	Nechama	MIRSKI	Chana
MATUSZEWICZ	Alte	MIRSKI	Gita Bejla
MATUSZEWICZ	Simka	MIRSKI	Itka
MATUSZEWICZ	Simka's husband	MOKOTOWICZ	husband
MATUSZEWICZ	Jochewet	MOKOTOWICZ	wife
MATUSZEWICZ	Jochewet's husband	MOKOTOWICZ	children
MECHIEL	Awram	MOKSI	Ben Zion
MECHIEL	Sara	MOKSI	Szoszana
MECHIEL	Jakow	MOKSI	Mirjam
MECHIEL	Mosia	MOKSI	Mosze
MEJEROWICZ	Masza	MOLCZADSKI	Roche Lea
MEJEROWICZ	Masza's children	MOLCZADSKI	Jidl
MEKEL	Berl	MOLCZADSKI	Batia
MEKEL	Meir	MOLER	Leib
MELZER	Alter	MOLER	Chana
MELZER	Chaja	MOLER	Eliezer
MELZER	Josef	MOLER	Reizl
MELZER	Dewora	MOLER	Jakow
MELZER	Dewora's 2 children	MOLER	Sasza
MENAKER	Alter	MOLER	Mosze
MENAKER	Jeszie killed in the partisans	MOLER	Mosze
		MOLER	Chana Rochl
MENAKER	Ester	MOLER	Alek
MENAKER	Szmuel	MOLER	Dowid
MIKOLAJEWICZ	(TILES) Eda	MOLER	Etka
MIKOLAJEWICZ	Chaim	MOLER	Mordrei
MIKOLAJEWICZ	Ester	MOLER	Szeina
MIKOLAJEWICZ	Mosze	MOLER	Rywka
MIKOLAJEWICZ	Amil	MOLODIECKI	Jidl
MIKULICKI	Izchak	MOLODIECKI	Dowid Berl
MIKULICKI	Mula	MOLOSZICKI	Mosze
MIKULICKI	Sonia	MOLOSZICKI	Fejga
MIRSKI	Jankl		

MOLOSZICKI	Izchak	MOWSZOWICZ	Ahron
MOLOSZICKI	Dewora	MOWSZOWICZ	Berl
MOLOSZICKI	Morduchai	MOWSZOWICZ	Chajcia Luba
MOLOSZICKI	Sara	MOWSZOWICZ	Cwi
MOLOSZICKI	Keila	MOWSZOWICZ	Chaja
MOLOSZICKI	Abram	MOWSZOWICZ	Chaja's child
MOLOSZICKI	Chaja	MOWSZOWICZ	Gitl
MOLOSZICKI	Chaja's son	MOWSZOWICZ	Eliezer Jona
MORDUCHOWICZ	Mordchai	MOWSZOWICZ	Szjne
MORDUCHOWICZ	Ester	MUCZNIK	Dinka
MORDUCHOWICZ	Michoel	MUCZNIK	Dinka's children
MORDUCHOWICZ	Rywka	**N**	
MORDUCHOWICZ	Rachel	NACHIMOWICZ	Szmuel
MORDUCHOWICZ	Cywia	NACHIMOWICZ	child
MORDUCHOWICZ	Osna	NAMIOT	Meier
MORDUCHOWICZ	Jakow Dowid	NAMIOT	Chana Rochl (WOLFOWICZ)
MORDUCHOWICZ	Rejne		
MORDUCHOWICZ	Szoszana	NAMIOT	Boruch Wolf
MORDUCHOWICZ	Batia	NAMIOT	Tzwi (paint shop)
MORDUCHOWICZ	Abram	NAMIOT	Tzwi's wife
MORIS	Jeszajohu	NAMIOT	Tzwi's daughter Lea
MOWSZOWICZ	Chaim Israel	NAMIOT	Herc
MOWSZOWICZ	Rachel		
MOWSZOWICZ	Szlomo	NAMIOT	Lea daughter of Herc
MOWSZOWICZ	Ester Malke	NARWER	Ruwen
MOWSZOWICZ	Dowid	NARWER	Baska nee BERKOWICZ
MOWSZOWICZ	Josef		
MOWSZOWICZ	Malke	NARWER	Musza
MOWSZOWICZ	Benzion	NARWER	Berl
MOWSZOWICZ	Michoel	NEWACHOWICH	Eliezer
MOWSZOWICZ	Mosze	NEWACHOWICH	Bejla
MOWSZOWICZ	Mosze's wife	NEWACHOWICH	Minia daughter
MOWSZOWICZ	Szlomo	NEWACHOWICH	Jakow
MOWSZOWICZ	Jente	NIANKOWSKI	Abram

NIANKOWSKI	Mosze	NISELEWICZ	Nisan's daughter
NIANKOWSKI	Eliezer	NISELEWICZ	daughter's 2 children
NIANKOWSKI	Luba		
NIANKOWSKI	Cipora	NIZEWICKI	Frejdl
NIANKOWSKI	Miriam	NOCHIMOWICZ	Hercl
NIANKOWSKI	Jakow	NOCHIMOWSKI	Aharon
NIANKOWSKI	Bezalel	NOCHIMOWSKI	Czerna
NIANKOWSKI	Mordchai	NOCHIMOWSKI	Chanele
NIANKOWSKI	Fryda	NOCHIMOWSKI	Esterl
NIANKOWSKI	Zisa	NOCHIMOWSKI	Heniele
NIANKOWSKI	Szlomo	NOCHIMOWSKI	Jechasiel
NIANKOWSKI	Silwa	NOCHIMOWSKI	Chana
NIANKOWSKI	Ada	NOCHIMOWSKI	Naomi
NIANKOWSKI	Rywka	NOCHIMOWSKI	Ruth
NIKOLAEWSKI	Chana	NOCHIMOWSKI	Chaim
NIKOLAEWSKI	Lea	NOCHIMOWSKI	Don
NIKOLAEWSKI	Gawriel	NOCHIMOWSKI	Sara
NIKOLAEWSKI	Rywka	NOCHIMOWSKI	Alter
NIEGNIEWICKI	Fejge Minie	NOCHIMOWSKI	Chaja Chana
NIEGNIEWICKI	Jehudit	NOCHIMOWSKI	Michoel
NIEGNIEWICKI	Awrom Itzchak	NOCHIMOWSKI	Sara
NIEGNIEWICKI	Itka	NOCHIMOWSKI	Jehoszua
NIEGNIEWICKI	Rachel	NOCHIMOWSKI	Fania
NIEGNIEWICKI	Jakow	NOCHIMOWSKI	Mirjam
NIEGNIEWICKI	Feidl	NOCHIMOWSKI	Sula
NIEGNIEWICKI	Rose	NOCHIMOWSKI	Sula's 2 children
NIEGNIEWICKI	Mejsze	NOCHIMOWSKI	Izchak ben Mordechaj
NIKOLOWSKI	Sara	NOCHIMOWSKI	Szlomo
NIKOLOWSKI	Bezalel	NOCHIMOWSKI	Elka
NIKOLOWSKI	Michael	NOCHIMOWSKI	Jakow
NISELEWICZ	Aharon	NOCHIMOWSKI	Jakow's wife
NISELEWICZ	Rachel	NOCHIMOWSKI	Jakow's 3 children
NISELEWICZ	Mosze	NOCHIMOWSKI	Rywka
NISELEWICZ	Nisan	NOCHIMOWSKI	Rywka's husband

NOCHIMOWSKI	Rywka's children	ORZECHOWSKI	Elka
NOCHIMOWSKI	Sonia	ORZECHOWSKI	Izchak
NOCHIMOWSKI	Szabsl's wife	ORZECHOWSKI	Mendl
NOCHIMOWSKI	Rochl	ORZECHOWSKI	Towa
NOCHIMOWSKI	Mordechai	ORZECHOWSKI	Sara
NOCHIMOWSKI	Towa	ORZECHOWSKI	Alter
NOTKOWICZ	Josef	OSTASZINSKI	Hersz
NOTKOWICZ	Sara	OSTASZINSKI	Rywka
NOTKOWICZ	Josze	OSTASZINSKI	Abraham
NOTKOWICZ	Rejzele	OSTASZINSKI	wife of Abraham
O		OSTASZINSKI	Chaim, family
OISTRACH	Israel	OSTASZINSKI	Yidl
OKANSKA	Dina	OSTASZINSKI	Josif, family
OKANSKA	Chana	OSTASZINSKI	Eliyahu, killed in forest
OKANSKI	Abraham Hirsz		
OKANSKI	Dawid	**P**	
OKANSKI	Natan	PARNES	Abram (teacher)
OKANSKI	Frejda Basza	PARNES	Abram's daughter
OKUN	Michla	PARNES	son of the solicitor
OKUN	Josef	PIERESIETSKI	Szyja
OKUN	Zimel	PIERESIETSKI	Abram
OKUN	Eliezer	PEREC	Fanie
OKUN	Guta	PERNIK	Welwl
OPENHEIM	Itka	PERNIK	Mejsze
OPENHEIM	Leib	PERNIK	Sara
OPENHEIM	Sonia	PERNIK	Arje
OPENHEIM	Szaul	PERNIK	Oszer
OPENHEIM	Chana, little daughter	PERNIK	Rywka
		PERNIK	Jechackel
ORINSKI	Jakow	PERNIK	Jente
ORLYNSKI,	family Yidishe gass	PERNIK	Mirjam
ORZECHOWSKI	Jehudit	PERNIK	Mirjam's husband
ORZECHOWSKI	Mosze	PERNIK	Mirjam's children
ORZECHOWSKI	Chaja Sara	PIKLIN	Lea
ORZECHOWSKI	Eliezer	PIKLIN	Baruch

PIKLIN	Chana Ester	POLONSKI	Zeldz
PIKLIN	Pnina	POLONSKI	Czerna
PIKLIN	Szlomo	POLONSKI	the tailor
PIKLIN	Chaja	POLONSKI'S	wife
PIKLIN	Szulamit	POLONSKI'S	daughters
PIKLIN	Israel	POLONSKI	Joel
PIKLIN	Szlomo	POLONSKI	Rochl
PIKLIN	Szolim Jojned	POLONSKI	Fejgl
PIKLIN	Perele	POLONSKI	Malka
PIKLIN	Dina	POLONSKI	Nechama
PIKLIN	Frume	POLONSKI	Ruwen
PIKLIN	Jechiel	POMIERCZIK	Mojsze
PIKLIN	Boruch	POMIERCZIK	Fajwl
PIKLIN	Chaje Gitl	POMIERCZIK	Gele
PIKLIN	Szulamit	POMIERCZIK	Malkijel
PINCHUK	Chaja	POMIERCZIK	Lea
PINCHUK	Sara	POZNIAK	Bezalel
PINCHUK	Cipora	POZNIAK	Bejla Feigl
PIONTEK	Lejb	POZNIAK	Dowid
PIONTEK	Luba	POZNIAK	Jerachamiel
PIONTEK	Malka	PRANIK	Jeszajahu
PIONTEK	Mejsze	PRANIK	Chana
PLOTKIN	Rywka	PRECNIK	Mordechaj
PLOTKIN	Mania	PRECNIK	Brejna
PLOTKIN	Fejga	PRECNIK	Hercl
PLOTKIN	Rywa	PRECNIK	Sara
PLOTKIN	Mania	PRESMAN	Oszer
PLOTKIN	Fela	PRISITZKI	S. teacher in Tarbut
POGORELSKI	Rachel	PRISITZKI	Jidl
POLONSKI	Faive Ele	PRISITZKI	Pesach
POLONSKI	Sara Bronia	PRISITZKI	Abram Izchak
POLONSKI	Ruwen	PRESMAN	Awrohom
POLONSKI	Awroham	PUPKE	Mejsze
POLONSKI	Aizik	PUPKE	Alte (RUDNICKI)

PUPKE	Jakow	RACZKOWSKI	Fejgl
PUPKE	Eliezer	RACZKOWSKI	Ziszka
PUTERMAN	Jehuda	RACZKOWSKI	Lejzer
PUTERMAN	Mosze	RAKOWSKI	Abraham
R		RARAKOWICZ	Dow
RABINOWICZ	Ester	RARAKOWICZ	Mirjam
RABINOWICZ	Zlata	RAWICZ	Dow
RABINOWICZ	Fejgl	RAWICZ	Chaja
RABINOWICZ	Alta	RAWICZ	Izchak
RABINOWICZ	Alta's husband	RAWICZ	Henia
RABINOWICZ	Alta's 3 children	RAWICZ	Ruwen
RABINOWICZ	Henia	RATNER	Chaim
RABINOWICZ	Rachel	RATNER	Risza
RABINOWICZ	Dwora	RATNER	Luba
RABINOWICZ	Jochewet	RATNER	Jakow
RABINOWICZ	Tajbele	RATNER	Risza
RABINOWICZ	Jehudit	REZNIK	Izchak
RABINOWICZ	Israel Mayer	REZNIK	Jona
RABINOWICZ	Benjamin	REZNIK	Kamela
RABINOWICZ	Jakow	REZNIK	Chaim
RABINOWICZ	Chana	RODNICKI	Gerszon
RABINOWICZ	Fryda	RODNICKI	Sara Rywka
RABINOWICZ	Fejga	ROTANSKI	Fruma
RABINOWICZ	Alta	ROTANSKI	Nechama
RABINOWICZ	Jankel	ROTANSKI	Lea
RABINOWICZ	Chava	ROTANSKI	Lea's children Sonia & Awremele
RABINOWICZ	Freidl		
RABINOWICZ	Szoszane	ROZANIK	Jakow
RABINOWICZ	Motl	ROZANIK	Rywka
RABINOWSKI	Ruwen	ROZANIK	Efraim
RABINOWSKI	Dora	ROZANIK	Hinda
RACHKOWICZ	Josef	ROZEN	Szmajahu
RACHKOWICZ	Ahron	ROZEN	Etl
RACZKOWSKI	Maks	ROZEN	Abraham
		ROZIANSKI	Zelig

ROZIANSKI	Chaja	SLUCKI	Leibl
ROZIANSKI	Szmuel	SLUCKI	Taibl
RUBIN	Sara	SLUCKI	Jakow
RUBIN	Mania	SLUCKI	Dowid
RUBIN	the watchmaker	SLUCKI	Awrhom
RUBIN'S	wife (nee PLOZYNSKI)	SLUCKI	Beines
		SLUCKI	Malka
RUBIN'S	daughter	SLUCKI	Reizl
RUDNICKI	Awrohom	SLUCKI	Dowid
RUDNICKI	Rywka	SLUCKI	Naomi
RUDNICKI	Mayer	SLUCKI	Rachel (SZLOSBERG)
S			
SACHAROWICZ	Kreine	SLUCKI	Dowid
SACHAROWICZ	Kreine's mother	SLUCKI	Kejla
SACHAROWICZ	Jente	SLUCKI	Szymen
SACHAROWICZ	Berl	SLUCKI	Mula
SEIFERT	Feigl	SLUCKI	Josef
SEIFERT	Hilel	SLUCKI	Izchok
SEIFERT	Wife	SLUCKI	Czerne
SEIFERT	Motl	SLUCKI	Jakow
SEIFERT	Nosn	SLUCKI	Joel
SIMCHOWICH	Bejle (WOLKIN)	SLUCKI	Jehudit
SKOROCHOD	Eliezer	SLUCKI	Nachmon
SKOROCHOD	Calke	SLUCKI	Luba
SKOROCHOD	Calke's family	SLUCKI	Luba's husband
SLODOWSKI	Elijahu	SLUCKI	Luba's son
SLOTER	Szlomo	SLUCKI	Chasia
SLOTER	Jakow	SLUCKI	Cipora
SLUCKI	Dowid	SMOLENSKI	Aharon
SLUCKI	Gola	SMOLENSKI	Mirjam
SLUCKI	Szmuel Milik	SMOLENSKI	Onia
SLUCKI	Luba	SMOLENSKI	Mejer
SLUCKI	Izchak	SNOWSKI	Dow
SLUCKI	Szlomo	SNOWSKI	Dow
SLUCKI	Rywka	SNOWSKI	Chaim

SNOWSKI	Sara	SUCHARSKI	Chaja
SNOWSKI	Jehudit	SUCHARSKI	Szejndl
SOFER	Idela	SUCHARSKI	Srolik
SOFER	Ciwa	SUCHARSKI	Jafa
SOFER	Dowid	SUCHARSKI	Isroel
SOFER	Baszka	SZABKOWSKI	Szpica
SOFER	Gitl	SZABKOWSKI	Ruwen
SOKOLOWSKI	Ajzik	SZACHOR	Mosze
SOKOLOWSKI	Ajzik's wife	SZALOWSKI	Ester
SOKOLOWSKI	Ajzik's 3 daughters	SZALOWSKI	Szmuel
SOLCINSKI	Jechaskel	SZALOWSKI	Rachel
SOLCINSKI	Jechaskel's parents	SZAPIRO	Mirjam
SOLCINSKI	Jechaskel's sister	SZAPIRO	Wolf
SOLOMON	Szmuel (teacher)	SZAPIRO	Dwora
SOLOMON	Chinke nee LUBECKI	SZAPIRO	Dwora's twins
		SZAPIRO	Elijahu
SOLOMON	Chinke's children	SZAPIRO	Sima
SOSNOWSKI	Noach	SZEWICKI	Rywka (OPENHEIM)
SOSNOWSKI	Noach's wife		
SOSNOWSKI	Michle	SZEWICKI	Szymon
SOSNOWSKI	Henie	SZIMANOWICZ	Riwka
SPUTNICKI	Izchak	SZIMANOWICZ	Gawriel
SPUTNICKI	Chana	SZIMANOWICZ	Jerachmiel
SPUTNICKI	Ruwen	SZIMANOWICZ	Mordchaj
SPUTNICKI	Cyrl nee CIRINSKI	SZIMANSKI	Izchak
SPUTNICKI	Berl	SZIMANSKI	Fruma
SPUTNICKI	of Hardielowke	SZIMANSKI	Arje
SREBRENIK	Leibl	SZIMONOWICZ	Mojsze
STOLOWICKI	Leib	SZIMONOWICZ	Rywka
STOLOWICKI	Leib's wife	SZIMSZELEWICZ	Szmuel
STOLOWICKI	Itzchak	SZIMSZELEWICZ	Malka
STOLOWICKI	Szmuel	SZKOLNIK	Zalman
STOLOWICKI	Frume	SZKOLNIK	Szlomo
STOLOWICKI	family of Baziljaner St.	SZKOLNIK	Gerszon
		SZKOLNIK	Sonia

SZLACHTMAN	Chaim	SZMULEWICZ	Izchak's 2 children
SZLACHTMAN	Sorke	SZMULEWICZ	Abraham Cwi
SZLACHTMAN	Josl	SZMULEWICZ	Zew
SZLACHTMAN	Mosze	SZMULEWICZ	Zlate
SZLACHTMAN	daughter of Chaim & Sorke	SZMULEWICZ	Cemach
		SZMULEWICZ	Chane Ester
SZLOBOWSKI	Jehuda	SZMULEWICZ	Abraham
SZLOBOWSKI	Rachel	SZMULEWICZ	Genia
SZLOBOWSKI	Ester	SZMULEWICZ	Mordechai
SZLOBOWSKI	Izchak	SZMULEWICZ	Chaja
SZLOSBERG	Elijahu	SZTEINBERG	Chana (BOGATIN)
SZLOSBERG	Fejgl	SZTEINBERG	Sara
SZLOSBERG	Raja	SZTEINBERG	Szulamit
SZLOSBERG	Eliezer	SZUSTER	Motl
SZLOSBERG	Chawa	SZULKLAPER	Elijahu
SZLOSBERG	Lolik	SZULKLAPER	Ola
SZLOSBERG	Izchak	SZULKLAPER	Ola's husband
SZLOSBERG	Boruch	SZULKLAPER	Ola's children
SZLOSBERG	Lonia	SZURC	Ahron
SZLOSBERG	Luba	SZURC	Ester
SZLOSBERG	Raja	SZURC	Dina (LEWIN)
SZLOSBERG	Baszke	SZURC	Mordechaj
SZLOSBERG	Dowid	SZURC	Chaja Golda
SZMERKOWICZ	Mola	SZURC	Chana
SZMUKLER	Abram Izchak	SZURC	Riwa
SZMUKLER	Nechama	SZUSTER	Abraham
SZMULEWICZ	Motl	SZUSTER	Gitl
SZMULEWICZ	Hinda	SZUSTER	Szlomo
SZMULEWICZ	Josef	SZUSTER	Pesia
SZMULEWICZ	Fejga	SZUSTER	Sara Fejgl (WOLFOWICZ)
SZMULEWICZ	Tewje		
SZMULEWICZ	Abram Dow	SZUSTER	Abraham
SZMULEWICZ	Batia	SZUSTER	Rochl
SZMULEWICZ	Izchak (WSIELUB)	SZUSTER	Chana
SZMULEWICZ	Izchak's wife	SZWARC	Chana

T

TAMARKIN	Jechezjel	TREIWISZ	
TAWARICKI	Dowid	TREIWISZ'S	wife
TWARICKI	Libe	TREIWISZ'S	daughter
TAWARICKI	Hanie (doctor)	TROJECKI	Zalman and family
TAWARICKI	Hanie's daughter	TROCKI	Mosia
TAWARICKI	Jehuda	TROCKI	Mosia's daughter
TAWARICKI	Jehuda's wife	TROCKI	Moisze Chaim
TAWARICKI	Jehuda's daughter	TROCKI	Moisze's wife
TCZESZLE	Josef Gerszon	TROCKI	Mosze's children
TCZESZLE	Abram Aharon	TROBOWICZ	Nachman
TCZESZLE	Hinda	TROBOWICZ	Motl
TCZESZLE	Chaja	TROBOWICZ	Josef
TCZESZLE	Marysia	TROBOWICZ	Rachel

W

TCZESZLE	Bencijon	WAGER	Mendl
TCZESZLE	Bela	WAGER	Sasza
TCZESZLE	Chasia	WAGER	Menasza
TCZESZLE	Gawriel	WAGER	(SPUTNICKI)
TCZESZLE	Sara Elke	WASILEWSKI	Chonie
TEITELBAUM	Tawaricki Klare	WASILEWSKI	Chonie's wife
TEITELBAUM	Beila	WASILEWSKI	Chonie's children
TILES	Israel	WASILEWSKI	Feigl
TILES	Debora Dowa	WASILEWSKI	Rajele
TILES	Chaja	WASILEWSKI	Rywka
TRACEWICKI	Chasza Leja	WASILEWSKI	Chajele
TRACEWICKI	Meier	WEINER	Malka
TRACEWICKI	Chasze Leje	WEINER	Lea
TRACEWICKI	Zelte	WEINER	Sonia
TRACEWICKI	Broche	WEINER	Miriam
TRACEWICKI	Abram	WEINER	Miriam's 3 children
TRACEWICKI	Lehoszua	WEISMAN	Itzchak
TRACEWICKI	Boruch	WEISMAN	Riwka
TRACEWICKI	Henie Mone	WIENER	Mirl (seamstress)
TRAJWUSZ	family of six people	WIENER	Mirl's children

WIERNIKOWSKI	Mosze	WISZNIEWSKI	Szoszana Golda
WIERNIKOWSKI	Batia	WISZNIEWSKI	Szimszon
WIERNIKOWSKI	Bejlka	WISZNIEWSKI	Abrahm Aba
WIERNIKOWSKI	Chaim Aharon	WISZNIEWSKI	Joel Chaim
WILENSKI	Jehuda Elijahu	WISZNIEWSKI	Izchak Dow
WILENSKI	Rachel	WISZNIEWSKI	(NIEGNEWICKI) Mojsze
WILENSKI	Perele	WOLFKIN	Leib
WILENSKI	Bejle	WOLFKIN	Sara
WILENSKI	Jehudit	WOLFOWICZ	Josze
WILENSKI	Aharon	WOLFOWICZ	Berl Leib
WILKIN	Rochl	WOLFOWICZ	Berl Leib's wife
WILKIN	Gitl	WOLFOWICZ	Berl Leib's children
WILKIN	Szmuel	WOLFOWICZ	Jakow Josef
WILKIN	Miriam	WOLFOWICZ	Cipa
WILNER	Misza	WOLFOWICZ	Cipa's 3 children
WILNER	Sara	WOLFOWICZ	Arie
WILNER	Feigl	WOLFOWICZ	Taiba
WILNER	Alter	WOLFOWICZ	Gita
WINER	Abram	WOLFOWICZ	Jakow
WINER	Chaja Sara	WOLFOWICZ	Brocha
WINER	Chaja Sara's 2 cildren (boys)	WOLFOWICZ	teacher
WINIK	Jakow	WOLFOWICZ	teacher's wife
WINIK	Jakow's wife	WOLFOWICZ	Lola (kindergarten teacher)
WINIK	Malka	WOLFOWICZ	Aharon
WINIK	Reizl	WOLFOWICZ	Baruch
WINIK	Abram (doctor)	WOLFOWICZ	Muska
WISZMMAN	Izchak	WOLFOWICZ	Lea
WISZMMAN	Sonia	WOLFOWICZ	Abram
WISZMMAN	Rywka	WOLFOWICZ	Szlomo
WISZMMAN	Israel Chaim	WOLKIN	Luba
WISZMMAN	Berl	WOLKIN	Luba's son
WISZMMAN	Abram Iser	WOLKIN	Gdaljahu
WISZNIEWSKI	Ziame	WOLKIN	Sara, children
WISZNIEWSKI	Gela		

WOLKIN	the barber & children	ZALMANOWSKI	Zelda's 4 young children
WOLKIN	Mosze	ZAMKOW	Rywka
WOLKIN	Lea and child (girl)	ZAMKOW	Abram Nisan
WOLKIN	Arie	ZAMKOW	Chana
WOLKIN	Sara	ZAMKOW	Jeszajahu
WOLKOWSKI	Chaim	ZAMKOW	Mosze
WOLKOWSKI	Hinda	ZAMKOW	Michael
WOLKOWSKI	Szlomo	ZAMKOWY	Elka
WOLKOWSKI	Cipora	ZAMKOWY	Szlomo
WOLONSKI	Hendl	ZAMKOWY	Cila
WOLONSKI	Hendl's wife	ZAMKOWY	Michala
WOLONSKI	Hendl's daughter Malka	ZAMKOWY	Dora
		ZAMKOWY	Szlomo
WOLTC	Sonia	ZAMKOWY	Chajka
WOLTC	Jeszajahu	ZAMOSZCZYK	Chaim
Z		ZAMOSZCZYK	Chaim's wife
ZABLOCKI	Chaim	ZAMOSZCZYK	Chaim's children
ZABLOCKI	Chana Riwka	ZAMOSZCZYK	Elijahu
ZACHAROWICZ	Chaja Mina	ZAMOSZCZYK	Dalia
ZACHAROWICZ	Izchak	ZAMOSZCZYK	Maier
ZACHAROWICZ	Rachel	ZAMOSZCZYK	Fryda
ZAJFERT	Hillel	ZAPOLSKI	Baruch
ZAJFERT	Hillel's wife	ZAPOLSKI	Moisze
ZAKCHAIM	Nataniel Rabbi from Wselib	ZASZWA	Mosze
ZALBIN	Alte	ZASZWA	Luba
ZALBIN	Alte's sisters	ZASZWA	Jehuda
ZALBIN	sisters children	ZASZWA	Cwi
ZALBINSKI	Hirsz	ZASZWA	Chaja
ZALBINSKI	Ita	ZELDOWICZ	Szaja
ZALMANOWSKI	Sara	ZELDOWICZ	Munia
ZALMANOWSKI	Rachel	ZELDOWICZ	Fima
ZALMANOWSKI	Nachama	ZILBERMAN	Dovid
ZALMANOWSKI	Zelda	ZILBERMAN	Herszl
		ZILBERMAN	Gitl

ZISKIND	David	ZLOTNIK	Jehudit
ZISKIND	Gerszon	ZLOTNIK	Jehudit's husband
ZISKIND	Dewora	ZLOTNIK	Jehudit's children
ZISKIND	Maier	ZLOTNIK	Rywka
ZISKIND	(SPUTNICKI) Rachel	ZUCHOWICKI	Rachel
		ZUCHOWICKI	Ruven
ZISKIND	Mosze (son)	ZUCHOWICKI	Dewora
ZISKIND	(FISZBACH) Rachel	ZUCHOWICKI	Cyla
		ZUCHOWICKI	Szmuel
ZISKIND	Lusia	ZUCHOWICKI	Liba
ZISKIND	Aleksander (Sasza) doctor	ZUCHOWICKI	Liba's children
		ZUCHOWICKI	Eliezer
ZISKIND	Eda (SZAPIRO)		
ZISKIND	Szejna	ZUCHOWICKI	Cypora
ZIZEMSKI	Israel	ZUCHOWICKI	Raja
ZIZEMSKI	Zlate	ZUCHOWICKI	Mendl
ZIZEMSKI	Mule	ZUCHOWICKI	Mendl's family
ZIZEMSKI	Josef	ZUCHOWICKI	Nisan
ZIZEMSKI	Chawa	ZUK	Cyla
ZIZEMSKI	Izchak	ZUK	Naftali
ZIZEMSKI	Gronia	ZUK	Sara
ZIZEMSKI	Jakow	ZUK	Bluma
ZIZEMSKI	Rejze	ZUK	Sima
ZLOTNIK	Jona	ZUK	Munia
ZLOTNIK	Chaja Beila	ZUK	Fryda
ZLOTNIK	Fajwl		

List of citizens of Novogrudok

Translated by Oskar Delatycki

A

ABERZANSKI	Moisiei
ABRAMOVICZ	Abram
ABRAMOVICZ	Chaja
ABRAMOVICZ	Chaja
ABRAMOVICZ	Chaja
ABRAMOVICZ	Chaja
ABRAMOVICZ	Chaja
ABRAMOVICZ	Chana
ABRAMOVICZ	Chania
ABRAMOVICZ	Chasia
ABRAMOVICZ	Cypa
ABRAMOVICZ	Dushka
ABRAMOVICZ	Gabriel
ABRAMOVICZ	Hirsh
ABRAMOVICZ	Iosif
ABRAMOVICZ	Iosif
ABRAMOVICZ	Isak
ABRAMOVICZ	Israel
ABRAMOVICZ	Leib
ABRAMOVICZ	Malka
ABRAMOVICZ	Moisiei
ABRAMOVICZ	Musia
ABRAMOVICZ	Nachama
ABRAMOVICZ	Naum
ABRAMOVICZ	Ovsiej
ABRAMOVICZ	Ovsiej
ABRAMOVICZ	Ryva
ABRAMOVICZ	Samuel
ABRAMOVICZ	Zejdel
ABRAMOVSKI	Mania
AJZIKOVICZ	Chaim
AJZIKOVICZ	Cylia
AJZIKOVICZ	Lolik
AJZIKOVICZ	Rosa
ARANOVSKI	Alter
ARANOVSKI	Chaim
ARANOVSKI	Elka
ARANOVSKI	Esther
ARANOVSKI	Frida-Beila
ARANOVSKI	Izak
ARANOVSKI	Rachel

ARANOVSKI	Shevah
ARANOVSKI	Tevel

B
BEGIN	Cyra
BEGIN	Eliash
BEGIN	Lida
BEGIN	Sara
BELIN	Cyra
BELIN	Gita
BELIN	Iosel
BELIN	Keila
BELIN	Mira
BELIN	Moisiei
BELIN	Morduch
BERENSTEIN	Iosif
BERENSTEIN	Leib
BERENSTEIN	Musia
BERENSTEIN	Rachela
BERENSTEIN	Ruva
BERENSTEIN	Shimon
BERENSTEIN	Somka
BERKOVICZ	Boruch
BERKOVICZ	Chana
BERKOVICZ	Chania-Chaja
BERKOVICZ	Chenia
BERKOVICZ	David
BERKOVICZ	Fania
BERKOVICZ	Iosif
BERKOVICZ	Musia
BERKOVICZ	Rocha
BERKOVICZ	Rocha
BERKOVICZ	Volf
BERKOVICZ	Zlata
BOLDO	Jankiel
BRESTLIN	Abram
BRESTLIN	Chaja
BRESTLIN	Fania
BRESTLIN	Salomon
BRESTLIN	Samson

C
CALKOVICZ	Boruch
CALKOVICZ	Naum
CALKOVICZ	Pinia
CALKOVICZ	Zlata
CALKOVICZ	Zysia

CHERTOK	Luba
CHERTOK	Mysia
CHITYN	Chaja
CHITYN	Chajm
CHITYN	Chana
CHITYN	Gitia
CHITYN	Jankiel
CIECHANOVSKI	Hirsh
CIECHANOVSKI	Klavia

D

DENTALSKI	Jakob
DENTALSKI	Minia
DENTALSKI	Mysia
DOBRYN	David
DOBRYN	Frida-Beila
DOBRYN	Iosif
DOBRYN	Nena
DVORECKI	Eliash
DVORECKI	Izak
DVORECKI	Sonia

E

EFRAIMOVSKI	Chana
EFRAIMOVSKI	Estera
EFRAIMOVSKI	Herz
ELIN	Berko
ELIN	Bliuma
ELIN	Echnia
ELIN	Ena
ELIN	Hecel
ELIN	Mera
ELIN	Mihail
ELIN	Mira
ELIN	Rachela
ELIN	Ryva
ELIN	Sheina
EPSTEIN	Boris
EPSTEIN	Luba
EPSTEIN	Maria
EPSTEIN	Ryva
EPSTEIN	Sara

F

FAJA	Chana
FAJA	Fania
FAJA	Isak

FAJA	Liba
FAJVELEVICZ	Chajm
FAJVELEVICZ	Chana
FAJVELEVICZ	Eliash
FAJVELEVICZ	Faja
FAJVELEVICZ	Genia
FAJVELEVICZ	Hiler
FAJVELEVICZ	Ida
FAJVELEVICZ	Shlena
FAJVELEVICZ	Sima
FAJVELEWICZ	Cylia
FAJVELEWICZ	Faivel
FAJVELEWICZ	Sonia
FISHBACH	Rachela
FLEISCHER	Judis
FLEISCHER	Majna
FLEISCHER	Morduch
FRIEDMAN	Alter
FRIEDMAN	Chaja
FRIEDMAN	Cyra
FRIEDMAN	Iosif
FRIEDMAN	Lea
FRIEDMAN	Sheina
FRIEDMAN	Shprinca

G

GABODYSKI	Mena
GABODYSKI	Shlena
GANCEVICZ	Dvora
GANCEVICZ	Isak
GANCEVICZ	Judel
GANCEVICZ	Luba
GANCEVICZ	Moisiei
GANCEVICZ	Zelik
GINZBURG	Fania
GINZBURG	Gusia
GINZBURG	Judel
GINZBURG	Rachela
GINZBURG	Roza
GOCZAHES	Fania
GOCZAHES	Godel
GOCZAHES	Nachama
GOCZAHES	Rachela
GOCZAHES	Shimon
GODELSALZ	Cypa
GODELSALZ	Elia
GOVDEN	Chasia

GOVDEN	Izak
GOVDEN	Mysia
GOVDEN	Rysia
GOVDEN	Zlata
GRINBERG	Moisiei
GRINBERG	Taiba
GULKOVICZ	Braina
GULKOVICZ	Chaja
GULKOVICZ	Fania
GULKOVICZ	Rocha
GULKOVICZ	Shlena
GUREVICZ	Estera
GUREVICZ	Falk

H

HERSHENOVSKI	Braina
HERSHENOVSKI	Chajm
HERSHENOVSKI	Gdalia
HERSHENOVSKI	Iosif
HERSHENOVSKI	Iosif
HERSHENOVSKI	Jasha
HERSHENOVSKI	Juda
HERSHENOVSKI	Liba
HERSHENOVSKI	Malka
HERSHENOVSKI	Moisiei
HERSHENOVSKI	Musia
HERSHENOVSKI	Rachela
HORODYSKI	Abram
HORODYSKI	Beniamin
HORODYSKI	Berko
HORODYSKI	Chana
HORODYSKI	Fania
HORODYSKI	Fania
HORODYSKI	Hinda
HORODYSKI	Niemika
HORODYSKI	Tamara

I

ICKOVICZ	Chana
ICKOVICZ	Isak
ICKOVICZ	Jankiel
ICKOVICZ	Moisiei
ISRABIENY	Lazar
ISRABIENY	Malka
IVIENSKI	Abram
IVIENSKI	Chaim
IZRAELIT	Hinda

IZRAELIT	Israel
J	
JOSELEVICZ	Aron
JOSELEVICZ	Belia
JOSELEVICZ	Felia
JOSELEVICZ	Getach
JOSELEVICZ	Moisiei
JOSELEVICZ	Pesia
JOSELEVICZ	Symka
JOSELEVICZ	Taiba
JANKIELEVICZ	Alter
JANKIELEVICZ	Belia
JANKIELEVICZ	Chajm
JANKIELEVICZ	Cyra
JANKIELEVICZ	David
JANKIELEVICZ	Mira
JANKIELEVICZ	Raja
JANKIELEVICZ	Sara
JANKIELEVICZ	Shmerko
JELEVICZ	Chaim Berko
JELEVICZ	Chaja
JELEVICZ	Klara
JOSELEVICZ	Aron
JOSELEVICZ	Belia
JOSELEVICZ	Beniamin
JOSELEVICZ	Chajm
JOSELEVICZ	Czerna
JOSELEVICZ	Ejser
JOSELEVICZ	Elojat
JOSELEVICZ	Faivel
JOSELEVICZ	Ida
JOSELEVICZ	Iosif
JOSELEVICZ	Luba
JOSELEVICZ	Rocha
JOSELEVICZ	Sara
JOSELEVICZ	Shlena
K	
KABAK	Ajzik
KABAK	Chajm
KABAK	Chana
KABAK	Doba
KABAK	Eta
KABAK	Isak
KABAK	Leiser
KABAK	Moisiei

KABAK	Moisiei-Leib
KABAK	Roza
KABAK	Sara
KABAK	Shlena
KAGAN	Chaja
KAGAN	Chaja
KAGAN	Chajm
KAGAN	David
KAGAN	David
KAGAN	Dora
KAGAN	Estera
KAGAN	Israel
KAGAN	Itka
KAGAN	Jankiel
KAGAN	Lazar
KAGAN	Majka
KAGAN	Mera
KAGAN	Musia
KAGAN	Nachama
KAGAN	Rachel
KAGAN	Roza
KAGAN	Rubin
KAGAN	Shulia
KAGAN	Sonia
KAPELEVICZ	Gutel
KAPELEVICZ	Rubin
KAPLAN	Abram
KAPLAN	Belia
KAPLAN	Chaja
KAPLAN	Chajm
KAPLAN	Gitia
KAPLAN	Iosif
KAPLAN	Levik
KAPLAN	Masha
KAPLAN	Roza
KAPLINSKI	Ajzik
KAPLINSKI	Judel
KAPLINSKI	Luba
KAPLINSKI	Raja
KAPLINSKI	Rysia
KAPLINSKI	Zelik
KAPUSHEVSKI	Alta
KIVIELEVICZ	Badana
KIVIELEVICZ	Berko
KIVIELEVICZ	Iosif
KIVIELEVICZ	Isser
KIVIELEVICZ	Judis

KIVIELEVICZ	Luba
KIVIELEVICZ	Nachama
KIVIELEVICZ	Nachama
KIVIELEVICZ	Zelda
KIZNER	Abram
KIZNER	Morduch
KIZNER	Rachela
KLOCKI	Chaja
KLOCKI	Isak
KLOCKI	Jankiel
KLOCKI	Lea
KOLCZYCKI	Chasia
KOLCZYCKI	Tevel
KOLEVNIK	Aron
KOLEVNIK	Faivel
KONCEVICZ	Faivel
KONCEVICZ	Liza
KONCEVICZ	Luba
KONCEVICZ	Mendel
KONCEVICZ	Naum
KORELICKI	Abram
KORELICKI	Enta
KORELICKI	Taiba
KRAVIEC	Pesia
KROLEVIECKI	Beniamin
KROLEVIECKI	Chaja
KROLEVIECKI	Doba
KROLEVIECKI	Grunia
KROLEVIECKI	Hirsh
KROLEVIECKI	Pesia

L

LAGATKOR	Beniamin
LAGATKOR	Estera
LAGATKOR	Majka
LAGATKOR	Marianna
LAGATKOR	Masha
LAGATKOR	Ryva
LEJBOVICZ	Isak
LEJBOVICZ	Leib
LEJBOVICZ	Minia
LEJBOVICZ	Nachama
LEJBOVICZ	Naum
LEJBOVICZ	Shera
LEV	Daja
LEV	Mera
LEV	Monus

LEVIN	Chaim
LEVIN	Dina
LEVIN	Eliash
LEVIN	Frida
LEVIN	Herz
LEVIN	Matlia
LEVIT	Judel
LEVIT	Shifra
LIDZKI	Zieja
LIPCHIN	Aron
LIPCHIN	Belia
LIPCHIN	Chania
LIS	Chana
LITVIN	Guda
LITVIN	Judia
LITVIN	Sonia
LUBCZANSKI	Chaja
LUBCZANSKI	Chajm
LUBCZANSKI	David
LUBCZANSKI	Israel
LUBCZANSKI	Roza
LUBCZANSKI	Syma
LUCKI	Eva
LUCKI	Isak

M

MASLOVATY	Chana
MASLOVATY	Rubin
MASLOVATY	Ryva
MASLOVATY	Shlena
MEIEROVICZ	Judel
MEIEROVICZ	Musia
MEIEROVICZ	Nachama
MEIEROVICZ	Rachela
MEIEROVICZ	Sonia
MENDELEVICZ	Iosif
MENDELEVICZ	Shifra
MICHALOJEVSKI	Chana
MICHALOJEVSKI	Faivel
MICHALOJEVSKI	Michail
MINIK	Abram
MINIK	Fira
MINIK	Jankiel
MINIK	Shiloka
MINIK	Shivia
MISCHIN	Chana
MISCHIN	Fania

MISCHIN	Lea
MISCHIN	Michail
MISCHIN	Osher
MLAMAJA	Chana
MLAMAJA	Ovsiej
MNAKER	Abram
MNAKER	Abram-Samuel
MNAKER	Alter
MNAKER	Belia
MNAKER	Benia
MNAKER	Chaja-Belia
MNAKER	Eska
MNAKER	Estera
MNAKER	Gita
MNAKER	Iosif
MNAKER	Isak
MNAKER	Markel
MNAKER	Shiffa
MOKOTOVICZ	Chana
MOKOTOVICZ	Moisiei
MOKOTOVICZ	Samuel
MOKOTOVICZ	Taiba
MORDUCHOVICZ	Asna
MORDUCHOVICZ	Braina
MORDUCHOVICZ	Chaim
MORDUCHOVICZ	Jankiel
MOVILEVICZ	Abram
MOVILEVICZ	Basia
MOVILEVICZ	Beniamin
MOVILEVICZ	Michail
MOVILEVICZ	Musia
MOVSHEVICZ	Aba
MOVSHEVICZ	David
MOVSHEVICZ	Mnicha
MOVSHEVICZ	Shena
MUCZNIK	Dinia
MUCZNIK	Eliash

N
NACHIMOVSKI	Abram
NACHIMOVSKI	Alter
NACHIMOVSKI	Herz
NACHIMOVSKI	Hinda
NACHIMOVSKI	Ryva
NAMYSLOVSKI	Elka
NAMYSLOVSKI	Focha
NAMYSLOVSKI	Iosif

NAMYSLOVSKI	Mera
NAMYSLOVSKI	Moisiei
NAMYSLOVSKI	Shlena
NIEGNIEVICKI	Abram
NIEGNIEVICKI	Chana
NIEGNIEVICKI	Doba
NIEGNIEVICKI	Frida
NIEGNIEVICKI	Gita
NIEGNIEVICKI	Icko
NIEGNIEVICKI	Ryva
NISELEVICZ	Ada
NISELEVICZ	Aron
NISELEVICZ	Aron
NISELEVICZ	Belia
NISELEVICZ	Chaja
NISELEVICZ	Chana
NISELEVICZ	David
NISELEVICZ	Faivel
NISELEVICZ	Fania
NISELEVICZ	Luba
NISELEVICZ	Masha
NISELEVICZ	Musia
NISELEVICZ	Necha
NISELEVICZ	Sara
NISELEVICZ	Sara
NISELEVICZ	Sonia
NISELEVICZ	Zalman

O

OBOVICZ	Bliuma
OBOVICZ	Genia
OBOVICZ	Jankiel
OBOVICZ	Martyna
OBOVICZ	Ryva
OBRYNSKI	Berko
OBRYNSKI	Chaja
OBRYNSKI	Sara
OCHANOVSKI	Aron
OCHANOVSKI	Estera
ORZECHOVSKI	Moisiei
OSTASHYNSKI	Fania
OSTASHYNSKI	Rubin

P

PERKOVICZ	Lea
PERKOVICZ	Morduch
PIEREVOLOCKI	Chaja

PIEREVOLOCKI	Elka
PIEREVOLOCKI	Hinda
PIEREVOLOCKI	Leib
PIEREVOLOCKI	Mendel
PIEREVOLOCKI	Rachela
PIEREVOLOCKI	Rachela
PIEREVOLOCKI	Rubin
PIEREVOLOCKI	Sheina
POLIMAKOVSKI	Isak
POLIMAKOVSKI	Morduch
POLONIECKI	Evel
POLONSKI	Chania
POLONSKI	Codik
POLONSKI	Luba
POLONSKI	Mashka
POLONSKI	Sonia
POLUZECKI	Berko
POLUZECKI	Bracha
POLUZECKI	Chaja
POLUZECKI	Chasia
POLUZECKI	Estera
POLUZECKI	Herman
POLUZECKI	Mera
POLUZECKI	Moisiei

R

RABEC	Genia
RABINOVICZ	Chana
RABINOVICZ	Dora
RABINOVICZ	Eda
RABINOVICZ	Iochava
RABINOVICZ	Jankiel
RABINOVICZ	Judis
RABINOVICZ	Lazar
RABINOVICZ	Meier
RABINOVICZ	Shelom
RABINOVICZ	Shmil
RABINOVICZ	Sonia
RABINOVICZ	Sonia
RABINOVICZ	Taiba
RACZKOVSKI	Chania
RACZKOVSKI	Make
RACZKOVSKI	Sonia
RACZKOVSKI	Zysia
RAJSIN	Cochot-Moisiei
RAJSIN	Iosif
RAJSIN	Mnucha

RAJSIN	Rosa
RAKOVICKI	Belia
RAKOVICKI	Chana
RAKOVICKI	Chana
RAKOVICKI	Hirsh
RAKOVICKI	Nissan
RAKOVICKI	Shlena
RAPAPORT	Abram
RAPAPORT	Moisiei
RAPAPORT	Sima
RAZOVSKI	Alter
RAZOVSKI	Chana
RAZOVSKI	Cyra
RAZOVSKI	Moisiei
RAZOVSKI	Sheitel
RAZOVSKI	Shirinca
REZNIK	Abram
REZNIK	Israel
REZNIK	Isser
REZNIK	Pesia
ROGATYNSKI	Frida
ROGATYNSKI	Ryva
ROZOVSKI	Beniamin
ROZOVSKI	Esther
ROZOVSKI	Frida
ROZOVSKI	Rafal
RUBIENCZIK	Zalman
RUTANSKA	Nachama

S

SALUCKI	Beniamin
SALUCKI	Chaja
SALUCKI	Hirsh
SAVICKI	Musia
SCHNEIDER	Maria
SCHNEIDER	Shlena
SCHNEIDER	Shlena
SHAPIRO	Maria
SHERESHEVSKI	Boruch
SHERESHEVSKI	Chana
SHERESHEVSKI	Hershen
SHERESHEVSKI	Lida
SHERESHEVSKI	Morduch
SHERESHEVSKI	Nissan
SHLACHTMAN	Chaim
SHLACHTMAN	Iosif

SHLACHTMAN	Moisiei
SHLACHTMAN	Sima
SILBERMAN	David
SILBERMAN	Hirsh
SLADKOVSKI	Belia
SLADKOVSKI	Doba
SLADKOVSKI	Elia
SLADKOVSKI	Jasha
SLOBOCKI	Etka
SLOBOCKI	Faivel
SLOBOCKI	Mira
SLOBOCKI	Rachela
SLOBOCKI	Velvel
SLOLEV	Iosif
SLOLEV	Isak
SLOLEV	Lea
SLUCKI	Aleksander
SLUCKI	Chasia
SLUCKI	David
SLUCKI	David
SLUCKI	Iosif
SLUCKI	Isak
SLUCKI	Jankiel
SLUCKI	Judis
SLUCKI	Kreina
SLUCKI	Liba
SLUCKI	Lipa
SLUCKI	Luba
SLUCKI	Noiman
SLUCKI	Rachela
SLUCKI	Ryva
SMILOVICZ	Braina
SMILOVICZ	Fiedia
SMILOVICZ	Moisei
SOLODUCHA	Eidel
SOLODUCHA	Jachka
SOSNOVSKI	Belia
SOSNOVSKI	Michlia
SOSNOVSKI	Naum
SOSNOVSKI	Sonia
SREBRNIK	Abram
STOCKI	Chaim
STOCKI	Sara
STOLER	Beniamin
STOLER	Chajm
STOLER	Gita
STOLER	Hirsh

STOLER	Meier
STOLER	Moisiei
STOLER	Moisiei
STOLER	Musia
STOLER	Shosel
SUCHARSKI	Chaja
SUCHARSKI	Israel
SUCHARSKI	Noma
SUCHARSKI	Sheina

T

TAVRYCKI	David
TAVRYCKI	Hinda
TAVRYCKI	Judis
TAVRYCKI	Luba
TAVRYCKI	Shuliama
TAVRYCKI	Sima

U

UGERT	Aliza
UGERT	Chaja

W

WERNIK	Aleksander
WERNIK	Chajm
WERNIK	Israel
WERNIK	Lea
WERNIK	Miriam
WERNIK	Ryva
WERNIK	Sonia
WOLFOVICZ	Abram
WOLFOVICZ	Berko
WOLFOVICZ	Chaja-Belia
WOLFOVICZ	Chana-Ryva
WOLFOVICZ	Golda
WOLFOVICZ	Leib
WOLFOVICZ	Libia
WAISS	Isak
WEINSTRAUB	Chaja
WEINSTRAUB	Chana
WEINSTRAUB	Grunia
WEINSTRAUB	Samuel
WIENER	Aron
WIENER	Chaja
WIENER	Judel
WOJMER	Fania
WOJMER	Mira

WOJMER	Zlata

Z

ZALAMANSKI	Finkel
ZALAMANSKI	Jankiel
ZALAMANSKI	Roza
ZALAMANSKI	Sara
ZAMOSHCHIK	Abram
ZAMOSHCHIK	Belia
ZAMOSHCHIK	Chaja
ZAMOSHCHIK	Chajm
ZAMOSHCHIK	Etka
ZAMOSHCHIK	Iosif
ZAMOSHCHIK	Leib
ZAMOSHCHIK	Nissan
ZAMOSHCHIK	Nissan
ZAMOSHCHIK	Sara
ZAMOSHCHIK	Sheina
ZAMOSHCHIK	Shelom
ZELIVIANSKI	Beniamin
ZELIVIANSKI	Molia
ZELIVIANSKI	Rosa
ZELIVIANSKI	Shimon
ZYSKIND	Dora
ZYSKIND	Herten
ZYSKIND	Jeda
ZYSKIND	Meier
ZYSKIND	Sacha

The List of Jews from Novogrudok, including members of the Bielski partisan group, killed in the Soviet armed forces in the Second World War. Most were killed in 1944, after the liberation of Novogrudok

ABRAMOVICH	Moisei Abramovich	killed in 1941
BIELSKI	Asoel	ex. Bielski partisan
BOLDO	Issak Moiseievich	killed on the 5.10.44 in Kelme Lithuania
BRUK	David	killed on the 22.7.44 in Poland
CHORNY	Chaim Moiseievich	killed on the 19.4.44, in Zabern, Germany
GILKIN	Abram Isaevich	killed on the 15.7.44
GRINDA	Chackel Berkovich	killed on the 3.5.45 in Germany
GUREWICZ	Cwi (Herszele)	ex. Bielski partisan
KAGAN	Ichke Moiseievich	killed on the 23,4.44 in Zabern Germany
KAGANOVICH	Michoel	killed on the 2.4.44 in Khadzi-Bulat Crimea
KAMENSKI	Michoel Yosifovich	died in 1945
KAMENSKI	Jehuda Yosifovich	killed in Zabern, Germany
PLOTNIK	Gersh Antonovich	killed on the 30.8.44 in Bialystok region
PLOTNIK	Cwi	ex. Bielski partisan
RAKOWSKI	Awrohom (Awremke)	ex. Bielski partisans
ROSIN	Awrohom (Bom)	ex. Bielski partisans
TROICKI	Zalmon	ex. Bielski partisan
ZAMKOWY	Jiszajahu (Szajke)	ex. Bielski partisan
ZLOTNIK	Faivl Yonovich	killed on the 17.9.44 near Warsaw
ZUCHOVICKI	Michoel Aronovich	killed on the 14.1.45 in Szczecin, Poland
ZUCHOVICKI	Nison Aronovich	buried in Starograd, Poland on the 5.9.44

Killed by the Poles soon after liberation

ZAMKOWY   Michoel

List of Jews from Novogrudok who were arrested or deported on the night of 19/20 June 1941 and died during the war in Russia.

BROIDO		Died probably on the train journey to prison
EFRON		Died in Saratov after the release from prison
GRAJWER	Isroel	Died in Tashkent after the release from prison
KIWELEWICZ		Died probably on the train journey to prison
KLUBOK		Died probably on the train journey to prison
LUBCZANSKI		Died in Achinsk Siberia soon after arrival from prison
NIANKOWSKI		Died probably on the train journey to prison
SZLOMOWICZ	Ester	Died in Achinsk Siberia after the amnesty

ZISKIND   Died probably on the train journey to prison

Of the above only Ester SZLOMOWICZ was deported, all others were arrested.

List of the Bielski Partisans Killed

BERKOWICZ	Mosze	Killed in May 1943
CHAJETOWICZ	Eliezer	Killed in Dobro-Polia March 1943
CZERNY	Mordechai	Killed in Naliboki Beginning 1942
EFROIMSKI	Herzl	Killed in Kharpenevo December 1942
EPSTEIN	Mark	Killed on the day of liberation 4.7.44
GERSZONOWSKI	Sara	Killed on the day of liberation 4.7.44
LEIBOWICZ	Itzchak	Killed in Kharpenevo December 1942
LEIBOWICZ	Cwi	Killed on the day of liberation 4.7.44
MENAKER	Jehoszua	Killed near Huta Beginning 1943
MOWSZOWICZ		Killed in 1944
MOWSZOWICZ	Ben-Zion	Killed in Naliboki Beginning 1942
OSTASZINSKI	Jehoszua	Killed in Dobro-Polia March 1943
OSTASZINSKI	Jehuda	Killed in Lipichanski forest
POLONSKI	Abraham	Killed in Dobro-Polia March 1943
POLONSKI	Ruven	Killed in Dobro-Polia March 1943
RAZEWSKI	Josef	Killed just before the liberation July 44
WOLFOWICZ	Aba	Killed in December 1942
WOLKIN	Arie (Lejbke)	Tortured and killed in Novogrudok jail 1942?
ZILBERMAN	Dowid	Killed in May 1943
ZILBERMAN	Cwi	Killed in May 1943
ZISKIND	Ada	Killed in Naliboki Beginning 1942

Karelich

Translated by Oskar Delatycki

A

ABRAMOWICZ	Duszka	BERKOWICZ	Chana
ABRAMOWICZ	Gavriel	BERKOWICZ	China, 2 children
ABRAMOWICZ	Jehoszua	BERKOWICZ	Szlomo, wife
ABRAMOWICZ	Jehoszua's wife	BERKOWICZ	Mirjam
ABRAMOWICZ	Cira	BERKOWICZ	Mojsze
ABRAMOWICZ	Rachel	BERKOWICZ	Chana Chaja
ABRAMOWICZ	Israel	BERKOWICZ	Zlata
ABRAMOWICZ	Chaja Dwora, 3 children	BERKOWICZ	Welwl
		BERKOWICZ	Mojsze
ABRAMOWICZ	Jehoszua Leib	BERKOWICZ	Ester Rochl
ABRAMOWICZ,	Jehoszua Leib's wife, children	BERKOWICZ	Josef
		BERMA	Abraham
ABRAMOWICZ	Leia	BERMA	Szejne
ABRAMOWICZ	Jehuda	BIGIN	Liba
ABRAMOWICZ	Jehoszua	BIGIN	Eliyahu
ABRAMOWICZ	Mosze	BIGIN	Cipa
ABRAMOWICZ	Chaja	BIGIN	Sara
ABRAMOWICZ	Alter	BOKER	Josef
ABRAMOWICZ	Riva, 3 children	BOKER	Nachum Izchak
ABRAZIANSKI	Abram Szmuel	BOLOTNICKI	Abram
ABRAZIANSKI	Hisz Leib	BOLOTNICKI	Grunia
ABRAZIANSKI	Mirjam	BOLOTNICKI	Raszel
ABRAZIANSKI	Szymon	BOLOTNICKI	Mojsze
ABRINSKI	Berl	BOLOTNICKI	Minia
ARCHONOWSKI	Izchak	BOROWSKI	Szifra
ARCHONOWSKI	Ester	BORENSZTEIN	Josef
ARCHONOWSKI	David	BORENSZTEIN	Rachel
ATLASKI	Fruma	BORENSZTEIN	Leibisz
ATLASKI	Josef	BORENSZTEIN	Sinaj
ATLASKI	Baruch	BOSEL	Chaim
ATLASKI	Rachel	BOSEL	Golda
ABRANSKI	Chisza	BOSEL	Berl
ABRANSKI	Sara	BOSEL	Pesach
AWISEWICZ	Michael	BOSEL	Sonia, child
		BOSEL	Bluma
B		BOTAINSKI	Ester Basza
BENIN	Mordechai	BOTAINSKI	Rejzl Rochl
BENIN	Gite	BOTAINSKI	Josef
BENIN	Josef	BOTAINSKI	Rochl
BENIN	Cypa	BRESLIN	Szmaj
BERKOWICZ	Davida	BRESLIN	Fejgl

BRESLIN	Abram	FAJWELEWICZ	his wife
BRESLIN	Sula	FAJWELEWICZ	Szlomo
BRESLIN	Chaja	FAJWELEWICZ	Henia, child
		FAJWELEWICZ	Eliyahu
C		FAJWELEWICZ	Sara Fejgl
CAROBODSKI	Minia	FAJWELEWICZ	Sara Fejgl's 2 children
CAROBODSKI	Minia's 2 children	FAJWELEWICZ	Herszl
CELKOWICZ	Pinchas	FAJWELEWICZ	Etka
CELKOWICZ	Zosia	FAJWELEWICZ	Abraham
CELKOWICZ	Baruch	FAJWELEWICZ	Chaim
CELKOWICZ	Zlata, child	FAJWELEWICZ	Zeidl
CHABARUK	Josef	FARBOLOCKI	Ruven
CHABARUK	Sara Feiga	FARBOLOCKI	Szejna
		FARBOLOCKI	Hadasa
D		FARBOLOCKI	Rachel
DAMASEK	Berl	FARBOLOCKI	Mendl
DAMASEK	Buza	FARBOLOCKI	Leib
DAMASEK	Jehudit	FARBOLOCKI	Elke
DAMASEK	Sula	FARBOLOCKI	Brocha
DUSZKIN	Abram	FARBOLOCKI	Chasia
DUSZKIN	Chaim	FRIDMAN	Chaja
DUSZKIN	Finkl	FRIDMAN	Josef
		FRIDMAN	Cirl
E		FRIDMAN	Mosze Dawid
EFROIMSKI	Hertz	FRIDMAN	Hodl Raizel
EFROIMSKI	Chana	FRIDMAN	Alter
EFROIMSKI	Fejgl	FRIDMAN	Szprinca
EFROIMSKI	Ester		
EPSHTEIN	David	**G**	
EPSHTEIN	Fajwl	GANCEWICZ	Zelig
EPSHTEIN	Duszka	GANCEWICZ	Dwosia
		GANCEWICZ	Izchak Berl
F		GANCEWICZ	Mojsze Dowid
FAJWELEWICZ	Cipa	GANCEWICZ	Jehuda
FAJWELEWICZ	Zejdl	GANCEWICZ	Luba
FAJWELEWICZ	Nochim	GERCOWSKI	Szlojma
FAJWELEWICZ	Sonia	GERCOWSKI	Shlojma's wife, child
FAJWELEWICZ	Etka	GERCOWSKI	Chasia
FAJWELEWICZ	Alter	GERCOWSKI	Leah
FAJWELEWICZ	Chana Yenta	GERCOWSKI	Szlomo
FAJWELEWICZ	Tiba	GERSZONOWSKI	Jehuda
FAJWELEWICZ	Rywka	GERSZONOWSKI	Brina
FAJWELEWICZ	Jenta	GERSZOWICZ	Noach
FAJWELEWICZ	Hilel	GERSZOWICZ	Mira
FAJWELEWICZ	Chana	GERSZOWICZ	Mosze
FAJWELEWICZ	Szjke	GERSZOWICZ	Batszeva
FAJWELEWICZ	his brother	GERSZOWICZ	Leibl

GERSZOWICZ	Minia	GOZICHEW	Godl's wife
GERSZOWICZ	Nechama	GOZICHEW	Noach
GERSZOWICZ	Hadasa	GOZICHEW	Szymon
GERSZOWICZ	Izchak	GRINBERG	Nisl
GERSZONOWSKI	Josef	GRINBERG	Tevl
GERSZONOWSKI	Mosia	GRINBERG	Jehuda
GERSZONOWSKI	Mosze	GRINBERG	Grisza
GERSZONOWSKI	Rachel	GRINBERG	Rejzl
GERSZONOWSKI	Gedalia	GRINFELD	Szymon
GERSZONOWSKI	Josef	GRINFELD	China
GERSZONOWSKI	Malka Riva	GRINFELD	Alter
GERSZONOWSKI	Mire	GRINFELD	Raszel
GERSZONOWSKI	Johewet	GRINFELD	David
GERSZONOWSKI	Chaim	GUREWICZ	Chana Gitl
GERSZONOWSKI	Liba	GURSZOWICZ	Aaron
GERSZONOWSKI	Chaja Bejla	GURSZOWICZ	Bronia
GITLIN	Jakow	GURSZOWICZ	Mojsze
GITLIN	Chajka	GURSZOWICZ	Mordechaj
GITLIN	Chajm		
GITLIN	Rochl	**H**	
GITLIN	Gitl	HORDUS	Mosze
GOLDSZMID	Mosze Ruven	HORDUS	Gitl
GOLDSZMID	Basia		
GOLDSZMID	Rachel	**I**	
GOLDSZMID	Guta	ICKOWICZ	Zisl
GOLKOWICZ	Szlomo	ICKOWICZ	Mosze
GOLKOWICZ	Rachel	ICKOWICZ	Sonia
GOLKOWICZ	Szlomo	ICKOWICZ	Izchak
GOLKOWICZ	Fajwl	ICKOWICZ	little girl
GOLKOWICZ	Brinia	IZRAELIT	Israel
GOREWICZ	Felka	IZRAELIT	Hinda
GOREWICZ	Ester Rochl	IZRAELIT	Henia
GOREWICZ	Dewora		
GOREWICZ	Josef	**J**	
GOREWICZ	Brajna Feigl	JANKELEWICZ	Szmerl
GOREWICZ	Chasia	JANKELEWICZ	Hinda
GORODENSKI	Berl	JANKELEWICZ	Alter
GORODENSKI	Niszka	JANKELEWICZ	Jehoszua Jakow
GORODENSKI	Freidl, child	JANKELEWICZ	wife
GORODENSKI	Abraham	JANKELEWICZ	Freidl
GORODENSKI	Heda Bejla	JANKELEWICZ	Baszka
GORODINSKI	Mosze	JANKELEWICZ	Eliahu
GORODINSKI	Mosze's 2 children	JANKELEWICZ	Devora
GORTONOWSKI	Jakow	JANKELEWICZ	Mosze
GORTONOWSKI	Sara Leje	JANKELEWICZ	Dovid
GORTONOWSKI	Sara Leje's child	JANKELEWSKI	Bejla
GOZICHEW	Godl	JANKELEWSKI	Hinda

JANKELEWSKI	Chaim	KAGAN	Chaja's small child
JANKELEWSKI	Rita	KAGAN	Itka
JANKELEWSKI	Cyra	KAGAN	David
JANKELEWSKI	Henia	KAGAN	David's 2 children
JELIN	Hercl	KAGAN	Miriam
JELIN	Jona	KAGAN	Ruven
JELIN	Szejna Feigl	KAGAN	Sula
JELIN	Ester Rochl	KAGAN	Sula's little girl
JELIN	Bacia	KALICKI	Towie
JELIN	Riva	KALICKI	Chasia
JELIN	Michl	KALMANOWICZ	Josef
JELIN	Sonia	KALMANOWICZ	Bejla
JELIN	Bluma	KALMANOWICZ	Izchak
JELIN	Miriam	KALMANOWICZ	Braine
JOSELEWICZ	Pinek	KALMANOWICZ	Szmuel
JOSELEWICZ	Szira, 2 children	KALMANOWICZ	Towa
JOSELEWICZ	Oszer Mosze	KALMANOWICZ	Szejna
JOSELEWICZ	Etl	KALMANOWICZ	Josef
JOSELEWICZ	Otrica	KALMANOWSKI	Szmuel Hirsz
JOSELEWICZ	Luba	KALMANOWSKI	Chana Etka
JOSELEWICZ	Symcha	KALMANOWSKI	Ruwen
JOSELEWICZ	Rachel	KALMANOWSKI	Hadasa
JOSELEWICZ	Josef	KAPLAN	Chaim
JOSELEWICZOYZER		KAPLAN	Chaja Lea
		KAPLAN	Szoszana
JOSELEWICZ	wife	KAPLAN	Meir
JOSELEWICZ	Chaim	KAPLAN	Mosze
JOSELEWICZ	wife	KAPLAN	Luke
JOSELEWICZ	Szlomo	KAPLAN	Chaja
JOSELEWICZ	Devora	KAPLAN	Josef
JOSELEWICZ	Moshe Rabbi	KAPLAN	Lipa
JOSELEWICZ	Moshe's wife	KAPLAN	Eyzer
JOSELEWICZ	Jenta	KAPLAN	Rywa
JOSELEWICZ	Sonia	KAPLAN	Chana
JOSELEWICZ	Maier	KAPLAN	Pesia
		KAPLAN	Fejga
K		KAPOSZEWSKI	Sara Golda
KABAK	Szlomo	KAPOSZEWSKI	Alta
KABAK	Dowa	KAUFMAN	Luba
KABAK	Mosze Leib	KAUFMAN	Jochewet
KABAK	Chaim	KAUFMAN	Idl
KABAK	Eliezer	KELECKI	Izchok Maier
KABAK	Rejzl	KELECKI	Chaja Cipa
KABAK	Mosze	KELECKI	Leja
KAGAN	Israel	KELECKI	Noach
KAGAN	Ester	KELECKI	Jakow
KAGAN	Chaja	KELECKI	Saul

KELECKI	Chaja Sara	LIPKIN	Bejla
KELECKI	Mirjam	LIPKIN	David
KELECKI	Izchak	LIPKIN	Mordechaj
KESLER	Arie	LIPKIN	Chana
KESLER	Ester	LIPKIN	Rachel
KESLER	Miriam	LIPKIN	Zalmon
KESLER	Tamara	LIPKIN	Chaim
KIWELEWICZ	Banda	LIPKIN	Mosze
KIWELEWICZ	Eska	LIPP	Szolem
KIWELEWICZ	Gite	LIPP	Kejla
KIWELEWICZ	Aaron	LIPP	Faigl
KOPERNIK	Aria	LIPSKI	Henach
KOPOLOWICZ	Gute	LIPSKI	Sonia, child
KOPOLOWICZ	Abram	LIPSZYC	David
KOPOLOWICZ	Ruwen	LOBIN	Chaskel
KORELICKI	Abram	LUBCZANSKI	Jakov Maier
KORELICKI	Jenta	LUBCZANSKI	Nechama, 2 children
KROLWACKI	Hirsz	LUBCZANSKI	Chaim
KROLWACKI	Pesia	LUBCZANSKI	Chasia Eta
KROLWACKI	Grunia	LUBCZANSKI	Symcha
KROLWACKI	Tamar	LUBCZANSKI	Rejzl
KUBANSKI	Szymon	LUBCZANSKI	Rachel
KUBANSKI	Jenta	LUDSKI	Zysia
KUBANSKI	Tamar		
KUBANSKI	Mojsze	**M**	
KUZNIC	Jehuda	MAYEROWICZ	Jehuda
KUZNIC	Rachel	MAYEROWICZ	Rachel
KUZNIC	Mosze	MAYEROWICZ	David
KUZNIC	Bajlke	MAYEROWICZ	Nechama
KUZNIC	Elke	MAYEROWICZ	Sara Minia
		MAZROWICZ	Mordechaj
L		MAZROWICZ	Fraidl
LESZCZYNSKI	David	MIRSKI	Nechamia
LESZCZYNSKI	Rywka	MIRSKI	Nachama
LEWIN	Mordchaj	MISZKIN	Lea
LEWIN	Sonia	MISZKIN	Chaim
LEWIN	Sonia's little child	MORDUCHOWICZ	Chaja Lea
LEWIT	Herc	MORDUCHOWICZ	Elka
LEWIT	Jehuda	MORDUCHOWICZ	Mordchaj
LEWIT	Szyfra	MORDUCHOWICZ	Etl
LEWIT	Luba	MORDUCHOWICZ	Chaja
LEWIT	Freidl	MORDUCHOWICZ	Godl
LIBOWICZ	Rywa Rejzl	MORDUCHOWICZ	Abram Izchak shoch
LIBOWICZ	David	MORDUCHOWICZ	Felka
LIBOWICZ	David's little girl	MORDUCHOWICZ	Uszer
LIPKIN	Chaim	MORDUCHOWICZ	Chasia
LIPKIN	Henia	MORDUCHOWICZ	Towa

MORDUCHOWICZ	Chaim		
		P	
N		PARSKI	Jehudit
NAMIOT	Herc	PILZANSKI	Ester
NAMIOT	Etl	PILZANSKI	Mosze
NAMIOT	Lea	PILOZOWSKI	Chasia
NAMIOT	Jakow	PILOZOWSKI	Mirjam
NAMIOT	Rywka	PILOZOWSKI	Brocha
NIEGNIEWICKI	Izchak	PILOZOWSKI	Chaja
NIEGNIEWICKI	Chana Sara	PILOZOWSKI	Berl
NIEGNIEWICKI	Eszka	POMIERCZIK	Ezra
NIEGNIEWICKI	Diva	POMIERCZIK	Luba
NIEGNIEWICKI	Rywa	POMIERCZIK	Berl
NIEGNIEWICKI	Abram	PORTNOJ	Mosze Hillel
NIEGNIEWICKI	Gitl	PORTNOJ	Mosze Hillel's wife
NISELEWICZ	David	PORTNOJ	Dawid
NISELEWICZ	Sara	PORTNOJ	Zalman
NISELEWICZ	Lova	PORTNOJ	Dewora
NISELEWICZ	Faigl	PUPKO	Sara Itka
NISELEWICZ	Fajwl	PUPKO	Aaron
NISELEWICZ	Mosze	PUPKO	Aaron's child
NISELEWICZ	Aaron		
NISELEWICZ	Aba	**R**	
NISLOWICZ	Sonia	RABINOWICZ	Szolim
NISLOWICZ	Zalmon	RABINOWICZ	Sonia
NISLOWICZ	Mosia	RABINOWICZ	Jakow
NISLOWICZ	Bejlka	RABINOWICZ	Lubcia
NISLOWICZ	Berl	RABINOWICZ	Noach
NOCHIMOWSKI	Alter	RAKOWICKI	Nisan
NOCHIMOWSKI	Sula	RAKOWICKI	Chana
NOCHIMOWSKI	Leibl	RAKOWICKI	Szyfra
		RAKOWICKI	Bejla
O		RAKOWICKI	Hirsz
OBOSIEWICZ	Tamar	RAKOWICKI	Szlomo
OKSIEWICZ	Chaja Lej	RAZOWSKI	Izchak
OLRAT	Chaja Leja	RAZOWSKI	Szprinca
ORZECHOWSKI	Chaja Sara	RAZOWSKI	Alter
ORZECHOWSKI	Chaja Sara	RAZOWSKI	Cipa
ORZECHOWSKI	Eliezer	RAZOWSKI	Szabatai
ORZECHOWSKI	Elka	RAZOWSKI	Mosze
ORZECHOWSKI	Mosze	RAZOWSKI	Rywa
OSZROWICZ	Josef Chaim		
OSZROWICZ	Eli Chaim	**S**	
OSZROWICZ	Eli's wife, 4 children	SARBARNIK	Alter
OTALSKI	Nisan	SARBARNIK	Lea
OWOSIEWICZ	Jehuda	SARBARNIK	Rejzl
OWOSIEWICZ	Benjamin	SARBARNIK	Mordechaj

SARBARNIK	Izchak	SLUCKI	Chaja
SARBARNIK	Sonia	SLUCKI	Benzion
SARBARNIK	Rafael	SOLOWICKI	Eliyahu
SARBARNIK	Golda	SOLOWICKI	Rachel
SARBARNIK	Sara	SOLOWICKI	Dowid
SAWICKI	Izchak	SOLOWICKI	Faitl
SAWICKI	Beilke	SOLOWICKI	Faitl's 2 children
SAWICKI	Idl	STOLAR	Izchak
SAWICKI	Chaim	STOLAR	Malka Rysia
SAWICKI	Lejbe	STOLAR	Mirjam
SKOROCHOD	Joel	STOLAR	Izchak
SKOROCHOD	Ciwja	STOLAR	Lea
SKOROCHOD	Bejlke	STOLAR	Jehuda
SKOROCHOD	Sonia	STOLAR	Mosia
SLOMINSKI	Fie	STOLAR	Josef
SLOMINSKI	Nisan	STOLAR	Nioma
SLOMINSKI	Diszka	STOLAR	Mira
SLOMINSKI	Mosze	STOLAR	Mosze
SLOMINSKI	Jakub	STOLAR	Kajla
SLOMINSKI	Finkl	STOLAR	Hirsz
SLOMINSKI	Sara	STOLAR	Grisza
SLOMINSKI	Reizl	STOLAR	Izchak
SLOMINSKI	Nisan	STOLAR	Lea
SLOMINSKI	Szaul	STOLAR	Chaim
SLOMINSKI	Hirsz	STOLAR	Luba
SLOMINSKI	Ruwen	STOLAR	Gitl
SLOMINSKI	Alter	STOLAR	Zelig
SLOMINSKI	Idel Fia	STOLAR	Szlomo
SLUBOCKI	Fajwl	STOLAR	Freidl
SLUBOCKI	Eszka	SZACKI	Malka
SLUBOCKI	Rachel	SZACKI	Israel
SLUBOCKI	Sara	SZACKI	Benjamin
SLUBOCKI	Welwl	SZACKI	Benjamin
SLUCKI	Jakow Leib	SZEROSZEWSKI	Jechiel
SLUCKI	Miriam	SZEROSZEWSKI	Sonia
SLUCKI	Chana	SZEROSZEWSKI	Jehuda
SLUCKI	Izchak	SZIMSZELEWICZ	Boruch
SLUCKI	Jehudit	SZIMSZELEWICZ	Chaja
SLUCKI	Jakow	SZIMSZELEWICZ	Lea
SLUCKI	Joel	SZIMSZELEWICZ	Mordchaj
SLUCKI	Dawid	SZIMSZELEWICZ	Nisan
SLUCKI	Dawid	SZIMSZELEWICZ	Gerszon
SLUCKI	Krejna	SZLIMOWICZ	Jechiskel
SLUCKI	Szura	SZLIMOWICZ	Sonia
SLUCKI	Josef	SZLIMOWICZ	Jehuda
SLUCKI	Lipe	SZMULEWICZ	Pinchas
SLUCKI	Hersz	SZMULEWICZ	Fruma, 2 children

SZUSTER	Mosia		
SZUSTER	Mosze Ele	**W**	
SZUSTER	Chedwa	WEINTRAUB	Gronia
SZUSTER	Nachum Bar	WEINTRAUB	Gronia's child
SZUSTER	Michoel	WERNIK	Rabbi
SZUSTER	Henia	WERNIK	Rabbi's wife
SZUSTER	Feigl	WERNIK	Chaim
SZUSTER	Ruwen	WERNIK	Sender
SZUSTER	Dowid Faitl	WERNIK	Mirjam
SZUSTER	Mosze	WERNIK	Riva
SZUSTER	Bejlke	WIENE	Kalman
SZUSTER	Dowid Faitl	WIENE	Kalman's wife
SZUSTER	Riwa	WIENE	Josef
SZUSTER	Chasia	WIENE	Aaron
SZYMONOWICZ	Szolim	WOLFIN	Mosze Abram
SZYMONOWICZ	Alte	WOLFIN	Johaved
SZYMONOWICZ	Hirsz		
SZYMONOWICZ	Bejle	**Z**	
SZYMONOWICZ	Jehuda	ZAMOSZCZYK	Abram
SZYMONOWICZ	Minia	ZAMOSZCZYK	Chaja, 3 children
SZYMONOWICZ	Benzion	ZLIWINSKI	Szymon
		ZLIWINSKI	Ruszka
T		ZLIWINSKI	Lea, 2 children
TAWARYCKI	Leib	ZLIWINSKI	Nioma
TAWARYCKI	Gersza Lei	ZLIWINSKI	Lipka
TAWARYCKI	Liula	ZLIWINSKI	mother
TROCKI	Mordechaj	ZLIWINSKI	Aaron
TROCKI	Beila	ZLIWINSKI	Masza
TROCKI	Basza	ZUSMAN	Rachel
TRUNKMAN	Hercl	ZUSMAN	Rejzl, 2 children
TRUNKMAN	Elka		

List of the Jews in the Ghetto of Karelich

Translated by Oskar Delatycki

As of the 20/5/1942.
Listing began 20.5.1942
Finished 20.6.1942
The list contains 888 names.

A

ABRAMOWICZ	Hirsz	ABRAMOWICZ	Gdala
ABRAMOWICZ	Mirka	ABRAMOWICZ	Duszka?
ABRAMOWICZ	Musza	ABRAMOWICZ	Jankel
ABRAMOWICZ	Chaja	ABRAMOWICZ	Gawriel
ABRAMOWICZ	Lea	AMALESKI	Sora
ABRAMOWICZ	Josl	AMALESKI	Iszka
ABRAMOWICZ	Anuel	AMALESKI	Josif
ABRAMOWICZ	Owsej Leiba	AMALESKI	Owsiej
ABRAMOWICZ	Chaja	AMALESKI	Basia
ABRAMOWICZ	Lea	AROL	Fruma
ABRAMOWICZ	Nachama	AROL	Falka?
ABRAMOWICZ	Chaja	AROL	Perec?
ABRAMOWICZ	Josl	AROL	Chana
ABRAMOWICZ	Abram	ABERZANSKI	Szloma
ABRAMOWICZ	Moisej	ABERZANSKI	Moisej ?
ABRAMOWICZ	Owsej	ABERZANSKI	Elka
ABRAMOWICZ	Izrael	ABERZANSKI	Mira
ABRAMOWICZ	Chaja (illegible)	ACHANOWSKI	Estera
		ACHANOWSKI	Dawid
		ABRAMOWICZ	Pesia
ABRAMOWICZ	Riwa	AROL	Lida
ABRAMOWICZ	Mojsej		
ABRAMOWICZ	Chana	**B**	
ABRAMOWICZ	Szmuel	BEJGIN	Luba
ABRAMOWICZ	Riwka	BEJGIN	Ela
ABRAMOWICZ	Abram	BEJGIN	Cyra
ABRAMOWICZ	Nison	BEJGIN	Sora
ABRAMOWICZ	Fejga	BEJGIN	Cyra
ABRAMOWICZ	Rachela	BEJGINSARA	
ABRAMOWICZ	Abram	BOLOTNICKI	Abram
ABRAMOWICZ	Rachela	BOLOTNICKI	Grunia
ABRAMOWICZ	Dowid	BOLOTNICKI	Roza
ABRAMOWICZ	Mowsza	BOLOTNICKI	Masza
ABRAMOWICZ	Chaim?	BOLOTNICKI	Minia
ABRAMOWICZ	Lea	BERKOWICZ	Ester
ABRAMOWICZ	Zusia	BERENSZTAIN	Rachela

BERENSZTAIN	Lejba	BRUK	Icko
BERENSZTAIN	?	BRUK	Brocha
BENIN	Jankel	BRZEZNICKI	Riwa
BENIN	?	BRZEZNICKI	Szewach
BENIN	Mowsza	**C**	
BRUDKA	Paulina	CANKIN	Fruma
BITENSKI	Josif	CALKOWICZ	Zlata
BITENSKI	Rosa	CALKOWICZ	Nachum
BERKOWICZ	Dawid	CIEPLOWODSKI	Minja
BERKOWICZ	Chaja	CIEPLOWODSKI	Fejga
BERKOWICZ	Genia	CIEPLOWODSKI	Zelda
BERKOWICZ	Beila	CIEPLOWODSKI	Abram
BERKOWICZ	Sonia	CHARLIN	Morduch
BERKOWICZ	Izko	CHARLIN	Judes
BERKOWICZ	Abram		
BEKER	Gdalia	**D**	
BEKER	Chana	DUSZKIN	Abram
BERKOWICZ	Wolf	DUDMAN	Sara
BERKOWICZ	Musza	DUSZKIN	Ruben
BERKOWICZ	Rocha	DUSZKIN	Mina
BERKOWICZ	Lejzer	DUSZKIN	Chaja
BERKOWICZ	Josel	DUSZKIN	Zisl
BERMAN	Szejna	DUSZKIN	Jankel
BERKOWICZ	Chana-Chaja	DUSZKIN	Genia
BERKOWICZ	Chaim	DUSZKIN	Ela
BERKOWICZ	Zlata	DUSZKIN	Chaim
BERKOWICZCYFRA		DUSZKIN	Finkl
BERKOWICZ	Genia	DUSZKIN	Dawid
BERKOWICZ	Josif	DUSZKIN	Chawa
BROJDA	Aron		
BROJDA	Itka	**E**	
BROJDA	Jechiel	EPSZTEIN	Duszka
BUSSEL	Bluma	EPSZTEIN	Faiwl
BUSSEL	Sara	EFROIMSKI	Ester
BUSSEL	Berta	EFROIMSKI	Chana
BOROWSKI	?	EFROIMSKI	Fania
BOROWSKI	?	EFROIMSKI	Roza
BOROWSKI	Szifra	EFROIMSKI	Adasa
BRASLIN	Feiga	EDELSZTAIN	Chaim
BRASLIN	Abram	EDELSZTAIN	Fruma
BRASLIN	Sola		
BRASLIN	Chaja	**F**	
BERKOWICZ	Morduch	FAIWELEWICZ	?
BERKOWICZ	Lea	FAIWELEWICZ	?
BERKOWICZ	Judes	FAIWELEWICZ	Nioma
BLOCH	Chaja	FAIWELEWICZ	Itka
BLOCH	Ruta	FAIWELEWICZ	Abram

FAIWELEWICZ	Rocha	GORODEJSKI	Genia
FAIWELEWICZ	Masza	GORODEJSKI	Sola
FAIWELEWICZ	Icko	GORODEJSKI	Icko
FAIWELEWICZ	?	GORODEJSKI	Abram
FAIWELEWICZ	Ela	GERSZENOWSKI	?
FAIWELEWICZ	Sara ?	GERSZENOWSKI	Malka
FAIWELEWICZ	Judel	GERSZENOWSKI	Jacha?
FAIWELEWICZ	Icko	GURDUS	Gita
FAIWELEWICZ	Efraim	GERSZENOWSKI	Chaim
FAIWELEWICZ	Szloma	GERSZENOWSKI	Liba
FAIWELEWICZ	Genia	GUREWICZ	Fanka
FAIWELEWICZ	Zlata	GUREWICZ	Ester Rosa
FRIDMAN	Roza	GUREWICZ	Dweira
FRIDMAN	Chaja	GERCOWSKI	Sadia?
FRIDMAN	Josl	GERCOWSKI	Lea
FRIDMAN	Lea	GERCOWSKI	Pera?
FRIDMAN	Mowsza	GERCOWSKI	Irma
FRIDMAN	Cyra	GERCENOWSKI	Masza
FRIDMAN	Abram	GERCOWSKI	Chasia
FRIDMAN	Szprinca	GELLER	Estera
FAIWELEWICZ	Cypa	GELLER	Naum
FAIWELEWICZ	Zeidl	GULKOWICZ	Szloma
FAIWELEWICZ	Nachum	GULKOWICZ	Feiga
FAIWELEWICZ	Sonia	GULKOWICZ	Broina
FAIWELEWICZ	Elka	GINZBURG	Judel
FAIWELEWICZ	Toiba	GINZBURG	Gisza
FARBER	Chaim	GINZBURG	Roza
FARBER	Minia	GINZBURG	Feiga
FARBER	Leiba	GINZBURG	Rachela
FARBER	Sara	GUREWICZ	Josel
FARBER	Frida	GUREWICZ	Broina
FARBER	Jankel	GUREWICZ	Nachama
FAIFER	Nachman	GUREWICZ	Chasia
FAIFER	Szewa	GERSZOWICZ	Merka
FAIFER	Lipa	GRINBERG	Jakov
FLESZER	Motka	GRINBERG	Taiba
FLESZER	Judis	GERSZOWICZ	Minia
FLESZER	Masza	GERSZOWICZ	Nachama
FAIWELEWICZ	Benjamin	GERSZOWICZ	Newach
FAIWELEWICZ	Chaim	GERSZOWICZ	Hadasa
	Zalmon	GERSZOWICZ	Pinchos
		GERSZOWICZ	Sorke?
G		GRINFELD	Szimon
GORODEJSKI	Eska	GRINFELD	Chana
GORODEJSKI	Szosza	GRINFELD	Roza
GOSZIN	Fejga	GITLIN	Jankel
GORODEJSKI	Mowsza	GITLIN	Chaja

GITLIN	Lea	GULKOWICZ	Chaja
GITLIN	Gita	GUREWICZ	Chana
GITLIN	haim	GUREWICZ	Liza
GITLIN	Rachela	GERSZOWICZ	Szlejma
GITLIN	Chackel	GERSZOWICZ	Elka
GITLIN	Zlata	GERSZOWICZ	Abram
GITLIN	Gita	GERSZOWICZ	Raisa
GERSZENOWSKI	Sara Roza	GERSZOWICZ	Dora
GERSZENOWSKI	Szloma	GERSZOWICZ	Sora Minia
GERSZENOWSKI	Roza	GUZUK	Sora
GERSZENOWSKI	Aliza	GILKOWICZ	Hilel
GOLDBERG	Chaim	GILKOWICZ	Chana
GORODISKI	Szloma	GILKOWICZ	Josif
GORODISKI	Taiba	GILKOWICZ	Elka
GORODISKI	Rachela	GEREWICZ?	Efroim
GERSZOWICZ	Basia	GEREWICZ?	Lida
GERSZOWICZ	Etka	GEREWICZ?	Sora
GERSZOWICZ	Mowsza		
GERSZOWICZ	Szloma	**I**	
GERSZOWICZ	Chana	IZRAELIT	Chaja Zusia
GERSZOWICZ	Josl	IZRAELIT	Pesia
GERSZOWICZ	Szaja	IZRAELIT	Izak
GERSZOWICZ	Berko	IZRAELIT	Hinda
GERSZOWICZ	Judel	ICKOWICZ	Sonia
GERSZOWICZ	Aron	ICKOWICZ	Jankel
GERSZOWICZ	Bunia	ICKOWICZ	Chana
GERSZOWICZ	Masza	ICKOWICZ	Zusia
GOCZICHES	Godel		
GOCZICHES	Nachama	**J**	
GOCZICHES	Feiga	JOSELEWICZ	Rachela
GOCZICHES	Szimon	JOSELEWICZ	Izer ?
GOCZICHES	Rachela	JOSELEWICZ	Cherna
GONCOWICZ	Dwosza	JOSELEWICZ	Ela
GONCOWICZ	Guta	JOSELEWICZ	Chaim
GONCOWICZ	Leiba	JOSELEWICZ	Rejza
GONCOWICZ	Luba	JOSELEWICZ	Bejla
GERSZOWICZ	Dwoira	JOSELEWICZ	Fajwel
GERSZOWICZ	Sonia	JOSELEWICZ	Benzion
GONCOWICZ	Josla	JOSELEWICZ	Itka
GERSZONOWSKI	Rachel	JOSELEWICZ	Gerszon
GERSZONOWSKI	Gdalia	JOSELEWICZ	Mira
GOLDSZMID	Mowsza	JOSELEWICZ	Sara
GOLDSZMID	Basia	JOSELEWICZ	Luba
GOLDSZMID	Rachela	JOSELEWICZ	Simcha
GOLDSZMID	Guta	JOSELEWICZ	Taiba
GULKOWICZ	Benzion	JOSELEWICZ	Pesia
GULKOWICZ	Judes	JOSELEWICZ	Beila

JOSELEWICZ	Benzion	KLECK	Hinda
JOSELEWICZ	Mowsza	KLECK	Majrim
JOSELEWICZ	Sonia	KOZAK	Wolf
JOSELEWICZ	Hirsz	KOZAK	Malka
JOSELEWICZ	Berko	KOZAK	Dwora
JOSELEWICZ	Efraim	KOZAK	Nison
JOSELEWICZ	Genia	KULIK	Nachama
JOSELEWICZ	Morduch	KULIK	Leiba
JOSELEWICZ	Jenta	KULIK	Chana
JOSELEWICZ	Mirjam	KULIK	Mera
JOSELEWICZ	Nachama	KULIK	Lea
JOSELEWICZ	Hirsz	KULIK	Feiga
JOSELEWICZ	Sara	KULIK	Szulamit
JOSELEWICZ	Mendl	KAGAN	Izrael
JOSELEWICZ	Roza	KAGAN	Estera
JOSELEWICZ	Malka	KAGAN	Braina
JOSELEWICZ	Nison	KAGAN	Chaja
JOSELEWICZ	Josl	KAGAN	Chaim
JEDIDOWICZ	Szloma	KAGAN	Benjamin
JEDIDOWICZ	Mera	KAGAN	Mowsza
JEDIDOWICZ	Minia	KAGAN	Rubin
JEDIDOWICZ	Judes	KOPERNIK	Berko
JEDIDOWICZ	Malka	KOPERNIK	Rachela
JEDIDOWICZ	Ester	KAGAN	?
JELIN	Fejga	KAGAN	Szula
JELIN	Rachela	KAGAN	Dweira
JELIN	Riwa	KAGANRACHELA	
JELIN	Sonia	KAPLAN	Masza
JELIN	Bluma	KAPLAN	Lewik
JELIN	Mirjam	KAPLAN	Bejla
JELIN	Mera	KAPLAN	Lipa
JANKELEWICZ	Sara	KOPURSKI	Maria
JANKELEWICZ	Mira	KALMANOWICZ	Taiba
JANKELEWICZ	Lida	KALMANOWICZ	Szejna
JANKELEWICZ	Dweira	KALMANOWICZ	Jela
JANKELEWICZ	Josif	KOPERNIK	Aron
JANKELEWICZ	Itka	KOPERNIK	Zelda
JANKELEWICZ	Dawid	KOPERNIK	Feiwl
JANKELEWICZ	Chaim	KOPERNIK	Chonia
JANKELEWICZ	Raja	KIWELEWICZ	?
JANKELEWICZ	Iser	KAGAN	Michel
JANKELEWICZ	?	KAGAN	Itka
JANKELEWICZ	Dawid	KAGAN	Dawid
JANKELEWICZ	Bejla	KAGAN	Malka
JANKELEWICZ	Cira	KAGAN	Estera
		KALMANOWICZ	Bejla
K		KALMANOWICZ	Icko

KALMANOWICZ	Fruma?	KIWELEWICZ	Nachama
KOPELOWICZ	Abram	KIWELEWICZ	Luba
KAFMAN	Lida	KIWELEWICZ	Judes
KAFMAN	Chawa	KIWELEWICZ	Zelda
KAFMAN	Ejdla	KUSZELEWICZ	Chaim Ruben
KAFMAN	Frida	KUSZELEWICZ	Bejla Rocha
KABAK	Leizer	KUSZELEWICZ	Josla?
KABAK	Roza	KUSZELEWICZ	Nachama
KABAK	Chana	KUSZELEWICZ	Szosza
KABAK	Chaja Sora	KUSZELEWICZ	Bluma
KABAK	Mowsza	KUSZELEWICZ	Hirsz
KABAK	Ajzik	KUSZELEWICZ	Cyra
KABAK	Doba	KOPELNICKI	Jeta
KABAK	Mowsza	KAPUSZEWICKI	Chaim
KABAK	Etka	KAPUSZEWICKI	Malka
KABAK	Jehoszua	KAPUSZEWICKI	Nachum
KABAK	Szejna	KIWELEWICZ	Etka
KLECKI	Chaja-?	KAPLAN	Chaim
KLECKI	Lea	KAPLAN	Chaja Lea
KLECKI	Jankel	KAPLAN	Roza
KRULEWIECKI	Pesia	KAPLAN	Abram
KRULEWIECKI	Grunia		
KRULEWIECKI	Tamara	**L**	
KRULEWIECKI?	Chasia	LESZCZINSKI	Riwa
KAZANOWICZ	Riwa	LUBCZANSKI	Nachama
KUZNIEC	Judel	LUBCZANSKI	Mejsza
KUZNIEC	Rocha	LUBCZANSKI	Mira
KUZNIEC	Bejla	LUBCZANSKI	Szifra
KUZNIEC	Elka	LEWIN	Morduch
KUZNIEC	Mowsza	LEWIN	Sonia
KANTOROWICZ	Rachela	LEWIN	Judes
KOWENSKI	Jenta	LEWIN	Doba
KOWENSKI	Tamara	LEWIN	?
KOWENSKI	Basia	LEWIN	Abram Icko
KAPLAN	?	LIBHABER	?
KAPLAN	Riwa	LIBHABER	Dowid
KAPLAN	Wolf	LIPCHIN	Mowsza
KAPLAN	Chana	LIPCHIN	Sara
KAPLAN	Feiga	LIPCHIN	Fania
KAPUSZEWSKI	?	LIPCHIN	Izak
KAPUSZEWSKI	Sora	LIPCHIN	Israel
KALMANOWSKI	Chawa	LIPCHIN	Szolem
KALMANOWSKI	Pesia	LIPCHIN	Chaim
KALMANOWSKI	Chaim	LIPCHIN	Chawa
KALMANOWSKI	?	LIPCHIN	Ela Chaim
KALMANOWSKI	Ela	LIPCHIN	Motl
KIWELEWICZ	Josl	LIPCHIN	Rachela

LIPCHIN	Hinda	MICKIN	Feiga
LEIBOWICZ	Dawid	MELAMED	Owsiej
LEIBOWICZ	Riwa	MELAMED	Chaja Roza
LEIBOWICZ	Lea	MELAMED	Hirsz
LEIBOWICZ	Mowsza-Sz.	MELAMED	Gehia
LEWIT	Lida	MELAMED	Masza
LEWIT	Freida	MELAMED	Moniek?
LEIBOWICZ	Estera	MELAMED	Mowsza
LEIBOWICZ	Roza	MORDUCHOWICZ	Chasia
LIP	Szolem	MORDUCHOWICZ	Rosa
LIP	Keila	MORDUCHOWICZ	Gita
LIFSZITS	Dowid	MORDUCHOWICZ	Chaikel
LEWIN	Sonia	MENAKER	Markel
LEWIN	Chasia	MENAKER	Szifra
LIDSKI	Zisia	MENAKER	Gerszon
LIPKA	Chackel	MIRSKI	Chaja
LIPKA	Szejna	MIRSKI	Sonia
LIPKA	Josif	MIRSKI	Mowsza
LUBCZANSKI	Chaim	MIRSKI	Nachum
LUBCZANSKI	Chaja	MIRSKI	Nachama
LUBCZANSKI	Rachela	MIRSKI	Gita
LUBCZANSKI	Israel	MIRSKI	Szimon
LUBCZANSKI	Roza	MORDUCHOWICZ	Motl
LUBCZANSKI	Dowid	MORDUCHOWICZ	Etka
LEJBOWICZ	Bejla	MORDUCHOWICZ	Godl
LUCKI	Estera	MORDUCHOWICZ	Chaja
LUCKI	Sara	MORDUCHOWICZ	Chaim
LUCKI	Hinda	MORDUCHOWICZ	Chaja Lea
LEW	Mera	MEJEROWICZ	Jawl?
LEW	Hadasa	MEJEROWICZ	Nachama
LOM	Jusla?	MEJEROWICZ	Sonia
LOM	Roza	MAZUREWICZ	Freida
LOM	Elka	MAZUREWICZ	Chaja Sora
LEWIN	Matla	MAZUREWICZ	Liba
LIPCHIN	Aron	MIRSKI	Ruben
LIPCHIN	Bejla	MORDUCHOWICZ	Oszer

M

N

MENAKER	Hirsz	NEGNIEWICKI	Aron
MENAKER	Chaja Bejla	NEGNIEWICKI	Duszka
MEJEROWICZ	Rachela	NISELEWICZ	Masza
MEJEROWICZ	Mowsza	NISELEWICZ	Lida
MEJEROWICZ	Morduch	NISELEWICZ	Sonia
MEJEROWICZ	Basia Rocha	NISELEWICZ	Dawid
MICKIN	Lea	NISELEWICZ	Feiga
MICKIN	Michoel	NISELEWICZ	Chaja
MICKIN	Oszer	NISELEWICZ	Chana

NISELEWICZ	Frida	ORZECHOWSKI	Chaja Sora
NACHUMOWSKI	Mejer	ORZECHOWSKI	Elka
NACHUMOWSKI	Szulka?	ORZECHOWSKI	Icko
NACHUMOWSKI	Lejba	ORZECHOWSKI	Lejzer
NACHUMOWSKI	Hirsz		
NACHUMOWSKI	Judel	**P**	
NISELEWICZ	Zalmon	POMERCZIK	Edra?
NISELEWICZ	Musza	POMERCZIK	Luba
NISELEWICZ	Necha	POLUZESKI	Estera
NISELEWICZ	Bejla	POLUZESKI	Mowsza
NISELEWICZ	Aron	PEREWOLOCKI	Elka
NOWICKI	Sara	PEREWOLOCKI	Rachela
NOWICKI	Eska	PEREWOLOCKI	Chasia
NOWICKI	Icko	PEREWOLOCKI	Szejna
NACHIMOWSKI	Elka	PEREWOLOCKI	Genia
NACHIMOWSKI	Mowsza	PEREWOLOCKI	Rachela
NACHIMOWSKI	Josel	PEREWOLOCKI	Mendel
NACHIMOWSKI	Leizer	PIK	Rosa Lea
NACHIMOWSKI	Gita	PIK	Izak
NACHIMOWSKI	Rocha	POLUZESKI	Chaja G.
NIEGNIEWICKI	Icko	POLUZESKI	Mera
NIEGNIEWICKI	Chana	POLUZESKI	Brocha
NIEGNIEWICKI	Chaja	POLUZESKI	Chaja
NIEGNIEWICKI	Doba	PILA	Sara
NIEGNIEWICKI	Riwa	PILA	Szloma
NIEGNIEWICKI	Abram	PORTNOJ	Mowsza
NIEGNIEWICKI	Gita	PORTNOJ	Dwora
NAMIOT	Rebeka	PORTNOJ	Sima
NAMIOT	Jakob		
		R	
O		RABINOWICZ	Chaim
OBRINSKI	Chasia	RAKOWICKI	Chana
OBRINSKI	Sara	RAKOWICKI	Bejla
OWSIEJEWICZ	Chaja ?	RAKOWICKI	Chasia
OWSIEJEWICZ	Michl	RABINOWICZ	Ida
OWSIEJEWICZ	?	RABINOWICZ	Aron
OWSIEJEWICZ	Judel	RABINOWICZ	Jacha
OSZEROWICZ	Ela Chaim	RABINOWICZ	Sora
OSZEROWICZ	Feiga	RAZOWKI	Icko
OSZEROWICZ	Szmuel Iser	RAZOWKI	Szprinca
OSZEROWICZ	Szoel	RAZOWKI	Cyra
OSZEROWICZ	Bluma	RAZOWKI	Szena?
OSZEROWICZ	Lea	RAZOWKI	Riwa
OSZEROWICZ	Elka	RAZOWKI	Masza
OSZEROWICZ	Lea	RAZOWKI	Sara
ORZECHOWSKI	Morduch	RABINOWICZ	Newach
ORZECHOWSKI	Judes	RABINOWICZ	Lida

RADUNOW	Dweira	STOLAR	Musza
RADUNOW	Gdalia	STOLAR	Josif
RADUNOW	Sonia	STOLAR	Nioma
RACHKOWSKI	Maks	STOLAR	Mowsza
RACHKOWSKI	Fania	STOLAR	Zelik
RACHKOWSKI	Isaak	STOLAR	Freida
RACHKOWSKI	Zusia	STOLAR	Josif
RACHKOWSKI	Sonia	STOLAR	Szloma
RACHKOWSKI	Chaim	STOLAR	Chaim
RYBAK	Elka	STOLAR	Lea
RYBAK	Josif	STOLAR	Josif
RAPPAPORT	Szimka	STOLAR	Mowsza
RAPPAPORT	Mowsza	STOLAR	Kejla
RACHOWSKI	Feiga	STOLAR	Gita
RACHOWSKI	Lea	STOLAR	Mejer
RUMANSKI	Nachama	SOLODUCHA	Eidla
RUMANSKI	Sonia	SOLODUCHA	Jacha?
RACHESZYCKI	Fruma	SKOROCHOD	Cywja
		SKOROCHOD	Bejla
S		SKOROCHOD	Sonia
SREBRENIK	Ajzik	SAWICKI	?
SREBRENIK	Sonia	SAWICKI	Chaim
SREBRENIK	Golda	SAWICKI	Lejba
SREBRENIKMOWSZA		SWERKOWSKI	Aleksandra
SREBRENIK	Rafael	SEREBRENIK	Sara
SLOBOCKI	Eszka	SEREBRENIK	Wolf
SLOBOCKI	Rachela	SEREBRENIK	Leiba
SLOBOCKI	Wolf	SLUCKI	Krejna
STOLOWICKI	Rachela	SLONIMSKI	?
STOLOWICKI	Michl	SLONIMSKI	Ejdla
STOLOWICKI	Roza	SZIMENOWICZ	Judl
SILOWICKI	Feina	SZIMENOWICZ	Minia
SLUCKI	Icko	SZIMENOWICZ	Benzion
SLUCKI	Jankel	SZIMENOWICZ	Hirsz
SLUCKI	Judes	SZIMENOWICZ	Michoel
SLUCKI	Dawid	SZIMENOWICZ	Lejba
SLUCKI	Chana	SZIMENOWICZ	Szolem
SLUCKI	Jankel	SZIMENOWICZ	Alta
SLUCKI	Chaja	SZIMENOWICZ	Szosza
SLUCKI	Mirka	SZIMENOWICZ	Dawid
SLUCKI	Luba	SZIMENOWICZ	Bejla
STOLAR	Icko	SZMULEWICZ	Pinchas
STOLAR	Malka	SZMULEWICZ	Fruma
STOLAR	Mera	SZMULEWICZ	Genia
STOLAR	Rachel	SZMULEWICZ	Izrael
STOLAR	Zejdl	SZMULEWICZ	Bejla
STOLAR	Judes	SZUSTER	Michl

SZUSTER	Genia	SZEWCZUK	Nisan
SZUSTER	Feiga	SZAPIRO	Jankel
SZUSTER	Feiga	SZAPIRO	Basia
SZUSTER	Ruwa		
SZUSTER	Dawid	**T**	
SZOFER	Etka	TURECKI	Sara
SZOFER	Dawid	TRINKMAN	Elka
SZOFER	Basia	TROCKI	Morduch
SZOFER	Chaja	TROCKI	Basia
SZMUSZKOWICZ	Ester	TROCKI	Bejla
SZMERKOWICZ	Jakob		
SZMUSZKOWICZ	Chaim	**U**	
SZMUSZKOWICZ	Riwka	ULERT	Izak
SZMUSZKOWICZ	Sonia	ULERT	Chaja Lea
SZEWRUK	Etka	ULERT	?
SZEWRUK	Abram		
SZKOLNIK	Hirsz	**W**	
SZILIK	Mowsza	WAKSER	Asna
SZILIK	Hinda	WOLFIN	Jechewet
SZILIK	Josif	WOLF	Maks
SZILIK	Hodes	WINTRAUB	Icko
SZILIK	Chaim	WINTRAUB	Grunia
SZUSTER	Dwejra	WINTRAUB	Mira
SZUSTER	Bejla	WERNIK	Lea
SZUSTER	Dawid	WERNIK	Chawa
SZUSTER	Riwa	WERNIK	Chaim
SZUSTER	Chasia	WERNIK	Aleksander
SZUSTER	Icko	WERNIK	Mira
SZLIMOWICZ	Guszel?	WERNIK	Riwa
SZLIMOWICZ	Sonia	WERNIK	Rosa
SZLIMOWICZ	Judel	WINER	Chaja
SZLIMOWICZ	Chaim	WINER	Judel
SZLIMOWICZ	Tamara	WINER	Aron
SZERESZEWSKI	Gitla	WOLFOWICZ	Szloma
SZERESZEWSKI	Lida	WOLFOWICZ	Szejna
SZIMSZELEWICZ	Boruch		
SZIMSZELEWICZ	Chana	**Z**	
SZIMSZELEWICZ	Morduch	ZALAMANSKI	Aron
SZIMSZELEWICZ	Gerszon	ZALAMANSKI	Masza
SZERER	Abus	ZALAMANSKI	Mowsza
SZNIDER	Szloma	ZALAMANSKI	Josif
SZNIDER	Michla	ZALAMANSKI	Sara
SZNIDER	Szulamit	ZALAMANSKI	Jankel
SZACKES	Benjamin	ZALAMANSKI	?
SZEWCZUK	Szejna	ZALAMANSKI	Faja
SZEWCZUK	Bejla	ZALAMANSKI	Sonia
SZEWCZUK	Sonia	ZALAMANSKI	Rosa

ZAMOSZCZIK	Chaja	ZUSMAN	Rosa
ZAMOSZCZIK	Zalmon	ZUSMAN	Icko
ZAMOSZCZIK	Rachel?	ZUSMAN	Sonia
ZAMOSZCZIK	Samuel	ZELEWIANSKI	Szimon
ZAPOLSKI	Izak	ZELEWIANSKI	Rosa
ZAPOLSKI	Sara Rocha	ZELEWIANSKI	Morduch
ZUSMAN	Herc		

Table of Contents of the Original Book

Translated by Solomon Manischwitz
and edited by Judy Montel and Oskar Delatycki

Note: [H] stands for Hebrew and [Y] for Yiddish

Introduction to the book

Introduction	the editors	[H]	
The prologue	the editors	[Y]	

History of the City

		[H]	11
The history of the Jews in Novogrudok	Yaakov Goldberg	[H]	11
The history of the town		[Y]	19
The Rabbis of Novogrudok	Rabbi V.Ch. Kancipolski	[Y]	25
The Musar movement	Mordechai Ginsburg (Montreal)	[Y]	33
What I remember of Novogrudok	Shlomo M. Gutman (Argentina)	[Y]	39
Leaders and ordinary members of the community	E. M. Yerushalmi	[Y]	42
The Bund in Novogrudok	H. Kaplan and Y. Maslow	[Y]	52
Memoirs from before the First World War	Wm Uris (New York)	[Y]	54
Old Novogrudok	Shimeon Yosifun	[Y]	61
Reminisces of Yischok Gurwitz: Rabbi Nachman Getzovhttp		[Y]	70
The Tailors' Synagogue		[Y]	72
The Seder night that was disrupted		[Y]	74
Dr. Benjamin Einhorn	Yaakov Gershovski	[Y]	76
Without a hammer, shears and a saw	Menashe Unger, US	[Y]	78
Alexander Harkavy	Prof. Nosun Ziskind, US	[Y]	79
Avrohom Eliyahu Harkavy		[Y]	82
The "eelui" (exceptional students of Tora) from Novogrudok (in memory of Reb Kalman Aharon Midler)	Chaim Noy	[H]	83
The big fire (blaze) in Novogrudok	Yaakov Gershovski	[Y]	84

The Jewish Souls (from the Old Pinkas Navaradok)	Dr. Eliezer Yerushalmi	[Y]	85

Between the Two World Wars

		[Y]	89
Hebrew education in Novogrudok	Moshe Steinberg-Sarig	[H]	89
The kindergarten	Sima Yonas-Portnoy	[H]	97
Music in Novogrudok	Menashe Rabina (Rabinovitz)	[H]	98
Politico-Communal life in Novogrudok	Shmuel Openheim	[Y]	100
The Novogrudok orphanage			107
The history of the orphanage		[Y]	107
Memories	Aharon Srebranik	[Y]	110
The first child in the orphanage	Aba Rutkovski	[Y]	112
The orphanage (1917-1919)	Shalom Cohen	[Y]	113
Shokdey melocho (the trade school)	Chaim Leibovich	[Y]	114
Volunteer Fire brigade	A. Shochor (Czarny)	[Y]	117
The theatre in Novogrudok	Zahava Rabinovich-Engel	[H]	118
Chaluts (Zionist scouts) movement	Yehoshua Brook (Kibbutz Negba)	[H]	119
Personalities	Shmuel Openheim	[Y]	126
The last of the Rabbis	Yehoshua Jaffe	[H]	129
People and Images	Yehoshua Yaffe	[Y]	130
Jewish Gardeners	Boruch Sapotnicki	[Y]	134
Peculiar types of people	A. Yerushalmi	[Y]	135
The public bath	A. Y.	[Y]	137
Schloss gass – a distinct township	Eliezer Berkovitch	[Y]	138
Yiddishe gass	Miriam Lipchin Negrevitski	[Y]	140
United Jewish Artisans Association	Samuel Nikolayevski	[Y]	141
The Professional Movement	Eliyahu Berkovitch	[Y]	143
"TOZ" (a Jewish Health Organization) activities	Majrim Ginzburg	[Y]	144
Aid for Jewish prisoners	Aharon Rudnicki	[Y]	148
Village Jews	D. Cohen	[Y]	149
Benjamin Kotlover	W. Uris	[Y]	152
Weekly papers in Novogrudok	Yehoshua Yaffe	[Y]	153

A native of Novogrudok in the Herzelia Gymnasium	Yishayahu Avi-Amots	[H]	154
Zeydl Bushelevits	Ch. Leibovitch	[H]	154
Extinguishing the fire of hatred	Noach Avni (Kamenitsky)	[Y]	155

Those Whom We Remember [Y] 156

Edna Kagan	Baruch Yakov and Meir Kagan	[Y]	156
Louie Zlotnik	Chaim Leibovich	[Y]	157
Ilia Aranovitch Gumener	Ch. L.	[Y]	157
Shmuel Solomon	Ch. L.	[Y]	158
Yitzchak Gurvitz	a fellow townsman	[Y]	159
Vager Family	Ch. L.	[Y]	159
Grandmother slept (in memory of the old woman Etl Goldberg)	D. C.	[H]	160
Alter Kamenetzki	N. K.	[Y]	161
Shmuel Goldberg	Lyuba Cohen	[H]	162
Yehuda Kaplinski	Lyuba Rudnicki	[Y]	162
My mother and sisters	Lyuba Valkin	[H]	163
Hersh Ostashinski	a fellow townsman	[Y]	164
With the coffin of Rabbi Yosef Yoyzl Hurvits in Israel		[H]	164

The Surroundings [H] 165

Karelich	Ch. T.	[H]	165
How I remember Selib (Wsielub)	Y. Y.	[Y]	167
My Shtetl Selib	Liba Shmulevits	[Y]	168
My shtetl Selub	Sara Shmulevits	[H]	170
Tsemach The Coachman (A type from the shtetl Selub)	Yehushua Yaffe	[Y]	170
Novoyelnie	Chana Kamin (Kaplan)	[Y]	171

Our Sisters and Brothers in the USA [Y] 172

The Alexander Harkavy Navaredker aid committee in US	Ya'akov Maslow	[Y]	172
Novogrudok Progressive Branch 146	B. Seltzer	[Y]	174

Yaakov Maslov	L.Ch.	[Y]	176
Committee of Emigrants from Novogrudok in Israel	Lyuba Rudnicki	[H]	178
About the editorial staff of the Pinkas Novogrudok (Yizkor) book	the Editors	[H]	181

Poetry and Prose in Novogrudok [H] 183

The song of Beseeching	Aharon Mirski	[H]	185
The Holy Ark Falls	Chaim Grade	[Y]	186
Mickiewicz and the Jews of Novogrudok	Prof B. Marc, Warsaw	[Y]	188
Adam Mickiewicz and his attitude to Jews	S. L. Shnayderman	[Y]	191
A Preacher in Siberia	Dr S. Shabbat	[H]	195
My home, poem	Bertha Kling	[Y]	196
A Friday in Novogrudok	Fruma Kamieniecki	[Y]	197
The first Rosh Hashona of the survivors of the Holocaust	Chaim Leibovich	[Y]	199
Three Kol Nidrei's	Chaim Leibovich	[Y]	201
Legends and fables	David Cohen	[Y]	203
The path to riches		[Y]	203
Belief in the Messiah		[Y]	205
"We will do and obey"– a legend		[H]	207
An Ethrog for Succoth		[Y]	208
A "Din Torah" a Jewish court		[Y]	209
Yitschok "Yom Suf"		[Y]	210
"Boze moyi"		[Y]	211
Letter from a mother	Edna Kagan	[Y]	213
The Shloss-barg	Dr. Avraham Ostashinski	[Y]	217
My home town	Emanuel Efron	[H]	220

Shoah and Bravery [Y] 227

Shoah [Y] 229

I fear and dread the consolation (poem)	Mirsky	[Y]	229
On the threshold of the shoah	Yaakov Kivelevich	[H]	230
A sea of troubles	Eliyau Berkovitz	[Y]	

A. Under the Soviets			237
B. The Tunnel			238
Under the German Yoke	Lyuba Rudnicki	[Y]	241
Outside of the Ghetto	Lyuba Rudnicki	[H]	246
In the days of annihilation	Shmuel Openheim	[Y]	251
In the Nazi hell			
The slaughter in Horodyszcze			
The 52 martyrs	Yehuda Slucki	[H]	257
The slaughter	Eshke Shor Levin	[Y]	258
The First Slaughter	Sima Yanos-Portnoy	[Y]	259
Slaughters	Chaim Kravets	[H]	263
Under the German whip	Sula Rubin-Wolozynski	[Y]	272
They burned the town	Yehoshua Yaffe	[Y]	274
The great destruction	Chaim Leibovitz	[Y]	287
A. How 300 Jews saved themselves			287
B. The last Passover			293
C. Three who were burned to death	(told by Chana Kirshner)		294
D. Escape through the tunnel			296
E. The heroic death of Berl Yoselevich			297
How I survived	Idl Kagan	[Y]	299
The Ghetto in Peresike	Frume Gulkovitz-Berger	[Y]	302
Chapters from the Holocaust	Y. Yaffe	[Y]	304
A. Escaping from the slaughter			304
B. The second slaughter			310
C. The final wandering			319
D. The tradesmen's Ghetto			322
E. The tar and pitch factory in the village of Karnyshi			327
The latest Kaddish (a poem)	Zelig Limon	[Y]	329
No Yahrzeit candle (a poem)	Nechama Layzerovski	[Y]	330
Where is my home? (a poem)	Miriam Ninkovski-Berkovich	[Y]	330

And the Bravery [H] **331**

The partisans' company of Tuvia Belski	Samuel Amarant	[H]	333
Jewish revenge	Chaim Leibovich	[Y]	346
A. Fight of the Jewish partisans			346
B. The Jewish Hero			349
C. Commander Shmatovich			350
Memories	Reyzl Volkin	[Y]	351
Jewish Partisan Intelligence	Moshe Reznick	[Y]	353
Jewish Bravery	Yehoshua Yaffe	[Y]	354
A. The first Jewish partisans			354
B. The partisans avoid slaughters			356
The four mass graves	Miriam Ninkovsky	[H]	357
People of Novogrudok after liberation	Yehoshua Yaffe	[Y]	357
Partisans of Novogrudok who fell in action	S. Openheim	[H]	359
Such were the Jewish partisans	Y. Yaffe	[H]	361
My brother Meir	Yaakov Rudnicki	[Y]	364
In memory of my father, Asoel Belski	Asoella	[H]	365
How does Novogrudok look now?	a townsman	[Y]	366
The Conclusion		[H/Y]	367
The Blood Bond with the Land of Israel		[H]	369
To Those Who Fell For Their Country		[H]	371
Osher Gorodisky	Ya'akov Ginenski	[H]	371
Yekuti'el (Kushi) Solchinski	Bilha	[H]	371
With Kushi in his last days	Shlomoleh Shvartz	[H]	372
Ruven Openheim	Shmuel Openheim	[H]	374
Eliezer Kriner		[H]	376
Luka Shapiro	a friend	[H]	376
A List: We will remember the Names of the Martyrs of Novogrudok, the Vicinity and Korelich		[H]	377

Novogrudok
List of citizens of Novogrudok
Killed in the Bielski partisans
A list of Jews from Novogrudok, including members of the Bielski partisan group
Killed by the Poles soon after liberation
List of Jews from Novogrudok who were arrested or deported on the night of 19/20 June 1941
Karelich
List of the Jews in the Ghetto of Karelich

INDEX

Please Note:

The index below does not include the names on pages 756 – 761.

Also due to technical difficulties, the index pages listed for pages 687 and greater may be off by up to three pages. If you do not find the name you are searching for on pages numbered 687 or greater, search on pages up to three lower. For example if you are searching for a name listed on page 710 and do not find it, extend your search to pages 707, 708 and 709. We apologize for this inconvenience.

A

Aberzanski, 718, 741
Abovich, 182, 227, 231, 242, 252
Abovitz, 227
Abowicz, 687
Abramit', 630
Abramovich, 194, 519, 652, 732
Abramovicz, 718
Abramovitch, 293
Abramovski, 718
Abramowicz, 687, 734, 741
Abramowski, 687
Abranski, 734
Abrazianski, 734
Abrinski, 734
Achanowski, 741
Aicher, 219, 243, 313, 661
Aizikowicz, 687
Ajzenberg, 75
Ajikovich, 182
Ajikovicz, 718
Ajikowicki, 687
Ajzykowicz, 538
Alchanan, 128, 227, 280
Alpersztein, 687
Alter, 56, 61, 116, 157, 159, 160, 176, 244, 281, 282, 481, 644
Amaleski, 741
Amarant, 572, 588, 590, 627
Amelung, 685
Amots, 267
Angelchik, 243
Angelczik, 687
Angelewicz, 468
Antek, 632
Aranovski, 718
Aranowicz, 687
Archonowski, 734
Arievich, 243
Ariovich, 17
Arjewicz, 687

Arlozorov, 214
Arol, 741
Aronowicz, 688
Aronowski, 688
Aspovich, 8, 9
Atlaski, 734
Auservitz, 285
Avni, 269, 316
Awisewicz, 734
Azikovich, 448, 451
Azriel, 66
Azrovich, 13
Azrowicz, 688

B

Baczynski, 688
Bakar, 688
Bakszt, 688
Bankaver, 178
Baranovich, 208, 211, 212, 295, 402, 403, 408, 508
Baretsky, 544
Barukh, 240, 316
Baumsztein, 688
Begin, 718, 719
Beigin, 293, 294
Bejgin, 741
Bejginsara, 741
Beker, 742
Bekolczuk, 688
Bel, 308
Belaus, 621, 624
Belin, 345, 719
Belski, 437, 439, 521, 572, 588, 590, 591, 592, 593, 594, 595, 599, 601, 604, 605, 606, 608, 611, 612, 613, 616, 621, 627, 641, 642, 644, 645, 646, 648, 649, 650, 652, 653, 688
Bencianovski, 157
Benin, 734, 741
Benzianovski, 243, 244
Benzianowski, 183, 385

Berenstein, 719
Berensztain, 741
Berger, 522, 555, 636
Bergman, 404, 435, 472
Bergner, 472
Berkman, 435, 437, 438, 439, 440, 441, 472
Berkovich, 242, 243, 586, 642, 732
Berkovicz, 719
Berkovitch, 250, 316, 627
Berkovitz, 417, 580
Berkovski, 238, 244, 296, 631
Berkowicz, 688, 689, 706, 732, 734, 741, 742
Berlin, 38, 42, 45, 50, 59, 60, 73, 90, 133, 135, 507
Berls, 116
Berma, 734
Berman, 649, 672, 689, 742
Beski, 422
Bezalel, 69, 70, 157, 229
Biber, 178
Bielski, 243, 296, 422, 452, 453, 474, 475, 477, 478, 562, 567, 572, 574, 575, 576, 579, 580, 581, 582, 589, 590, 618, 619, 621, 624, 625, 628, 629, 630, 631, 655, 686, 732
Bielsky, 588, 600, 617
Bigin, 734
Bigun, 689
Bilha, 667
Bitanski, 155
Bitenski, 689, 741
Blacher, 347
Blech, 689
Bloch, 171, 183, 189, 219, 244, 650, 689, 742
Bloser, 50, 55, 59
Bodjung, 241
Bogatin, 155, 689, 713
Bokatowich, 689
Bokatowicz, 689
Boker, 734
Boldo, 415, 599, 689, 719, 732
Bolotnicki, 734, 741
Bolszowicz, 689
Borecki, 420, 468, 689
Borensztein, 734
Borkowski, 689, 690
Borowski, 689, 690, 734, 742
Borski, 690
Borsztein, 690
Bortski, 689, 690
Boruchovich, 283
Bosel, 690, 734
Botainski, 734
Botwinik, 690

Bramson, 37
Braslin, 742
Breslerman, 690
Breslin, 734
Brestlin, 719
Brikner, 162
Brodna, 559
Brodner, 297
Broido, 84, 732
Brojda, 742
Brojdo, 223, 254, 483
Brolnicki, 690
Bronshtein, 632
Brook, 202
Broydo, 691
Bruchovich, 68, 325
Brudka, 741
Brudne, 690
Bruk, 168, 206, 212, 244, 643, 661, 690, 691, 701, 732, 742
Brzeznicki, 742
Brzozovski, 13
Burshtain, 61, 270
Burshtein, 500, 557
Burshten, 45
Bursztyn, 539
Buselevich, 266
Buselevitch, 224, 268
Bussel, 742
Buszel, 691
Butenski, 73

C

Calkovicz, 719
Calkowicz, 742
Cankin, 742
Carobodski, 734
Celkowicz, 734
Chabaruk, 734, 735
Chaitovich, 642
Chajetowicz, 691, 732
Chamiec, 270
Chanan, 350, 510, 513, 539
Chananies, 116
Charlin, 742
Charney, 6
Charny, 448, 630
Chasovschik, 71
Chasovshchik, 182
Chavivi, 170
Chernichovski, 516
Cherny, 644
Chernyshev, 592, 593
Chertok, 106, 580, 719
Chesly, 176, 691
Chimesz, 690

Chisin, 99
Chityn, 719
Chiz, 157, 178
Chodosz, 700
Chorny, 732
Churgin, 691
Ciechanovski, 719
Ciechanowski, 266, 429, 444, 448, 691
Cieplowodski, 742
Cimerinski, 691
Cimerman, 691
Cirinski, 712
Cohen, 1, 2, 5, 155, 182, 191, 192, 193,
    194, 204, 221, 222, 259, 273, 283, 291,
    319, 355, 358, 359, 364, 367, 369, 499,
    500, 501, 505, 507
Cukernik, 691
Cyitlin, 691
Cymerman, 691
Cyres, 68
Cyrinski, 691
Czarny, 198
Czernichowski, 500, 507
Czerny, 732
Czertok, 691, 692, 699
Czorny, 692
Czyz, 692

D

Damasek, 735
Dambrowski, 335, 336
Damesk, 616
Daniel, 21, 316, 536, 670
Danilovich, 26
Dawidow, 692
Dawidòwka, 335
Dawidowski, 692, 698
Delatycki, 4, 19, 30, 46, 58, 63, 82, 85, 96,
    110, 111, 114, 117, 120, 124, 125, 133,
    137, 138, 171, 183, 188, 189, 191, 192,
    194, 196, 197, 198, 217, 228, 235, 237,
    240, 242, 245, 247, 250, 251, 257, 259,
    265, 266, 268, 269, 272, 273, 275, 277,
    278, 281, 285, 287, 295, 297, 301, 303,
    304, 307, 309, 329, 335, 344, 345, 348,
    351, 355, 358, 364, 367, 372, 375, 381,
    417, 423, 441, 446, 455, 457, 463, 477,
    480, 498, 507, 510, 512, 514, 517, 522,
    525, 533, 546, 551, 559, 583, 585, 586,
    620, 625, 626, 628, 631, 632, 635, 638,
    654, 656, 683, 692, 718, 734, 741
De-Lion, 68, 325
Dentalski, 719
Dinerstein, 627
Dirlewanger, 572
Diskin, 36, 41

Dobrin, 100, 108, 212, 444, 448, 487, 692
Dobryn, 720
Dodowicz, 692
Dodowski, 692
Domb, 201
Donic, 692
Dorogow, 692
Dowidiche, 335
Drabski, 9
Drinski, 692
Dudman, 742
Dulsin, 692
Dunitz, 157
Duszkin, 735, 742
Dvorecki, 720
Dworches, 106
Dworecki, 504, 692
Dzentsolski, 414
Dzienciolski, 316, 599, 692, 693

E

Edelsztain, 742
Edida, 109
Efraimovski, 720
Efraimski, 693
Efroimski, 157, 439, 641, 648, 732, 735,
    742
Efron, 155, 156, 206, 230, 345, 384, 386,
    387, 391, 693, 732
Eherlich, 693
Eicher, 182, 252, 314, 693
Einhoren, 291
Einhorn, 120, 121, 122, 123, 124
Eisenstadt, 37
Eizenberg, 182
Eizikovich, 183
Elchanan, 69, 154, 155
Elchanon, 86
Elchonon, 50, 55, 137
Eliash, 103
Elin, 720
Engel, 199
Epshtein, 66, 99, 234, 735
Epshtin, 56, 60, 61, 86, 89, 91
Epstein, 41, 44, 109, 227, 234, 608, 614,
    643, 720, 732
Epsztein, 693, 742
Erlich, 196, 559, 693

F

Factornik, 467
Faifer, 743
Faigenberg, 61
Faiwelewicz, 742, 743
Faja, 720
Fajvelevicz, 720

Fajvelewicz, 720
Fajwelevich, 176
Fajwelewicz, 735
Falkovitz, 316
Fantal, 313
Farber, 743
Farbolocki, 735
Feigenberg, 694
Feigenberg', 85
Feigin, 150
Fidler, 72
Finman, 305
Firkes, 474
Fishbach, 720
Fishman, 249
Fiszbach, 717
Fleischer, 720
Fleszer, 743
Florent, 510
Frankfovitz, 661
Freedland, 39
Fridberg, 308, 472, 601
Fridman, 157, 735, 742
Friedberg, 623, 628
Friedman, 720, 721
Frumkes, 109
Fuks, 694
Furman, 694
Fus, 106

G

Gabodyski, 721
Gafkin, 546
Gancevicz, 721
Gancewicz, 735
Gancik, 465
Garcewski, 694
Gatzov, 283
Geler, 694
Geller, 743
Genikow, 694
Gerber, 204
Gercowicz, 694
Gercowski, 735, 743
Gerewicz, 744
Gershenovich, 28
Gershenowski, 248
Gershon, 33, 59, 63, 66, 70, 125, 219, 296, 313, 314, 316, 420, 421, 661
Gershonovich, 11, 102, 244
Gershonovski, 202, 294, 459, 643
Gershonowski, 448
Gershovich, 510
Gershovski, 120, 137
Gerszenowski, 743
Gerszonowicz, 694

Gerszonowski, 704, 732, 735, 743, 744
Gerszowicz, 735, 743, 744
Getzov, 86, 92, 111, 112
Getzvan, 75
Gilkin, 732
Gilkowicz, 623, 744
Gimolski, 694
Ginienski, 482, 688, 700
Ginsburg, 46
Ginski, 694
Ginzburg, 196, 251, 252, 694, 721, 743
Gitlin, 735, 743
Goczahes, 721
Gocziches, 743
Godelsalz, 721
Goldberg, 7, 42, 279, 283, 743
Goldfine, 111
Goldin, 694
Goldman, 307
Goldshmit, 157
Goldszmid, 694, 735, 744
Golkowicz, 694, 695, 735, 736
Golowicki, 694
Golub, 695
Golvicki, 432
Goncewicz, 695
Goncowicz, 743
Gorcowski, 695
Gordieyski, 249
Gordin, 695
Gordon, 134, 135, 136, 156, 208, 228, 385, 601, 614, 657, 695
Gorewicz, 736
Gorodechno, 260, 264
Gorodejski, 743
Gorodenski, 736
Gorodinski, 581, 666, 695, 736
Gorodiski, 665, 666, 743
Gorsztein, 695
Gortonowski, 736
Goszin, 743
Gotfrid, 695
Gotlib, 695
Govden, 721
Gozichew, 736
Grade, 325, 329
Grajwer, 732
Grasbowski, 88
Grinberg, 721, 736, 743
Grinda, 732
Grinfeld, 736, 743
Grodzienski, 73
Gromov, 432
Grossman, 181
Grynberg, 110, 354, 683
Gudsvirk, 286
Gulkovicz, 721

Gulkovitz, 522, 636
Gulkowicz, 743, 744
Gumener, 145, 155, 181, 183, 189, 195, 196, 218, 266, 275, 277, 444, 695
Gurcowski, 695
Gurdus, 743
Gurevich, 7, 21, 206, 266, 645
Gurevicz, 721
Gurevitz, 277
Gurewicz, 695, 732, 736, 743, 744
Gurszowicz, 736
Gursztein, 695
Gurvich, 277, 278, 297
Gurwitz, 111, 117
Gushkovich, 13
Guskind, 695, 696
Gutman, 58, 61, 62, 311
Gutswort, 155
Guzuk, 744

H

Haimovich, 9, 13
Halperin, 696
Hammurabit, 233
Harakavi, 157
Harakavy, 283, 663
Harbuna, 105
Harkavy, 33, 61, 63, 64, 65, 66, 67, 68, 69, 70, 86, 99, 102, 109, 110, 125, 126, 127, 128, 130, 131, 133, 182, 194, 219, 221, 255, 274, 304, 305, 307, 310, 325, 483, 660, 696
Harkawy, 696
Heine, 336
Helfand, 696
Helhonon, 34, 35, 36, 38, 39, 40, 139, 141
Hershenovski, 721
Hertz, 30
Hertzkes, 80
Hindl, 202
Hirsh, 30, 38, 58, 61, 62, 72, 83, 108, 194, 288
Hordus, 736
Horodyski, 721, 722
Horovich, 100, 101, 288
Horovitch, 313, 314, 316
Horovitz, 66
Horowicz, 696
Horvitz, 101
Hurovitz, 47, 49, 52, 53, 58
Hurvits, 315

I

Ibinitzki, 157
Iches, 116
Ickovicz, 722
Ickowicz, 696, 736, 744
Ikhelovich, 26
Isakow, 696
Iser, 35, 69
Israbieny, 722
Israelit, 83, 101, 118, 157, 198, 202, 251, 286, 313, 448, 487
Isrolik, 468, 475, 632
Itzkovich, 9, 192, 244
Iveniecki, 253
Ivienski, 722
Iviniecki, 202
Iwieniecki, 445
Iwiniecki, 696
Izaelit, 696
Izakson, 255
Izik, 13, 101, 107, 172, 219, 261
Izikovich, 191
Izikowicki, 696
Izraelit, 104, 182, 183, 188, 192, 196, 197, 270, 286, 444, 459, 473, 644, 689, 696, 697, 722, 736, 744
Izraelovich, 13, 16

J

Jabotinsky, 181
Jacubovitz, 570
Jaffa, 1, 178, 268
Jaffe, 106, 196, 231, 697
Jakubovich, 419
Jakubowski, 499, 505, 507
Jankelewicz, 468, 476, 623, 697, 736, 744
Jankelewski, 736
Jankielevicz, 722
Jankowski, 697
Japoniec, 83
Jarmowski, 689, 697, 698
Jasilinski, 698
Jawnowicz, 698
Jedidowicz, 698, 744
Jelen, 305, 523
Jelevicz, 722
Jelin, 70, 736, 744
Jerusalimski, 265
Jesofovich, 26
Jewelewicz, 698
Joselevich, 194
Joselevicz, 722, 723
Joselewicz, 424, 507, 698, 736, 744
Joselewiczoyzer, 736
Joselowski, 698
Judelewicz, 698

K

Kabak, 61, 63, 65, 99, 109, 444, 448, 457, 459, 698, 723, 736, 737, 745

Kac, 698
Kacenelenboign, 31
Kafelman, 471
Kafman, 745
Kagan, 3, 5, 6, 128, 172, 229, 272, 317, 318, 348, 375, 422, 508, 517, 518, 559, 563, 564, 582, 589, 663, 664, 678, 683, 685, 686, 698, 723, 732, 737, 745
Kaganovich, 632, 732
Kaganowicz, 698
Kahn, 372
Kaldfine, 116
Kalicki, 698, 699, 737
Kalinin, 574, 621
Kalmanovski, 294
Kalmanowicz, 699, 737, 745
Kalmanowski, 737, 745
Kalpanicki, 82, 83, 85
Kaltenhauer, 504
Kamai, 291
Kamen, 661, 685
Kamenetsky, 281
Kamenetzki, 244
Kamenietsky, 269
Kamenski, 732
Kamieniecki, 252, 345, 699
Kamil, 1, 6, 7, 46, 114, 134, 142, 162, 164, 182, 199, 202, 225, 267, 279, 283, 287, 288, 290, 300, 313, 317, 320, 340, 363, 369, 386, 399, 432, 453, 588, 637, 641, 646, 655, 663, 665, 667, 668, 675, 679, 681
Kamin, 1, 2, 5, 303, 319
Kaminetzki, 157, 159, 160
Kaminiecki, 5, 232, 233, 281, 283, 385, 433
Kaminietzki, 2
Kaminski, 212, 232, 313
Kancipolski, 30
Kandibe, 241
Kantorovich, 71, 220
Kantorowicz, 699, 745
Kapelevicz, 723
Kaplan, 82, 85, 244, 294, 303, 314, 699, 723, 737, 745
Kaplanski, 157, 234, 235
Kaplinski, 156, 223, 285, 426, 434, 695, 699, 700, 703, 723
Kaplinsky, 284
Kaposzewski, 737
Kapushevski, 723
Kapuszczewski, 700
Kapuszewicki, 745
Kapuszewski, 745
Kapuszowski, 700
Karajinski, 700
Karenski, 183

Karkur, 294
Karliner, 37
Kasmajewicz, 700
Kaspi, 293
Katrashinski, 207
Katsenelson, 291
Katz, 103
Katzenelson, 39, 222
Kaufman, 737
Kazan, 700
Kazanowicz, 745
Keidrel, 651
Kelecki, 737
Kemplowski, 623
Kesler, 593, 737
Kevelevicz, 470
Khaimovich, 26
Kirshner, 116, 117, 510, 511
Kirsner, 216
Kirzner, 653, 700
Kisner, 116
Kitaevitch, 313
Kitajewicz, 700
Kivelevich, 2, 5, 83, 85, 108, 196, 202, 399, 416
Kivelevitz, 1, 319, 400
Kivielevicz, 724
Kiwelewicz, 253, 345, 657, 700, 732, 737, 745
Kizner, 724
Klachko, 194
Klavoriski, 214
Kleck, 744
Klecki, 745
Kling, 307, 344
Klinicki, 700
Klitelnik, 243
Klitnik, 700
Klocki, 724
Klubok, 183, 194, 196, 208, 216, 700, 732
Kmitich, 26
Kodelman, 700
Kohen, 219
Kohn, 700
Koidanower, 30
Kolczycki, 724
Koldicki, 700
Kolevnik, 724
Koncevicz, 724
Kopelman, 403, 404, 414, 415
Kopelnicki, 745
Kopelowicz, 745
Kopernik, 737, 745
Kopls, 116
Kopolowicz, 737
Kopurski, 745
Korelicki, 724, 737

Koren, 155, 205
Korenski, 189
Korman, 309, 700, 701
Korn, 270, 271, 286
Korzuchovski, 500
Koshlen, 155
Koszelewski, 701
Kotlar, 623
Kotlover, 265
Kotlower, 94
Kowenski, 701, 745
Kowner, 701
Kozak, 744
Kozlovsky, 627
Kozlowski, 441
Koznietski, 314
Koznitch, 293
Kozuchowski, 507
Kraikenborn, 572
Krakowski, 45
Kramie, 336
Krant, 155
Krantz, 462
Krasinski, 334
Krasnopiurka, 61
Kravets, 243, 446
Kraviec, 724
Kraviets, 463
Krawiec, 701
Krimer, 701
Kriner, 679, 680
Kroleviecki, 724
Krolwacki, 737
Krulewiecki, 701, 745
Kubanski, 737
Kube, 572
Kulachek, 421
Kulik, 744, 745
Kupelman, 701
Kushi, 433, 667, 668, 669, 670, 671, 672, 673, 674, 679
Kushner, 447, 580, 582
Kushnir, 308
Kuszczynski, 701
Kuszelewicz, 745
Kuznic, 737
Kuzniec, 745
Kvak, 642

L

Lagatker, 701
Lagatkier, 243
Lagatkor, 724
Lageza, 83
Lagocki, 701, 702
Laibovich, 17

Landau, 487, 509
Langleben, 155
Layzerovski, 585
Lazerovich, 10
Lazowski, 702
Leib, 30
Leibovich, 3, 5, 117, 180, 194, 196, 273, 278, 348, 351, 439, 553, 641, 643, 648
Leibovitch, 268, 620, 626
Leibovitz, 318, 498, 507, 510, 512, 514
Leibowicz, 702, 732, 746
Leikin, 153, 154, 155, 702
Leipuner, 78, 345, 346, 347
Leizaerowski, 702
Leizerovski, 104, 200
Leizerowski, 297, 425, 452, 461, 472, 657
Lejbovich, 468
Lejbovicz, 724
Lejbowicz, 746
Leszczinski, 746
Lev, 724
Levin, 55, 61, 150, 154, 155, 268, 414, 455, 620, 632, 724, 725
Levit, 725
Levy, 336
Lew, 702, 746
Lewin, 426, 468, 702, 713, 737, 746
Lewit, 702, 737, 746
Liber, 307
Libhaber, 746
Libowicz, 737
Lidski, 86, 155, 204, 286, 387, 702, 746
Lidzki, 725
Liebovitz, 581
Lifszits, 746
Limon, 278, 437, 583, 702, 703
Lintz, 83
Lip, 746
Lipchin, 725, 746
Lipka, 746
Lipkes, 6, 30
Lipkin, 703, 737, 738
Lipp, 738
Lipshits, 35, 40, 188, 189
Lipski, 155, 738
Lipszyc, 738
Lis, 155, 161, 469, 545, 703, 725
Lishanko, 592
Lisowski, 703
Liszinski, 703
Litman, 703
Litovski, 157
Litowski, 703
Litvin, 116, 725
Litwin, 703
Lizerowski, 104, 444, 445
Lobin, 738

Lom, 746
Lubacki, 703
Lubaczanski, 703, 704
Lubchanski, 61, 121, 156, 170, 175, 176, 219, 248, 249, 465
Lubczanski, 725, 732, 738, 746
Lubecki, 712
Lucki, 704, 725, 746
Ludski, 421, 471, 704, 738
Lurie, 39
Luszanski, 704
Lutski, 157

M

Magid, 704
Mairi, 30
Maker, 298
Makil, 704
Makoliveski, 157
Malachowski, 704
Malbin, 156, 601, 623, 628
Malchacki, 116
Maluszicki, 704
Mandelbaum, 704
Mandelevich, 11
Mandri, 500
Maniszewicz, 699, 704
Manusevich, 155
Marc, 329
Margolit, 31
Markl, 30
Marmurshtain, 186
Marmurshtein, 252
Marmurshtin, 286
Marmurstein, 145
Marmursztein, 704
Marmursztin, 253
Mas, 308
Maskil, 704
Maslov, 3, 5, 308, 309, 310, 311, 312
Maslovaty, 85, 155, 156, 244, 725
Maslow, 82, 304, 305
Maslowaty, 430, 496, 497, 704
Maslowski, 704, 705
Matis, 71
Matuses, 61
Matuszewicz, 705
Mayerovich, 231
Mayerowicz, 738
Mazrowicz, 738
Mazurewicz, 746
Mazurkiewicz, 513
Mechiel, 705
Mecklenburg, 37
Meierovicz, 725
Meilach, 116, 355, 525, 526, 527, 528, 529, 533
Meirovich, 225, 226, 227, 242
Meirovitch, 294
Mejerowicz, 705, 746
Mek, 238
Mekel, 705
Melamed, 746
Melzer, 705
Menaker, 174, 515, 517, 523, 644, 705, 732, 746
Mendelevicz, 725
Mendelovich, 28
Mendelson, 68, 505, 506, 570, 573
Metatshiz, 10
Metropolitanski, 182
Michalewicz, 421
Michalojevski, 725
Michalovich, 420
Michalski, 207, 472
Miches, 103
Mickiewicz, 19, 86, 139, 329, 330, 331, 332, 333, 334, 335, 336, 337, 338, 339, 340, 385, 426, 657
Mickin, 746
Midler, 134, 135, 136
Mikolajewicz, 705
Mikulicki, 243, 705
Milchiker, 155
Miller, 457, 461, 478
Minik, 725
Minsker, 38
Mircelevski, 85
Mirski, 1, 2, 5, 204, 313, 315, 319, 320, 346, 384, 387, 399, 705, 738, 746
Mirsky, 320
Mischin, 725
Miszkin, 738
Mitkobatshes, 594
Mitskewitz, 333, 334, 384
Mlamaja, 725
Mnaker, 725, 726
Mockiewicz, 332
Moiseyevich, 26
Mokotovicz, 726
Mokotowicz, 705
Moksi, 705
Molczadski, 705
Moler, 705
Molodiecka, 335
Molodiecki, 705
Moloszicki, 705, 706
Montel, 202
Mordechovich, 155
Morduchovicz, 726
Morduchowicz, 706, 738, 746, 747
Moris, 706
Moscalov, 540

Moskovski, 85
Motkes, 198
Motkies, 347
Movilevicz, 726
Movshevicz, 726
Movshovich, 13, 61, 94, 196, 243, 252, 265, 296, 407, 424, 432, 560, 643, 644, 645
Mowszowicz, 425, 448, 706, 732
Mucznik, 706, 726
Muler, 248
Murdoch, 16

N

Nachimovski, 255, 430, 447, 482, 726
Nachimowicz, 706
Nachimowski, 623, 747
Nachumovski, 156, 157
Nachumowski, 747
Nairovich, 10
Namiot, 706, 738, 747
Namyslovski, 726
Narwer, 706
Negniewicki, 747
Negrevitski, 245
Nekrich, 61
Nevachovich, 500
Newachowich, 706
Newachowicz, 507
Niankovski, 264, 382, 405
Niankowski, 448, 489, 706, 707, 732
Niegnewicki, 715
Niegnievicki, 581, 726
Niegniewicki, 707, 738, 747
Nikolaewski, 707
Nikolayevski, 229, 247, 248, 249
Nikolowski, 707
Nimenchik, 154, 155
Ninkovski, 586, 637
Niselevicz, 726, 727
Niselewicz, 707, 738, 747
Nislowicz, 738
Nizewicki, 707
Nochimovski, 465, 467, 468
Nochimowicz, 707
Nochimowski, 707, 708, 738
Noske, 241
Notkowicz, 708
Nowicki, 747
Noy, 134
Nyevski, 653

O

Obelinski, 67
Obosiewicz, 738
Obovicz, 727
Obrinski, 747
Obrynski, 727
Ochanovski, 727
Oistrach, 708
Okanska, 708
Okanski, 708
Okonski, 582
Oksiewicz, 738
Okun, 708
Olrat, 738
Openhaim, 641, 665
Openheim, 157, 171, 262, 358, 441, 442, 446, 675, 678, 688, 708, 712
Openhiem, 517, 518
Openhim, 176, 217
Orinski, 708
Orlanski, 500, 507, 516
Orlinski, 155, 156
Orlynski, 708
Orzechovski, 727
Orzechowski, 708, 738, 747
Osataszinski, 448
Oshman, 581
Ostashinski, 85, 157, 159, 160, 179, 194, 214, 217, 243, 255, 287, 288, 381, 405, 560, 580, 642, 645, 649, 650
Ostashynski, 727
Ostaszinski, 688, 708, 732
Ostshinski, 614
Oszerowicz, 747
Oszrowicz, 738
Otalski, 738
Owosiewicz, 738
Owsiejewicz, 747

P

Panchenko, 590, 646
Pargowicka, 435
Parnes, 204, 708
Parski, 738
Parsman, 155, 156, 157
Pashovich, 9, 11, 13
Pasveler, 31
Patzovski, 614
Pejsachovich, 26, 28
Percig, 299
Perec, 708
Peresetzki, 244
Peresiecki, 204
Perewolocki, 747
Perkovicz, 727
Pernik, 346, 347, 708
Pesies, 107
Peterburger, 59
Pieresedski, 286
Pieresietski, 708

Pierevolocki, 727
Pik, 747
Piklin, 708, 709
Pila, 747
Pilecki, 179
Pilozowski, 738
Pilsudski, 163, 295, 563
Piltski, 155, 208, 211
Pilzanski, 738
Pinchuk, 106, 709
Pinczuk, 657
Pinski, 194
Piontek, 709
Plazenski, 433
Plebaner, 196
Plotkin, 709
Plotnik, 643, 732
Plozynski, 711
Pluzanski, 293
Pogorelski, 709
Polanski, 476, 621
Polimakovski, 727
Poloniecki, 727
Polonski, 75, 641, 642, 709, 727, 732
Poluzecki, 727, 728
Poluzeski, 747
Pomerczik, 747
Pomierczik, 709, 738
Portnoi, 151, 419
Portnoj, 738, 747
Portnoy, 155, 162, 164, 216, 457, 570, 571, 580
Pozniak, 709
Pranik, 709
Precnik, 709
Presman, 709
Pressman, 217, 465
Prisitzki, 155, 179, 709
Prochiner, 291
Pupke, 709, 710
Pupko, 738
Purkuls, 116
Puterman, 710

R

Rabec, 728
Rabina, 2, 5, 164, 209
Rabinovich, 72, 106, 109, 149, 155, 157, 160, 164, 167, 178, 180, 199, 201, 202, 221, 252, 254, 286, 387, 392
Rabinovicz, 728
Rabinovitch, 149, 167, 209
Rabinovitz, 173
Rabinowicz, 183, 190, 523, 710, 739, 747
Rabinowski, 710
Racheszycki, 748

Rachkowicz, 710
Rachkowski, 748
Rachowski, 748
Raczkovski, 728
Raczkowski, 710
Radunow, 747, 748
Raisin, 421
Rajsin, 728
Rakovicki, 728
Rakovski, 208, 500, 645
Rakowicki, 739, 747
Rakowski, 507, 710, 732
Ram, 69, 70, 101, 126
Rapaport, 728
Rappaport, 748
Rarakowicz, 710
Ratner, 243, 710
Rauter, 494, 497
Rawicz, 710
Razevski, 645
Razewski, 732
Razovski, 728
Razowki, 747
Razowski, 739
Redrovich, 293
Reine, 559
Reines, 61, 91
Reisen, 86
Reuter, 452, 461, 501, 502, 558, 684
Reuveni, 294
Reznick, 631
Reznik, 623, 630, 710, 728
Ribinski, 595
Rifkin, 448
Rivak, 605, 606, 607
Robinovich, 13
Rodnicki, 710
Rogatynski, 728
Rosenbloom, 422, 441
Rosenhouse, 573, 578
Rosin, 732
Rotanski, 710
Rozanik, 710
Rozen, 710
Rozianski, 710, 711
Rozovski, 728
Rubienczik, 728
Rubin, 70, 477, 711, 723, 725, 727, 745
Rudnicki, 1, 5, 243, 257, 285, 313, 315, 384, 423, 428, 430, 432, 435, 438, 472, 641, 654, 655, 661, 709, 711
Rudnidski, 207
Rudnitsky, 316, 319
Rudnitzki, 2
Rudski, 482
Rukovski, 570, 571, 576
Rumanski, 748

Runicki, 661
Rutanska, 728
Rutkovski, 191
Rybak, 512, 513, 748

S

Sacharowicz, 711
Sakovich, 26
Salander, 37, 49, 53, 59, 60
Salomon, 145, 155, 218, 275, 277, 445
Salter, 6
Salucki, 729
Samsonovich, 505
Sapotnicki, 65, 194, 235, 244, 382
Sarbarnik, 739
Sarig, 2, 5, 142, 155, 285, 319
Savicki, 729
Sawicki, 739, 748
Sazyner, 59
Schmitt, 492
Schneider, 729
Seifert, 711
Seltzer, 307
Selubski, 520
Sensentus, 155
Serebrenik, 748
Shabakovski, 557, 570
Shabbat, 96, 149, 209, 340, 370, 371, 389, 391, 395
Shaffer, 505
Shalit, 183, 190, 196
Shalita, 155
Shapira, 294, 616
Shapiro, 50, 105, 208, 424, 432, 444, 645, 681, 729
Shelemovich, 26
Shemyatoviec, 598, 627
Shepsl, 73, 115
Shepsman, 579
Shereshevski, 729
Sheroshevski, 37
Shimanovich, 223
Shimen, 83, 96, 115, 198
Shimonovich, 85
Shimonovitz, 194
Shkolnik, 194
Shlachtman, 729
Shlachtovic, 610
Shlobovski, 405
Shlomovich, 13
Shlosberg, 156, 157, 163
Shmatovich, 626, 627
Shmelke, 30
Shmerkovich, 116, 117
Shmoilovich, 9
Shmuelevich, 11

Shmulevich, 243, 295, 297, 300
Shmulevits, 297
Shmulovich, 28, 56
Shnayderman, 335
Shocher, 170
Shochor, 198
Shor, 455
Shteihoise, 72
Shteinberg, 2, 319, 459
Shtesnovitz, 606
Shtrik, 121
Shvartz, 182
Shwartz, 168, 202, 216, 668
Sielubski, 571
Silberman, 729
Silowicki, 748
Simchovich, 287
Simchowich, 711
Skakun, 116
Skleser, 139
Skobelev, 102
Skolnik, 570
Skorochod, 711, 739, 748
Sladkovski, 729
Slobocki, 729, 748
Slodowski, 711
Slolev, 729
Slominski, 739
Slonimski, 689, 748
Slosberg, 202
Sloter, 711
Slubocki, 739
Slucki, 453, 711, 729, 739, 748
Slutski, 652, 653
Slutzker, 38
Slutzki, 218, 453, 454
Smilovicz, 729
Smolenski, 711
Smolski, 443
Smuelevich, 13
Snichin, 592
Snowski, 711, 712
Sofer, 712
Soker, 85
Sokolowski, 697, 712
Solchinski, 667
Solcinski, 712
Soloducha, 729, 748
Solomon, 170, 174, 196, 218, 261, 266, 276, 370, 404, 405, 454, 712
Soloveichik, 38, 56
Solowicki, 739
Sosnovski, 729, 730
Sosnowski, 517, 519, 712
Spector, 34
Spiter, 632
Sputnicki, 712, 714, 717

Srebranik, 188
Srebrenik, 712, 748
Srebrnik, 730
Stanislavovicz, 9
Steinberg, 1, 5, 142, 155, 163, 174, 190, 285, 286
Stocki, 730
Stolar, 739, 748
Stoler, 651, 652, 730
Stolowicki, 712, 748
Strashun, 69
Stratovicz, 9
Sucharski, 248, 517, 521, 570, 579, 644, 712, 730
Sucharsky, 220
Sukarski, 157
Swerkowski, 748
Szabkowski, 712
Szachor, 712
Szackes, 749
Szacki, 739
Szalowski, 712
Szapiro, 712, 717, 749
Szerer, 749
Szereszewski, 749
Szeroszewski, 739, 740
Szewczuk, 749
Szewicki, 712
Szewruk, 748
Szilik, 749
Szimanowicz, 381, 385, 712
Szimanski, 712
Szimenowicz, 748
Szimonowicz, 712
Szimszelewicz, 712, 740, 749
Szkolnik, 712, 749
Szlachtman, 713
Szlimowicz, 740, 749
Szlobowski, 713
Szlomowicz, 732
Szlosberg, 711, 713
Szmerkowicz, 713, 748
Szmukler, 713
Szmulewicz, 694, 713, 740, 748
Szmuszkowicz, 748
Sznider, 749
Szofer, 748
Szteinberg, 713
Szulklaper, 713
Szumski, 495
Szurc, 713
Szuster, 713, 740, 748, 749
Szwarc, 253, 470, 471, 474, 475, 476, 687, 713
Szymonowicz, 740

T

Tabakovski, 469
Tamara, 263, 347, 435, 436, 437, 439, 551
Tamarkin, 714
Tavrycki, 730
Tawaricki, 714
Tawarycki, 740
Tchernichovski, 267, 268, 393
Tczeszle, 714
Tiles, 447, 477, 705, 714
Tracewicki, 714
Trajwusz, 714
Traub, 422, 447, 462, 510, 624, 685
Treitl, 79
Treiwisz, 714
Trinkman, 749
Trobowicz, 714
Trocki, 714, 740, 749
Troicki, 732
Troitski, 644
Trojecki, 714
Trunkman, 740
Tsemach, 301
Tsesya, 610
Tsires, 116
Tubishovich, 13
Turecki, 749
Twaricki, 714

U

Ugert, 730
Ulert, 749
Unger, 124
Uris, 69, 85, 265

V

Vager, 278
Valkin, 287
Vasilevitch, 626, 627
Vasserman, 182
Vigacki, 296
Vilenski, 116, 117
Vilner, 30, 325, 326, 327, 328
Viner, 435, 437, 674
Vinnick, 176, 222
Volfkind, 182
Volfovich, 243, 244, 641
Volfovitz, 316, 661
Volkin, 439, 628, 641, 647, 648
Volkovyski, 596, 601
Volozhinska, 581
Voloziner, 31
Volozyner, 42

W

Wager, 183, 714
Wagers, 116
Wagier, 85
Waiss, 730
Wakser, 749
Waldrich, 556
Walowski, 490
Warsaw, 8, 11, 20, 55, 100, 101, 104, 175, 176, 184, 189, 192, 201, 213, 251, 255, 288, 329, 345, 428, 435, 437, 503, 508, 509, 557, 653, 732
Wasilewski, 714
Wasserman, 61
Weiner, 714
Weinstraub, 730
Weintraub, 740
Weisman, 714
Wenze, 106
Wernik, 730, 740, 749
Wiene, 740
Wiener, 714, 730, 731
Wiernikowski, 715
Wilenski, 715
Wilkin, 715
Wilner, 715
Winer, 715, 749
Winik, 715
Wintraub, 749
Wiszmman, 715
Wiszniewski, 559, 560, 561, 562, 622, 715
Wojmer, 731
Wolf, 69, 154, 155, 240, 478, 749
Wolfin, 740, 749
Wolfkin, 715
Wolfkind, 183, 202
Wolfmayer, 511
Wolfovich, 155, 174
Wolfovicz, 730
Wolfowicz, 706, 713, 715, 732, 749
Wolkin, 711, 715, 716, 732
Wolkowski, 716
Wolobrinski, 183
Wolonski, 716
Wolozynski, 477
Woltc, 716
Wsielub, 713

Y

Yafe, 319
Yaffe, 2, 5, 44, 56, 62, 131, 225, 228, 230, 266, 267, 268, 282, 301, 449, 480, 511, 525, 533, 546, 551, 559, 635, 638, 646
Yankelevitch, 652
Yanovski, 307
Yarmovski, 414, 579
Yavnovich, 649
Yecerov, 183
Yedida, 74, 115
Yehilevich, 9
Yelen, 182, 192
Yelin, 70, 155
Yerushalmi, 1, 3, 5, 6, 63, 68, 138, 237, 265, 317, 319, 664
Yofe, 632
Yoffe, 61, 62
Yoine, 109, 116
Yorman, 286
Yoselevich, 286, 419, 500, 504, 514, 515, 516
Yoselevitz, 569
Yosifun, 96, 114
Yshayhu, 298
Yudkovich, 13

Z

Zablocki, 716
Zacharowicz, 716
Zahakis, 32
Zajfert, 716
Zakchaim, 716
Zalamanski, 731, 749
Zalatuche, 100, 110, 253, 426, 472
Zalbin, 716
Zalbinski, 716
Zalmanowski, 716
Zalmon, 96
Zaloga, 412
Zamko, 630
Zamkovy, 644
Zamkow, 716
Zamkowe, 183
Zamkowy, 418, 468, 692, 716, 732
Zamoshchik, 731
Zamoszczik, 749
Zamoszczyk, 716, 740
Zamshnik, 84
Zapolski, 716, 749
Zarkain, 295
Zaszwa, 716
Zdienciolski, 448
Zeldowicz, 270, 444, 487, 716
Zelewianski, 749
Zeliks, 115
Zelivianski, 731
Zelkind, 39
Zellinger, 503
Zeltser, 308
Zelzer, 39
Zeshukovski, 216
Zilberman, 483, 642, 716, 732
Zion, 176

Zipert, 159
Ziskind, 33, 63, 125, 219, 223, 424, 432, 435, 437, 438, 441, 472, 560, 645, 717, 732
Zizemski, 717
Zliwinski, 740
Zlotnik, 273, 274, 717, 732
Zubarski, 519
Zubarsky, 220

Zuchovicki, 104, 208, 732
Zuchovicki', 104
Zuchovitski, 650
Zuchowicki, 717
Zuk, 405, 717
Zukerman, 632
Zundel, 31
Zusman, 740, 749
Zyskind, 196, 731

www.ingramcontent.com/pod-product-compliance
Lightning Source LLC
Chambersburg PA
CBHW082002150426

42814CB00005BA/194